Encyclopedia
of British Sport

Encyclopedia
of British Sport

Edited by Richard Cox, Grant Jarvie
and Wray Vamplew

ABC-CLIO
Oxford, England
Santa Barbara, California
Denver, Colorado

© Copyright 2000 by ABC-CLIO Ltd.

British Library Cataloguing in Publication Data

Encyclopedia of British Sport
    1. Sports – Great Britain – Encyclopedias
    I. Cox, Richard William, 1953-   II. Jarvie, Grant, 1955-   III. Vamplew, Wray
    IV. British Sport
796'.0941'03

ISBNs 1–85109–334–6 (Paperback)
        1–85109–344–3 (Hardback)

ABC-CLIO Ltd,
Old Clarendon Ironworks,
35A Great Clarendon Street,
Oxford OX2 6AT, England.

———————————————

ABC-CLIO Inc.,
130 Cremona Drive,
Santa Barbara,
CA 93117, USA.

Typeset by ABC-CLIO Ltd., Oxford, England.
Printed and bound in Great Britain by
MPG Books Limited, Bodmin, Cornwall.

This book is dedicated to
The British Society of Sports History

Contents

FOREWORD, *BY TIM HENMAN* ix

FOREWORD, *BY LORD ASA BRIGGS* xi

PREFACE xiii

INTRODUCTION xv

LIST OF ENTRIES xxi

LIST OF CONTRIBUTORS xxv

LIST OF ABBREVIATIONS AND ACRONYMS USED............................... xxxiii

A-Z ENCYCLOPEDIA OF BRITISH SPORT 1

INDEX 431

Contents

Foreword

Few people in Britain today are unaware of the importance attached to sport by all sections of society. Indeed, sport takes up an ever increasing amount of air time on television and a growing number of pages in both the national and local press. We now have television and radio channels entirely devoted to sport and thousands of people walk the streets in 'trainers', track-suits and the strip of their favourite team.

Whilst sporting competition can generate intense rivalry, especially between fans of opposing teams, it can also break down prejudices and bring otherwise bitterly opposed individuals together. Many of you will have seen the picture of Tony Banks and David Mellor, two ideologically opposed politicians, sitting side by side at Stamford Bridge pledging their allegiances to their favourite football team – Chelsea. The same principle is also true of Irish Rugby, with residents of both Eire and Northern Ireland passionately united behind the national team.

Even the British public, who have not had a lot to cheer about in recent years, are united under the Union Jack when it comes to sport. We have all heard about the positive impact which England winning the World Cup in 1966 had on the nation as a whole. Although I cannot remember that occasion, I certainly remember very vividly the good feeling which resulted from Linford Christie winning the 100-metre sprint at the Barcelona Olympic Games in 1992. As a tennis player, I can certainly tell you that there is no greater thrill than performing well on the Centre Court at Wimbledon in front of a home crowd willing you on for every point. When you win your joy is shared, not only with the many fans surrounding you in the stadium, but also with the hundreds of thousands sitting at home watching the match on television.

Given the importance of sport both to the individual and society as a whole, it is fitting that *The Encyclopedia of British Sport* has set out to achieve more than most traditional encyclopedias. This invaluable reference work is not simply a listing of scores, dates, other facts and feats, it provides the reader with informed insights into a broad range of other aspects of British sport. There is something here for everyone, even the minority who have little, or no, interest in sport. At least here, they can read about some of its foibles and problems, as well as its good points.

Tim Henman

Foreword

I am glad to have been given the opportunity to write a brief foreword to this lively encyclopedia. The ramifications of sport in contemporary society are so wide that they cover most subjects of study, from physiology and psychology through to economics and history. Newspapers, radio and television provide daily fare, the latter often minute by minute, almost instantaneously, from all parts of the globe. Sports news consists of information, commentary, gossip and entertainment. The boundary lines between play and work, performance and business are blurred and are always changing. An encyclopedia of sport must encompass much more than encyclopedias of particular sports. It has to take account of the social and cultural context within which all sports are pursued.

Sport, which once was local, is now global, and this encyclopedia is a sequel to ABC-CLIO's recently published *Encyclopedia of World Sport*. Its focus on British sport is justifiable, however, for global sport draws on national loyalties and rivalries and the sporting life of no two countries is quite the same. There are notable differences in the British Isles between England, Scotland, Wales and Ireland. They reflect other differences, but also bring out common passions. They cluster round both individuals and teams, and they express styles as well as follow rules. There have been enormous changes, both in particular sports and in the whole pattern of sport, during the last thirty years. Yet, as long ago as 1936 when conditions were quite different, the editor of *Encyclopaedia of Sports, Games and Pastimes*, explaining the need for 'a work of reference devoted exclusively to sporting topics', described what he called 'the new and world wide interest in sport' (it was not all that new) as 'not casual and desultory, but rather intensive and concentrated'. Since then, as sports have become more professionalized, studies of sport, including histories, have become more specialized, and there is a need now to draw them together.

One of the merits of this new encyclopedia is that its editors, supported by knowledgeable contributors, state very clearly in their Preface and Introduction how they set about their task. Faced with the need to be selective, they quite deliberately left out some relevant and interesting matter. They state the reasons why, and they also helpfully state where what they have left out can be found. Because there is relentless change, there can be no finality in these pages as they stand, but they constitute an impressive record of editorship and scholarly achievement. I am impressed by the range of new areas examined by the editors and contributors and, above all, their willingness and capacity to communicate in a readable fashion. Of course, it is the sportsmen and sportswomen themselves who make the whole academic exercise possible and worthwhile. How they relate to sponsors, managers, spectators and journalists – and how these groups relate to them – is as much the stuff of contemporary sports as the games themselves.

Lord Asa Briggs

Preface

The initiative for this encyclopedia came from Dr Bob Neville, Editorial Director of ABC-CLIO Ltd. Following the success of the recently published *Encyclopedia of World Sport*, he suggested that there might be sufficient demand for a separate encyclopedia of British sport, especially given the popularity and importance attached to it in today's society. More pertinent for such a work from our point of view was the fact that Britain was the cradle of modern sport and has had a unique and enduring influence on the rest of the world. Moreover the volume would have many interesting and special features and would consider the many profound and significant changes which had taken place since the publication of John Arlott's *Oxford Companion to Sports and Games* (1975), J. A. Cuddon's *International Dictionary of Sports and Games* (1979), Marshall Cavendish's *The Game: Marshall Cavendish's Encyclopedia of World Sports in 126 Weekly Parts* (1974-76), the *Purnell's Encyclopedia of Sport* (1974) and the Robert Hale series (1970s) (which were arguably the most significant sports reference works of this nature to be published in recent years). For example, we were provided with the opportunity to discuss such developments as: the introduction of the Premier League; the professionalization of Rugby Union; the increasing role of technology in determining overall performance in some sports; the increased use of drugs; Britain's demise in the world of sport (both in terms of influence in governance and performance on the field of play); the impact of National Lottery funding; the introduction of the *Sky Sports* television channel; and the Taylor Report into safety at sports grounds. None of the works listed above, nor the more recent encyclopedias of sport such as M. Tyler's *The Encyclopedia of Sports: the Rules, Champions, Histories and Great Moments* (1975), have tackled these broader socio-economic and political issues surrounding sport in a thematic, or scholarly, way.

Having said this, it should be emphasized that this encyclopedia should not be regarded as the definitive source which supersedes everything published hitherto. Whilst it introduces some new topics and a novel approach to satisfy the new dimensions of sport and a better informed public, it does not aim, nor ever claim, to replace all of its predecessors. Although Joseph Strutt's *The Sports and Pastimes of the People of England* published in 1801 was not strictly an encyclopedia of sport, it was none the less a valuable and entertaining mine of information concerning antiquarian lore. Included in that volume are many old sporting customs and practices we have not even attempted to embrace.

Blaine's *Encyclopedia of Rural Sports* published in 1840 aimed to describe 'the progress of each sport to its present state of perfection', added considerable new material and remained in print for thirty years. By 1898, the Duke of Suffolk and Berkshire felt compelled to 'bring the story up-to-date' and produced another excellent exposition in the two-volumed *Encyclopedia of Sports and Games*. Like Blaine, this work went into considerable depth on the then highly popular 'gentleman's field sports' such as angling and game shooting. However, ten years on the Duke decided it was desirable to produce an updated second version. This time the encyclopedia ran to four volumes.

There were no significant encyclopedias of sport published after that date until the 1970s. Two intervening world wars no doubt slowed down the rapid commercialization of sport but, the fact that by the late 1960s we were able to watch live sport on television, put it back on track. John Arlott's *Oxford Companion to Sports and Games*, the lavishly illustrated Marshall Cavendish's *The Game*, and the Guinness and Robert Hale series were all published within a short time of each other and were soon followed up with new editions and series.

In a perhaps unusual fashion, all these volumes tend to complement rather than duplicate each other. All have their own strengths and weaknesses and, as you might expect, include many of the same headwords. However, you will not find mention of the ancient and obscure games included in Strutt here in this present volume; nor the in-depth factual detail of many of the popular modern sports included in *The Game*. On the other hand, you will not find thematic essays on advertising, art, the cinema, commercialism, costume, journalism, music, myths, racism, spectators, technology or violence in any of the other volumes mentioned. Nor will you find details of newly-founded institutions such as the National Coaching Foundation, the Youth Sport Trust, and the Women's Sports Foundation. This is also the first encyclopedia of sport which, to our knowledge, includes details of internet websites, an increasingly valuable source of up-to-date information.

We will have to wait and see how soon our encyclopedia becomes out of date. There is no doubt that sport continues to change at an ever faster pace as more competitions are introduced, rules are changed, new personalities make their mark, and institutions are founded. Naturally, we hope to keep pace with these developments and to update you with a second edition in years to come. However, gone are the days when there could be a gap of between ten and thirty years before a new edition was required.

We hope that the progressive improvements and changes that ran through the earlier encyclopedias outlined above are continued in this volume. It has certainly been our aim to satisfy the broader, and overall more informed, audience of readers and to inform them about the wider issues of sport.

It is intended that the *Encyclopedia of British Sport* will provide journalists, librarians, students, scholars, teachers and sports enthusiasts, as well as members of the general public, with an authoritative source of information about a comprehensive range of subjects embracing the history and culture of sport in Britain. Altogether, there are over 300 entries written by over 100 contributors focusing on individual sports (identifying significant landmarks, key organizations or individuals, famous clubs, major competitions, events, venues and incidents), institutions and organizations. The volume also analyses key concepts such as amateurism and fair play; examines themes such as sporting eccentrics; discusses contemporary concerns and issues such as commercialization, drugs, ethics, gender, racism and professionalism; and considers theoretical perspectives such as sociology and psychology, as well as important relationships such as alcohol and sport, language and terminology. Sport as reflected in drama, film, literature, painting and other arts is also included.

Introduction

Methodology

Determining the individual headings to be included in this encyclopedia, even within the confines already outlined above, stimulated much debate amongst the editors. Clearly, there were many sports and related topics that could have been justifiably included in an *Encyclopedia of British Sport*. If we were to add all the entries in the Robert Hale series of sports encyclopedias, for example, the present volume would have contained several thousand headwords. However, we were restricted to no more than two hundred thousand words (for the main section), only a tenth of those in Marshall Cavendish's *The Game*. At the request of the publishers, our first major task was to compile the list of headwords that would comprise the encyclopedia. Between ourselves, we agreed to list these under the following headings: individual sports; biographies; competitions; concepts; incidents; institutions; terminology; and venues. Despite our attempts to be prudent, we still came up with a short list of around 1,000 headings. Given our word limit, however, we soon realized that we could not do justice to even this number of entries.

Ultimately, it was the biographical entries which were omitted *en masse*. We had considered placing them under broader headings such as Famous Administrators, Broadcasters, Exceptional Talents, People's Heroes and Celebrities. Unfortunately, there was a never-ending argument about which individuals were most worthy for inclusion. Should it be British-born nationals, or British citizens at the time of their achievements or prowess? Is it a sportsperson's positive contributions to sport throughout his or her life that should count most (in which case should he or she be dead before an accurate assessment can be made?), or should achievements on the field of play, or in a similar capacity (administration, coaching, commentating, refereeing, talent scouting, etc.) be the determining factor? In the case of performers, should it be their achievements on the domestic, or international stage (national champion, Olympic gold medal winner, etc.)? Should other factors justify a person's inclusion? Feats (records, averages, number of caps, etc.), life-time earnings, popularity, or even notoriety (in which case would Arthur Wharton, England's first professional black footballer, who died a pauper, or Eddie 'the Eagle' Edwards qualify?)? Are outstanding amateur sportsmen and women equally as worthy for inclusion as their professional counterparts? Are those involved in minority sport as important as those involved in our national games? Should only those playing in an era when the standard of play was of a high standard be considered? Peter Matthews and Ian Buchanan in their *All-Time Greats of British and Irish Sport* (1995) experienced difficulties in limiting their list for inclusion to 1,500 individuals, and several newspapers and television programmes which attempted to assess Britain's most outstanding athletes over the years, as part of the Millennium celebrations, met with strong differences of opinion. In the end, we dropped the idea of including biographical entries on the basis that in some cases we felt there was little more we could say in relatively few words about the significance and sporting lives of George Best, Lord Burghley, C. B. Fry and W. G. Grace, for example, than had already been written in numerous full-length specialized biographical studies. Moreover, in the interim we were commissioned to compile an *Encyclopedia of British Football* and it was decided that some of those entries could be included in that volume, and possibly in some of the other specialist encyclopedias on individual sports in this series. This does not mean that an individual's achievements and contributions to British sport do not get a mention but simply that they are discussed only in wider contexts such as the development of the sport as a whole, as key achievements, turning points, etc. Thus, Ian Botham's outstanding achievement in the Ashes test match of 1981 does not get a separate entry but is alluded to in the entry on Headingley. Likewise Fred Archers' achievements on the racetrack are not listed but his suicide is discussed as both a reflection of his personality and in the context of the problems facing a professional sportsman. A similar philosophy has been adopted in relation to some individual associations, clubs, events, institutions and venues. There are separate entries dealing with the Football Association and Jockey Club, but not the Hockey Association, or the Rugby Football Union. Apart from these exceptions (exceptional because of their long and important history), we have tried to tackle the matter of 'governance' within the entries for the individual sports. In terms of individual clubs, the M.C.C. receives an entry of its own but not the highly successful Manchester United Football Club, or the controversial Yorkshire County Cricket Club. Similarly, Badminton Horse Trials do not get a separate entry but are mentioned as part of the entries on Badminton House and Eventing. We acknowledge that there are sound reasons for including separate entries on the contributions of such organizations as the Outward Bound Trust and the Y.M.C.A.; on the football World Cup as well as the cricket and Rugby world cups; on the Professional Golfers' Association as well as the Professional Footballers' Association; on the Oval as well as Headingley; on Roger Bannister's four-minute mile as well as Frankie Dettori's seven wins; etc. Although we have our reasons for what we did, and did not, include in the space available to us, and have attempted to summarize most of these, we would be interested to hear readers' views and will take these into consideration when planning future editions. We accept that our approach of subjugating many institutions, individuals and events within broader headings is a reversal of what some readers might expect in an encyclopedia of sport, especially if their primary purpose is to obtain facts and figures to help them win quizzes, or impress their friends, but it reflects our policy of both attempting to provide contexts to events and our aim of complementing rather than competing against existing publications.

Once we had agreed a list of headwords, we assigned each one a rating: A (250 words); B (500 words); and C (1,000 words). In addition, some of the major sports were broken down into several sub-sections focusing on origins, governance and administration, personalities, competitions and incidents. The size of each entry was determined by the editors and it should be appreciated that those charged with the task of writing on 'bigger subjects' sometimes found it difficult to stay within the word limits. Squeezing the history, or politics of sport, for example, into 1,000 words is problematical, especially when the editors remained firm on this point.

Finally, details of all the short-listed headwords were circulated to members of the British Society of Sports History (B.S.S.H.), both for comment, and also in an effort to commission authors to write specific entries. After several weeks, details were posted on the B.S.S.H. internet website and circulated via the SportHist Listserv to solicit further contributors. In the end, approximately one quarter of the entries remained uncommissioned. Ray Physick kindly agreed to act as 'sweeper' for the least popular entries, for which even hard-pressed volunteers could not be found.

Coverage

Our aim in this volume has not been to provide hundreds of separate entries on every conceivable sporting topic but rather to provide a reasonably comprehensive overview of British sport, past and present, within a broad social, economic and political context.

We are aware that there are some sports played in Britain whose recent origins are in another country and that their history in Britain is not particularly significant. No real attempt has therefore been made to include entries on Lacrosse or Ten Pin Bowling. Nonetheless, we have included an entry on Gridiron Football because this is an example of a sport which, although enormously popular in one country, has failed to transplant itself in a foreign culture. Although darts, knurr and spell, and quoits are included, we are also very conscious of the fact that there are other bar, folk and parlour games, such as skittles, which do originate in Britain and are still played today in certain parts of the country, but which we have not been able to cover in detail. The same is true of many of the so-called 'animal baiting sports' and certain purely recreational sporting activities such as cruising and rambling. However, we have covered angling; this we regarded as an exception because of its enormous popularity and its long history. Notwithstanding this, we have also been mindful of other reference works recently published, or currently in preparation, and have attempted to avoid unnecessary duplication. Hence, we thought it more important to tackle hitherto uncovered subjects, or topics which are the subject of rapid and constant change (such as advertising, drugs, language and the development of the academic disciplines of sport) as opposed to well-documented topics such as the rules of cricket, or England's progress in the World Cup (see, for example, the series and titles listed above).

Finally, we do admit that there are a few topics which we would have liked to include, notwithstanding all of the above considerations. However, in some cases expert contributors were not available, or there were insufficient sources of information available to the researcher to do the subject justice. Typical examples which fell into this category were sport in the Civil Service and sport in the Police service.

We have not attempted to provide a comprehensive bibliography of the literature available. Instead, we would refer the reader to *Sport in Britain: a Bibliography of Historical Publications to 2000* (Frank Cass, 2001). This can be supplemented with R. W. Cox's other publications documenting the literature of British sport: *History of Sport: a Guide to the Literature and Sources of Information* (Sports History Publihing, 1995) and *Index to Sporting Manuscripts in the UK* (Sports History Publishing, 1996), which lists primary sources. All three are regularly updated in *The Sports Historian*. Recommended sport specific bibliographies covering a selection of both primary and secondary source material include: J. Jenkins, *A Rugby Compendium* (British Library, 1998); E. W. Padwick, *A Bibliography of Cricket* (Library Association for the Cricket Society, 1984) and its supplement, compiled by S. Ely and P. Griffiths, *Padwick's Bibliography of Cricket, volume II* (Library Association, 1991); P. J. Seddon, *Football: a Comprehensive Guide to the Literature of Association Football* (British Library Publications, 1999. 2nd ed.). Although we had intended to include a chronology of significant dates in the history of British Sport, it grew to such a size that it became no longer practical to include it in the present volume. It will now be published as a separate volume by Frank Cass in 2001 under the editorship of R. W. Cox. Lack of space also prevented the inclusion of detailed breakdowns of facts and figures, such as record scores, league tables and averages. Several useful publications already exist in this field, however (see, for example, H. Russell, *Carling 10,000 Football Facts and Questions* [Arcturus Press, 1999], or the many compilations of the Association of Track and Field Statisticians, the Association of Football Statisticians, the Association of Cricket Statisticians and Historians, etc., and some of the encyclopedias listed above). Those interested in the rules of sport should refer to *Rules of the Game: the Complete Illustrated Encyclopaedia of all the Sports of the World* (Collins, 1990). Another important reference source covering sport throughout the world is D. Levinson and K. Christensen,

Encyclopedia of World Sport (ABC-CLIO, 1996). Finally, a list of internet websites has been included for a large number of entries. These have been confined to what might be regarded as 'official sites' in that they are maintained by the governing body for that sport or event. However, since this is a rapidly evolving area, addresses may soon change and the quality of information prove variable. An introductory booklet on this subject has been published by R. W. Cox, *Sport and the Internet* (Coxburn Press, 1995).

It should be pointed out that from an early stage we were conscious of ABC-CLIO's plans to publish more specialized encyclopedias on individual sports such as British football (scheduled for 2001), extreme sports (2002), golf (2003) and horseracing (2002) and Oxford University Press's plans for an encyclopedia of women and sport (2001). We have, nevertheless, attempted to provide sources for further reading in relation to these sports and especially in the case of the less documented sports.

Our hope is that this encyclopedia will become the automatic first port of call for a researcher wanting an overview of British sport, or an insight into a particular aspect. For many needing only limited information, we hope that this volume alone will provide them with what they require.

Structure

Given these objectives and our intended audience, we decided in the end to structure the encyclopedia largely around individual sports using an alphabetical arrangement. Key individuals, important competitions, memorable events, if appropriate, are incorporated within these sections as stand alone paragraphs. Major multiple sporting organizations (for example, the Sports Council [now Sport England]), events (for example, the Olympic Games), venues (for example, Wembley) have been provided with their own entry alongside other topics of a more general nature. At the foot of most entries the contributor has supplied a list of sources used to complete the entry and a list of bibliographic references as a guide for further information. Again, these are not meant to be exhaustive but rather helpful and reliable 'next ports of call' for further details.

We appreciate that there will be readers disappointed to find that there is no entry on their favourite club, event, sport, or venue. There will certainly be those who fail to see why there is a separate entry on the Football Association and the M.C.C. but not on the Badminton Association, or Amateur Swimming Association. Similarly, there will be readers who will note that there are entries on Bedford, Chelsea, Dartford and Dunfermline women's P.E. colleges but not Anstey, Lady Mabel or Nonington; that there are entries on Carnegie, Jordanhill and Loughborough colleges for men but not Cardiff, St Luke's or Madeley; that Murrayfield has an entry but Meadowbank stadium does not, Old Trafford has an entry but not Villa Park; that the Wembley Experience has a main entry but not the Theatre of Dreams (i.e., Old Trafford) museum; that the Waterloo Cup for coursing has its own entry but the Queen's Medal for Target Shooting does not. We also accept that there are some topics and issues more thoroughly researched and addressed than others. Had the pressure of time not been an issue, had sources on some sports been more readily available and had experts been available on all sports, then this particular problem would not have arisen. However, we have tried to adopt a logical, as well as a pragmatic, approach to what we have included, excluded and condensed into the space available to us. Ultimately, we hope that you will agree that our approach has been justified and we trust that those disappointed this time around will be satisfied with the more specialist volumes on individual sports which will follow.

Illustrations

Sport provides the inspiration, and subject matter, for many art forms from drama, through painting and print-making, to sculpture and verse. Many of our contributors have recommended numerous interesting and exciting pictures to illustrate the subjects on which they had written. Unfortunately, for a variety of reasons it was not possible to reproduce these images in the present volume. However, we have chosen illustrations which provide a balanced coverage and which depict several sports, events, issues, personalities and venues from different geographical locations (England, Ireland, Scotland and Wales) and periods of history (early, modern). We have also endeavoured not to reproduce a number of well-known illustrations (good as they might be) which have already been published many times in one book, or encyclopedia, after another.

Acknowledgements

This project has been an exciting and stimulating one with which to be associated. It has demanded taking an overview of the whole of British sport, past and present, and has helped identify the gaps in our knowledge. As well as exposing areas in need of future research, it has also stimulated new ideas and themes for further investigation.

As fellow officers of the British Society of Sports History (B.S.S.H.), we wanted members to have a sense of ownership of this encyclopedia and so at all stages we attempted to involve them in some capacity. Details of the short-listed headwords were published in the B.S.S.H. *Newsletter* and on the website for comment, and all members were invited to offer their services in writing entries. We appreciate the enthusiasm they expressed for the project, the contributions they made and especially the occasions when they agreed to bail us out with less popular topics when already under pressure.

The project has also helped bring together a vast number of individuals hitherto unknown personally to the editors, each with their own talents and insights, to help document this very important aspect of the British way of life and culture. It never ceases to amaze us how many unsung heroes and heroines are 'out there' working in isolation but with a vast knowledge of their 'pet subject'. Their expertise is based on many years of painstaking research during which they have accumulated not only facts and figures, but also, in many cases, artefacts and memorabilia. Our hope is that they will continue their good work and not hide their work under such big bushels.

We would like to specifically thank Bob Neville, Editorial Director of ABC-CLIO Ltd, for commissioning the encyclopedia in the first place, and for his continued friendly support together with that of his staff. We are particularly grateful to Dan Nunn, whose painstaking editing and fact checking have greatly improved the overall accuracy and quality of the work. Our gratitude also goes to Tim Henman, a modern icon of British sport, and Lord Asa Briggs for writing the Forewords; and to all the many members of the British Society of Sport History for their contributions. We also thank the many organizations granting us permission to make use of their illustrations.

Finally, it should be noted that the responsibility for all errors and omissions ultimately lies with us, the series editors.

Richard Cox
Grant Jarvie
Wray Vamplew

1.8.2000

List of Entries

Admiral's Cup, *1*
Advertising, *2*
Aikido, *3*
Aintree, *3*
Alcohol, *4*
Amateurism and
  Professionalism, *6*
Angling, *8*
Archery, *11*
Army Physical Training
  Corps, *13*
Army Sport Control Board, *14*
Ascot, *14*
Ashes, *15*
Association Football, *16*
Athletics – Indoor Athletics, *23*
Athletics – Track and Field, *25*
Australian Rules Football, *27*
Badminton, *29*
Badminton House, *30*
Basketball, *31*
Bedford College, *33*
Belfry (The), *33*
Benefit, *34*
Birmingham Athletic
  Institute, *35*
Birmingham University, *35*
Bisham Abbey, *36*
Bobsleigh, *36*
Bowls (Indoor and
  Outdoor), *37*
Boxing, *40*
Brands Hatch, *44*
British Association for Shooting
  and Conservation, *45*
British Association of Sport
  and Exercise Medicine, *46*

British Association of Sport
  and Exercise Sciences, *47*
British Olympic Association, *48*
British Society of Sports
  History, *48*
British Sporting Art Trust, *49*
British Universities Sports
  Association, *51*
Brooklands Circuit, *52*
Calcutta Cup, *55*
Cambridge University, *55*
Canoeing, *57*
Cardiff Arms Park, *58*
Carnegie College, *59*
Central Council of Physical
  Recreation, *60*
Channel Swimming, *61*
Chelsea College, *63*
Cheltenham, *64*
Chester Roodee, *65*
Children, *65*
Class, *67*
Classics (The), *69*
Coaching, *69*
Commercialism, *71*
Commonwealth (formerly
  Empire) Games, *73*
Commonwealth Games:
  London, 1934, *74*
Commonwealth Games:
  Cardiff, 1958, *74*
Commonwealth Games:
  Edinburgh, 1970, *75*
Commonwealth Games:
  Edinburgh, 1986, *75*
Community, Civic Pride and
  Sport, *76*

Corinthians, *77*
Costume and Clothing, *78*
Cotswold Games, *78*
Countryside Alliance, *79*
Cricket, *80*
Croquet, *93*
Cross-country Running, *93*
Crystal Palace, *94*
Curling, *95*
Cycling, *96*
Cyclo-cross, *99*
Dartford College, *101*
Darts, *102*
Deer Stalking, *103*
Derby Matches, *104*
Disability Sports, *105*
Disasters, *107*
Diving, *110*
Doggett's Coat and Badge, *111*
Donington Park, *112*
Drama, *113*
Drugs, *115*
Dunfermline College, *116*
Economics of Sport, *119*
Education – Commissions
  and Reports, *121*
Education – Public School
  Sport, *123*
Education – Teacher
  Training, *125*
Epsom, *127*
Ethics, *128*
Eton Versus Harrow, *130*
Eventing, *130*
F.A. Cup, *133*
Fair Play, *133*
Fastnet Race, *134*

Fell Running, *135*
Fencing, *136*
Field Sports, *138*
Films, *139*
Fives, *140*
Foundation for Sport and the Arts, *141*
Fox-hunting, *142*
Gaelic Football, *143*
Gambling, *144*
Game Laws, *146*
Game Shooting, *147*
Gay Sport, *148*
Gender, *149*
Geography, *151*
Gillette Cup, *152*
Glenmore Lodge, *153*
Gliding Sports, *153*
Globalization, *154*
Golf, *156*
Goodwood, *162*
Grand National, *163*
Grasmere Sports, *164*
Grass Track Racing, *165*
Greyhound Racing, *165*
Gridiron Football, *166*
Gymnastics, *167*
Hampden Park, *169*
Handball, *169*
Hare Hunting and Coursing, *170*
Hat Trick, *172*
Head to Head, *172*
Headingley Sports Ground, *172*
Henley Royal Regatta, *173*
Hickstead, *175*
Highland Games, *176*
Hill Climbing (Motor Car), *178*
History, *178*
Hockey (Field), *180*
Holme Pierrepont, *182*
Horse of the Year Show, *183*
Horse-racing – The American Invasion, *184*
Horse-racing – Breeding, *184*

Horse-racing – Flat-racing, *186*
Horse-racing – Governance and Administration, *187*
Horse-racing – Jockeys, *188*
Horse-racing – National Hunt, *190*
Horse-racing – Terminology, *192*
Hurling, *192*
Ice Hockey, *195*
Isle of Man T.T. Races, *196*
Jordanhill College, *199*
Journalism, *199*
Judo, *201*
Karate, *203*
Kick Boxing, *204*
Knur and Spell, *204*
Kung Fu, *205*
Land and Water Speed Records, *207*
Landyachting, *208*
Language, *209*
Law, *211*
Law – The Kerry Packer Trial, *212*
Law – Overseas Players, *213*
Law – Restraint of Trade, *214*
Lawn Tennis, *214*
League Against Cruel Sports, *224*
League Cup, *225*
Lilleshall, *226*
Literature, *226*
Liverpool Gymnasium, *228*
Liverpool Olympics, *229*
London Marathon, *230*
London Polytechnic, *231*
Lord's Cricket Ground, *232*
Loughborough University, *233*
Management, *235*
Manx Grand Prix, *237*
Marathon Racing, *237*
Marketing, *238*
Mascots, *240*

M.C.C. (Marylebone Cricket Club), *241*
Media, *242*
Media – *Athletic News*, *244*
Media – Fanzines, *244*
Media – Radio 5, *245*
Media – Sky Sports, *245*
Media – *Sporting Chronicle*, *246*
Media – *Sporting Life*, *246*
Media – Sports Personality of the Year, *247*
Media – *Sportsman*, *248*
Memorable Events – Death of Tommy Simpson, *248*
Memorable Events – Frankie Dettori's Seven, *249*
Memorable Events – Fred Archer's Suicide, *249*
Milk Race, *250*
Morpeth Olympic Games, *250*
Motor Boat Racing, *251*
Motor Racing, *251*
Motorcycle Racing, *253*
Mountain Biking, *255*
Mountaineering, *256*
Much Wenlock Games, *257*
Murrayfield, *259*
Muscular Christianity, *260*
Museums and Halls of Fame, *260*
Museums and Halls of Fame – British Golf Museum, *262*
Museums and Halls of Fame – Cheltenham Hall of Fame, *262*
Museums and Halls of Fame – The Football Musuem, Preston, *263*
Museums and Halls of Fame – Lord's Cricket Museum, *263*
Museums and Halls of Fame – National Horseracing Musuem, Newmarket, *264*
Museums and Halls of Fame – River and Rowing Musuem, *264*

Museums and Halls of Fame
– Rugby Museum,
Twickenham, 265
Museums and Halls of Fame
– Scottish Football
Association Museum, 266
Museums and Halls of Fame
– Wembley Experience, 266
Museums and Halls of Fame
– Wimbledon Lawn Tennis
Museum, 267
Museums and Halls of Fame
– York Racing Museum, 268
Music, 268
Myths, 270
National Coaching
Foundation, 273
National Equestrian Centre, 274
National Lottery, 275
National Playing Fields
Association, 275
Nationalism, 276
Netball, 278
Newmarket, 279
Odsal Stadium, 281
Offside, 281
Old Trafford Cricket
Ground, 282
Old Trafford Football
Stadium, 282
Olympic Games, 283
Olympic Games –
London 1908, 284
Olympic Games –
London 1948, 285
Olympic Games –
Olympic Bids, 287
Open Championship, 288
Orienteering, 289
Oulton Park, 290
Oxford University, 291
Parachuting, 293
Pedestrianism, 295
Physical Education
Association of the United
Kingdom, 296

Pigeon Racing, 297
Plas Menai, 298
Plas Y Brenin, 299
Player Violence, 300
Politics and Government, 301
Politics and Government –
The Suffragette Movement
and Sport, 303
Polo, 303
Professional Footballers'
Association, 305
Professional Golfers'
Association, 305
Psychology, 306
Pugilism, 307
Punting, 310
Quoits, 313
Racism and Ethnicity, 315
Rackets, 316
R.A.F. Cosford, 317
R.A.F. Sports Board, 318
Rallying, 319
Real Tennis, 320
Religion, 321
Rhythmic Gymnastics, 323
Ritual and Superstition, 324
Road Running, 324
Rock Climbing, 326
Roller Hockey, 328
Roller-skating, 328
Roses Matches, 329
Rounders, 330
Rowing, 331
Royal International Horse
Show, 333
Royal Navy Sports Control
Board, 334
Royal Patronage, 335
Rugby League, 336
Rugby Union, 339
Ryder Cup, 345
Sailing, 347
St Andrews, 348
Scrambling, 349
Services Sport, 349
Shinty, 350

Showjumping, 351
Silverstone, 352
Skating – Figure, 353
Skating – Speed, 354
Skiing, 355
Snooker, 356
Sociology of Sport, 357
Softball, 359
Sophia Gardens, 360
Spectators, Fans and Crowd
Disorder, 360
Spectators, Fans and Crowd
Disorder – Hampden Park
Riot 1909, 362
Spectators, Fans and Crowd
Disorder – Record Crowds, 363
Speedway, 363
Sporting Art, 365
Sporting Eccentrics, 367
Sporting Heroes, 368
Sports Acrobatics, 370
Sports Announcing and
Commentating, 371
Sports Council (now Sport
England), 372
Sports Industry, 373
Sports Medicine, 374
Sports Science, 376
Sports Sponsorship, 379
Sprinting (Motor Car), 380
Squash, 381
Stock-car Racing, 382
Stoke Mandeville, 383
Stoolball, 383
Strathclyde Water Park, 384
Surfing, 385
Swimming, 385
Table Tennis, 391
Target Shooting, 393
Taylor Reports, 393
Technology, 394
Television, 396
Test Matches, 398
Trampolining, 399
Triathlon, 400
Triple Crown, 401

Tug Of War, *401*
Turnhalle, *402*
Twickenham, *403*
U.K. Sailing Academy,
Cowes, *405*
Unions and Strikes, *406*
University Boat Race, *408*
Volleyball, *411*
Water Polo, *413*
Water-skiing, *414*
Waterloo Cup, *414*

Weightlifting, *414*
Welsh Handball, *416*
Wembley Stadium, *417*
White City, *418*
Wightman Cup, *419*
Wild Pigeon Shooting, *419*
Wildfowling, *420*
Wimbledon, *421*
Windsurfing, *422*
Wisden Cricketers'
Almanack, *423*

Wolfenden Report, *424*
Women's Sports
Foundation, *425*
World Cup Cricket, *425*
World Cup Rugby
League, *426*
World Cup Rugby
Union, *426*
Wrestling, *427*
Youth Sport Trust, *429*

List of Contributors

John Allen
University of New
  Hampshire, Plymouth,
  United States of America
Skiing

Julie Anderson
De Montfort University,
  Leicester
Disability Sports
Skating – Figure
Skating – Speed
Stoke Mandeville
Technology

John Bale
University of Keele
Geography

Michaela Baxendale
British Horse Society
National Equestrian Centre

Mrs G. Benyon
The Foundation for Sport
  and the Arts
*Foundation for Sport and the
  Arts*

Toby Beardsall
U.K. Sailing Academy
U.K. Sailing Academy, Cowes

Peter Bilsborough
University of Stirling
Channel Swimming
Swimming
Water Polo

Gherardo Bonini
Historical Archives of
  European Communities,
  Florence, Italy
Corinthians
Cycling
Diving
Weightlifting

Dr Bernard F. Booth
Visiting Professor, C.A.R.E.,
  University of East Anglia,
  Norwich
Grasmere Sports

Ian Buchanan
Burgh-next-Aylsham,
  Norfolk
British Olympic Association

John Burnett
National Museum of
  Scotland
Archery
Bowls (Indoor and Outdoor)
Curling
Motor Racing

Peter M. B. Cahusac
University of Stirling
Fives
Real Tennis
Squash

Nigel Cameron
University College London
Grass Track Racing

Tim Chandler
Kent State University, Ohio,
  United States of America
Cambridge University
*Education – Public School
  Sport*

Patrick Chaplin
Malden, Essex
Darts

Elinor Clarke
Golf

John H. Clegg
Honorary Secretary, British
  Association of Sport and
  Exercise Medicine
*British Association of Sport
  and Exercise Medicine*

Tony Collins
De Montfort University,
  Leicester
Headingley Sports Ground
Odsal Stadium
Rugby League
World Cup Rugby League

Eugene Connolly
University of Edinburgh
Hockey (Field)

Richard William Cox
UMIST, Manchester
Basketball
Brands Hatch
British Society of Sports
  History
Canoeing
Central Council of Physical
  Recreation
Holme Pierrepont
Knur and Spell
Liverpool Gymnasium
Motor Boat Racing
National Lottery
Orienteering
Sailing
Stock-car Racing
Target Shooting
Water-skiing

Jennifer Crabb
Seattle, United States of
  America
Sports Announcing and
  Commentating

Garry Crawford
University of Salford
Ice Hockey

John Crawford
Perth, Scotland
Admiral's Cup
Fastnet Race
Hickstead
Royal International Horse
  Show

Scott Crawford
Eastern Illinois University,
  United States of America
Admiral's Cup
Commonwealth Games:
  London, 1934
Commonwealth Games:
  Cardiff, 1958
Curling
Eventing
Fastnet Race
Films
Gridiron Football
Hickstead
Isle of Man T.T. Races
Manx Grand Prix
Museums and Halls of Fame –
  Wimbledon Lawn Tennis
  Museum
Parachuting
Pigeon Racing
Royal International Horse
  Show
Silverstone
Snooker
Triple Crown
Twickenham
World Cup Rugby Union

Mike Cronin
De Montfort University,
  Leicester
Bobsleigh
Gaelic Football
Nationalism
Rock Climbing

Sheila Cutler
Reigate, Surrey
Dartford College

Brian Davies
Royal Navy Sports Control
  Board

Elsa Davies
The National Playing Fields
  Association
National Playing Fields
  Association

Kevin Dicks
Welsh Handball Association
Welsh Handball

Steve Dobson
University of Hull
Economics of Sport

Chris Dodd
River and Rowing Museum,
  Henley-on-Thames
Doggett's Coat and Badge
Henley Royal Regatta
Museums and Halls of Fame –
  River and Rowing Musuem
Rowing
University Boat Race

Lynne Duval
Staffordshire University,
  Stoke-on-Trent
Athletics – Indoor Athletics
Fell Running
Marathon Racing
Road Running

Alun Evans
De Montfort University,
  Leicester
British Universities Sports
  Association
Plas Menai
Plas Y Brenin

Nicky Fossey
University of Bath
Gender
Netball

Graham Fraser
Stirling
Speedway

Ann Furtado
Oxford
Cycling
Mountain Biking

Frank Galligan
Droitwich, Worcestershire
Army Physical Training Corps
Army Sport Control Board
Badminton
Gymnastics
Rhythmic Gymnastics
Sports Acrobatics
Trampolining

Edward Gillespie
The Steeplechase Co.
  (Cheltenham) Ltd
Museums and Halls of Fame –
  Cheltenham Hall of Fame

Heiner Gillmeister
University of Bonn, Germany
Lawn Tennis
Wightman Cup
Wimbledon

Steve Greenfield
University of Westminster
Game Laws
Law
Law – Overseas Players
Law – Restraint of Trade
Test Matches
Unions and Strikes

Gerald Gurney
Colchester, Essex
Table Tennis

Mike Haggerty
Clydebank
Strathclyde Water Park

Sally Hall
Sport England
Sports Council (now Sport
  England)

John Harding
Hornsey
Professional Footballers'
  Association

Lew Hardy
University College of Wales,
  Bangor
Psychology

Mark Hathaway
Kellogg College, Oxford
Goodwood
Oxford University
Punting
Sporting Art

Murray Hedgcock
London
Australian Rules Football

Andrew Hignell
Wells, Somerset
Cardiff Arms Park
Eton Versus Harrow
Gillette Cup
Sophia Gardens
World Cup Cricket

Jeff Hill
Trent University, Nottingham
Class
Museums and Halls of Fame –
  Wembley Experience
Wembley Stadium

Richard Holt
De Montfort University,
  Leicester
Amateurism and
  Professionalism
Sporting Heroes

Adam Hornbuckle
Olympic Games – London
  1908
Olympic Games – London
  1948

Dave Hudson
De Montfort University,
  Leicester
Marketing

Lorna Jackson
University of Edinburgh
Dunfermline College
Education – Commissions and
  Reports
Education – Teacher Training
Jordanhill College
Murrayfield

Trevor James
Lichfield, Staffordshire
Athletics – Track and Field
Cross-country Running
Horse of the Year Show
Lilleshall
London Marathon
London Polytechnic
R.A.F. Cosford
Royal Patronage
Services Sport
Showjumping
Triathlon
Tug Of War

Grant Jarvie
University of Stirling
Community, Civic Pride and
  Sport
Globalization
Highland Games
Racism and Ethnicity
Rugby Union
Sociology of Sport

xxvii

Charles Jenkins
University of Birmingham
Birmingham Athletic Institute
Wolfenden Report

John Jenkins
Aberystwyth
Calcutta Cup

Martin Johnes
St Martin's College, Lancaster
Advertising
Commercialism
Sports Industry

Sam Johnstone
University of Liverpool
Disasters
F.A. Cup
League Cup
Spectators, Fans and Crowd
Disorder – Record Crowds

Rob Jones
Loughborough University of
Technology
Loughborough University

Joyce Kay
Edinburgh
Cheltenham
Media – Sports Personality of
the Year
Music
Politics and Government – The
Suffragette Movement and
Sport
Sports Sponsorship

Arnd Krüger
Universitaet Göettingen,
Germany
Gay Sport

Daniel Laurent
Université de Bretagne-Sud,
Lorient, France
Hare Hunting and Coursing

Marigold Lawton
The British Sporting Art
Trust
British Sporting Art Trust

Peter Lewis
The British Golf Museum
Golf
Museums and Halls of Fame –
British Golf Museum
Open Championship
Ryder Cup
St Andrews

Robert Lewis
Rossendale, Lancashire
Disasters
Old Trafford Football Stadium
Spectators, Fans and Crowd
Disorder
Spectators, Fans and Crowd
Disorder – Hampden Park
Riot 1909

Malcolm Lorimer
Sale, Manchester
Old Trafford Cricket Ground

John Lowerson
University of Sussex
Angling
Stoolball

John Lyle
University of Northumbria
Volleyball

Eric Macintyre
Loughborough College
Badminton House

Callum Mackenzie
University of Strathclyde
Waterloo Cup

Hugh Dan MacLennan
University of Stirling
Hurling
Shinty

Graham McMillan
University of Central
Lancashire
Media – Radio 5

Mike McNamee
Cheltenham and Gloucester
College of Higher
Education
Ethics

John Martin
De Montfort University,
Leicester
British Association for Shooting
and Conservation
Countryside Alliance
Deer Stalking
Field Sports
Game Shooting
Hare Hunting and Coursing
League Against Cruel Sports
Wild Pigeon Shooting
Wildfowling

Tony Mason
De Montfort University,
Leicester
Association Football
Media – Athletic News
Media – Sporting Chronicle
Media – Sporting Life
Media – Sportsman

Gavin Mellor
Liverpool Hope University
  College
Benefit
Fair Play
Hat Trick
Roses Matches

Ian Moir
University of Birmingham
Birmingham University

Kevin Moore
The Football Museum,
  Preston
Museums and Halls of Fame –
  The Football Musuem,
  Preston

Roger Munting
University of East Anglia,
  Norwich
Aintree
Gambling
Horse-racing – National Hunt

Donna Musgrove
University of Edinburgh
Kick Boxing

Rex Nash
University of Liverpool
Disasters
Media – Fanzines
Politics and Government
Taylor Reports

The National Coaching
Foundation
National Coaching Foundation

Ged O'Brien
Scottish Football Association
  Museum
Museums and Halls of Fame –
  Scottish Football Association
  Museum

Guy Osborn
University of Westminster
Game Laws
Law
Law – Overseas Players
Law – Restraint of Trade
Test Matches
Unions and Strikes

Geoffrey Page
National Water Sports Centre
Holme Pierrepont

Andrew Parr
Broadhaven, Dyfed
Landyachting

Benny Peiser
Liverpool John Moores
  University
Religion

Kyle Phillpots
P.G.A. National Training
  Academy
British Association of Sport
  and Exercise Sciences
Carnegie College
Head to Head
Mascots
Offside

Ray Physick
De Montfort University,
  Leicester
Aikido
Basketball
Central Council of Physical
  Recreation
Cyclo-cross
Fencing
Fox-hunting
Gliding Sports
Handball
Judo
Karate
Kung Fu
Motorcycle Racing
Roller Hockey
Roller-skating
Rounders
Scrambling
Showjumping
Softball
Sports Acrobatics
Stock-car Racing
Surfing
Windsurfing

Brian Pluckrose
National Water Sports Centre
Bisham Abbey

Martin Polley
King Alfred's College,
  Winchester
Croquet
Greyhound Racing
Polo

Nigel Quincey
R.A.F. Sports Board
R.A.F. Sports Board

Peter Radford
Brunel University
Boxing
Pugilism

Tom Reilly
Liverpool John Moores
  University
Sports Science

Tony Rennick
Boston, Lincolnshire
Children
Coaching
Costume and Clothing
Derby Matches
Films
Hampden Park
Land and Water Speed Records
Milk Race
Muscular Christianity
Ritual and Superstition
Sporting Eccentrics

Huw Richards
London
Journalism

Norman Rosser
University of Stirling
Rackets

Joachim Ruhl
Deutche Sporthochschule
  Köln, Germany
Cotswold Games
Liverpool Olympics
Morpeth Olympic Games
Much Wenlock Games
Turnhalle

Dave Russell
University of Central
  Lancashire, Preston
Disasters

Kelvin Street
Luton
Bedford College

Swantje Scharenberg
Georg-August University,
  Göttingen, Germany
Channel Swimming

Trevor Slack
De Montfort University,
  Bedford
Management

Jed Smith
The Museum of Rugby,
  Twickenham
Museums and Halls of Fame –
  Rugby Museum, Twickenham

Michel Tailland
Université de Toulon et du
  Var, France
Mountaineering

Elizabeth Taplin
De Montfort University,
  Leicester
Women's Sport Foundation

Matthew Taylor
De Montfort University,
  Leicester
Commonwealth (formerly
  Empire) Games
Commonwealth Games:
  Edinburgh, 1970
Commonwealth Games:
  Edinburgh, 1986

Hamish Telfer
St Martins University College
Pedestrianism

Dave Terry
National Union of Track
  Statisticians
Crystal Palace
White City

Jonathon Thomas
De Montfort University,
  Leicester
Olympic Games
Olympic Games – Olympic
  Bids

David Thoms
Kenilworth, Warwickshire
Brooklands Circuit
Donington Park
Hill Climbing (Motor Car)
Oulton Park
Rallying
Sprinting (Motor Car)

John Tolson
De Montfort University,
  Leicester
Ascot
Chester Roodee
Epsom
Horse-racing – Flat-racing
Museums and Halls of Fame –
  National Horseracing
  Musuem, Newmarket
Newmarket

Neil Tranter
University of Stirling
Quoits

Michael Tripp
De Montfort University,
  Leicester
Wrestling

Wray Vamplew
De Montfort University
  Leicester
Alcohol
Belfry (The)
Classics (The)
Disasters
Drugs
Grand National
History
Horse-racing – The American
  Invasion
Horse-racing – Breeding
Horse-racing – Flat-racing
Horse-racing – Governance
  and Administration
Horse-racing – Jockeys
Horse-racing – Terminology
Language
Memorable Events – Death of
  Tommy Simpson
Memorable Events – Frankie
  Dettori's Seven
Memorable Events – Fred
  Archer's Suicide
Museums and Halls of Fame
Museums and Halls of Fame –
  York Racing Museum
Myths
Player Violence
Professional Golfers' Association

Ivan Waddington
University of Leicester
Sports Medicine

Tim Walker
Sport Scotland
Glenmore Lodge

Barrie Watkins
Manchester
Wisden Cricketers' Almanack

Ida Webb
Willingdon, East Sussex
Chelsea College
Physical Education Association
  of the United Kingdom

Paul Wells
De Montfort University,
  Leicester
Media
Media – Sky Sports

Garry Whannel
London
Television

Gareth Williams
University College of Wales,
  Aberystwyth
Rugby Union

Glenys Williams
M.C.C. Library
Ashes
Law – The Kerry Packer Trial
Lord's Cricket Ground
M.C.C. (Marylebone Cricket
  Club)
Museums and Halls of Fame –
  Lord's Cricket Museum

Jack Williams
Liverpool John Moores
  University
Cricket

Jean Williams
De Montfort University,
  Leicester
Drama
Literature

Anna Windmill
The Youth Sport Trust
Youth Sport Trust

List of Abbreviations and Acronyms Used

A.A.A.	Amateur Athletic Association
A.B.A.	Amateur Boxing Association
A.C.C.C.	Advisory County Cricket Committee
A.C.U.	Auto-cycle Union
A.D.A.	Amateur Diving Association
A.E.W.H.A.	All England Women's Hockey Association
A.F.A.	Amateur Fencing Association
A.I.B.A.	Amateur International Boxing Association
A.P.T.C.	Army Physical Training Corps
A.R.A.	Amateur Rowing Association
A.S.A.	Amateur Swimming Association
A.S.C.B.	Army Sport Control Board
A.T.P.	Association of Tennis Professionals
A.V.A.	Amateur Volleyball Association
B.A.A.	British Aikido Association
B.A.E.	Badminton Association of England
B.A.F.A.	British American Football Association
B.A.G.A.	British Amateur Gymnastics Association
B.A.I.	Birmingham Athletic Institute
B.A.N.C.	British Association of National Coaches
B.A.R.R.	British Association of Road Runners
B.A.S.C.	British Association for Shooting and Conservation
B.A.S.E.S.	British Association of Sport and Exercise Sciences

B.A.W.L.A.	British Amateur Weight Lifters' Association
B.B.B.C.	British Boxing Board of Control
B.B.C.	British Broadcasting Corporation
B.C.A.F.L.	British Collegiate American Football League
B.C.C.A.	British Cyclo-Cross Association
B.C.F.	British Cycling Federation
B.C.U.	British Canoe Union
B.D.C.	British Darts Council
B.D.O.	British Darts Organisation
B.E.C.	British Equestrian Centre
B.F.R.S.	British Federation of Roller Skating
B.F.S.L.Y.C.	British Federation of Sand and Land Yacht Clubs
B.F.S.S.	British Field Sports Society
B.H.S.	British Horse Society
B.I.H.A.	British Ice Hockey Association
B.L.D.S.A.	British Long Distance Swimming Association
B.L.R.C.	British League of Racing Cyclists
B.M.C.	British Mountaineering Council
B.O.A.	British Olympic Association
B.P.A.	British Parachute Association
B.S.A.	British Surfing Association
B.S.A.F.A.	British Student American Football Association
B.S.F.	British Softball Federation
B.S.J.A.	British Show Jumping Association

B.T.F.	British Trampoline Federation	F.I.F.A.	Fédération Internationale de Football Association (International Association Football Federation)
B.U.S.A.	British Universities Sports Association		
B.U.S.F.	British Universities Sports Federation	F.I.H.	Fédération Internationale de Hockey (International Hockey Federation)
C.C.P.R.	Central Council of Physical Recreation		
C.W.F.W.	Cumberland and Westmorland freestyle wrestling	F.I.L.A.	Fédération Internationale des Luttes Amateurs (International Amateur Wrestling Federation)
C.I.P.	Commission Internationale de Parachutisme (International Parachuting Commission)		
		F.I.M.	Fédération Internationale de Motorcyclisme
C.P.S.A.	Clay Pigeon Shooting Association	F.I.M.S.	Fédération Internationale de Médicine Sportive (International Federation of Sports Medicine)
C.T.C.	Cyclists Touring Club		
C.W.F.W.	Cumberland and Westmorland freestyle wrestling		
E.A.S.M.	European Association for Sport Management	F.I.N.A.	Fédération Internationale de Natation Amateur (International Amateur Swimming Federation)
E.B.A.	English Bowling Association		
E.B.F.	English Bowling Federation		
E.K.G.B.	English Karate Governing Body	F.I.R.S.	Fédération Internationale de Roller Skating (International Roller Skating Federation)
E.L.P.G.A.	European Ladies Professional Golf Association		
E.W.C.B.	England and Wales Cricket Board	F.I.S.A.	Fédération Internationale des Sociétés d'Aviron (International Rowing Federation)
F.A.	Football Association		
F.A.I.	Fédération Aéronautique Internationale (International Aeronautical Federation)	F.I.S.S.	Federation of Inline Speed Skating
F.A.J.K.O.	Federation of All Japan Karate-do Organisations	F.I.S.U.	Fédération Internationale du Sport Universitaire (International University Sport Federation)
F.A.R.S.	Federation of Artistic Roller Skating		
F.C.	Football Club	F.I.T.	Fédération Internationale de Trampoline (International Trampoline Federation)
F.E.I.	Fédération Equestre Internationale (International Equestrian Federation)		
		F.I.V.B.	Fédération Internationale de Volleyball (International Volleyball Federation)
F.I.B.T.	Fédération Internationale de Bobsleigh et de Tobogganing (International Bobsleigh and Tobogganing Federation)		
		F.R.A.	Fell Runners Association
		F.R.S.	Federation of Roller Skating
		G.A.A.	Gaelic Athletic Association
F.I.G.	Fédération Internationale de Gymnastique (International Gymnastic Federation)	I.B.F.	International Badminton Federation
		I.B.F.	International Boxing Federation

I.B.S.A.	Inanimate Bird Shooting Association	N.O.A.	National Olympian Association
I.C.A.	International Cyclist Association	NPFA	National Playing Fields Association
I.C.C.	International Cricket Council	N.R.A.	National Rounders Association
I.C.F.	International Canoe Federation	N.R.F.U.	Northern Rugby Football Union
I.F.S.A.	International Federation of Sports Acrobatics	N.S.A.	National Skating Association
I.F.W.H.A.	International Federation of Women's Hockey Associations	N.S.C.	National Sailing Centre
		N.S.C.	National Sporting Club
		N.S.M.I.	National Sports Medicine Institute of the United Kingdom
I.L.A.M.	Institute of Leisure and Amenity Managers		
I.L.T.F.	International Lawn Tennis Federation	P.B.A.	Professional Boxers' Association
		P.E.	Physical Education
I.O.C.	International Olympic Committee	P.F.A.	Professional Footballers' Association
I.R.F.B.	International Rugby Football Board	P.G.A.	Professional Golfers' Association
		R.&A.	Royal and Ancient Golf Club
I.S.A.	Independent Supporters Associations	R.A.C.	Royal Automobile Club
		R.A.S.E.	Royal Agricultural Society of England
I.T.F.	International Tennis Federation		
I.T.T.F.	International Table Tennis Federation	R.F.L.	Rugby Football League
		R.F.U.	Rugby Football Union
I.T.V.	Independent Television	R.L.S.S.	Royal Life Saving Society
L.D.A.	Ladies Diving Association	R.O.R.C.	Royal Ocean Racing Club
L.G.U.	Ladies' Golf Union	R.R.C.	Road Runners Club
L.P.G.A.	Ladies' Professional Golf Association	S.B.A.	Scottish Bowling Association
		S.F.A.M.T.	Scottish Football Association Museum Trust
L.T.A.	Lawn Tennis Association		
M.C.C.	Marylebone Cricket Club	S.I.H.A.	Scottish Ice Hockey Association
N.A.R.A.	National Amateur Rowing Association	S.O.S.	Shropshire Olympian Society
		S.R.U.	Scottish Rugby Union
N.A.S.C.A.R.	National Association for Stock Car Auto Racing	T.C.C.B.	Test and County Cricket Board
		T.P.C.	Thames Punting Club
N.A.S.S.M.	North American Society for Sport Management	T.T.	Tourist Trophy
		U.A.U.	Universities Athletic Union
N.B.A.	National Boxing Association	U.C.I.	Union Cycliste Internationale (International Cycling Union)
N.C.A.	National Cricket Association		
N.C.F.	National Coaching Foundation		
N.C.U.	National Cycling Union	U.E.F.A.	Union des Associations Européennes de Football (European Football Associations Union)
N.D.A.	National Darts Association		
N.E.C.	National Equestrian Centre		
N.F.F.S.C.	National Federation of Football Supporters' Clubs		
N.F.L.	(American) Nation Football League	U.E.G.	Union Européenne de Gymnastique (European Gymnastics Union)

W.B.A.	World Boxing Association	W.O.S.	Wenlock Olympian Society
W.B.C.	World Boxing Council	W.R.R.A.	Women's Road Racing
W.B.O.	World Boxing Organisation		Association
W.D.F.	World Darts Federation	W.S.C.	World Series Cricket
W.I.B.F.	Women's International Boxing	W.S.F.	Womens' Sports Foundation
	Federation	W.T.A.	Women's Tennis Association
W.L.T.M.	Wimbledon Lawn Tennis	W.U.G.S.	World University Games
	Museum	Y.M.C.A.	Young Men's Christian
W.O.C.	Wenlock Olympian Class		Association
W.O.G.	Wenlock Olympian Games		

A

Admiral's Cup

The Admiral's Cup yacht race series was first held in 1957 off Cowes, Isle of Wight. Organized by the Royal Ocean Racing Club (R.O.R.C.), the competition was devised by five club members. The objective was to encourage international sailors to race against British yachts in British waters. Held every two years, the competition culminates with the awarding of a silver gilt trophy named after Sir Myles Wyatt, who was Admiral of R.O.R.C. at that time.

While the inaugural series (1957) attracted only two yachts, by the late 1970s the Admiral's Cup had become established as one of the world's premier sailing competitions. For example, in 1979, fifty-seven yachts from nineteen countries participated. One of the significant reasons behind the competition's increasing recognition and appreciation by British audiences was the pivotal role played by Edward Heath. In 1969, his yacht, *Morning Cloud*, won the Sydney to Hobart Race with Heath at the helm. As a result, Heath skippered both *Morning Cloud* and the British team at the 1971 Admiral's Cup. At the time he was also a Member of Parliament, leader of the Conservative Party, and British Prime Minister.

The Admiral's Cup comprises a series of eight races, with each participating country allowed a maximum of three yachts. The races include one in the Solent, two races over an Olympic-type course in Christchurch Bay, a 220-mile Channel Race, a long inshore race, and the legendary, gruelling 605-mile Fastnet race, amongst others.

The Complete Book of Sailing notes that the Admiral's Cup was the world's first inshore/offshore event and 'since its inception many other yacht racing organizations around the world have copied its successful formula'. During the 1980s, helped by television coverage of the America's Cup, the Admiral's Cup found itself 'grabbing prime-time coverage on television world wide'.

Sponsorship has been critical to the success, and survival, of the Admiral's Cup. Originally, the tobacco company, Dunhill, was a primary supporter. In recent years, major sponsorship support has come from French champagne producers, G. H. Mumm. Indeed, Timothy Jeffery, the yachting historian, asserts that the Admiral's Cup is synonymous with Mumm champagne.

References:

Bond, B., Clark, J., Grant, B., Morgan, A. and Pelly, D., *The Complete Book of Sailing* (London: Hamlyn Publishing, 1990), pp. 176-177.

Further reading:

Jeffery, T., *The Champagne Mumm Admiral's Cup - The Official History* (London: Bloomsbury Publishing, 1994), pp. 13-15.

Websites:

Champagne Mumm Admiral's Cup – http://mummadmiralscup.org/
Royal Ocean Racing Club – http://www.rorc.org/

See also:
Sailing

-John Crawford/Scott Crawford

Advertising

Advertising is the publicizing of goods with a view to increasing sales. In sport this can be split into two broad categories: the advertising of sports equipment and the use of sporting stars and events to sell non-sporting commodities. Today, sport is awash with advertising, from the product logos on team-shirts to the hoardings at and around stadiums. It is the most visible sign of sport's commercialization.

The relationship goes back to the late 19th century when sportsmen were used on cigarette cards as a way of selling the brand. This quickly diversified with, for example, W. G. Grace endorsing a variety of products from cricket equipment to mustard. It was in the inter-war years that advertisers began to exploit more fully the lucrative potential of sport. By 1934, the F.A. Cup finalists were promoting trousers, shoe-polish and Shredded Wheat. Not all sports were able to take advantage of these new opportunities. Snooker, for instance, suffered from a seedy reputation and found it difficult to attract endorsements. However, for the stars of the more popular spectator sports, endorsement provided a lucrative sideline which went someway to make up for economic disadvantages such as short careers and maximum wages.

It was the large audiences generated by the increasing role of television in sport that developed sport's relationship with advertising and led to its other manifestation, sponsorship. The lure of televised football was actually used in the advertising of television sets themselves during the 1950s and satellite dishes in the 1990s. By the 1970s, advertising's increased interest in televised sport had become a way for the stars of amateur sports such as athletics or Rugby Union to earn money more openly from their talents, and this accelerated the drive towards professionalism in these two sports. Advertising non-sporting commodities on television is especially important for the most famous sports stars. It offers income and continued fame after retirement and has helped to create public personalities for stars such as Frank Bruno, shifting their careers away from sport and towards the wider entertainment sector.

Today, sports clothing is used as much for fashion as its intended purpose. However, sporting stars are still used in the advertising of such goods in an attempt to associate the success of the individual with the product he or she is endorsing. Similarly, playing equipment is rarely advertised without the endorsement of a famous sportsperson. Given the reputation of certain stars for misbehaviour and with image being all-important in marketing, the choice of sportsperson for an advertising campaign is a matter of careful decision.

Sport has been particularly important for tobacco products because of the ban on the latter advertising on television. Advertising at sporting events has offered tobacco manufacturers access to markets otherwise usually denied to them. Alcoholic products too extensively use sport to advertise because of the access it provides to young, male markets. The contradiction between sport's healthy message and the unhealthy connotations of some products associated with sport through advertising has caused some concern. The European Union has directed that all tobacco advertising should cease in the hope of reducing the numbers who smoke. Consequently, it has banned all tobacco sponsorship in sport from July 30th, 2003, with the exception of specified 'global events' that have until 2006. Formula One motor racing is one such global event and was granted the European-wide extension after controversial political pressure in the United Kingdom.

References:

Holt, R., *Sport and the British: a Modern History* (Oxford: Oxford University Press, 1990).

Mason, T., *Sport in Britain* (London: Faber & Faber, 1988).

2

Mason, T. (ed.), *Sport in Britain: a Social History* (Cambridge: Cambridge University Press, 1989).

Polley, M., *Moving the Goalposts: a History of Sport and Society Since 1945* (London: Routledge, 1998).

Further reading:

Mason, T., *Only a Game?* (Cambridge: Cambridge University Press, 1993).

The resources of the History of Advertising Trust, Gloucester Docks

See also:

Commercialism; Sports Sponsorship

-Martin Johnes

Aikido

Aikido, a self-defence martial art that resembles ju-jitsu and judo, probably originates from *c.* 14th-century Japan. Its aim is to subdue an opponent, not injure, maim or kill, and it places great emphasis upon mental preparation as well as physical prowess.

Modern Aikido was founded by Morihei Ueshiba in 1942, and is based on the ethic of self-defence, as Ueshiba believed that the fundamental principle of the martial arts was universal love not combat. Indeed, the very name 'Aikido' means 'the way of harmony'. Aikido's primary objective is to unify the mind and body with the mysterious force *ki*.

Aikido's sporting form, which is also known as Tomiki Aikido, was developed by Tomiki Kenji, who gave the sport its name. Bouts take the form of mock fighting between two opponents, a defender and an attacker. The two main sporting bouts are called *tanto randor* and *randori ryoghi*. The former involves an attacker with a rubber knife, who aims to score points by striking the defender on the chest with the point of the knife. The latter is an unarmed contest based on free fighting. Both bouts concentrate on defensive techniques, which are the essence of Aikido. Throughout the bouts, in common with all martial arts, contestants are expected to be courteous and respectful to their opponent. These values underpin the spirit of Aikido.

The British Aikido Association (B.A.A.) was formed in 1966 to promote and maintain the ethical and technical standards of Aikido in Britain. Aikido clubs approved by the B.A.A. can be found all over the United Kingdom and, through the auspices of the B.A.A., top-class international instructors are regularly brought to Britain to further promote and develop the sport. Recognized by Sport England, the Association also organizes local, national and international competitions – in 1991, for example, the B.A.A. hosted the biannual international tournament. On this occasion, British teams came first, beating Japan and sixteen other national teams.

References:

The British Aikido Association website – http://www.aikido-baa.org.uk/

Lewis, P., *The Martial Arts: Origins, Philosophy, Practice* (London: Prion Books, 1996).

Webster's Sports Dictionary (Springfield, Massachusetts: Merriam, 1976).

Websites:

The British Aikido Association – http://www.aikido-baa.org.uk/

-Ray Physick

Aintree

Aintree racecourse, near Liverpool, is world famous as the home of the Grand National. The first course at Aintree was set out in 1829 by William Lynn, a publican, on land rented from the Earl of Sefton. Apart from war years, races have been held continuously ever since, including, until 1975, flat-racing. In 1949, Mrs Mirabel Topham (whose family had been associated with Aintree since 1857) bought the racecourse but some years later ran into financial difficulty, threatening its future. In an attempt to make more use of the land, in 1953 she opened an additional, conventional steeplechase course and a motor-racing circuit. The British Grand

Prix was run here on five occasions between 1955 and 1962. It ceased to be a grand prix circuit in 1964, though for some years enthusiasts continued to operate the track.

Mrs Topham sold the course in 1973 and, after continuing uncertainty about its future, the course was sold again, in 1983, to the Aintree Racecourse Co., a subsidiary of Racecourse Holdings Ltd, itself wholly owned by the Jockey Club. Most of the money, however, was raised by public subscription.

The course has changed over the years. It was not fully turfed until 1885 and the distinctive fences have been altered on several occasions in recent years to make them safer for the horses. It is otherwise ideal, being completely flat with an excellent racing surface. Recent improvements to facilities for spectators have added to its attractions.

References:

Court, W., *Power and Glory: the History of Grand Prix Motor Racing. Vol. 2, 1952-1973* (Wellingborough: Stephens, 1990).

King, P., *The Grand National: Anybody's Race* (London: Quartet Books, 1983).

Smyly, P., *The Encyclopaedia of Steeplechasing* (London: Hale, 1979).

Websites:

Aintree – http://www.aintree.co.uk/

See also:

Grand National

-Roger Munting

Alcohol

It is a paradox that sport, generally considered as health promoting, is also closely associated in Britain with the alcohol industry, not normally regarded in the same light. Undoubtedly the alcohol industry has brought benefits to British sport: at the élite level via major sponsorships of events, teams and leagues; and lower down the sporting pyramid through assistance to the construction of club premises and the support of junior coaching. At the same time, however, there have been less positive aspects to the relationship through crowd disturbance from 'lager louts', the promotion of drinking to excess, and the risk of alcoholism to sportspersons and others.

The relationship is a long-standing one. Historically, the public house played an important role by organizing sporting events, providing a meeting place for sports teams (often sponsoring them), and offering a results service. During the 19th century, attempts to reform sport and render it less disreputable forced the drinks trade to realign itself with new forms of 'respectable' sport. Darts, snooker and lawn bowls, among other public house sporting activities, replaced brutal animal and human blood sports as an attraction to a drinking clientele. As team sports emerged among the working class, sponsorship came from landlords and hoteliers and, at the élite level, as sports clubs adopted limited liability company status, those in the drinks trade came to the fore as shareholders and directors. In the 20th century, the alcohol sector has promoted its wares through sport via media advertising; promotion at the event itself on perimeter boards, shirt fronts and the actual playing area; and in the naming of leagues, races and other competitions. However, in associating itself with sport, the alcohol industry has exhibited selectivity: whereas 15-20 per cent of racing sponsorship is alcohol-related, little such involvement has featured in women's hockey and netball. Alcohol-related income has been important to many sports and clubs. In the late 19th century, horse-racing relied on beer booth rents for significant contributions to the race fund and in the 1890s, Leicestershire County Cricket Club claimed that 'it was impossible to carry on a cricket ground without an hotel'. Today the bar is an integral feature of most clubhouses and has often been provided via a tied agreement with a particular brewery, often in return for a loan.

Alcohol consumption and watching sport are two important social pastimes that have often come together, though over time the nexus has been influenced by attempts to curb the excesses associated with the package of alcohol, violence and gambling, the unholy trinity allied to sport. There is a class aspect to this: the hip-flask and stirrup cup appear to have been more acceptable than crates of ale. Although some sports crowds, notably modern horse-racing, have developed a culture in which alcohol is important without necessarily leading to disorderly conduct, historically in football, Rugby League and 19th-century racing, alcohol was often a trigger mechanism to spectator disturbances.

Today it is recognized that alcohol depresses the nervous system, impairs both motor ability and judgement, reduces endurance, and, as a diuretic, can cause dehydration, none of which are conducive to sports performance. In the past, however, the drinking of alcohol, particularly ales and porters, was positively encouraged as a perceived aid to strength and stamina. In the 1880s, adverts professing the fitness-aiding qualities of alcohol were common and even in the interwar years, Bass advertised its beers as health and fitness promoting. As this suggests, the use of alcohol by sports participants was licit in the 19th and early 20th centuries: today this is less so. The U.K. Sports Council has legislated against the use of alcohol as a performance-enhancing drug in those areas where there is an advantage to be gained from its use as an anti-anxiety drug, an isometric muscular strengthener, and as an aid to improving steadiness in 'aiming' sports. Other bodies, notably the Jockey Club, are more concerned with the deleterious effects of drink on sportspersons, including the fact that alcohol-affected activity can have dangerous effects on other participants. What cannot be determined is the extent to which performance improvement has come indirectly through the use of drinking sessions to bond team members and create team spirit.

Sportspersons do not turn to alcohol solely for reasons of performance enhancement. Like other members of society they use it for relaxation, to relieve stress, and for convivial recreational purposes. Also like other members of society, sportspersons can abuse alcohol. Historically there was a high rate of alcoholism amongst élite jockeys. County cricket committees constantly complained about fans buying drinks for their players, and several football clubs have disciplined their players for drunkenness. Others, like West Ham United F.C., held wages in trust for those professionals deemed to have a drinking problem. Some of this alcohol abuse arose for sport-specific reasons such as the stress of an occupation dominated by insecurity and the free time available for drinking in an occupation where relatively little time was needed for training and playing. The relaxation of wage restrictions in professional sport and the consequent increased affluence among sportsmen may also have influenced their consumption of alcohol, though this may have been modified as fitness has assumed growing importance and made alcohol less compatible with the needs of élite sport. This may be less true of those sports played in an alcohol-friendly environment, such as darts and snooker.

There have been many attempts to sever the link between sport and alcohol, sometimes individually as when Sheffield Wednesday's chairman banned his players from holding public house tenancies, and at other times more collectively via the temperance movement opposed to any sporting link with alcohol, local authorities fearful of crowd disturbances, and sports associations anxious about the public image of their sport. A distinction should also be drawn between opposition from within the sport by clubs, their members, and governing bodies such as the Northern Union's proscription of bar work as a recognized occupation under their 'working clause' eligibility to play, and opposition which came externally from medical authorities, local councils, temperance advocates and the police.

References:

Stewart, D., *Alcohol: the Ethical Dilemma*, MA Dissertation, University of Warwick, 1997.

Vamplew, W., *Pay Up and Play the Game: Professional Sport in Britain* (Cambridge: Cambridge University Press, 1988).

Further reading:

Marsh, P. and Fox Kibby, K., *Drinking and Public Disorder* (Oxford: Portman, 1993).

Stainback, J., *Alcohol and Sport* (Champaign, Illinois: Human Kinetics, 1998).

See also:

Class; Commercialism; Sports Sponsorship

-Wray Vamplew

Amateurism and Professionalism

These two interdependent terms have determined much of the distinctive character of modern British sport. Amateurism involved not only the prohibition of payment but also the banning of gambling, the creation of disciplinary codes, the setting up of organizing bodies and the encouragement of 'sportsmanship' and 'fair play'. Professionalism was subsequently defined as anything that contravened either the rules or the ethos of amateurism. Amateurism was a fusion of that which was perceived as the best of the old aristocratic sporting code of honour with a new middle-class moral preoccupation with exertion for its own sake – hence the term 'amateur', meaning a 'lover' of sport rather than a paid performer. For all that, amateur enthusiasts, especially influential Victorian headmasters, saw the practical value of sport as training for a life of strenuous business or imperial competition, in keeping with the social Darwinian ideas of racial vigour and national rivalry which spread rapidly in the late 19th century.

New amateur bodies emerged from the 1860s to the 1880s to organize new sports in the four constituent nations of the United Kingdom. Voluntary association independent of state control or subsidy was the preferred Victorian form of social action, in sport as in other spheres. This took the form of setting up bodies such as the Football Association (F.A.) in 1863, the Rugby Football Union (R.F.U.) in 1871 and the Amateur Athletic Association (A.A.A.) in 1880 to re-define and supervise team ball games adapted to the needs of the greatly expanded Victorian middle classes, who sent their sons to be privately educated and to play with boys from older landed families. These new amateur bodies, which soon included swimming, hockey and tennis amongst other sports, did not formally exclude manual workers as the Amateur Rowing Association did. This was, after all, the age of political democracy and free competition. On the other hand, they did not promote contact between social classes and often left clubs free to draw up their own fixture lists. Working men did not tend to share the sporting idealism of the middle classes, especially their distaste for payment, although there were plenty of examples of manual workers making their mark in amateur sports like athletics. The biggest challenge to amateurism came from the sudden upsurge of popular interest in football and Rugby, which soon led to some northern industrial-based clubs charging spectators and paying players. The F.A., run by Charles Alcock, the son of a Sunderland shipowner who had been sent to Harrow and who became secretary of Surrey County Cricket Club, favoured a kind of internal segregation by setting up the Football League (1888), which would control the professional game but leave disciplinary control in the hands of the amateurs of the F.A. As Rugby grew in popularity, especially in Yorkshire, gate money supported the recruitment of the best players and led to a split between the predominantly working-class northern clubs and the more southern public school sides over the issue of compensation for loss of wages ('broken time'). This caused the split of 1895 between the R.F.U. and the Northern Union, which eventually became the Rugby League in 1923.

6

Professionalism embraced both the continuity of older practices in racing, cricket, golf and pugilism (boxing) and the new league structures in football and Rugby. The old tradition of professional athletics (pedestrianism) was marginalized by the A.A.A. as amateur influence grew, reinforced by the success of the Olympic Games, which had been partly inspired by a French nobleman's admiration for public school sport. Walter George, the great runner of the early years of the A.A.A., found the new constraints unbearable and turned professional but those who came after broadly kept to the amateur path, earning fame instead of money. This was fine for the middle-class university man such as Harold Abrahams or Roger Bannister, but far more difficult for a railwayman and veteran of the trenches like Albert Hill, who won two track gold medals at Antwerp in 1920 and later emigrated to Canada.

In cricket, the 'Gentlemen' and 'Players' distinction provided for separate changing rooms and hotels, placed the initials of the professional 'player' after his name and prevented a 'player' from captaining his county or his country. The abandonment of this social division between cricketers did not come until the early 1960s, when there was a shortage of amateurs of sufficient ability and a general decline in the deference paid to the amateur 'gentleman'. In 1961, professional footballers, using the threat of strike action, finally overturned the imposition of the 'maximum wage', which had arbitrarily determined their earnings at a level slightly above a skilled manual rate since the turn of the century. The amateur F.A. had kept market forces out of football, partly to protect smaller clubs and partly to keep professionals as 'obedient servants'. This state of affairs was even more firmly entrenched in Rugby League, which was run by northern businessmen who paid part-time wages based on results.

The position of the professional in sport has been transformed since the 1960s. Television and tabloid journalism have turned the professional into a highly marketable commodity. High-level sport is exceptionally attractive to sponsors and advertisers, who have steadily invested more and more in spectator sport. The 1960s saw top footballers begin to earn much higher incomes – £100 a week for the best, which was five times more than the previous maximum. This was nothing, however, compared to what was to come through league, club and shirt sponsorship, culminating in the advent of satellite television in the 1990s, revolutionizing sport. Athletics is now fully professional and so is Rugby Union. The vast sums available through Sky Sport's satellite television coverage have turned Rugby League into a summer sport and introduced the Premier League into football, permitting top professionals to earn vast sums. As bookmakers spread their activities right across sport, the contemporary professional in some ways resembles the jockeys and pugilists of old more closely than the 'honest pro' who worked for fixed wages in the heyday of British amateur sport. Amateur has come to mean 'unprofessional' and amateurism has been finally laid to rest.

References:

Holt, R., *Sport and the British: a Modern History* (Oxford: Oxford University Press, 1990).

McIntosh, P., *Fair Play: Ethics in Sport and Education* (London: Heinemann, 1980).

Mason, T., *Association Football and English Society, 1863-1915* (Brighton: Harvester, 1980).

Tranter, N., *Sport, Economy and Society in Britain 1750-1914* (Cambridge: Cambridge University Press, 1998).

Vamplew, W., *Pay Up and Play the Game: Professional Sport in Britain* (Cambridge: Cambridge University Press, 1988).

See also:

Class

-Richard Holt

American Football (*see* Grid-iron Football)

Angling

Fishing with a rod and line, hence the 'angle', rather than a net has been practised in Britain since the late Middle Ages. The earliest writing on the subject is ascribed, conventionally, to Dame Juliana Berners' *The Treatyse of Fysshynge Wyth an Angle* of 1496 and the classical work is *The Compleat Angler*, first published by Izaak Walton (1593-1683) in 1653. Many of its earliest practitioners practised fishing for food and indeed some of the catch in game and sea fishing is still eaten, but the majority of anglers now fish for recreation in a symbolic contest with nature where the prey is often anthropomorphized. The sport grew rapidly in Victorian Britain after railway building opened up access to waters away from industrial pollution for townspeople to escape either for short breaks or more distant holidays; rural Britain offered a wide range of sites for anglers whose sport was often divided on class lines, with the gentry and middle classes dominating game and sea fishing.

The advent of mass car ownership in the 1960s gave a further boost to the sport, and changes in the disposable wealth of skilled workers in particular allowed much wider access to all its various branches. Participation peaked in around 1980, with some 3.7 million people taking part; with the subsequent recession and competition from a growing variety of leisure opportunities, that figure fell by about 18 per cent. At the end of the 20th century, some 2.3 million follow coarse fishing, 0.8 million game fishing and 1.1 million sea fishing, although some practise more than one discipline; only one angler in eight is a woman, however. Since the Second World War, all branches of the sport have been affected by rapid technological changes. Wood and bamboo as rod materials have given way to steel, fibreglass and carbon fibre; gut and silk lines have been replaced by nylon; and the range of bait and lures has expanded hugely. This has made angling a major industry in itself – it is estimated that annual expenditure on the sport is about £3.5 billion.

Each branch has its own central federations and competitive networks, often sponsored by large multinationals and followed by full-time and semi-professional anglers, but the vast majority fish for pleasure. Their angling is bolstered by a growing range of books, magazines, television programmes and instructional videos. Much of the sport, particularly the holding of freshwater fishing rights, is managed by clubs and associations, but many of their members join only to gain access to fishing. Record fish for each species are recognized by the British Record (Rod Caught) Fish Committee.

Coarse Fishing

The quarry of course fishing comprises all those freshwater fish not pursued by game anglers. With rare exceptions, coarse fishing has historically been regarded as a socially inferior sport, if not a less challenging one. Coarse fish were farmed and netted in ponds during the Middle Ages as part of the diets of landowners, while working-class river anglers continued to eat their catch well into the 19th century. This gave way, however, to a 'catch and return' convention, with rare exceptions when large fish were stuffed and mounted as trophies.

The Victorian years saw a massive expansion in the number of anglers, who used the sport as an escape from urban work and pollution and often organized themselves into clubs and federations in order to negotiate river rights and lower transport costs, for example by chartering 'anglers' special' trains. These often carried 3,000 or more men and their families for a day's fishing 90 miles away from their homes and powerful bodies such as the Sheffield Anglers' Association became major examples of working and lower-middle class leisure associations. To match local water conditions, a number of distinctly regional angling styles evolved, using different rods, tactics and bait – these included the 'Thames', the 'Sheffield', the 'Nottingham-Trent' and the 'Clydeside'. A key part of this growth was the angling match, often organized by publicans or clubs, in which the winners with the largest weight of fish received prizes in kind. Slowly these gave way to cash prizes, which led to many complaints that it would encourage bad sportsmanship. This pattern survived the decline of industries and the railways and emerged into a complex network of regional, national and international tournaments, the most prestigious of which in England are under the aegis of the National Federation of Anglers, founded in 1903; Wales and Scotland have their own, similar structures. Many matches are now sponsored by tobacco firms, breweries and tackle manufacturers and dealers, since 'stars' such as Ivan Marks and Bob Nudd, who won his fourth world championship in 1999, can design and endorse products with high sales returns. The levels of reward have encouraged the emergence of a small group of wholly professional and semi-professional match anglers but the rewards from sponsorship are significantly smaller than in higher-profile sports.

The targets of both match and pleasure anglers were the small 'silver' fish of river and occasional flooded gravel pit but this changed significantly after 1980 when the predominantly still-water carp became the most favoured quarry. This shift can be ascribed to the influence of one man, Richard Walker (1918-1985), an engineer who brought 'scientific method' to 'specimen hunting'; he caught the then record carp (44 pounds – 20 kilos) in 1952, using the first electric bite indicator. Eventually, an enormous demand for still-water carp fishing emerged and many property developers, leisure entrepreneurs and farmers, seeking to diversify, opened up artificial lakes all over the country, stocked with increasingly heavy specially-bred fish. The irony was that Walker's solitary skills became a mass activity,

and many of these waters now organize carp-fishing matches. Similarly, pike, much sought by specimen hunters aiming to catch those weighing over 20 pounds (9 kilos), are now often fished for competitively.

Much of the shift in emphasis has been accompanied by the use of materials imported from the aerospace industry, including carbon fibre rods, and alloys and polymers for other tackle. Perhaps the most significant influence has been the reintroduction of fishing poles, tied directly to lines, as used before the invention of reels in the 17th century. These had remained popular in Europe but re-emerged in Britain in the 1980s when new materials made greater lengths – up to 50 feet (15 metres) – possible. The changes have made the relative costs of the sport significantly higher, which may account for its partial decline. Recruiting the young has become difficult and women are still largely segregated. The days of whole families accompanying father to the river-bank are long gone.

Game Fishing

Game fishing is traditionally the peak of angling, both socially and economically. The quarry – salmon, sea trout, trout and grayling – thrive only in clean waters, often at a premium during industrial pollution. Although artificial man-made spinners are occasionally used, the preferred, often mandatory method is to fish using artificial flies, which may bear little resemblance to real ones. Early fly-fishers occasionally used real flies, but the construction of artificials using hair, wool, indeed anything to hand, was well developed by the late Middle Ages. Unlike the use of netting, such methods far from guaranteed success, hence the sense of sporting uncertainty. Salmon and sea trout have always been limited in their distribution and trout have thrived most in the chalk streams of southern England as well as northern streams and Scottish lochs and Welsh waters. Industrialization meant that these were usually annexed by the urban upper-middle classes, able to buy up fishing rights by forming syndicates. Only in some parts of Scotland was game fishing more 'democratic'.

Social exclusivity was accompanied by a fierce ethical and regional debate over fly-fishing methods. Northerners usually employed sunken flies, southerners the surface-floating dry fly. In the late Victorian period, arguments about this exploded into a savage debate as to which method represented 'purity'. The dry-fly camp was dominated by the irascible F. M. Halford (1844-1915), the wet-fly camp by the more reflective G. E. M. Skues (1858-1949); on the southern chalk streams it was Halford who won.

An alternative to scarce river fishing emerged in still waters, particularly the new reservoirs flooded for urban water supplies, but this was severely limited until the 1960s, when increased disposable income amongst car workers in the English Midlands combined with the creation of new reservoirs, such as Cambridgeshire's Grafham water, covering 1000 acres (400 hectares), and low-cost mass-produced tackle to make fly-fishing much less socially exclusive. In succeeding decades, farmers with surplus land opened smaller fisheries, as did enthusiasts such as Roger Daltry, the lead singer of 'The Who'. Guidance was offered by writers such as Richard Walker (see below) and Bob Church (who was active during the 1970s) through books and specialist magazines. Most of these waters were stocked from fish farms with imported breeds such as the Rainbow Trout and huge hybrid fish. Native Brown Trout are also farmed but these indigenous fish of the chalk streams remain the preferred quarry of the wealthy, who often follow a 'catch and return' policy. Competition has always existed in this branch of the sport, largely unofficially between individuals, but a regional, national and international competitive structure has emerged. The magazine *Trout Fisherman* sponsors the annual English Troutmasters' National, fished on reservoirs. Meanwhile, threats to salmon and sea-trout stocks from environmental pollution and commercial netting have reached almost crisis proportions, with significant consequences for landowning and tourist incomes in parts of Scotland, Wales and the English West Country. On still waters in particular, the traditional 'close' season, which allowed for natural breeding stocks to replenish themselves, has given way to year-round angling. These issues are monitored by the Salmon and Trout Association (founded in 1903), an English research and pressure group, and there are similar bodies in Scotland and Wales.

Sea Fishing

Sea fishing often arouses images of well-wrapped, lonely figures on all-night vigils on winter beaches. Many do fish that way, since shore fishing is very dependent on tide and season. Sea fishing as a sport emerged amongst middle-class visitors to late Victorian seaside resorts, which often formed clubs for their own inhabitants; beach piers, jetties and rocks all offered attractions. Unlike the other branches of angling, sea fishing has never required licenses and, although it has shared the same technological revolution, beach fishing has remained relatively cheap. It is now followed by many who drive to the coast throughout the year and it has largely lost its dependence on holidays. Some resorts do still sponsor matches but these are more often underwritten by magazines and tackle makers; there are regular weekly matches with £1000 in prize money throughout the country, and a national competition, sponsored by the tackle firm, Penn, is organized regionally. Overall bodies, the National Sea Anglers' Federation and Scottish Federation of Sea Anglers, act as negotiators and environmental watchdogs. The shore quarry includes all close-feeding fish – sole, cod, bass and so on, but the sport is very much affected by the impact of European-wide fishing policies.

The other main branch of sea fishing is boat fishing, both inshore (up to 20 miles or 30 kilometres) and deep-sea. Much of this takes place near rocks or the abundant number of wrecks around Britain – more recently, oil rigs have become great magnets for fish. The quarry is often general – cod, wrasse, conger and so on, but there are also specialist groups, fishing particularly for shark in western areas. For a coastal fishing industry beleaguered by decline and politics, providing transport for amateurs has proved to be a valuable source of secondary employment, although the craft used are increasingly specialist, requiring heavy investment in electronics and safety equipment – it is no coincidence that many of their owners also run the local tackle shop. Sea fishing is, perhaps, the most pan-class of all the branches of angling.

References:

Angling Times (Peterborough, weekly).

Koller, L., *The Treasury of Angling* (London: Hamlyn, 1966).

Lowerson, J., 'Brothers of the Angle: Coarse Fishing and Working-Class Culture' in J. A. Mangan (ed.), *Pleasure, Profit, Proselytism: British Culture and Sport at Home and Abroad, 1700-1914* (London: Frank Cass, 1988), p. 105-127.

Lowerson, J., 'Angling' in Tony Mason (ed.), *Sport in Britain: a Social History* (Cambridge: Cambridge University Press, 1989).

Lowerson, J., *Sport and the English Middle Classes, 1870-1914* (Manchester: Manchester University Press, 1993).

National Rivers Authority, National Angling Survey 1994 (London: HMSO, 1994).

Voss Bark, C., *A History of Flyfishing* (Ludlow: Merlin Unwin Books, 1992).

Yates, A. and Entwistle, T., *The Complete Book of Sea Fishing* (Newton Abbot: David & Charles, 1992).

Websites:

The National Federation of Anglers – http://www.fire.org.uk/nfa/

The Salmon and Trout Association – http://www.brucepub.com/sata/index.htm

The Scottish Federation of Sea Anglers – http://www.sfsa.freeserve.co.uk/

–John Lowerson

Archery

The bow is tens of thousands of years old; the English longbow made its first impact on history – and on the Scots – at the battle of Falkirk in 1298. From the 13th century, the men of England were required to practise on Sundays and holidays: bowmen had a decisive role at Crécy (1346) and later battles in the Hundred Years' War.

Archery was encouraged by many European monarchs. In England, the first Act which prohibited other sports in favour of archery practice was passed in 1363, and in Scotland in 1424. With the spread of the use of gunpowder between 1450 and 1550, archery became a leisure pursuit, though archers fought in a Scottish clan battle as late as 1664. At the same time, the bow was dying out as a hunting weapon; hunting with bow and arrow is now illegal in Britain.

An archery society, the Guild of St George, was established in 1537 in London by Henry VIII; it was similar to earlier archery guilds in the Low Countries. From it stemmed the Finsbury Archers, who last met in 1761. Its members raised money to pay for the Bragança Shield, a trophy dedicated to Catharine of Bragança, consort of Charles II, and now on loan to the Victoria and Albert Museum. In 1688, the first Kilwinning Papingo was held. Also derived from Continental practice, the aim was to dislodge a wooden parrot from the top of the Abbey tower at Kilwinning in Ayrshire, shooting from directly below. Today, a model dove is used.

For most of the 17th and 18th centuries, archery was enjoyed by only a tiny minority, though it was in this period that the oldest surviving British archery society was formed, the Company of Scottish Archers (1676), who were granted a Royal Charter by Queen Anne. Its members were drawn from the aristocracy, landed classes, and Edinburgh professional men. In 1776, the Company built Archers' Hall, which now contains the finest collection of archery trophies in Britain. On the occasion of George IV's visit to Edinburgh in 1822, the Royal Company was appointed the King's bodyguard in Scotland. Other clubs were small and selective in their membership.

The founding of the Toxophilite Society in London in 1781 was a sign of the new interest in archery; it became the Royal Toxophilite Society in 1844. The individuals behind the Tox were the antiquary, naturalist and eccentric Sir Ashton Lever (1729-1788), and the bow-maker Thomas Waring (1729-1788). The decisive power of the English longbow in battle made it a patriotic symbol, and it acquired romance with the late 18th-century growth in interest in the medieval. During this period, archery had a self-consciously antiquarian atmosphere – Roger Ascham's *Toxophilus* (1545) was republished in 1788.

The Prince of Wales (later King George IV) was an enthusiast and active patron; the growth of archery can be attributed partly to a desire to emulate royalty. From this period came the standard layout of the target in Britain, which works outwards from the gold worth nine points in the centre, and was called 'The Prince's Colours'. The standard lengths of 60, 80 and 100 yards were 'The Prince's Lengths'. Many of the new clubs were socially highly exclusive; one, the Royal British Bowmen, admitted women as shooting members in 1787. The Napoleonic Wars brought a decline, and many clubs dwindled away.

Walter Scott made the winning of an archery competition by Locksley (otherwise known as Robin Hood) a central element in the plot of his fabulously popular novel, *Ivanhoe* (1819). The revival of archery in the 1820s was coloured by Scott's enthusiasm for the medieval, and each society shot in a variant of a medieval uniform. Archery was taken up by the middle classes, including women, without initially altering the sport.

However, the history of archery changed direction when the first Grand National Archery Meeting was held in 1844 at York, the result of an initiative taken by the Hull Archers. The Grand National was the focus for a rapid improvement in levels of performance, directed particularly by the analytical mind of a Welsh solicitor, Horace Alfred Ford (1822-1880). Ford was champion for eleven consecutive years from 1849. At his best, in the late 1850s, Ford's scores in major events usually fell little short of double that of his nearest rivals. The Grand National Archery Society was founded in 1861 and it is now the governing body for the sport in Great Britain. Archery reached a peak of popularity between 1840 and 1860; its subsequent decline was due to croquet and later tennis, both of which could be enjoyed by women, to the Volunteer movement and its rifle shooting competitions, and perhaps also to changes in fashion.

Archery was an Olympic sport from 1900 to 1908, in 1920, and since 1972. Sybil 'Queenie' Newall won the women's event in 1908 at the age of fifty-three, the oldest woman to win an Olympic gold medal. The Fédération Internationale de Tir à l'Arc (International Archery Federation) was founded in 1931; Great Britain joined the following year.

In field archery, archers shoot at 14 or 28 targets, at various distances, as they walk round a course – it is thus partially derived from golf, but also from the idea of archery as hunting. Field archery is catered for by the Grand National Archery Society, and also by the more specialized English Field Archery Association and the National Field Archery Society.

For target archery the traditional bow was replaced in the 1940s, first by one of tubular steel and then by a composite bow of wood, plastic and fibreglass.

Archers, more than most sportsmen, are aware of the historic dimension of their sport. The British Longbow Society encourages shooting with the traditional wooden bow and wooden arrows with feather fletchings. Ancient competitions such as the Scorton Arrow, a Yorkshire competition held since 1673, and the Kilwinning Papingo in Ayrshire, dating from 1688, are still held. The Society of Archer-Antiquaries was founded in 1956.

Further reading:

Hardy, R., *Longbow: a Social and Military History* (Sparkford: Patrick Stephens, 1992).

Heath, E. G., *History of Target Archery* (Newton Abbot: David & Charles, 1973).

Longman, C. J. and Walrond, H., *Archery* (London: Longmans & Co., 1894).

Websites:

The English Field Archery Association – http://www.fieldarcher.com/

The Grand National Archery Society – http://www.gnas.org/

The National Field Archery Association – http://www.clark-1.demon.co.uk/nfas/

-John Burnett

Army Physical Training Corps

The Army Physical Training Corps (A.P.T.C.) was founded under the command of Major (later Colonel) W. J. Hammersley at the Aldershot garrison in June 1861. Its purpose was to form a corps of non-commissioned officers capable of preparing British soldiers for the rigours of the battlefield. Although based at Aldershot, the Corps first assembled, in September 1860, at the University Gymnasium in Oxford under the tutelage of Archibald MacLaren. MacLaren was a civilian instructor in both fencing and gymnastics and was asked by the War Office to undertake this task. Losses in the many campaigns of the mid-19th century had caused concern over fitness in the ranks and the high number of rejections at recruiting stations.

Known as the Army Gymnastic Staff and later the Army Physical Training Staff, the Corps did not appear in the Army List as a School of Instruction until 1885. It has operated under its present title since the Second World War. The first two groups of instructors were trained by MacLaren at Oxford, though subsequently, all army physical training instructors have been trained only at Aldershot, with the exception of schools abroad in times of war. Wartime has seen the only occasions when instructors were not trained directly from the ranks, with the acceptance of well-known sportsmen into the Corps. Many international sportsmen, such as the late Sir Matt Busby, were accorded such a distinction. Hammersley commanded the Corps until his retirement in 1871. Since then, perhaps Colonel Cleather and Colonel Fox have done most to forge the traditions and standards still maintained today.

Colonel Cleather was largely responsible for the adoption of Swedish gymnastics by the army in 1881, a move highly significant in the history of physical education. Colonel Fox, who was knighted in 1910 for his service to the army and to education, is perhaps the most notable. 'Fox Gymnasium' was built in 1893 and the present Aldershot military stadium was financed from Fox's own purse following War Office reluctance to provide funds. He is probably better known as the author of the 1909 syllabus of Physical Training, for which task he was seconded to the Board of Education and, it is generally held, received his knighthood.

Although gymnastics, fencing and drill were the early tools of instruction, sport has been a major medium of activity for many years. All physical training instructors are qualified to coach in several sports and some in adventurous and mountain activities. In the days of amateur sport, members of the Corps figured largely in teams at international and Olympic level. The Corps is perhaps best known for the international gymnasts it has produced over the years – Kriss Akabusi and Kelly Holmes are just two of the more recent stars to have followed in the footsteps of the long line of military sportspersons who have also been A.P.T.C. members.

The small museum adjacent to Fox Gymnasium contains a fascinating documentary and material record of the Corp's activities, both sporting and otherwise. The Corps is based at the Army School of Physical Training, Fox Lines, Aldershot.

References:

Hammersley, W. J., *The Hammersley Scrap Book* (Aldershot: Army School of Physical Training, Museum and Archives, 1861-1869).

Oldfield, E. A. L., *History of the Army Physical Training Corps* (Aldershot: Gale & Polden Ltd, 1955).

Taylor, D., *Archibald MacLaren: His Work and Influence in Physical Education from 1850 to 1884* (M.Ed. thesis, University of Manchester, 1980).

Personal interviews with Lt. Col. (retired) A. A. Forbes between 1992 and 1996.

-Frank Galligan

Army Sport Control Board

The Army Sport Control Board (A.S.C.B.) was formed on November 20th, 1918, just a few days after the cessation of hostilities of the First World War, with the aim (amongst others) of controlling sport in the army in accordance with the strictest amateur principles.

The ravages of the First World War had impressed upon officials in the War Office the need to relax the men, and the limited opportunities for such recreation that had presented themselves during this time had convinced the War Office that such activity should be an ongoing morale-boosting programme in peacetime also. A programme of inter-unit and inter-regimental activities was thus initiated. This eventually embraced inter-services competition in a range of sporting activities and contests, of which the Military Tournament, held annually at the Albert Hall, was just one example.

In the days of strict demarcation between amateur and professional sportsmen, Army sport was unique in that it dispensed with such distinctions during the period of military service. This allowed, for instance, many Rugby League professionals to play alongside amateur Rugby Union internationals, without censure from either of the Rugby authorities.

The range of activities embraced by the A.S.C.B. today encompasses almost every sport imaginable and the administration is now based in Aldershot rather than run directly from the War Office. The relationship between the A.S.C.B. and the Army School of Physical Training is invaluable and the programme of the A.S.C.B. embraces a range of sports coaching awards for members of all military units and ranks.

References:

Oldfield, E. A. L., *History of the Army Physical Training Corps* (Aldershot: Gale & Polden Ltd, 1955).

Games and Sports in the Army (London: Army Sport Control Board, various years).

Websites:

Army Sport –
http://www.army.mod.uk/army/life/sport/sprt_top.htm

See also:

R.A.F. Sports Board; Services Sport

-Frank Galligan

Ascot

Founded in 1711 by Queen Anne, Ascot is the only English course owned by the Crown, being assigned for this purpose in 1813, when much of the Heath was enclosed. In 1825, its royal connections were emphasized by the procession along the course, which still remains a feature of the June meeting.

The railway was to change Ascot's nature from an upper-class outing to a spectacle for the middle classes, but the formality of the Royal Enclosure remains.

Until 1939 there were generally only four days of racing each year, but the war years saw the beginning of year-round racing at Ascot. The courses were renewed in the early 1950s, the Queen Elizabeth II stand was completed in 1961, and a new steeplechase course was opened four years later.

Ascot is now a Grade I course with more than twenty days of flat and National Hunt fixtures. The centrepiece of Royal Ascot in June is still the 2-mile Gold Cup, inaugurated in 1807. Another attraction is the *Queen Alexandra Stakes*, inaugurated in 1865 and won no less than six times by Brown Jack, who is commemorated by a handicap race at the late July meeting. The main event at this meeting is the *King George VI and Queen Elizabeth Stakes*, which in 1973 became the first £100,000 race in Britain. The Festival of British Racing takes place in late September, and these events, together with the jump meetings, provide a comprehensive test for horse and jockey over the triangular undulating course.

References:

Mortimer, R., Onslow, R. and Willett, P., *Biographical Encyclopaedia of British Flat Racing* (London: Macdonald & Jane's Ltd, 1978).

Tyrrel, J., *Racecourses on the Flat* (Marlborough: Crowood Press, 1989).

See also:

Horse-racing

Websites:

Ascot Racecourse – http://www.ascot.co.uk/

-John Tolson

Ashes

Standing only 11 cm high and made of pottery, the Ashes urn, displayed in the Marylebone Cricket Club (M.C.C.) Museum at Lord's Cricket Ground, is the most famous trophy in cricket.

The story began on August 29th, 1882, when Australia narrowly defeated a strong England side at the Oval in what remains one

of the most dramatic test matches ever played. This first Australian victory on English soil was considered a national calamity and the following day an obituary notice, written by Shirley Brooks, appeared in the *Sporting Times*, which read 'In affectionate remembrance of English Cricket which died at the Oval, 29th August 1882. Deeply lamented by a large circle of sorrowing friends and acquaintances. R.I.P. N.B. – The body will be cremated and the ashes taken to Australia.'

That winter, the Hon. Ivo Bligh (later Lord Darnley) took a side to Australia to recover these mythical ashes. Following England's victory in two of a three match series, a group of Melbourne ladies burned a bail and placed the ashes inside a pottery urn, which was presented to the England captain. Thus the real Ashes came into being.

The Ashes were a personal gift to Bligh and remained in his possession until his death in 1927, when his widow, who was one of the donors, presented them to the M.C.C. Although the term 'winning the Ashes' has

The Ashes Trophy (M.C.C.)

become common sporting parlance, the urn has never been competed for as a trophy and remains permanently in the M.C.C. Museum.

References:

Arnold, P. and Wynne-Thomas, P., *The Ashes: a Complete Illustrated History* (London: Brian Trodd, 1990).

Munns, J., *Origin of the Ashes* (privately published, 1995).

Rice, T. M. B., *Treasures of Lord's* (London: Willow, 1989).

See also:

Cricket

-Glenys Williams

Association Football

Origins and Development

Football is found in most cultures and can be traced back to the 12th century in Britain. It was certainly being played in some of the schools for the sons of the better off in the 16th century, although how regularly and in what circumstances we do not know. It was also played in some places in the 17th century, provoking attempts from Evangelicals and Puritans to stop it. Joseph Strutt in his famous book *Sports and Pastimes of the People of England* (1801) suggested football was little practised in his time. Among the fashionable and well off this may have been true but its disappearance among male youths of the lower orders seems doubtful. Only twenty years after Strutt, a writer in the *Gentleman's Magazine* in 1822, in an article about Herefordshire, named football as the most common sport, especially on Sunday afternoons.

The growing pressures of urbanization and industrialization undoubtedly undermined the old Shrovetide game in which large numbers of men had wildly pursued the ball through crowded streets. But football on a smaller scale, either the casual kick-about in working-class neighbourhoods or more organized games in public house paddocks probably had a more continuous history. This is important because it meant that when a rationalized version of this ancient sport was innovated in the public schools and universities in the mid-19th century, it did not appear dangerously different to ordinary folk, hence the speed with which a new generation of young men fell in love with it.

Public school football varied from school to school. Such rules as existed were passed on orally, those at Rugby School not being written down until 1846. Games were encouraged in an attempt to discipline unruly boys and worked so well that by the 1860s they had become an essential part of the curriculum. Two types of football gradually emerged – one with the emphasis on handling, the other characterized by kicking. Some of the more upper-class schools clung to their own versions of the game. None of this would have mattered much if football had been confined to the public schools. But the expanding number of school leavers who wanted to continue playing as young adults posed a problem: which version of football should be played? A group of students at Cambridge wrote down some rules in 1848. There must have been a lot of talk about the need to produce a single game with a single rulebook.

The turning point appears to have come in the early 1860s. Charterhouse School wrote down the rules of its own game for the first time in 1861. The next year, the headmaster of Uppingham issued his 'rules of the simplest game'. Clubs began to be formed by better-off young men in a variety of places, such as London, Nottingham and Sheffield. In 1863, John Cartwright wrote a letter to the sporting newspaper, *Bell's Life*, suggesting a meeting between representatives of different schools and colleges in order to see if one set of rules for football could be agreed. A meeting was held at Cambridge, which seemed to suggest that some thought the Rugby game too dangerous for adults. A further meeting between representatives of eleven London clubs and schools in October 1863 established what was called the Football Association (F.A.). However, this did not resolve whether hacking and the use of the hands should be allowed and in fact this could not be resolved. Several 'Rugby' clubs withdrew from the F.A. and in January 1871 formed the Rugby Football Union. One game had become divided into two.

Football grew slowly during the rest of the 1860s. Sheffield set up its own football association in 1867 but it was 1875 before Birmingham followed suit, soon copied by Lancashire in 1878. An important stimulus to growth was the institution of a knockout cup by the F.A. in 1871. Other associations soon established their own local cups, including those of Scotland and Wales. Cup-tie football changed the nature of the game, building on existing local rivalries and providing opportunities for excitement and sociability. Newspapers began to reflect and promote the new sport and the urge to defeat opponents led teams to try to recruit the best players, if necessary by poaching them from other clubs with offers of jobs and money.

Football was supposed to be a rational recreation not a job or a business. The young men who had established the F.A. had not expected this sudden growth in the game and the intensity of competition that accompanied it, particularly in the industrial towns and cities of the Midlands, northern England and central Scotland. In 1883, a team of Lancashire working men called Blackburn Olympic won the F.A. Cup having undergone special training at Blackpool prior to the final rounds, paid for by a local manufacturer. Football outside London and the South attracted big crowds of working men prepared to pay to see the best teams play cup-ties. Local businessmen began to take control of the leading clubs. Scotsmen left their homes and jobs to play football for English clubs.

The F.A.'s response was to outlaw the paid player, but a threatened breakaway by many of the leading clubs led to a compromise solution whereby professionalism was legalized in 1885 under the control of the F.A. The conflict had been social, regional and emotional, with competing notions about the nature of football and how it might evolve. However, this was an important turning-point and only one major step remained before the foundations of the modern game had been clearly laid.

The leading clubs wanted a more predictable programme of attractive, competitive games. In 1888, twelve of the leading English professional clubs, six from the Midlands and six from Lancashire, arranged a regular schedule of home and away matches with each other, at the end of which the club with the best record was declared the champion. This was the Football League. Regular training and practice for the best players, and the enhanced competition that the League stimulated, further guaranteed quality and promoted interest. In Scotland, where professionalism was resisted until 1893, a Scottish League was formed in 1890. Soon there would be second divisions in both countries and leagues would spring up everywhere from the Professional Southern League in 1894 to the hundreds of semi-professional and recreational leagues that provide the competitive structure of football to this day. By 1914, a modern national sport had been created out of an inchoate if popular game.

Leaders and Personalities

The founding fathers of football were generally young men who had to learn all of the skills needed to manage a modern sport as they went along. They often combined the roles of player, referee, administrator and journalist. None was more important in the early development of football than Charles William Alcock (1842-1907). He went to school at Harrow, where he played football and cricket for his house. In 1857, he was among the founders of the Forest Football Club, out of which grew the famous Wanderers. He was not one of the founders of the F.A. in 1863 but he was elected to its committee in 1866. By 1870, he was both Secretary and Treasurer. He would remain in the first post until 1895, although he was only paid during the last ten years. He earned his living partly by being Secretary to the Surrey County Cricket Club from 1872 until his death, but mainly by writing about sport for many papers, including the *Sportsman* for fourteen years from 1866, and the *Field*. In 1882, he became owner and editor of *Cricket*, and there must have been times during the 1870s when even his enthusiasm found a life of reporting, sub-editing, doing the secretarial duties for two sporting organizations and looking after a young family a little stressful. Perhaps this was reflected in the brusqueness of personality that led to his nickname 'the Baron'.

He was a useful forward who both organized and played in the first unofficial international between England and Scotland in 1870, and scored in the official match in 1875. He will probably be best remembered for inventing the F.A. Cup, the knockout competition, which was based on one among the houses at Harrow.

If Alcock will be always associated with the Cup, it was a Scottish migrant to Birmingham, William McGregor (1847-1911), who pioneered the formation of the League. He ran a draper's shop close to Birmingham city centre and although not much of a player himself, was interested enough to close his shop on Saturday afternoons so he could watch. He was invited to join the committee that ran Aston Villa in the late 1870s, did some umpiring for them and began to sell football shorts and shirts.

As football developed as a spectator sport after the acceptance of professionalism in 1885, McGregor recognized the need for a regular programme of fixtures between the strongest teams, along the same lines as the county cricket championship. This was what he suggested in a letter that he wrote to five of the leading clubs in March 1888. At a meeting in Manchester the following month, the Football League was born, with six clubs from

Lancashire and six from the Midlands. McGregor was Chairman of the Management Committee between 1888 and 1892, President between 1892 and 1894, and a Life Member between 1895 and 1911. He was also an F.A. Councillor, wrote regularly in the newspapers, and allowed his name to be used for the sale of balls and boots. Cheerful though teetotal, he was optimistic in his forecast of the relationship between the new league and the old F.A., saying '...The League must be a selfish body. Its interests are wholly bound up in the welfare of its affiliated clubs... The League has its work to do; the Association has its work to do and there need be no clashing.'

John James Bentley (1860-1918) was another of the pioneers of modern football who made a living from it through his off-the-field activities. He was a good enough player to represent his home village of Turton and play for Lancashire, but it was as a referee, administrator and journalist that he became probably the most powerful man in football around the turn of the century.

He had begun sending in reports of Turton's matches to local newspapers while he was still playing in them in the early 1880s. In 1884, he began writing for the *Bolton Cricket and Football Field* and then in 1886 became assistant editor of the *Athletic News*. He was editor from 1895 to 1900, by which time the weekly had a circulation close to 200,000 and a readership of many more.

Bentley had become Secretary of Bolton Wanderers in 1885 and he was one of those who received McGregor's letter in 1888 suggesting the formation of a football league. He served on its Management Committee for the next thirty years and held a wide variety of other positions including the first League official to be a Vice-President of the F.A., in 1905. When Newton Heath was reconstructed into Manchester United following financial mismanagement he became Chairman and was Secretary from 1912 to 1916. He was not much of an orator and his thousands of journalistic words were eminently unquotable, but he was a tough leader of professional league football during its formative phase.

Although there was money to be made out of professional football, for most of its first century it depended largely on the time and energy of volunteers. None of these were more committed nor more influential than Charles Edward Sutcliffe (1864-1939). Born in Burnley the son of a solicitor, Sutcliffe went into his father's practice. He was keen on cricket and football, playing for both his home-town clubs, and was also a fearless referee. It was as an administrator and organizer, however, that he was to make his mark. A committee-man at Burnley, Sutcliffe was one of its first directors in 1897. He was elected to the Management Committee of the Football League in 1898, beginning a forty-year association culminating in the Presidency in 1936. For most of that period he was the most powerful man in the League. He travelled many a mile on its business and his business was the Football League rather than the law.

Sutcliffe was a passionate defender of the maximum wage and the retain-and-transfer system, which stipulated that players could not join a new club without permission from their existing club, as long as they were being paid the maximum wage. He believed that this would allow small as well as big clubs to remain in the same competition and successfully defended the League in the 1912 Kingsby case on this very same issue. He drew up the emergency regulations which kept the clubs afloat during the First World War, and after the war he organized the appointment of referees to matches and advised the system which produced the league fixtures. Every summer, he locked himself away with his son and daughter for two or three days until the mysterious process was complete. After he died, his son Harold took over and it was only after *his* death that computers were brought in, in 1968. Sutcliffe masterminded the League's Jubilee celebrations in 1938, out of which came a fund,

later the Provident Fund, to help players whose careers were over. He also found time to preside over the Lancashire F.A., write its jubilee history, sit on several F.A. committees, sit on the Appeal Committees of twenty different leagues as well as becoming a Liberal councillor in Rawtenstall. In addition to all this, he was a prolific journalist. With the exception of Alan Hardaker, no one made a deeper impact on the League.

Soon after Alan Hardaker (1912-1980) became Secretary of the Football League in 1957, both the football world and the world in which football was played showed signs of rapid change. In football, the number of matches was increasing as European and international competition grew. Television began to undermine the traditional relationship between the fans and the clubs. Attendances at league games were falling while costs were rising, especially after the abolition of the maximum wage in 1961. A more affluent British society provided more choices of leisure and recreation.

Hardaker was the first League Secretary to have been on the books of a football league club, though as an amateur with Hull City. His work experience had been in local government, where he had been the Lord Mayor's Secretary in Hull and Portsmouth before being appointed Assistant Secretary at the Football League in 1947. He found a small organization deeply reluctant to accept change but once he became Secretary in 1956, he set about a programme of modernization, moving the offices from Preston to Lytham and increasing the size of the staff from six to thirty. After this he turned to the structure of the game itself.

Although a reformer, he was in essence a conservative who saw that if the League was to survive, it had to adapt to the changing circumstances. The public did not want more football but better and more competitive football. With this in mind, he devised the 'Pattern of Football' which advocated a league of five divisions, each of twenty clubs with four promoted and four relegated each season. This

19

would reduce the number of games, but the introduction of a knock-out league cup was intended to sugar the pill. There was a good deal of support for the plan but not enough to obtain the necessary three-quarters majority.

Hardaker was an outspoken man who, like Sutcliffe, wanted to keep the League together rather than create an élite within it. Although his rhetoric was often couched in terms of the League as a family, he saw clubs and their managers as selfish as they refused to see that managed change would be for the good of all. He fell out with Stanley Rous at the F.A., whose vision of a Super League moving towards a European League he did not share. For Hardaker, as for most football supporters, club was more important than country.

In 1977 his title was changed to Chief Executive and General Secretary and he published a spiky autobiography called simply *Hardaker of the League*. He was still struggling with the problem of its reform when he died suddenly of a heart attack on March 4th, 1980.

Sir Stanley Rous (1895-1986) could not be called a radical either, but in some important respects he did have wider horizons than either Sutcliffe or Hardaker. Rous had been a teacher at Watford Grammar School and, after the early end of his playing days due to injury, qualified as a football referee. He was placed on the Football League list and was soon in demand to referee international matches in Europe. He officiated in thirty-four games between 1927 and 1934. His educational background helped to stimulate an interest in the educational and technical side of the game. He was an early advocate of coaching and the scheme he pioneered at the Football Association in the 1930s was one of the earliest in any British sport.

He was also impressed by the way football was developing in Europe and elsewhere and the part coaching was playing in its progress. His foreign trips and friendships made him more sensitive to international issues and after

1945 he not only took England back into F.I.F.A., the International Football Federation, and therefore into the World Cup for the first time, but was also a prime mover in the setting up of U.E.F.A., its European equivalent. He helped to set up the Inter-Cities Fairs Cup (the forerunner of the U.E.F.A. cup) and had a vision of a European League.

Rous was less insular than many other leaders of British sport. He felt that sport required a forum through which it could speak to the world with a single voice, and was a founder member and Executive Committee Chairman of the Central Council of Physical Recreation. His wartime fundraising for the Red Cross earned him a C.B.E. in 1943 and a Knighthood in 1949. He cut an impressive figure, 6 feet 3 inches tall, with a husky voice and jovial personality. He was a powerful man who may have had ambitions of taking over the Football League. Certainly he and Hardaker approached the problems of English football in the late 1950s from different directions. The struggle between them would have become more colourful if Rous had not been elected President of F.I.F.A. in 1961.

Famous Venues

There are few British towns without a football ground. Since the 1890s, the football ground has been an urban landmark like the cathedral, hospital, railway station or theatre. The grander ones have often been compared to churches, with Saturday as the day of worship. Many British football grounds were cold and uncomfortable with minimum protection against the weather, but the football supporter found them exciting, each having its own special history and identity.

As bigger crowds were attracted by football in the late 19th century, the clubs followed athletics, cricket and racing by enclosing their grounds and charging admission. Sloping banks of earth were built to give a better view and, as these hardened, steps or terracing could be cut into them. Grandstands and pavilions were put up so that the better off could sit under cover.

Investment in grounds grew after the formation of the Football and Scottish Leagues in 1888 and 1890. The first modern football stadium in England was Everton's Goodison Park. In the 1890s it often housed crowds of 30,000. A double-decker stand was constructed behind one of the goals in 1907 and a new main stand on the Goodison Road side in 1909, which remained in use until 1971. Another double-decker was built in 1926, by which time it was one of the most impressive stadiums in Britain, its four double-deckers and extensive terracing often filled by crowds exceeding 60,000.

Across Stanley Park, Anfield had been the home of Everton before the split which led to the formation of Liverpool F.C. in 1892, and their rivalry quickly became a passionate one. Liverpool actually won the championship in 1901 and 1906 and it was after this latter success that the notorious Kop terracing was built. The name was taken from a bloody battle fought for a hill, Spion Kop, by Lancashire troops during the Boer War in 1900. In 1928 it was extended and covered, by which time it was the largest behind-the-goal terracing in the country, with room, though not much, for 30,000 people to stand. Other grounds also built their Kops, although they could not outstrip the fame of the one at Anfield, which spread as a result of the series of successful Liverpool teams between 1963 and 1991 and the growth of football on television. The first Match of the Day was shown from Anfield in 1964.

By this time, many grounds had become well known parts of a town's culture and identity. Schoolboys knew that Bolton Wanderers played at Burden Park, built in 1895, and that Aston Villa boasted Villa Park, constructed two years later. Sunderland enclosed their Roker Park ground in 1898, the same year that Southampton began operations at the Dell. Manchester United moved into the monumental Old Trafford in 1909, ten years after

Sheffield Wednesday had gone from the pastoral-sounding Olive Grove to the imposing Hillsborough, where the first length-of-the-pitch cantilever stand would be built in 1961, making it the only Football League ground to be listed in Pevsner's *Buildings of England*. In the 1930s, Arsenal re-developed their Highbury ground with what critics called the two most advanced and architecturally dazzling grandstands in Britain.

But it was the size of grounds which made the most impact on spectators, and for most of the 20th century it was Glasgow which contained the three largest stadiums in Britain. Celtic Park was built in the Parkhead district of the city in 1892 at the same time as Goodison Park, but it was much bigger. It incorporated running and cycle tracks and after the re-development of the South Stand in 1929 it was larger than any club ground in England. A crowd of 92,000 saw the New Year game with Rangers in 1938. By 1967, three sides of the ground were covered, more than on any other ground in Britain, although there were few seats. When the Taylor report recommended all-seater stadiums for the leading clubs in 1990, change was inevitable, and between 1994 and 1998 a spectacular modern stadium was built on the site of the old ground. With an all-seated capacity of 60,294, it has reclaimed its former position as one of the largest club stadiums in Britain.

The largest crowd ever to watch a league football match in the United Kingdom was not at Celtic Park but at Ibrox Park, home to Celtic's rivals, Rangers, when 118,567 squeezed in to see the 'old firm' game in 1939. Ibrox had been rebuilt in 1902, but new wooden terracing behind one of the goals had collapsed during the Scotland-England match that year causing twenty-six deaths. Further redevelopment followed, including the splendid South stand opened in 1928. Another disaster in 1971, when crushing on a stairway at the end of the match against Celtic cost a further sixty-six lives, led to the *Safety of Sports*

Grounds Act (1975) and a reduction in capacity to 65,000. During the late 1970s, the ground was further reconstructed with many more seats, thus reducing the capacity to 45,000. Work in 1994 completed its makeover to an all-seater stadium with a capacity of 50,500.

By the 1920s, the most spectacular ground in Glasgow was neither of these but Hampden Park, home to the amateur Queen's Park F.C. and venue for all Scotland-England games between 1906 and 1989 and most Scottish Cup Finals since 1904. By 1937, this huge elongated oval had uncovered standing room for 150,000. Records unlikely ever to be broken were set when 149,415 saw the international game against England in 1937 and 144,303 saw the Scottish Cup Final in the same year. 135,000 watched the European Cup Final as late as 1960. No wonder the Hampden Roar, first identified in 1929, was supposed to be Scotland's twelfth man. By the 1960s, Hampden's ash and timber terracing was looking shoddy and old-fashioned. The West End was covered in 1967 and safety concerns gradually diminished the capacity. Concrete terracing replaced the ash and wood in the 1980s and, following the Taylor Report (1990), it was rebuilt as an all-seater stadium with a 52,000 capacity in the 1990s.

In England it was the Cup Final which gradually emerged as the biggest football occasion of the season. As the demand to see it grew, a suitable venue in London for the climax of this national competition had to be found, once it became clear that the Oval was too small. In 1895, the game moved to Crystal Palace, where a football pitch was laid out in the well-known pleasure park. Every cup final was played there until 1914 and it was in these years that the event was established as a day-out for the thousands of supporters. This picnic-like atmosphere was just as well, because a considerable proportion of an increasingly large crowd – it exceeded 100,000 in 1901, 1905 and 1913 – stood on sloping grass banks not only giving poor views of the game, but

becoming slippery and dangerous in the wet. The Crystal Palace athletics stadium now occupies the site of the pitch.

It was to be Wembley, however, which became the Mecca of English football when it was built as the centrepiece of the British Empire Exhibition in 1922-1923. The Cup Final has been held there ever since, England against Scotland every second year between 1924 and 1986, many other England games, the World Cup Final of 1966, several European Cup Finals and, most recently, the final of Euro 96. Wembley also hosted the 1948 Olympic Games. When the stadium opened for the Cup Final of 1923 there were only 25,000 seats and 91,000 standing places. 200,000 people turned up producing chaotic scenes and leading to subsequent finals being ticket only, with a limit of 100,000. Wembley was owned by a private company which, through most of its history, has made more money out of greyhound racing and speedway than football. The ground was only slowly modernized. In 1963, the stands got new roofs and the ends were covered for the first time. By the end of the 1990s, Wembley had reached her seventies and was looking shabby and out of date. In the year 2000, the twin towers are to be demolished and a new stadium is to rise from the rubble. It remains unclear whether it will be the English national sports stadium or merely the English national football stadium.

On April 15th, 1989, the worst disaster at a British football ground took place at Hillsborough, Sheffield, before the F.A. Cup semi-final between Liverpool and Nottingham Forest. Ninety-six Liverpool supporters were crushed to death in pens behind the goal at the Leppings Lane End. The official inquiry produced the Taylor Report (1990), which recommended a timetable for the top fifty clubs to convert to all-seater stadia. In the budget of 1990, the Treasury made available £100 million to the Football Trust to allocate to the clubs for ground improvements. The result has been a period of stadium building, modernization and re-location unknown since the previous turn of the century. At least thirteen clubs, Bolton Wanderers, Brighton and Hove Albion, Derby County, Huddersfield Town, Middlesborough, Millwall, Northampton Town, Reading, Scunthorpe United, Stoke City, Sunderland, Walsall and Wigan Athletic have moved to new stadiums. It remains to be seen whether the fans will find them as excitingly welcoming as their predecessors.

The formation of the Premier League

In 1992, the twenty-two teams in the English First Division broke away from the Football League to form the F.A. Carling Premiership. The 1980s had been a disastrous decade for football. It had begun with falling crowds, hooliganism and the exclusion of English teams from European competition, and had culminated in the catastrophe at Hillsborough in 1989. The Taylor Report in January 1990 had called for reforms in the way that football was run and in October of that year, the Football League had proposed a joint board with the Football Association to oversee all football, both professional and recreational. The F.A. had been opposed to such a power-sharing scheme and in 1991 had produced their own 'Blueprint for the Future of Football'. At the same time, a small number of leading clubs keen to break away from the Football League in order to maximize revenue from television had approached the F.A. for support. The result was the mass resignation of the twenty-two teams in the First Division of the Football League in 1992 and the formation of the F.A. Carling Premiership, for which the F.A. agreed to provide referees, a disciplinary system and an organization for the registration of players. The idea of mutuality, which had sustained the Football League for over a century, was irretrievably destroyed.

References:

Mason, T., *Association Football and English Society 1863-1915* (Brighton: Harvester, 1980).

Russell, D., *Football and the English: a Social History of Association Football in England 1863-1995* (Preston: Carnegie, 1997).

Websites:

The Football Association – http://www.thefa.org/
The Football League –
http://www.football-league.co.uk/
F.I.F.A. – http://www.fifa.com/

See also:

Amateurism and Professionalism; Disasters – Burnden Park; Disasters; F.A. Cup; League Cup; Hampden Park; Old Trafford; Wembley Stadium

-Tony Mason

Athletics – Indoor Athletics

It would appear that credit should be given to the United States for pioneering indoor athletic meetings. In 1861, the Young Men's Gymnastic Club of Cincinnati, Ohio, arranged a meeting. Seven years later, in 1868, the first indoor meeting to be held in New York was arranged in a skating rink. Much later, in 1927, the U.S. organized the first women's indoor championships, continuing their role as pioneers in this sphere of the sport.

The history of indoor athletics is linked to the tradition of pedestrianism that developed in the late 19th century. 'Peds', as they were known to the public, took their name from the 17th-century footmen who walked and ran alongside the coaches.

The first reported meeting in England was held in April 1877, at Ashbourne Hall in Chelsea. This was organized for the West London Rowing Club. There were several other meetings held before 1878, namely those in Liverpool, at Lambeth Baths and in the Royal Agricultural Hall, Islington.

The Agricultural Hall hosted the vast majority of pedestrian meetings in Britain during the late 19th century. The first match was between an American athlete, Edward Payson

Weston, and Daniel O'Leary, who walked 520 miles and 420 yards in 139 hours and 30 minutes. The rules governing style had been relaxed the previous year and the athletes could now walk and run. Subsequent meetings were organized, with the longest distance recorded at the Agricultural Hall being 623 miles in 1888.

In 1888, twenty-three men competed for the Astley Belt, which was provided by Sir John Astley, who promoted such events. He was keen to see an English Challenger to the Americans. The competitors walked on wooden board, with eight laps of the hall making 1 mile. After a series of competitions at the Agricultural Hall and in the United States, the Astley belt returned to England in 1879 thanks to Charles Rowell.

Sporadic indoor meetings were held in England during the early 20th century, including several during 1919 at Regent Street Polytechnic. The popularity of the sport diminished, especially once the amateur athletic governing bodies gained control of the development of track and field.

The first Amateur Athletic Association (A.A.A.) indoor championship was held in 1935 at the Empire Pool, Wembley. They were held annually until 1939 and were notable for the fact that they were organized jointly between the men and women's governing bodies. The facilities reflected the general poor standard in Britain at this time and consisted of a wooden track that was only 142.5 yards round, something that athletes reportedly found hard to negotiate.

Indoor athletics struggled to become established in Britain and, after the Second World War, competitions were still held only sporadically. They were primarily seen as providing sprinters with competition just prior to the summer track season and were unable to attract the degree of public interest that indoor racing in America enjoyed. However, competitions did increase in number as the fifties progressed, particularly once R.A.F. Cosford was established as an indoor venue in the 1950s.

Cosford was to become the home of British indoor athletics. The first meeting was held on November 9th, 1955, and was a joint venture between the Midland A.A.A., the A.A.A. Coaching Committee and the R.A.F.'s physical education staff. At this stage, track events were competed for on a 160-yard, unbanked track that was simply marked out on the wood floor. Evening competitions were organized by Dan Davies, who was a squadron leader at the base and coach to Derek Ibbotson. Ibbotson later set a new British two-mile record in 1965. From 1961, the competitions were held in a hanger, which was big enough to allow 100-yard races to be organized. In November 1961, R.A.F. Cosford witnessed its first world record, courtesy of Brenda Cook who ran 880 yards in 2:19.5.

The A.A.A. Championship was resurrected in 1962, with the support of the *Daily Herald*. These were again jointly arranged by the A.A.A. and W.A.A.A. and held at the Empire Pool. The newspaper's sponsorship enabled a new portable track to be purchased, the former wooden one having been destroyed during the war. Three years later, Cosford hosted the Midland and A.A.A./W.A.A.A. Championships. A new wooden 220-yard banked track had been purchased, with the support of the Department of Education and Science. It was used for the first time at the Midland Championships, where Mary Campbell of Birchfield set a new world best for 660 yards.

The first international meeting that Britain competed in was against West Germany in 1962. Britain was victorious and a return match was arranged for the following year. In 1965, the Cosford track was converted to 200 metres and the first full international was held on this facility. The match was against West Germany but this time the visitors won.

Although indoor athletics has never gained the support that it has outdoors, there have been some notable performances from athletes during the indoor season. In 1972, Britain gained a synthetic track at Cosford and the following year, Margaret Beacham set a world best for 1500 metres at the European Championship in Sofia. Verona Elder won the European 400 metres Championship three times and recorded a world best over 600 metres in 1974. Sebastian Coe used the indoor season to good effect in 1981, when he set a world record of 1:46.0 for 800 metres. That was the year that he set world records outdoors for 800 metres, 1,000 metres and the mile. Linford Christie must also be mentioned. He broke through into the international ranks at the 1986 European Championships, when he won the 200 metres.

Scotland gained an indoor facility in 1987, when the refurbished Kelvin Hall was opened in Glasgow. Cosford remained the primary venue in England until the National Indoor Arena in Birmingham was opened in 1992. The last event to be held at Cosford was a Dairy Crest Invitational International in February 1991. Both Kelvin Hall and the National Indoor Arena now hold regular inter-national and domestic meetings.

Internationally, the inaugural European Indoor Championships were held in Dortmund, Germany in 1966 and Indianapolis hosted the first World Indoor Championships in 1987.

References:
Crump, J., *Running Round the World* (London: Hale, 1966).

Dillon, M., 'Crooked Bookies, Drugs and Mobs', *Marathon and Distance Runner* (August, 1983).

Lovesey, P., *The Official Centenary of the Amateur Athletic Association* (Enfield: Guinness Superlatives Limited, 1979).

Quercetani, R. L., *Athletics: a History of Modern Track and Field Athletics (1860-1990) Men and Women* (Milan: Vallardi & Associates, 1990).

Watman, M., *History of British Athletics* (London: Hale, 1968).

Further reading:
Grajewski, T. T., *The Building That Would Not Go Away: the Story of How Sam Morris Rescued the Royal Agricultural Hall* (London: The Royal Agricultural Hall, 1989).

Mackay, D., 'Goodbye To All That', *Athletics Today* (Surrey: Athletics Today Publications Limited, February 1991).

Websites:
U.K. Athletics – http://www.ukathletics.org/

See also:
R.A.F. Cosford

-Lynne Duval

Athletics – Track and Field

Track and field athletics is an essentially English contribution to the sports world. It had its origins in hundreds of village and town celebrations or 'wakes'. One of the greatest of these was the Cotswold Games, organized by Robert Dover during the reign of James I. At such events people enjoyed jumping and throwing but their greatest admiration was reserved for runners. This preference, or prej-udice, was still evident in the writing of the contributors of 'Athletics' articles in the Victoria County History between 1905 and 1912, who discussed only running and run-ners in their reports, a prejudice, or prefer-ence, still exercised by modern-day television editors.

Most of the first half of the 19th century was dominated by professional athletics in the form of pedestrianism, but when William 'Penny' Brookes launched his influential Much Wenlock Olympian Games in 1850 he was as much reflecting a change of mood and emphasis as changing it. The military colleges at Woolwich, Sandhurst and Addiscombe had already introduced track and field 'sports days', the characteristics of which were very similar to modern-day programmes, with sprints, middle-distance running, hurdles, jumps and throws. They were joined in 1850 by Exeter College, Oxford, and thereafter by a succession of Oxbridge Colleges and public schools, culminating in 1864 with the first

Oxford-Cambridge fixture and in 1866 with the first Amateur Athletic Club championship.

These were the years during which much of the form of athletics took shape: a standard take-off line in the long jump; a throwing line in the shot; standardized heights and distances in the hurdles; and a standard weight for the shot. Much of the metricized form of modern athletics disguises the fact that they are based on English measurements – 3 feet 6 inches (hurdles); 120 yards (hurdles); 440 yards (tracks); 16 pounds (shot).

There was, however, a merging of traditions and this is well exemplified by the shot. By 1850, there was fairly common consensus that it should weigh about 16 pounds, but three distinctive names were applied, betraying three different traditions – shot or shell (from the military tradition); stone (used in rural sports); and weight (used in schools and colleges). Shot finally became the accepted term, although it is still occasionally referred to as 'the weight' even today.

The development of the form of athletic competition was in a sense shaped by the upper-middle classes, who had experienced athletics in the colleges, public schools and army, but even in the early 1860s other enthusiasts were being drawn away from pedestrianism to the wider attractions of track and field. This was true for spectators who not only flocked to Beaufort House and Lillie Bridge to see spectacular competitions, but also to provincial athletic meetings all over the country. It was true also for the competitors: people were drawn to this sport by the unique individualism that athletics encourages. They formed and joined clubs. London Athletic Club (which was started in 1863 as Mincing Lane Athletic Club) can still claim to be the club with the longest continuous history, but the fact is that the 1860s saw the emergence of many different clubs, some of which, through a process of constant renewal and name change, still exist today.

The clubs, many of which held open meetings, were run by committees, and the club committee was to become the power-base of English athletics. The Amateur Athletic Club, which was formed in 1866 to organize a national championship, possibly as a deft response to William Brookes' National Olympian movement, was only the principal club amongst many. It was representatives of club committees in the North in 1879 and the Midlands in 1880 who formed the Northern Counties A.A.A. and the Midland Counties A.A.A. respectively, and it was this that led Montague Shearman to intervene with his now famous meeting in 1880 at the Randolph Hotel in Oxford, where the Amateur Athletic Association (A.A.A.) was founded to provide co-ordination and leadership to this movement of clubs and the now burgeoning sport. At this stage athletics was seen as a sport for men – it was not until the 1920s that women entered the sport in any numbers and their separate organizations developed about fifty years behind those of the men.

In 1880, amateur athletics and professional pedestrianism stood in competition with each other, and the A.A.A. took over from the Amateur Athletic Club the role of ensuring that professionalism, and the betting associated with it, was kept separate from amateur athletics. There was a mixed response to 'amateurism' across the country – in Middlesex and Yorkshire it was widely practised and respected but in other places, in particular Kent, a wholly anarchic situation prevailed. In Essex, the early introduction of a county association helped to regulate the sport at a local level and other counties began to adopt this approach. Indeed, after the First World War, the A.A.A. imposed county associations everywhere as part of that regulatory process.

One hundred years later the amateur-professional separation has been discarded and the separate men's and women's organizations have been merged, but the clubs remain the bulwark of British athletics. Successive leaders of British athletics in the 1980s and 1990s have discovered, to their cost, that they need the support of clubs because athletics in Britain is nurtured by clubs. Sometimes athletes are poached from one club to another, but generally they exhibit strong club loyalty. It is certainly through clubs that the great Olympian successes of British athletics have emerged.

Track and field athletics has become a popular worldwide sport, heavily influenced by its origins in England, but its character tends to be different elsewhere. In the United States it is dominated by educational establishments, and in many other countries the sport is managed as part of a national recreational strategy. Its mass foundation in Britain, based on voluntary groups of enthusiasts in clubs, is a unique characteristic.

References:

Lovesey, P., *The Official Centenary of the Amateur Athletic Association* (Enfield: Guinness Superlatives Limited, 1979).

Quercetani, R. L., *Athletics: a History of Modern Track and Field Athletics (1860-1990) Men and Women* (Milan: Vallardi & Associati, 1990).

Watman, M., *History of British Athletics* (London: Hale, 1968).

Websites:

U.K. Athletics – http://www.ukathletics.org/

See also:

Crystal Palace; London Marathon; Marathon Racing; Pedestrianism; R.A.F. Cosford; Road Running; White City

-Trevor James

Australian Rules Football

Australian Football ('Aussie Rules' or 'footy' to devotees) was established in 1858 as a proposed winter exercise for Melbourne cricketers, but has since become Australia's dominant football code. It is played eighteen-a-side on grounds measuring 135-185 metres by 110-155 metres, matches lasting four twenty-minute quarters, and play moving fast because there is no offside rule.

The oval ball is kicked or hand-passed, goals (worth six points) being scored between tall goalposts and behinds (worth one point) being scored when the ball is forced between smaller posts on either side.

Australians at Scottish universities imported the code late last century, and a seventeen-team league existed on the Clyde at the outbreak of the First World War. Australian servicemen played the game here during both wars, notably in exhibition matches in aid of the Red Cross at the Queen's Club, London, in 1916.

The travel boom after World War Two saw London-based Australians numerous enough to sustain a league which played a visiting Australian select side at Crystal Palace in 1967. In 1972, the leading Melbourne club, Carlton, played an all-star team at The Oval, watched by the Prince of Wales. Sponsorship of The Foster's Oval by the Australian-based brewer in 1984 began the Foster's Cup series, contested regularly by teams from the Australian Football League. Growing television coverage of Australian matches helped the British Australian Rules Football League, set up in 1989 by expatriates and converted Britons, to win further converts. The League runs a summer competition based in London, but is hampered by the regular loss of homeward-bound Australian supporters.

References:

Mulle, C. C., *History of Australian Rules Football, 1858-1958* (Melbourne: The Author, 1958).

Pascoe, R., *The Winter Game: the Complete History of Australian Football* (Melbourne: The Text Publishing Company, 1995).

Further reading:

Ross, J., *100 Years of Australian Football* (Melbourne: Viking, 1996).

Websites:

The British Australian Rules Football League – http://www.barfl.co.uk/

-Murray Hedgcock

27

B

Badminton

The Badminton Association of England (B.A.E.) was formed in 1893 by fourteen clubs attending a meeting in Southsea, Hampshire. The game has, however, a rather longer history than this might suggest. The first clubs in England had been formed in the 1870s, largely in the resorts of southern England, including an officers' club in Folkestone in 1875.

The most commonly quoted origin of the game is its appearance at Badminton House, home of the Duke of Beaufort, where a version was played in 1874. A connection with India is quite clear and evidence suggests that the game was played there in the mid-1860s. The nature of the court has changed, both in the court markings and its shape, which at one period had a 'v'-shaped segment in the middle of each sideline. This hourglass-shaped court has been ascribed to the need to allow room for the doors opening inwards in the officers' mess in Madras, where the game was played in the 1870s. The game was played largely outdoors as a social activity, much in the same way that tennis also commandeered the modest gardens of middle-class suburbs during the 1880s and 1890s. By 1883, the centre line of the court stopped at the service line, and some play had moved indoors, allowing the game to be played other than during the summer.

Courts varied considerably in size, as did rules, and it was for this reason that the B.A.E. was formed in 1893, mirroring the process that had standardized play in both football codes some twenty or thirty years earlier. The hour-glass court lasted until 1901, by which time both the court and the rules had been standardized. The first All-England Championships took place at the London Scottish Drill Hall at Buckingham Gate in 1899, lasting for one day and consisting of doubles matches only. By 1910, four days were needed to complete an increasingly popular championship, by which time the Royal Horticultural Hall in Westminster had become the venue.

By 1907, the *Badminton Gazette* had been launched and the Ealing club had built its own three-court hall by forming a limited company. In the following year, the North Kensington Club also built its own hall, with a tearoom overlooking the courts. Middlesex held its own County Championships in 1905, quickly followed by other counties in the South, and Hampshire and Surrey played inter-county matches prior to the First World War. The game had spread to Ireland and Scotland by 1900 and the first international match had taken place in Dublin between England and Ireland in 1903. By 1908, the game had spread to South Africa, France, Germany, British Columbia and New York, but the game did not expand nationally in England until the 1930s, by which time it had spread to the north and north-east, commandeering every available drill hall and village hall in its path.

Such players as Frank Devlin, G. S. B. Mack and Frank Hodge graced the 1920s and 1930s, with Margaret Tragett and the McKane sisters notable amongst the ladies. By 1928, the Welsh Badminton Union had been born out of the North Wales Badminton Union and Wales played its first international against Scotland at Llandudno in 1929.

The issue of professionalism first surfaced in 1921, and a motion that anyone 'who had competed against a professional', had 'accepted expenses from a body other than the Badminton Association' or was 'a professional in any other branch of sport', should be declared a professional was defeated, it being decided that cases should be judged individually. The endorsement of racquets had been commonplace but the issue became a real one in 1931, when Devlin turned professional by becoming a full-time coach.

In 1925 the game spread to Denmark and to Sweden, and by 1935 it was also becoming very popular in the U.S. The spread of the game in Europe led to the formation of the International Badminton Federation (I.B.F.) in 1934, and a significantly influential development was its growing popularity in Malaysia. Frank Devlin visited the Malay States in 1937 and noted that 'The Malayan players are very good and amazingly active' – a sign of things to come.

By the end of the 1930s, the lack of adequate facilities had begun to hold the game back in Britain and the Danish invasion of 1939, which resulted in only one title being won by an English player, did little to help. Following the Second World War little changed in either respect, perhaps an early sign that a purely amateur approach did little to move the game out of drill halls or generate press coverage. The game had exploded into a world game and although the number of clubs affiliated to the B.A.E. had risen to 1,500 by 1946, the level and amount of competition was insufficient to enable parity to be maintained with other leading countries.

The All England Championships had remained the world's most popular tournament and it was perhaps Iris Cooley and June White's victory in the ladies doubles in 1953 which saw feint glimmerings of a climb back from the doldrums. The Thomas Cup games of the early 1950s also saw the beginnings of the Malaysian domination of the world game until the arrival of the Indonesians in the 1960s and the Chinese in the following decade.

In the 1970s, the arrival of better facilities in the form of local and regional sports centres and competition in the Commonwealth Games began to give British players something of a more level playing field on which to perform. Such players as Mike Tredgett of Gloucestershire, and Gillian Gilks, Norah Perry and Jane Webster in the ladies game, began to help English badminton climb slowly back on to the world stage. The game in Britain dispensed with the differentiation between amateurs and professionals in 1980.

References:

Adams, B., *The Badminton Story* (London: British Broadcasting Corporation, 1980).

Davis, P., *Badminton: the Complete Practical Guide* (Newton Abbott: David & Charles, 1988).

Websites:

The Badminton Association of England – http://www.baofe.co.uk/

The Welsh Badminton Union – http://www.welshbadminton.force9.co.uk/

The International Badminton Federation – http://www.intbadfed.org/

-Frank Galligan

Badminton House

Badminton House, the seat of the Dukes of Beaufort in the county of Avon, has had an illustrious association with sport in Britain. Built in 1692, it hosts the famous Badminton

Horse Trials event and also gave its name to the game of Badminton, which is said to have been first played there.

The eighth Duke, Henry Charles Fitzroy Somerset (1824-1899), became editor of the *Badminton Library of Sports and Pastimes*, published by Longmans, the first volume of which he co-wrote on *Hunting* in 1885. The aim of the series was to 'supply to lovers of field sports and of our national games and pastimes' books which 'should be, before all things, thoroughly practical, but the subjects will be diversified with anecdotes and incidents of sporting life'.

The Duke was an assiduous editor, but after his death it was Alfred E. T. Watson (1849-1922) who continued the task and also produced the *Badminton Magazine*, which derived from the book series.

Between 1885 and 1920, thirty books were published on activities ranging from field sports to golf and tennis and new pursuits such as motoring, with the authors being experts or personalities in the subject.

The *Badminton Library* books are profusely illustrated and provide a major source of information and comment on the growth and development of sports and pastimes in a crucial period in British sporting history. They fetch high prices on the second-hand book market and some volumes were re-printed by Ashford Press in the 1980s.

References:

Briggs, A., 'The View from Badminton' in A. Briggs (ed.), *Essays in the History of Publishing in Celebration of the 250th Anniversary of the House of Longman, 1724-1974* (London: Longman, 1974), pp. 187-218.

Further reading:

Watson, A. E. T., *A Sporting and Dramatic Career* (London: Macmillan, 1918).

See also:

Badminton; Eventing

-Eric Macintyre

Basketball

Basketball is an indoor handball game played between two teams, each team consisting of five players. Goals are scored when a player successfully throws the inflated ball through a stringed net. Nets are located at each end of the court and are mounted on a backboard 10 feet above the ground.

The ancient Central and South American civilizations played a form of basketball, which they called *pok-tapok*, with a rubber ball filled with sacred plants. The game was played during religious festivals and in honour of their gods; the playing area was decorated with symbols associated with their religious beliefs.

The origins of the modern game lie in the United States. Indeed, basketball remains the only major international sport with origins in North America. Following a request in 1891 by the Y.M.C.A., James Naismith developed the fundamentals of the modern game. Initially the game was played with an association football, but this was soon abandoned for a bigger, harder and bouncier ball. During play, no physical contact is allowed. What is more, players are not allowed to hold onto the ball, the ball being moved around the court via passing movements and dribbling. The art of dribbling is performed by the player bouncing the ball whilst running. The laws of the game have been designed to give it great movement. In 1895, the Y.M.C.A. developed a less energetic form of the game for women. This became known as netball, a sport that became very popular in British schools.

Until 1900, a peach basket was used as a goal. This was disadvantageous to the fast movement of the game as each time a goal was scored a ladder was required to retrieve the ball. Consequently, the bottomless net secured on an iron ring was introduced. This allowed the game to restart immediately after a goal was scored.

Basketball was introduced to Britain in 1892 by C. J. Procter, President of Birkenhead Y.M.C.A., following a business trip to Canada. From here it spread to other Y.M.C.A.s in the Merseyside region, but remained essentially a local initiative until 1911, when a Y.M.C.A. instructor took the game to Birmingham. Soon after, other teams were established playing to a simplified set of rules adapted from the American game.

The arrival of American personnel in Britain during the course of the First World War helped to spread the game further and to promote a version more akin to the American rules and styles of play.

In 1936, a meeting was called at the London Central Y.M.C.A. to form a governing body for the sport. The new association, the Amateur Basket Ball Association of England and Wales, was established with Herbert Naylor, National Physical Director of the Y.M.C.A., as chairman. The first National Championship, held later that year, was won by Hoylake, who beat Polytechnic in the final. They also won the next two finals, the 1938 final being broadcast live on radio.

The first composite England international team was selected to play in an international tournament in Berlin in 1938.

The Second World War also gave an impetus to the development of basketball in Britain. Many conscripts were introduced to the game for the first time, and those with some experience of basketball were introduced to a higher standard of play through the graded competitions in the services, the influx of French and Polish servicemen into Britain and, more especially, the arrival of the American forces in 1942-1943. Basketball was played extensively throughout the United States and most Americans had a good grounding and enthusiasm for the sport, which they took with them wherever they went. American forces remained at bases throughout Britain for many years and therefore continued to have an impact through their involvement in local leagues and competitions.

The rules used in Britain were the rules adopted by the International Basketball Federation founded in 1932 and have been revised at every World Championships. Separate associations now exist for the four countries making up the United Kingdom, with separate schools associations administering the game for the under-fifteens.

A National League was organized in England in 1960, but this failed to attract entries from the leading clubs so the sport had to wait until 1972-1973 for a truly National League competition to commence. Today, it comprises three men's and two women's divisions.

Although the televising of live matches on a Monday night on Channel 4 in the 1980s helped to promote the profile of basketball in Britain, it is probably true to say that it has still failed to attract the number of players, spectators and sponsors aspired to, especially compared with certain other European countries.

'Mission 2000', a National Lottery-funded initiative of the English Basketball Association (renamed in 1994), aimed to install several thousand basketball courts and hoops throughout the country in order to make it the most popular indoor game in Britain by the 21st century. Although this target has not been achieved, the initiative did help promote the sport within new communities.

The professional 'Budweiser League' was established in the early 1990s and appears to have established a solid financial base. Unfortunately, the professional game is not overseen by the English Basketball Association, and many of the players in the competition are foreign imports from North America.

References:

Arlott J. (ed.), *Oxford Companion to Sports and Games* (London: Oxford University Press, 1976).

English Basketball Association, *A Guide to English Basketball* (Leeds: English Basketball Association, 1999), pp. 5-10.

Websites:

The English Basketball Association – http://www.basketballengland.org.uk/

-Richard William Cox/Ray Physick

Bedford College

Bedford Physical Training College specialized in the training of young women to be physical educators.

It was founded in 1903 by owner and principal, Margaret Stansfeld O.B.E. (1860-1951), at Lansdowne Road, Bedford. The college was one of a small group of pioneer institutions established at a time when higher education and vocational training for women was frowned upon by Edwardian society.

Students had to prove their worth at a demanding range of disciplines. Theoretical subjects included the study of Anatomy, Physiology, and Hygiene. Practical work involved Swedish gymnastics, dancing, and various sports including cricket, hockey, netball and tennis. Teaching practice took place in secondary schools. Most students went on to become physical educators.

The college diploma was replaced in 1935 by a national qualification, The Diploma in the Theory and Practice of Education from the University of London. In 1952, the college became maintained by Bedfordshire County Council under its new title of Bedford College of Physical Education. Students took the University of Cambridge Certificate of Education, until B.Ed. degrees were introduced in 1968. The College was incorporated into the Bedford College of Higher Education in 1976. Since 1992, the site has been part of De Montfort University and still specializes in sport and education work at undergraduate and postgraduate level.

The Bedford Physical Education Old Students' Association meets regularly and has a current membership of over 1,000 old students.

References:

Smart, R., *On Others' Shoulders: an Illustrated History of the Polhill and Lansdowne Colleges, now De Montfort University Bedford* (Bedford: De Montfort University Bedford, 1994).

Further reading:

Fletcher, S., *Women First: the Female Tradition in English Physical Education 1880-1980* (London: Athlone Press, 1984).

See also:

Chelsea College; Dartford College; Dunfermline College; Education – Teacher Training; Physical Education Association of the United Kingdom

-Kelvin Street

Belfry (The)

One of the newest British championship golf courses, the Belfry opened in 1977 at Sutton Coldfield, close to the heart of the motorway system. It was severely criticized in its early years – Mark James, recent Ryder Cup captain, once described it as 'not fit to hold a Lincolnshire ladies' monthly medal'. It was improved and, in 1985, hosted the Ryder Cup, at which Europe claimed its first victory against the United States, the first American defeat for twenty-eight years. The Ryder Cup was successfully defended there in 1989 but the Americans proved victorious in 1993. Lord Derby resigned as President of the Professional Golfers Association after having to make the casting vote between the Belfry and the Spanish course, Club de Campo, for the site of the latter match. Although not a great course for spectators, because of its relatively flat terrain, or a really challenging one for the players, it has a two-hole finish as difficult and as exciting as any. The seventeenth is a long dog-leg to an elevated green (i.e., the players cannot aim directly at the green from the tee), followed by a par four final hole which necessitates two shots over water hazards with the second demanding accurate judgement of length to a three-tiered green. Recently, £2.4 million has been spent remodelling the Brabazon course, with the 2001 Ryder Cup to be held there, an event that coincides with the centenary of the Professional Golfers Association, whose headquarters and academy are at the course.

References:

Sunday Telegraph (30 August 1998).

Barrett, T. and Hobbs, M., *The Ultimate Encyclopedia of Golf* (London: Carlton, 1995).

Websites:

The Belfry – http://www.thebelfry.com/

See also:

Golf

-Wray Vamplew

Benefit

A benefit is a sports match from which all proceeds are paid to one player. Benefits originated in cricket and other sports during the 19th century as money-raising events for veteran professionals nearing retirement.

Benefit matches developed slowly in Victorian England, as there was no tradition of paying pensions to ordinary workers. Nevertheless, by the 1840s, cricketers such as William Clarke had staged benefits for themselves to earn extra income as retirement loomed.

By the end of the 19th century, benefits in many sports had developed established structures. In county cricket, players were offered the choice of a match, from which they would retain the gate receipts less the county's expenses. These were usually awarded after about fifteen years of service, but only at the behest of club committees. Unfortunately, this left players at the mercy of clubs, who could fail to provide benefits. William Scotton, who played for Nottinghamshire between 1875 and 1890, was one player who never received a benefit, and subsequently committed suicide in 1893.

Even when awarded, benefits could offer players a poor financial return, as matches were susceptible to poor weather and other factors affecting attendance. To counter this problem, a number of supplementary fund-raising events developed alongside benefit matches to generate more income for players and to spread financial risk.

Benefits are today organized with a high degree of professionalism to offer players the greatest possible financial rewards. Players now commonly employ accountants, agents, lawyers and professional fund-raisers to arrange and run their benefit events.

References:

Sandiford, K., *Cricket and the Victorians* (Aldershot: Scolar Press, 1994).

Vamplew, W., *Pay Up and Play the Game: Professional Sport in Britain, 1875-1914* (Cambridge: Cambridge University Press, 1988).

Further reading:

Sissons, R., *The Players: a Social History of the Professional Cricketer* (London: Kingswood, 1988).

See also:

Amateurism and Professionalism

-Gavin Mellor

Betting (*see* Gambling)

Bicycle Grass Track Racing (*see* Grass Track Racing)

Birmingham Athletic Institute

The Birmingham Athletic Institute (B.A.I.) was founded in 1889 by a group of philanthropists, including Sir George Dixon M.P., George Kenrik, Henry Mitchell, Dr H. Carter and Lord Beresford, who wanted to inspire civic development and social reform in Birmingham. The objectives of the Institute were to provide sporting facilities and instructors, and to encourage the formation of boys' and girls' clubs for all kinds of healthy exercise and recreation.

In 1891, the responsibilities of the Birmingham School Board Physical Exercises Committee were transferred to the B.A.I., which had appointed instructors trained in Europe and by 1896 was officially recognized by the Department of Education as a training centre for teachers of physical exercise in elementary schools.

By 1900, the B.A.I. was playing an important part in education, in community sport and physical training and in the general area of health promotion and heath education.

References:

Waterman, M. I. (ed.), *B.A.I.: Birmingham Athletic Institute Remembered* (Birmingham: Brewin Books, 1992).

-Charles Jenkins

Birmingham University

In 1939, the University of Birmingham, with personal encouragement from the Vice-Chancellor, Sir Raymond Priestley (a member of Scott's Antarctic expedition), developed a range of sports facilities on the Edgbaston campus. In the same year, A. D. (Dave) Munrow was appointed Director of Physical Education. The stimulus for such pioneering developments in British universities was a general concern about the health and fitness of students.

Two further innovations contributed to the unique status of physical education at Birmingham. Firstly, a physical recreation course was compulsory for all undergraduates from 1940 to 1968. More significantly, in 1946, Birmingham became the first British university to offer a non-vocational degree course in Physical Education.

Following the 1956 publication by departmental staff of the influential booklet *Britain in the World of Sport*, Munrow became a member of the Wolfenden Committee (1957-1960). In 1972, he was succeeded by W. J. (Bill) Slater, the former Wolves and England soccer captain. The Department's reputation was further enhanced by the contributions of Peter McIntosh (sociology) and Barbara Knapp (psychology). Slater's departure in 1984 heralded a radical change of direction. In 1986, C. T. M. (Mervyn) Davies was appointed as Professor of Applied Physiology and head of the newly entitled 'School of Sport and Exercise Sciences'. The School was located in the Science Faculty and a sports science degree was instituted. A dramatic increase in both student numbers and research activity has enabled Birmingham to retain its position as one of the leading British universities in the field of sport and exercise sciences.

References:

The Physical Education Department, *Britain in the World of Sport* (Birmingham: University of Birmingham, 1956).

The Wolfenden Committee on Sport, Sport and the Community (London: The Central Council of Physical Recreation, 1960).

Further reading:

Campbell, L., *An Analysis of the Evolution of Master's Degrees in Physical Education and Associated Areas in British Universities* (M.Ed. Dissertation, University of Glasgow, 1988).

See also:

British Universities Sports Association; Cambridge University; Oxford University; University Boat Race

-Ian Moir

Bisham Abbey

For 800 years, Bisham Abbey, set in beautiful grounds on the banks of the river Thames, was both a home and a place of refuge for the English nobility and aristocracy.

In 1780, Bisham was bought by the Vansittart family and was their home until 1947, when Phyllis Vansittart-Neale loaned and then sold the building to the Central Council of Physical Recreation in memory of her two nephews who were killed in the Second World War. It then became the first National Recreation Centre in Britain.

More recently, it has become one of five centres of excellence for the country's leading sportsmen and women and is part of the network of sites that comprise the U.K. Sports Institute. It is the training centre for England's football and hockey teams, the British Amateur Weight Lifters' Association, and is extensively used by the Lawn Tennis Association for coaching up-and-coming players.

As a centre of sporting excellence, the Abbey is equipped with a modern gymnasium, with extensive free weights training facilities. There are four indoor and ten outdoor tennis courts, including three clay courts; four outdoor football and Rugby pitches as well as two floodlight astroturf pitches marked out for hockey; two squash courts; and a dance studio where aerobics and other activities take place. There is also a 9-hole par 3 golf course within the Abbey grounds, which is exclusively a members-only course. In the early 1970s, residential accommodation blocks were built within the grounds for sportsmen and women using the facilities.

-Brian Pluckrose

Bobsleigh

Bobsleigh was invented by wealthy English tourists in St Moritz, Switzerland, in 1890. It is now one of the most exciting of Alpine sports.

It is a sport based on a mixture of speed and ice. The aim is for the two-man or four-man teams to drive their sled down a 1500-metre course in the quickest combined time from four runs.

The British Bobsleigh Association was formed in 1927 in New York and is the national governing body for the sport. It is recognized by the Fédération Internationale de Bobsleigh et de Tobogganing (F.I.B.T. – International Bobsleigh and Tobogganing Federation), which was formed in 1923. The F.I.B.T. governs the rules for Bobsleigh and controls all world championships. Bobsleigh was included in the first Winter Olympics in 1924, and has been a common feature ever since.

Bobsleigh has been Britain's most successful winter team sport. In 1964, Tony Nash and Robin Dixon took gold in the two-man event. In 1994, both Britain's teams finished in the top ten. At the 1998 Olympics in Nagano (Japan), Britain won bronze in the four-man event. This was despite the fact that there are no bobsleigh runs in Britain.

Women's bobsleighing began as a recognized sport in the 1990s, and Britain was one of the leading nations in pushing the F.I.B.T. to acknowledge the women's event. Recognition was achieved in 1995, and women's bobsleigh is expected to be an event

The Great Britain Bobsleigh team at the 1998 Winter Olympics in Nagano, Japan (Credit: Action Images / Stuart Franklin)

at the 2002 Olympics. Britain's women's team is highly successful and finished second in the 1997 and 1998 World Cups.

References:

Kotter, K., 'Le bobsleigh et la fédération internationale de bobsleigh et de tobogganing', *Message-Olympique* (June 1984), p. 59-66.

Mallon, B., 'On Two Blades and a Few Prayers', *Olympian* (vol. 18, no. 6, 1992), p. 54-55.

O'Brien, A. and O'Bryan, M., *Bobsled and Luge* (Toronto, Canada: Colban, 1976).

Wallechinsky, D., *The Complete Book of the Winter Olympics* (London: Aurum, 1998).

Websites:

International Bobsleigh and Tobogganing Federation – http://www.fibt.com/

The British Bobsleigh Association – http://www.british-bobsleigh.com/

-Mike Cronin

Bowls (Indoor and Outdoor)

Bowling games came to England from northern France, no later than the 13th century, and are closely related to skittles, an import from Germany. Many local forms have been played and some survive – however, only flat and crown green bowls will be discussed here.

The origin of modern bowls lies in two developments in the 16th century – the introduction of the jack (a moveable target) and the bias bowl (a bowl with an irregular shape). Half-bowls, which had a large bias, had been used in skittles games in the Middle Ages. The new bowls had a small bias and increased the subtlety of the game.

Most of the important developments in the creation of modern bowls took place in

37

Scotland between 1771 and 1892. The first rules were written in 1771 by the Edinburgh Society of Bowlers. They wished to gain a 'seal of cause' from the city, enabling the Society to own property, and the city required that they submit their rules for approval. The oldest surviving bowling trophy, a silver jack, was made for the Society in 1781. The game developed further in the west of Scotland through an insistence on the use of the finest quality of turf, emphasizing the players' skill. In 1848/9, William Mitchell, a Glasgow solicitor, wrote new rules at the request of the Scottish clubs. These were used immediately in Scotland, standardizing the game, and over succeeding decades were taken up by some English clubs.

The idea of a bowling club was central to the development of the game. Good turf is expensive to lay and needs continued maintenance – the club was the mechanism for funding this. The Victorian bowling green was costly, so members of clubs were usually professionals and tradesmen. The expansion of the

game to the working classes followed the development of municipal greens. The first was probably at Leith (1857), and many others followed by 1914.

The institutional structure of bowls was created between 1882 and 1904. The Northumberland and Durham Bowling Association, the first county body, was set up in 1882. The most important of the early organizations was the Scottish Bowling Association (S.B.A.), founded in 1892 – its first tasks were the clarification and expansion of the laws and the organization of national competitions. Parallel associations followed in England (1903), Wales (1904), and Ireland (1904). From the beginning, the S.B.A. set its face against cash prizes and thus created the strictly amateur sport that survived until the 1980s. The International (later Imperial) Bowling Association was set up in 1899 – it was supplanted by the International Bowls Board (now the World Bowls Board) in 1905. The first series of international matches between all four

Bowlers on the green of the Spread Eagle, Turton, near Bolton. Photograph by T. Calvert, Turton, c.1890s. (Documentary Photography Archive, Manchester. Ref: 540/1 J1/39)

home nations at one venue was played in London in 1903, and the series has continued annually since then. The leading figure in setting up the internationals was Dr W. G. Grace.

The nature of the game is such that few bowlers, before the era of professionalism, have been consistent winners at the highest level. Percy Baker of Dorset won the English Bowling Association (E.B.A.) singles title four times between 1932 and 1955. His record was beaten by David Bryant, who was singles champion on six occasions between 1960 and 1975, and indoor champion an amazing nine times.

Indoor bowling using outdoor bowls was tried, unsuccessfully, at Edinburgh in 1888 – matting provided far too fast a surface. The use of a heavier carpet made possible the formation of the Edinburgh Winter Bowling Association in 1905. The indoor game spread in England, and was already widespread when an indoor section of the E.B.A. was created in 1933. Internationals, similar to those for the outdoor game, started in 1935. England dominated indoor bowls, both in numbers of players and in international success, until after 1960.

The early history of women's bowls is shadowy. When, in 1906, London County Council laid out greens in public parks, they specified that one rink on each should be reserved for women. The first women's club was Kingston Canbury (1910). The first national tournament for women was held at Eastbourne in 1931. A month later, the English Women's Bowling Association was set up and the organizer of the tournament, Mrs Clara E. Johns, elected president. Similar bodies followed in Wales (1932), Scotland (1936) and Ireland (1947).

The English Bowling Federation (E.B.F.) supervises a game with slightly different rules, the most important of which is that no bowl counts unless it is less than 2 yards from the jack. The Federation game emerged in public parks in Newcastle in the 1890s. It spread down the east coast of England, growing rapidly after the First

World War. A number of county associations combined in 1926 to form the Midland and East Anglia Bowling Association, which in 1945 transformed itself into the English Bowling Federation. Federation bowls is less formal than the E.B.A. game – there is not the same insistence on wearing whites for matches, greens are often beside public houses, and mixed play has been encouraged since the 1920s. The E.B.A., on the other hand, did not allow mixed competition until 1985.

Crown green bowls grew up in the North of England, chiefly on small greens beside public houses. The green is higher in the middle than at the edges, and the jack, as well as the bowls, is biased. It also differs from the E.B.A. game by allowing professionalism and betting. The first county organization, covering Lancashire and Cheshire, was formed in 1888. The first major competition was the Talbot Handicap, organised by Robert Nickson, landlord of the Talbot Arms at Blackpool. It ran from 1887 to 1975, when the Talbot green was turned into a car park. The Waterloo Handicap (established 1907), also at Blackpool, is now the premier event.

The manufacture of an accurately biased bowl is a skilled task, carried out by wood turners. In the middle of the 19th century some began to concentrate exclusively on bowl making. The most successful material was lignum vitae, a very dense wood from San Domingo. Although bowls made of a rubber-based compound were developed in Australia during the 1920s, they were little used in Britain until after the Second World War – the manufacture of the de Havilland Mosquito, an aircraft with all-wood fuselage and wings, had used up all the stocks of lignum vitae. Wooden bowls are now rarely used.

Further reading:

Haynes, A. H., *The Story of Bowls* (London: Sporting Handbooks, 1972).

Pilley, P. (ed.), *The Story of Bowls: From Drake to Bryant* (London: Stanley Paul, 1987).

Pretsell, J., *The Game of Bowls: Past and Present* (Edinburgh: Oliver & Boyd, 1908).

Sullivan, P., *Bowls: the Records* (Enfield: Guinness Books, 1986).

Websites:

The English Bowling Association – http://www.bowlsengland.com/

The English Indoor Bowling Association – http://www.eiba.co.uk/

The British Crown Green Bowling Association – http://www.bowls.org/

-John Burnett

Boxing

Fighting with the fists for sport and spectacle is probably as old as sport itself. The word 'boxing' first came into use in England in the 18th century to distinguish between fighting to settle disputes, and fighting under agreed rules for sport. It is now used to describe a sport in which two contestants (boxers) wearing padded gloves face each other in a 'ring' and fight an agreed number of 'rounds' under recognized rules. Although men have always been the most numerous participants, there are some references to fights between women during the 18th century, and women's boxing was organized again at the end of the 20th century.

Throughout the latter part of the 19th century and the whole of the 20th century, amateur and professional boxing operated in parallel. In the final quarter of the 20th century, however, amateur boxing lost much of its popular support. Traditional concerns about bruises and black eyes gave way to more serious concerns about long-term eye and brain damage, and medical checks on boxers, and medical supervision of their fights, became an increasingly important feature of both amateur and professional boxing.

Origins

18th- and early 19th-century pugilism (bare-knuckle fighting) was an important precursor of boxing in Britain. Boxing, however, proba-bly grew most specifically out of the demonstrations held at the Fives Court and the Tennis Court in London in the early 19th century. These promotions had several features that anticipated the future sport of boxing. The boxers wore 'mufflers' (padded gloves), and 'time' was called after a set period, and the length of the fight was predetermined. Wrestling throws were also barred. None of these features were present in bare-knuckle pugilism (see 'Pugilism').

'Boxing' as distinct from any other form of fist fighting can be dated from 1867, when John Graham Chambers drafted new rules. There were twelve rules in all, and they specified that fights should be 'a fair stand-up boxing match' in a 24-foot ring. Rounds were to be of three minutes duration with one minute between rounds. Ten seconds were allowed for a man to get up if he had gone down during a round. New gloves of 'fair-size' were to be worn and 'wrestling or hugging' was specifically forbidden. These rules were published under the patronage of the Marquess of Queensberry, whose name has always been associated with them. The first fighter to win a world title under these rules was Jim Corbett, who defeated John L. Sullivan in 1892 at the Pelican Athletic Club in New Orleans.

The success of boxers has always been associated with their size. In the early days of pugilism, however, there was only one 'Champion', who always tended to be one of the heaviest. The term 'light weight' was in use from the early 19th century and fights were sometimes arranged between the lighter men, but there was no specific Championship for them. The terms 'lightweight', 'welterweight', 'middleweight' and 'heavy weight' became common during the late 19th century, but there were no universally recognized definitions of weight class. Throughout the 20th century, new weight classes were added, extending the range down to 'strawweight' and up to 'super-heavyweight' but with varying agreement over their definitions.

In the early days of pugilism, all fighters were 'professional' in the sense that few would fight for 'love' rather than money. No distinct 'amateur' sport existed until 1867, when amateur championships under Marquess of Queensberry Rules were held at Lillie Bridge in London for Lightweights, Middleweights and Heavyweights. By this date, the old professional bare-knuckle 'Prize Ring' was in terminal decline. It had always been against the law, but in the early part of the century it survived because it had widespread popular support and because there were many influential men who supported it. By 1867, however, the results of fights were increasingly suspect, and sometimes boxers even failed to turn up for fights. Less money came into the sport and bare-knuckle pugilism slowly died out.

Conversely, the amateur side of the sport flourished, not only in schools, universities and in the armed forces, but also in the working-class areas of the expanding urban centres.

With the gradual acceptance of Marquess of Queensberry Rules, two distinct branches of boxing emerged, professional and amateur, and each produced its own local, national and international governing bodies and its own variation of the rules.

Governance – Professional

For a generation following the creation of the Queensberry Rules, bare-knuckle and glove-fights were both promoted. The bare-knuckle fights were usually held under the 'New Rules' produced by the Pugilistic Benevolent Society in 1866, which had superseded the 'Pugilistic Association's Revised Rules' of 1853. They were often popularly referred to as the 'Rules of the London Prize-Ring'.

In 1891, the National Sporting Club (N.S.C.), a private club in London, began to promote professional glove fights at its own premises, and created nine of its own rules to augment the Queensberry Rules. These rules specified more accurately the role of the officials, and produced a system of scoring that

enabled the referee to decide the result of a fight. Previously, all fights ended with a knock-out or, more usually, when one fighter was too exhausted to continue. It was thanks to the N.S.C. Rules that the sport emerged into one of skill rather than of endurance. The British Boxing Board of Control (B.B.B.C.) was first formed in 1919 with close links to the N.S.C., and was re-formed in 1929 after the N.S.C. closed.

In 1909, the first of twenty-two belts were presented by the fifth Earl of Lonsdale to the winner of a British title-fight held at the N.S.C. In 1929, the B.B.B.C. continued to award Lonsdale Belts to any British boxer who won three title-fights in the same weight division. The 'title fight' has always been the focal point in professional boxing. In the 19th and early 20th centuries, however, there were relatively few. As weight divisions became increasingly recognized, however, there were title-fights at each weight. Promoters who could stage profitable title-fights became influential in the sport. So, too, did boxers' managers. The best promoters and managers have been instrumental in bringing boxing to new audiences and provoking media and public interest. The most famous of all three-way partnerships (fighter-manager-promoter) was that of Jack Dempsey (Heavyweight Champion, 1919-1928), his manager Jack Kearns, and the promoter Tex Rickard. Together they grossed US$ 8.4 million in only five fights between 1921 and 1927 and ushered in a 'golden age' of popularity for professional boxing in the 1920s. They were also responsible for the first live radio broadcast of a title-fight (Dempsey v. Carpentier, in 1921). In Britain, Jack Solomons' success as a fight promoter helped re-establish professional boxing after the Second World War and made Britain a poplar place for title-fights in the 1950s and 1960s.

In the first part of the 20th century, the United States became the centre for professional boxing. It was generally accepted that the 'world champions' were those listed by the

Police Gazette. After 1920, the National Boxing Association (N.B.A.) and the New York State Athletic Commission (N.Y.S.A.C.) began to sanction 'title-fights'. The N.B.A. was renamed in 1962 and became the World Boxing Association (W.B.A.). The following year, a rival body, the World Boxing Council (W.B.C.), was formed. The influence, internationally, of the N.Y.S.A.C. declined. In 1983, another world body, the International Boxing Federation (I.B.F.) was formed, and in 1989, this was followed by yet another, the World Boxing Organisation (W.B.O.). Each body sanctions its own title-fights and recognizes its own 'champions'. By the end of the 20th century, a boxer had to be recognized by four separate bodies to be the 'undisputed champion' of the world, and each year saw over 100 'title-fights' take place in up to seventeen weight divisions.

Although women fought professionally in many countries, in Britain the B.B.B.C. refused to issue licenses to women until 1998. By the end of the century, however, they had issued five such licenses. The first sanctioned bout was in November 1998 at Streatham in London, between Jane Couch and Simona Lukic.

Governance – Amateur

The Queensberry Amateur Championships continued from 1867 to 1885, and so, unlike their professional counterparts, amateur boxers did not deviate from using gloves once the Queensberry Rules had been published. In Britain, the Amateur Boxing Association (A.B.A.) was formed in 1880 when twelve clubs affiliated. It held its first championships the following year. Four weight classes were contested, Featherweight (9 stone), Lightweight (10 stone), Middleweight (11 stone, 4 pounds) and Heavyweight (no limit). By 1902, American boxers were contesting the titles in the A.B.A. Championships, which, therefore, took on an international complexion. By 1924, the A.B.A. had 105 clubs in affiliation.

Boxing first appeared at the Olympic Games in 1904 and, apart from the Games of

Soldiers boxing in France during the First World War (Documentary Photography Archive, Manchester, Ref: 600/19 J23/35)

1912, has always been part of them. Internationally, amateur boxing spread steadily throughout the first half of the 20th century, but when the first international body, the Fédération Internationale de Boxe Amateur (International Amateur Boxing Federation), was formed in Paris in 1920, there were only five member nations. In 1946, however, when the International Amateur Boxing Association (A.I.B.A.) was formed in London, twenty-four nations from five continents were represented, and the A.I.B.A. has continued to be the official world federation of amateur boxing ever since. The first World Amateur Boxing Championships were staged in 1974.

In the late 19th and early 20th century, amateur boxing was encouraged in schools, universities and in the armed forces, but the champions, in the main, came from among the urban poor.

Women's boxing first appeared in the Olympic Games as a demonstration bout in 1904. For most of the 20th century, however, it was banned in most nations. Its revival was pioneered by the Swedish Amateur Boxing Association, which sanctioned events for women in 1988. The British Amateur Boxing Association sanctioned its first boxing competition for women in 1997. The first event was to be between two thirteen year olds, but one of the boxers withdrew because of hostile media attention. Four weeks later, an event was held between two sixteen year olds.

The A.I.B.A. accepted new rules for Women's Boxing at the end of the 20th century and approved the first European Cup for Women in 1999 and the first World Championship for women in 2001.

Personalities

Among British amateur boxers, only those who won Olympic gold medals tended to achieve recognition beyond the limits of boxing enthusiasts. They included Harry Mallin (Middleweight, 1920 and 1924), Terry Spinks (Flyweight, 1956), Dick McTaggart (Lightweight, 1956) and Chris Finnegan (Middleweight, 1968). In 1908, at the Olympic Games in London, five weight divisions were contested, Bantamweight, Featherweight, Lightweight, Middleweight and Heavyweight. British boxers won them all, and four of the finals were all-British!

It is the professional side of boxing, however, that has produced the celebrities whose activities the public have generally followed. In the period between bare-knuckle pugilism and post-Queensberry boxing, Jem Mace was important. He carried many of the traditions of the old London Prize-Ring, but promoted the use of gloves and helped to popularize the sport in the United States and Australia. In the post-Queensberry era, the first British fighter to achieve superstar status was Bob Fitzsimmons. He weighed less than 12 stone but won world titles at Middleweight (1891), Light-heavyweight (1903) and Heavyweight (1897), and fought his last bout at the age of fifty-two.

Successful fighters have provoked fierce local pride. The best example was Jimmy Wilde, a Welsh Flyweight who won the world Flyweight Championship in 1916 and held it until 1923. He once had a sequence of eighty-eight fights without defeat. Between 1911 and 1923, he won seventy-five of his fights by a knockout. He was idolized in Wales, where they commonly believed him to be the best boxer, pound-for-pound, that ever lived. He was described as the 'Mighty Atom' and 'the ghost with a hammer in his hand'. Freddy Welsh (Freddy Hall Thomas), from Pontypridd, won the Lightweight title in 1912.

The Scots had a similar pride in Benny Lynch, a Flyweight from Glasgow, who held the world Flyweight title in 1935 and again in 1937. Over the years, Scots have had great success at this weight; Jackie Paterson won the title in 1943 and Walter McGowan in 1966. Ken Buchanan won the Lightweight title in 1971 and Jim Watt in 1980. In Northern Ireland, Rinty Monahan held the Flyweight title from

1947 to 1950 and Barry McGuigan won the W.B.C. Featherweight title in 1985.

England, too, has had its successes at the lighter weights. Among the Flyweights, Jackie Brown won the title in 1932, Peter Kane in 1938 and Terry Allen in 1950. Jim Driscoll won the Featherweight title in 1909 and Naseem Hamed in the 1990s.

Britain has had other popular world champions. In the 1930s, Jackie Berg won the Light-Welterweight title; in the 1940s, Freddie Mills won the Light-Heavyweight title; in the 1950s and 1960s, Randolph Turpin and Terry Downes won Middle-Weight titles; and in the 1970s, John Conteh and John Stracey won the Light-Heavyweight and Welterweight titles respectively. With so many title-awarding bodies in the 1980s and 1990s, the public became unsure about who actually was the champion. Nevertheless, the successes of Nigel Benn, Chris Eubank and Joe Calzaghe continued to bring extensive media coverage to boxing and sustained a considerable public following.

The most popular boxers, however, have not always been the world title-holders. Just fighting for the world title in the Heavyweight division can bestow celebrity status, as was shown by Henry Cooper, who twice unsuccessfully fought Mohammed Ali in the 1960s, and Frank Bruno, who twice unsuccessfully fought Mike Tyson, once in 1989 and again in 1996.

Britain had to wait 100 years to have its first Heavyweight champion since Bob Fitzsimmons lost his title in 1899. Lennox Lewis became undisputed champion in 1999, having first gained the W.B.C. title in 1993.

Sue Atkins (alias Sue Catkins) helped to pioneer women's boxing in Britain in the 1980s, but without any official recognition. The first British woman to be issued with a license was Jane Couch from Fleetwood, who won the Women's International Boxing Federation (W.I.B.F.) Welterweight title in 1996.

References:

Andre, S. and Fleisher, N., *A Pictorial History of Boxing* (London: Hamlyn, 1998).

Hartley, R. A., *History and Bibliography of Boxing Books* (Alton: Nimrod Press, 1988).

Sugden, J. P., *Boxing and Society: an International Analysis* (Manchester: Manchester University Press, 1996).

Weston, S., *The Best of The Ring: the Bible of Boxing* (Chicago: Bonus Books, 1996).

Further reading:

McIlvanney, H., *McIlvanney on Boxing: an Anthology* (London: Stanley Paul, 1990).

Mailer, N., *The Fight* (Harmondsworth: Penguin, 1991).

Fraser, G. M., *Black Ajax* (London: HarperCollins, 1997).

Websites:

The International Amateur Boxing Association – http://www.aiba.net/

The World Boxing Association – http://www.wbaonline.com/

The World Boxing Council – http://www.wbcboxing.com/

The World Boxing Organization – http://www.wbo-int.com/

The International Boxing Federation – http://www.ibf-usba-boxing.com/

See also:

Pugilism

-Peter Radford

Brands Hatch

One of Britain's most prestigious motor-racing circuits, Brands Hatch is said to have been discovered by a group of cyclists in 1926 whilst travelling on the A20 London-Maidstone road, near Farningham, 20 miles south east of London. The cyclists noticed a stretch of farmland that formed a natural amphitheatre, which would be ideal for spectators. They asked the farmer for permission to use it and began organizing competitions around the kidney-shaped track. Two years later, they were joined by motor-cycling enthusiasts.

During the Second World War, the army moved in, and although one or two bombs were exploded there, damage was not too serious and by 1947 racing had recommenced.

In 1947, ex-speedway ace Joe Francis bought the land from the farm, and formed a limited company. Plans went ahead to surface the cinder track with tarmacadam. The 1-mile track (later extended to 1.24 miles) was officially opened on April 16th, 1950. In 1954, an extra loop was added to the circuit.

By 1960, the circuit had been purchased by Grovewood Securities Ltd. It was under their management that the Grand Prix circuit was built – extending the distance to 2.65 miles.

In the motor-cycling world, Brands Hatch became famous as the nursery of talent. John Surtees (one-time world motor-car and motor-cycle champion) won his first race there and other well-known drivers were said to have cut their racing teeth at the Hatch.

Some of the events became as famous as the names associated with them. One such was the Hutchinson '100', which was always run in an anti-clockwise direction. Another, the Guard's Trophy, produced a long string of memorable six-hour saloon car races. The first British Grand Prix to be held at the Hatch took place in 1964 and was repeated in 1966, 1968 and 1970, alternating with Silverstone. Regarded as an exceptionally tricky circuit because of its changes in gradient and tight corners, the Hatch was the scene of several fatalities in the 1960s, which contributed to its decline as a popular course for competitions. Although it played second fiddle to Silverstone throughout the 1970s, the 1980s and the 1990s, plans were announced in 1999 to upgrade the track and to use it for the British Grand Prix once again in the 21st century.

References:

Georgano, G. N., *The Encyclopaedia of Motor Sport* (London: Ebury Press & Michael Joseph, 1971).

Hamilton, M., *British Grand Prix* (Swindon: Crowood, 1990).

Websites:

Brands Hatch Leisure Group – http://www.brands-hatch.co.uk/

See also:

Motor Racing

-Richard William Cox

British Association for Shooting and Conservation

The British Association for Shooting and Conservation (B.A.S.C.) is the main organization responsible for fostering and safeguarding shooting, with particular emphasis on wildfowling (a specialist branch of shooting, which traditionally involves the pursuit of wild ducks and geese on marshes and foreshores) and roughshooting (which involves the pursuit of a multitude of species, including game birds and rabbits). It represents the interests of wildfowlers on numerous national and international committees. Until the 1970s, it was known as the Wildfowlers Association of Great Britain and Ireland (W.A.G.B.I.), which had been founded in 1908 by Stanley Duncan. It has several hundred affiliated wildfowling clubs, which are responsible for controlling wildfowling on their local marshes.

One of its most important functions is to monitor political activity at local, governmental and European levels. Draft legislation affecting land use, wildlife conservation or firearms is reviewed and the appropriate representations made. Its staff provide advice and services covering all aspects of shooting and practical conservation to both individual members and wildfowling clubs. Practical conservation measures have included The Duck Conservation Scheme in 1954; the establishment of the Wildfowl Trust's experimental reserve at Sevenoaks in 1958; and assisting the Icelandic government's research into Pink-footed Geese, threatened by a proposed hydroelectric development in the 1970s. The B.A.S.C.'s Wildlife Habitat Trust has provided resources for purchasing the freehold of some marshes. The designation of Sites of Special Scientific Interest (S.S.S.I.s) and Special Protection Areas (S.P.A.s) have posed a threat to the survival of wildfowling in many localities. Work by its research staff includes investigations into the effects of harsh weather upon wildfowl and joint projects with other organizations into the effects on wildfowl of the ingestion of lead shot.

Until the 1980s, the rise of wildfowling clubs was not universally popular, since some wildfowlers were reluctant to accept a degree of regulation. Membership, for most shooters, is now a necessary prerequisite to securing access to suitable wildfowling foreshore. There has been a gradual realization that self-regulation and the voluntary acceptance of sensible and moderate codes of conduct is the most effective way of avoiding more draconian statutory regulations.

References:

WAGBI, *Nature Conservancy and the Wildfowl Trust* (Chester: WAGBI, 1970).

WAGBI, *The Story of a Triumvirate: Wildfowl Conservation in Great Britain* (Chester: WAGBI, 1970).

Websites:

The British Association for Shooting and Conservation – http://www.basc.org.uk/

See also:

Field Sports; Game Shooting; Wildfowling

-John Martin

British Association of Sport and Exercise Medicine

The British Association of Sport and Exercise Medicine (formerly the British Association of Sport and Medicine) was founded as the representative professional body in sports medicine in 1953, when a group of doctors, mostly the medical officers of the governing bodies of sport, met at the Westminster Hospital in London at the instigation of Sir Adolphe Abrahams and Sir Arthur Porritt. In the early stages, meetings were held in various London hospitals, and some special committees were set up on an ad hoc basis to give guidance on specific matters relating to medical and physiological aspects of sport.

By 1961, there was a membership of around 100, mostly doctors, but a few national coaches and physiotherapists were brought in as associated members in an advisory capacity. By that time it was realized that sports medicine, like many other branches of medicine, was becoming an interdisciplinary subject, so full membership was opened to dental surgeons, veterinary surgeons, physiotherapists, physiologists, physical educationalists and other pure and applied scientists whose interests or work overlapped into sports-related fields of study. Membership rapidly rose to 300 – medical membership alone was doubled in two years – and there are now approximately 1,000 members, including podiatrists, chiropodists and osteopaths who hold a qualification acceptable as a condition of employment in a United Kingdom National Health Service Hospital.

The Association is divided into three home countries – Northern Ireland, Scotland and Wales; and nine regions – Eastern, East Midlands, London and South East, Northern, North West, Southern, South West, West Midlands, and Yorkshire, according to the U.K. Sports Council and English Sports Council Boundaries.

The British Association of Sport and Exercise Medicine seeks to promote public health and fitness as well as to conduct research into the causation and treatment of medical problems aligned with sport and exercise.

As a vehicle of communication between the Executive Committee and members, as well as an outlet for the publication of the proceedings of scientific meetings, the *Bulletin of the British Association of Sports Medicine* was established in 1965. By the spring of 1969, with a policy of accepting only original articles, the *Bulletin* was incorporated into a new journal, the *British Journal of Sports Medicine* (this title is copyright), although the volume numbers established for the *Bulletin* were continued. The first issue of the *Journal* was therefore vol. IV no. 1.

In 1996, the Association entered into a joint partnership with the British Medical Journal Publishing Group. The *British Journal of Sports Medicine*, published bi-monthly, also has a new appearance and a new editor, and the quality of presentation and content is continually improving. Attachment to a professional medical publishing house has brought rewards in the form of increased international recognition and access to new technologies. The journal is now on the Citation Index and there are plans to make it available on the internet.

The annual congress is a three- or four-day event organized by and for the members in October or November of each year. There is a great deal of input from the organizers of the home countries and regions, with the financial management of the conference being monitored and controlled by the national executive. This is the leading British sports medicine congress and it attracts sponsorship from major companies who wish to make contact with people actively involved in sport and exercise medicine. The conference is held in a different home country or region each year.

The British Association of Sport and Exercise Medicine runs a national medical educational programme, with the financial and administrative aspects of the courses being serviced by the National Sports Medicine Institute in a partnership agreement.

See also:

Sports Medicine

-John H. Clegg

British Association of Sport and Exercise Sciences

The British Association of Sport and Exercise Sciences (B.A.S.E.S.) aims to promote the scientific study of sport and exercise in the United Kingdom. Since its inception in the early 1980s, it has spearheaded developments that have affected not only sport and exercise scientists but also coaches and performers.

B.A.S.E.S. supports and monitors sport and exercise research and consultancy. It also disseminates sport and exercise science knowledge to its members through a quarterly newsletter and to the wider sport and scientific community through the *Journal of Sports Sciences*.

Originally named the British Association of Sport Scientists (B.A.S.S.), the organization was established to enable sport scientists from different disciplines to collaborate more easily. The name change to B.A.S.E.S. in 1993 reflected more accurately the interests of the members involved in the science of exercise as well as sport.

Specialist interests are recognized within the Association. The disciplines of physiology, biomechanics and psychology have their own sections. The interdisciplinary section enables the social scientists and members with multi- or interdisciplinary interests to play an active role within the association. Each section of B.A.S.E.S. runs regular workshops and there are also annual conferences for both members and students.

B.A.S.E.S. has various categories of membership. Many sports science posts now require applicants to be accredited by B.A.S.E.S. Accreditation involves a process of peer review within the particular section. The highest category of membership is Fellowship, which is awarded to individuals who have made a substantial contribution to academic research in sport and exercise sciences.

References:

The British Association of Sport and Exercise Sciences, *Members' Handbook* (Leeds: British Association of Sport and Exercise Sciences, 1995).

Websites:

The British Association of Sport and Exercise Sciences – http://www.bases.co.uk/

See also:

Sports Science

-Kyle Phillpots

References:

'The British Olympic Association and its Role in the Olympic Movement', *Olympic Review* (January-February 1976).

Websites:

The British Olympic Association – http://www.olympics.org.uk/

See also:

Olympic Games

-Ian Buchannan

British Olympic Association

On the initiative of Sir Howard Vincent, MP and the Reverend de Courcy Laffan, the British Olympic Association (B.O.A.) was founded at a meeting at the House of Commons on May 24th, 1905. Representatives of the governing bodies of all major sports were elected to the council and Lord Desborough was appointed as the first President.

After playing only a minimal role in Britain's participation at the Intercalated Olympic Games of 1906, the B.O.A. successfully organized the Games of 1908, which Britain agreed to host at short notice after the Italians withdrew. The B.O.A. again played a pivotal role when Britain hosted the Olympic Games for a second time in 1948.

In more recent times, the B.O.A. has become one of the most influential sporting bodies in Britain. The National Olympic Committee is made up of elected officials representing each Olympic sport and the Association provides many facilities for competitors who have reached Olympic standard. A medical centre has been established at Harrow, there are training centres throughout the country and at selected locations abroad, and help is given in finding employment for potential Olympians. Fund-raising has been an ever-present task and through appeals, sponsorship and licensing, the B.O.A. raises the funds required to send teams to every Summer and Winter Olympic Games.

British Society of Sports History

The British Society of Sports History was founded by Richard Cox. It emerged, to some extent, out of a History of Physical Education Study Group that had established itself within the History of Education Society in the mid-1970s, led by David McNair and Nick Parry. As interest in the broader area of sport started to take precedent, a new group with the name British Society *for* Sports History was formed in 1981. After a number of informal meetings, the inaugural conference was organized and took place at the University of Liverpool in March 1982. Peter McIntosh, Tony Mangan, John Lowerson and Richard Holt were invited as the main speakers, with additional contributions on the second day of the conference from Derek Benning, Beryl Furlong, Joachim Rühl and Peter Treadwell. At this conference, the British Society *of* Sports History was more formally constituted, with Tony Mangan as Chairman. He was succeeded by Tony Mason in 1985, Richard Cox in 1991, and Grant Jarvie in 1996.

Membership grew to around sixty in the first year and has since grown steadily to peak at around 250 by the end of the 20th century.

Annual conferences, at first focused on specific themes to encourage new research, took place in Keele (Religion) 1983, Chester

(Women) 1984, Glasgow (Nationalism) 1985, Stoke-on-Trent (Imperialism) 1986, Cardiff (Images) 1987, Brighton (Local History) 1988, Coventry (Economics) 1989, Birmingham (Military) 1990, Manchester (Art) 1991, Nottingham (Media) 1992, Manchester (Cricket) 1993, London (Youth) 1994, Huddersfield (Rugby) 1995, London (Youth) 1996, Keele 1997, Edinburgh 1998, Brighton 1999 and Liverpool 2000. Since 1994, the keynote address to the conference has been sponsored by the Sports Pages Bookshop in London.

As well as conferences, publications have always been an important feature of the Society's activities. *The British Journal of Sports History* (founded in 1984 under the editorship of Richard Cox, John Lowerson and Tony Mangan), later to become *The International Journal of the History of Sport* (1987), emerged out of the society, although an agreement with a publisher could not be reached which limited subscriptions to members of the society. A *Newsletter* which started in 1982 (first edited by Richard Cox, followed by Jack Wiliams) developed into the *British Society of Sports History Bulletin* in 1984 (edited by Tony Mason then Russell Potts) and finally *The Sports Historian* in 1994 (edited first by Russell Potts, then by Sir Derek Birley, Richard Cox, Tony Mason, Benny Peiser and Wray Vamplew, and, from 2000, by Martin Polley). This was supplemented with a new format *Newsletter* in 1994 (edited by Martin Polley and Dave Terry). As well as publishing papers from the annual conference, the editorial policy of *The Sports Historian* has always been to maintain an open approach as to what should be considered for inclusion. Given the composition of the membership, the focus in the past has tended to be on the history of sport in Britain, although recently articles on sport in the ancient world and other countries such as Finland and Canada have been included. *The Sports Historian* and its predecessor has also always included an annual bibliography of theses and publications on the history of sport in Britain and a listing of recent accessions of sporting manuscripts in British record offices.

Sports History Publishing was founded in 1994 as the publishing arm of the Society and has so far produced four monographs.

Another way of promoting and recognizing achievement in sports history research has been the annual Aberdare Literary Prize. Sponsored by Lord Aberdare, whose family name has long been associated with the development and administration of sport in Britain, the prize is awarded to the best book on British sports history or the best book on sports history published by a British scholar. Prizewinners to date include Mark Marquesse (1995), John Sugden and Alan Bairner (1996), John Bale and Joe Sang (1997), Tony Collins (1998) and Jack Williams (1999).

Early in 1994, the Society made history itself by launching the very first sports history internet site and electronic conference; it was also one of the very first sports websites in the world. With more than 1,500 pages in 2000, this site is the world's premier site for information on sports history courses, publications and much more besides.

Websites:

The British Society of Sports History – http://www.umist.ac.uk/sport/bssh.html

See also:

History

-Richard William Cox

British Sporting Art Trust

The British Sporting Art Trust is a charity dedicated to the continuing development and exhibition of paintings, engravings, bronzes and associated objects that together comprise sporting art. Its complementary activity is to encourage and promote research and the dissemination of information on the subject through its activities, publications and library.

Two examples of paintings from the British Sporting Art Trust Collection. Top: The Stewards Stand after The Derby, 1844 (Artist: F.C. Turner). Bottom: Anglers in action (Artist: Henry Alken Senior). Pictures courtesy of The British Sporting Art Trust/Ackermann Photographic Archive)

The term 'sporting art' embraces not only field sports but also rural pastimes and recreations. In the collection, there are items, for example, relating to coaching, archery, croquet, cricket, pugilism and fencing.

It was thanks to the support of the then Director of the Tate Gallery, Sir Norman Reid, that a group of enthusiasts set up the Trust. The dream became reality when Mr Paul Mellon gave to the Tate Gallery, through the Trust, a group of thirty major sporting paintings.

The initial ambition of the Trustees was to procure quality sporting paintings for the Historic British Collection at the Tate Gallery. Two truths soon became evident; first that with the best will in the world no Director of the Tate could bind his successor to a policy of permanently exhibiting sporting art, and secondly that the paintings would be divorced from the associated engravings, bronzes and other objects that gave the subject such a universality through the centuries. The Trustees concluded, after they had donated a second tranche of seventeen paintings from the bequest of Mr Ambrose Clark to the Tate Gallery, that the principles on which the Trust had been founded would be best served by a permanent independent gallery.

In 1989, the decision was made to add a wing to the National Horseracing Museum at Newmarket, where the Trust had rented a room for three years. Two galleries, a library and storeroom were completed in 1991, a venture made possible by contributions from Mr Edmund Vestey and many others.

The Trustees have always had an onward-looking policy of exhibiting sporting art nationwide. They have exhibited their collection in six major cities outside London, and have arranged five loan exhibitions, which have visited Leicester, London, Sussex and Paris.

The Trustees realized that for a full appreciation of sporting art, more knowledge of both its practitioners and origins were needed. With this in mind, the Trust has produced *An Inventory of British Sporting Art* (by Gerald Pendred), a *Bibliography of British Sporting Artists* (by Norah Titley), and thirty-five illustrated essays. It has also initiated twenty-one annual Paul Mellon lectures in London and has a slide collection and a large photo archive. Students have received sponsorship, and an annual sculpture prize has been awarded for the last ten years.

The Trust currently holds 40 paintings, 130 engravings, 5 bronzes and about 500 books. Their permanent collection is complemented by regular loans from both the Tate Gallery and private sources.

Aims for the future are to expand the collection to include both a wider range of subjects and more 20th-century artists, to encourage young artists who wish to carry forward the great British tradition of sporting art in new ways, to continue to encourage research, and 'to publicise the delights and surprises of sporting art, that golden thread of our heritage which has run through country life for the last three centuries'.

See also:
Sporting Art

-Marigold Lawton

British Universities Sports Association

The British Universities Sports Association (B.U.S.A.) provides competition in forty-four sports to students through the organization of national championships, representative fixtures and the selection and funding of British teams for international events. The Association has 148 members and its simple central structure belies the complex administration of student sport prior to its foundation in 1994.

B.U.S.A. was formed through a merger of the two most powerful bodies, the Universities Athletic Union (U.A.U.) and the British Universities Sports Federation (B.U.S.F.). The

U.A.U. was founded in 1919, but Oxford and Cambridge remained largely aloof from its activities, partly due to their focus on the annual 'Blues' contests and partly due to their inability to meet the affiliation fees (the U.A.U. was funded from members' student union fees, a situation which did not exist in the collegiate Oxbridge system). Funding problems led to London's withdrawal also, and the absence of the three senior universities complicated British team selection for the World Student Games.

International selection became more problematic with the development of separate bodies in Scotland and Wales, and at U.A.U.'s instigation the British Universities Sports Board was formed in 1953, with representation from the other national bodies and the three English universities. However, it was obvious that the structure was unsustainable without guaranteed funding, and this was eventually secured from the vice-chancellors' committee in 1962, enabling a separate permanent administration to be provided for the B.U.S.F.

B.U.S.F. assumed responsibility for international events, while U.A.U. concentrated on the domestic programme for the universities of England and Wales. Although they were effectively concerned with different strands of student sport, relations were sometimes strained as issues of national identity intruded on policy-making. When changes in the eligibility rules of the World Student Games opened up participation to other higher education students, the need to give a voice to the British Polytechnics Sports Association and the British Colleges Sports Association led to the formation of an umbrella organization, the British Students' Sports Federation, in 1974.

The proliferation of voices in student sport was accompanied by increasing disputes over territorial rights, and although the need for a unified body was recognized, several working parties failed to find a solution. In 1992, the funding of higher education, allied to the upgrading of polytechnics and colleges of education to university status, brought a sense of realism to discussions, and the U.A.U. and the B.U.S.F. agreed to amalgamate to form B.U.S.A. Their financial muscle, together with their established programmes of sporting competition, forced the other organizations to close down and release their members to the new body.

B.U.S.A.'s birth was timely. Many governing bodies had begun to incorporate student sport into their performance plans, and the new organization was able to dovetail its programme with these proposals to ensure that it retained the status of its competitions and representative teams. The recent introduction of merit leagues instead of regional groupings in cricket, hockey, lawn tennis, Rugby Union and squash recognized the establishment of centres of excellence and sports scholarships within designated universities.

References:

British Universities Sports Association, *Annual Handbooks and Annual Reports*, 1994- .

Palmer, R. W., *The Development of Student Sports Bodies in Britain since 1919*, M.Ed. thesis, Leicester University, 1974.

Further reading:

Kerslake, R. F., *50 Years of University Sport* (London: Universities Athletic Union, 1969).

Websites:

The British Universities Sports Association – http://www.busa.org.uk/

See also:

Birmingham University; Cambridge University; Oxford University; University Boat Race

-Alun Evans

Brooklands Circuit

Brooklands Motor Course near Weybridge in Surrey was opened in 1907 as the world's first purpose-built motor racetrack. It was funded by H. F. Locke-King, a wealthy local landowner, to circumvent the speed restrictions which applied on public roads. The track was constructed in the shape of a large concrete oval, 2.75 miles long and 100 feet wide and banked at the curves, which gave spectators a clear view of the cars for almost the entire circuit. It was itself a major engineering achievement, for it involved diverting the River Wey in two places as well as the removal of a variety of other natural obstacles. The course proved valuable for test purposes but was less successful as a popular venue for motor racing, partly because of the nature of the track, which failed to convey the impression of speed and became very bumpy once it settled, but also because of the somewhat exclusive view of the sport taken by its sponsors, the Brooklands Automobile Racing Club. During the Second World War, Brooklands was used as a site for aircraft production and this brought its eventual demise as a motor racetrack.

The first race meeting was held on July 6th, 1907 but prior to this, S. F. Edge, one of the leading drivers of the period, used the circuit for an endurance event, travelling 1,581 miles over 24 hours in his 60-horsepower Napier, at an average speed of 65.9 miles per hour. Brooklands hosted the British Grand Prix in 1926 and 1927, both won by the French manufacturer, Delage. However, the circuit became

noted for the diverse nature of its meetings, including long-distance races for sports cars and other club events, promoted by a system of handicapping designed to allow maximum participation. The speed record at Brooklands is held by John Cobb's Napier-Railton, which in 1935 covered a flying kilometre at 151.97 miles per hour.

References:

Brendon, P., *The Motoring Century. The Story of the Royal Automobile Club* (London: Bloomsbury, 1997).

Georgano, G. N., *The Encyclopaedia of Motor Sport* (London: Ebury Press & Michael Joseph, 1971).

Nye, D., *Motor Racing in Colour* (Poole: Blandford Press, 1978).

Further reading:

Richardson, K., *The British Motor Industry, 1896-1939* (London: Macmillan, 1977).

Websites:

The Brooklands Society – http://www.brooklands.org.uk/

See also:

Motor Racing

-Dave Thoms

Calcutta Cup

The Calcutta Cup is awarded to the victors of the annual England versus Scotland Rugby Union fixture. Although the inaugural international match between the two countries was played at Raeburn Place, Edinburgh on March 27th, 1871, a further seven matches were played before the introduction of the Calcutta Cup in the game, again at Raeburn Place, on March 10th, 1879.

On Christmas Day, 1872, two teams consisting of Irish, Scottish, Welsh and English players, drawn from the public schools and military garrisons, arranged a game of Rugby in Calcutta. At the beginning of the following year they formed the Calcutta Football Club and, in 1874, joined the Rugby Football Union (R.F.U.).

In 1877, the club decided to disband owing to a loss in membership, an absence of new blood, a dearth of opposing clubs, the emergence of other sports such as polo, and a climate not conducive to playing Rugby. In order to dispose of its funds, something in the order of £60, the club decided to fashion a trophy using local craftsmanship and to offer it to the R.F.U. for the 'lasting good of Rugby football'. It was to be competed for annually, and was intended to keep alive the memory of the club.

The offer was sent to the R.F.U. in December 1877, and was duly accepted by its President, A. G. Guillemard. In his reply, he outlined that the trophy would be competed for annually by England and Scotland, the cup remaining the property of the R.F.U.

A total of 270 solid silver rupees were melted down in order to make the cup. Standing about 18 inches high, its three handles in the form of snakes and an elephant on the lid, the trophy as it now stands has a wooden base which was added at a later stage in order to record the date of each match, the winning country, and the names of the two captains.

Apart from three matches not played in the 1880s, and the intervention of the two World Wars, the annual match for the Calcutta Cup continues, with England enjoying a clear lead.

References:

Titley, U. A. and MacWhirter, R., *Centenary History of the Rugby Football Union* (London: Rugby Football Union, 1970).

Further reading:

Thorburn, A. C. M., *The Scottish Rugby Union Official History* (Edinburgh: Collins, 1985).

See also:

Rugby Union

-John Jenkins

Cambridge University

Cambridge University, like Oxford, was not made – it grew. References to it as a 'studium generale' or University first appear in state documents in the 13th century. The University grew in prosperity and power during the 16th century and by the 18th century had developed its familiar group of colleges. During the 18th century, sport became a more prominent feature of university life, but it was during the 19th century that Cambridge developed its reputation as a significant sporting institution. It is now considered one of the world's leading universities, noted for its expertise in the fields of mathematics, science and technology. It is also widely known for its sporting contests with Oxford, in particular the Boat Race, which was first rowed in 1829.

Royal patronage during the 16th century brought with it the development of tennis courts. Ten of the sixteen colleges could boast a ball court by 1690. The courts were used for a variety of fives and tennis-type games. Other activities included bowls and archery. In the 18th and early 19th centuries, walking dominated the recreational habits of Cambridge men, although amongst some of the wealthier undergraduates the pleasures of Newmarket were not unknown.

The increasing influence of boys educated in the public schools in the early years of the 19th century meant that activities such as rowing and cricket, already part of public school life, were quickly organized as inter-collegiate and inter-university activities. The Cambridge University Cricket Club was founded in 1820, the University Boat Club in 1829. In both cases this was to enable Cambridge to meet challenges from Oxford. Athletics, rackets, and tennis were all similarly organized throughout the course of the century, as 'moral and manly' sport increasingly garnered support, guidance, and even leadership from dons such as Leslie Stephen.

Football was slower to be organized because of rule difficulties caused by boys from each of the major public schools wanting to play by 'their' rules. As a compromise, a group of undergraduates offered a set of Cambridge rules for 'association' football in 1846. Again,

in 1863, Cambridge men produced a simple set of rules 'fair to all the schools' in an attempt to codify and unite the various forms of the game. Out of these efforts developed the rules of football and its governing body the Football Association.

All of these activities were for men only. With the founding of Girton College in 1869, women began to take part in tennis, the first inter-collegiate competition being against Newnham College in 1878, followed by inter-university competition in 1892. More vigorous activities followed – notably hockey, but also golf, swimming, and lacrosse – fuelled by the enthusiasm of girls from the new girls' public schools. Justifications for such activities were based on health and teamwork. The 'separate spheres' of male and female activity were finally broken with the inclusion of a female cox in the 1981 Boat Race. It is also the Boat Race against Oxford which remains 'unchallenged as the pinnacle of publicity, public attention and university patriotism'.

References:

Chandler, T., 'The Development of a Sporting Tradition at Oxbridge, 1800-1860', *Canadian Journal of History of Sport and Physical Education*, 19, 2 (1988), p. 1-29.

Money, T., *Manly and Muscular Diversions: Public Schools and the Nineteenth-Century Sporting Revival* (London: Duckworth, 1997).

Searby, P., *A History of the University of Cambridge* (Cambridge: Cambridge University Press, 1997).

Further reading:

McCrone, K., *Playing the Game: Sport and the Physical Emancipation of Women, 1870-1914* (London: Routledge, 1988).

Websites:

Cambridge University – http://www.cam.ac.uk/

See also:

British Universities Sports Association; Birmingham University; Oxford University; University Boat Race

-Tim Chandler

Canoeing

The history of the sport of canoeing goes back thousands of years to when log canoes and dugouts were used for fishing, hunting and transportation. Canoes are defined as open craft propelled by a single blade, and appeared in many early Egyptian illustrations. Kayaks, on the other hand, are completely covered craft propelled by a double-bladed paddle, and have long been a common feature of the Inuit way of life in Greenland.

The credit for the birth of modern canoeing goes to a Scottish-born, London-based lawyer, John MacGregor. In 1865, he designed and built a unique craft, the *Rob Roy*, which became a legend in its time. It measured 4.57 metres long and was 76 centimetres wide at its beam. In this craft, MacGregor toured extensively on the lakes and rivers of northern and central Europe. His travel book, *One Thousand Miles in the Rob Roy Canoe,* aroused wide interest, not only in Britain but in the rest of Europe as well.

The first ever canoe club was the Royal Canoe Club, established in 1866, which continues to thrive at its original site on Thurlock island in the river Thames, near Kingston.

Today, the sport has seven competitive divisions, as well as life-saving and recreational elements. These include canoe-orienteering, canoe-polo, marathon, rodeo, sailing, sprint and surf canoeing.

Canoe-polo has its origins in a game designed by Oliver Cock to help learners overcome their fears and inhibitions in a canoe. Since the 1970s, it has grown into a popular sport with leagues and competitions throughout the British Isles. The first world championships were held in Sheffield, in 1994.

Marathon canoeing has its origins in some of the long-distance races that evolved in Britain, the most famous of which is the 125-mile Devizes to Westminster race. Races can vary in distance from 3 to over 100 miles and

usually involve some form of portaging past natural obstacles. The course can take in canals, estuaries, open lakes and rivers up to Grade III. Nottingham was host to the first ever International Canoe Federation (I.C.F.) World Marathon Championships in 1988.

Rodeo is the latest discipline to emerge and entails performing tricks on a set piece of water in a given time frame, performance being judged on points of technical merit.

Canoe-sailing in Britain goes back to John MacGregor's days, when he employed a small 'lug sail' to propel his *Rob Roy* whenever there was a following wind. Over the years, more specialized craft have evolved and as a result standards have improved. In 1946, the I.C.F. adopted a 10-square-metre sail canoe for international competition and, in 1955, a sliding seat. The first World Championships were held at Hayling Island in 1961.

Surf canoeing did not become properly established as a separate discipline until the 1950s. The first British Championships took place at Bude in 1967. Today, surf kayaks are very specialist designs capable of riding waves and at the same time performing a wide range of tricks.

White-water racing established itself as a separate discipline in the 1950s and entails racing straight down rivers with sections of grade III and above rapids, usually over a distance of 3 to 5 miles. Individuals set off at intervals, the winner being the person to cover the course in the shortest time.

Slalom canoeing has its origins on the continent in the 1920s and entails navigating a craft through 'gates' as they make their way down fast-flowing rivers. The first canoe slalom to be held in Britain was in 1939. This was held at Trevor Rock on the river Dee, near Llangollen. World championships were introduced in 1949 and have since been held in Britain twice, at Bala in 1981 and Nottingham in 1995. Although Britain has many fine rivers for slalom canoeing, providing there has been sufficient rainfall, a great lift to the sport in

Britain was given with the creation of artificially created dam-controlled courses at Bala (1981), Holme Pierrepont (1986) and Middlesborough (1997).

Sprint racing also developed extensively on the continent. It was first included in the Olympic programme in Berlin in 1936. When the Games came to London in 1948, the canoeing events were staged on the regatta course at Henley. In 1953, the *News of the World* sponsored the first annual sprint regatta on the Serpentine in Hyde Park but, unfortunately, the sport struggled to survive. Sprint canoeing was given a boost in Britain with the creation of the Sports Council's National Water Sports Centre at Holme Pierrepont in 1972. This nine-laned, purpose-built course hosted the World Championships in 1981.

A British Canoe Association was formed in 1887, primarily for touring canoeists, but this was short-lived, quietly disappearing sometime in the 1920s. The Canoe Camping Club was formed in 1933, alongside a number of independent clubs around the same time. Soon it became important to establish a national governing body and the British Canoe Union (B.C.U.) was founded in 1936. Separate associations were formed for Scotland in 1939, Northern Ireland in 1944 and Wales in 1978.

Proficiency tests were introduced by the B.C.U. in 1949 and the first full-time national coach (Oliver Cock) was appointed in 1962.

Perhaps the most notable individual in the development of canoeing in Britain is John Dudderidge, who over three decades played a leading role in many aspects of the sport, primarily as an administrator.

Britain has also produced some notable paddlers in recent years. For more than a decade, Richard Fox dominated the international slalom scene, winning the individual world title on five occasions between 1981 and 1993. Liz Sharman won the ladies' equivalent in 1983 and 1987 and she was followed by Lynn Simpson in 1995. In the marathon discipline, Ivan Lawler has won a total of five world

championship titles to date. Britain has also had individual world champions in canoe-sailing (Alan Emus, Robin Wood) and sprint (Jeremy West).

Finally, it would be unfair not to mention the leading role some British paddlers have played in pioneering expeditions down uncharted rivers and across open seas. A notable example was Dr Mike Jones, who was tragically killed on the river Bradu, in the Himalayan Mountains, in 1978.

References:

Good, G., 'A Short History of Canoeing in Great Britain', in *British Canoe Union Canoeing Handbook* (Nottingham: British Canoe Union, 1991), pp. 1-26.

Toro, A., *Canoeing: an Olympic Sport* (San Francisco: The Author, 1986).

Further reading:

Roberts, K. G. and Shackleton, P., *The Canoe: a History of the Craft from Panama to the Arctic* (Toronto: Macmillan of Canada, 1983).

Townes, J., 'Canoeing and Kayaking', in D. Levinson and K. Christensen (eds.), *Encyclopedia of World Sport* (Santa Barbara, California: ABC-CLIO, 1996), vol. I, p. 173.

Websites:

The British Canoe Union – http://www.bcu.org.uk/

See also:

Holme Pierrepont

-Richard William Cox

Cardiff Arms Park

Cardiff Arms Park and the National Stadium are synonymous throughout the sporting world as the home of the Welsh Rugby Union, and the scene of some of the greatest triumphs by the Welsh Rugby team, including their victories in 1905 and 1935 over New Zealand. However, the ground, in the heart of Cardiff, has also staged other sports – up until 1966 there was a cricket ground in the north-west corner, which was used by Glamorgan County

Cricket Club, as well as tennis courts and hockey pitches. The Rugby ground, used by Cardiff Rugby Football Club as well as by Wales, has also hosted greyhound racing, Association Football, athletics (especially those in the 1958 Commonwealth Games) and boxing, in particular the 1993 W.B.C. bout between Lennox Lewis and Frank Bruno.

The name 'Arms Park' is derived from the Cardiff Arms Hotel (or Inn) which stood alongside the east bank of the Taff, close to the town centre. A plaque with the civic crest stood above the main doorway to the coaching inn and, during the mid-19th century, the gardens and river meadows behind the Inn were used for recreation.

Like much of Cardiff, the Park was owned by the Bute family, and the Marquis encouraged healthy recreation on his 18 acres of parkland. In 1867, Cardiff Cricket Club began playing in the northern part, followed in 1876 by Cardiff Rugby Football Club in the southern part. In 1882, the Cardiff Arms Hotel was demolished, and on April 12th, 1884, the Welsh Rugby team played their first ever international at the Arms Park, recording a victory over Ireland.

By the post-war period, the Arms Park had become a victim of its own success, and there was no room for further expansion. The overuse of the Rugby ground also led to complaints about the playing surface, so in 1963 the Welsh Rugby Union, who had long treasured the idea of owning their own stadium, secured the ground from Cardiff Athletic Club. Many changes have subsequently taken place, with the removal of the cricket ground and tennis courts, and their replacement by 1970 by a National Stadium for the Welsh team and a smaller ground for Cardiff R.F.C.

Further changes have occurred in the late 1990s, transforming the Arms Park into a multi-purpose Millennium Stadium, with a seating capacity of 72,500, a retractable roof and an adjoining retail and leisure plaza. The official opening ceremony took place on June 26th, 1999, when Wales played the then World Champions, South Africa. On November 6th, 1999, it hosted the final of the 1999 Rugby World Cup between Australia and France.

References:

Parry-Jones, D., *Taff's Acre: a History and Celebration of Cardiff Arms Park* (London: Willow Books, 1984).

Smith, D. and Williams, G., *Fields of Praise: the Official History of the Welsh Rugby Union 1881-1981* (Cardiff: University of Wales Press, 1981).

Hignell, A. K., *Cricket Grounds of Glamorgan C. C. C.* (London: Christopher Helm, 1988).

Websites:

Cardiff Stadium – http://www.cardiff-stadium.co.uk/
The Welsh Rugby Union – http://www.wru.co.uk/

See also:

Rugby Union

-Andrew Hignell

Carnegie College

Carnegie Physical Training College was first opened in 1933, the first college to train male physical education teachers in England. Since that time, it has been responsible for the training of several generations of P.E. teachers.

The need for specialist teachers of physical education had arisen after the First World War. The Chief Medical Officer to the Board of Education suggested that there was an urgent need for specialist teachers of physical training who would 'look at their work through the eyes of teachers rather than drill sergeants'. In 1933, the curriculum at Carnegie included the history of P.E., anatomy and physiology as well as grounding in the major sports and games. The name Carnegie College of Physical Education (from 1947) reflected the broadening of the curriculum away from 'PT and Drill'.

The College's influence was further extended in 1952 with the introduction of a supplementary course, which recruited overseas teachers for the Advanced Diploma in Physical Education. From 1960, the College offered specialist three-year training courses for secondary physical education teachers. It continued to offer one-year specialist diploma courses for teachers or lecturers who had at least five years teaching experience. In 1974, Bachelor of Education degree courses were offered for the first time.

Women were admitted in 1968, during the merger to become the City of Leeds and Carnegie College. In 1976, this institution merged with Leeds Polytechnic, which in 1995 became Leeds Metropolitan University. Carnegie Hall remains the centre for physical education and numerous other sports-related courses.

References:

Connell, L., *Carnegie: a History of Carnegie College and School of Physical Education, 1933-1976* (Leeds: Leeds University Press, 1983).

Further reading:

Furlong, B. A. F., *Carnegie 1933-1983: College and School* (Leeds: Carnegie School of Physical Education, Leeds Polytechnic, 1983).

McIntosh, P., Dixon, J. G., Munrow, A. D., and Willetts, R. F. (eds.), *Landmarks in the History of Physical Education* (London: Routledge & Kegan Paul, 1981).

See also:

Education – Teacher Training; Jordanhill College; Loughborough University; Physical Education Association of the United Kingdom

-Kyle Phillpots

Central Council of Physical Recreation

The Central Council of Recreative Physical Training, from 1944 known as the Central Council of Physical Recreation (C.C.P.R.), was formed in 1935. Its Scottish equivalent was established in 1944. The C.C.P.R. brought together a coalition of health, educational and sporting bodies to promote physical recreation amongst Britain's youth. The first executive was made up of representatives from bodies such as the British Medical Association, the National Union of Teachers, the Football Association, Marylebone Cricket Club (M.C.C.), the Rugby Football Union and the Amateur Athletics Association: all of whom had some link with Britain's young people and an interest in promoting their physical well-being..

The formation of the C.C.P.R. should be placed in the context of the social and economic situation of the 1930s. Mass unemployment had led to the physical deterioration of a high proportion of Britain's youth. Moreover, with the threat of war never far away, the government was keen to promote physical recreation and welcomed the establishment of a voluntary body that would work in conjunction with bodies such as the Y.M.C.A., Girl Guides and the Boys Brigade.

The C.C.P.R. played an important role during the Second World War, collaborating with the Football Association to run 'Fitness for Services' courses. These proved very successful, and by 1940, over 35,000 people had attended 230 fitness events. Inevitably, some pre-military training underlining its contribution to the war effort was included in the courses.

In the post-war period, the C.C.P.R. increased its stature and became responsible for establishing national physical recreation centres at Bisham Abbey in 1946, Lilleshall Hall in 1951, Plas y Brenin in 1954, Crystal Palace in 1964, Cowes National Sailing Centre in 1968, the National Sports Centre for Wales in 1972 and Holme Pierrepont Water Sports Centre in 1973. Its Scottish equivalent established an outdoor leisure activities centre at Glenmore Lodge in 1948.

Following the establishment of the Sports Council in 1965 to promote amateur sport and physical recreation, the C.C.P.R. was invited to play a key role. However, in 1972, following the Conservative Government's decision to enhance the powers of the Sports Council, the future role of the C.C.P.R. was placed into doubt. At one point, its Executive Committee resigned itself to accepting the idea of going into voluntary liquidation. However, at the A.G.M. meeting in 1971, the President, the Duke of Edinburgh, opposed the move on the grounds that as an independent voluntary body it was ideally placed to represent the collective view of the Governing Bodies of Sport to Government and other interested parties. In effect, the C.C.P.R. took on a new role. It transferred all its assets, namely the National Sports Centre, its staff and its resources, including financial reserves, to the Sports Council. Its objectives were amended thus:

– to constitute a standing forum where all national governing and representative bodies of sport and physical recreation may be represented and may collectively, or through special groups where appropriate, formulate and promote measures to improve and develop sport.

– to support the work of the specialist sports bodies and to bring them together with other interested organisations; and

– to act as a consultative body to the Sports Council and other representative or public bodies concerned or interested in sport and recreation.

In return for the transfer of its assets, the C.C.P.R. and the Sports Council entered into a contract in which the Sports Council agreed to reimburse the C.C.P.R. such costs as may be 'reasonably required' to implement is objectives.

The six divisions of the C.C.P.R. are Games and Sports, Major Spectator Sport, Movement and Dance, Outdoor Pursuits, Water Recreation, and the division of Interested Organisations. The C.C.P.R. lobbies for sport by recommending legislative measures affecting sport, submitting views on relevant items of legislation at different stages of the Parliamentary process (from consultation to enactment), and by briefing MPs and Ministers on sports-related issues.

In 1982, the C.C.P.R. established an extensive training programme to encourage volunteers to help individuals get involved in sports. At the beginning of the 21st century, the 'leadership programme' (currently sponsored by Royal and Sun Alliance) trains in the region of 50,000 leaders each year. Some of these programmes are jointly run in conjunction with the Youth Sport Trust (see separate entry).

In 1998, the C.C.P.R. established the British Sports Trust, a wholly owned charity of the C.C.P.R., to fund-raise and then finance the Community Sports Leaders Award.

References:
Evans, H. J., *Service to Sport: the Story of the CCPR, 1935-72* (London: The Sports Council, 1974).

See also:
Sports Council

-Richard William Cox/Ray Physick

Channel Swimming

Swimming the English Channel is an essentially British fascination. French men and women have swum the channel but they do not have the British tradition of constant endeavour to achieve the feat. The shortest distance is 20.5 miles from Dover to Cap Gris-Nez, but tides and currents can increase this distance significantly while wind, waves, fog and the cold can be additional hazards. Timing is the most important factor. Swimmers start on an outgoing tide and land on the opposite shore on an in-going tide. Those swimming too slowly or too fast may lose the right tide and be thrown miles off course.

Englishman Captain Matthew Webb made the first crossing of the Channel from Dover to Calais on August 24th-25th, 1875. Using a breast-stroke of twenty strokes per minute, Webb covered a distance of roughly 39.5 miles, from Dover's Admiralty Pier to Calais, in 21 hours 45 minutes. He became a national hero overnight. The feat was interpreted as conclu-

Captain Matthew Webb, the first man to swim the English Channel, is assisted out of the water at Calais on August 25th, 1875 (The Illustrated London News Picture Library)

sive proof of the close link between achievements in shipping and navigation, and the swimming ability of the English nation. Unfortunately, Webb drowned in 1883 attempting to swim the rapids and whirlpools below Niagara Falls.

More than seventy unsuccessful attempts by both sexes were recorded in the newspapers between 1875 and 1911; one man, Jabez Wolffe, made twenty attempts. The second successful swimmer was Thomas William Burgess. After fifteen previous attempts, he finally succeeded in 1911, using a left overarm-stroke of twenty-four per minute to swim from South Foreland to Griz-Nez in 22 hours 35 minutes. Like the swimmers of today, he was wearing a swimming costume for physical protection only, had to be properly acclimatized and had to deal with problems like jellyfish and unreliable weather forecasts. Once in the water

he was totally dependent on the experienced boatman accompanying him. Orientation and navigation, today done with the help of a computer, in those days relied on fixed points of light on the coast. Because there was a lack of lights on the French coast, swimming from France to England was regarded as the 'easy way'. Burgess took the hard route and had to expend about 1,500 calories an hour. His body had to be prepared for a sea temperature of roughly 17° C, in spite of his skin being well greased.

The first woman to cross was German-American Gertrude Ederle, an Olympic swimming medallist, who crossed from France to England in 1926. She was also the first to swim the crawl-stroke exclusively. On August 6th, 1926, she succeeded in a new record time of 14 hours and 23 minutes (faster than any man up to that point).

The press fanned the hunger for records and stimulated competition by offering prize money. It was only a matter of time until someone made a bogus claim. In October 1927, Dr Dorothy Cochrane Logan claimed to have swum the Channel in a new record time for women of 13 hours and 10 minutes, proved by four English witnesses. Shortly after she had received the £1,000 prize money, Logan told the press that her swim was a deliberately planned and well-organized fake.

In 1927, the Channel Swimming Association was founded, fixing rules and regulations and overseeing attempts and authenticating claims. Every swimmer attempting the Channel has to have completed a medical examination, a six-hour swim in cold water and must undertake the crossing with a licensed boat and observer. An attempt costs about £1,500.

The current record holder is Chad Hundeby (U.S.). It took him 7 hours and 17 minutes to swim the Channel. By 1995, there had been 761 successful crossings by 485 individuals (324 men and 161 women) from 42 different countries – 708 solos, 22 two-ways and 3 three-ways. More than 6,000 people have tried to complete the crossing. Englishwoman Alison Streeter has made the crossing a record thirty-eight times. Another British swimmer, Kevin Murphy, holds the men's record for the greatest number of successful crossings.

References:

Besford, P. *Encyclopaedia of Swimming* (London: Robert Hale and Co., 1971).

Elderwick, D., *Captain Webb – Channel Swimmer* (Studley: K. A. F. Brewin, 1987).

Jarvis, M. A., *Captain Webb and 100 years of Channel Swimming* (Newton Abbot: David & Charles, 1975).

Keil, I. and Wix, D. *In the Swim: the Amateur Swimming Association from 1869 to 1994* (Loughborough: Swimming Times Ltd, 1996).

Scharenberg, S., 'Cross-Channel Swims – A Matter of National Pride, Gender and Money?', in: A. Krüger and A. Teja (eds.), *La Commune Eredità dello Sport in Europa (Proceedings of the First European Congress on Sports History, Rome 1996)* (Rome: Scuola dello Sport – CONI, 1997), p. 286–296.

Further reading:

Thomas, R., *Swimming* (London: Samson Low, Marston & Company, 1904).

Webb, Captain M., *The Art of Swimming* (London: Ward, Lock & Tyler, *c.* 1875).

Websites:

The Channel Swimming and Piloting Federation – http://www.channelswimming.co.uk/

See also:

Swimming

-Peter Bilsborough/Swantje Scharenberg

Chelsea College

Chelsea School (1976-), formerly Chelsea College of Physical Education (1920-1976), was founded by Dorette Wilke in 1898, within the South Western Polytechnic, as a Department (later College) for the training of women as gymnastic and games teachers in girls' schools.

Its founder, a pioneering personality of great vision, remained in office as Head Mistress until 1929. She was followed by seven outstanding women Principals/Heads: May Fountain (1929-1950), Gwyneth Cater (1950-1953), Annie Rogers (1954-1958), Audrey Bambra (1958-1976), Patricia Kingston (1976-1979), Gillian Burke (1979-1984) and Elizabeth Murdoch (1985-1998).

Four authorities have governed the College/School – London County Council (1889-1947), Eastbourne Education Authority (1947-1974), East Sussex Education Authority (1974-1989) and Brighton Polytechnic/ University of Brighton (1989-1992/1992-1998).

The College remained in London from 1898 to 1939, when it was evacuated to the Grand Hotel, Borth, Wales. After the war,

Chelsea Polytechnic was unable to re-accommodate the College. Following protracted discussions involving the Ministry of Education, the College moved to Eastbourne, into Hillbrow, St Winifred's and Granville Crest in 1948.

The College/School grew from five students to 850 by 1998; recruitment changed from all female to equal members of women and men by 1997; courses developed from the College Diploma (1898-1952) to under and postgraduate awards from London (1930-1967), Sussex (1965-1984), the Council for National Academic Awards (1981-1995) and Brighton (1992-1998).

The focus diversified from teacher training to current courses in education, sport and leisure. Teaching, learning, and research in academic, practical and professional strands continue as key aspects of Chelsea's programme.

References:

Archives, Chelsea School, University of Brighton
Webb, I. M., *The History of Chelsea College of Physical Education with special reference to Curriculum Development 1898-1973*, PhD thesis, University of Leicester, 1977.

Further reading:

Webb, I. M., *The Challenge of Change in Physical Education – Chelsea College of Physical Education – Chelsea School, University of Brighton – 1898-1998* (London: Falmer Press, 1999).

See also:

Bedford College; Dartford College; Dunfermline College; Education – Teacher Training

-Ida Webb

Cheltenham

Cheltenham considers itself to be the home of National Hunt racing. Although flat-racing was held intermittently at Prestbury Park from 1831 to 1898, it was the building of the steeplechase course there in 1902 that heralded the rise of Cheltenham to its present position as the premier jumping track in Britain.

Hosting sixteen race days each year on its undulating courses, including a new cross-country course of natural obstacles, it is best known for its National Hunt Festival in March, at which nine of the season's twenty-four Grade 1 National Hunt races, such as the Gold Cup and the Champion Hurdle, are run. Prize money for the three-day festival now tops £1 million and attracts strong British and Irish fields together with thousands of spectators, especially on Gold Cup day.

The Gold Cup, a prestigious race for five-year-olds and upwards over 3 miles and 2 furlongs, was first run in 1924 and was won by the legendary Golden Miller in five consecutive years from 1932 to 1936. His achievement has been commemorated in bronze at the course together with statues of two great Irish horses, Arkle, winner of the Gold Cup on three occasions (1964-1966), and Dawn Run, the only horse to date to have won both the Champion Hurdle (1984) and the Gold Cup (1986).

The participation of Irish horses, trainers and punters is a hallmark of the Cheltenham Festival, perhaps sealed in the post-war period by Vincent O'Brien's successes with Cottage Rake in the Gold Cup (1948-1950) and Hatton's Grace in the Champion Hurdle (1949-1951).

References:

Cranham, G., and Pitman, R., *The Guinness Book of Steeplechasing* (Enfield: Guinness, 1988).

Websites:

Cheltenham Racecourse –
http://www.cheltenham.co.uk/

See also:

Horse-racing

-Joyce Kay

Chester Roodee

Chester racecourse, which is just over 1 mile in circumference and nestles between the city walls and the River Dee, is the oldest in England where racing still takes place in the same location. There are documented records of a race for a silver ball in 1511, and for silver bells around 1540, an event which ultimately became the City Plate and survived until 1836. Twelve years earlier, a major new race over 2.25 miles had been inaugurated, which in due course became the Chester Cup, and during the 19th century was second only to the Derby in the interest it aroused in the betting fraternity.

Chester suffered a decline in both sporting and social terms from the 1860s, until a new management took over and the course was enclosed in 1893. A new grandstand was built in 1899, by which time Chester was one of the leading courses in the country in providing money for prizes.

The course went through a difficult patch in the 1960s, but dealt well with the problems of additional fixtures, the destruction by fire of its County Stand in 1985, and an ongoing modernization programme. Chester is now a Group I course with its main meeting in May, when runners in the Chester Cup pass the stands no less than three times. Among other attractions is the Chester Vase (1907) – a 1.5-mile race widely regarded as a trial for the Derby. With the parade ring inside the course, Chester has a life and bustle often lacking in more spacious surroundings, while there is still a superb free view of the racing from the city walls.

References:

Curling, B. W. R., *British Racecourses* (London: H. F. & G. W. Witherby Ltd, 1951).

Magee, S. (ed.), *The Channel Four Book of the Racing Year* (London: Sidgwick & Jackson, 1990).

Tyrrel, J., *Racecourses on the Flat* (Marlborough: Crowood Press, 1989).

Further reading:

Bevan. R. M., *The Roodee – 450 Years of Racing in Chester* (Northwich: Cheshire County Publishing Ltd, 1989).

See also:

Horse-racing

-John Tolson

Children

Sport has positive advantages for children. It can provide enjoyment and promote physical fitness; it can result in improved posture and a healthier lifestyle; and it can help develop hand-eye co-ordination and motor skills. In addition, there are the perceived social goals of sportsmanship, teamwork, responsibility, commitment, and self-discipline. Learning to obey rules and to respect figures of authority is an important part of a child's upbringing and a necessity for taking his or her place in society. In this respect sport can be taken as a metaphor for life: it has rules, it has officials who control things; it can bring disappointment and success. Most of all, if approached in the right way it can be enormous fun. If sport provides children with enjoyment then they are more likely to put an effort into it and to stay in the sport after leaving school.

A major problem with children's sport is the adults associated with it, the pushy parents and the coach who seeks victory rather than fun and participation. School sports teachers and coaches should be wary of well-meaning parents who often inadvertently put pressure on children to excel; this can place extreme strain on a child, especially if that child is eager to please. The attitude that winning is all-important can be both discouraging and destructive. An educational video released by the National Coaching Foundation in the 1990s illustrated this point in respect of the parent and showed how a caring coach can offset it. A father showed disappointment in his daughter's school's poor showing in an athletics match and was especially displeased

65

to hear that she herself had not earned any points for her school. The girl's abject look of failure was only dispelled when her coach appeared, praising her for achieving a personal best and telling her father he should be proud of her. A smile returned to the youngster's face and the father seemed suitably chastened. It could well be that the father was merely seeking reflected glory. A more mature approach would have been for him to encourage his daughter to enjoy sport for sport's sake, not merely to please a frustrated athlete. In an ideal world parents and coaches work together in the interests of the child. The coach sets realistically attainable goals, giving the child something to aim for. If the demands are reasonable then there is less chance of perceived personal failure discouraging the child, possibly from any future participation in any sport. Emphasis should be placed on sportsmanship, support and personal improvement, rather than on winning at all costs. If parents remember that participation in sport is not only an end in itself but a grounding in the social skills needed later in life, they will be sharing in an invaluable part of their children's development.

Schools have a major role in assisting this sporting development of the child. When a child starts school, part of the education process teaches the difference between organized sport, with its structure and rules that have to be learned, and unstructured play which will have been his or her previous experience of physical exercise. The family kick-about in the garden will seem a world away from a child's first formal game of soccer with a referee, a properly marked pitch and strict rules to adhere to, but the enjoyment should not be diminished. Participation in sport, still seen in young eyes as play or fun, can help ease a child into the unfamiliar territory of full-time schooling. To this end, primary school P.E. co-ordinators (full-time P.E. teachers are not encountered until secondary school) will do their best to make sport as informal as they can. Activities will, whenever possible, take place outside and involve girls as well as boys. Size of playing area and numbers in a team will be flexible

and rules will be simplified. The purpose of the game will be explained, together with pupils' individual roles. Children will be encouraged to do their best and to maintain a sense of fair play. Involvement and activity should be kept to a maximum; children have a very low boredom threshold. If the ball doesn't come near them for a while they have a habit of finding something else to do. Fortunately a major development of the past two decades has been the introduction of games with modified rules, which has assisted participation as sport has spread down the age scale to the physically immature. Progressively these special rules are eliminated as the children gain the necessary skills so that when old enough they can play fully competitive sport.

Outside the school, sport for children is a 20th-century phenomenon. Prior to that, and indeed well into the century, the maxim was that if they were big enough they were old enough to participate in adult sport. Increasingly, over the past decade, the provision of sport for children has switched from the education sector to the voluntary and private sectors. This has followed the withdrawal of many teachers from extracurricular activities after the union disputes of the 1980s, and the imposition of the National Curriculum without adequate additional resources, which led to both a reduction in the overall time devoted to sport and physical education in schools and also a restricted choice of physical activities made available. In cricket, for example, the loss of playing fields as schools have sold off land to finance educational activities now means that it is the clubs, both first class and further down the scale, that promote cricket for children in the community. Unfortunately, in most sports the number of teams being run by clubs has been reduced, which often results in only the most talented youngsters getting regular opportunities to play.

Nevertheless, perhaps too much critical emphasis can be placed on the negative aspects of children's sport. There are coaches who are trying to improve their qualifications to teach young persons and who set realistic targets for their charges and there are parents who want their off-spring to enjoy their sport irrespective of the result.

References:

Grisognono, V., *Children and Sport* (London: John Murray, 1991).

Marmion, M., *The Effect of Government Intervention on the Development of Physical Education in State Schools Since 1970*, MA Dissertation, De Montfort University, 2000.

Maulden, E., and Redfern, H. B., *Games Teaching: an Approach for the Primary School* (Plymouth: MacDonald & Evans, 1981).

See also:

Education

-Tony Rennick

Cinema (*see* Films)

Class

The development of sport in most countries has been influenced by a variety of social relationships – class, gender, ethnicity and age. In Britain, social class has been of paramount importance. Not only have many sports been confined to particular social classes, and the administration of sport invariably been restricted to a narrow élite, but sport itself has often acted as a marker of status and honour. Until the 20th century, the very word 'sport' described the recreation of leisured gentlemen who participated in the famous trinity of hunting, shooting and fishing. The 'sportsman' thus maintained an essentially aristocratic and pre-industrial tradition of outdoor pastimes, exemplified in the great Scottish landed estates. The burgeoning public schools of the 19th century, though they pioneered Association Football and other ball games, continued to find a place for field sports. As late as the 1960s, the Prime Minister, Harold Macmillan, still personified this tradition on his outings to the grouse moor.

Though restricted, at its leading edge, to the upper classes, sport of this kind was only possible with the support of a vast army of domestic helpers who prepared, fetched and carried. Out of this servile relationship developed a number of sporting activities in which the practitioners were often members of the lower classes dependent upon the patronage and finance of the wealthy. Horse-racing, cricket and boxing each developed in this way during the 18th century, and each could claim to be a sport capable of drawing together all social groups: 'prince and peasant in cricket are united' claimed a Victorian proverb.

It was only in the 20th century that a significant fracturing began to occur. In boxing, for example, the rise of professionalism saw a large area of the sport pass under the control of small to middling urban entrepreneurs, of which the London-based promoter Jack Solomons was a leading example. Even in amateur boxing most clubs were in working-class areas, though often run by middle-class people. J. W. H. T. Douglas was probably the last person from a well-connected background to achieve national renown as a boxer, and this was before the First World War, by which time Douglas had switched his attentions to cricket. Cricket did not shed its upper-class image and control until after the Second World War. County clubs remained firmly wedded to a semi-commercial form of development under the guidance of their moneyed members, whose power in the committee room was extended on to the field of play in the person of the ubiquitous amateur captain. Few counties (and none through choice) felt able to dispense with this system until the 1950s, and no paid player captained England until 1952, when the leading professional batsman, Len Hutton (later Sir Leonard), was given the job. It reverted to an amateur in 1955 when Hutton retired. Only in the early 1960s, when the supply of amateur players was drying up (and when many 'amateurs' were in any case covert professionals), was the social distinction abolished. Horse-racing, though traditionally associated with 'new money', was nevertheless the sport most closely linked to the monarchy, and this assured it of the highest social profile.

Social attitudes had conventionally scorned the idea that 'sport' could be paid work, or even a pastime for waged people. Friction broke out in the British team at the 1896 Olympic Games in Athens when two servants at the Embassy were drafted in to make up numbers. By this time, however, the meaning of sport was starting to change as a result of the related processes of mass culture and commercialization. This is best illustrated by the development of Association Football, which, from the 1860s through to the 1910s, underwent a major social transformation. Having begun as primarily a participatory sport of the public schools it became the 'people's game' – the subject of immense interest and enjoyment at all social levels, at the apex of which was professional football based on middle-class commercial businesses ('clubs') attracting a large number of working-class male spectators. Association football in this form succeeded in harmonizing strong proletarian characteristics with control vested in other social groups, thus becoming a genuinely national game. It was only in the latter part of the 20th century, with the rise of alternative forms of leisure and the desire by leading clubs to capitalize on revenue from the televising of matches, that some of the working-class image began to fade. This caused some younger supporters to seek to reclaim 'their' game through violent behaviour, often referred to as 'football hooliganism'.

By contrast with football, the development of other sports was marked by sharp class tensions. Rowing offers a prime example – until the 1950s, there were two rival rowing associations for different social groups. In Rugby too, class difference resulted in hostility between Rugby Union, a game which succeeded in shedding its middle-class, suburban image only in South Wales, and Rugby League, confined to the North of England and, like Association Football, primarily to the working class. This was because Rugby Union shared a characteristic with several other sports, such as tennis and golf – each managed to exclude, either deliberately or through cost factors, a section of the population.

A contributory factor to the success of any sport among the working class was the opportunities it offered for betting. The football pools, begun in the 1920s but only fully established after the Second World War, were immensely popular until affected by the establishment of the National Lottery in the 1990s. Betting was responsible for other ventures which captured, at least for a time, a working-class following – greyhound and speedway racing became popular commercial sports in the interwar years, though neither had the following of angling, a male sport based on voluntary associations which attracted much betting and could lay claim to being the largest participant sport in the country. Aside from betting, sports with a working-class following often exhibited a degree of spectator passion, hero-worship and 'win-at-all-costs' mentality that went against the grain of polite society. There was, therefore, a sense in which a person's choice of sport defined his or her status; it was a marker of respectability and of whom one wished to be associated with.

An emphasis on social class cannot explain all aspects of the development of British sport – it tends, for example, to preclude the place of women in sport – but there is good reason for believing that sport and class have been mutually reinforcing categories in British society for a long time. Indeed, the claim that the decline of British sport in the international arena during the 20th century can be explained in part by the exclusionary nature of sport in Britain is one that cannot lightly be dismissed.

References:

Holt, R., *Sport and the British: a Modern History* (Oxford: Oxford University Press, 1990).

Holt, R. (ed.), *Sport and the Working Class in Modern Britain* (Manchester: Manchester University Press, 1990).

Mason, A. (ed.), *Sport in Britain: a Social History* (Cambridge: Cambridge University Press, 1989).

Further reading:

Hargreaves, J., *Sport, Power and Culture: a Social and Historical Analysis of Popular Sports in Britain* (Cambridge: Polity Press, 1986).

McKibbin, R., *Classes and Cultures: England, 1918-1951* (Oxford: Oxford University Press, 1998).

Polley, M., *Moving the Goalposts: a History of Sport and Society Since 1945* (London: Routledge, 1998).

See also:

Sociology of Sport

-Jeff Hill

Classics (The)

In chronological order of their development in British horse-racing, the five classic races, all for three-year-olds, are the Saint Leger (1776), the Oaks (1779), the Derby (1780) and the Two Thousand (1809) and One Thousand Guineas (1814). All of these races did away with the concept of heats, which had been standard practice at 18th-century race meetings. Since their establishment, the names have been adopted by race clubs worldwide for their own premier events, such as the Oaks d'Italia and the Kentucky Derby.

The Saint Leger was named after Lieutenant General Anthony Saint Leger (originally pronounced 'Sellinger'), a Park Hill (Doncaster) resident. It is run over 1 mile, 6 furlongs and 132 yards, almost a complete circuit of the Doncaster Town Moor course. The Oaks, named after Lord Derby's hunting lodge, is a 12 furlong race for fillies and the Derby, initially run over a mile but later 12 furlongs also, gained its title when the Twelfth Earl of Derby won the toss of a coin with Sir Charles Bunbury. Both are run at Epsom. The Guineas events are run over the Rowley Mile course at Newmarket, the racing home of the Jockey Club, and were established as the Club sought to have some prestige events under its own, immediate control.

There have been many multiple classic winners, but only Sceptre (1902) has won four classics outright, though Formosa (1868) won the Oaks, Saint Leger and One Thousand Guineas, and dead-heated in the Two Thousand Guineas.

References:

White, J., *The Racegoers' Encyclopedia* (London: Collins Willow, 1997).

Magee, S., *The Channel Four Book of Racing* (London: Sidgwick & Jackson, 1989).

Further reading:

Mortimer, R., *The History of the Derby Stakes* (London: Michael Joseph, 1973).

See also:

Horse-racing

-Wray Vamplew

Clay Pigeon Shooting (*see* Wild Pigeon Shooting)

Coaching

Modern coaching has, thankfully, progressed from the dark days of the late 18th and early 19th centuries when a trainer would fill his mouth with cold water (to take the chill off it), blow it onto his athlete's back and follow this up with a quick rub down with a rough towel. If the skin shone after such treatment, this was considered a sign of fitness. The sport was foot-racing or 'pedestrianism'.

Dietary regimes could be equally bizarre. Prize-fighters or 'pugilists' were fed raw meat and eggs to 'strengthen their wind and increase their savagery' and were likely to be revived between rounds with swigs of brandy. Jockeys found themselves under increasing pressure to keep their weight down as younger, lighter horses were developed. If tramping cross-country wearing half a dozen waistcoats and an extra overcoat did not do the trick, then virtual starvation was necessary.

Meanwhile, in the public schools and universities, coaching was developing along two

69

distinct and less extreme lines. Talented 'Blues' (students who had represented their places of learning in a sport) often returned as teachers and acted as coaches in sports such as Rugby or the more esoteric school games of Eton Fives and Harrow Football. Cricket and rowing, however, employed professional coaches such as the working-class bowlers paid to provide net practice for their young masters and the professional watermen who coached, and coxed, boat race crews.

By the last quarter of the 19th century, as sport became more and more organized, many individual sports set up their own governing bodies, although these were more concerned with combating corruption and crusading against the dreaded professionalism than putting the still haphazard area of coaching on a more efficient footing. Sporting excellence was thought to be achievable by the traditional British custom of 'mudding through'.

This illusion was shattered when the prestigious London Athletic Club crossed the Atlantic to take on their New York counterparts in 1895. They returned humiliated, having failed to win a single one of the eleven events. Worse was to come in 1912, when the country on whose Empire the sun never set was shocked at the poor performance of the British team at the Stockholm Olympics. Despite finishing third in the medal table, with ten gold, fifteen silver and sixteen bronze medals, the team was slated in the sporting press for their perceived 'failure'.

This criticism was sufficient to galvanize the Council of the British Olympic Association into launching a public appeal for financial support in an attempt to improve matters; £3,000 was raised for the Amateur Athletic Association (A.A.A.), £600 for the Amateur Swimming Association and £250 for the National Cycling Union in 1914 to help raise standards. The A.A.A. invested this windfall by engaging one professional coach, W. R. Knox, and nine regional part-timers. Knox's programme was abandoned

with the outbreak of the First World War, however, and was not revived when hostilities ceased.

Nevertheless, records show that the British team that attended the Paris Olympics took seventeen coaches, although the more common name was still 'trainers'. In the following years, various sports tinkered with the idea of coaching but no overall strategy existed. Universities and the bigger athletics clubs employed old 'pros' but only to act as masseurs and to train runners – the concept of the modern track and field coach was unheard of. Professional football still languished in the era of the bucket-and-sponge trainer and the professional foot-racers of the North of England and Southern Scotland were no better served than they had been a century earlier.

Gradually, however, coaching began to be taken more seriously. The A.A.A. set up its first Summer School in athletics in 1934 and the Loughborough School of Sport and Games was established two years later. By 1946, the A.A.A. was running a National Coaching Scheme, with G. H. G. Dyson as chief coach. He was joined by four more national coaches in 1948 and the 1950s were years of rapid expansion, although the growing army of national coaches was less enthusiastically received by the national bodies' administrators than by the performers they served so well. This lack of appreciation led to low morale and to the formation of a coaches' forum, the British Association of National Coaches (B.A.N.C.) in 1965. The National Coaching Foundation followed in 1983 and is now recognized as one of the world's leading sources of coaching knowledge. In 1988, following a B.A.N.C. initiative, the British Institute of Sports Coaches came into being, representing not only the professional coaches but also the approximately 100,000 others, mainly volunteers, working at grass-roots level. A job had finally become a profession.

Today, a top coach needs to be well versed in biomechanics, physiology and psychology as well as being an expert at dealing with people of all ages and abilities, earning their trust and respect. In other words, his work is both a science and an art.

Appreciation of these skills is acknowledged by the National Coaching Foundation, which offers courses at various levels up to a B.Sc. (Hons) degree in Applied Sports Coaching. Professional coaches are often ex-players reluctant to give up daily contact with the sport that has been their livelihood; these are the coaches who normally work with their fellow professionals. Some amateur sports, via their governing bodies, employ full-time coaches and similar positions can be found in this leisure-conscious age with local authorities, health farms, private hotels, holiday camps, leisure centres and the larger sports clubs.

References:

Paish, W., *The Complete Manual of Sports Science* (London: A. & C. Black, 1998).
Coaching Matters (London: Sports Council, 1991).

Websites:

The National Coaching Foundation – http://www.ncf.org.uk/

See also:

Central Council of Physical Recreation; National Coaching Foundation

-Tony Rennick

Commercialism

Commercialization is the process through which sport has been subjected to commercial forces in order to yield income for sport itself and associated agencies. It is the most significant structural change to affect sport in the second half of the 20th century and has resulted in all levels of sport becoming irredeemably entwined with commercial transactions.

Historically, commercialism has long been a force in sport. Its first stirrings were the placing of wagers on sporting contests. By the 16th century, gambling had become a driving motive in the staging of such events. Pugilism, pedestrianism, horse-racing, animal baiting and even cricket were all accompanied by betting, despite barriers of class. This, and the general spectacle and excitement, drew in spectators who were sometimes charged admission fees by profit-seeking promoters. Even where no such fees were charged there were attempts to profit from sport through the selling of victuals and food. Innkeepers in particular took advantage of such opportunities and began organizing sporting events in order to sell their wares. Competitions were advertised by posters and handbills in order to attract competitors and, more importantly, spectators. By the mid-18th century, even town corporations were encouraging sporting events in order to attract business and custom. In short, money and sport had become irreversibly linked and the sums involved were instrumental in the development of standardized rules.

As industrialization and urbanization changed the structure of traditional sport, new opportunities arose for their commercial exploitation, most notably with the growth of the weekly half-day holiday. Pedestrianism was the first sport to switch its contests to a Saturday afternoon to profit from workers in search of entertainment beyond drinking. Other sports soon followed and Saturday afternoon became established as the central date of the sporting calendar in order to maximize the number of spectators and the money they paid to be entertained. The desire to attract paying spectators also contributed to the beginnings of professionalism, as the most talented sportsmen were able to demand fees or jobs in return for their services.

The mid- to late 19th century witnessed a hostile reaction to commercial forces within sport as the middle classes and public schools attempted to distance themselves from the leisure of the masses. Being paid was seen as tainting the beneficial effects of playing games, while spectating was seen as having no moral

71

benefits. Thus, the élite attempted to exclude commercial forces from sport and professionalism was banned in sports such as football that had their organized roots in the public schools.

However, professionalism was legalized in football in order to counter the threat of teams from working-class areas breaking away from the fledgling ruling bodies. Thus, commercial forces were tolerated by middle-class administrators in order that they might retain control of their sports. It was this toleration of professionalism that led to a growth in the commercialization of sport in the Victorian period. Soccer clearly illustrates this trend. By the turn of the 20th century, professional clubs were usually registered as limited liability companies with shareholders and directors. Crowds of thousands were generating large sums of gate money and players were being bought and sold as commodities.

Yet, despite this, profit was rarely the motive of sport's patrons and controls continued to limit commercialism's impact. Maximum wages, distinctions between gentlemen and professional players, and limits on dividends were among the controls utilized in soccer and cricket. Profits in both sports were small if existent at all and used to improve the team or ground rather than financially benefit their owners. Nor were there attempts to cut entry prices to compete with other clubs, sports or new entertainments such as the cinema. In contrast though, pugilism and horse-racing could sometimes generate significant profits for competitors and patrons alike. However, in the world of mass spectator sport such overt commercialization remained the exception.

By the interwar period, the popularity of sport had brought new avenues of commercialism. Famous sportsmen were being used to advertise goods, new sports such as speedway and greyhound racing were introduced to Britain by entrepreneurs seeking to make profits, while the football pools brought gambling on sport to new levels of popularity that incor-

porated those not even interested in the game itself. However, a moral disdain to overtly prioritizing profit remained. This was illustrated by the Football League's refusal to accept the offer of money from the pools companies for use of their fixture lists in 1936. As Holt points out, such relationships were evidence that commercialization and professionalism were not synonymous.

It was from the 1960s onwards that commercialism in sport began to reach new levels. Changes in wider social attitudes and legal challenges saw the old controls in sports fall one by one. Consequently, from the abolition of soccer's maximum wage and retain-and-transfer system to the eventual professionalization of Rugby Union, sport has gradually become further intertwined with market forces. Income and expenditure have risen significantly in all sports as competitors' wages and the prizes offered have grown alongside the new riches that sponsorship and, in particular, television generate. The latter has brought huge new audiences, making sport an attractive proposition for advertisers. The money television is thus willing to pay for the right to broadcast events has commercialized sport to the extent that its timing, location and even rules and names are all subject to change and compromise. Aligned to this rising audience is the growth in merchandising, which has become more important for the largest clubs than gate receipts. The profits now possible for sport's competitors, owners and sponsors have grown to levels their predecessors could never have imagined.

This level of commercialism has led to contemporary concerns that sport has lost its soul and sold out to financial interests. Yet commercialism in sport has a long history. Nevertheless, it was a halting and slow development before sport fully took up its place as part of a commercial leisure industry. Today, sport is clearly a commercial concern that is about far more than just games.

References:

Brailsford, D., *British Sport: a Social History* (Cambridge: Lutterworth Press, 1992).

Holt, R., *Sport and the British: a Modern History* (Oxford: Oxford University Press, 1990).

Sleap, M., *Social Issues in Sport* (Basingstoke: Macmillan, 1998).

Further reading:

Vamplew, W., *Pay Up and Play the Game: Professional Sport in Britain, 1875-1914* (Cambridge: Cambridge University Press, 1988).

See also:

Marketing; Sports Sponsorship

-Martin Johnes

Commonwealth (formerly Empire) Games

The Commonwealth Games are second only to the Olympics in the hierarchy of 20th-century multi-sports gatherings, even if of late its significance on the international sporting calendar has diminished. Its origins can be traced to an article written in 1891 by a young Englishman, John Astley Cooper, outlining proposals for a Pan-Britannic Festival incorporating industrial, cultural and athletic contests and designed 'to draw closer the ties between the Nations of the Empire'. The idea was widely debated throughout the Empire and received some support but was ultimately overtaken by the successful attempt of Baron de Coubertin to revive the Olympic Games in a modern form.

The 1911 Festival of Empire provided the first practical demonstration of Cooper's proposal with the inclusion of an Inter-Empire Sports Meeting. However, relatively few athletes were involved and attendances were disappointing, so the idea of a more permanent gathering was not seriously discussed for another seventeen years, when Bobby Robinson and other Canadian sports administrators began developing plans for a British

Empire Games to be staged in Hamilton in the summer of 1930. Despite financial and logistical difficulties, the Games went ahead with some 400 competitors from eleven countries competing in six sports. A British Empire Games Federation was established to oversee and organize future Games, which were to be held every four years.

Though modelled on the Olympics, the Games have been different in purpose and style. Unofficially titled the 'friendly games', they eschewed the apparent lack of sportsmanship and the emphasis on winning, as well as the increasing nationalism and commercialization, associated with the larger event. The number of sports has been restricted so as to allow smaller nations to compete on equal terms, team games were not, until recently, included and there has been no official medals table. Moreover, in the oath of allegiance to the British monarch, the singing of the British national anthem and the releasing of doves at the opening ceremony, there was a conscious effort to establish the Games as a symbol of imperial unity at a time when formal political control was weakening.

Despite this, the Games have been forced to adapt to broader political developments. In 1952, they were renamed the British Empire and Commonwealth Games, but in 1966 and 1974 respectively, the words 'Empire' and 'British' were dropped, leaving simply the Commonwealth Games. The Games have also incorporated the increasing role of the newly independent, non-white African, Caribbean and Asian nations, although only Jamaica in 1966 and Malaysia in 1998 have actually hosted the event. It has also been subject to boycotts by black members over sporting links with South Africa.

While they were never envisaged as a competition to rival the Olympics in sporting excellence, the Games have been witness to a number of outstanding performances and world records. However, in an era of increasing globalization and international sporting competition, the status of an event based essentially on 19th-century imperial relationships may continue to wane.

References:

A Historical Record of the Games leading up to the Commonwealth Games of 1978 (Edmonton, Canada: History Committee of the XI Commonwealth Games Canada (1978) Foundation, 1978).

Moore, K., 'The Pan-Britannic Festival: a Tangible but Forlorn Expression of Imperial Unity', in J. A. Mangan (ed.), *Pleasure, Profit, Proselytism: British Culture and Sport at Home and Abroad, 1700-1914* (London: Frank Cass, 1988), pp. 144-162.

Websites:

The Commonwealth Games Federation – http://www.commonwealthgames-fed.org/

-Matthew Taylor

Commonwealth Games: London, 1934

The 1934 Empire Games ran from August 4th to August 11th. These games marked the first occasion of a political crisis within the Empire Games umbrella of sporting nations. They had originally been awarded to Johannesburg, South Africa, but Canada persuaded the young Empire Games Federation to talk London into hosting the event because of concerns over the way South Africa might treat the black and Asian athletes.

The site for the track and field events was the White City Stadium in West London, which had been specially constructed for the 1908 Olympics. At the opening ceremonies, 50,000 spectators greeted 500 competitors and 100 officials from sixteen countries. Women competed for the first time and India, Rhodesia, Jamaica, Trinidad (a team of one) and Hong Kong made their first appearance. R. L. Howland, England's team captain and shot-putter, took the Games oath and trumpet blasts framed the celebratory release of thousands of pigeons.

The star performer at the 1934 Games was New Zealand's Jack Lovelock. He carried his country's flag on the opening day and won the mile by a margin of 6 yards. Phil Edwards of Guiana, competing for Canada, became the first black gold medallist in the history of the Empire Games with his victory in the 880 yards. Godfrey Rampling of England achieved a double gold medal with wins in the 440 yards and the final leg of the 4 by 440 yards relay. The swimming events at the Wembley Games Empire Pool were dominated by a seventeen-year-old Canadian, Phyllis Dewar. She won four gold medals. Another Canadian, Ed Clayton, showed extraordinary powers of endurance by winning medals in three cycling events (the 1000 metres time trial, the 1000 metres sprint and the 10 mile race) on the same day.

In the medal count, Australia had eight gold medals, Canada seventeen and England twenty-nine. *The Times* newspaper of August 6th, 1934, underscored the collegial spirit of the Games by commenting in an editorial on 'keen sportsmanship', 'good fellowship' and 'friendly rivalry'.

References:

Dheensaw, C., *The Commonwealth Games: the First 60 Years, 1930-1990* (Victoria, British Columbia: Orca Publishing, 1994).

-Scott Crawford

Commonwealth Games: Cardiff, 1958

The 1958 Games were hosted by Wales and attracted a record thirty-five countries, over 1,100 athletes and 228 officials, the biggest sporting event ever undertaken by the Welsh people. The dramatic centre stage was Cardiff Arms Park, the spiritual home of Welsh Rugby, which had a red cinder running track configured around the grass pitch. A new Empire Pool was built at a cost of £700,000; boxing, wrestling and lawn bowls were sited at the Sophia Gardens Pavilion; cycling was based at Maindy Stadium; weightlifting went to Barry, a small town on the outskirts of Cardiff; fencing took place at Cae'r Castile School; and the rowing venue had to be Lake Padarn in Snowdonia, a distance of 180 miles from Cardiff.

Prior to the opening of the Games, and during the Games itself, there were significant protests and demonstrations regarding the fact that the South African team had been selected according to an exclusive and racist philosophy of 'whites only'. This apartheid-driven athletics selection programme generated strong antagonism from multiracial Commonwealth countries. South Africa eventually withdrew from the Commonwealth in 1961. They returned to the Commonwealth Games arena in 1994 (Victoria, Canada), two years after their return to the Olympic stage. Ironically, it was at Cardiff that new Third-World African countries emerged – Uganda, Kenya and Tanzania, for example – that have since become major forces in sports such as boxing and track athletics.

References:

Dheensaw, C., *The Commonwealth Games: the First 60 Years, 1930-1990* (Victoria, British Columbia: Orca Publishing, 1994).

See also:

Sophia Gardens

-Scott Crawford

Commonwealth Games: Edinburgh, 1970

Held in Edinburgh, the 1970 Commonwealth Games were regarded as a success both in organizational and sporting terms. In many ways it represented the culmination of the growth of the Games following the postwar era of British decolonization. By far the largest at that time (it also surpassed the 1974 Christchurch Games), Edinburgh played host to 1,383 competitors and 361 officials from 42 countries, including

for the first time teams from Grenada, Guernsey, Malawi, Swaziland and the Gambia.

The Games were marked by a heavy royal presence. Various members of the royal family attended events, and Prince Philip, as always, presided at the opening ceremony. Significantly, however, for the first time the Queen herself was present at the closing ceremony. In addition, the event has been portrayed as a particularly celebratory and unifying occasion, symbolized by 'the spontaneous show of friendliness' of competitors at the closing ceremony and described subsequently as the archetypal 'friendly games'.

Aided by financial support from central government, the events were centred around Edinburgh's new Meadowbank Stadium complex, which was specifically designed for use in future competitions. With their decisions to use metric measurements for the Athletics and Swimming events and to adopt the photo finish to decide placings on the track, the organizers were also recognizing the Games' place as an international event comparable with the Olympics.

References:

A Historical Record of the Games leading up to the Commonwealth Games of 1978 (Edmonton, Canada: History Committee of the XI Commonwealth Games Canada (1978) Foundation, 1978).

-Matthew Taylor

Commonwealth Games: Edinburgh, 1986

The 1986 Commonwealth Games, held for the second time in Edinburgh, were plagued by financial difficulties and a mass boycott. The commercial success of the Los Angeles Olympics of 1984 had heralded a new vision of self-funding through television rights, sponsorship and advertising revenue, which the Edinburgh organizers were keen to adopt. However, conflict between the organizing committee and the city council and the failure to secure the expected

75

backing from major sponsors led to a crisis which threatened the viability of the Games.

Barely months before the opening ceremony, Robert Maxwell, the millionaire publisher and owner of Mirror Group Newspapers, stepped in to assume financial and fund-raising control. However, despite assurances that the Games would not make a loss, Maxwell failed to persuade the British government to join himself and a Japanese businessman in paying off a £3 million deficit and, barely two months after the closing ceremony, the Games were officially declared bankrupt.

The Games were also seriously affected by the largest boycott of competing nations in its history. Infuriated by the British government's rejection of sanctions against the South African apartheid regime, thirty-two national teams – mainly from Africa, Asia and the Caribbean – withdrew, leaving just twenty-six teams to compete. Further controversy came when England included two South Africans, the athlete Zola Budd and the swimmer Annette Cowley, in its team. In an unprecedented decision, the Games Federation subsequently overturned the decision of the national selectors and decided that Budd and Cowley were ineligible to compete.

References:

Bateman, D. and Douglas, D., *Unfriendly Games: Boycotted and Broke. The Inside Story of the 1986 Commonwealth Games* (Edinburgh: Mainstream, 1986).

-Matthew Taylor

Community, Civic Pride and Sport

The word community has often been associated with British sports policy. It has been suggested that sport contributes to community in at least two ways. First there is the notion of a distinct sports community in its own right and second the notion that sport itself contributes to the re-generation of, for example, urban communities.

Sport is viewed as contributing to Civic as opposed to Ethnic pride, although it contributes to both. Cup-winning teams are often provided with the freedom of the home city because sporting success is shared by both the community and the local politicians, who use sport to reinforce notions of civic pride and loyalty to the town or area.

The relationship between West Ham Football Club and the community is borne out in the work of Korr, who describes the meaning of the club to one of the poorest inner-city areas of London in the early 1920s. Graham Walker's account of swimming in Motherwell in the 1940s shows how the swimming club tapped into notions of local civic pride and the need to swim well for the community, whether it be Motherwell, Scotland or Great Britain. Jeff Hill's research highlights the town of Nelson in the North West of England and the place of sport in the process of building civic identity between 1870 and 1950.

The history of British sport shows that an often idealized notion of community has overlooked the fact that there has nearly always been a tension between sport for its own sake and sport as a means to an end. Historically, the provision of sports facilities in Britain has often been rationalized on the grounds that sport will promote healthy communities, reduce crime rates, help with urban regeneration or promote community integration and social inclusion. For example, the New Labour Agenda for Sport states that 'Sport can make a unique contribution to tackling social exclusion in our society.' Rarely is sport viewed in terms of sport for sports sake but rather because it is a means to an end and is seen to deliver something else other than just sport.

References:

Hill, J., *Nelson: Economy, Politics, Community* (Keele: Keele University Press, 1999).

Korr, C. P., 'A Different Kind of Success: West Ham United and the Creation of Tradition and Community', in R. Holt (ed.), *Sport and the Working Class in Modern Britain* (Manchester: Manchester University Press, 1990).

Walker, G., 'Nancy Riach and the Motherwell Swimming Phenomenon', in G. Jarvie and G. Walker (eds.), *Scottish Sport in the Making of the Nation* (Leicester: Leicester University Press, 1994).

Further reading:

New Labour, *A Sporting Future for All* (London: HMSO, 2000).

Sugden, J., *Boxing and Society: an International Analysis* (Manchester: Manchester University Press, 1996).

Watson, N., 'Football in the Community' in J. Garland (ed.), *The Future of Football: Challenges for the Twenty-First Century* (London: Frank Cass, 2000).

See also:

Class

-Grant Jarvie

Concepts (*see* Amateurism; Fair Play; etc.)

Corinthians

Now a little-known amateur club, the Corinthians Football Club has a remarkable history, largely due to what it stood for and its remarkable achievements on the field of play.

In 1882, following several poor results by the national England team, Norman A. Jackson, Assistant-Secretary of the Football Association (F.A.), created a team he called the Corinthians, this being a name borrowed from classical antiquity. The England team had been composed mainly of university players; the idea of establishing the Corinthians club was to create more opportunities for these players to come and play together.

The team played only friendly matches and did not participate in the F.A. Cup, but they often defeated teams that had recently won the competition. Eighty-three of the team's players received

Corinthians Football Club, 1924. Once one of the top clubs in the country, Corinthians are now a little-known amateur club (Hulton Getty Picture Collection)

full international honours, three of them, L. H. Gay, C. B. Fry and R. E. Foster, also playing for England at cricket. In two England international matches against Wales in 1894 and 1895, all the English team were Corinthians. From 1897, the Corinthians toured overseas, taking with them their tremendous passing skills and open style of play. At the same time, they espoused amateur values, a sense of sportsmanship and an unselfish joy of the game at a time when professionalism was very much on the increase.

Between 1907 and 1914, the Corinthians adhered to the amateur spirit of the game and, in 1909, beat Bohemia. After the First World War, the legendary success of the Corinthians started to wane. From 1922, the team participated in the F.A. Cup, but rarely achieved the results for which they had previously been renowned. A Corinthians player, Howard Baker, was capped for England during this period and later become President of the F.A. In 1939, the Corinthians merged with the Casuals and were banished to the amateur leagues.

References:

Butler, B., *The Official History of the Football Association* (London: McDonald & Queen Anne Press, 1991).

Grayson, E., *Corinthians and Cricketers: and Towards a New Sporting Era* (Harefield: Yore Publications, 1996).

Further reading:

Golesworthy, M., *Encyclopedia of Football* (London: Robert Hale & Co., 1973).

Young, P. M., *A History of British Football* (London: Arrow Books, 1973).

Websites:

Corinthian-Casuals Football Club – http://www.corinthians.freeserve.co.uk/

See also:

Amateurism and Professionalism

-Gherardo Bonini

Costume and Clothing

Sports clothing can be either of practical value, worn as protection, or merely colour-coded as a guide to identification.

Examples of the first category are the gloves right-handed golfers wear on the left hand to aid grip, or the lightweight boots, with various lengths of studs to suit different playing conditions, favoured by modern footballers.

Protective clothing in its most extreme form is, not surprisingly, worn by Formula One drivers, who share their tiny cockpit space with whole-body fireproof suits, space-age crash helmets and oxygen masks. Soccer players make do with shin-guards, the brainwave of Nottingham Forest player Sam Widdowson in 1874. By the 1940s, these leg-preservers were thought so essential that the Bolton Wanderer's team, arriving at Middlesborough railway station only to find their shin-guards missing, invested in twenty-two romantic novels from the station bookstall as replacements.

The modern footballer's strip is not only a visual aid to the referee but a sartorial advertising hoarding for his club's sponsor and kit manufacturer. Nor are a club's colours sacrosanct. In 1996, Manchester United manager Alex Ferguson blamed his side's poor performance at Southampton on their new grey strip, because the players had difficulty picking one another out. The grey outfit was never seen again, but fans had already seen 'The Reds' perform in green and yellow, black, blue and blue and white. All very confusing for the television viewer, as were John Motson's immortal words, 'For those of you watching in black and white, Spurs are playing in yellow.'

References:

Cunnington, P. E. and Mansfield, A., *English Costume for Sports and Outdoor Recreation from the 16th to the 19th Century* (London: A. C. Black, 1969).

Morrison, I., *Rules and Equipment of the Game* (London: Pelham, 1987).

-Tony Rennick

Cotswold Games

The Cotswold Games were instituted in *c.* 1611 or 1612 by Robert Dover (1582-1652) on Dover's Hill (near Chipping Campden in Gloucestershire) and, after a possible interruption from 1622 to

COTSWOLD GAMES.

A poster advertising the Cotswold Games, from M. Walbancke, Annalia Dvbrensia *(London: R. Roworth, 1636).*

1624, were revived in 1625. According to Mr Walbancke's *Annalia Dubrensia* of 1636, a collection of thirty-three poems in praise of Dover, the Games were staged at yearly intervals on Thursdays and Fridays during Whitsun week. 'Mr. Robert Dovers Olimpick Games vpon Cotswold-Hills', with their classical touch, were instituted to revive and preserve good old English folk-festivals, as well as to stem the influence of the Puritans who were trying to crush them root and branch. With the support of his influential local friends, B. Hicks and E. Porter, as well as that of James I, Charles I and Bishop G. Goodman of Gloucester (all of whom were no admirers of the Puritans), Dover was able to stage a programme with sports disciplines for all social ranks. There was horse-racing, coursing and hunting by scent for the landed gentry; irish, cent, balloon, and shovelboard for the lesser ranks; wrestling, the quintain and barriers for townspeople; and the cudgel-play, shin-kicking, running, jumping,

throwing the hammer, spurning the bar, football, tumbling, skittles, dancing and music for the rural population. The Civil War brought the original Games to a close in 1642, but after 1660 they were resumed under the name of 'Dover's Meeting', organized by the innkeepers of the vicinity. The Games were discontinued in 1851 after the Enclosure Act came into force (dividing the hill into enclosures), however, they were taken up again properly in 1965 as 'Robert Dover's Games', organized by the Robert Dover's Games Society. This final incarnation is still celebrated to this day.

References:

Rühl, J. K., *Die 'Olympischen Spiele' Robert Dovers* (Heidelberg: C. Winter Universitätsverlag, 1975).

Rühl, J. K., 'The 'Olympic Games' of Robert Dover, 1612-1984', in M. Müller and J. K. Rühl (eds.), *Olympic Scientific Congress 1984. Official Report. Sport History* (Niedernhausen, Germany: Schors, 1985), p. 192-203.

Walbancke, M., *Annalia Dubrensia* (London: R. Raworth, 1636).

Whitfield, C., *Robert Dover and the Cotswold Games. Annalia Dubrensia* (London: H. Sotheran, 1962).

Wood, A., *Athenae Oxonienses* (London: Tho. Bennet, 1691-1692).

Further reading:

Burns, F. D. A., *ANNALIA DVBRENSIA. Vpon the yeerely celebration of Mr. ROBERT DOVERS Olimpick Games vpon Cotswold-Hills; with a History of the Cotswold Games*, MA dissertation, Sheffield University, 1960.

Clarke, S., 'Olympus in the Cotswolds: the Cotswold Games and Continuity in Popular Culture, 1612-1800', *The International Journal of the History of Sport*, vol. 14, no. 2 (August 1997), p. 40-66.

Grosart, A. B. (ed.), *Annalia Dubrensia* (Manchester: C. E. Simms, 1877).

See also:

Liverpool Olympics; Morpeth Olympic Games; Much Wenlock Games

-Joachim Ruhl

Countryside Alliance

The Countryside Alliance, formally established in March 1977, is an omnibus organization which aims to ensure the promotion, protection and preservation of traditional country sports and related activities in a thriving countryside that is properly cared for. It is an amalgamation of the Countryside Movement, the Countryside Business Group and the British Field Sports Society (B.F.S.S.). The best known of these was the B.F.S.S., which was formed in 1930 to safeguard fox hunting by uniting all field sports under one banner. The group was instrumental in successfully mobilizing opposition to a series of Private Members' Bills to outlaw hunting. The B.F.S.S. made strenuous efforts to maintain the fragile unity that existed between the hunting and shooting factions of the alliance.

The broad aims of the Alliance encompass the formulation of countryside initiatives to safeguard its vitality, viability and heritage. It operates as a pressure group representing the interests of its members at all levels of government and in the media. Its 'Listen to Us' meeting on July 10th, 1997, led to an estimated 120,000 people meeting in Hyde Park to draw public attention to the threatened way of life of country people. The Countryside March on March 1st, 1998, brought nearly 300,000 people on to the streets of London in protest. The Alliance's concerns focused on the Private Member's Bill to ban hunting with hounds and the government's proposal to introduce a statutory 'Right to Roam' Bill, in addition to the parlous state of the farming industry. The Alliance's defence of field sports is based on the preservation of civil liberties.

References:

Thomas, R. H., *The Politics of Hunting* (Aldershot: Gower, 1983).

Websites:

The Countryside Alliance –
http://www.countryside-alliance.org.uk/

See also:

Field Sports; Game Shooting; Wildfowling

-John Martin

Coursing (*see* Hare Hunting and Coursing)

Cowes (*see* U.K. Sailing Academy, Cowes)

Cricket

Cricket is a field ball sport played in summer, usually by teams of eleven players. In recent years, an indoor version of cricket has been played in winter.

The complexities of cricket make a simple description of its laws an impossibility. Cricket is played with a wooden bat and a hard leather ball. In the middle of a cricket field are two sets of three sticks or stumps, also called the wickets, which are 9 inches wide and 28 inches high, and set 22 yards apart. Whilst one team bats, the other team fields. One member of the fielding team bowls, that is, propels the ball with the hand towards one set of the wickets. One of the batting team attempts to hit the ball with the bat and, if the ball travels a sufficient distance, is then able to run to the other set of stumps and score one run. If the ball is hit far enough, a batsman may run two, three or even four runs. When the ball is hit over the boundary of the field, the batsman is awarded four runs, or six if it has not bounced. There are nine ways in which the fielding side can cause the batsmen to be 'out' (or stop batting), but the most common are to be bowled (the bowler propelling the ball so that it hits the stumps), caught (when a fielder catches the ball after it has been hit with the bat but not touched the ground) or l.b.w. (leg before wicket – where the batsman's body prevents the ball from hitting the stumps). A team stops batting when ten of its players are out, and the team that was fielding then bats. The side whose batsmen score the most runs are the winners of the match, but if not all the batsmen have been out during the time scheduled for the match, it is declared drawn, meaning that neither side has won.

Even at the lowest levels of recreational cricket, matches are usually scheduled to last four hours. The scheduled period for a test match is now five days. County championship matches are scheduled for four days. Despite having so many days of play, many test and county games are drawn or unfinished. Rain and poor light cause play to be suspended.

Traditionally, more people have played and watched cricket in England than elsewhere in Britain. Indeed, cricket has often been regarded as a symbol of England and, in particular, as part of the English pastoral tradition. Apologists for cricket have claimed that village cricket represents the truest form of cricket and even in the late 20th century, cricket matches played on a village green against a backdrop of the village inn and church are frequently employed to evoke immediately recognizable images of England. The distribution of population, however, means that more teams are based in towns than the countryside.

Far more men than women have played cricket. Teams including men and women are very unusual. Media coverage of the highest levels of women's cricket has rarely been more than minimal. Many women watch men's cricket and much of men's recreational cricket depends upon women performing domestic-style tasks such as preparing teas for players and looking after children whilst the men play.

In the late 19th century and for at least the first half of the 20th century, cricket was often thought to be pervaded by class distinctions. Many clubs were socially exclusive. The Marylebone Cricket Club (M.C.C.) and the county clubs were dominated by the economically and socially privileged. Until the 1963 season, first-class cricketers were divided into amateurs, usually with wealthy backgrounds, and professionals, who generally had working-class origins. Traditionally, county and England

sides were captained by amateurs, whose playing skills and experience were often inferior to those of the professionals under their command. Before 1939, at many grounds amateurs and professionals had separate dressing rooms and entrances to the field of play. On score cards amateurs were referred to as 'Mr', or had the initials of their forenames printed before their surnames, whereas the initials of professionals' forenames were printed after their surnames. In the 20th century, no professional captained England until 1952. During the last third of the 20th century, county cricket retained links with the social and political establishment but cricketing expertise rather than social background become the decisive qualification in cricket administration and authority.

By the last quarter of the 19th century, white trousers or flannels and white shirts and sweaters had become accepted as cricket clothing and have remained so in county championship and test match cricket. Coloured clothing has been worn in some forms of limited overs international cricket since the late 1970s, and in Sunday League cricket since 1993.

Use of the term 'It's not cricket' in everyday speech to condemn anything morally suspect indicates how widely it was believed, at least until the middle of the 20th century, that levels of sportsmanship in cricket were higher than those of other sports and that playing cricket promoted moral qualities which could be transferred to other areas of social activity. Assumptions that amateurs would be more likely to defend standards of sportsmanship were often used to justify the appointment of amateur captains. The sportsmanship of cricket was probably always exaggerated, but in the 1980s and 1990s there was much concern that at all levels of cricket, the traditions of sportsmanship were being increasingly flouted.

In the 19th century and for much of the 20th century, cricket was thought to have closer connections with churches than other sports. Between 1860 and 1900, a third of Oxbridge cricket blues became ordained. By

1914, many towns in Northern England had church cricket leagues. Traditionally, the vicar or curate was seen as a vital member of a village team and, in the first half of the 20th century, clergymen were often the presidents of village clubs. During the final third of the 20th century, cricket was less frequently represented as an expression of Christian morality.

Origins and Development

Scraps of evidence have led to claims that cricket was played in medieval England, but not all cricket historians accept these claims. The description of a game played in Essex in 1562 as 'clykett' and dictionary references to cricket in 1598 and 1611 suggest that a form of cricket was played in the 16th century. Use of the terms 'bat', 'cricket ball' and 'wicket' in the 17th century, and the account of cricket provided in William Goldwin's Latin poem of 1706, indicate that modern cricket is descended from a game played in the 17th century. Written rules survive from 1744 and the laws drawn up by the M.C.C. in 1788 seem to have been generally accepted as those by which the game should be played. All bowling in the 18th century was underarm. The M.C.C. legalized roundarm bowling in 1835 and overarm bowling in 1864 and, since then, changes to the game's laws have been matters of detail rather than fundamental reforms. In the late 17th century, cricket was largely restricted to the Sussex Weald and adjoining areas of Kent and Surrey. By 1700, cricket had probably spread to London and to all parts of England by the early 19th century. The first recorded game in Wales was played in 1783, Scotland in 1785 and Ireland in 1792. The earliest firm evidence of a match between women in England dates from 1745.

In the 18th century, cricket was played by men from all social groups, and aristocrats such as the Duke of Richmond patronized teams on whose matches vast sums were wagered. Watching cricket became so popular that spectators paid for admission to a match in 1744.

Initially, teams were organized on an ad hoc basis for particular matches, but clubs began to emerge in the 1720s. By the 1770s, the Hambledon club in Hampshire had become the strongest team in England. The Marylebone Cricket Club (M.C.C.), a club for the social élite that became the dominant power within cricket for much of the 19th and 20th centuries, is generally thought to have been formed in 1787. Some cricketers were paid to play cricket in the 18th century. In the mid-19th century, the strongest teams were the troupes of professionals, such as the All England Eleven and the United All England Eleven, who toured the country playing against local club sides often composed of fifteen or twenty-two players. The expansion of county championship cricket in the 1860s and 1870s, in which teams were usually captained by amateurs but included professionals, contributed to the eclipse of these touring professional teams. League cricket, a form of cricket especially strong in the industrial North and Midlands, began in 1889 with the creation of the Birmingham League. Other prestigious leagues include the Lancashire League (formed 1892), the Central Lancashire League (formed 1892) and the Bradford League (formed 1903).

The game soon spread to the British colonies. The reference in the diary of William Stephen or Stephens to cricket being played in Georgia in 1741 is usually taken to be the earliest reliable recorded instance of cricket being played in North America. A military history of India by Lieutenant Clement Downing mentions that British sailors played cricket at Cambay, Gujerat, India in 1721. The Calcutta Club, formed in 1792, was the first cricket club established in India. Reports in the *Sydney Gazette* of matches between civilians and the military at Sydney in 1803 are the first references to cricket being played in Australia. A meeting of the St. Ann's Club shows that cricket was being played in Barbados in 1806. An advertisement for a match between two military sides in 1808 in *The Cape Town*

Gazette and African Advertiser is the first reliable evidence of when cricket was first played in South Africa. In his account of the Beagle voyage, the scientist Charles Darwin mentions seeing Maoris play cricket in 1835. A club had been formed in Wellington, New Zealand, by Christmas 1842.

Governance and Administration

Until 1968 cricket did not have an administrative structure embracing all levels of the sport. The M.C.C., although a private club, dominated first-class cricket and was recognized as the supreme authority in English cricket, but had no formalized control over recreational cricket. The M.C.C. selected officials and players for the overseas tours on which England played test matches. The Board of Control, established in 1898, administered test matches played in England. The M.C.C. president was the chairman of the Board, which included five other representatives of the M.C.C., although these were outnumbered by those representing the county clubs. In 1904, the Advisory County Cricket Committee (A.C.C.C.) was established to administer the County Championship, but the M.C.C. was able to veto A.C.C.C. resolutions. The M.C.C. also represented England on the Imperial Cricket Conference, created in 1909 to decide the procedures of test cricket. In 1965, the Imperial Cricket Conference became the International Cricket Conference, which in 1989 became the International Cricket Council. The M.C.C. remained responsible for the administration of the International Cricket Council until 1993.

The Cricket Council, an administrative structure representing all levels of cricket in the British Isles, was established in 1968. The Board of Control and the A.C.C.C. were abolished and the Test and County Cricket Board (T.C.C.B.) was set up to control test match and county cricket. The National Cricket Association (N.C.A.) was formed to represent the interests of cricket outside the first-class game. The T.C.C.B., the N.C.A. and the M.C.C. were all represented on the Cricket Council. In 1983, a restructuring of the Cricket Council gave the T.C.C.B. eight votes on the Cricket Council, the N.C.A. five and the M.C.C. three. This reorganization of cricket stemmed in part from concerns that the M.C.C. as a private club wielded too much influence over first-class cricket and in part from the belief that a structure representing all levels of cricket would be required in order for cricket to become eligible for government funding.

Another major reform of cricket administration took place in 1997 when the Cricket Council, T.C.C.B. and N.C.A. were abolished. A new organization, the England and Wales Cricket Board (E.W.C.B.), became the governing body for all cricket in those two countries. This new structure recognized, and is intended to foster, the interdependency of a strong England test team and interest in all levels of cricket. The E.W.C.B. consists of the chairmen of the eighteen first-class counties and the twenty Minor Counties plus the M.C.C. treasurer. Its First-class Cricket Forum superintends first-class cricket whilst the Recreational Forum considers policy for the non-first-class counties, league, club and school cricket. The First-class Forum consists of two representatives from each first-class county. The Recreational Forum consists of representatives from the Minor Counties Cricket Association (which has retained control over minor counties cricket), the thirty-eight County Cricket Boards and other sections of non-first-class cricket. Each County Board includes representatives from all levels of cricket within its county area. The Irish and Scottish Cricket Unions are providing more unified structures for all levels of cricket outside England and Wales.

The Women's Cricket Association was established in 1926 to administer women's cricket. It disbanded in 1998 when the E.W.C.B. assumed responsibility for women's cricket.

Leaders and Personalities

The absence of detailed score cards from the early 18th century makes it difficult to be certain about who were the best cricketers at that time. More is known about the cricket personalities from the second half of the 18th century. Two Hambledon professional bowlers, Edward 'Lumpy' Stevens (1735-1819), who demonstrated the importance of bowling to a length, and David Harris (1755-1803), who bowled fast and made the ball rise from the pitch, did much to raise the standard of underarm bowling. William Beldham (1766-1862), another Hambledon player, was recognized as the leading batsman of the late 18th and early 19th centuries and a pioneer of playing forward to meet length bowling. Thomas Walker (1762-1831) was reputed to be the best defensive batsman of his day and a pioneer of round-arm bowling.

Alfred Mynn (1807-1861), nicknamed 'the lion of Kent' and 'Alfred the Great', was the most famous cricketer of the first half of the 19th century. A very large man of massive strength, he was a great all-round cricketer and for twenty years was a mainstay of the Gentlemen's teams. He was equally famed for his upright character and good humour and perhaps the first cricketer to achieve a celebrity that extended beyond the world of cricket. Fuller Pilch (1804-1870), a professional, was regarded as the best batsman of the 1830s and 1840s. His batting had great elegance and by playing forward and placing the ball through off-side he was reputed to have discovered how to master round-arm bowling. James Broadbridge (1796-1843) and Frederick Lillywhite (1792-1854) are usually regarded as the first successful exponents of round-arm bowling. Dominant figures of the touring professional elevens in the 1840s and 1850s were William Clarke (1798-1856), George Parr (1826-1891), considered to be the best batsman of the 1850s, and John Wisden (1826-1884).

William Gilbert Grace (1848-1915) was the most eminent cricketer of Victorian England and possibly the most famous Englishman of his time. Even today, his image is immediately recognized by English people who know little about cricket. In first-class cricket he is usually thought to have scored 54,896 runs and 126 centuries and as a bowler to have taken 2,876 wickets. Only four men have scored more runs and only five have taken more wickets. His score of 344 in 1876 was the first triple century. He was the first to score a hundred centuries and the first to score 2,000 runs in one season and also the first to score 1,000 runs and take 100 wickets in one season. In test match cricket, his record was not so impressive but he was perhaps past his peak when test cricket began to be played regularly. His appeal to spectators did much to establish county cricket as the major form of domestic cricket in England. Nominally an amateur, Grace was in fact a 'shamateur' and was often reputed to have indulged in sharp practice contrary to cricket's supposed traditions of fair play.

In the late 19th century, Arthur Shrewsbury (1856-1903) of Nottinghamshire and England was the leading professional batsman. Jack Hobbs (1882-1963), the Surrey and England professional batsman who played between 1905 and 1934, made the highest aggregate of runs – 61,270 – and the highest number of centuries – 197 – in first-class cricket. He was called 'The Master' because of the perfection of his batting technique whilst his gentle, modest nature and unquestioned sportsmanship helped to confirm perceptions of cricket as an expression of English moral worth. Walter Hammond (1903-1965) was the leading English batsman in the late 1920s and 1930s and would perhaps have been one of cricket's greatest all-rounders had he chosen to bowl more frequently. Len Hutton (1916-1990) and Denis Compton (1918-1997) were the leading English batsmen in the mid-20th century. Hutton was a classical stylist whereas Compton was unorthodox and an improviser. In 1952, Hutton became the first professional in the 20th century to captain England. Peter May (1929-1994) is often described as the best batsman of the post-1945 period but Geoffrey Boycott (1940-) in a much longer career scored more runs. Graham Gooch (1953-) and David Gower (1957-) are usually regarded as the best English batsmen of the 1980s and 1990s.

Wilfred Rhodes (1877-1973), a left-arm spin bowler, is the English bowler to have taken most wickets – 4,187 – and 'Tich' Freeman (1888-1965), a right-arm leg spinner, took the highest number of wickets in a season – 304. In 1932, Hedley Verity (1905-1943), another left-arm spin bowler, had the best bowling analysis for one innings – 10 wickets for 10 runs. In a test match against Australia in 1956, the off-spinner Jim Laker (1922-1986) took 19 wickets, the highest number of wickets ever taken by a bowler in a first-class match. Harold Larwood (1904-1995) and Frank Tyson (1930-) are usually thought to have been the fastest bowlers to play for England. Fred Trueman (1931-), another fast bowler, in 1963 was the first bowler to take 300 test wickets in test cricket. Brian Statham (1930-), John Snow (1941-) and Bob Willis (1949-) have been other outstanding England fast bowlers. Maurice Tate (1895-1956) and Alec Bedser (1918-) have been the leading English medium-pace bowlers and played with great success against Australia. Ian Botham (1955-) took most wickets for England and was also a flamboyant batsman who scored 14 test centuries. Herbert Strudwick (1880-1970), George Duckworth (1901-1966), Leslie Ames (1905-1990), Godfrey Evans (1920-1999), Alan Knott (1946-) and Bob Taylor (1941-) are usually considered to have been England's best wicket-keepers.

'Molly' Hide (1913-1995), England captain from 1937 until 1954, did much to establish the credibility of women's cricket. Rachel Heyhoe-Flint (1939-) was a member of the England women's cricket team from 1960 until 1983 and was probably the first English woman cricketer to become known to the general public. Janette Brittin (1959-) has played in more test and one-day matches for England than any other female player and scored the highest aggregate of runs – 4,056.

Famous Venues

The Artillery Ground in Finsbury was the leading cricket ground in London in the 1730s and 1740s. It was developed for cricket by George Smith, a cricketer and landlord of the Pied Horse public house in Chiswell Street, which adjoined the ground. The first recorded match was played there in 1730. In the 1740s, seventy major matches were played on the Artillery Ground. Ten thousand were thought to have watched a three-a-side game between Kent and an All-England side at the Artillery Ground in 1743. The first match at which spectators were charged for admission was held there in 1744.

Lord's, the ground of the M.C.C., is generally regarded as the most prestigious cricket venue in England. It is often perceived as the headquarters of cricket and the word 'Lord's' is used frequently to denote those who control cricket. Since 1877, Lord's has also been the home ground and administrative headquarters of Middlesex County Cricket Club. The bodies which have controlled national cricket since 1968 – the Cricket Council, the National Cricket Association, the Test and County Cricket Board, and the England and Wales Cricket Board – as well as the International Cricket Council have had their offices at Lord's. Because of the M.C.C.'s connections with the social élite, Lord's has often been seen as part of cricket's associations with privilege and class distinction. Women have only been admitted to the pavilion during matches since 1998, when the M.C.C. finally decided that women could become full members. Lord's is situated in St John's Wood, near Regent's Park in London. It is the third ground that was owned by Thomas Lord, a professional bowler, and was bought by the M.C.C. in 1866. The pavilion, built in 1889-1890, was designed by Thomas Verity, architect of the Albert Memorial. A test match was first played at

Lord's in July 1884, and every year since then, when test matches have been played in England, one has been held at Lord's. The Oxford and Cambridge University match, Eton versus Harrow and other public school games are played at Lord's. Until 1962, a Gentlemen and Players match was held there each year too, as were the cricket World Cup finals in 1975, 1979, 1983 and 1999. The finals of the English limited overs competitions and of the village and club competitions are also staged at Lord's.

The Oval is the headquarters and ground of Surrey County Cricket Club. In 1845, more than 100 cricket clubs from Surrey met after a match at The Oval and decided to set up Surrey County Cricket Club. The county club played its first match at The Oval in 1846. The Oval soon became one of the major sporting venues of London, largely due to the initiatives of C. W. Alcock, a Harrovian, who was secretary of Surrey County Cricket Club from 1872 to 1907 and the honorary secretary and then secretary of the Football Association from 1867 until 1896. The first test match played in England took place at The Oval in September 1880, as did the test match of 1882 in which Australia defeated England, thus giving rise to the Ashes tradition. The first F.A. Cup Final and the finals from 1874 until 1892 were played at The Oval, and the first Association Football and Rugby Union internationals played in England were held there as well. Gentlemen/Players matches and the annual game between the county champions and a side selected from other counties were also played at the ground. In 1938, England made the record test match score for a side in one innings of 903 runs, in which Len Hutton set a new test match individual score record of 364 runs, at The Oval. England's winning of the Ashes at The Oval in 1926 and in 1953 were occasions of national rejoicing. The Oval was renamed The Fosters Oval in 1988 after the Elders IKL brewing conglomerate financed an extensive re-building programme.

Old Trafford, just outside Manchester, is the main cricket venue in north-west England. The Manchester Cricket Club began playing matches at Old Trafford in 1857. Since its formation in 1864, Lancashire County Cricket Club has used Old Trafford as its principal ground and its administration is based there. In July 1884, Old Trafford became the second ground in England to stage a test match. In 1956, the bowler Jim Laker took nineteen wickets for England in the test match against Australia at Old Trafford. Yorkshire County Cricket Club have played county cricket at Headingley, Leeds, since 1891 and a test match was first played there in 1899. In 1962, the administration of Yorkshire C.C.C. moved to Headingley. In 1930 and 1934, Don Bradman scored triple centuries for Australia in test matches at Headingley, and at Headingley in 1981, England, inspired by Ian Botham and Bob Willis, became the first team since 1894 to win a test match after having to follow on. In 1902, a test match against Australia was played at Bramall Lane, Sheffield, where cricket had been played since 1856 and which was the administrative headquarters of Yorkshire C.C.C. between 1863 and 1903. Sheffield United, a Football League club, also played at Bramall Lane and in 1973, Yorkshire C.C.C. ceased playing there.

In the Midlands, test matches are played at Trent Bridge, Nottingham and at Edgbaston in Birmingham. Cricket was first played at Trent Bridge in 1838 on a ground laid out behind the Trent Bridge Inn by William Clarke, the professional cricketer who had married the landlady of the Inn. Nottinghamshire played a county match at Trent Bridge in 1840 and a test match was staged there for the first time in 1899. Warwickshire C.C.C. first played a county match at Edgbaston in 1894, although an England XI had played the Australians there in 1886. Edgbaston was first used for a test match in 1902, but only four test matches had been played there by 1929. After 1929, no test matches were staged at Edgbaston until 1957.

Since 1957, Edgbaston has been a regular test match venue.

Famous Clubs and Teams

The Marylebone Cricket Club is often regarded as having been formed in 1787, but it is possible that a cricket club for 'Noblemen and Gentlemen', which met at the Star and Garter from around the 1750s, and the White Conduit Club, which existed from 1785 until 1788, were different names for the same club. Peter Wynne-Thomas, in his *The History of Cricket from The Weald to The World*, claims that the club could have existed as early as 1744. The White Conduit Club played on the White Conduit Fields three days a week, where Thomas Lord, a professional cricketer, acted as the club's general factotum. In 1786, Lord Winchilsea, Colonel Lennox (later the Duke of Richmond) and Sir Peter Burrell (later Baron Gwydyr) promised to patronize Lord if he could find a more private ground for them. He found a ground near Dorset Square and the name Marylebone Cricket Club (M.C.C.) was adopted when the club started to play matches on Lord's ground. No doubt because of its members' social eminence, the M.C.C. soon became the most prestigious cricket club in England and to this day is perceived as a club for the social élite and especially those with inherited wealth. The laws which it drew up in 1788 for the matches it played became the rules by which almost all cricket was played and the M.C.C. retains the copyright for the laws of cricket (for details of the M.C.C.'s powers over first-class cricket, see the section on *Administration and Governance*). The M.C.C. remains a private members' club and it voted to admit women as members only in 1998. In 1999, it had 19,831 members and played 406 matches, but only one was first-class.

Hambledon, a Hampshire village, had perhaps the first cricket club with a national reputation. It was founded in the 1750s and/or the early 1760s, and from the 1760s until the 1780s it was reputed to have the strongest side in England, often defeating sides representing counties and sometimes the rest of England. Most of its players had relatively humble origins and were paid to play cricket, but the club had aristocratic patrons such as the Duke of Chandos, the Duke of Richmond, Lord Winchilsea and Lord Darnley. By the end of the 1780s, leading players were being attracted to London and the Hambledon Club disbanded in the early 1790s. The club played first on Broadhalfpenny Down and later on Windmill Hill. Its players are thought to have made a major contribution to the evolution of playing techniques by emphasizing the need for application and method as well as strength and co-ordination.

The All England Eleven was formed in 1846 by the professional cricketer William Clarke, whose party of leading professionals agreed to play matches against club and district sides in return for a guaranteed fee. To ensure reasonably even matches, the All England Eleven often played against teams of fifteen or twenty-two players. In 1852, John Wisden and other professionals who objected to Clarke's handling of the All England Eleven formed the rival United All England Eleven, but both elevens were able to arrange sufficient fixtures. When Clarke died in 1856, he was succeeded as captain and manager of the All England Eleven by George Parr. In 1865, a breakaway from the United All England Eleven led to the creation of the United South of England Eleven. In the North, Roger Iddison of Yorkshire formed the United North of England Eleven. W. G. Grace played for the United South of England Eleven in 1866. In the 1870s, the touring elevens began to fade with the expansion of county cricket.

Since the acceptance of rules for determining places in the county championship in 1890, Yorkshire has won the championship the most times, being champions almost twice as often as any other county. Between 1890 and 1968, Yorkshire were outright champions in twenty-nine seasons and joint champions in another season, which meant that nearly half of these championships had been won by Yorkshire. At the time of writing, in 2000, Yorkshire have not won the championship since 1968. Yorkshire's dominance in the county championship was strongest in the 1930s, when the championship was won in seven seasons. Surrey have been outright champions in sixteen seasons and joint champions once. Surrey won the championship each season from 1952 until 1958, a record unequalled by any other county. Middlesex, outright champions in ten seasons and joint champions in two seasons, are the only other county whose county championships reach double figures. Durham, Gloucestershire, Northamptonshire, Somerset and Sussex have never won the championship since its re-organization in 1890.

Lancashire has been the most successful county in limited overs cricket. The Gillette Cup/Natwest Trophy has been won seven times by Lancashire and five times by Warwickshire. Lancashire's four wins in the Benson and Hedges Cup are also a record, while Kent and Leicestershire have won the competition three times. Lancashire have been the Sunday league champions five times, Kent four times and Essex, Hampshire, Lancashire, Warwickshire and Worcestershire have each been champions in three seasons.

In test matches against Australia, England's most sustained period of success was between 1882-1883 and 1896, when England won or drew eleven out of twelve test series played. England lost or drew five successive test series against Australia from 1934 to 1950-1951 and from 1989 until 1997. Since 1973, England have played twelve test series against the West Indies. Three were drawn and the rest lost by England. Australia in 1920-1921 and the West Indies in 1984 and in 1985-1986 have been the only teams to defeat England in all five matches of a test series. Only against India in 1959 have England won all five matches of a test series. The England test record in the 1990s was especially dismal. Fifteen series were

played against Australia, the West Indies, South Africa and Pakistan, generally considered to be the four strongest countries playing test cricket, but only that against South Africa in 1998 was won.

Famous Competitions

The Ashes test match series between England and Australia is traditionally held to determine which country holds the Ashes. The country that wins the series is said to have won the Ashes. If a series is drawn, the country which already held the Ashes retains them.

The County Championship is regarded as the major cricket competition in the United Kingdom. Cricket historians disagree about when the championship started. In the 1820s, teams representing the best cricketers in a county could challenge the county which was regarded as the champion county for the title of champion county in much the same manner as challenges were issued to champion boxers. By the 1860s, several counties were playing against other counties and in 1873, rules governing the residential qualifications of those eligible to play county cricket were drawn up. In the 1870s and 1880s, journalists began to place counties in a championship table but in some seasons there was no general agreement about which was the champion county. After the 1889 season the counties agreed on how to determine positions in the championship. In 1890, Gloucestershire, Kent, Lancashire, Middlesex, Nottinghamshire, Surrey, Sussex and Yorkshire were recognized as competing for the championship. Somerset joined in 1891 and Derbyshire, Essex, Hampshire, Leicestershire and Warwickshire in 1895. Worcestershire was admitted in 1899, Northamptonshire in 1905, Glamorgan in 1921 and Durham in 1992.

The Oxford University versus Cambridge University match, or the 'varsity' match as it is known, is the oldest first-class cricket fixture. It was first played in 1827 and, except for the war years, has been played annually since 1838. Since 1851 it has been played at Lord's. Cricket blues are awarded only to those who play in the 'varsity' match. The University match was among the most prestigious matches of the cricket season but its importance has declined over the last thirty or so years. By 1999, Cambridge had won fifty-six of the matches, Oxford forty-eight and fifty had been drawn.

The first match between the Gentlemen (the leading amateurs) and the Players (the leading professionals) was played in 1806 and the last in 1962, the final year when a distinction was made in first-class cricket between amateurs and professionals. Until the rise of test cricket, these were the most prestigious matches of the cricket season. From 1806 an annual match was played at Lord's but in many years, Gentlemen and Players matches were also held at The Oval, Scarborough and occasionally at other grounds.

The Minor Counties Championship was first contested in 1895 by counties not playing in the county championship. Second elevens of county championship clubs were allowed to compete in 1899. The Championship was organized as a league but not all teams played every other team in each season. In seasons when the top two teams had not played each other, a challenge match could be played to decide the championship. In 1959, most first-class county second elevens withdrew when a separate Second Eleven Championship was introduced. Somerset Second XI in 1987 were the last second eleven to play in the Minor Counties Championship. From 1983, teams have been divided into Eastern and Western Divisions with the championship being decided by a final between the winners of each division. The M.C.C. Trophy, a limited overs knockout competition, has been contested by Minor Counties teams since 1983. In 1999, this became the E.C.B. 38-County Competition.

The National Club Championship, a knockout competition for club cricket, was first held in 1969. The early rounds are contested on a regional basis with the final at Lord's. Scarborough, with five wins, have won it most often.

The National Village Championship, a knockout competition for teams representing villages, was first played in 1972. The early rounds are contested on a regional basis with the final at Lord's.

The NatWest Bank Trophy, introduced in 1963, was the first limited overs competition for county clubs. It has always been a knockout competition. The final is held at Lord's each September. From 1963 until 1980 it was called the Gillette Cup.

The Benson and Hedges Cup, a limited overs competition, was introduced in 1972. By 1998, all first-class counties, Ireland, Scotland, a British Universities XI and a Minor Counties XI were taking part. Teams are divided into groups whose placings are decided on a league basis. The top two teams from each group then play in a knockout competition, with a final held at Lord's in the middle of the season. In 1999, the format was changed to a knockout competition for the clubs finishing in the top eight positions of the county championship in 1998. The competition was due to revert to its earlier format in 2000.

The C.G.U. National League is usually known as the Sunday League. It began in 1969 as a limited overs league competition for the first-class counties, but matches are no longer restricted to Sundays. It has also been called the John Player's County League (1969), the John Player League (1970-1983), the John Player Special League (1984-1986), the Refuge Assurance League (1987-1991), the Sunday League (1992), the AXA Equity and Law League (1993-1996), the AXA Life League (1997) and the AXA League (1998). In 1999, the league was divided into a first and second division with promotion and relegation. Counties were given new names such as Lancashire Lightning and Sussex Sharks.

The Texaco Trophy has been awarded since 1984 to the winners of the series of limited overs matches played between England and the test sides touring England. From 1972 until 1982, the Prudential Trophy was awarded to the winners of these series.

The (Men's) World Cup is a limited overs competition for international teams and has been held in 1975, 1979, 1983, 1987-1988, 1991-1992, 1996 and 1999 by the countries playing test cricket. In addition to the nine countries playing test cricket, Bangladesh, Canada, East Africa, Holland, Kenya, Scotland and the United Arab Emirates have played in some of the World Cups. The first three World Cups and that of 1999 were played in England, and England were the losing finalists in 1979 and 1988. The Prudential Cup was awarded to the winners of the World Cups in 1975, 1979 and 1983, the Reliance Cup to the winners in 1988, the Benson and Hedges Cup to the winners in 1992 and the Wills Cup to the winners in 1996. The name of no single sponsor was attached to the 1999 cup.

The Women's World Cup is a limited overs competition for international teams. The competition has been held in 1973, 1978-1979, 1981-1982, 1988-1989 and 1993. England were the winners in 1973 and 1993 and losing finalists to Australia in the other three competitions.

Memorable Events

1709 – The first reference to a match between teams representing counties can be found in the *Post Man* of 25 June, 1709. Kent played Surrey at Dartford Brent.

1745 – the first recorded women's cricket match was played between the 'maids' of Hambleton and Bramley. The first recorded women's county match, between teams from Hampshire and Surrey, was arranged in 1811 by an unknown aristocrat for stakes of 500 guineas.

1769 – John Minshull is thought to have made the first century when he scored 107 runs for the Duke of Dorset's XI versus Wrotham. In 1895, W. G. Grace became the first batsman to score 100 centuries in first-class cricket. In 1925, Jack Hobbs exceeded Grace's total of 126 centuries.

1859 – George Parr, an English professional cricketer, organized the first overseas cricket tour when his party of English professionals visited North America. The first English tour of Australia occurred in 1861-1862.

1864 – The first issue of *Wisden's Cricketers' Almanack* appeared. It has been published each year since 1864 and includes cricket records and detailed scores of all first-class matches played in England during the previous year. 'Wisden' is synonymous with the accurate keeping of cricket statistics and has become the standard against which similar volumes for other sports are judged.

1868 – The Australian Aboriginal cricketers were the first party of overseas cricketers to tour England.

1877 – A match played at Melbourne in Australia between a combined Melbourne and Sydney XI and a team of English professionals, led by James Lillywhite, subsequently became accepted as a match between England and Australia and is regarded as the first test match. Australia won by 45 runs. Charles Bannerman's 165 runs in Australia's first innings are considered the first test match century. The first match in England accorded test match status was played between England and Australia at The Oval in 1880.

1882 – The Beginning of the Ashes. At the Oval in 1882, Australia defeated England in England for the first time by the narrow margin of seven runs. The Australian fast bowler 'The Demon' Spofforth took fourteen wickets in the match. England's defeat led *The Sporting Times* to print a mock obituary stating 'In affectionate remembrance of English Cricket which died at the Oval, 29th August 1882. Deeply lamented by a large circle of sorrowing friends and acquaintances. R.I.P. N.B. – The body will be cremated and the ashes taken to Australia.' When England defeated Australia in 1882-1883, the England captain, the Honourable Ivo Bligh, was presented with the ashes of a bail and this is regarded as having started the tradition that the winning of test series between Australia and England decides which country holds the Ashes. The urn containing the 'Ashes' is kept permanently at Lord's.

1912 – The Triangular Tournament – In 1912, nine test matches were played in England between Australia, England and South Africa. England won the tournament but disappointing gate receipts in a wet summer meant that it was not repeated.

1926 – Establishment of the Women's Cricket Association (W.C.A.). By encouraging the formation of clubs and county associations, the W.C.A. did much to boost the playing of cricket among women. It insisted that its affiliated teams could not include men or play against men's teams. The W.C.A. held county matches in the early 1930s and in 1934 sent a touring party to play test matches in Australia and New Zealand. In 1937, an Australian team toured England.

1932-1933 – The Bodyline Series – On this tour of Australia the England captain, Douglas Jardine, was believed to have instructed his professional fast bowlers, Larwood, Voce and Bowes, to bowl short balls aimed at the batsmen's bodies as a means of counteracting the Australian batting strength and particularly Don Bradman, who had scored 974 runs against England in the 1930 series. These tactics were described as 'bodyline bowling'. Many Australians felt that 'bodyline' was physical intimidation that could cause serious injury to batsmen. Australian spectators were outraged and the Australian Board of Control threatened to abandon playing test matches against England. The ill feeling generated by bodyline was said to have 'almost cost us a Dominion'. England won the series but 'direct attack bowling' was not employed in subsequent inter-war test matches between England and Australia.

1968 – The D'Oliveira Affair – The England tour of South Africa, scheduled for 1968-1969, was called off when the South African government declared that Basil D'Oliveira, a non-white born in South Africa but who had played for Worcestershire and England, would not be acceptable to South Africa as a member of the touring party. D'Oliveira had not originally been chosen for the tour party, which was selected immediately after a test match against Australia in which he had scored a century for England. He was subsequently selected for the tour when another player dropped out of the tour party because of injury.

1968 – The Cricketers' Association, a trade union for county cricketers, was formed.

1970 – The cancellation of the South African tour of England – In 1970, public protests against the retention of sporting links with the apartheid regime in South Africa, pressure from the South African Non-Racial Olympic Committee (S.A.N.R.O.C.) and the Stop the Seventy Tour campaign, fears about protesters disrupting matches and advice from the government caused the Cricket Council to cancel the South African tour of England. The Cricket Council followed this by announcing that no further test matches would be played against South Africa until cricket in South Africa became multiracial. England resumed playing cricket against South Africa in 1994 after the abandonment of apartheid in South Africa. In 1982, English cricketers took part in a 'rebel' tour of South Africa without the approval of the T.C.C.B. In 1989-1990, a second rebel tour was abandoned and one planned for 1990-1991 was cancelled because of protests in South Africa.

1994 – Brian Lara set a world record first-class individual score when he made 501 runs for Warwickshire against Durham at Edgbaston.

Terms and Concepts

Ball – The term 'ball' can refer to the ball with which the game is played or also one attempt by the bowler to bowl the ball at the wickets.

Bouncers – Bouncers are also known as bumpers or short-pitched fast bowling, and are attempts to make the ball bounce up towards the batsmen's upper body or head.

Innings – The period which an individual batsman or a team spends batting is called an innings. In first-class matches sides usually have two innings each.

Limited Overs Cricket – In limited overs matches, each side is permitted to bat for only an agreed number of overs. The team which scores more runs in its allocation of overs wins the match. As limited overs matches are scheduled for one day, they are often called 'one day cricket'. Limited overs matches played by county and international teams are not accorded first-class status. It is often argued that limited overs cricket undermines the techniques required for test match cricket.

Over – Six successive balls bowled by the same bowler. After completing one over, six balls are then bowled from the opposite set of stumps by another bowler. A maiden over is one from which a batsman scores no runs.

Pitch – The pitch can mean the turf between the two sets of stumps and also the point where a ball from a bowler hits the turf.

Round arm bowling – This occurs when the bowler does not raise the arm above the shoulder.

Seam bowling – This consists of fast- or medium-paced bowling where bowlers try to make the seam of the ball hit the pitch and so move either towards or away from the batsmen.

Spin bowling – This is a form of bowling whereby a bowler tries to make a ball change direction after it has hit the pitch. Spin bowling is nearly always slow bowling. Leg spinners are bowlers who make the ball bounce away from the batsman. Off spinners make the ball bounce into a batsman.

Straight bat – Coaching manuals have traditionally recommended batsmen to hit the ball with a straight bat, i.e. with the bat held vertically. In everyday speech 'playing with a straight bat' has come to mean acting in a reliable and correct manner.

Swing bowling – A form of bowling in which the bowler attempts to make the ball swerve either away from or towards the batsman. Swing is obtained more easily with a new ball or a ball with shine on one side.

Test matches – Test matches are international cricket matches in which each side has two innings. The countries playing test match cricket and seasons when they first played test cricket are Australia (1876-1877), England (1876-1877), South Africa (1888-1889), the West Indies (1928), New Zealand (1929-1930), India (1932), Pakistan (1951-1952), Sri Lanka (1981-1982) and Zimbabwe (1992-1993).

Wicket – Three wickets form the stumps. 'The wicket' is also another name for the pitch. The bowler responsible for ending a batsman's innings is said to have taken a wicket.

Further reading:

Annual issues of *Wisden Cricketers' Almanack* (1988 edition published by John Wisden & Co., Guildford).

Birley, D., *A Social History of English Cricket* (London: Aurum, 1999).

Eley, S. and Griffiths, P. (comps.), *Padwick's Bibliography of Cricket*, volume II (London: Library Association, 1991).

Marqusee, M., *Anyone But England: Cricket and the National Malaise* (London: Verso, 1994).

Padwick, E. W. (comp.), *A Bibliography of Cricket*, volume I (London: Library Association, 1984).

Sandiford, K. A. P., *Cricket and the Victorians* (Aldershot: Scolar, 1994).

Swanton, E. W., Plumptre, G. and Woodcock, J. (eds.), *Barclays World of Cricket: the Game from A to Z* (London: Willow Books, 1986).

Websites:

The England and Wales Cricket Board – http://www.ecb.co.uk/

Hambledon – Cradle of Cricket – http://hambledon.parish.hants.gov.uk/notemain.htm

The International Cricket Council – www-uk1.cricket.org/link_to_database/NATIONAL/ICC/

Lancashire County Cricket Club – http://www.lccc.co.uk/

Lords and Marylebone Cricket Club –
http://www.lords.org/

Middlesex County Cricket Club –
http://www.middlesexccc.co.uk/

Surrey County Cricket Club –
http://www.surreyccc.co.uk/

Yorkshire County Cricket Club –
http://www.yorkshireccc.org.uk/

See also:

The Ashes; Headingley Sports Ground; Lord's Cricket Ground; Old Trafford Cricket Ground; Test Matches; World Cup Cricket

-Jack Williams

Croquet

Croquet is a lawn game involving the ordered propulsion of balls through designated hoops, using mallets. The game emerged in an organized form in Ireland in the 1830s, and spread to England in the 1850s. It was promoted by a number of individuals, including the sports goods manufacturer John Jaques, and it soon gained a keen following as a game played at country houses. In 1867, Walter Jones Whitmore promoted a championship at Evesham, and in 1868 the All-England Croquet Club was formed, promoting its own national championships at Wimbledon from 1870. However, croquet's early success was soon undermined by the spread of lawn tennis – seen most obviously in the All-England Club's adoption of the new sport – and it was not until 1896 that its enthusiasts formed the Croquet Association. By 1914, the Association had 170 affiliated clubs and 2,300 members. Croquet was damaged by the First World War, but it revived in the inter-war period, notably through the innovation of international tournament play between England and Australia from 1925. Croquet declined again during and after the Second World War, and by the early 1960s registered players and affiliated clubs had dropped to an all-time low. Its revival thereafter was linked to its attraction to a new generation of young players, to its spread in some universities, and to a modest amount of corporate sponsorship. The promotion of two shorter versions – golf croquet and short croquet – have also helped to attract more players, while the fact that it is played on equal terms by men and women has also been an advantage.

References:

Prichard, D. M. C., *The History of Croquet* (London: Cassell, 1981).

Further reading:

Gill, A. E., *Croquet: The Complete Guide* (London: Heinemann, 1988).

Smith, N., *Queen of Games: the History of Croquet* (London: Weidenfeld & Nicolson, 1991).

Websites:

The Croquet Association –
http://www.croquet.org.uk/

-Martin Polley

Cross-country Running

Competitive racing across the countryside can be traced back to Stuart and Hanoverian England. In 1663, Samuel Pepys witnessed a 'great foot race' on Banstead Down, near Croydon; and Daniel Defoe in his *Tour* made several references to foot races, including a description written in mid-Staffordshire where he reported that 'running foot-races seems to be the great sport or diversion of the country'.

By the early 19th century, the excitement of man-against-man or man-against-the-clock racing, known as pedestrianism, had begun to attract popular support, but the challenge of racing across the countryside still attracted its adherents. Cross-country running was not, and has never become, however, an essentially spectator sport – it is a sport for enthusiasts.

When the 'Crick Run', immortalized in *Tom Brown's Schooldays*, was started at Rugby School in 1837, it was mirroring a widespread but informal activity; and by 1850, various public schools and Oxbridge Colleges had 'runs' such as the 'Grind' at Exeter College, Oxford. It was then known as 'steeplechasing' because of its tendency to follow such landmarks and, in those environmentally unaware days, paper chasing was the method used to establish the course, unlike the biodegradable sawdust of modern times.

Early clubs which concentrated just on cross-country running were formed. These included Thames Hare and Hounds (1868), an offshoot of the West London Rowing Club; Ranelagh Harriers (1881); and the Cheshire Tally-Ho Hare and Hounds (1871). However, the commonplace use of the word 'Harriers' amongst 19th-century athletic clubs' names confirms that cross-country running was the prime focus of many others. From the 1860s to the 1880s, like track and field athletics, cross-country running broke away from a narrow class focus. By 1903, the International Cross-Country Union existed and, for over half a century, the four home countries were permitted to compete as separate teams in the 'international' championship, partly in recognition of the cross-country traditions that existed and partly because of Britain's part in its formation. By the 1920s, women's cross-country running was beginning to occur, but its formal organization really only commenced after the Second World War.

The English Cross-Country Championships started in 1877 and the roll of honour of winners since that time is a record of the greatest distance runners of modern times, from Walter George (1882 and 1884) and Alfred Shrubb (1901-1904) in the early years to Gordon Pirie (1953-1955) and Brendan Foster (1977) in more recent times. It is one of the largest championships held anywhere and it regularly attracts enormous fields, with a very strong focus on the team competition. This popularity accords with the very strong club basis of athletics generally in Britain.

References:

Bright, M. (ed.), *Diary and Correspondence of Samuel Pepys*, volume II (London: Bickers, 1876), p. 287.

Defoe, D., *A Tour Through the Whole Island of Great Britain*, volume II (London: Dent, 1962), p. 79.

Lovesey, P., *Centenary History of the Amateur Athletic Association* (Enfield: Guinness Superlatives, 1979).

Further reading:

Hartley, A. M. and Crighton, A. M., *History of the Tally-Ho Hare and Hounds Club: 80 years of Cross-Country Running* (Manchester: Tally-Ho Hare and Hounds, 1952).

James, T. M., *Bibliography of British Athletic Club Histories* (Sutton Coldfield: Distance Learning, 1998).

Richardson, L. N., *History of the International Cross-Country Union, 1903-1953: Jubilee Souvenir* (Birmingham: International Cross-Country Union, 1953).

Ryan, J. and Fraser, I. H., *The Annals of Thames Hare and Hounds 1868-1968* (London: Thames Hare and Hounds, 1968).

See also:

Athletics

-Trevor James

Crowd Behaviour (*see* Spectators, Fans and Crowd Disorder)

Crystal Palace

Originally built in Hyde Park, London to house the Great Exhibition of 1851, Crystal Palace was subsequently taken down and rebuilt on the top of a hill at Sydenham and opened on June 10th, 1854. Its main purpose was to hold shows and exhibitions, although many sports were also catered for. Historical records show evidence of the following activities taking place: cricket in 1849, on what had previously been Penge Common; rowing, paddle and motor boats from 1855; archery between 1858 and 1902; football from 1861; athletics from 1864; snowshoe-racing in 1867; croquet during the 1860s; and cycling from 1869. In around 1875, a running/ cycling track was added, and in 1878 sixty tennis courts were constructed, two of which were replaced by squash courts in 1920. A 150,000-capacity football stadium was built in 1894. Bowls (1901) and indoor bowls, for which a large shed was erected in 1905, followed. The Canada Building provided indoor accommodation for badminton (c. 1920-1936). There is also evidence of Rugby being played in 1905 and a massed-start road cycling race in 1926.

In 1927, a 2-mile road circuit for cars, motor bikes and cyclists was constructed, but this was reduced in length to 1.39 miles in 1953. A speedway circuit was added in 1929.

Other indoor sports were gymnastics (c. 1867-c. 1875), roller skating (c. 1880-1914), roller hockey (1885-1914) and amateur boxing (1900-1914).

The Sports Council added a host of new facilities in the 1960s when Crystal Palace became a national centre of sport (see entry for the Sports Council). A national running track appeared in 1964 and a year later, Olympic-size swimming and diving pools, in addition to teaching and training pools, were constructed. Also built were a sports hall, a gymnasium, an indoor running track, Astroturf hockey pitches, an artificial ski slope and residential accommodation.

International events have been held at Crystal Palace in athletics, swimming, diving, water polo, synchronized swimming, gymnastics, weightlifting, fencing, table tennis, badminton, tennis and cyclo-cross, with world records being set in many of these sports.

-Dave Terry

Curling

Curling is a target sport in which granite stones are slid across ice towards a fixed point at a distance of 40 yards (36.58 metres).

The origins of curling probably lie in simple stone-throwing games on ice. Morris Mott, in his essay on curling, notes that there is evidence – from 15th- to 17th-century paintings, printed documents and playing artefacts – that curling evolved in Scotland and/or continental Europe. It was certainly played all over Lowland Scotland in the 18th century, and used irregular stones taken from riverbeds, which were known as *channel stones*. In the latter half of the 18th century, the first clubs were formed. The most historically important of these was the Duddingston Curling Society (1795), whose members wrote the first rules in 1803-1804 – these were printed in 1811 and soon became widely accepted. Duddingston encouraged the use of circular stones, whose behaviour on impact was more predictable, increasing the element of skill in the game. Curling became the most popular 18th-century sport in Scotland after 1780.

The Grand Caledonian Curling Club was founded in 1838 and received its Royal Charter in 1843. It is an association of clubs and probably the oldest national body of its kind in Britain. The Royal Caledonian Curling Club supervises the rules of curling, organizes competitions between clubs and, in a winter of sufficient frost, holds a Grand Match. It has published an *Annual* since 1838.

The modern game of curling was developed in Scotland and subsequently exported to North America by Scottish emigrants between the mid-18th and early 20th centuries. Two Scottish clergymen, the Reverend J. Ramsay and the Reverend J. Kerr, wrote seminal studies on the history of curling in 1811 and 1890 respectively. Sir Walter Scott mentions curling in *Guy Mannering* (1815), and in his *Tom*

Samson's Elegy (1786), Robert Burns describes a celebrated curler who played like a 'King'.

The sport of British curling was greatly advanced by the invention of artificial ice in England in the late 1800s. The first indoor ice rinks were opened at Manchester and Stockport in 1877, and in Scotland at Glasgow in 1907. According to Mott, several more were constructed in Scotland and England before the Second World War. Membership in British curling has fluctuated considerably during the 20th century. While England had thirty-seven curling clubs in 1914, Mott points out that 'the sport nearly disappeared between the two world wars and when men or women from England curled they usually did so in Scotland or at a resort hotel in the Alps'.

International Scotland-Canada curling competitions, especially the Strathcona Cup, contributed to the sport's modern renaissance and today in Scotland there are more than 30,000 curlers. One of the most impressive indoor ice rinks in Europe is based at Aviemore, Scotland. A major feature of British contemporary curling is the proliferation of ladies and junior youth clubs.

The game was established in Switzerland by British holiday-makers, and indeed the Winter Olympics included curling for the first time at Chamonix in 1924, albeit as a demonstration sport. On that occasion, Great Britain won the championship. In 1959, the first world curling championships were hosted, with the Scotch Whisky Association sponsoring the tournament and providing the grand prize – the Scotch Whisky Cup.

The game slowly moved indoors. In Canada, the smooth ice of indoor arenas facilitated the sliding delivery, in which the curler slides with his stone for a few yards before releasing it, making the game more skilful and precise.

More than any other Scottish game, curling produced a host of songs. Many of the songs celebrated nothing more – or nothing less – than a wholehearted enjoyment of the game and the socializing afterwards. There was little relationship between teetotalism and curling.

Curling became a full Olympic Sport at the 1998 Games in Nagano, Japan.

References:

Arlott, J. (ed.), *Oxford Companion to World Sports and Games* (London: Oxford University Press, 1975).

Burnett, J., *Sporting Scotland* (Edinburgh: National Museums of Scotland, 1995).

Cuddon, J. A., *The Macmillan Dictionary of Sports and Games* (London: Macmillan, 1980).

Smith, D. B., *Curling: an Illustrated History* (Edinburgh: Donald, 1981).

Further reading:

Mott, M., 'Curling', in D. Levinson and K. Christensen (eds.), *Encyclopedia of World Sport* (Santa Barbara, California: ABC-CLIO, 1996), vol. I, pp. 226-232.

-John Burnett/Scott Crawford

Cycling

Britain has played an important role in the development of cycling as a recreation, sport and, more recently, sustainable form of transport.

Bicycles emerged in the late 18th and early 19th century with the invention of the *draisienne*, or dandy horse. A rigid, wooden-framed machine with no means of steering and no cranks or pedals, the dandy horse was a fashionable toy for wealthy young men who scooted their machines around the streets of London and Paris.

Kirkpatrick Macmillan, a Scottish blacksmith, produced a machine that used treadles and rods to drive the rear wheel in 1839, but it was not until the 1860s that French coachmaker Pierre Michaux added pedals and cranks to the front wheel of a hobbyhorse and produced the velocipede, or boneshaker as it was known in Britain. (This was hotly disputed by a former employee of Michaux, Pierre Lallemont, who also claimed credit for this innovation.) In 1870, James Starley enlarged the size of the front wheel to produce the bicy-

The National Cycling Centre, Manchester: a statue of Reg Harris looks down over the track as Chris Boardman sets a new 1 hour time trial world record (Painting by Rod Holt)

cle known as the Ordinary (later called the Penny Farthing). The larger wheel offered more speed per revolution and a smoother ride on the rough roads of the day. In 1888, Scotsman John Byrd Dunlop patented pneumatic tyres, allowing the Safety Bicycle, which also had equal-sized wheels, to become the first unique standardized machine on the market. The invention of the derailleur gear in 1899 marked the last major technical innovation until the introduction of the small-wheeled folding bike by Alex Moulton in the 1960s and the fat-tyred, multiple-geared, go-anywhere mountain bike in the last quarter of the 20th century.

From the 1870s, cycling boomed in Britain, especially among the middle classes. The Pickwick Cycling Club, founded in 1869, is the oldest cycling club in existence anywhere in the world. The Bicycle Touring Club (later the Cyclists Touring Club – C.T.C.), formed in 1878, represented recreational cyclists and

later that year had 189 member clubs and an estimated 50,000 individual members. The club provided a forum for the exchange of information about machines, roads and routes, as well as negotiating agreed rates for bed and breakfast nationwide for their members, who were regularly riding 80 miles a day and undertaking longer tours in Britain and Europe. The proliferation of tricycles in the late 1870s, and of the 'safety' bicycle in 1884/85, opened up cycling to all. Despite prohibitive clothing and moral strictures, women also took to the wheel with alacrity and the bicycle had a significant effect on the liberation of Victorian women from the home and also on relations between the sexes and between the classes. H. G. Wells's novel, *Wheels of Chance* (1896), portrays a cycling romance between a draper's assistant and a young lady and captures perfectly the new social possibilities offered by the bicycle.

97

The bicycle became the height of fashion amongst the upper classes during the late 1890s and Hyde Park in London would be filled with hundreds of cyclists on a fine Sunday. C.T.C. membership peaked at 60,449 in 1899, when there were an estimated one million cyclists in Britain, but the arrival of the motor car around the turn of the century distracted the wealthy and the élite. Thereafter, the bicycle became largely a means for the urban middle and working classes to get out of the towns and into the countryside.

In terms of competitive cycling, the Bicycle Union founded in 1878 was the first national federation in the world. Organizations for Ireland, Scotland and Wales soon followed. In 1883, the Bicycle Union became the National Cycling Union (N.C.U.) and encompassed also the League of Tricyclists. Unofficial world championships were held in Leicester and Birmingham between 1883 and 1888, and Britain surpassed the rest of the world in honours. In Berlin in 1886, Edward Hale of the Lainsborough Bicycle Club was the first (unofficial) European Champion.

On November 23rd, 1892, in London, under the direction of the N.C.U., the International Cyclist Association (I.C.A.) was created. All four British federations affiliated to it. The first British cyclist to win a world crown was the Englishman James Michael in the 100 kilometres paced race for professionals in 1895. In 1897, Scotland hosted the World Championship, but problems ensued later with the existence of four separate British federations, and this was one of the reasons for the rebellion of other countries which led to the formation of the Union Cycliste Internationale (U.C.I. – International Cycling Union) in Paris in 1900. British federations reacted by transforming the I.C.A. into a British Empire League, but, in February 1903, they also agreed to affiliate to the U.C.I. as one federation. The first British Empire Championships were organized in 1911, on the occasion of the Empire Games. Britain was the most successful nation in world track championships before 1914.

In 1896, a law forbidding open road races changed the fortunes of British cycle racing. Only time trials or limited town circuits were permitted, although in 1922, Liverpool hosted the Amateur Road World Championship on a time trial basis, a unique exception in the history of the competition. Sporadic attempts were made to end the marginalization of road cyclists. In 1937, a mixed team composed of British, Australian and Canadian riders took part in the Tour de France. In 1943, a group of riders founded a British League of Racing Cyclists (B.L.R.C.), creating road time trial championships ranging from 25 miles up to 24 hours. In 1951, a Tour of Britain (see also separate entry) was organized, sponsored by *The Daily Express*. The juxtaposition of the B.L.R.C. and the N.C.U. ended on February 1st, 1959, with the formation of a new British Cycling Federation (B.C.F.).

A Women's Road Racing Association (W.R.R.A.) developed women's racing in Britain after several decades of exclusion. The first women's championships were held on roads in 1944 and on track in 1947. The W.R.R.A. played a decisive role in persuading the U.C.I. to include official women's races in 1955. Beryl Burton was the first British woman to win a world title in the individual pursuit, in 1959. She won another four world titles and was the first woman allowed to compete internationally in a men's race, the Grand Prix of Nations.

British prowess on the track re-established itself after the Second World War, when the sprinter, Reginald Harris, won five world titles between 1947 and 1954. Tommy Simpson also became a great figure in road cycling by being the first Briton to wear the yellow jersey at the Tour de France (1962) and the first Briton to win the world road race professional championships (1965).

In 1974, Britain hosted a stage of the Tour de France for the first time and in the 1980s a new generation of world-class riders started to emerge. The Scotsman Robert Millar twice came second in the *Vuelta a Espana* (1985 and 1986), and in 1987 he also finished second in the *Giro d'Italia*.

With the introduction of the much-publicized Kellogg's Tour of Britain in 1986, there has been increased coverage of cycling on television, especially on *Channel 4*. Chris Boardman's success in winning the Olympic gold medal for individual pursuit in 1992 has also helped to raise the sport's profile. He later won both time trial road championships and track pursuit championships and in 1996 established a new world record for the greatest distance travelled in one hour. Following the collapse of the Kellogg's Tour in 1994, a new stage competition called the Prudential Tour was initiated in 1998.

Cycling in Britain steadily declined during the first half of the 20th century and it was not until the beginnings of 'green' ecologically-aware thinking and the oil crises of the 1970s, which sparked renewed interest in sustainable transport, that the decline was halted. The civil engineering charity SUSTRANS (SUStainable TRANSport) is currently in the process of creating a 5,000-mile national network of routes for cyclists and walkers. Backed by £43.5 million of National Lottery money, this network is likely to be a key factor in the continued resurgence of cycling as a recreation and a source of enjoyment for individuals and families. In addition, the introduction of a government-backed National Cycling Strategy in 1996, which aimed to double bike usage by 2002, gave official backing to cycling as a health-promoting and socially desirable activity. The introduction of the folding bicycle and mountain bikes has also helped to encourage greater recreational and commuter usage of the bicycle.

References:

Dragoslav, A., *Two Centuries of Bicycle* (Lucerne, Switzerland: Bessa Publishing & Motovun, 1990).

England, H. H., 'Cycling', in Charles Harvey (ed.), *Encyclopaedia of Sport* (London: Sampson Low, Marston & Co. Limited, 1959).

McGurn, J., *On Your Bicycle: an Illustrated History of Cycling* (London: John Murray, 1987).

Ritchie, A., *King of the Road: an Illustrated History of Cycling* (London: Wildwood, 1975).

Woodforde, J., *The Story of the Bicycle* (London: Routledge & Kegan Paul, 1977).

Further reading:

Dew, J., *The Wind in My Wheels* (London: Little, Brown & Co., 1993).

Matthews, P. and Buchanan, I., *The All Time Greats of British and Irish Sport* (Enfield: Guinness Publishing Limited, 1995).

Murphy, D., *Full Tilt* (London: John Murray, 1965).

Selby, B., *Pilgrim's Road: a Journey to Santiago de Compostela* (London: Abacus, 1995).

Websites:

The British Cycling Federation – http://www.bcf.uk.com/

The Cyclists Touring Club – http://www.ctc.org.uk/

The International Cycling Union – http://www.uci.ch/

The Internet Bicycling Hub – http://www.cycling.org/

SUSTRANS – http://www.sustrans.org.uk/

See also:

Milk Race

-Gherardo Bonini/Ann Furtado

Cyclo-cross

Cyclo-cross is cross-country bicycle racing, which often takes place over rough terrain. Because of this, riders are often forced to dismount and carry their bicycles. The sport resembles scrambling and moto-cross, though in cyclo-cross the bikes are propelled manually. Its origins date back to early 20th-century France and the use of cycles in military manoeuvres.

Road race cycling was very popular in France and, following a suggestion by Daniel Gousseau in 1902, the French cycling federation organized off-road racing through fields and forests. Off-road racing proved popular with riders preparing for the Tour de France. Indeed, Octave Lapize, winner of the 1910 Tour de France, attributed his superior fitness to his participation in cyclo-cross events during the winter. This, in turn, gave the sport a big boost, as many more riders adopted Lapize's winter training schedule. The technique of carrying the cycle over the shoulder when the terrain gets too rough is also attributed to Lapize.

Following the sport's growing popularity, world championships were initiated in 1925. After 1950, these were organized by the Union Cycliste Internationale (U.C.I. – International Cycling Union). Until 1967, amateurs and professionals competed on equal terms. Today, however, they are separated in competition, though they still compete in the same races.

Cyclo-Cross arrived in Britain in 1921, but it was 1954 before the British Cyclo-Cross Association (B.C.C.A.) was formed. The following year, the B.C.C.A. organized the first British Championships. The sport is most popular in the north of England, especially in the Pennine towns of Lancashire and Yorkshire.

The International Amateur Cycling Federation is the governing body of the sport and is responsible for overseeing its laws.

References:

Trayers, N., 'Cyclo Cross', in P. Ligget (ed.), *The Complete Book of Performance Cycling* (London: Collins Willow, 1992).

Arlott, J. (ed.), *Oxford Companion to Sports and Games* (London: Oxford University Press, 1976).

Websites:

The British Cyclo-Cross Association – http://www.cyclo-cross.co.uk/

See also:

Cycling; Mountain Biking

-Ray Physick

D

Dartford College

Dartford College holds a unique position in the history of Physical Education. Established in Hampstead in 1885, twelve years before any similar college, it gave a new profession to women – that of the specialist physical education teacher.

Founded by Martina Bergman Österberg (1849-1915), the college moved to Dartford in 1895. The course was based on Madame Österberg's training at the Royal Central Gymnastic Institute in Stockholm. It included practical and teaching skills with a strong emphasis on the medical side, particularly remedial gymnastics, which required a thorough understanding of anatomy and physiology.

Whilst promoting the Swedish system, Madame Österberg, astutely aware of their importance in Britain, gave games a prominent position. This is reflected in the number of

'Madame's Girls on College Pitch, circa 1914', from the Bergman Österberg Archive
(The Bergman Österberg Archive: The Dartford Campus of the University of Greenwich)

international players trained at Dartford. Even more significantly, netball evolved here as a new game suitable for girls. Madame's students took this into the schools and it ultimately developed as an international sport. Another innovation was the gymslip, daringly designed at the college in 1892 and worn by schoolgirls in this country and abroad throughout the 20th century.

Following Madame Österberg's death, Dartford was administered by the Bergman Österberg Trust until 1961, when it was transferred to London County Council. In 1976 it became part of Thames Polytechnic, now the University of Greenwich. Astonishingly, Government policy caused its closure in 1986.

A flourishing association, the Bergman Österberg Union, and a comprehensive Archive, generously accommodated by the University of Greenwich, ensure that Dartford's contribution to Physical Education and Sport will not be forgotten.

References:

The Bergman Österberg Archive, University of Greenwich, Dartford Campus Library

Further reading:

May, J., *Madame Bergman-Österberg* (London: George G. Harrap and Co. Ltd, 1969).

Pomfret, A., *Dartford College 1885-1985* (Dartford: Thames Polytechnic, 1985).

See also:

Bedford College; Chelsea College; Dunfermline College; Education – Teacher Training; Physical Education Association of the United Kingdom

-Sheila Cutler

Darts

Darts is a target sport involving two or more players throwing three darts in turn. The standard dartboard is usually constructed of bristle (sisal). Some dartboards are still made from elm or poplar wood, but these are now less com-

mon. Other materials used in the past include clay and compressed paper.

The dartboard consists of twenty segments numbered 1 to 20 (but situated randomly around the board), an outer bull's-eye (worth 25 points), and an inner bull's-eye (worth 50 points). There is also an outer ring, scoring double the value of the segment, and an inner ring, between the double ring and the outer bull, scoring treble the value. In standard games, players usually begin on any double score (a dart thrown into the outer ring). This and subsequent scores are then subtracted from a previously chosen number, usually 301, 501 or 1,001. To win the game, a player must reach exactly zero on his last throw. There are also a number of regional dartboards that still exist, including the Yorkshire and Manchester Boards.

Darts, in one form or another, has been played in English inns and public houses since the 16th century. However, the modern game only developed during the latter part of the 19th century. The rules of play were first standardized with the foundation of the National Darts Association (N.D.A.) in 1924, which included representatives from the brewery trade, the darts industry and licensees. The N.D.A. set up the first major individual darts championship in 1926. Within a year this had evolved into the *News of the World* Individual Darts Championship, a competition that would be regarded by all darts players as *the* competition to win over the next fifty years, attracting anything up to 250,000 entrants in the post-war years. The championship was originally restricted to the Metropolitan area (1927-1935) but, by the outbreak of war, regional finals were being contested in London and the South, Lancashire and Cheshire, Yorkshire, the North of England, the Midland Counties and Wales. After 1947, the competition became national and later international.

Darts became fashionable during the mid-1930s and temporarily appeared to have broken through class barriers, further interest being stimulated after the King and Queen played a game at a community centre in Slough in 1937. The short-lived British Darts Council (B.D.C.) reported a tremendous influx of enquiries, particularly from women, asking for details of the rules of the game. Neither the N.D.A. nor the B.D.C. remained active after the Second World War.

After the Second World War, the playing of darts began to spread across the globe. This was primarily due to ex-patriots settling in other countries, such as Holland, and forming darts clubs and leagues. In addition, servicemen from, for example, the United States, Australia and New Zealand, having been stationed in England and experienced the game, returned home and took darts with them. Darts gradually became established as a worldwide sport.

With the formation of the British Darts Organisation (B.D.O.) in 1973, the phenomenon of darts changed out of all recognition. The B.D.O. succeeded in encouraging television companies to cover the sport. New split-screen television techniques made darts more 'watchable' and transmissions drew millions of viewers. The B.D.O. established county leagues, organized home internationals and introduced the first darts world championship. The work of the B.D.O. also led the way to the formation of the World Darts Federation (W.D.F.).

However, the further development of darts has been stymied by the image of the archetypal darts player – beer-bellied and lager-swilling – and the inability of the sport to make itself more interesting. Although this image was, to an extent, created by the media, it has remained a millstone around the neck of the sport, especially during the 1990s when the B.D.O. strived to obtain recognition of darts from the Sports Council.

References:
Chaplin, P., 'You Can Take the Darts Out of the Pub…', *Darts World* (May 1998).

Chaplin, P., 'Those Regional Boards Just Won't Go Away', *Darts Player 97* (1997).

Further reading:
Brown, D., *The Guinness Book of Darts* (Enfield: Guinness Superlatives Ltd, 1981).
Croft-Cooke, R., *Darts* (London: Geoffrey Bles, 1936).
Taylor, A. R., *The Guinness Book of Traditional Pub Games* (Enfield: Guinness Publishing Ltd, 1992).

Websites:
The British Darts Organisation – http://www.bdodarts.com/

-Patrick Chaplin

Deer Stalking

Conducted on horseback, deer stalking entails the pursuit of red deer in the wild, with hounds that hunt by scent. Historically, stag hunting was regarded as the noblest of sports, being reserved exclusively for the aristocracy and royalty, who retained large deer parks protected by foresters. Following the Norman Conquest, the Forest Laws of William I imposed barbaric punishments on those found guilty of killing deer and other game, and legislation was further refined by William's successors.

The English followed the Norman tradition of hunting on horseback with scenting hounds, but in Scotland deer were coursed with specialist deer-hounds. In addition, the so-called *tainchell*, or deer drive, was used, where large numbers of beaters drove deer into gorges for the aristocracy to kill. This sport provided a diversion for the nobility whilst enabling their clansmen to be supplied with meat.

Following the demise of royal stag hunts, the hunting of deer on horseback with hounds survives only in the West Country. Before hunt meets, the harbourer, working in conjunction with local landowners, identifies the animals to be culled, a process known as harbouring. In autumn hunts, it is usually the old or weak animals that are destined to be killed. Occasionally, a stag in his prime or one that has been with the same group of hinds (females) for several years is selected for culling in order to prevent inter-breeding. In contrast, stag hunting in the spring concentrates on the younger stags with inferior antlers. In the hind-hunting season during the winter, the herd is chased until one of the animals breaks away from the rest.

Another popular method of killing deer is by using long-range high-calibre rifles. Stalking deer in this way is a highly developed craft because of the deer's acute hearing and their sensitive scenting ability, which brings a constant stream of information on the breeze. In Scotland, where it became the only legitimate way of killing deer, professional gillies assist their deer-stalking clients, helping the shooter to locate the deer and decide which ones to shoot, gut the animals and arrange for transportation.

Apart from controlling the population levels, shooting magnificent adult stags commands premium trophy fees from paying sportsmen guests. Following the Second World War, the stalking of roe deer in the lowlands became fashionable amongst a small band of dedicated enthusiasts. The development of modern flat-trajectory calibre rifles with telescopic sights improved the accuracy of shooting in the poor light of early dawn and late dusk, when it was possible to get closer to the deer.

The Deer Act of 1963 forms the legislative and, in many respects, philosophical foundation of deer control and stalking, prescribing how the activity may be legally undertaken and who may participate in the sport.

References:

Coles, C., *Shooting and Stalking* (London: Stanley Paul, 1988).

Further reading:

Beaver, D., 'The Great Deer Massacre: Animals, Honor, and Communication in Early Modern England', *Journal of British Studies* (April 1999), pp. 187-217.

Parkes, C., *Fair Game: the Law of Country Sports and the Protection of Wildlife* (London: Pelham Books, 1994).

See also:

Field Sports

-John Martin

Derby Matches

Nothing is guaranteed to inflame the passions of a football supporter more than a contest with 'the enemy', the team from down the road. This happens for various reasons.

Religious division lies at the heart of the 'Old Firm' conflict in Glasgow, where the game, not just in the city but in Scotland, has long been dominated by Rangers, heroes of the Protestant establishment, and Celtic, formed in 1888 as representatives of the Irish immigrant community. In 1989, both camps were stunned when Rangers signed Maurice Johnston from French club Nantes, narrowly beating Celtic, who had been trying to re-sign their ex-player. Crowds besieged Ranger's ground, Ibrox, in an orgy of shirt-burning, incensed that Rangers had finally signed a Catholic. In the words of Jonathan Swift, 'We have just enough religion to make us hate but not enough to make us love each other.'

The North London friction can be traced back to 1913, when Arsenal crossed the river from Woolwich and set up home near Tottenham. When league football resumed after the First World War, Tottenham, who had finished bottom of the First Division in 1915, expected to be safe from relegation as both First and Second Divisions were to be extended from twenty to twenty-two teams. Not so; following secret negotiations between Arsenal chairman, Sir Henry Norris, and League president, John McKenna, the two top Second Division sides, Derby and Preston, were promoted, along with Arsenal, who had finished sixth. Spurs went down. Bitter rivalry was cemented by such shenanigans, to such an extent that many Spurs fans consider their team's greatest achievement not the historic Cup and League double of 1960/61 but the 3-1 defeat of Arsenal in the first Wembley F.A. Cup semi-final in 1991.

The Merseyside rivalry has just as strange an origin. When the Football League was founded in 1888, Everton were one of the origin twelve clubs. When Chairman and Landlord John Houlding tried to raise the rent of the ground where they played, the club moved across Stanley Park to Goodison. Houlding responded by forming a new club. Both claimed the right to the name Everton; Houlding finally lost and Liverpool F.C. was born. Fans of both teams can be found to this day in the same family and were allowed to mix at Wembley for the League Cup Final of 1984. A drawn match resulted in the famous old stadium ringing to cries of 'Merseyside, Merseyside'.

In 1998, with Manchester United preparing for a crucial game against Bayern Munich that could put them into the quarter-finals of the Champion's League, their rivals, Manchester City, were scraping a draw with Third Division Darlington in the second round of the F.A. Cup. City fan Colin Shindler could be forgiven for describing in *Manchester United Ruined My Life* how it felt to be a little boy with his nose pressed up against the sweetshop window watching United supporters take all the wine gums. Who said it was only a game?

References:

Barwick, B., and Sinstadt, G., *The Great Derbies 1962-1988: Everton v Liverpool: a celebration of the Merseyside Derby* (London: BBC Books, 1988).

Inglis, S., *The Football Grounds of Great Britain* (London: CollinsWillow, 1996).

Shindler, C., *Manchester United Ruined My Life* (London: Headline, 1998).

See also:

Roses Matches

-Tony Rennick

Colin Shindler's team, Manchester City, during a 5-1 derby victory over neighbours United in 1989 (Action Images)

Disability Sports

The term 'disability' refers to a physical or learning difficulty. This may take the form of cerebral palsy, visual impairment, or the inability to move without assistance. Disabilities may be a result of birth defects, disease or accident. For some, this may seem like the end of an active life. This does not mean, however, that the disabled do not participate in sport. In the second half of the 20th century, the disabled have not only participated in sport, but have also taken it to new élite levels.

As with all people, whether able-bodied or disabled, sport provides not only competition, but also recreation and a social life. This is particularly important for disabled people, as it is not always easy to gain acceptance within the

105

community. Sport allows for communication and shared experiences that can increase self-esteem and confidence.

Disabled sport takes many forms. Some sports are adapted from the able-bodied version, and others are developed specifically for the disabled. As with most sport, an effort to ensure fair competition exists. With that in mind, a fairly intricate classification system has been adopted. Disabilities can vary widely, so it is important to ensure that people of the right classification are competing against each other.

Britain has a long association with disability sport. Although there were sporting groups for the disabled in existence before the 1940s, it was in 1944 that the Stoke Mandeville Hospital for the Spinal Injured was opened, and the more official organization of disabled sport began. Prior to this, there were particular associations such as the British Society of One-Armed Golfers, which was established in 1932,

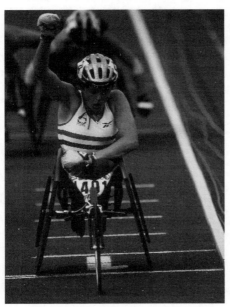

Great Britain's Tanni Grey in the 800m wheelchair race at the 1998 European Championships in Budapest (Action Images)

and the Disabled Drivers Club, which had been in existence since 1922. During the Second World War, the use of sulpha drugs meant that many more service-people survived their injuries, including those to the spine. Unlike those injured in the First World War, whose life expectancy had been very short, these spinal injured of the 1940s had a greater life expectancy thanks to the new treatments available. The pioneer of this new regime was Sir Ludwig Guttmann, who was the founder of the Stoke Mandeville Hospital for the Spinal Injured. Part of Sir Ludwig's rehabilitation treatment consisted of sport. Other countries began to copy this British example. In 1948, it was decided to have an archery competition in the grounds of the Hospital. There were sixteen competitors, two women and fourteen men. From those sixteen original competitors, the Stoke Mandeville Games have become a yearly fixture, except in Olympic years. In 1952, ex-servicemen from the Netherlands took part and the Stoke Mandeville Games became international. In 1998, the Games had approximately 450 competitors from 30 countries.

Government interest in the disabled and aspects of their lives increased throughout the 1960s. In 1961, the British Sports Association for the Disabled was established. Out of this association grew many others, which all assisted with the development of disabled sport in Britain. In 1969, the Disabled Living Foundation was set up and one of their first enquiries was an investigation into sport and recreation for the disabled. The House of Lords produced a White Paper in 1975 where disability sport was highlighted in the enquiry into sport and recreation. Disability sport was being included as part of sport in Britain. This subject was investigated again in 1976 by the Snowdon Working Party.

The first Paralympics was in Rome in 1960, although it did not have the official title 'Paralympics' until 1984. Until 1972, Paralympics were only open to those with a spinal injury. In 1976, visually impaired and amputee athletes competed, and in 1980, those athletes with cerebral palsy were included in the programme. In 1984, *les autres* ('the others', those that did not fit under the standard classes of disability) were added. Britain has had a long history of success in the Paralympics. It is a fallacy to believe that the disabled simply have to attend the Paralympics in order to win a medal – Paralympians are élite athletes and have to train as such. Athletes such as wheelchair racer Tanni Grey spend many hours per week training for their events. At the 1996 Paralympic Games in Atlanta, Britain took home 122 medals, 39 of them gold, coming fourth in the medal tally. Compare that achievement to the able-bodied Olympics in the same year, when Britain won 15 medals and came 36th in the medal rankings!

The Paralympics should not be confused with the Special Olympics, which were developed by the Schriver family in the United States in 1968 and are a more recreational event, where people with learning difficulties can have fun simply by participating, as opposed to competing in serious athletic competition.

As well as performing at the élite level, many disabled people enjoy recreational sport. Organizations such as Disability Sport England provide disabled children with sporting events to attend. The Mini Games are for those disabled children who are between the age of eight and eleven, and aim to increase their participation in sport. The Junior Games are open to those between twelve and twenty who have qualified through regional finals. Amongst these children may be Paralympians of the future.

For those adults who are interested in sport on a more recreational level, there are many associations, mainly staffed by volunteers, that provide opportunities for participation. Problems do exist for disabled people regarding facilities. Some sporting facilities are not built with the disabled in mind and therefore access, especially for those in wheelchairs, can be problematic.

Throughout history, disabled sport has been somewhat marginalized by the media. Although as exciting and emotive as any sport, disabled sport has not received much media coverage. With the acceptance of the disabled as part of the community, hopefully this will change, as it has for other minority groups.

References:

Disability Sport England Information Pack (London: Sport England, 1998).

Sainsbury, T., 'The Paralympic Movement' (paper given at the British Olympic Academy, March 1998).

Scruton, J., *Stoke Mandeville: Road to the Paralympics. Fifty Years of History* (Aylesbury: Peterhouse Press, 1998).

Conference University of Stirling, *Sport for All Disabled People* (Edinburgh: The Scottish Sports Council, 1982).

Further reading:

Guttmann, L., *A Textbook of Sport for the Disabled* (Aylesbury: HM+M, 1976).

Humphries, S., and Gordon, P., *Out of Sight: the Experience of Disability, 1900-1950* (Plymouth: Northcote House Publishers, 1992).

Websites:

Disability Sport England –
http://www.euroyellowpages.com/dse/dispengl.html
The British Paralympic Association –
http://www.paralympics.org.uk/

See also:

Stoke Mandeville

-Julie Anderson

Disasters

Triumph and disaster, Kipling's two imposters, have been rendered even more fraudulent by the media's treatment of sporting events. They have become much abused words in an inflationary sporting language. Last-minute victories are lauded as triumphs; a third successive defeat labelled a disaster. Real triumphs, however, are won by those sportspersons who come back from serious injury to participate again. Similarly, a failure to put the ball in the net, hit winning runs or not choke over a putt cannot be equated with a plane crash that destroys a team or collapsing walls, fires or police inefficiencies that take the lives of those who came to see a game.

Ibrox, Glasgow, 1902

The disaster of April 5th, 1902, was the first major British football disaster, resulting in 540 casualties, 25 of whom were killed and 163 seriously injured. The match was a Scotland versus England international staged at Glasgow Rangers' recently expanded 68,000 capacity stadium. In fact, the actual attendance was 68,114, 33,000 of whom were in the Western end. Here a 50-foot-high bank of terracing was erected, formed of wooden planks on a steel framework. During the game, the crowd surged, and a section of terracing swayed and collapsed like a trapdoor, through which hundreds of spectators fell. Fans caught in the crush fled on to the pitch, and the match was temporarily stopped.

Casualties were attended to by doctors from the crowd, and carried into the changing rooms. Most of the crowd and players were unaware of the scale of the disaster, and the authorities thought it was best to continue the game. The second half was, however, a 'mechanical charade', as the players had been affected by the casualties laid out in the pavilion.

Experts examined the scene as police sealed off the stadium, and an enquiry into the incident was held. A relief fund was set up for the victims and their dependants, and the Scottish F.A. offered to donate £5,000 if it were relieved of all responsibility. As a result of the disaster, further improvements were made to Ibrox under engineer Archibald Leitch, with solid earth banking being constructed. This signalled the end of wooden terracing as a viable alternative for large crowds.

Burden Park, Bolton 1946

On March 9th, 1946, 65,000 gathered to see Bolton Wanderers play Stoke City in a sixth round F.A. Cup tie at Burnden Park. The gates were closed, but at least 2,000 of the estimated 15,000 fans locked outside found their way in. The ground, although boasting a record attendance of 69,212, was poorly maintained and not yet up to full capacity following its wartime requisition. Shortly after 3 p.m., a crowd surge at the packed Railway End collapsed two crush barriers, resulting in the deaths of 33 people and injuries to over 400 others.

A public enquiry by Justice R. Moelwyn Hughes defined the major cause as the simple presence of a crowd far larger than expected. However, the enquiry heard plentiful evidence suggestive of a disaster rooted in a fatal marriage of interests. Football clubs, and to some degree the police, placed a low priority on the safety and comfort of fans (it was widely assumed locally that the game, featuring Stoke's Stanley Matthews, would draw a huge crowd) while fans were often prepared to watch key matches in the most uncomfortable conditions. It is indeed remarkable that this was England's first major football disaster. Justice Hughes's recommendation that Parliament introduce formal ground licensing was defeated by a combination of football's lack of enthusiasm and the Labour Government's unwillingness to be seen attacking a major working-class pastime at a delicate political juncture. A less than watertight voluntary code was adopted in March 1949.

Ibrox, Glasgow, 1971

The second Ibrox disaster, on January 2nd, 1971, was one of the most serious football-related incidents in British history. There had been three accidents prior to 1971 on stairway thirteen, resulting in some ground improvements. However, upgraded barriers could not prevent large numbers of spectators tumbling down the steps towards the end of a match between Glasgow Rangers and Celtic. According to eyewitnesses, the crowd collapsed halfway down, apparently after some hesitation when various spectators celebrated Stein's late equalizer for Rangers. One man claimed that he had attempted to rescue a fallen boy but was himself pushed over, and others fell on top of him as the crowd continued to surge down the steps. Many people were crushed in the fall. The barriers held, but buckled, leaving 66 people dead and over 200 injured. Players, ground staff, officials and supporters all helped the emergency services with the injured.

For an 'Old Firm' match (i.e., Rangers versus Celtic), there had been little trouble in the crowd, and the attendance of 80,000 was not unusually large for this fixture. The enquiry into the disaster did not apportion blame, but found that Rangers had been complacent following previous incidents, despite having made improvements. The incident prompted wider enquiries into football crowd safety, and highlighted the lack of established standards for improvements. This eventually led to the Wheatley Report on football ground safety, culminating in the Safety of Sports Grounds Act 1975. Ibrox itself was fully remodelled from 1978, and the dangers of stairway 13 were removed forever.

Munich, 1958

On the evening of February 5th, 1958, Manchester United's famous 'Busby Babes' – the young side created by manager Matt Busby – drew 3-3 in the second leg of their European Cup tie with Red Star Belgrade, a result sufficient to put them into the semi-finals for the second successive year, following their earlier 2-1 home win. The following afternoon, their chartered B.E.A. Elizabethan airliner crashed in snow on take-off from Munich-Riem airport after a refuelling stop on the way home. Two previous attempts to take-off had been aborted because of fluctuations in engine pressure. Twenty-three people died including three club officials and eight players, five of whom had played in the match.

Although they lost to A.C. Milan in the European tournament, a combination of survivors, reserves and experienced players recruited from other clubs (the F.A. had suspended the 'cup tied' rule) carried United through to the F.A. Cup Final on a wave of emotion. Four players who had been in the crash, Bobby Charlton, Bill Foulkes, Dennis Viollett and Harry Gregg, played in the team that lost 2-0 to Bolton Wanderers at Wembley.

In 1968, United finally won the European Cup, the first English side to do so. Years later, Matt Busby and Bobby Charlton were knighted for services to football, as manager and international player respectively.

Valley Parade, Bradford, 1985

Bradford City supporters had expected May 11th, 1985, to be a day of celebration. Their team had just clinched promotion to Division Two, and the last game of the season against Lincoln City was to be a party. Just before half-time, however, a small fire started beneath the main stand and, within ten minutes, flames had engulfed the area. Despite acts of heroism from police officers and supporters alike, the fire claimed the lives of 56 supporters, with at least 200 more badly injured through smoke inhalation and burns. The subsequent Popplewell enquiry found the cause of the fire to be a discarded cigarette which had fallen through the wooden structure of the main stand setting light to years of discarded debris beneath. The enquiry focused on the lack of adequate safety precautions taken by the club, and referred to the 'Green Guide', a government publication used by the Football Licensing Authority for safety issues. The previous year had seen a safety inspection by West Yorkshire Council at the club, and the inspectors had noted the piles of rubbish beneath the main stand, some of it dating from the 1960s. A letter to the club from the Council had stated that 'a carelessly discarded cigarette could give rise to a fire risk'.

Hillsborough, Sheffield, 1989

The worst disaster in British sport, Hillsborough in April 1989 was the epitome of football's decline and its incompetence, greed and disinterest in supporters. Following a series of operational mistakes by South Yorkshire Police, ninety-six Liverpool fans were crushed to death on the Leppings Lane terrace at Sheffield Wednesday's ground.

The F.A. Cup semi-final between Liverpool and Nottingham Forest became a disaster after the police failed to regulate the flow of Liverpool fans arriving at the Leppings Lane end. The ensuing crush outside the ground led senior police to open a gate into the ground to relieve the pressure. Fans then made their way through a central tunnel into Pens three and four of Leppings Lane. These pens were already overfull and badly maintained and, caged by the steel perimeter fences, the inflow of extra fans caused a fatal crush. The failure to regulate the flow of fans outside, close the tunnel or direct supporters towards the empty side pens proved deadly.

The game was stopped at 3.06 p.m. as fans clambered over the fences to escape the crush, and the police finally reacted, but the damage was done. The death toll was worsened by the emergency services' slow response, the state of the ground and the lack of basic safety facilities. Yet within half an hour, Chief Superintendent Duckinfield, in charge on the day, was telling the world that Liverpool fans had broken down the gate into the ground, an entirely false accusation exacerbated by *The Sun* newspaper in the days after the disaster.

References:

Athletic News (14, 21 April 1902).

Scotsman (4, 5, 6, 7 January 1971).

Times (7, 8, 9, 10 April 1902; 4, 5, 6, 7 January 1971).

'The Busby Babes: End of a Dream', ITV, 1 February 1998.

Final Report of the Committee of Enquiry into Crowd Safety and Control at Sports Grounds (Popplewell Report) (London: HMSO, 1986).

Baker, N., 'Have They Forgotten Bolton?', *The Sports Historian* (May 1998), pp. 120-151.

Inglis, S., *The Football Grounds of Great Britain* (London: Willow, various editions).

Scraton, P., *Hillsborough: the Truth* (Edinburgh: Mainstream, 1999).

Taylor, Lord Justice, *The Hillsborough Stadium Disaster: Interim Report* (London: HMSO, 1989).

Taylor, R., Ward, A., and Newburn, T., *The Day of the Hillsborough Disaster* (Liverpool: Liverpool University Press, 1995).

Further reading:

Glasgow Herald (7-18 April, 8 July 1902).

Safety of Sports Grounds Act (London: HMSO, 1975).

Wheatley Report Command Paper 4952 (1975).

Goodwin, C., 'The Darkest Hour: Manchester United and the Munich Air Disaster', *Total Sport*, no. 26 (February 1998), pp. 46-49.

Inglis, S., *The Football Grounds of Great Britain* (London: Willow, various editions).

Mason, T., *Association Football and English Society 1863-1915* (Brighton: Harvester, 1980), pp. 155-156.

See also:

Spectators, Fans and Crowd Disorder

- Wray Vamplew/Robert Lewis/ Dave Russell/Rex Nash/Sam Johnstone

Diving

According to *Master Digbie's Book of the Art of Swimming* (1595), the British innovated the plunge in which the diver enters the water hands first. After the 1850s, by which time swimming baths had become more common, competitions with measured dives developed. In this distance diving, one calculated the length accomplished by the diver from the take-off to the emersion after gliding underwater. Later, in what became known as 'plunging', a time limit of one minute was enforced, during which time the body had to remain motionless while underwater.

An unofficial English plunging championship was first organized in the summer of

1867, and from 1883 to 1937 official championships were held under the auspices of the governing body of English swimming, the Amateur Swimming Association (A.S.A.). In the 1904 Saint Louis Olympics, plunging was included in the programme, but British divers did not compete, which was unfortunate in the respect that the American winner was well below the top standards in Britain.

At the beginning of the 20th century, divers from Germany and Sweden were the best in the world. The Swedish divers Johannson, Hagberg and Mauritzi came to London and entertained spectators with exhibitions of what was termed 'fancy diving', because of the variety of shapes, body positions and aerial movements executed by the divers. These exhibitions led directly to the foundation of the Amateur Diving Association (A.D.A.) in 1901, the first diving governing body in the world. When the A.D.A. was founded, there was an urgent need for strict controls – diving was popular but also dangerous, at times even deadly, with some divers jumping from high bridges, although this was strictly illegal. In 1908, a Ladies Diving Association (L.D.A.) was established, and in 1912, the English diver, Bella White, gained the bronze medal when 'plain diving' was introduced to the Olympics for the first time. Although a diving championship did take place in Scotland in 1889, a national fancy diving championship did not develop until the A.S.A. organized a competition in 1907, though the Royal Life Saving Society (R.L.S.S.) had already inaugurated a national graceful diving championship in 1895. The A.S.A. instituted an official women's championship in 1924. In 1925, the International Amateur Swimming Federation (F.I.N.A.) merged plain and fancy diving, scheduling the different forms in a unique programme that combined diving from platforms of different heights with springboard events.

In the 1930s, both the A.D.A. and the L.D.A. found it impossible to continue all their activities, so on December 31st, 1935, the A.S.A. took over their respective duties. In 1936, the A.S.A. started an educational programme in order to develop diving activities among the younger generation, and young divers soon became frequent participants at international events. In 1993, the management of British diving was reorganized. The various national bodies merged to form the Great Britain Diving Federation, with governors appointed for each of England, Wales and Scotland.

Britain dominates diving among Commonwealth countries, but has had limited success internationally. The best British male diver was Brian Phelps, twice European champion and Olympic bronze medal winner at the 1960 games in Rome.

References:

Crawford, S. A. G. M., 'Diving', in K. Christensen and D. Levinson (eds.), *Encyclopedia of World Sport* (Santa Barbara, California: ABC-CLIO, 1996), vol. I, pp. 260-265.

Keil, I. and Wix, D., *In the Swim: the Amateur Swimming Association from 1869 to 1994* (Loughborough: Swimming Times Ltd, 1996).

Further reading:

Bilsborough, P., *One Hundred Years of Scottish Swimming* (Glasgow: Scottish Amateur Swimming Association, 1988).

Websites:

The Great Britain Diving Federation – http://www.diving-gbdf.com/

-Gherardo Bonini

Doggett's Coat and Badge

Doggett's Coat and Badge is the surviving link between rowing as a way of life and rowing as a sport. An annual race for single scullers from London Bridge to Chelsea, about 5 miles on the Thames, Doggett's was first run in 1715, originally for six watermen in their first year of freedom from apprenticeship to obtain a license to work on the river.

When the actor-manager Thomas Doggett offered a scarlet coat and silver badge for the winner, London Bridge was the only bridge in the capital. Thousands of watermen made a meagre living ferrying passengers across the Thames in wherries, the forerunners of the 'black cab'. Winners were the cream of the wherrymen, and their badges inscribed 'Liberty' served as the license which all watermen needed to ply their trade. Doggett founded it to support watermen and to celebrate the Hanoverian succession – Handel's *Water Music* is also associated with the race.

Doggett's is the only coat and badge race to survive to this day, and it remains a challenge of speed and endurance in a sculling boat as well as a great test of watermanship in steering unassisted on a crowded river through the numerous bridges which now traverse the course. Sometimes competitors encounter unusual obstacles – in the 1999 race, London's millennium Ferris wheel, under construction at the time, occupied much of the river.

The original rule restricting the number of times any individual was allowed to compete to one has now been relaxed by Fishmongers' Company, the executors of Doggett's will, because of the sharp decline in numbers of apprentices. A second attempt is now permitted for those unsuccessful first time around.

References:

Cleaver, H., *A History of Rowing* (London: Herbert Jenkins, 1957).

Cook, T. A. and Nickalls, G., *Thomas Doggett Deceased* (London: Constable, 1908).

Dodd C., *The Story of World Rowing* (London: Stanley Paul, 1992).

See also:

Rowing

-Chris Dodd

Donington Park

Donington Park Circuit is located close to the village of Castle Donington, some 10 miles to the south east of Derby. It was created within the grounds of the 17th-century Donington Hall as a joint venture between the landowner, J. W. Shields, and Fred Cranmer of the Derby and District Motor Club. The first meeting, which was restricted to motorcycles, was staged in May 1931 and attracted some 22,000 spectators. The track was widened and laid with tarmac in 1933 to create the first road-racing circuit for cars in Britain. With the outbreak of war in 1939, Donington Park was requisitioned by the War Office and used as a vehicle depot. Although released from government control in 1956, the restoration of Donington was delayed until 1971 when the site was bought by Tom Wheatcroft, a Leicester builder and racing enthusiast. Wheatcroft invested heavily in improving and extending the track, creating hospitality facilities and a museum housing a world-renowned collection of historic Grand Prix cars.

The first Donington Grand Prix, held in 1935, was run by Richard Shuttleworth who completed the 120 laps (300 miles) in an Alfa Romeo at an average speed of 63.97 miles per hour. The race was given full international status in 1937, with the last pre-war meeting being held the following year. Other significant events during this period included the Nuffield Trophy (1934-1939), consistently won by English Racing Automobiles, and the R.A.C. T.T. (1937). Racing of international calibre was restored to Donington under Wheatcroft's patronage, including the British Motorcycle Grand Prix in 1987. Two years later, the circuit was awarded rounds of the Sportscar World Championship and in 1993 hosted the European Grand Prix, won by Ayrton Senna in a McLaren-Ford.

References:

Georgano, G. N., *The Encyclopaedia of Motor Sport* (London: Michael Joseph, 1971).

Rendall, I., *The Chequered Flag. 100 Years of Motor Racing* (London: Weidenfeld & Nicolson, 1993).

Rendall, I., *The Power and the Glory. A Century of Motor Racing* (London: BBC Books, 1991).

Further reading:

Dugdale, J., *Great Motor Sport of the Thirties* (London: Wilton House Gentry, 1977).

Websites:

Donington Park Grand Prix Circuit – http://www.donington.co.uk/

See also:

Motor Racing

-David Thoms

Drama

Sport may appear to share several features of what could be called dramatic action. In professional and amateur sport there is conflict (in which the participant is challenged by time, one or more aspects of three-dimensional space and, in some cases, an opponent) before resolution; there are clear demarcations of audience and participant by dress, costume or numerical classification; there is often spatial and physical separation between those who watch and those who are viewed; and there are certain conventions which need to be followed in order for the spectacle to be performed and consumed. Indeed, a link that might be made between sport and other primarily visual and aural media is the existence of an audience, who simultaneously share an event with others (previous, present or future observers) and who view that event in their own idiosyncratic way according to their surroundings, previous experience, cultural beliefs and other experiences. However, the major difference between sport and other forms of dramatic entertainment, with the exception of mime, is the primacy of action rather than language.

In plays, films, television and other dramatic forms, the importance of the spoken word is linked with choreographed action, stage setting and sound to produce an overall 'style' which might be said to be naturalistic, metaphysical or somewhere in between. In sport, on the other hand, it is the action of the participants that acquires symbolic significance – the act of winning or losing; of behaving in a sporting or cheating manner; of personal courage and the demonstration of excellence – all derive from the feat itself rather than the interpretation of it. A sporting event may have a commentator in an apparently similar way that a play has a chorus, but the interpretation of the commentator in sport is contingent upon the event, not an integral part of it. Exceptions to this principle are usually more expressive forms of sport (for example, ice dance, gymnastics or skateboarding), which can provide philosophical illustrations of when sport ends and entertainment begins and strike a balance between professional sport's quantitative emphasis on a winner and entertainment or art's qualitative emphasis on the experience.

This freedom from language enables sporting participants to construct their own persona and, unlike actors, who reproduce the characters that they are assigned to play through rehearsal and performance, the creativity of sporting players resides in their ability to read each situation and adapt their physical and psychological movements to maximum benefit.

Bertolt Brecht's analysis of the relationship between theatre and sport, written in 1926, may idealize both the sportsperson and the spectator at the expense of the actor and the theatre. He writes, 'When people in sporting establishments buy their tickets they know exactly what is going to take place; and that is exactly what does take place once they are in their seats: viz. highly trained persons developing their peculiar powers in the way most suited to them, with the greatest sense of responsibility yet in such a way as to make one feel that they are doing it primarily for their own fun.'

In contrast, throughout *Beyond a Boundary*, the author C. L. R. James draws a direct link between the spectacle and experience of classical Greek drama and cricket in his efforts to maintain that each is equally an art. He notes, 'Once every year for four days the tens of thousands of Athenian citizens sat in the open air on the stone seats at the side of the acropolis and from sunrise to sunset watched the plays of the competing dramatists. All that we have to correspond is a Test match'. However, the view that the audience constitutes a vital part of the meaning of sport is one with which both writers concur. This is in contrast, in the case of cricket, to Neville Cardus, who agreed with the representation of the game as an art form but felt that this precluded both its understanding and appeal to the masses. Thus there is a conflict between sport as 'low' and 'high' culture.

The relative lack of drama pieces concerned with sport at a time when other literary media have grown enormously requires further investigation. On the one hand, it may be that real sport offers more drama than fiction ever could. On the other hand, it may be that drama is a specialized, exclusive world with an idiom and manner not easily accessible to those not involved in it. The latter would seem not to be so, because of the success of the cinema over the last two decades, which, like football, went through a period of low interest in the early 1970s before repackaging itself for new kinds of audiences. Shaw recognized the importance of the cinema and added scenes to *Pygmalion* specifically with the possibility of a cinematic production in mind; subsequently, the musical version used the racing scene to make points about middle-class culture to great effect.

In the early decades of the 20th century, the link between popular theatre and sport as forms of entertainment can be seen in the form of journals such as the *Illustrated Sporting and Dramatic News*, which reviewed music hall shows and contained sports reports. In more recent times, the ubiquity of television and the advent of satellite and digital technologies means that audiences have more experience and are more sophisticated viewers of certain types of drama, although theatre audiences have continued to fall. In this way it is possible to see music hall production values of amusing with a spectacle, rather than educating the consumer, as preceding television. Both have influenced the way that sport has been turned into a drama for the consumption of the audience, in competition with, and drawing reference from, other kinds of entertainment. For example, in his essay 'What happened at Munich', Raymond Williams suggests that television made a living drama out of the massacre of Israeli athletes by the Black September movement at the 1972 Olympic Games.

Much more frequent than drama about sport is the use of sport as a metaphor or symbol within drama, for example, Harold Pinter's *No Man's Land* uses the names of old cricketers for characters who are obsessed with validating their pasts and *The Dumb Waiter: a Play in One Act* has a sequence in which the two main characters ponder the implications of 'Playing Away'. Three plays with football themes are popular school productions – Andrew Bethell's adaptation of Bill Forsythe's original film script *Gregory's Girl*; Peter Terson's *Zigger Zagger* and *Ooh Aah Showab Khan*; and *An Evening with Gary Lineker*, which is perhaps the most recent popular piece to earn box office success.

References:

Berkoff, S., *The Trial; Metamorphosis; In the Penal Colony: Three Theatre Adaptations from Franz Kafka* (Oxford: Amber Lane Press, 1988).

Brecht B., 'Emphasis on Sport', in J. Willett (ed. and translator), *Brecht on Theatre: the Development of an Aesthetic* (London: Methuen & Co., 1986).

James, C. L. R., *Beyond a Boundary* (London: Hutchinson, 1963).

Further reading:

Ganzl K., *The British Musical Theatre, vol. 2 1915-1984* (London: Macmillan, 1986).

O'Connor, A. (ed.), *Raymond Williams on Television: Selected Writings* (London: Routledge & Kegan Paul, 1989).

See also:

Film; Literature

-Jean Williams

Drugs

It should not be assumed that sportspersons resort to drug-taking simply to cheat. Like the rest of us, athletes suffer from colds and allergies and have a need for therapeutic drugs. The problem here is that some of the medications contain banned substances, so the Sports Council has produced a guide on 'allowable medicines'. Additionally, restorative drugs can be legitimately used to overcome injury and to continue performing whilst recovering from injury. Some athletes also use 'recreational drugs' for relaxation, though most governing bodies take a dim view of this and wish to project an image of their sport as free from the 'social drugs culture'. Nevertheless, most objections to drugs in sport lie in the area of performance enhancement, in which sportspersons take drugs either to give them an advantage over their rivals or to prevent their rivals gaining a drug-assisted advantage over them.

Objections to performance-enhancing drugs in sport are raised both for moral reasons and on health grounds, and indeed, these factors are cited by the International Olympic Committee (I.O.C.) and supported by various British sporting bodies. The I.O.C. official policy document states, 'The use of doping agents in sport is both unhealthy and contrary to the ethics of sport. It is necessary to protect the physical and spiritual health of athletes, the values of fair play and of competition, the integrity and unity of sport, and the rights of those who take part in it at whatever level.'

In many respects, the moral argument follows the line of 19th-century Muscular Christians, who saw sport as having a major utilitarian function by helping to build character. The health argument is based on the side-effects of drug-taking. In the case of anabolic steroids, for example, there is overwhelming evidence that females may undergo masculinization, resulting in hair growth on the face and body, irreversible voice changes and serious disturbances to the menstrual cycle; adolescent males may experience stunting of growth; older males can get heart disease, hypertension, liver toxicity and premature baldness; and all users can suffer from severe acne on face and body.

Currently, the I.O.C.'s list of banned drugs (which has been adopted by most sports) covers five categories of drug-taking. First, there are stimulants, which improve performance by reducing tiredness and increasing alertness and aggression. They can thus help in endurance events and explosive power activities, because of the increased capacity to exercise strenuously. Second are narcotics, which act on the brain to reduce the amount of pain felt from injury or illness, so enabling athletes to pass through the pain barrier. Third are anabolic agents, by which athletes seek to increase performance by modifying muscle size. Fourth come diuretics, which eliminate fluid from the body thus facilitating acute weight reduction by jockeys and in sports with weight divisions, such as boxing and wrestling. Diuretics can also be used to dilute the doping agent in urine prior to testing. Finally there are peptide and glycoprotein hormones and analogues, in essence hormone substances which can increase size, strength or height. There is also an additional list of classes of drugs subject to certain restrictions in sports where they could secure an advantage. This covers alcohol, marijuana, local anaesthetics, corticosteroids (anti-inflammatory substances) and beta-blockers.

The I.O.C. have also banned the activities of blood doping, which increases the oxygen carrying capacity of the blood, and any

115

attempts to use pharmacological, chemical or physical manipulation to affect the results of drug tests, for example by secreting a clean urine sample in or around the body to switch for one's own.

There are major difficulties to be confronted in attempting to eradicate drugs from sport, not least the legal barriers of ensuring that restrictive clauses are watertight and test procedures rigorously adhered to. Such is the earning power of the modern sportsperson that a successful suit could bankrupt many of the governing bodies. Testing systems have improved and become more sophisticated, though the more effective blood testing has yet to replace urine testing. However, detection is now more likely since the introduction of out-of-competition testing.

Arraigned against the drug eradicators is the powerful pharmaceutical industry whose ingenuity has created a menu for the athlete and a goldmine for the chemist: sport at the élite level has in some instances become a one-sided race between the pharmacists and the sports authorities. That is not to say that governing bodies, especially at the national level, can be exonerated. As well as state-sponsored sports drug programmes in China and previously in East Germany and the Soviet Union, there are allegations that western nations have failed to pursue a strict anti-drugs policy because of a reluctance to tarnish their sport by admitting that positive tests have occurred. Others require world champions to keep their audiences and sponsors. Hence, athletes are warned when they will be tested, samples are mislaid and results forgotten.

There is also the problem of the athletes themselves. Doping on a significant scale came first in horse-racing, but horses had no option but to have the drugs imposed on them. For most athletes, taking drugs is a matter of choice and for some the benefits of winning outweigh any possible adverse effects on health. The side effects of anabolic steroids are well documented but do not appear to have checked their use.

Punishment may be a greater deterrent, though when the desire to win is so strong, ways will be found to beat the system and, furthermore, bans and suspensions are rarely for life.

It should be noted, however, that there is, on the other hand, an alternative argument that sees little difference between athletes receiving nutritional information on what diet might give them the most energy and athletes getting advice on what drugs could improve their performance. It is also suggested by some that pharmacology is a form of technology, so what is the difference between receiving aid from the chemist and adopting such technological improvements as air-cushioned running shoes and disk wheels on bicycles? Why is gaining an advantage through the assistance of a sports psychologist or by a biomechanical analysis met with approval, but taking a pill or injecting a drug regarded as cheating?

References:

Houlihan, B., *Sport, Policy and Politics: a Comparative Analysis* (London: Routledge, 1997).

Mottram, D. R., *Drugs in Sport* (London: Spon, 1996).

Further reading:

Goldman, B., Bush, P. and Klatz, R., *Death in the Locker Room* (London: Century Publishing, 1984).

See also:

Memorable Events – Death of Tommy Simpson

-Wray Vamplew

Dunfermline College

Dunfermline College was the first college in Scotland for the training of specialist teachers of physical education. It was founded in Dunfermline in 1905 by the trustees of a fund provided by Andrew Carnegie, the Scottish-born American philanthropist, to ameliorate the lives of the people of the town. The national College of Hygiene and Physical Training for women and men students replaced (from 1908) an earlier venture at Aberdeen Training College.

The centre was used primarily for training women teachers until after the end of the First World War, when the male side of the institution re-opened to provide courses for returning ex-servicemen. During the 1920s, the principle of separate training became accepted, and in 1931 male training moved to a new site at Jordanhill College in Glasgow. In the 1940s, Dunfermline dropped the remedial gymnastics element of training, and practical work focused on games and Rudolf Laban-based dance and gymnastics. After two spells in Aberdeen during and after the Second World War, the college moved to purpose-built premises in Cramond, Edinburgh in March 1966.

Through validation by the Council National Academic Awards, Dunfermline College of Physical Education introduced a B.Ed. Honours degree in Physical Education in 1973. Following the report of the Scottish Tertiary Education Advisory Council in 1987, Jordanhill's training facility closed and the two separate programmes merged into one institution within Moray House Institute of Education, offering the sole training course in physical education in Scotland (with a duration of four years). 'Dunf' is now part of the Faculty of Education of the University of Edinburgh.

References:

Cruickshank, M., *A History of the Training of Teachers in Scotland* (London: University of London Press, 1970).

Fletcher, S., *Women First: the Female Tradition in English Physical Education 1880-1980* (London: Athlone Press, 1984).

McIntosh, P. C., *Physical Education in England since 1800* (London: G. Bell and Sons Ltd, 1968).

MacLean, I. C., *The History of Dunfermline College of Physical Education* (Edinburgh: William Blackwood and Sons, 1976).

Scotland, J., *The History of Scottish Education* (London: University of London Press, 1969).

Further reading:

Cruickshank, M., *A History of the Training of Teachers in Scotland* (London: University of London Press, 1970).

Fletcher, S., *Women First: the Female Tradition in English Physical Education 1880-1980* (London: Athlone Press, 1984).

McIntosh, P. C., *Physical Education in England since 1800* (London: G. Bell & Sons Ltd, 1968).

See also:

Bedford College; Chelsea College; Dartford College; Dunfermline College; Education – Teacher Training

-Lorna Jackson

E

Economics of Sport

The economics of sport came to prominence as a branch of the economics discipline in 1956 with Rottenberg's analysis of the labour market in baseball. Since his work, sports economists across the globe have found the sports industry a fertile area for research. Economists have focused their attention on, amongst other things, the link between player salaries and player productivity, the structure and operation of sporting leagues, the nature of (as well as the demand for) the product produced by sporting leagues, the operation of player transfer markets, the performance of team managers/coaches, and racial discrimination in team sports.

A key issue in the economic analysis of sports is whether government should treat the sports industry as just another industry. The economics of sport is peculiar to the extent that rival producers (or teams) must combine together to produce a saleable product (individual matches). Without co-operation between the member clubs of a league, it would not be possible for matches to be played. The product (matches) is therefore produced co-operatively. In many countries, open collusion between the producers in an industry is forbidden. But in team sports, the authorities allow anti-competitive practices; in U.S. baseball, for example, the industry receives special exemption from the government's anti-monopoly legislation. Sporting leagues are cartels where entry and exit are rigidly controlled. They are not competitive industries in which firms can freely come and go.

Professional sports in Britain, especially Association Football, have undergone rapid change during the 1990s. Professionalism has been extended into other sports and deeper within sports where it already existed, clubs have floated on the stock exchange, investment in new stadia is commonplace, and television revenues have grown tremendously. While many football clubs are experiencing growing revenues, they are also having to live with larger and larger wage bills. The likelihood is that wage costs will further escalate as a result of the Bosman ruling in December 1995, which established the principle of complete freedom of movement for out-of-contract players, with no transfer fee payable to the former club if the player moves to a club in another European Union member-state. Furthermore, domestic transfer fees in England have also been abolished for out-of-contract players over the age of twenty-four since the 1998/99 season. The result of this is that bargaining power has shifted in favour of the player, allowing player salaries to rise. The ability of the smaller clubs to survive financially through trading their better (more marketable) players has therefore been reduced, although to counter this, clubs are now likely to try and sign players on longer-term contracts (to which the players will agree provided the terms are more favourable).

The economic analysis of team sports raises a number of public policy issues. Across the world, sporting authorities have introduced many regulations designed to maintain competitive balance. That is, the authorities have taken measures to ensure that on the field, competition is not too unequal. It is believed that the greater the uncertainty of outcome (each match or over a whole season), the greater will be the spectator interest, and, hence, the greater the chance of industry profit maximization. Belief in the uncertainty of outcome idea explains to a large extent why sporting authorities restrict competitive behaviour in a way that would not be possible in 'normal' industries.

To some extent the rules adopted reflect the fact that the sporting league is a cartel. Rules are needed in order to maintain 'good practice' and for the league to operate effectively. Thus, sporting authorities have to establish playing rules and generate a fixture list. The league may also be required to rule on the selection and employment of players by clubs and control the number of clubs in a league, and their precise location. Sporting leagues also determine rules for the allocation of revenues. Certain restrictions, however, have gone beyond the basic rules for 'good practice'. Most notably, the reserve clause in North American sports and the retain-and-transfer system in English Association Football served to restrict the mobility of labour and keep down player salaries.

Restrictions on the mobility of footballers were first introduced in 1891. From this time until 1963, the transfer market operated under the regime of the 'retain-and-transfer system'. Any player wishing to move to another club had to make a transfer request. If the club holding the player's registration refused the request, the player, if he wished to remain in the Football League, had no option but to stay with that club. If the request was granted, the player could leave providing a satisfactory fee was paid to the selling club. Where players were placed on the retained list, the terms offered had to be at least as favourable as the current minimum wages and conditions. This system effectively tied a player to his club until the club gave him permission to move elsewhere. In 1963, the system was amended to allow players limited freedom of movement.

At the beginning of the 1977/78 season, the rules were further modified with the establishment of 'freedom of contract'. At the end of his contract, a player was able to negotiate a move to another club. As before, the holding club had to offer terms at least as good as in the final year of the contract. If this was not done, the player was allowed to move without a fee being paid. If the club offered terms at least as good as in the final year of the contract and these were rejected by the player, then he was allowed to move to another club provided that the holding club received a fee as compensation for loss of service. The rights of clubs were further reduced in 1995 when the Bosman ruling established the principle of complete freedom of movement for out-of-contract players moving to another European Union country (see above). In such cases, no transfer fee was payable to the former club.

The retain-and-transfer system was a player reservation system, motivated by a desire to ensure competitive balance by reducing the concentration of star players in a few clubs. Freedom of contract (and the Bosman ruling) allows out-of-contract players to move to another club if they so desire. According to economic theory, free movement of players should not alter the distribution of playing talent in a league, but it will increase the rewards to players. The allocation of (human) resources is thus central to the economic analysis of team sports.

References:

Scully, G. W., *The Market Structure of Sports* (Chicago: Chicago University Press, 1995).

Further reading:

Noll, R. (ed.), *Government and the Sports Business* (Washington, DC: Brookings Institution, 1974).

Rottenberg, S., 'The Baseball Player's Labour Market', *Journal of Political Economy*, 64 (1956), pp. 242-258.

See also:

Commercialism

-Steve Dobson

Education – Commissions and Reports

The history of physical education does not figure prominently in official commissions and reports of the 19th century, but the impact of sport on character as well as health can be traced from mid-century in official enquiries into education. The earliest body in Britain for governmental provision and supervision of education, the Committee of Council on Education, had offered encouragement in its first circular of 1839 for the place of physical activity in schools, but there is little evidence that this had much impact.

The Clarendon Commission (1864) investigating the English public schools (the private sector) reported that boys at Eton devoted more than twenty hours a week to playing cricket, but this was not appreciated in terms of bodily training, rather as a form of character training through the playing of athletic team games. The subsequent Taunton Commission exploring middle-class schools reported in 1868 and included evidence from Miss Buss, pioneering headmistress of North London Collegiate School (a school for middle-class girls), asserting that mental exertion and bodily exercise should go together in a balanced curriculum for educating the young. The third level of educational provision, state elementary education for the working classes, was scrutinized by the Cross Commission (1888); among the individuals giving evidence was Madame

Bergman Österberg on her work in the elementary schools of the London School Board. The rising importance of physical exercise in education is evidenced in the Day School Code of 1895 (regulations governing payment of grants to elementary schools), which required schools to include 'Swedish or other drill or suitable physical exercises' in the curriculum before the higher grant for discipline and organization would be paid.

The impact of the Boer War on Victorian Britain had repercussions for the place of physical education: the poor physical condition of recruits raised official concerns about the health of the nation, and a Royal Commission began work in 1901 to investigate. A model course of exercises based on the army system was drawn up by the English Board of Education in 1902, but was rejected by the teaching profession as being too military in content. A Scottish commission had come out against military drill, and noted the significance of environment and nurture to children's health. The outcome was the setting up in 1904 of the Inter-departmental Committee on Physical Deterioration to examine the model course and develop a new syllabus based on educational and medical justifications. In practice, however, the Scottish 1905 syllabus drew more on military exercises than from the remedial or educational aspects of the Swedish system. Physical education was linked with child health concerns but within a very prescribed system of exercising. The basic approach remained until the Fisher Education Act of 1918 extended the concept of educational access and curricula – a revised syllabus of 1919 emphasized the educative role of physical activity, rather than militaristic drill, and suggested the incorporation of games.

Since the educational philosophy of the 1926 Hadow report, with its emphasis on the developmental role of schools, set the context within which the landmark 1933 syllabus of physical education was produced, the subject of physical education in schools became quite

121

definitely educational as opposed to military. Beyond the educational sphere, social changes in work time, attitudes to leisure and an ongoing concern with national health and fitness led to the establishment of official bodies to promote sport and physical activity among the wider population. Hadow had argued for an expansion of facilities for sport – one response was the creation of the National Playing Fields Association. Subsequently, the Central Council for Recreation and Physical Training began to develop and support the provision of sporting activities and facilities for young people.

After the Second World War, attention focused on other aspects of societal regeneration. The Ministry of Education, in the spirit of easing restrictions, produced curriculum guides in 1952 and 1953 that further encouraged the incorporation of games and the expressiveness of educational gymnastics into the school curriculum. On top of this, the 1960 Wolfenden report on sport in the community gained a higher profile for the reconstituted Central Council of Physical Recreation by urging greater spending on sports facilities for young people, independent of school provision.

The move in educational philosophy towards 'discovery and exploration' for primary school children peaked with two reports, *Primary Education in Scotland* (1965) and *Children and their Primary Schools* (Plowden, 1967), where physical activities formed an integrated part of the curriculum (linked with the expressive arts of art, music and drama). Increasing pressure on secondary school curricula gradually diminished the amount of time for physical education, and the role of physical education in schools declined.

In response to increasing discussion, not to say condemnation, of the claimed failure of school physical education to improve standards of personal fitness or to increase success in international sports competitions, the Physical Education Association in 1987 instituted a commission of enquiry into physical education in schools. Its belated acknowledgement that there was contention and ongoing debate about the role of physical education had relatively little impact on trends in schools. More recently, Sport 21 (a series of policy documents produced by the Strategy Advisory Group of the Scottish Sports Council) has raised discussion of a task force to promote physical education, and there has been talk of the need to revise the National Curriculum in England and Wales. The Scottish Sports Council, with its Scottish school sport co-ordinator programme to manage and facilitate extracurricular school sporting programmes, illustrates how school sport is now being seen as distinct from education.

Although reports and commissions on educational matters provide evidence on the historic role and status of physical education, the likelihood grows that future discussions on the nature, role and status of sport will increasingly focus on schemes within the local community rather than in schools.

References:

Kirk, D., *Defining Physical Education: the Social Construction of a School Subject in Postwar Britain* (London: Falmer Press, 1992).

Kirk, D., *Schooling Bodies: School Practice and School Disorder, 1880-1940* (London: Leicester University Press, 1998).

McIntosh, P. C., *Physical Education in England since 1800* (London: G. Bell & Sons Ltd, 1968).

McIntosh, P. C., Dixon, J. G., Munrow, A. D., and Willetts, R. F. (eds.), *Landmarks in the History of Physical Education* (London: Routledge & Kegan Paul, 1981).

Penn, A., *Targeting Schools: Drill, Militarism and Imperialism* (London: Woburn Press, 1999).

See also:

Muscular Christianity

-Lorna Jackson

Education – Public School Sport

The significance of the public schools by the mid-19th century is summed up by Leslie Stephen who, in 1868, wrote, 'Neither the British jury, nor the House of Lords, nor the Church of England, nay scarcely the monarchy itself, seems so deeply enshrined in the bosoms of our countrymen as our public schools.' The 'Sacred Seven' public schools – Charterhouse, Eton, Harrow, Rugby, Shrewsbury, Westminster and Winchester – had been joined by new schools such as Cheltenham, Marlborough and Wellington, and endowed grammar schools such as Repton, Sherborne, Tonbridge and Uppingham, to form the core of those educational establishments thought of as public schools by 1868. These schools, which became centres for the development of organized games as educational tools promoting 'godliness and good learning', were to inspire the founder of the modern Olympic Games and generate an ideology of athleticism which spread throughout the British Empire.

Winchester, founded in 1382 with seventy scholars, was the first of these schools to experience the need for providing space for physical activity. Forms of football and cricket appear to have been played by the scholars from the mid-17th century onwards, although forms of tennis and fives were played before this. Eton (1440), and Westminster (1560), developed many of the same activities. The great increase in the number of boarders throughout the 18th century encouraged the further development of team games in all seven of these schools.

Eton played cricket matches against Westminster, and later Winchester and

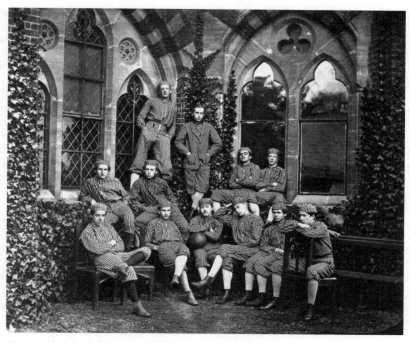

Harrow School Football Team, 1867 (Hulton Getty Picture Collection)

Harrow, from 1796 onwards, with Eton versus Harrow being the oldest continuous fixture on today's cricket calendar. Matches at cricket spawned other contests, notably in rowing between Eton and Westminster. Detailed records of cricket and rowing at both schools are to be found from the early years of the 19th century. These were boy-organized and boy-run activities. The head of each sport collected subscriptions, engaged professional coaches and organized contests. The increasing interest, influence and (finally) control of masters was a feature that did not emerge until mid-century and was more typical of the newer public schools, with little or no history of boy-organized and boy-controlled activities.

As a game with a central organizing body and an established set of laws, cricket was an ideal summer activity for inter-school matches. It was a standardized and regulated activity. The same was not true of the major winter activity, football. As such, each school developed its own variety (or varieties) of football. Local conditions framed such games and provided a context for a wide number of variations, some of which (e.g., the Eton Wall Game, Harrow Football and Winchester Football) have survived alongside the two major forms played at the time – the Association's football and Rugby's football.

Despite their somewhat casual acceptance by the aristocracy in the late 18th century, by the mid-19th century the public schools had become the centres of education for the upper-middle classes by absorbing the sons of the emerging business and professional classes. They became 'social agencies' and were described by one contemporary as furnishing neither 'the best moral nor the best mental discipline... but they are the theatres of athletic manners and the training places of a gallant, generous spirit for the English gentleman'. In addition, the English middle classes, influenced by the Evangelical movement, were religious, and their aim in education was largely 'godliness and good learning'. The increased empha-sis on gentlemanly character and strong moral principles propounded by Thomas Arnold, headmaster of Rugby (1828-1842), quickly permeated all of the schools, which were increasingly in competition with each other for students.

The critical decade in the development of organized games was the 1850s, as Cheltenham, Harrow, Marlborough, Uppingham and others – each under new, vigorous headmasters in the Arnold mould – promoted organized games and developed very successful schools. This was a complete change from the early years of the century when headmasters tried to prevent activities such as football, rowing and cross-country running. By mid-century, the publication of *Tom Brown's School Days* and the promotion of Muscular Christianity had provided exemplars and an ideology to support a philosophy of education which was grounded in the belief that competitive sport, and notably team games, had a basis in moral as well as physical health, and that training in moral behaviour on the playing field was transferable to life beyond school. Manliness, morality, health and even nationalism could be taught through team games. By the end of the 19th century, the playing field was seen as a training ground for, and even the moral equivalent of, the battlefield. Darwinist notions of 'strength through struggle' further underpinned this ideology of athleticism and gave credence to the belief that football (and particularly Rugby's football) would produce 'toughness of muscle and toughness of heart' for a rising generation of national leaders and imperial rulers.

By the 1890s, sport had ceased to be a means to an end and was an end in itself. The cult of athleticism dominated much of public school and even upper-middle class life. The close links between the public schools and Oxbridge meant that similar effects were felt there also. And while the 'diffusion thesis' for the growth of organized games across Britain is at best only a partial explanation for the spread of sport, there is evidence that public school and university-educated young men were indeed responsible for diffusing sport by carrying their games to all parts of Britain and the Empire by the early years of the 20th century. The development of public schools for girls in the second half of the 19th century, often as direct parallels to boys schools, where organized games such as hockey, cricket, tennis and lacrosse were the favoured activities, is also indicative of the strength of the public school model and its ideology of athleticism. Even today, the public schools games-playing legacy can be observed in the enormous emphasis placed on games in the National Curriculum for Physical Education.

References:

Chandler, T., 'The Structuring of Manliness', in J. Nauright and T. Chandler (eds.), *Making Men: Rugby and Masculine Identity* (London: Frank Cass, 1996), pp. 13-31.

Mangan, J., *Athleticism in the Victorian and Edwardian Public School: the Emergence and Consolidation of the Educational Ideology* (Cambridge: Cambridge University Press, 1981).

Money, T., *Manly and Muscular Diversions: Public Schools and the Nineteenth-Century Sporting Revival* (London: Duckworth, 1997).

Further reading:

Gathorne-Hardy, J., *The Old School Tie: the Phenomenon of the English Public School* (New York: Viking, 1977).

Holt, R., *Sport and the British: a Modern History* (Oxford: Clarendon Press, 1989).

Honey, J., *Tom Brown's Universe: the Development of the Victorian Public School* (London: Millington, 1977).

See also:

Eton Versus Harrow

-Tim Chandler

Education – Teacher Training

In the context of teacher training, the physical education profession was late in getting off its marks. The first attempts to train teachers came through the early 19th-century monitorial systems promoted by religious-sponsored societies' schools in England and by the national church in Scotland, and in neither instance was physical activity seen as an important constituent of the curriculum. Exceptions to this general position came in the work of Robert Owen, who encouraged the teaching of dance and games in his pioneering community school at New Lanark, and in the educational practices of David Stow in Glasgow, who included games in the training programme of his Normal School (from the Latin *norma*, a rule) for intending teachers. The institution of formalized training for trainee teachers by the Committee of Council on Education (from 1846) strengthened the position of training colleges.

With the increasing provision of education during the 19th century, differences emerged in the practice of physical education (and hence in the preparation of teachers/instructors) in the various sectors of education. The English public schools (the private sector) had seen games as an appropriate activity, but this depended on the individual interests of masters until later in the century, when the ideology of athleticism gained the upper hand. Even then, though, there was no specialist preparation of masters to teach games.

The British view of physical activity was out of step with developments in Europe, where the work of Pehr Henrik Ling in Sweden and Friedrich Jahn in Germany had focused attention on systems of gymnastic exercise. This began to change in the 1860s, when Archibald Maclaren reorganized physical training in the British Army to include a form of military gymnastics. Maclaren favoured the German system of exercising based on the work of J. C. Guts Muths, which involved the structured use of apparatus rather than the callisthenics favoured by the other main school of the time, the Swedish system. Thus, army personnel gained expertise in instruction and, with the institution of State-supported mass education

School children participating in a physical exercise drill at a London school, date unknown (London Metropolitan Archives)

from 1870 onwards, army drill sergeants were employed in the new large elementary schools to provide instruction in physical exercises. The motive here was arguably control not health – drill trained the children in obedience to instruction as well as in basic physical manoeuvres.

London School Board was one of the first to promote physical training, exercise and drill, developing different programmes for boys and girls. While the former were instructed by army drill sergeants, women were appointed to develop programmes for girls and infants, and early appointees were trained in the Swedish system of remedial and educational gymnastics. In 1881, Miss Martina Bergman (later Madame Bergman Österberg) was appointed superintendent of the girls' and infants' programme, but she soon moved into the developing sector of schools for middle-class girls and, in 1885, opened a training college in

Hampstead. Bergman Österberg's innovation was to combine Ling gymnastics with team games for girls (modelled on the English public school tradition), and she began to offer specialist training for women to work in the middle-class girls' day and boarding schools. Following a move to Dartford, other training colleges were soon set up by her students to spread the message, and thus the earliest specialist training colleges were for women training in the Bergman Österberg / Ling system (Dartford, 1895; Chelsea, 1898; Anstey, 1899; I. M. Marsh, Liverpool, 1900; Bedford, 1903; Dunfermline, 1905).

In the state elementary system, the Day School Code of 1895 had acknowledged the role of physical activity in the curriculum, but the testing of recruits at the time of the Boer War (1899-1902) had shown how unfit the majority of young men were. This raised serious questions about the role of military drill, and the Royal Commission of 1905 acknowledged the role that physical education could play in remedial health. However, little effort was made before the First World War to alter the training of elementary teachers, or to develop male specialist training.

During the 1920s, a new factor appeared – the influence of Rudolf Laban, whose stress on freedom of expression fitted well with the popular educational philosophies of the 1930s. This was taken up in the women's colleges, but the newly developed courses for men focused their training on games and the skill-based elements of Swedish gymnastics – thus, the split in the definition of physical education grew. It was also the case that male trainees were already graduates, while the specialist women's colleges were private and independent of the national training system.

Teacher training in general underwent a tremendous expansion after the Second World War, in line with the McNair report (1944). For physical education, this resulted in the development of physical education wings (specialist streams) in general colleges. However, not until the Robbins report (1963) resulted in the creation of a two-sector system of higher education was there a possibility of students gaining degrees in physical education: the Council for National Academic Awards was set up to validate non-university awards. This led to the growth of the B.Ed. (Bachelor of Education) degree, but also a need for the subject to fit into an 'academic' mould. Simultaneously, college staff seeking to improve their own qualifications led to a growth in postgraduate degree awards at universities.

The James report on teacher training (1972) sounded a death-knell for specialist colleges in England by arguing that teacher education should be 'end on' to subject study (i.e. follow consecutively); the report had no effect in Scotland, where the General Teaching Council for Scotland, which controlled teacher education and entry to the profession, contin-

ued to favour the traditional concurrent pattern (personal education and learning to teach the subject undertaken simultaneously). In England the separate identity of the specialist colleges began to disappear in mergers and closures, and by the mid-1980s, few were still in existence. With the declining numbers, the debate about the focus of training intensified, and in the spirit of the times, sports studies and the scientific approach to physical activity gained ground over the free approach of the Laban ethos. The decline of specialist teacher training in physical education may be seen as mirroring a decline in the subject itself.

References:

Cruickshank, M., *A History of the Training of Teachers in Scotland* (London: University of London Press, 1970).

Fletcher, S. *Women First: the Female Tradition in English Physical Education, 1880-1980* (London: Athlone Press, 1984).

Kirk, D., *Defining Physical Education: the Social Construction of a School Subject in Postwar Britain* (London: Falmer Press, 1992).

McIntosh, P. C., *Physical Education in England since 1800* (London: G. Bell & Sons Ltd, 1968).

McIntosh, P. C., Dixon, J. G., Munrow, A. D. and Willetts, R. F. (eds.), *Landmarks in the History of Physical Education* (London: Routledge & Kegan Paul, 1981).

See also:

Bedford College; Carnegie College; Chelsea College; Dartford College; Dunfermline College; Jordanhill College; Loughborough University

-Lorna Jackson

Epsom

The inauguration of the Oaks (1779) and the Derby (1780) at Epsom Downs, Surrey, gave impetus to the modern style of deciding races without preliminary heats and the emphasis on young horses. The summer meeting quickly developed into a gigantic folk festival for London and the surrounding area, with reported attendances of 80,000 on Derby Day in the 1820s.

A grandstand was erected in 1829-1830, but neither the Grandstand Association nor the Dorling family, who dominated Epsom for much of the 19th century, always acted in the best interests of racing, and even the Derby lost out against the new enclosed courses in terms of its prize money. In 1890, the Jockey Club finally persuaded the Grandstand Association to make a sizeable contribution to the race fund, and thereafter it adopted a more realistic attitude and set about obtaining control of the Downs.

A new grandstand was built in 1927, but the Association had to wait for a further nine years before it had an unrestricted freehold of the Downs. Even then, the course, apart from entrance to the stands and enclosures, still remained free of access, and Frith's famous painting, 'Derby Day 1858', still captured the essence of Epsom over a century later. In 1985, legislation was passed which allowed the course to be enclosed and, since then, gate-money, coupled with an increasing level of sponsorship, has enabled Epsom to maintain its pre-eminence with the public. However, the relentless market-ing of the Derby meeting as the 'world's greatest picnic' and the plethora of other attractions can sometimes divert attention from the all-round excellence of the racing.

References:

Wright, H., *The Encyclopaedia of Flat Racing* (London: Robert Hale Ltd, 1986. 2nd ed.).

Wynn Jones, M., *The Derby – A Celebration of the World's Most Famous Horse Race* (London: Croom Helm, 1979).

Further reading:

Hunn, D., *Epsom Racecourse, its Story and its People* (London: Davis-Poynter, 1973).

Websites:

Epsom Downs Racecourse – http://www.epsomderby.co.uk/

See also:

Horse-racing

-John Tolson

Ethics

When most people think about ethics and sport, it is likely that they will visualize first and foremost an image of an individual doing something against the rules. For example, they might remember Ben Johnson, the Canadian sprinter, head hung low, an object of scorn and derision, trundling through an airport, kit-bag over shoulder, without an apparent friend in the world after his expulsion from the Seoul Olympic Games for taking drugs. British sports fans may recall footballer Vinnie Jones reaching behind to grasp Paul Gascoigne's testicles, so that the thought would be left with him for the rest of the game. Others may recollect England captain Michael Atherton's ball tampering, captured on camera in the 1997 cricket test between England and the Australians.

Indeed, many of our perceptions as to what constitute ethics in sport are dominated by media representations – the kind of incidents referred to above understandably make for good copy. However, if unethical behaviour seems everywhere to follow sport, what, if any-thing, is positively ethical about it? It might be helpful here to distinguish between two senses of the term 'ethics' employed by academics.

First, there is 'ethics' with a small 'e'. This is the social scientific study of behaviour, prac-tices or policies thought to be good or bad, right or wrong, fair or foul and so on. Early sociologists noted how sport functioned as a kind of social glue, which helped to bind peo-ple to the dominant norms and values of a given culture or society. More recently, scholars have investigated the tendencies of sport to give rise to and sustain sexist and autocratic forms of organizations and subcultures. Psychologists have observed the tendencies of certain sports such as Rugby and American football to foster aggression and violent attitudes towards the opposing team. A noteworthy aspect of this research into 'ethics' and sport has been the fact that the very meaning of the term 'ethics' has largely been taken for granted in two distinct ways. First, some think of ethics as a set of universal action-guiding rules that apply to all persons in all places and can be thought of in terms of duties, obligations and rights. Others have taken the opposite view that ethics are merely a set of codified norms that are group or culture-specific.

'Ethics' with a capital 'E' – if one can think of it without prioritizing one over the other – is a branch of philosophy, commonly referred to as moral philosophy. It deals with questions regarding what we mean by concepts such as 'good' and 'evil', 'virtue' and 'vice', 'right' and 'wrong'. Those who study 'Ethics' also raise questions as to the role that these concepts play in the different moral traditions that have existed down from Socrates and the ancient Greeks in the West and Confucius and his followers in the East, on through the entire history of civilization. Crucially, each of these traditions belong to and operate from different starting points, which lead them to differ in their evaluations of the precise nature of right and wrong, acceptable and unacceptable behaviour. This can be clarified by considering an example taken from British sport.

In 1998, in an F.A. Cup football match between Arsenal and Sheffield United, an Arsenal player became injured. In accordance with the ethos of the game, a Sheffield United player kicked the ball out of play so that the player could receive medical treatment. It is customary, once the player has been taken from the field of play or is able to continue, for the ball to be thrown back to the opposition without challenge, so that the state of affairs prior to the stoppage of play can be resumed. In this match, an Arsenal player threw the ball back in the direction of the Sheffield defence. Then, a new player to the Arsenal team (a recent recruit from an African nation) intercepted the ball and crossed it to one of his team-mates, who instinctively (so it is said) struck the ball and scored a goal. The referee blew his whistle and

signalled a legal goal. The Sheffield United players, fans and coach were outraged. Even the Arsenal players seemed embarrassed. Here we have an instance where no formal rule appeared to have been broken, though a widely shared and popular convention clearly had been ignored. How we are to think of this type of conduct and its presupposed concepts is the object of ethics and sport.

Sociologists might investigate the socialization of the players involved – whether they had understood the local conventions of professional English soccer, or whether commercial interests were now so predominant that even this last attempt to preserve fair play in football had fallen by the wayside. Psychologists might conduct interviews with the players to assess their levels of moral reasoning or to uncover latent models of ethical decision making. Historians could consider the players' actions in the context of changing patterns of late 20th-century global football culture and their influences on a hitherto homogenous game. Moral philosophers (or ethicists if you prefer) might enquire into how evaluations of 'fair' and 'foul' can be formulated, what criteria should be used to guide the judgements and whether they should judge the character of the players first and foremost, the consequences of their actions, or the obligations that players have (or do not have) to keep to the spirit and the letter of the law.

Issues such as this, old and new, about human conduct are becoming part of a new line of academic enquiry – ethics and sport. Whether sports ought to ban or embrace performance enhancing drugs, whether men and women ought to compete in mixed events, whether sport ought to be free from politics, whether coaches ought to have such high degrees of power over their athletes, are all questions that are being addressed by philosophers of sport just as they are by fans and aficionados the world over. To those who look unhistorically for a time when sport was pure, some correctives are required. Sportsmen and women have played foul as long as they have played fair. The naive would do well to remember Woody Allen's celebrated quip, 'nostalgia ain't what it used to be'.

See also:
Fair Play

-Mike McNamee

Ethnicity (*see* Racism and Ethnicity)

Eton Versus Harrow

The annual fixture at Lord's between Eton College and Harrow School has been the highlight of the public school cricket calendar since the early 19th century. Eton was one of the first public schools to regularly play fixtures, with matches against Harrow dating back to 1805. Since 1805, their annual encounter has been staged at Lord's – the oldest of the fixtures at the ground. Since 1982 it has been a one-day rather than a two-day contest, yet it retains a special kudos, eagerly awaited by past and present pupils, and remains part of London's social calendar. Until recently, horse-drawn carriages would line the boundary rope, with many convivial parties staged around the ground.

A measure of the importance of the Eton-Harrow match is that over 320 Oxbridge Blues have taken part in the games, besides numerous county players. Twenty-one players have subsequently won test caps, and the list of scholars to have played in the annual fixtures reads like a Who's Who of cricket, including Gubby Allen, B. J. T. Bosanquet, A. N. Hornby, F. S. Jackson, A. C. MacLaren, Lord Tennyson, the Hon. Ivo Bligh and Lord Hawke. Out of the 162 encounters between the two famous schools, those in 1900 and 1910 stand out. The 1900 contest saw Harrow win by one wicket, whilst in 1910, R. St. L. Fowler, the Eton captain, single-handedly turned the match around, with an innings of sixty-four as Eton followed on, before taking eight wickets for twenty-three runs in Harrow's second innings, as they were dismissed for just forty-five, leaving Eton victorious by nine runs.

References:
Titchener-Barrett, R., *Eton and Harrow at Lord's* (London: Quiller Press, 1996).

Further reading:
Gordon, H., *Eton v. Harrow* (London: Williams & Norgate, 1926).
Lyon, W. R. (ed.), *The Elevens of Three Great Schools, 1805-1929* (London: Spottiswoode, 1930).
Lyttleton, Hon. G. W., Eton and Anson, Hon. R. and Leaf, F. A., 'Harrow', in W. N. Roe, (ed.), *Public Schools Cricket, 1901-1950* (London: Max Parrish, 1951), pp. 64-76, 89-102.

Websites:
Eton College – http://www.etoncollege.com/
Harrow School – http://www.harrowschool.org.uk/

See also:
Education – Public School Sport

-Andrew Hignell

Eventing

Three-day eventing, originally called combined training, is the supreme test of the rider and horse tandem combination. It is analogous to the decathlon or heptathlon in track and field. The three testing environments – dressage (the training of a horse in obedience and deportment), a timed cross-country course and stadium showjumping – reward the all-round horse that has both precision and discipline in its gait; tremendous stamina, endurance, speed and courage for the cross-country stage; and jumping ability. Two very special features of eventing concern age and gender. Eventing has seen significant numbers of competitors continue to be successful into middle age, as indeed has showjumping. For example, Major Derek Allhusen represented Great Britain at the 1948 Olympics aged thirty-four. In 1968, he was again an Olympian and at the age of fifty-four won a team gold and an individual silver. In terms of gender, eventing is one of only a handful of sports (others are dressage, show jumping and rifle shooting) in which women have won world and Olympic titles in open competition with men.

Mary Conti, in the *Encyclopedia of World Sport* (1996), describes the origins of the sport: 'The tradition of three-day eventing began as a test of the cavalry mount, which needed to gallop long distances, negotiate the natural obstacles found on cross-country trips, and perform demanding parade movements, and the cavalry rider, who required strong riding abilities, control, and sharp reflexes.'

The sport of eventing is controlled by the Fédération Equestre Internationale (F.E.I. – International Equestrian Federation). Europe, United States and Australia are the three geographic regions in which eventing has built up its strongest following. The highlights of British eventing are the Burghley, Blenheim and Badminton Horse Trials, the latter being arguably the world's most prestigious tournament prize.

Commercial sponsorship has played a key role in developing and popularizing British eventing. The 1999 Badminton Horse Trials, for example, were known as the Mitsubishi Motors Badminton Horse Trials. The event was first started by the Duke of Beaufort in 1949, and is held on his estates near the village of Badminton, Gloucestershire.

The high point of Badminton eventing for the spectators is undoubtedly the cross-country stage. At the 1998 Badminton event, which took place from May 5th to May 9th, the gates opened at 7.00 a.m., with the first horse going out on the course at 11.15 a.m. and the last horse completing the course at around 5.00 p.m. Vast numbers of spectators, upwards of a

quarter of a million, were able to camp, walk and picnic along and around the famous, and at times, notorious, course.

Olympic equestrian activity does not get the media coverage devoted to sports such as track and field or gymnastics. For example, in *The Olympic Spirit: 100 Years of the Games* (1996), the only photographic references to horses are pictures of archaeological artefacts connected with chariot-racing at the Ancient Olympics and a ride-by performed by a platoon of Royal Canadian 'mounties' at the opening of the Calgary Winter Olympics in 1988. Nevertheless, it is the Olympic Games that have consistently witnessed eventing at its very best. In 1972, Richard Meade took gold for Britain in the three-day individual event and led the British eventing team to a second gold medal in the three-day team competition, beating the United States and West Germany in second and third. The British team was Richard Meade (on Laurieston), Mary Gordon-Watson (on Cornishman), Bridget Parker (on Cornish Gold) and Lieutenant Mark Phillips (on Great Ovation). Great Britain also won gold in the 1968 Olympic three-day team event, and has won the team title at the World Championships (first held in 1966) on three occasions – 1970, 1982 and 1986.

Eventing, especially in the sense that it moves across and through three different dramatic stages, lends itself to modern and innovative analyses. The work of Karl B. Raitz and his notions of theatre and sports landscape seem most appropriate in, for example, the context of Badminton with a galaxy of celebrities (Princess Anne is a former participant!) and occasional jumps that are literally death defying.

Britain's premier eventer in the halcyon years of eventing, the 1970s and 1980s, was Lucinda Green (née Prior Palmer). By 1984, she had won six Badminton victories (1973, 1976, 1977, 1979, 1983 and 1984), two European titles and a world championship. She succeeded in many respects because of her professionalism, saying 'Sport today is all-consuming if you want to reach the top. There is no means of earning a living in a normal way and at the end of say, ten or fifteen years, competitors can go out of sport without money or a job.'

References:

Conti, M., 'Horseback Riding, Eventing', in D. Levinson and K. Christensen (eds.), *Encyclopedia of World Sport* (Santa Barbara, California: ABC-CLIO, 1996), vol. I, pp. 457-460.

Raitz, K. B. (ed.), *The Theater of Sport* (Baltimore, Maryland: Johns Hopkins University Press, 1995).

Further reading:

Emery, D. and Greenberg S. (compilers), *World Sports Record Atlas* (Oxford: Facts on File, 1986).

Wels, S., *The Olympic Spirit: 100 Years of the Games* (Del Mar, California: Tehabi Books/Time Warner, 1996).

Websites:

Badminton Horse Trials –
http://www.badminton-horse.co.uk/
The British Equestrian Federation –
http://www.bef.org.uk/
Burghley Horse Trials –
http://www.burghley-horse.co.uk/

-Scott Crawford

F

F.A. Cup

The English Football Association Challenge Cup (commonly known as the F.A. Cup) was the first knockout competition of its type in the world. Introduced in 1871 by the then F.A. Secretary, C. W. Alcock, the first competition saw the Wanderers beat the Royal Engineers at the Oval by a single goal. For the next decade, a succession of southern amateur sides won the trophy until 1883, when Blackburn Olympic became the first non-amateur and northern club to succeed. Tottenham Hotspur became the last non-league side to take the Cup in 1901; they also stopped an eighteen-year run of victories by northern teams. The Cup Final moved to the newly built Empire Stadium, Wembley, in 1923, a location that has become synonymous with the 'magic' of the F.A. Cup. The 1923 final saw an estimated crowd of 200,000 (the official figure was 126,047 but many thousands more entered without tickets) watch Bolton Wanderers beat West Ham United 2-0, and became known as the 'White Horse' Final, referring to a police horse named Billy that herded many thousands of supporters off the pitch.

For many, the road to Wembley is an opportunity to see less-fancied teams compete against the giants of the English game. Notable Cup Final giant-killings have included Sunderland's 1-0 victory over the strong Leeds United side of 1973; second division Southampton's defeat of Manchester United in 1976; and the Wimbledon victory over Liverpool in 1988. Perhaps the most remarkable giant-killing side in F.A. Cup history is Yeovil Town, a non-league club who have over twenty victories against League opposition to their credit.

References:
Butler, B., *The Official History of the Football Association* (London: Queen Anne Press, 1993).

Further reading:
Seddon, P., *A Football Compendium* (Wetherby: The British Library National Bibliography Service, 1995).

See also:
Association Football

-Sam Johnstone

Fair Play

The term 'fair play' refers to a distinctive style and spirit of approaching sports that developed among 'gentleman amateur' sportsmen in England during the second half of the 19th century. Gentleman amateurs were individuals from the middle and upper classes who not only respected the written rules of sports, but also sought to abide by what they thought to be the 'spirit of the game'. The ethic of amateurism was based on fair competition that decreed that the true amateur should never seek to gain an unfair advantage over an opponent. Moreover, it ordered that the amateur should play with style and most certainly not for the pecuniary rewards received by professionals. While amateurs rarely lived up to these ideals, it was thought that a person's approach to sport revealed something about their character and class, and that sports were the perfect spheres in which to express the moral values befitting a middle- or upper-class gentleman.

This connection between sports and moral values developed among the middle and upper classes in the English public schools from the mid-1800s onwards. It arose from the theory that competitive sport had an ethical basis, and that moral training on the sports field was transferable to the outside world. In the first part of the 19th century there was growing concern about the absence of moral education both within and outside the English Public Schools. To breach this gap, headmasters such as G. E. L. Cotton of Marlborough College deliberately promoted games to encourage moral fortitude. He taught that sports provided opportunities for mental as well as physical health, and that they could teach pupils 'religious goodness, unselfishness, right principles and justice'. This philosophy came to be known as 'Muscular Christianity'.

As the 19th century proceeded, a growing number of values came to be associated with sports and the concept of fair play. As a new definition of Victorian masculinity developed, it was assumed that sports could teach boys loyalty, bravery, control of temper, and an abhorrence of homosexuality and masturbation. Similarly, in the context of concerns over Britain's economic and imperial strength, it was thought that sports could teach patriotic values, a unity of purpose across classes, and the discipline of learning to fail before you succeed. It was also believed that sports could teach values relevant to war, as expressed by the Duke of Wellington's oft-quoted (but probably apocryphal) remark that the battle of Waterloo was won on the playing fields of Eton.

The ideology of fair play was so pervasive in Victorian England that it came to represent one of the central tenets of the English national character. It was believed that English people's approach to sport represented something in their wider personality that was expressed in everyday social and political life. This may explain why phrases such as 'to play with a straight bat' and 'to face the bowling' still indicate approval in England today, and why the concept of fair play, though stripped of some of its amateur connotations, also remains common in English sporting and non-sporting language.

References:

Holt, R., *Sport and the British: a Modern History* (Oxford: Clarendon, 1989).

McIntosh, P., *Fair Play: Ethics in Sport and Education* (London: Heinemann Educational Books, 1979).

Further reading:

Holt, R., *Sport and the British: a Modern History* (Oxford: Clarendon, 1989).

McIntosh, P., *Fair Play: Ethics in Sport and Education* (London: Heinemann Educational Books, 1979).

Mangan, J. A., *Athleticism in the Victorian and Edwardian Public School: the Emergence and Consolidation of the Educational Ideology* (Cambridge: Cambridge University Press, 1981).

See also:

Ethics

-Gavin Mellor

Fastnet Race

Sailing has been likened to a beguiling open-air painting of white wings on blue water. C. Fox Smith, writing in 1927, further develops this analogy. Smith talks of 'epic fights', of a sailor as 'the fighting man doing battle with the elements', and of oceans and seas 'haunted by the pale and lovely shadow of fair ships departed'.

Smith foreshadowed the Fastnet Race (established in 1957) with rare prescience. The Fastnet is acknowledged to be amongst the most severely taxing ocean races in the world. The 605-mile race, one of six that make up the Admiral's Cup series, starts at the Royal Yacht Squadron, Cowes, on the Isle of Wight. Boats sail west to go round the Fastnet Light, a beacon atop a rocky outcrop at the southern end of Ireland, and then return to the finish line at Plymouth.

In the late 1960s, a new order in international racing was established when the Australians won the Fastnet in 1967, to be followed in 1969 by an American triumph with Dick Carter's space-age gadgetry allowing his 'Red Rooster' to pioneer a radical keel design that proved to be unbeatable. In 1971, sponsorship by Dunhill, the tobacco company, popularized the Fastnet by enabling proper press facilities to be set up at Cowes. As a result, journalists and photographers helped what had previously been simply an ocean race metamorphose into an international, front-page celebration and carnival. In 1979, these reporters found themselves eyewitnesses to the greatest yachting tragedy of all time. In terms of outdoor 'athletic' disasters, the August 1979 Fastnet race ranks on a par with the infamous Everest saga of May 1996. On August 14th and 15th, 1979, a horrendous storm picked up speed crossing the Atlantic and literally lashed, and bashed, the Fastnet fleet. Fifteen people died, plus four more on board a trimaran accompanying the racing vessels. Out of 303 starting vessels, only 85 completed the race. Twenty-five boats were abandoned and 136 sailors were rescued. Tim Jeffery describes a fleet in which one third were laid flat and a quarter 'were inverted, many of them rolling through a full 360 degrees'. In *The Official History*, sailor and parliamentarian Edward Heath is quoted as saying, 'It was the worst experience I have ever had. We were fighting massive seas. It was very frightening – the sort of thing you would never want to experience again.'

John Rousmaniere's *Fastnet Force 10* (1980) records the tragedy in much the same manner as Jon Krakauer's *Into Thin Air* (1997) documents the May 1996 Mount Everest disaster, when twelve climbers perished in the so-called 'Death Zone' above 25,000 feet. *Fastnet Force 10* is a tale of courage, daring and human tenacity in the face of awesome natural forces. It also raises questions about misunderstandings and miscalculations. The court of inquiry report, following the 1979 Fastnet race, stressed that the sea 'can be a deadly enemy'. Despite all of this, it should be noted that the 1979 Fastnet was not called off, and that Admiral's Cup participants continued to race and set new records.

References:

Jeffery, T., *The Champagne Mumm Admiral's Cup – The Official History* (London: Bloomsbury Publishing, 1994).

Further reading:

Bond, B., Clark, J., Morgan, A. and Pelly, D., *The Complete Book of Sailing* (London: Hamlyn Publishing, 1990), p. 164.

Rousmaniere, J., *Fastnet Force 10* (London: W. W. Norton, 1993).

Smith, C. F., 'Introduction', in B. Lubbock (ed.), *Sail: the Romance of the Clipper Ships* (London: Blue Peter Company, 1927), pp. ix-x.

Websites:

Fastnet – http://www.fastnet.org/

See also:

Admiral's Cup; Sailing

-John Crawford/Scott Crawford

Fell Running

While the Lake District is commonly believed to be the home of fell racing, the earliest reported event is in 1064 in Scotland. King Malcolm Canmore organized a race up Creag Choinnich, above Braemar, to select the best runner to take dispatches over the rough terrain. Although records were not kept until the mid-1800s, many Highland Games included hill racing, as did rural village sports and fairs in northern England. Several professional events were first held in the late 19th century, including the Grasmere Guides Race (1868), Ben Nevis Race (1899), the Rivington Pike Race (1893), and those at Lothersdale (1847), Kilnsey Crag and Coniston Gullies. The establishment of the Amateur Athletic Association (1880) meant that many events in the South Pennines were subsequently organized as amateur events.

Today, events are held all year, although most races take place in the summer months. Distances range from approximately 1.5 miles to over 40 miles and do not always have a formal course. As in orienteering, a compass and map can be used on more severe routes. Races are graded 'A' to 'C', with 'A' equalling the most climbing. The Three Peaks, inaugurated in 1955, is perhaps the best-known post-Second World War event. Further developments in the calendar occurred in the 1960s, which witnessed the resurgence of long-distance racing. The renowned Karrimor two-day event was established in 1968. There are championship races for all the home countries and, in addition, there is an annual World Trophy event, inaugurated by the Italians in 1985.

The Fell Runners Association (F.R.A.) was founded by fell runners on April 4th, 1970, and governs the sport. In addition, it organizes the British and English Championships. The English Championship consists of six races, two short (less than 6 miles), two medium and two long (over 12 miles). Four races, which must include one from each distance, are added together to work out the overall position of each runner. The British Championship is run along similar lines and in both competitions there are full junior, senior and veteran programmes. Although they participated unofficially before this, women's races have been organized by the F.R.A. since 1977, with the first championship held two years later.

References:

Fell Runners Association, *Welcome to Fell Running* (The Fell Runners Association information leaflet, [n.d.]).

Matthews, N., and Quinlan, D., *Fell and Hill Running* (Birmingham: British Athletic Federation, 1996).

Further reading:

Fell Runners Association, *1999 Handbook and Fixtures Calendar* (The Fell Runners Association, 1999).

Smith, B., *Stud Marks on the Summits: a History of Amateur Fell Racing, 1861-1982* (Preston: SKG Publications, c. 1985).

Websites:

The Fell Runners Association – http://www.ae401.dial.pipex.com/

See also:

Athletics; Road Running

-Lynne Duval

Fencing

Modern fencing has its roots in the ancient practice of swordsmanship, which was practised as essential preparation for warfare in practically all ancient civilizations. The ancient origins of fencing were confirmed following the discovery of an Egyptian fresco, dating from circa 1200 BC, which depicts a fencing bout. Modern day competitive fencing, however, began during the 19th century, taking the form of a bout between two contestants who use one of three weapons – a foil, an épée or a sabre.

During the Middle Ages, swords were heavy and cumbersome and were used as much to bludgeon an opponent as to fence. They also had to be held with two hands, making delicate swordplay impossible. However, following the invention of gunpowder, the role of swords in warfare changed, the heavy bludgeon-type sword giving way to lighter weapons. From this point onward can be traced the skilful art of fencing. Such skills were promoted by guilds, which were established during this period to teach fencing. Indeed, many of the strokes associated with modern fencing can be traced to this time.

The ability to fence skilfully was further enhanced following the development of the rapier in Italy during the 16th century. Prior to this, fencing bouts often resulted in the two opponents wrestling each other in an attempt to overcome their opponent by brute strength. The rapier, however, allowed for the emphasis to be placed upon skill not strength and wrestling was abandoned in favour of dextrous swordplay. However, the reign of the rapier was short lived, as changing fashions within the courts of European monarchs ushered in a smaller, lighter sword that looked less out of place with the lightweight clothing of silk and satins popular at the time. It was this sword which in effect laid the foundations for modern-day fencing techniques. Now, one-handed fencing became still more practical, which in turn allowed for the development of evermore complicated swordplay skills.

In England, the development of fencing also centred on the needs of the monarch and his court. During the reign of Edward I, fencing schools were places of brawling and duelling for the nobility. Edward became concerned that such debauchery would further undermine his unstable regime and for this reason he banned fencing and fencing schools within the city of London in 1285. Edward's decree remained in place until the reign of Henry VIII, with the result that English fencing did not keep apace of developments in Europe. Consequently, the traditional broadsword and buckler form of fencing remained in place until 1540, when Henry revoked the 1285 Statute. This allowed the Corporation of the Masters of Defence a monopoly to teach fencing, which in turn allowed the Masters of Defence to introduce the more skilful European style of fencing into England. Soon after the passing of the 1540 Act, lighter swords belatedly made their way into English fencing and revived what had been a decaying pastime. With the introduction of European techniques, English sword fencing was also free to abandon wrestling tricks and develop its own dextrous techniques, such as the lunge to strike an opponent.

Despite its long tradition, English fencing went into decline in the early 19th century. Some schools survived, however, most notably the London Fencing Club. The revival of fencing began in 1861, following the introduction of fencing into the curriculum of the Army School of Physical Training. The sport was further popularized by Captain Hutton, an acknowledged expert on ancient weapons, who was responsible for increasing awareness of fencing amongst the wider public. Increasing popularity led to the formation of the Amateur Fencing Association (A.F.A.) in 1902. Keen to trace its roots back to the Tudor monarchy, the A.F.A. asked Edward VII for permission to adopt the Tudor Rose as its emblem. This was duly granted and today British fencers compete with an English monarch's emblem on their costumes.

Modern fencing's three weapons, the foil, épée and sabre, were all introduced before the modern sport was established. Protective clothing is worn to minimize injury, and the rules of the sport are also designed with safety in mind. The foil, for example, has been modified to reduce its sharpness, while the blunt épée was introduced in the mid-19th century to encourage a freer style of fencing, more in keeping with fencing as it was during traditional duels. The sabre, used by the Hungarian cavalry in the 18th century, was modified during the 19th century by the Italians, making it a lighter and more suitable weapon for tournament fencing.

Fencing was included in the first modern Olympics Games in 1896. Although records demonstrate that women's fencing has been extant since the 18th century, it was 1924 before women were allowed to compete in an Olympic event. Then, the International Olympic Committee allowed a women's foil event to take place, but it was 1960 before women's teams were allowed to compete.

Given the speed of a fencing bout, the task of accurately recording scores has often proved difficult. Hence, the use of electrical scoring has been actively encouraged as technology has developed. Electrical scoring was introduced for the épée in 1936, the foil in 1955 and the sabre in 1992 (at the 1992 Olympic Games), thus allowing the arrival and judgement of hits to be registered by electrical apparatus.

Historically, skill and dexterity with the sword was an indication of manliness. Today, however, fencing is an Olympic sport for both sexes and is one of the few sports in which males and females compete on equal terms. It is also a major sport in disabled competitions and Britain has won many medals for fencing at the Paraplegic Games. Indeed, fencing is one of the few combat sports that can be practised from a wheelchair. During combat the wheelchair is clamped, thereby ensuring that the distance between the two opponents remains constant. This allows for an intensive bout requiring high levels of concentration, as contestants are always within reaching distance – hence, the slightest mistake can result in defeat. Combat rules for paraplegics are similar to the rules for able-bodied fencers, with additional rules applied only to cover complications arising from the participation of two wheelchair fencers.

References:

Arlott, J. (ed.), *Oxford Companion to Sports and Games* (London: Oxford University Press, 1976).
British Fencing Association leaflet

Websites:

The British Fencing Association – http://www.britishfencing.com/

-Ray Physick

Field Sports

Field Sports is the collective term used to describe the rural activities involving the pursuit and killing of wild animals and birds. There are two main branches – the hunting of wild animals using dogs; and the use of firearms to shoot birds and animals. Of the two, hunting with dogs has the longest history, dating back to the pre-mediaeval period when wealthy lords indulged in deer hunting on horseback using specialist deer-hounds. By the 18th century, the shortage of deer compelled huntsmen to pursue hares, and eventually foxes, which had previously been despised as vermin. The sport reached its heyday in the Midland shires during the mid-19th century, when the prevailing system of pastoral farming enabled long chases over hedges to take place. At this time, packs of dogs were usually owned by a single landowner and meets were held early in the morning. By the latter part of the century, mid-morning meetings prevailed whilst subscription packs funded by donations from members were commonplace. The agricultural depression of the late 19th century adversely affected hunting not only in terms of reducing the income of the hunt's patrons, the landed aristocracy, but also through the use of barbed wire for fencing, which made long chases more difficult. Hunting continued to play an important part in the rural economy of the 20th century by creating employment for a multitude of occupations.

The other main branch of the sport, involving the pursuit of animals and birds with firearms, takes a variety of forms. In the case of deer, this usually involves the stalking of the animals and the use of high velocity rifles to kill them. In the case of shotgun shooting, the activity entails the covert shooting of game-birds after lines of beaters have driven the quarry towards the stationary guns. Rough shooting, or walking-up, involves the use of dogs to flush out a variety of species for the guns. Legally prescribed close seasons (during which the killing of game is illegal) are designated by the government and shooters are encouraged to abide by a voluntary code of conduct.

All blood sports have historically been hotly debated. Supporters have consistently argued that it constitutes an integral and functional part of rural life. To their opponents, blood sports should be prohibited because of the suffering they impose on defenceless animals. Opposition in the late 1990s reached such an extent that the Labour government actually threatened to prohibit the hunting of wild animals with dogs altogether.

References:

Willock, C., *The ABC of Shooting* (London: André Duetsch, 1975).

See also:

Angling; Fox-hunting; Game Shooting

-John Martin

Films

In any overall assessment of sports movies it is essential to come to terms with the fact that films about sport play a minor, if not insignificant, role in the pantheon of cinema 'classics'. The American Film Institute's 1998 'Top 100 American movies of the last 100 years' (headed by *Citizen Kane*, *Casablanca* and *The Godfather*) contains only two sports movies – both on boxing – *Raging Bull* (no. 24) and *Rocky* (no. 78). This is not to say that athleticism is absent from the list. Marlon Brando's fighting persona in *On the Waterfront* (no. 8), the basketball game in *One Flew Over the Cuckoo's Nest* (no. 20), the inspiring Jerome Robbins choreography of the Jets and the Sharks in *West Side Story* (no. 41), the assorted sporting roles of Tom Hanks as table-tennis player and Alabama running back in *Forrest Gump* (no. 71), the breathtaking char-

iot race in *Ben-Hur* (no. 72) and Jimmy Cagney's gymnastic tap dancing in *Yankee Doodle Dandy* (no. 100), all serve as a reminder that sports and athletic activity have the potential to enrich cinema. Outside of the Top 100, British actress Elizabeth Taylor shot to fame after starring with Mickey Rooney in *National Velvet*. This film centred around her horse National Velvet, ridden by her co-star, winning the Grand National.

Britain's film history is in many respects different from that of Hollywood. While both countries have produced a whole host of sports films, the British tradition is one steeped in the tradition of treating sport as a 'serious' art form, even when, paradoxically, the topic has comedic qualities.

In 1981, director Hugh Hudson saw his *Chariots of Fire* win the Oscar for Best Picture. It also won Oscars for Best Score (Greek composer, Vangelis Papathanassiou), Best Costume Design (Milena Canonero) and Best Original Screenplay (Colin Welland). The true-life story of two British track athletes at the 1924 Olympics in Paris, Harold Abrahams (an English Jew) and Eric Liddell (a Scottish evangelical Presbyterian), succeeds wonderfully well because of an intelligently crafted, part-fact, part-fiction, story line, and a series of accomplished acting performances. Ian Holm's performance as the eccentric coach, Sam Mussabini, is extraordinary. His feisty manner, theatrical gestures and pointed phrases are a telling vignette on English class, culture, manners and mores. Not surprisingly, Holm won the 1981 British Academy Award for Best Supporting Actor. *Chariots of Fire* is the twelfth-ranked top-grossing sports movie (North American revenues only) of all time, with a take of $62,471,886.

The acme of British sports films is consistently held by critics to be Tony Richardson's *Loneliness of the Long Distance Runner* (1962) and Lindsay Anderson's *This Sporting Life* (1963). Nevertheless, while the stark black-and-white photography and the taut dialogue dispensed by Allan Sillitoe (*Loneliness*) and David Storey (*Life*) are memorably timeless, the pacing and the action sequences seem, today, to be hopelessly anti-

139

quated and artificial. More recent is *Champion* (1981), based on the life story of Bob Champion who overcame cancer to win the Grand National.

The film *Once a Jolly Swagman* (1949), however, demonstrates remarkable resilience. Buoyed up by superior acting performances from Dirk Bogarde, Bill Owen, Cyril Cusack, Thora Hird and Moira Lister, this rags-to-riches story is a nuanced picture of late-1940s motorcycle speedway racing, a boom sport in post-Second World War England.

As a vivid and compelling example of contemporary British sports cinema, the talented interplay of producer/director Jim Sheridan, writer Terry George and actor Daniel Day-Lewis deserves analysis. In the film *In the Name of the Father* (1993), sporting motifs are secondary but striking. The film's opening monologue – a soccer litany – acknowledges the magic of Manchester United's Georgie Best; the Gerry Conlon prison cell is adorned by a Benfica and European Cup Final pennant; and when the Conlons, father and son, realize that they were framed by the British police, the joint cry of metaphorical triumph is – 'they fouled the ball.'

Jim Sheridan's most recent work, *The Boxer* (1997), is another highly charged story of the Irish Troubles. Once again, Sheridan, George and Day-Lewis work together to try and make some sense out of a country's tortured past and present. Daniel Day-Lewis, playing a former I.R.A. member released from prison after fourteen years, gives up one violent life and takes up another. He founds a boxing club that will admit both Protestant and Catholic children. Barry McGuigan, the Irish former W.B.A. champion, served as the movie's technical consultant. *Newsweek's* David Ansen liked the 'explosive drama' of *The Boxer* but lamented its melodrama. In *Sports Illustrated*, Richard O'Brien wrote of 'a gritty, startlingly realistic fight film that avoids the usual Hollywood excesses'.

An intriguing athlete-as-actor character to explore, in terms of sports history, would be Tunbridge Wells-born Victor McLaglen (1886-1959). He was a boy soldier in the Boer War,

who emigrated to Canada and became a prize-fighter and then a vaudeville and circus performer. He fought Jack Johnson for the world boxing heavyweight championship (he lost after six rounds) and received a 1935 Oscar for his title role as Gypo Nolan in *The Informer*. The movie also earned director John Ford an Oscar.

References:

Ansen, D., 'Oh, Danny Boy', *Newsweek*, vol. CXXXI, no. 2 (12 January 1998), p. 61.

Barr, C., *All Our Yesterdays: 90 Years of British Cinema* (London: British Film Institute, 1986).

Murphy, R., *The British Cinema Book* (London: British Film Institute, 1998).

O'Brien, R., 'My Left Hook', *Sports Illustrated*, vol. 87, no. 26 (29 December 1997 - 5 January 1998), p. 24.

Pym, J., *Time Out Film Guide* (London: Penguin, 1998).

Zucker, M. Z. and Babich, L. J. (eds.), *Sports Films: a Complete Reference* (Jefferson, North Carolina: McFarland, 1987).

Further reading:

Crawford, S. A. G. M., 'Movies', in D. Levinson and K. Christensen (eds.), *Encyclopedia of World Sport* (Santa Barbara, California: ABC-CLIO, 1996), vol. II, pp. 663-667.

-Scott Crawford/Tony Rennick

Fishing (*see* Angling)

Fives

Fives is a British form of handball in which a ball is propelled against the walls of a special court using gloved hands. The name may be derived from the slang expression 'a bunch of fives' (meaning a fist), or possibly from an early version of the game where there were five players on each side. The game has also been known as hand-tennis and historically was often played against church buildings in England. There are links between Fives and the Irish and North American handball games and indeed, in recent years, British clubs have begun to establish ties with clubs in those countries.

There are two main forms of the game, Eton Fives and Rugby Fives. Eton Fives is played competitively as a doubles game, while Rugby Fives is played as both a singles and a doubles game. The rules for Eton and Rugby Fives were both published in 1931.

The Eton Fives court is modelled on part of Eton College's Chapel and is enclosed on three sides and open at the back. A small step splits the court into upper and lower sections, and sloping ledges run horizontally across the walls, one of which forms the 'line'. The first courts at Eton were built in 1840.

Rugby Fives uses a simpler court, more like a small squash court, and has a back wall. A variation of Rugby Fives, known as Winchester Fives, differs by the addition of a buttress (resembling the tambour of a real tennis court) on the left-hand wall.

Fives is a minority sport played by enthusiasts numbering perhaps 4,000 active adult players in the United Kingdom. A similar number play in schools. About forty schools are affiliated to the Eton Fives Association (the governing body of the Eton Fives variation), and there are a number of Old Boys' and university clubs. There are some well-established clubs overseas, such as the Zuoz Fives Club in Switzerland, and the game is also vigorously pursued in northern Nigeria. Like the Eton Fives Association, the Rugby Fives Association (the governing body of Rugby Fives, founded in 1927) has affiliations from over forty schools and thirty-two clubs, from Edinburgh to Tavistock, and there are also a number of clubs overseas, for example in South Africa and the United States.

The first match on record between schools was when one Eton pair played at Harrow in 1885 (F. Thomas and C. Barclay of Eton beat E. M. Butler and B. R. Warren of Harrow).

Although the image of Fives has been dominated by the well-known eponymous public schools, courts do exist at state schools, and in recent years many of these have been brought into full use. The advantages of economy of space and low playing costs (ball and gloves) make it an attractive sport for schools. Fives continues to develop in England and has started to attract interest from the wider community.

There are numerous championships, notably the (doubles) Eton Fives Kinnaird Cup and the Rugby Fives Singles Open championship (The Jesters' Cup). Other events include school, university, age-group, Winchester and (recently) ladies championships.

Exceptional players in recent times have included John Reynolds and Brian Matthews (Old Citizens, Kinnaird Cup) and Wayne Enstone (Manchester Y.M.C.A., Rugby Fives).

References:

Aberdare, Lord (ed.), *Rackets, Squash Rackets, Tennis, Fives and Badminton* (London: Seeley, Service & Co. Ltd, 1933).

Egerton, D. and Armitage, J., *Eton and Rugby Fives* (London: Seeley, Service & Co. Ltd, 1935).

Strutt, J., enlarged and updated by Cox, J. C., *The Sports and Pastimes of the People of England* (London: Methuen & Co., 1903).

See also:

Welsh Handball

Websites:

Eton Fives – http://www.etonfives.co.uk/

Rugby Fives – http://www.btinternet.com:81/~naustin/

-Peter M. B. Cahusac

Foundation for Sport and the Arts

The Foundation for Sport and the Arts was established in July 1991 by members of the Pool Promoters Association – Littlewoods, Vernons and Zetters. Assisted by the Government's agreed reduction in the rate of Pool Betting Duty, the Pool Promoters passed subscriptions to the Foundation of around £20 million per year in 1999.

The Foundation aims to encourage outstanding initiative, enterprise and creativity, with a portion of the funding directed towards the pursuit of excellence. The main target, however, is to encourage community participation and the 'grass roots'. The Trustees are free to make a number of adventurous decisions in order to give the younger generation an opportunity to show what it can do.

References:
Annual Reports, 1991 to date.

See also:
Sport Sponsorship

-Mrs G. Beynon

Fox-hunting

Fox-hunting is a blood sport conducted in the countryside. Horse-riders, along with a pack of trained hounds, chase foxes across country with the aim of the hounds catching and killing the fox. Until the 18th century, the main sport for the aristocracy was deer and hare hunting. However, during the 18th century fox-hunting was revolutionized following the development of sophisticated dog breeding by Hugo Meynell. The hounds bred by Meynell were able to keep track of a fox using the fox's scent. Moreover, the dogs were bred with speed and endurance in mind and this gave the sport a big boost. Alongside dog breeding techniques, the breeding of thoroughbred horses also took place, and this in turn impacted upon horse riding. Moreover, better breeding techniques coincided with the enclosure of common land, which prepared the way for big landowners and large tenants. This was the social foundation for the growth of fox-hunting. As the sport developed, it became regulated by the Master of Foxhounds Association.

By the middle of the 19th century, fox-hunting was the most popular of the hunting pastimes. However, the increasing cost associated with dog and horse breeding, as well as maintaining the animals, proved too costly for all but the wealthiest landowners. To overcome this enormous expense, a system of subscription packs was developed, in which a group of people joined together to maintain a pack of hounds. Wealthy people from the cities, many with recent links to the countryside, were keen subscribers to such packs, which usually consisted of fifteen to twenty matched pairs. This option became more viable as the railways improved accessibility to the countryside. The sport went into relative decline following the First World War, as the shooting of game birds became a popular and cheaper option.

Costumes reflect the aristocratic past of the hunt and costume colours are steeped in the hierarchical structures of aristocratic society. The general uniform for the master, huntsman and whippers-in consists of a scarlet coat, which is embellished with a white cravat, and a black velvet cap. More prestigious huntsmen can wear the hunt's individualized buttons on their coat and also wear a top hat. Ordinary followers of the hunt wear plain black coats and can wear top hats or bowlers. Noble families, who still participate in the hunt, use their ancestral colours, which are usually green, yellow or grey.

Whether fox-hunting will survive the 21st century is open to doubt, as in the year 2000 the Labour government was threatening to introduce, or at least support, a Parliamentary Bill to outlaw the sport. Meanwhile, the whippers-in sitting in the House of Lords have promised to oppose the Bill.

References:
Carr, R., *English Fox Hunting: a History* (London: Weidenfeld & Nicolson, 1976).

'Fox hunting', in *Britannica.com* (http://www.britannica.com/)

Holt, R., *Sport and the British: a Modern History* (Oxford: Clarendon, 1989).

Itzkowitz, D. C., *Peculiar Privilege. A Social History of English Fox Hunting* (Hassocks: Harvester, 1977).

See also:
Field Sports

-Ray Physick

142

Gaelic Football

Gaelic football is Ireland's most popular team sport. It has been organized under the auspices of the Gaelic Athletic Association (G.A.A.) since 1884. It is played in Northern Ireland and the Irish Republic, and remains popular with members of the Irish community living in Britain.

The earliest records of the game date from the 1670s, when a ball game that allowed catching and kicking was popular. Prior to the Irish famine of the 1840s, a game similar to Gaelic football was universally popular, and it appears that areas such as East Munster had developed a game with a clear set of rules. However, the effects of the famine, and the popularity of the imported English games of Rugby, Soccer and Cricket, severely dented the development of Gaelic football.

In 1884, the G.A.A. was formed, specifically to promote Irish sports and pastimes. The first rules of Gaelic football were published at the beginning of 1885 and, although refined since that date, mark the arrival of the modern game. The G.A.A. played an important role in the political as well as sporting sphere. Irish nationalists were fighting to be free from British rule, and the playing of national games such as Gaelic football was important. By playing Gaelic football, Irish men were able to reject English sports, embrace Irish culture and

also be physically prepared to fight for Ireland on the battlefield.

The game itself is contested between two teams of fifteen players each. The players are allowed to catch and carry the ball, or alternatively they can kick it. The goals at either end of the pitch are similar to Rugby posts, but with the bottom section netted. Teams are awarded three points for getting the ball into the net, and one point if the ball is kicked over the crossbar.

The major competition, the All-Ireland series, is contested by teams from each of the four historical Irish provinces (Ulster, Munster, Leinster and Connacht), and is played during the summer. The finals are held in September and the winner is awarded the Sam Maguire Cup. The National Football League, the secondary competition, runs through the winter, and is based around county and club sides.

Gaelic football has always been popular in Britain, especially amongst Irish immigrants and their descendants. The first official clubs that were affiliated to the G.A.A. were founded in London and Manchester in 1895. London has always remained the main focus of the G.A.A. in mainland Britain, and competes as a County in the All-Ireland series. The current headquarters are in Ruislip, although there are other grounds across Britain, most notably in Birmingham, Liverpool and Glasgow.

The various club and county sides of Northern Ireland continue, as they always have, to play in the various Gaelic football competitions organized by the G.A.A., as part of a 32 County organization that transcends the border between north and south.

Gaelic football is currently the fastest growing women's sport in Ireland. The Ladies' Football Association was set up in 1974. The games are organized on the same basis as the men's equivalent, and the finals are similarly held at Croke Park, the home of Gaelic Football.

References:

de Búrca, M., *The G.A.A. A History of the Gaelic Athletic Association* (Dublin: Cumann Lúthchleas Gael, 1980).

Prior, I., *The History of Gaelic Games* (Belfast: Appletree Press, 1997).

Further reading:

Bradley, J. M., *Sport, Culture, Politics and Scottish Society: Irish Immigrants and the Gaelic Athletic Association* (Edinburgh: John Donald, 1998).

Cumann Lúthchleas Gael, *A Century of Service* (Dublin: Cumann Lúthchleas Gael, 1984).

Websites:

The Gaelic Athletic Association – http://www.gaa.ie/

-Mike Cronin

Gambling

People have always been inclined to gamble, on a variety of uncertain events. Today, gambling is usually associated with betting (principally on horse-racing but also on many other sporting and non-sporting events), the football pools, gaming (bingo and casino games) and lotteries. Historically, gambling has always been popular in Britain, although throughout the 19th century it became increasingly subject to restriction. In more recent years, overt gambling has become both socially and politically acceptable. Horse-racing was a popular betting medium well before the end of the 18th cen-

A thousand clerks check coupons in one of Littlewoods' six pools buildings, 1954 (Hulton Getty Picture Collection)

tury and gradually a cohort of bookmakers, offering odds on all runners in a race, emerged early in the 19th century. Acts of Parliament put an end to cash betting offices in 1853 and to 'common' gaming houses (casinos) in 1854. Denied legal access to gambling venues other than on bona fide racecourses, ordinary people took to betting on the street (or in pubs and the workplace). This too was banned in 1906. The Street Betting Act, which outlawed any cash betting other than on a racecourse, was class discriminatory, as the well-to-do were able to bet on credit with respectable bookmakers. Bookmakers operated legally on-course or by offering credit betting, or frequently illegally as 'street bookies'. Casinos were not legal, however.

Paradoxically, the inter-war years brought an expansion of popular gambling opportunities. Football pools were developed in the 1920s, the most famous company, Littlewoods, being founded by John Moores in Liverpool in 1923. It was soon followed by Vernons (set up by Vernon Sangster) in 1925, also in Liverpool. These two companies came to be the largest of the many hundreds that were operating in the 1930s.

Greyhound racing, on enclosed tracks with an electric hare, began in 1926 at Belle Vue, Manchester. Within a year, sixty-two companies were operating tracks in towns throughout the country. Greyhound racing subsequently grew to become the second most popular spectator sport after football, almost exclusively as a betting medium. Also in the late 1920s, the totalizator, known as the Tote, began as an alternative to bookmakers for betting on horse-races. The Tote was a pool betting scheme, following examples in France and New Zealand, specifically designed to provide some revenue for racing by making deductions from the pool before paying out winnings. In contrast to many other countries, however, this form of betting never proved as popular with punters as taking known odds with bookmakers. (Greyhound racetracks also operated their own totalizators, which had no connection with the horse-racing Tote.)

The principle of making such a deduction from betting turnover to help support sport was extended from 1960 with the introduction of the betting levy – a deduction taken from bookmakers' turnover. This marked a turning-point in popular betting for it accompanied the legalization of cash betting shops and an end to the discredited Street Betting Act. Bookmakers were now able to offer legal off-course betting – a commercial opportunity that in the longer term allowed a few large firms to dominate the market, especially the 'Big Four' of Ladbrokes, Hills, Corals and Mecca Bookmakers (although these were reduced to three through amalgamation and take-over in 1989). The Tote also entered the off-course betting market, effectively as a publicly owned bookmaker. The shops owned by these few companies accounted for most off-course betting.

The 1960s were thus a watershed in gambling law and practice. As well as betting shops, bingo clubs and casinos were also permitted, for a few years with little control before the Gaming Act of 1968 limited numbers and restricted play to bona fide members. By this time, Britain had become one of the largest gambling markets in Europe and London, with around twenty casinos, had become a major gaming centre. Further legal relaxation in the 1990s allowed casinos to open in more locations throughout the country. A recent development is spread betting, in which punters gamble whether bookmakers' estimates of winning margins, number of free kicks and other quantifiable aspects of sport are too high or too low – the amount of loss or gain depends on the degree of error not just the stake.

Not surprisingly, the government welcomed the opportunity for taxation presented by a burgeoning gambling market. A 10 per cent tax on football pools and greyhound track on-course totalizators was introduced in 1948. The rates on pools increased markedly in later years. In 1966, a general betting duty was introduced to take a share of the money staked with book-makers and the Tote. Similarly, duty was charged on bingo and casino gaming. In addition to such taxes were various forms of transfer or quasi-tax. The betting levy helped fund horse-racing; similarly, a levy was deducted from football pools to help meet the cost of football ground improvements. In 1991, the pools companies took the initiative to set up the Foundation for Sport and the Arts. This, of course, was not mere altruism but rather an attempt to stave off the next great step in mass gambling, a National Lottery, which they correctly saw as threatening direct competition.

After long political resistance to such an idea the government introduced a National Lottery in 1994, to raise money for 'good causes' including extra funding for the Sports Council and Arts Council. Receipts from the lottery quickly became a staple form of income for these bodies. The 12 per cent tax on the lottery levied by government soon exceeded other gambling taxation receipts. The popularity of the lottery confirms a widespread interest in gambling, though it has captured a new market as well as eating into established ones. It is also a politically desirable form of tax – or quasi-tax – for public expenditure on 'good causes' because it is paid both voluntarily and with enthusiasm. Curiously, many players do not regard the lottery as gambling proper. The real importance of the lottery in raising public expenditure and the continuing liberalization – 'deregulation' in the jargon – of other gambling media suggests that mass gambling is here to stay. It is both socially acceptable and politically necessary.

References:

Chinn, C., *Better Betting with a Decent Feller: Bookmaking, Betting and the British Working Class, 1750-1990* (London: Harvester Wheatsheaf, 1991).

Clapson, M., *A Bit of a Flutter: Popular Gambling and English Society, c. 1823-1961* (Manchester: Manchester University Press, 1992).

Dixon, D., *From Prohibition to Regulation: Bookmaking, Anti-gambling and the Law* (Oxford: Clarendon Press, 1991).

Further reading:

Dixon, D., 'Class Law, the Street Betting Act of 1906', *International Journal of the Sociology of Law*, vol. 8 (1980), pp. 101-128.

Munting, R., *An Economic and Social History of Gambling in Britain and the USA* (Manchester: Manchester University Press, 1996).

Websites:

The National Lottery –
http://www.nationallottery.co.uk/

See also:

Foundation for Sport and the Arts

-Roger Munting

Game Laws

Game laws are concerned with the legal rights and controls that exist with respect to a variety of animals. There is no overall definition of game; rather it has been defined by a number of Acts of Parliament. For example, the Game Act 1831 included hares, pheasants, partridges and grouse. Deer were added for the purposes of the Game Licences Act 1860, whilst the phrase 'ground game' refers to hares and rabbits. Wild animals are not considered to be goods or chattels and accordingly there are no absolute property rights in living wild animals. However, a landowner or occupier has certain rights over game whilst it is alive on the land and absolute rights if it is dead. Such rights are referred to as Game Rights. Generally, such rights are bound with the ownership or possession of land and may be passed with occupation of the land or may be reserved even though there is a new occupier of the land. Thus, a landowner may grant a lease to another person to occupy the land but reserve the 'sporting rights' for himself. If the sporting rights are not reserved they will pass on to the tenant. A tenant will, provided the lease is after 1880, always have the right to kill the ground game. The rights to kill the game will be determined by the agreement between the landlord and tenant but will also be restricted by any of the protective legislation that applies to certain classes of wild animals.

See also:

Field Sports

-Steve Greenfield/Guy Osborn

Game Shooting

In the early decades of the 19th century, the shooting of game birds was a high status leisure activity, restricted by law to the landowning classes. Game birds were protected by a succession of game laws that imposed draconian sentences on those caught poaching. Gamekeepers sometimes used spring-guns attached to trip wires and mantraps to deter poachers. Specially trained dogs or pointers were used to locate the quarry but the flintlock muzzle-loading guns of the era were ill-suited for rapid firing or even shooting flying birds.

Improvements in firearm technology following the invention of the breech-loader with self-priming cartridges, the choke bore and smokeless powder revolutionized the sport. These technological changes pre-empted *battue* shooting in the late Victorian and Edwardian periods, in which grouse, partridges or pheasants were driven in military fashion by a line of beaters towards waiting guns in their camouflaged butts (or shooting stands). Each sportsman had an assistant to reload his guns and a gun dog handler who was responsible for retrieving the birds.

During the heyday of formalized game shooting, some of the country's most celebrated pheasant and partridge shoots were located on the Brecklands of Norfolk and Suffolk. Here, the light sandy soils were used more as game reserves than for conventional farming. Large bags were the order of the day and great estates vied with each other to kill the most birds, the details of which were recorded for posterity in meticulously kept game books. In order to ensure high densities of gamebirds, farming on these estates was entirely subsidiary to shooting and geared towards maintaining abundant nesting sites and a diversity of crops such as roots to provide essential cover for partridges in the autumn and early winter. Preservation measures involved the ruthless culling of birds of prey and other animals, which were believed to attack gamebirds. Up to the First World War, the grey partridge was the premier sporting game bird in Britain.

Conventional game shooting declined during the early part of the 20th century, partly because of rising costs and partly due to the break-up of the large estates. The number of gamekeepers declined rapidly as an indirect result of the two world wars. Population levels of partridges and grouse plummeted following the post-war revolution in farming practices. These changes ensured the ascendancy of the pheasant, whose population was able to remain relatively static because of the dramatic increase in the artificial rearing and release each summer of captive-bred poults. Driven game shooting survived as an expensive leisure activity for the select few. The 1980s witnessed a revival in the popularity of traditional *battue* shooting for pheasants, with its emphasis on maximizing the number of birds killed. It was a short-lived phenomenon, quickly supplanted by a return to more modest bags of high, fast-flying birds providing testing shots.

In the 20th century, game shooting continued in the guise of 'rough shooting', or the 'walking up' of the quarry in fields, woods and hedgerows. Quarry included gamebirds, hares, rabbits, pigeons and several other species. Throughout the period, game continued to be protected by legally prescribed close seasons and, more recently, by a series of advisory codes drawn up by shooting and conservation organizations.

References:

Brander, M., *A Concise Guide to Game Shooting* (London: The Sportsman Press, 1986).

147

McKelvie, C., *A Future for Game?* (London: George Allen & Unwin, 1985).

Munsche, P. B., *Gentlemen and Poachers: the English Game Laws, 1671-1831* (Cambridge: Cambridge University Press, 1981).

Further reading:

Howkins, A., 'Economic Crime and Class Law: Poaching and the Game Laws 1830-1880', in S. Burman and B. Harrell Bond (eds.), *The Imposition of Law* (New York: Academic Press, 1979).

See also:

Target Shooting; Wild Pigeon Shooting

-John Martin

Gay Sport

Gay culture in sport has existed since antiquity. In classical Greece, neither male nor female homosexual behaviour was considered unusual or discriminated against, provided that it occurred by mutual consent. Indeed, in ancient Greece, there was a clear connection between manliness, homosexuality and hero worship.

Following the June 1969 'Stonewall Revolt' in New York, during which American gays and lesbians vigourously defended their right to assemble in private, many U.S. athletes came out and revealed their gay or lesbian orientation. Although such openness at the élite level has not occurred in Britain, many openly gay teams and societies have emerged in recent years, such as Foothold (a Northern Irish gay outdoor group), the Kings Cross Steelers Rugby Football Club and the Dynamo Dykes (a lesbian volleyball club). There is also a branch of the Frontrunners Club in London (Front Runners was the first gay and lesbian sports club to join the Amateur Athletic Union of North America in 1980).

A major international gay and lesbian sporting event is the Gay Games, which were first organized by Dr Tom Waddell, a San Francisco gay activist. The Gay Games were modelled on the modern Olympics, and at first they were called the Gay Olympic Games. However, the United States Olympic Committee, as sole owner of the rights to the name 'Olympic' in the United States, objected and so the event became known as simply the Gay Games.

The first Gay Games were held in San Francisco in 1982, and over eight days, 1,350 athletes from twelve countries took part in fourteen events. There were also 600 gay volunteers and judges. The Gay Games II, in August 1986, also lasted eight days and was again held in San Francisco (the city of San Francisco actually subsidized the games). This time there were 3,500 participants (40 per cent of them women) from nineteen countries. The number of events was increased to nineteen. In 1989, the Federation of Gay Games was formed as a permanent body. Great Britain is represented on this body by the British Gay and Lesbian Sports Federation. The most recent games, the Gay Games V, were held in August 1998 in Amsterdam with 12,500 participants in the sports and 2,500 more in cultural events drawn from all five continents. The Gay Games VI have been awarded to Sydney for the year 2002, presenting the interesting possibility that Olympic cities in the future may continue to host the Gay Games using their athletic facilities. Meanwhile, more and more international sports federations of gays and lesbians are being founded, such as the International Association of Gay and Lesbian Martial Artists.

Gay sport has had a considerable influence in Europe. From the very beginning, British and other European gays participated in the United States, came home and often started their own gay sports clubs, although in many cases sports were just one activity of a general gay club. In 1992, the first Gay Eurogames, which were modelled on the Gay Games, were held in The Hague. The 1999 Eurogames, which were supposed to have been staged in Manchester, did not receive enough local support and were thus cancelled. One dilemma for the organizers of future Eurogames is whether

148

to limit the competition to the sporting élite, who would have to first qualify in national competition, or whether to maintain the Eurogames as a major sports-for-all event.

References:

Griffin, P., 'Homophobia in Women's Sports. The Fear that Divides Us', in G. L. Cohen (ed.), *Women in Sport: Issues and Controversies* (London: Sage, 1993), pp. 193-203.

Krüger, A., 'The Homosexual and Homoerotic in Sport', in J. Riordan and A. Krüger (eds.), *The International Politics of Sport in the Twentieth Century* (London: Spon, 1999), pp. 191-216.

Pronger, B., *The Arena of Masculinity: Sports, Homosexuality and the Meaning of Sex* (New York: St. Martin's, 1996).

Further reading:

Guttmann, A., *The Erotic in Sports* (New York: Columbia University Press, c. 1996).

Lenskyj, H., 'Sports Literature: Lesbian', in C. J. Summers (ed.), *The Gay and Lesbian Literary Heritage* (New York: Henry Holt, 1995), pp. 678-681.

Websites:

The Federation of Gay Games – http://www.gaygames.org/

-Arnd Krüger

Gender

On Saturday, July 10th, 1999, the women's football world cup final was played before a sell-out 92,000 capacity crowd in Pasadena, in the United States. The three-week tournament attracted more than 650,000 fans, and brought unprecedented publicity for women's sport. Unfortunately, no British team qualified for the tournament. Unlike women's soccer in the United States, netball and women's hockey in Australia, or women's tennis in France and the United States, women's sport still remains the poor relation of British sport, and as such British sportswomen have achieved comparatively little success on the world stage. There are many reasons to account for this gender imbalance and, as such, gender is an important issue in present-day sport.

In the early 19th century, the balance of power between men and women in society, and consequently in sport, was desperately uneven. The Victorian period gave rise to modern sports, and the British boys' public schools provided the setting for their codification and organization. Victorian images of masculinity and character building were paramount, and these ideals became fundamental to the future development of sports both in Britain and the world.

In her book, *Sporting Females*, Jennifer Hargreaves extensively examines critical issues in the history and sociology of women's sports in Britain and concludes that 19th-century attitudes to women's participation in sports were consolidated by attitudes to women that were pervasive throughout society. Martin Polley argues that such attitudes and indeed 'norms' had been established during 19th-century debates over medicine and anatomy. In 1887, the Chairman of the British Medical Association proposed that, 'in the interest of social progress, national efficiency and the progressive improvement of the human race, women should be denied education and other activities which would cause constitutional overstrain and inability to produce healthy offspring'. There were vigorous protests against such claims, but the view of the 'physically limited' female was institutionalized in the scientific and medical establishments. The result was that women were pushed into certain sports deemed appropriately feminine and, although team games developed in a limited way in parallel to Rugby and football at boys' schools, these typically involved less direct physical contact between players than the male team games. Thus, netball, hockey and lacrosse became the main sports played by women in Britain, and attempts to establish women's football and Rugby teams were resisted by the male authorities in these sports.

Developments in female education during the last third of the 19th century were probably the greatest factor behind the increasing legitimization of more active forms of sports and exercise for women. Increasing numbers of physicians were adopting the view that gentle forms of physical exercise would aid women's health and their ability to bear healthy children. The development of education for women was, in fact, the prerequisite for the development of sport for women. The majority of women's sports, in their institutionalized forms, developed in the education system and in the specialist colleges of physical education. Several historians note that a number of public boarding schools for girls modelled themselves on the boys' public schools. The original prospectus for Roedean (1885) prioritized physical education. Indeed, games-playing provided the setting for girls to emulate certain physical and moral characteristics previously ascribed exclusively to males. However, as Hargreaves observes, 'since the girls were not educated with the boys and they did not play games with them, the male sporting role was not directly challenged'. It should be noted that, although in 1887 Madame Österberg, founder of Dartford College and a leading exponent of physical education, introduced the Swedish system of physical training into the London elementary girl schools, for the bulk of the 19th century, there was no form of physical activity for working-class girls.

Thanks to Österberg and trained physical educators, middle-class girls experienced Swedish gymnastics as part of a wider range of activities. Similarly, competitive women's sports were associated with the expansion of the physical education profession and the 1920s witnessed the acceleration of competitive games for women. This period was characterized by a growing acceptance of women's physicality, largely as a result of the role played by women during the First World War, when they undertook work previously seen as men's work and consequently challenged stereotypes about women's physical capabilities. In 1926, the British Women's Cricket Association was developed, as was the All England Netball Association. Netball, unlike other team sports, was not a 'male' sport copied by women. Women's football, on the other hand, was severely curtailed when the Football Association banned women playing football on league grounds in 1921, despite the fact that women's matches regularly drew crowds of over 50,000 people.

Several developments since the mid-1960s have led to the emergence of women's sport on a significant scale. Firstly, there has been increased provision of leisure activities and trends towards individual health and fitness. For example, Kenneth H. Cooper's 1968 book, *Aerobics*, caught the attention of the public and made aerobics a household word and, following the publication of *Aerobics for Women* in 1972, jogging became seen as an activity beneficial to both sexes for cardiovascular health and weight loss. In 1984, the Women's Sports Foundation was developed. It is the only organization in the UK that is solely committed to improving and promoting opportunities for women and girls in sport at all levels. Nevertheless, as late as 1993 and despite the growth of women's sport, a Sports Council survey found that women's sport received, on average, between 0.5 and 5 per cent of the newspaper space given over to men's sport. In the same year, the Sports Council called for newspaper editors to 'eliminate sexist references and photographs in the coverage of women's sport'.

Women's sport still remains the poor relation of British sport, but times are changing and multimillion-dollar sportswear firms are now portraying active, dynamic, sports-playing females in their commercials. Nike, for instance, recently produced a television advertisement of very athletic, highly competitive female basketball players accompanied by the slogan, 'Just Do It!'

References:

Fletcher, S. *Women First: the Female Tradition in English Physical Education, 1880-1980* (London: Athlone Press, 1984).

Hargreaves, J., *Sporting Females: Critical Issues in the History and Sociology of Women's Sports* (London: Routledge, 1994).

Polley, M., *Moving the Goalposts; A History of Sport and Society Since 1945* (London: Routledge, 1998).

See also:

Education – Teacher Training; Politics and Governance – The Suffragette Movement and Sport; Women's Sports Foundation

-Nicky Fossey

Geography

Compared with other sport-related disciplines, the geography of sport is rather undeveloped in Britain. It possesses neither a national association nor a specialized journal. There are, nevertheless, a small number of geographers working in this potentially important sub-discipline whose numbers are slowly growing. In addition to these, there are scholars from other disciplines whose work is implicitly geographical and some geographers who, while not regarding themselves as specialists in the geography of sports, nonetheless make insightful allusions to it as part of their broader work.

There are three broad areas that arguably best typify a British approach to the geography of sport. These focus on (i) 'regional variations', (ii) 'landscapes of sport', and (iii) a 'welfare geography' approach. Each of these will now be discussed in turn.

Regional variations and sports

A characteristic of British sport is the uneven distribution of a variety of sporting attributes. Such variations can be mapped and geographical patterns can be identified. For example, in the mid-1980s it was established that considerable regional variations existed in the 'production' (i.e. the birthplaces) of Football League

players. Although Greater London was the major source of talent in absolute terms (accounting for 13.4 per cent of the total), it was the North that, in relative terms, confirmed itself as the traditional heartland of English football culture. It produced over twice as many professional footballers than would be expected given its population. At the county level, Tyne and Wear supplied over two-and-a-half times as many as would be expected, whereas Greater London's figure was at just above the national average. Similar studies for other sports reveal equally marked variations. For example, South Wales provided the largest number of professional boxers per capita, the county of South Glamorgan supplying over four times the national per capita average.

It would be possible to recognize a number of other geographical variations that exist, for example, in the provision of facilities for sports. The provision of sports centres varies dramatically from place to place. Inner cities have a substantial deficit while the more remote rural areas also suffer from under-provision.

Landscapes of sports

Sport has changed the landscape of Britain in a variety of ways. As the sites on which sport takes place have become more specialized, sport has become enclosed. Whereas pre-modern sports took place on multifunctional sites such as commons and streets, modern sport is frequently contained within sites that are used solely for sport. The football stadium can be interpreted as a triumph of sport over nature and over space. The application of 'turf science' makes the football field, cricket pitch and golf course examples of the blending of nature and artifice. Consider the concrete surrounds of the stadium and it can clearly be seen that the modern sports venue is one where architecture and horticulture triumph over the natural landscape. Golf illustrates the way in which sport can colonize a very wide variety of natural landscapes. In Scotland, the early courses were usually built on natural linksland. Since then, they

151

have progressively utilized a wide variety of landforms and can no longer be solely recognized by the underlying soil types.

In other activities, such as athletics and swimming, venues have witnessed a change from specialized facilities to multifunctional resources. The synthetic running track permits uses other than athletics; the rectangular swimming pool which satisfied the serious swimmer is now often but part of a 'water world' where more fun-oriented pursuits can take place.

Sports landscapes also illustrate the way in which sports segment landscapes. They are increasingly separate from other land uses and are themselves highly compartmentalized. The football stadium illustrates this tendency. Originally, the football field was unenclosed. The inscribing of a white line around the pitch initially separated spectator and players. Since then, football grounds have witnessed a progressive process of segmentation until today spectators each have their own seat, separated from each other in a fixed spot. This is an extreme example of the control of spectators at sports venues, though the need for crowd restraint is not unknown in other sports.

Welfare geographies

The impact of a sports event can be felt well beyond the specific site at which it is held. In Britain, these spillover effects have been mainly associated in the popular psyche with football stadiums. This is in large part the result of many football stadiums being located among land uses which are considered incompatible with an activity which generates a variety of negative spillover effects. Residents living around football grounds have been found to suffer from nuisances such as traffic congestion, parking, crowds, noise and hooliganism to a greater extent than those residents living further way. It is perhaps significant that research into this problem has consistently found that residents living near stadiums rarely refer to hooliganism and vandalism as the most frequently perceived nuisance.

At the same time, it should be recognized that football and other sports may also generate positive spillover effects on local communities. Many of these may be of a 'psychic' nature (for example, a local 'feelgood' condition following a major sporting success), but economic gains to some local businesses through additional income generation on match days should not be ignored. The new, post-Hillsborough, generation of relocated football grounds should, in theory, be more sympathetically sited and, as a result, reduce the number of negative effects on local communities. It cannot be said, however, that all new stadiums necessarily satisfy this ideal.

References:

Bale, J., *Sport and Place: a Geography of Sport in England, Wales and Scotland* (London: Hurst, 1981).

Bale, J., *Sport, Space and the City* (London: Routledge, 1993).

Patmore, A., *Recreation and Resources: Leisure Patterns and Leisure Places* (Oxford: Blackwell, 1983).

Price, R., *Scotland's Golf Courses* (Aberdeen: Aberdeen University Press, 1989).

Further reading:

Bale, J., *Sports Geography* (London: Spon, 1989).

Bale, J., *Landscapes of Modern Sport* (London: Leicester University Press, 1995).

Hague, E. and John M., 'Geographical Memory and Urban Identity in Scotland: Raith Rovers F. C. and Kirkaldy', *Geography*, vol. 83, no. 2 (1998), pp. 105-116.

Mason, C. and Moncrieff, A., 'The Effect of Relocation on the Externality Fields of Football Stadia: the Case of St. Jonstone F. C.', *Scottish Geographical Magazine*, vol. 109 no. 2 (1993), pp. 96-105.

-John Bale

Gillette Cup

Falling attendances at County Championship games during the 1950s prompted the cricketing authorities to consider the introduction of a one-day competition. After a pilot scheme in 1962, the seventeen first-class counties competed in a sixty-five overs 'Knock–out Competition' during

1963, and Sussex duly became the first winners of what became known as the Gillette Cup until 1980, and subsequently the NatWest Trophy.

The full house at the first Lord's final in 1963 confirmed that the new competition had succeeded in capturing public imagination, and the competition, which since 1966 has been staged over sixty overs, has become the highlight of the one-day calendar. 1964 saw the introduction of Minor Counties into the first round, with five teams playing first-class opposition. However, it was not until 1973 that any beat their Championship counterparts, with Durham recording a five-wicket win over Yorkshire.

Further changes occurred in 1983 when thirty-two teams participated in the competition, including thirteen Minor Counties plus Ireland and Scotland in the first round. In 1993, they were joined by Wales Minor Counties, followed by Holland in 1995. Yet more changes were due to be made from 1999 onwards, with fifty-over contests involving County Board teams to be held in the first two rounds, after which most of the first-class counties would enter in the third round.

Highlights of the competition so far include Lancashire's hat trick of Cup final wins in 1970, 1971 and 1972 (all under the inspirational captaincy of Jack Bond), plus Alvin Kallicharran's 206 for Warwickshire against Oxfordshire at Edgbaston in 1984, and Michael Holding's 8-21 for Derbyshire against Sussex at Hove in 1988.

References:

Isaacs, V. H. and R., *The Gillette Cup / NatWest Trophy Record Book 1963-1996* (Nottingham: Association of Cricket Statisticians and Historians, 1997).

Further reading:

Lemmon, D., *One Day Cricket* (London: Century Benham, 1988).

Laker, J., *One-Day Cricket* (London: Batsford, 1977).

See also:

Cricket

-Andrew Hignell

Glenmore Lodge

Glenmore Lodge is the Scottish Sports Council's National Outdoor Training Centre, delivering outdoor adventure activities and courses. As a centre of excellence it offers some of the best training facilities and staff in the United Kingdom.

The Lodge was established by the Central Council of Physical Recreation in 1948 and is situated at the foot of the Cairngorm mountains, near Aviemore, Scotland.

The Lodge has been operated by the Scottish Sports Council since 1972. It offers a wide range of mountain- and water-based courses, including mountaineering, climbing, skiing and canoeing. The priority is to train those who wish to instruct, lead or coach others in a range of outdoor activities. Many of the courses lead to professional and national governing body awards.

The Lodge is home to the Scottish Mountain Leader Training Board, British Association of Ski Instructors, The Uphill Ski Club, National Orienteering Centre, British Biathlon Union Olympic Centre, the Scottish Avalanche Information Service and a Sport and Exercise Medicine Centre.

Websites:

Glenmore Lodge – http://www.glenmorelodge.org.uk/

See also:

Plas Y Brenin

-Tim Walker

Gliding Sports

Hang-gliding and paragliding are sports in which pilots use aerodynamics and thermals to keep their craft airborne. Humans have been fascinated with the flight of birds for thousands of years. Hence, man often attempted to mimic bird flight, attempts that usually led to disaster for the person concerned. Attempts at flying were greatly advanced when the Chinese discovered that fixed wings were far superior for gliding than the traditionally used flexible flapping wings, at least as far as humans were concerned. However, even with this advance humans could still only glide if they had access to a hilltop from which they could launch themselves. Furthermore, pilots had no real control over their descent and could only glide to the bottom of the hill, albeit with greater safety.

Towards the end of the 19th century and at the beginning of the 20th century, the first manned gliders, as opposed to wings fixed on a person's arms, appeared. Otto Lilienthal designed the first such glider in 1893, while the Wright brothers were the first to power gliders with the aid of an engine. Between these innovations and the 1960s, however, hang-gliding all but disappeared. The revival of hang-gliding emerged out of experiments by Francis Rogallo, a scientist at the American space agency, N.A.S.A. N.A.S.A.'s aim was to land its spacecraft on earth without the aid of a parachute. These experiments eventually bore fruit with the development of the space shuttle. Rogallo developed a triangular design, thereby creating a foil that enabled the craft to be in control of its descent. Having been developed from space technology, modern hang-gliders are very strong.

Since the 1970s, hang-gliding has become a well-established sport internationally. European championships were inaugurated in 1974 and were followed by the first world championships in 1975. Technological development and hang-gliding have gone hand-in-hand, especially since the development of mechanically powered hang-gliders. These have been admitted into hang-gliding competitions since 1979, thus serving to increase the popularity of hang-gliding yet further.

Paragliding emerged in the late 1960s following the development of square parachutes. A paraglider uses forward speed to inflate an aerofoil, which in turn generates lift. The pilot also uses thermals, which allow him or her to raise and lower the craft, thus facilitating a controlled descent.

Hang-gliding and paragliding are both dependent upon certain weather conditions so pilots have to have a good understanding of meteorology, which enables them to understand and locate rising air currents. Another essential requirement for pilots is an understanding of aerodynamics.

Hang-gliding and paragliding in Britain are governed and promoted by the British Hang Gliding and Paragliding Association (B.H.P.A.). Based in Leicester, the B.H.P.A. licences flying schools and coaching clubs in order to ensure that rigorous flying safety standards are applied and maintained. The Association also organizes competitive flying for the more experienced pilot and is responsible for selecting the highly successful national team.

References:

Sollom, D. and Cook, M., *Paragliding: From Beginner to Cross Country* (Marlborough: The Crowood Press, 1998).

Tomlinson, J., *The Ultimate Encyclopaedia of Extreme Sports* (London: Carlton, 1996).

The British Hang Gliding and Paragliding Association Website – http://www.bhpa.co.uk/

Websites:

British Hang Gliding and Paragliding Association Website – http://www.bhpa.co.uk/

See also:

Parachuting

-Ray Physick

Globalization

The term globalization is used to indicate that in the late 20th century, global developments have made it meaningful to talk of a global economy and, to a lesser extent, a global culture. In sport, the term globalization is usually used to explain the fact that sport has become a global phenomenon. As elsewhere in the world, the effects of this globalization process can be clearly seen in British sport.

The process of globalization has been brought about by a variety of economic and cultural developments which might include: the existence of a world satellite information system; the emergence of global patterns of consumption and consumerism; the cultivation of more cosmopolitan lifestyles; the emergence of global sports competitions such as the Olympic Games, the Football World Cup, the Rugby World Cup, and the World Athletic Championships; the decline in the sovereignty of nation-states; the recognition of a world-wide ecological crisis; and world health problems, amongst others. The relationship between sport and globalization can be thought of in at least two ways – first, the globalization of sport itself; and second, the contribution that sport makes to other processes of globalization.

Making sport available to viewers around the world is a critical step in the globalization of sport. For example, many British football teams have popular fan bases in other parts of the world. Manchester United and Glasgow Celtic Football Clubs, for instance, are increasingly viewed as global clubs, while Newcastle United Football Club have a popular fan base in Thailand. Internationally, U.S. baseball games can now be viewed on television in 205 countries around the world.

The contribution that sport makes to other processes of globalization can be seen if one considers the sports company Nike's recent ten-year deal with the Brazilian national soccer team, worth 200 million dollars: Nike clearly views soccer as a universal commercial language that will unite consumers globally. Indeed, it has been estimated that by the year 2000, the football industry will be worth more than 250 billion dollars annually world-wide.

In *The Global Sports Arena: Athletic Talent Migration in an Interdependent World*, Bale and Maguire outline five different aspects of the relationship between sport and globalization – sporting *ethnoscapes*, sporting *technoscapes*, sporting *financescapes*, sporting *mediascapes* and sporting *ideoscapes*.

'Sporting *ethnoscapes*' refers to the international movement of sports workers and migrant labourers across continents. This category includes both the professional and non-professional sports person that moves from sports club to sports club, whether by transfer or in search of work. The term 'ethnoscape' is used to depict the international movement of people such as tourists, exiles, migrants and guestworkers across the globe.

'Sporting *technoscapes*' refers to the transfer of machinery, equipment or agencies between countries. Examples of this could include objective cultural artefacts produced for sporting consumption, such as Nike or Adidas sports goods, which are available in the majority of countries throughout the world; the building of golf courses on different continents, which involves the transfer of technology and sports knowledge; the movement of squash courts around the world in order to provide sporting spectacles; and the global presence in every continent of the major sporting agencies.

'Sporting *financescapes*' refers to the global flow of money brought about through international sport. A sports-specific flow of money is brought about through the international movement of players, prize-money and sporting endorsements. Certain British football clubs, such as Manchester United, Glasgow Celtic and Glasgow Rangers, have their market values displayed on the stock exchanges of the world. Sport itself provides a global arena for the flow of international finances.

'Sporting *mediascapes*' refers to the sports-media complex which transports sport across the globe, determines the television timing of major sporting events and provides a constant flow of information linked to films, television, newspapers, radios and computer screens. It produces and destroys sporting heroes and heroines depending upon their level of performance. British sport is literally mediated by the various forms of media and is packaged and sold around the world. The recent

155

proposed take-over by BSkyB of Manchester United Football Club illustrates the desirability to the media of sports involvement.

'Sporting *ideoscapes*' refers to the flow of ideas and philosophies often associated or expressed through sport. Many different bodies of knowledge or ideas struggle to represent different groups and ideologies. Examples of these sporting ideoscapes might include professionalism, amateurism, sport for all, fair play, equal sporting opportunities and liberal or critical notions of the values of sport.

It must be recognized that there is no common consensus in the debate about the globalization of sport. The export of British sport overseas during the Victorian period, for example, was a form of global cultural expansion, and can be viewed in two different ways. On the one hand it involved the export of British culture, but on the other hand it might also be viewed as cultural imperialism or the diffusion of Western sport at the expense of indigenous forms of sport. To what extent was imperialism a form of globalization?

Finally, the antithesis of global sport is local sport and any discussion of global sport ought to acknowledge the relationship between the global and the local, and Western sport and indigenous non-western forms of sport. It should also consider the spread of American, Japanese or Gaelic forms of sport. These are all issues closely connected to the globalization of sport.

References:

Bale, J. and Maguire, J., *The Global Sports Arena: Athletic Talent Migration in an Interdependent World* (London: Frank Cass, 1994).

Maguire, J., *Global Sport: Identities, Societies, Civilizations* (Cambridge: Polity Press, 1999).

-Grant Jarvie

Golf

Origins and Development

The earliest known written reference to golf dates from 1457, but remarkably little is known about the game from that date until the late 17th century. There is also much evidence of golf being played on an informal basis in the early decades of the 18th century, however, there are no surviving rules or records of golfing societies before 1744, when the first Challenge for the Silver Club was played by what later became the Honourable Company of Edinburgh Golfers. A similar competition began at St Andrews in 1754.

Organized golf grew very slowly in Britain. By 1800, there were only about seven active clubs. This had increased to about fifteen by 1819 and eighteen by 1831. There were still only about thirty-five active clubs in 1859 but ten years later, this had increased to about fifty-four, of which eight were in England. By 1879, this number had grown to 111 clubs with 22 in England, and then the great golf boom began in the 1880s. In 1885, there were about 161 clubs and by 1895 this had grown to 959. Almost another thousand were founded in the following ten years.

The earliest known type of ball was leather-cased and stuffed with feathers. The durability of the ball depended on the thickness of the leather or hide covering. The feather ball was replaced by one made from gutta-percha in about 1848. In turn, the solid gutta-percha ball was superseded by the wound rubber-cored ball, which first came to Britain in late 1901.

The change in ball type led to changes in club design. During the feather ball era, iron clubs were large and unwieldy implements, which were only used as a last resort to hit the ball out of very rough ground. There was always a danger that the heavy iron head would split the leather-cased ball. The gutta-percha ball was much harder than its predecessor and was solid. The necks of the existing wooden clubs needed to be strengthened and the shape of the club head was altered from the 'long-nosed' type to a more rounded type. The gutta-percha ball was much more durable and iron clubs came into general use for shots off the fairway, replacing the array of 'spoons'.

There were no rules about the form and make of golf clubs until 1909 and ball specification until 1920. Indeed, there was no overall governing body for the game until 1897. That year, the Royal and Ancient Golf Club, which was viewed as the de facto ruling body but not the *de jure* one, responded to external pressure and formed the Rules of Golf Committee. Its responsibilities have grown from that date.

The Royal and Ancient (R.&A.) was not the first royal golf club. That honour went to the Perth Golfing Society in 1833, six months before the Venerable Society of St Andrews Golfers became the R.&A.

Until 1857, in the amateur game most golfers competed only in competitions for club team medals. The first Grand National Tournament held that year at St Andrews was a team competition between clubs. The 1858 Grand National was the first individual amateur championship and this was held again in 1859 and then discontinued. The idea of an amateur championship was then revived by the Royal Liverpool Golf Club in 1885.

The earliest known professional tournament was played at St Andrews in 1819 and there were recorded tournaments there in the 1830s and 1840s. The Open Championship was started by the Prestwick Golf Club in 1860.

The tremendous growth of golf at the end of the 19th century vastly increased the potential employment opportunities for professionals. What soon became the Professional Golfers' Association (P.G.A.) was formed in 1901. As well as looking after the welfare of its members, the P.G.A. organized a growing number of tournaments, based on its regional sections. The *News of the World* tournament began in 1903 and was second in importance only to the Open until the 1960s.

Although there are various references to ladies playing golf dating back to Mary, Queen of Scots, the first ladies' clubs were formed in the 1860s, starting in St Andrews in 1867. References to them playing with a set of clubs on short courses were first seen in the 1870s. The number of ladies' clubs had grown to thirty by 1890 and there were eighteen courses

listed as specifically for ladies. By 1914, there were over 450 ladies' clubs, of which more than 10 per cent had courses of their own. The Ladies' Golf Union was founded in 1893 and the first Ladies' Amateur Championship was played that same year.

The Walker Cup, played between men's amateur teams from Great Britain and the United States, was first played in 1922. This competition had been preceded by an informal tournament at Hoylake in 1921, in which the United States had defeated Great Britain. The Curtis Cup, played between ladies' amateur teams from Great Britain and the United States, was first competed for in 1932. The first Ryder Cup match between professionals from Great Britain and America was played in 1927. In 1979, team selection was expanded to include players from Europe. The equivalent competition for ladies, the Solheim Cup, was first played in 1990.

In 1946, there were thirteen tournaments in Britain and Europe, in which competitors played for about £23,500. The number of tournaments and their prize funds gradually increased until, in 1972, the European Tour was formed with twenty-seven events and a prize fund of £442,000. The number and wealth of tournaments have continued to rise ever more rapidly – by 1997 there were thirty-four events for a total purse of close to £29 million.

Governance and Administration

Golf in Britain is organized at various levels. The Royal and Ancient Golf Club of St Andrews (the R.&A.) is the governing authority for the game throughout the world, except in the United States and Canada. The R.&A. is a private club, with a membership heavily endowed with past and present golf administrators who bring their experience to the club's various functions. The Rules of Golf Committee and the United States Golf Association, with representation from golfing bodies at home and abroad, constantly review the game's laws and make decisions on their interpretation. The Open and Amateur Championships and other national and international events played in Britain are administered by the R.&A.'s Championship Committee. Profits from the Open Championship are used to subsidize the other championships and internationals administered by the R.&A., but the bulk of funds are ploughed back into golf at all levels, to improve access to golf for present and future golfers.

The Golf Foundation is the national body for the development of junior golf. It provides coaching services, runs a Merit Award Scheme and provides funding to promising youngsters. In addition, it runs team and individual competitions.

There are national Home Unions for England, Scotland, Ireland and Wales. These bodies work to further amateur golf within their countries, to administer handicapping and to run national, international and other competitions. They are constituted in slightly different ways, but are associated with regional unions, clubs, societies and associations within their countries and recognize the R.&A. as their ruling authority.

The Ladies' Golf Union (L.G.U.) works to uphold the rules of the game, as published by the R.&A., to advance and safeguard the interests of women's golf and to maintain, regulate and enforce the L.G.U. system of handicapping. In addition, the L.G.U. also administers various international events, championships and competitions. The L.G.U. in Britain is made up of constituent Home Unions and their affiliated ladies' societies, schools and clubs. Also affiliated are ladies' golf unions and clubs from around the world.

The Professional Golfers' Association (P.G.A.) promotes interest in the game of golf, protects and advances the mutual and trade interests of its membership, arranges and holds meetings and tournaments for its members and assists them in obtaining employment. To become a club professional and a member, three years must be spent in registra-

tion before qualifying through the P.G.A. Training School.

The P.G.A. European Tour organizes a series of annual events for which players must originally qualify and then maintain the minimum standards set by the Tournament Committee. A Ranking or Order of Merit is kept, based on winnings in recognized tournaments, with a winner being declared at the end of the playing year.

The European Ladies Professional Golf Association (E.L.P.G.A.) Tour bears similar responsibilities in ladies' professional golf. An amateur wishing to join the E.L.P.G.A. Tour must be eighteen and have a handicap of one or less. Within her first eight rounds in tournaments, the player must maintain certain standards to retain her place.

Leaders and Personalities

Many individuals have made their mark in the history of golf. Allan Robertson was the greatest golfer of the 1840s and 1850s. He died in 1858, two years before the Open Championship was first played. Tom Morris Senior won this four times and, as a clubmaker and Keeper of the Green at St Andrews, he became a revered figure, known as the 'Grand Old Man of Golf'.

His son, Tom Morris Junior, won the Open Championship in 1868, 1869 and 1870, thus gaining possession of the original trophy, the Challenge Belt. There was no championship in 1871 and he won again in 1872. He might have achieved much more, but he died on Christmas Day, 1875, at the age of twenty-four.

In 1894, the Open Championship was won by J. H. Taylor, heralding an era that came to be dominated by three great players, namely Taylor, Harry Vardon and James Braid. Called the 'Triumvirate', between them they were to win sixteen Open Championships in twenty-one years. Harry Vardon remains the only player to have won the Open six times. All three were influential in the early development of the Professional Golfer's Association.

Two great women golfers who dominated the early decades of the 20th century were Cecil Leitch and Joyce Wethered.

Bernard Darwin was a good player, but above all a writer. Twice a semi-finalist in the Amateur Championship and a last minute substitute in the 1922 Walker Cup, Darwin brought a fresh look to golf journalism with his knowledge of, and enthusiasm for, the game. He wrote for *The Times* and *Country Life*, as well as publishing many books on the subject.

Henry Cotton won the Open in 1934, 1937 and 1948. Cotton, from a middle-class background, played an important part in increasing the status of the professional and was also involved in teaching, writing and course architecture. In 1987, just before his death, he heard that he was to be awarded a knighthood for his services to golf.

Scottish golfer Colin Montgomerie in action. Montgomerie led the European Order of Merit between 1993 and 1997 (Action Images)

Michael Bonallack won the Amateur Championship five times between 1961 and 1970. Active in golf administration since the 1970s, he became the Secretary of the Royal and Ancient Golf Club in 1983. In 1998, he became the second person to be awarded a knighthood for services to golf.

Tony Jacklin won the Open Championship in 1969 and the U.S. Open in the following year. Victories in the Open for Sandy Lyle in 1985 and Nick Faldo in 1987, 1990 and 1992 marked a resurgence in British golf. Lyle became the first Briton to win the U.S. Masters, in 1988. Colin Montgomerie led the European Order of Merit for a record five consecutive years between 1993 and 1997.

Laura Davies has been a prominent figure in ladies' professional golf since the 1980s. She topped the Order of Merit four times, in 1985, 1986, 1992 and 1996. In 1996, Laura Davies became the first woman golfer to win £1 million world-wide in one season.

Famous Venues

Golf courses can be divided into two broad classes, famous examples of both being used for tournaments today. Links courses only are used for the Open Championship, golf's oldest and premier tournament. These courses are based on rough open ground by the sea, naturally undulating, treeless and beset by winds. The most prestigious of all is the Old Course, St Andrews. This course has been played over since before 1552, its main features being crafted by nature. Like all links courses, thick gorse bushes, hidden bunkers and, above all, subtle undulations make the course deceptively difficult. These, combined with the strength and variability of the wind, call for skill and adaptability. Winning at St Andrews needs a combination of local knowledge and accuracy to avoid hazards such as Hell Bunker, the Road Bunker and the Valley of Sin.

Muirfield, home of the Honourable Company of Edinburgh Golfers, is laid out with the clockwise front nine encircling the anticlockwise back nine, adding extra difficulty to the challenge of the wind, and set with cruelly deep bunkers. Other venues for the Open Championship are Royal St Georges on the Kent coast, a driver's course known for its blind shots, and Royal Troon, with its infamous 8th hole, the short but punishing Postage Stamp. Royal Lytham and St Annes, an oasis of links golf surrounded by modern housing, Carnoustie, known for its tricky water hazards, Royal Birkdale, played between sand-dunes moulded for spectator access, and Turnberry, reconstructed from an R.A.F. base after World War II, all add their unique challenges to the Open Championship.

Several links courses, including Prestwick, the originator of the Open, have been dropped from the Open Championship rota largely because they cannot cope with the volume of visitors and traffic generated by the Championship. Today, Prestwick's route between and over sand hills still provides sufficient challenge to host the Amateur Championship and other major amateur events. The 9-hole course at Musselburgh, which staged the Open Championship six times between 1874 and 1889, was replaced by Muirfield in 1892. Hoylake, home of the Royal Liverpool Golf Club and the first Amateur Championship, held its first Open in 1897 and its last in 1967. Hoylake staged its eighteenth Amateur Championship in 2000 (jointly with Wallasey).

Inland courses are far more prolific than links courses and have a very different character. They range from heathland or cliff-side to manicured parkland courses, but generally fairways are sweeping and trees provide definition and challenge on the courses. Sunningdale (Old Course) is a heathland course characterized by raised sloping greens and well-placed bunkers, while Wentworth (West Course), the home of the World Match Play Championship, is a long and challenging course nicknamed 'Burma Road'. Gleneagles (King's Course),

once home of the Scottish Open, offers excellent, interesting golf in a beautiful setting, while The Belfry (Brabazon Course), home of the P.G.A. and three times the venue for the Ryder Cup, is an American-style course with lakes, trees and long carries.

Famous Competitions

The intensely competitive game of golf today can be traced back to fairly humble beginnings. The first organized 'national' tournaments were held in the 1850s. The first Grand National Tournament was held in 1857 at St Andrews and was a team event between eleven clubs. In 1858 and 1859, further Grand National Tournaments were held, but the format was changed to make them individual events. No more were held after 1859, because it was felt that they drew interest away from the more important club medals. In 1860, the first formal competition for professionals was staged at Prestwick. There were eight entrants, all 'known and respected caddies'. The following year, the competition was made 'open to all the world'. This was to become the Open Championship.

The next amateur national event was held in 1885, when the Royal Liverpool Golf Club organized a Grand Golf Tournament over their links at Hoylake. A rule regarding amateur status was drafted and the format used was match-play, with any ties proceeding to the next round to play again. The winner was A. F. Macfie. The following year, a format for playing the Amateur Championship in a rota between St Andrews, Hoylake and Prestwick was established, with a revised definition of an amateur. Twenty-four clubs subscribed to the trophy, which is still played for today. In 1922, the 1885 tournament was retrospectively recognized as the first Amateur Championship.

In 1903, the first *News of the World* Match Play Tournament was played. Limited to P.G.A. members, this was second in status only to the Open until the 1960s. It was last played in 1979. From 1911, the Sphere and Tatler

Cups were also contested. Both of these events were backed up by regional qualifying events. These events provided the foundations for today's P.G.A. European Tour, which was officially set up in 1971.

The first British Ladies Amateur Championship was played in 1893, but it was not until the mid-1970s that professional tournament golf for ladies in Britain developed. In 1975, the Ladies Professional Golf Association Championship was inaugurated and the first Women's British Open Championship took place in 1976.

International team events have always held a particular appeal. The Walker Cup was inaugurated in 1922 between amateurs from Britain and the United States. When first played in 1927, the Ryder Cup was contested by teams of professionals from Britain and the United States, but from 1979 European players were made eligible for the once all-British team. The Curtis Cup, established in 1932, was initially meant to be contested by 'women golfers of many lands', but it, too, was to be an event between Britain and the United States. It was not until 1990 that a comparable ladies' professional event was established – the Solheim Cup, played between Europe and the United States.

Memorable Events

Throughout the history of competitive golf there have been many memorable moments. In 1839, a sweepstake tournament was held in St Andrews and won by Allan Robertson. In 1842, a similar event was held, but as reported in *The Fifeshire Journal*, 'Allan Robertson was prohibited by his brethren from competing for these stakes on account of his superior play, it being their impression that they would have no chance in any contest in which Allan took part'. Tom Morris was the victor.

A photograph survives of Robert Chambers, the winner of the 1858 Grand National Tournament at St Andrews, on the final green. This event was the first amateur championship.

In 1905, an international foursomes match for the stake of £200 was held over four greens, played cumulatively over 144 holes. These were St Andrews, Troon, St Anne's and Deal. Harry Vardon and J. H. Taylor represented England and James Braid and Sandy Herd represented Scotland. This event received unprecedented coverage in the journals of the time. Scotland led after the first leg at St Andrews, but England won thirteen up with twelve to play. An estimated 26,000 spectators witnessed the four matches, 10,000 of these being at St Andrews.

Two great shots are commemorated by plaques on Open Championship courses. At Lytham, on the penultimate hole of the 1926 Open, Bobby Jones hit a shot from sand on to the green, 175 yards away. Jones went on to win his first Open. In the final round of the 1961 Championship, Arnold Palmer played a 6-iron shot from heavy rough on the 15th to reach the green. He made his par and went on to win the Championship by one stroke.

In the modern era of golf, certain moments are remembered by so many because of the medium of television. Stirring moments from the Open Championship include Tony Jacklin's win in 1969, which he followed with the U.S. Open the following year, the play-off between Doug Sanders and Jack Nicklaus in 1970, and the epic battle between Jack Nicklaus and Tom Watson at Turnberry in 1977.

In 1970, Michael Bonallack won his third consecutive Amateur Championship, his fifth in all. This run of three Championships is unparalleled and only John Ball Junior, Champion eight times, has won more.

In 1969, the Ryder Cup ended with a gesture of supreme sportsmanship. On the final green of the final match, Jack Nicklaus holed out for four. His opponent, Tony Jacklin, had to hole his putt to draw the Cup. Nicklaus lifted Jacklin's marker and offered his hand. An abiding image of European victory at the 1985 Ryder Cup is of Sam Torrance on the final green with his hands aloft.

Victory in the 1986 Curtis Cup for Great Britain and Ireland was a landmark in the history of ladies' amateur golf. Following a long period of American domination, this resounding victory, the first on American soil, marked a new era in which the British team could match and better the Americans.

Terms and Concepts

There are a number of fundamental concepts that make up the game of golf. It is defined as playing a ball from the teeing ground into the hole by a stroke or successive strokes in accordance with the rules. There are two basic methods of play. In match play, the game is played by holes, a hole being won by the side that holes its ball in the fewer strokes. With stroke play, the competitor who plays the stipulated round or rounds in the fewest strokes is the winner. Variations on these formats allow players to participate either individually or in partnership.

Stroke play is the norm for professional competition and scores tend to be measured against par, where par is the standard scratch score for each hole. The following terms describe position against par: an 'albatross' is three under par, an 'eagle' two under, a 'birdie' one under and a 'bogey' is one over par.

'Bogey' also refers to a method of play where the competitor competes against a fixed score for each hole, reckoning as in match play. The competitor with the most holes won is the winner. In Stableford, play points are allocated in relation to a fixed score at each hole, with the most points winning the match.

Other terms with meanings peculiar to golf and defined in the Rules are 'casual water', 'hazard', 'honour', 'loose impediments' and 'rub of the green'. The playing of the game itself has its own extensive vocabulary – terms include 'to drive', 'pitch' or 'putt' the ball.

References:

Alliss, P., *The Who's Who of Golf* (London: Orbis Publishing, 1983).

Browning, R., *A History of Golf: the Royal and Ancient Game* (London: Dent, 1955).

Cousins, G., *Golf in Britain: a Social History from the Beginnings to the Present Day* (London: Routledge & Kegan Paul, 1975).

Davies, P., *The Historical Dictionary of Golfing Terms: From 1500 to the Present* (London: Robson Books Ltd, 1993).

Geddes, O. M., *A Swing Through Time: Golf in Scotland 1457-1743* (Edinburgh: HMSO, 1992).

Johnston, A. J. and Johnston J. F., *The Chronicles of Golf: 1457 to 1857* (Cleveland: International Merchandising Corporation, 1998).

Laidlaw, R. (ed.), *The Royal and Ancient Golfer's Handbook 1998* (London: Macmillan Press, 1998).

Lewis, P. N., *The Dawn of Professional Golf: the Genesis of the European Tour, 1894-1914* (New Ridley: Hobbs & McEwan, 1995).

Lewis, P. N., Clark, E. R. and Grieve, F. C., *A Round of History at the British Golf Museum* (St Andrews: Royal and Ancient Golf Club Trust, 1998).

The Royal and Ancient Golf Club of St Andrews, *Rules of Golf* (St Andrews: Royal and Ancient Golf Club of St Andrews and the United States Golf Association, 1995).

Viney, L., *The Royal and Ancient Book of Golf Records* (London: Macmillan Press, 1991).

Ward-Thomas, P., *The World Atlas of Golf* (London: Mitchell Beazley, 1976).

Websites:

The Ladies Golf Union – http://www.lgu.co.uk/
The Professional Golfers' Association – http://www.pga.org.uk/
The Royal and Ancient Golf Club – http://www.randa.org/

See also:

Belfry (The); Open Championship; St Andrews

-Elinor Clarke/Peter Lewis

Goodwood

'Glorious Goodwood', on the Sussex Downs 4 miles north of Chichester, is one of the world's most striking flat horse-racing courses, its looped track ascending and descending about a natural amphitheatre. The seat of the Dukes of Richmond since 1697, private racing began in 1801 and a public three-day event followed the next year. After 1813, the main meeting moved to the end of July (or the beginning of August) where it remains to this day.

The fifth Duke (1791-1860), assisted by Lord George Bentinck (1802-1848), oversaw the alteration and improvement of the course (1829), construction of a new grandstand (1830), and a steady increase in prize money. Four main races were established by 1840, the Gold Cup (1812), Goodwood Stakes (1823), Goodwood Cup (1840) and Stewards' Cup (1840). Meetings were unusually well organized, Bentinck instituting improvements in racecourse management subsequently adopted elsewhere, for example flag starts, public saddling of runners, and starting places decided by lot.

By the 1890s, the July raceweek – described by King Edward VII in 1906 as 'a garden party with racing tacked on' – was central to the London social season and its immediate postwar popularity continues. Its highlight is now the Sussex Stakes, a mile-long race for horses of three years and over. Attendance in 1999 totalled 98,000 for the July festival and 221,000 for all twenty racing days from May to September. A £4 million development scheme, due for completion by the start of the 2001 season, will further improve facilities on this Grade I course.

References:

Barker, J. (ed.), *A Day at the Races: a Guide to Britain's Major Racecourses* (Basingstoke: A.A. Publishing, 1997).

Gill, J., *Racecourses of Great Britain* (London: Barrie & Jenkins, 1975).

Tyrrel, J., *Racecourses on the Flat* (Marlborough: Crowood Press, 1989).

Websites:

Goodwood Racecourse – http://www.goodwood.co.uk/

See also:

Horse-racing

-Mark Hathaway

Grand National

The Grand National steeplechase, run over 4.5 miles at Liverpool's Aintree course, is considered to be Britain's toughest horse-race. Although the name was not used until 1847, the 1839 Grand Liverpool Steeplechase at Aintree has always been regarded as the first Grand National. In that 1839 race, Captain Martin William Becher gained racing immortality. His mount, Conrad, fell at a specially constructed jump in which a brook had been dammed. Becher landed in the water and crouched in safety until the rest of the horses had passed by. Such was his celebrity that the fence at which he fell thereafter became known as Becher's Brook.

Other famous incidents include Devon Loch, the Queen Mother's horse, falling in 1956 for no apparent reason when in the clear only 50 yards from the winning post. Eleven years later, Foinavon, a 100-1 outsider, won the race when almost every other horse became involved in a pile-up at the twenty-third fence. Then came the emotional win of Bob Champion on Aldaniti in 1981. Both horse and rider were making comebacks, Aldaniti from a breakdown and Champion after major treatment for cancer.

The 1990s witnessed two major incidents. In 1993, a false start was not recalled and, after six horses completed the two circuits, the race was declared void. In 1997, an I.R.A. bomb threat forced the abandonment of the meeting, though it was rerun on the following Monday with the winner being ridden by the appropriately named Tony Dobbin.

References:

Green, R., *The History of the Grand National: a Race Apart* (London: Hodder & Stoughton, 1993).

Further reading:

Payne, N. and Hart, D., *Everyone Must Leave: the Day They Stopped the National* (Edinburgh: Mainstream, 1998).

Websites:

Aintree – http://www.aintree.co.uk/

See also:

Aintree; Horse-racing

-Wray Vamplew

Grasmere Sports

The Grasmere Sports, although founded in 1865, had their origins partly in legendary ancient Viking and Saxon contests at Dunmail Raise, and partly in traditions of localized Lakeland sports, which occurred at annual rush-bearing services (when parishioners carried rushes to church to strew upon the floor) and at sheep fairs. Cumberland and Westmorland freestyle wrestling (C.W.F.W.), with its tradition of awarding leather belts to victors, can be dated from an edict in the 15th century forbidding wrestling on Sundays, but which allowed attendance at church wearing the belt. C.W.F.W. reached its pinnacle at Flan How and Windermere Ferry and created a legend in the champion, Thomas Longmire, in 1825. With the exception of some gentry sponsorship of C.W.F.W. at their manors, these competitions were organized and run locally.

Grasmere Sports are unique in Lakeland because from 1870 they enjoyed gentry support from the Sandys and Machell families. The programme of events drew on the same traditions of C.W.F.W. and leaping contests, but added a new Grasmere creation, namely the guides' race, which evolved from guiding Victorian tourists over the fells.

The other main attraction was hound trailing, which replaced the outlawed cockfighting in the 1830s, and which had evolved from Lakeland copper and iron ore mining culture. In hound trailing, hounds race over the fells following an aniseed trail; betting is normative. Grasmere reflected the intertwining of business and gentry interests to promote a spectacle second to none on the social calendar. Under the patronage of the Earls of Lonsdale, the Games attracted the London social élite, and the *Westmorland Gazette* has recorded these events for posterity. The Games were modified constantly to enhance their visitor appeal. In 1870, the day was changed from a Saturday to a Thursday; in 1904, the field was changed; and in 1919, the guides' race was altered to provide a better view of the runners. Prizes grew as attendances increased, but so did incentives to cheat. Grasmere became an important stage for both social display and for the making of champions. Rationalization of the sports led to the formation of wrestling (1900) and hound-trail (1906) organizations to police their sports. In 1930, gambling on the course was evident.

The effect of the Sports has been to provide a model of sporting respectability which has permeated Lakeland sport culture generally, aided the hotel industry, and created legendary champions such as fell racing's J. Greenop (1876-1881) and E. Dalzell (1905-1910), pole leaping's Tom Ray (1882-1887) and G. Steadman, fourteen times a winner of the C.W.F.W. (heavyweight) (1872-1900). The Games are still run today. In 1998, the day was moved to a Sunday for the first time. Sky Television records the Games.

References:

Machell, H. W., *Some Records of the Annual Grasmere Sports* (Carlisle: Charles Thurnam & Sons, 1911).

Miller, M., *See the Conquering Hero Comes: an Illustrated History of the Grasmere Sports Senior Guide's Race* (Kendal: Bland, 1973).

North, C., 'Professor of Wrestling', *Wrestliana* (1811-1815; 1823-1848).

Rawnsley, H. D., *Months at the Lakes* (Glasgow: James MacLehose & Sons, 1906)

Wilson, J., *Reminiscences in the Life of Thomas Longmire* (circa 1857).

Woods, R., *Grasmere's Giants of Today* (Liss: Spur Publications Co., 1975).

Wrestling, (Edinburgh: Blackwood, 1823).

-Dr Bernard F. Booth,
with the assistance of Dr Chris Laing

Grass Track Racing

Bicycle grass track racing is a summer sport, typically associated with athletics events at town, village and factory fêtes and sports days, agricultural and flower shows, miners' galas, and Highland games. Races take place on oval circuits marked temporarily on sports fields, running tracks, or on dedicated bicycle grass tracks that have banked bends. The courses vary in length from approximately 250 metres to 400 metres, and are marked on the inner perimeter with angled pegs. Grass track meetings include scratch and handicap competitions, with sprint, elimination (devil take the hindmost), points, and pursuit races. The effort required to ride at speed on grass usually restricts distance events to a maximum of 8 kilometres. The bicycles used are similar to those ridden on velodromes, having a single fixed gear, a high bottom bracket and short cranks to give maximum inside pedal clearance when cornering. Lightweight tyres with a suitable tread pattern are required.

Grass track racing continues to form a significant part of open and league track events organized under British Cycling Federation (B.C.F.) rules. Currently, British amateur championships for men are held at distances of 400 metres, 800 metres and 8 kilometres, and for women at 800 metres. The British Schools Cycling Association and a number of national and regional cycling organizations affiliated to the B.C.F. also hold championship events. Bicycle grass track racing at many Highland games is now administered by the Scottish Professional Cycling Association. Infamously, professional grass track events have attracted amateur riders to compete incognito.

Websites:

The British Cycling Federation –
http://www.bcf.uk.com/

Nigel Cameron

Greyhound Racing

Modern greyhound racing has its origins in coursing. The first recorded attempt at racing greyhounds on a track was made at Hendon in 1876, but this experiment did not develop. The sport emerged in its recognizable modern form, featuring circular or oval tracks, an artificial hare as quarry and on-course betting, in the United States during the 1920s. In 1926, it was introduced to Britain by an American, Charles Munn, in association with Major Lyne-Dixon, a key figure in coursing, and Brigadier-General Critchley. They launched the Greyhound Racing Association, and held the first British meeting at Manchester's Belle Vue. The sport was successful in cities and towns throughout the U.K. – by the end of 1927, there were forty tracks operating. The sport was particularly attractive to predominantly male working-class audiences, for whom the urban locations of the tracks and the evening times of the meetings were accessible, and to patrons and owners from various social backgrounds. Betting has always been a key ingredient of greyhound racing, both through on-course bookmakers and the totalizator, first introduced in 1930.

In common with many other sports, greyhound racing enjoyed its highest attendances just after the Second World War – for example, there were 34 million paying spectators in 1946. The sport experienced a decline from the early 1960s, when the 1960 Betting and Gaming Act permitted off-course cash betting, although sponsorship, limited television coverage and the later abolition of on-course betting tax have partially offset this decline.

References:

Genders, R., *The NGRC Book of Greyhound Racing: a History of the Sport* (London: Pelham, 1990. Rev. ed.).

Greyhounds racing in the William Hill Grand National at Wimbledon Stadium, March 1999. (Action Images)

Further reading:

Baker, N., 'Going to the Dogs: Hostility to Greyhound Racing in Britain: Puritanism, Socialism and Pragmatism', *Journal of Sport History*, vol. 22, no. 2 (1996), pp. 97-119.

Thompson, L., *The Dogs: a Personal History of Greyhound Racing* (London: Chatto & Windus, 1994).

See also:

Coursing; Gambling

-Martin Polley

Gridiron Football

One of the sporting tourist attractions of visiting London, England, in the 1990s is the paradox of seeing a huge store owned and operated by the (American) National Football League (N.F.L.). The notion of Green Bay Packer sweat tops rubbing shoulders with Arsenal or Manchester United strips on the London underground is an intriguing cultural mix. In actual fact, American football, or gridiron, developed something of a following in the 1980s when for several years it was featured on Channel 4 television on Sunday evenings.

The N.F.L. set up a World League for American football in Western Europe. This group of professional teams played in the spring and early summer, thus avoiding any scheduling conflict with the N.F.L. In 1998, the World League was renamed the N.F.L. Europe League. Its World Bowl (official championship match) was held on June 14th, 1998. Alton Byrd, the general manager of the now disbanded England Monarchs, was optimistic that this new league could attract other sports fans, saying 'It is tough because [American football] is not a sport that's indigenous to European sports fans. It's soccer, soccer, more soccer, a bit more soccer, and then a little of everything else. I think we fit firmly in that bit of everything else that people will watch when they get tired of watching soccer.'

Currently, the N.F.L. Europe League comprises six teams, the Amsterdam Admirals, the Barcelona Dragons, Berlin Thunder, Frankfurt Galaxy, Rhein Fire and the Scottish Claymores. The Scottish Claymores have twenty-five cheerleaders, including names such as Siobhan Ring, Lois Mackenzie, Fiona Hunter and Isla Brown. The World League, and now the N.F.L. Europe League, is like a nursery school or 'minor league' farm school for the N.F.L. In September 1998 there were sixteen former Claymores on N.F.L. team rosters.

Within Great Britain there is another organization that promotes American football. This semi-professional league is organized by the British American Football Association (B.A.F.A.). With a record B.A.F.A. crowd of 10,000 spectators, good gates are relatively meagre – normal attendances are closer to one or two thousand spectators.

Tertiary education American football in Britain is governed by the British Collegiate American Football League (B.C.A.F.L.) and the British Student American Football Association (B.S.A.F.A.). The latter sponsors the Great Britain Bulldogs, the official national student American football team, representing all the university teams in Great Britain. Membership is restricted to British nationals.

Both B.A.F.A. and B.S.A.F.A. team names are rich in symbolism and share an 'animal' connection with the N.F.L. – note, for example, the Bath Killer Bees, the Cambridge Pythons, the Glasgow Tigers and the Sunderland Wearwolves.

References:

The British Collegiate American Football League website – http://www.bcafl.org/

The Scottish Claymores website – http://www.claymores.co.uk/

Websites:

The British Collegiate American Football League – http://www.bcafl.org/

Gridiron U.K. – http://www.gridironuk.com/

N.F.L. Europe – http://www.nfleurope.com/

The Scottish Claymores – http://www.claymores.co.uk/

-Scott Crawford

Gymnastics

The origins of gymnastics can be traced to the ancient civilizations of China, Greece, Persia and India. Exercises such as rope-climbing were included in the ancient Olympic games. Gymnastic exercise was also practised by the Romans in military preparation. Following the demise of the ancient Olympic games in AD 393, and the subsequent fall of the Roman Empire, the sport disappeared until its revival in the 19th century.

The first gymnastic club in Britain was formed in 1860 by German immigrants. Over the next twenty years, most major cities established gymnastic clubs. The sport boomed internationally during this time, leading to the establishment of the International Gymnastic Federation (F.I.G.) in 1881.

The British Amateur Gymnastics Association (B.A.G.A.) was formed in 1888. The first British championships were held in 1896 at Northampton. In 1899, an international match between England, Scotland and Ireland was held in Dublin. Following the match, William Adam JP, from Birmingham, proposed that the countries should compete every year, for which he donated a trophy. The 'Adam Shield' is still in existence and is the most coveted award within British gymnastics.

At the 1908 London Olympics, Walter Tysall won a silver medal on floor. The only other Olympic medals won by Britain for Gymnastics were in 1912, when the men's team won bronze, and 1928, when women's teams equalled the achievement of 1912.

In common with the Roman Empire, Britain has used gymnastic training to improve the physical fitness of its army. During the Crimean War, the realization that soldiers needed to be fit for war resulted in army gymnastic clubs being formed, many of which joined the B.A.G.A. in 1890. The Aldershot Army School came onto the national gymnastics scene in the 1950s. Nick Stuart, M.B.E. for services to gymnastics, was a product of this school and was many times a national champion. He also won the silver medal on floor at the 1957 European Championships.

The British Amateur Gymnastics Association became a limited company in 1982. In 1996, as a result of a thorough review, it evolved into British Gymnastics for all operational purposes. Its current headquarters, since 1989, are at Lilleshall National Sports Centre. The Association is the only recognized governing body for the sport of gymnastics within the U.K. and has over 100,000 members.

The Association is a member of the International Gymnastic Federation, the world governing body for the sport, as well as its European equivalent, the European Gymnastics Union (U.E.G.). The Association is also a member of the British Olympic Association (B.O.A.) and the Central Council of Physical Recreation (C.C.P.R.), and is also represented, both locally and nationally, on many other sporting bodies.

In 1998, the international success of British gymnasts reached a new peak. The English men's team won the team title at the Commonwealth Games in Kuala Lumpur, Annika Reeder retained the Commonwealth gold medal on Floor, and Lisa Mason became champion on vault. Mason also won a full collection of medals (gold, silver and bronze) at the Grand Prix series of competitions during the same year. Britain's most outstanding gymnast in world terms is probably Neil Thomas who won the silver medal in the floor exercise event at the World Championships in 1993.

References:

Goodbody, J., *The Illustrated History of Gymnastics* (London: Stanley Paul, 1982).

Hunn, D., *The Complete Book of Gymnastics* (London: Ward Lock, 1978).

Prestidge, J., *The History of British Gymnastics* (Slough: British Amateur Gymnastics Association, 1988).

Websites:

British Amateur Gymnastics Association website – http://www.baga.co.uk/

See also:

Rhythmic Gymnastics; Sports Acrobatics

-Frank Galligan

H

Hampden Park

Hampden Park is Scotland's national stadium, and until 1950 was the world's largest football ground. It is also the home of Queen's Park, not only the oldest Scottish club but still determinedly amateur as well.

Hampden Park was opened on October 31st, 1903, when Queen's Park beat Celtic 1-0 in the Scottish First Division. The following April, the ground hosted the Cup Final, when Celtic beat Rangers before a record crowd of 65,000.

This was the first of many attendance records to be shattered as the ground was extended over the years. The highest crowd ever at a British ground was for Scotland versus England on April 17th, 1937. The official figure of 149,415 (or 149,547, depending on the source) is said to have been augmented by some 10,000 gatecrashers. A week later, 144,303 (or 147,365) watched the Aberdeen versus Celtic Cup Final. Celtic versus Leeds in the European Cup semi-final in 1970 attracted 136,505, while even a friendly between Rangers and Eintracht Frankfurt in 1961 saw 104,494 in attendance. Lowly Queen's Park's best effort was a mere 95,772 against Rangers in 1930!

Such crowds are now a thing of the past, however. Hampden began a modernization programme in 1994 that temporarily reduced the capacity to 9,000. In 1998, pending completion of a 21st century 52,000-capacity stadium,

Queen's Park's first team used the adjacent Lesser Hampden, opened in 1923 to cater for the club's junior sides. With room for only 800 fans, this at least gave the Division Three amateurs a chance to play in front of a full house.

At the start of the new millennium the new stadium is almost completed. It staged its first international match in 1999 and now houses the Scottish Football Museum.

References:

Inglis, S., *The Football Grounds of Great Britain* (London: CollinsWillow, 1996).

See also:

Association Football; Mueums and Halls of Fame – Scottish Football Association Museum

-Tony Rennick

Handball

Handball is a non-physical contact sport played between two teams. Two versions of the game, indoor and outdoor, exist. The sport has ancient origins – a tombstone carving, *c.* 600 BC, of handball players was unearthed in Athens in 1926. Moreover, a reference to the game is made in Homer's *Odyssey* and the game was also popular with the Romans. Following the fall of the Roman Empire, the game seems to have survived in what is today modern Spain and France.

The sport also has a long tradition in Ireland, dating back over 1,000 years. Indeed, it is in Ireland that the modern origins of the game can be found. Around the middle of the 19th century, town and county championships were organized in Ireland and the game achieved semi-professional status. This resulted in the withholding of recognition by the Gaelic Athletic Association (G.A.A.) (founded in 1884 to promote Irish pastimes) until 1924, as the G.A.A. only recognized amateur sports.

Mass emigration from Ireland took the game to the United States, where Irish immigrants erected the first indoor handball court in 1886. The sport thus became both an indoor and an outdoor pastime. The modern game was developed by Konrad Koch, a German gymnastics teacher, while two other Germans, Hirschmann and Dr. Karl Schelenz, helped to popularize the sport by adapting it to Association Football-type rules. This, in turn, led to the founding of the International Amateur Handball Federation in 1928. Handball was included in the modern Olympics for the first time at the Berlin games in 1936.

Until 1952, the outdoor eleven-a-side version of the game was the most popular, but since then the seven-a-side indoor version has grown in popularity and become the favoured form of the sport.

In Britain the game was slow to take off. The first club was not formed until 1957 and it was not until 1967 that a national association, the British Handball Association, was formed. Handball in Britain is an amateur sport.

References:

Arlott, J. (ed.), *Oxford Companion to Sports and Games* (Oxford: Oxford University Press, 1976).

Websites:

The British Handball Association – http://www.britsport.com/handball/

See also:

Welsh Handball

-Ray Physick

Hangliding (*see* Gliding Sports)

Hare Hunting and Coursing

The pursuit of the brown hare with packs of beagles, basset-hounds or harriers is a very ancient sport, predating fox-hunting as an appropriate leisure activity for the aristocracy.

Beagles and basset-hounds are usually followed on foot, while harriers are usually followed on horseback. Although basset-hounds lack the speed of the other breeds, they have excellent scenting ability and impressive 'voice'. Like in fox-hunting, each hunt has a master who organizes activities and staff to control the hounds whilst hunting. As hares are very territorial, the followers can sometimes travel in circles. Whilst there are no legal close seasons for hares, hunting starts in September and ends in March. The sport's governing bodies, the Association of Masters of Harriers and Beagles, and the Masters of Basset Hounds Association, regulate hare hunting with a code of conduct.

Hare coursing, or the chasing of live hares with greyhounds or lurchers, is one of the world's oldest field sports, out of which developed greyhound racing with a mechanical hare. Purportedly invented by a Roman philosopher and historian of Greek extraction going by the name of Flavius Arrianus at the beginning of the Common Era, the sport, as well as the dog, originated in Great Britain. Indeed, in all probability, the sport was devised by the aristocratic and merchant élites of the second part of the 16th century. Ownership of greyhounds remained the preserve of the rich, as dogs were very expensive. Furthermore, ordinary people were discouraged from owning greyhounds, as landowners were concerned that they would be used for poaching. The Forest Laws legislated against this threat, specifying, for example, that claws had to be removed so that the greyhounds would be unable to catch the hares. First documented at Robert Dover's Cotswold Games, the sport was codified by the Duke of Norfolk somewhere between 1560 and 1571, before being revised at the command of Queen Elizabeth, as the legend has it, in 1591.

The vast majority of coursing takes place under National Coursing Club Rules. Beaters either drive the hares, one at a time, onto the running ground or, like rough shooting, the participants and their dogs put up the hares as they walk the fields. Under National Coursing Club Rules, when the hare is at least 80 yards in front of the two competing dogs held by the slipper, a trained official licensed by the Club is allowed to release or 'slip' the hounds. The first part of the chase consists of a run up to the hare. The second part begins when the greyhounds, which are much quicker, break her and try to catch her. As the hare is much more agile and has much greater stamina, however, the pursuit is not invariably fatal. Moreover, the sport is not solely about killing the hare, and a horse-mounted judge in hunting attire ensures that the more meritorious qualifies for the next round, awarding each hound points for speed, stamina and the ability to turn the hare in a competition that may rally up to sixty-four greyhounds.

The present variant of the sport has its origins in the first public coursing club, established at Swaffham, Norfolk, in 1776. The most prestigious event is the Waterloo Cup, the annual blue riband event, which has been organized at Altcar, near Liverpool, since 1836. All greyhounds participating in any events have to be registered in a studbook that was established by the National Coursing Club in 1882. Others coursing breeds are regulated by their own clubs and associations.

Hare coursing is also undertaken on a more ad hoc basis with lurchers, which are a cross between a greyhound and a herding dog, such as the Irish wolfhound, Bedlington or collie. The legends and folklore of the 18th century record accounts of amazing beasts that were brave, bold, cunning, loyal and adept at scent hunting. Lurchers and their owners were depicted as 'roguish' figures that were involved in illicit hunting. This popular view was encouraged by the belief that the word 'lurcher' originated historically from the Romany word 'lur', meaning 'thief'. Daytime sport involves the pursuit of hares or even rabbits, with ferrets being used to persuade them to vacate their subterranean refuges, which are marked by the lurchers. The use of lurchers at night also takes place, using powerful lamps to spot the quarry, a practice known as 'lamping'. Lurcher owners are encouraged to become members of local clubs and to abide by a nationally agreed code of conduct, which involves a close season for their quarry.

Despite constant parliamentary lobbying by animal rights' organizations, coursing managed to struggle along in the 20th century, and the National Coursing Club currently presides over the activities of some 20 clubs, down from more than 150 at its peak in the 1880s.

References:

Cox, H., 'Coursing', in Duke of Beaufort (ed.), *Coursing and Falconry* (Southampton: Ashford Press Publishing, 1986. 2nd ed.), pp. 1-213.

Grant-Rennick, R. (ed.), *Coursing: the Pursuit of Game with Gazehounds* (London: Saul & the Standfast Sporting Library, 1977).

Plummer, D. B., *Lurcher and Long Dog Training* (London: Robinson Publishing, 1993).

Further reading:

Stable, O. and Stuttard, R. M., *A Review of Coursing* (London: British Field Sports Society, 1971).

Websites:

The National Coursing Club – http://www.nationalcoursingclub.freeserve.co.uk/

See also:

Greyhound Racing; Waterloo Cup

-Daniel Laurent/John Martin

Hat Trick

The term 'hat trick' originally described the act of a cricket bowler who took three wickets in three successive balls. It appears to have derived from the practice of cricket clubs who presented bowlers with new hats or some equivalent whenever they performed such a feat.

The most prestigious hat trick in cricket is one achieved during a test match. The Australian player, F. R. Spofforth, produced the first of these against England at Melbourne in 1879, when he dismissed Royle, Mackinnon and Emmett in the first innings.

Having taken a lead from cricket, the term has also come to describe a threefold feat in other sports and activities. This is particularly true of Association Football, where it is used to describe the scoring of three goals by the same player in one match.

One of the rarest hat tricks in English football is one scored during the F.A. Cup Final. Blackburn Rovers' Billy Townley scored the first of these against Sheffield Wednesday at the Kennington Oval in 1890. Blackpool's Stan Mortensen scored the first (and so far only) hat trick in a Wembley cup final in 1953.

Probably the most famous hat trick produced by an English player in any sport was scored by Geoff Hurst in the football World Cup final of 1966. It included one of the most controversial goals ever scored in the World Cup, and won the tournament for England. Hurst remains the only player to have scored three goals in a World Cup final.

References:

Cashman, R. et al. (eds.), *The Oxford Companion to Australian Cricket* (Melbourne: Oxford University Press, 1997).

Glanville, B., *The Story of the World Cup* (London: Faber & Faber, 1997).

See also:

Cricket

-Gavin Mellor

Head to Head

The term 'head to head' normally refers to competition between two teams or individuals where the result has more significance than would normally be the case. This could be a competition between two unbeaten teams in a league or between champion boxers, tennis players with contrasting styles or top athletes in a race where the participants have established strong credentials. 'Head to head' is a term also used to compare the performance statistics of individuals or teams before they compete, inviting the reader to form a judgement as to the likely outcome.

There have, in recent years, been a number of staged races where the intention has been to maximize public interest by bringing together athletes who have a special reason to want to win the race. One example of this was the 'grudge' match between Mary Decker and British athlete Zola Budd after their clash in the 1984 Olympics. In 1996, the Champions of the two Rugby codes, Bath and Wigan, faced each other in a two-match head to head, one match under league rules, the other under union rules.

There has been some disquiet in sporting circles as to whether these competitions spoil the purity of sport. The most notable head to head of recent years was a race to find the fastest human. Olympic Champions and World Record holders Michael Johnson (200 metres) and Donovan Bailey (100 metres) raced over the hybrid distance of 150 metres for a cash prize of $1.5 million. Bailey won a disappointing and ultimately meaningless race.

-Kyle Phillpots

Headingley Sports Ground

The home of Leeds Rugby League Club and spiritually, if not officially, Yorkshire County Cricket Club (who only lease, not own, the ground), Headingley was opened in May 1890, after being bought for £25,000 as Lot 17a, a 22-acre site from Cardigan Estates. Designed to be the best sports stadium in the North of England, it had a capacity of 30,000 and its facilities were quickly expanded to include athletics, bowling, tennis, cycling and soccer.

On September 20th, 1890, its first Rugby match, between Leeds and Manningham, took place and on June 6th, 1891, county cricket began when Yorkshire played Derbyshire. In 1893, the ground staged international Rugby Union for the first and only time when Scotland defeated England. The 1895 F.A. Amateur Cup final was also staged there.

Before the 1895 Rugby split, Headingley also staged three Yorkshire Rugby Union cup finals and hosted an English Rugby Union club record crowd when 27,654 saw Leeds play Halifax in 1892. In 1996, Rugby Union returned to the ground when Leeds Rugby Union club made it their permanent home.

Its test cricket debut came in 1899 when Middlesex's J. T. Hearne became the first Englishman to take a hat trick against Australia. Three years later, Yorkshire dismissed the Australians there for just 23. But from then on, Headingley became a happy hunting ground for Australian batsmen: in 1926, C. G. MacCartney scored a test century for lunch; in 1930, Don Bradman repeated the feat and scored 309 in a day, eventually setting a new test record of 334; on the 1934 tour he scored 304; and on his last appearance in 1948, in front of an English record crowd of 158,000 over five days, he hammered an undefeated 173 to win the Fourth Test.

In 14 months spanning 1931 and 1932, Yorkshire's Hedley Verity twice took all ten wickets in an innings on the ground, the latter occasion for just 10 runs against Nottinghamshire. Peter Loader took a hat trick against the West Indies in 1957, becoming only the second English bowler to do so at home. In 1981, Headingley saw one of the most dramatic test wins ever when Ian Botham dragged England back from the brink of an innings defeat with

149 not out, leaving Bob Willis to take 8 for 43 as Australia were skittled out for 111, 18 runs short of the English total. Sadly, it was also the scene of the only test match wicket sabotage, when in 1975 vandals poured petrol over the popping crease at one end.

Its status as a Rugby League ground is no less historic. It hosted the first ever Northern Union Challenge Cup final in 1897 between Batley and St Helens, and a further eleven before the cup final was moved permanently to Wembley; eleven championship finals; and over thirty international matches since the first New Zealand tourists played a test match there in 1908. In January 1943, a Rugby League XV defeated a Rugby Union XV 18-11 playing under Rugby Union rules. In 1970, it hosted the Rugby League World Cup final between Great Britain and Australia. The ground's record attendance of 40,175 was set at the 1947 Leeds versus Bradford league match.

References:

Dalby, K., *The Headingley Story* (Leeds: The Author, 1955-1985. 6 vols.).

Delaney, T., *The Grounds of Rugby League* (Keighley: The Author, 1991).

See also:

Cricket; Rugby League

-Tony Collins

Henley Royal Regatta

Henley Royal Regatta was founded in 1839 when the dignitaries of the town sought ways of relieving economic depression in the area. Remembering the crowds attracted to the first Oxford versus Cambridge Boat Race, which had been held on their reach of the Thames ten years previously, they put up 100 guineas (£105) for a Grand Challenge Cup open to eight-oared boats. Trinity College, Cambridge, carried it off to London to have their names engraved upon it, and the regatta has been run annually ever since, except for the years of the two world wars.

Rowing at Henley Royal Regatta, July 3rd, 1999 (Action Images/Brandon Malone)

One hundred and fifty regattas later, Henley Regatta, which acquired royal patronage in 1851, is held over five days and attracts more than 500 entries for its sixteen challenge trophies. The original course was 1 mile 550 yards, the longest distance of open water obtainable in 1839. It was straightened by removing part of Temple Island and trimming the Berkshire bank near the start in time for the 1924 regatta, and remains the original length. In 9,560 races held from 1946 to 1998 inclusive (excluding dead heats and races not rowed out), 51.2 per cent of races have been won on the Berkshire station and 48.8 per cent on the Buckinghamshire station.

The early establishment of the regatta and its rules of racing gave it considerable influence in the development of rowing and amateur sport. It is controlled by Stewards elected for life, most of whom are drawn from the sport. When Oxford University won the Grand with seven men in 1843, rowing began to be taken seriously as a sporting activity. The Diamond Sculls, probably Henley's best known trophy after the Grand, was introduced in 1844. In 1879, the Stewards barred men who worked with their hands from competing, a bar which lasted until 1938. Germania of Frankfurt were the first foreign entry for the Grand in 1880, and the first foreigners to win it were Club Nautique de Gand of Belgium in 1906.

The regatta established itself as part of the upper classes' social scene during the Victorian era, boosted by the arrival of the Great Western Railway in the town in 1857. In 1919, the Stewards capitalized on the popularity of their event by establishing the Stewards' Enclosure, where exacting standards of dress and behaviour are still enforced. In the year 2000, it had more than 6,000 members, while up to 100,000 people visit the regatta freely along the towpath or as guests in hospitality areas.

The regatta has quietly updated its rules to comply with the aspirations and requirements of competitors. Milestones include the admittance of women as coxes in 1975, the introduction of the Princess Royal Challenge Cup for women scullers in 1993, and invitation women's eights in 1998. It has a range of events covering open, restricted and junior categories, and is recognized by the International Rowing Federation (F.I.S.A.) even though the course does not comply with its requirements. The annual turnover has passed £1.5 million, and the Stewards Charitable Trust makes large donations to junior rowing in Britain.

References:

Burnell, R., *Henley Royal Regatta: a celebration of 150 years* (London: William Heinemann, 1989).

Burnell, R., and Page, G., *The Brilliants: a History of Leander Club* (Henley-on-Thames: Leander Club, 1997).

Dodd, C., *Henley Royal Regatta* (London: Stanley Paul, 1981, 1989).

Halladay, E., *Rowing in England: a Social History* (Manchester: Manchester University Press, 1990).

Websites:

Henley Royal Regatta – http://www.hrr.co.uk/

See also:

Museums and Halls of Fame – River and Rowing Museum

-Chris Dodd

Hickstead

Hickstead is Britain's premier showjumping venue, but its origins are comparatively recent.

Douglas Bunn was a British showjumper of the 1950s who was part-time lawyer (a barrister) and part-time equestrian. While not as well known as Captain Harry Llewellyn and Pat Smythe, Bunn competed in an era, the late 1940s to early 1960s, in which British showjumping flourished. At the 1948 London Olympics, 80,000 spectators cheered on the national team as they won a bronze medal. Four years later, at Helsinki, the British showjumping team took gold. Llewellyn's horse, Foxhunter, became something of a national icon. The showjumping success was, after all, Great Britain's solitary Olympic gold medal.

Bunn was well aware that British showjumping suffered from a desperate shortage of demanding and challenging courses within the shores of Great Britain. With this in mind, Bunn bought Hickstead Place in 1959 which, together with additional land near the growing Gatwick Airport, totalled around 30 acres. His first show, on May 6th, 1960, was, very nearly, a disaster – it conflicted with Princess Margaret's marriage to Lord Snowdon. Nevertheless, Bunn displayed his inimitable charm and bulldog tenacity. Eventually he secured thirty entries.

Bunn, ably helped by forestry worker, and later show manager, Ernie Fish, crafted the All England Jumping Course with an assortment of stone walls, water jumps, dykes and ditches. Its most celebrated and controversial aspect was a Derby Bank. He took the model of the Flottbeck (Hamburg) Derby, at a height of 3 metres, and then added 9 inches to make the Hickstead bank the biggest, and most daunting, in the world.

Peter Jeffery notes, 'When he [Bunn] introduced his Derby Bank – very much as it is today – riders were outraged and many refused to present a horse to it. But Douglas's confidence, plus a stunning clear round of the first Derby course in 1961 by Seamus Hayes, proved the challenge that many have undertaken but only a comparative few achieved.'

Over the years the Hickstead complex, known generally as the Showground, has grown considerably. There are now six arenas, permanent seating for over 5,000 spectators, and twenty-six corporate hospitality suites.

In 1997, Hickstead's future was threatened when the tobacco/cigarette company 'Silk Cut' ended fourteen years of sponsorship. However, German businessman and showjumper Paul Schockemohle stepped in with significant financial support, which has since been formalized into a long-term arrangement.

Hickstead is to showjumping what Badminton is to three-day eventing. It has staged many major events including six European and two World Championships. From August 25th to August 29th, 1999, Hickstead hosted the European Showjumping Championships and British Jumping Derby. The Showground has marketed itself as a modern entertainment centre. For example, the 1999 season membership at the All England Jumping Course, Hickstead, at a cost of £90, provided thirty-four days of top-class sport – ten days of international showjumping, twenty-one days of racing and high-goal polo, and three days of county cricket.

References:

Jeffery, P., Personal communication received May 7th, 1999.

Further reading:

Barnett, S. *Games and Sets: the Changing Face of Sport on Television* (London: British Film Institute, 1990), pp. 48-49.

Clayton, M. (ed.), *The Complete Book of Show Jumping* (London: Heinemann, 1975).

Official Traxdata European Showjumping Championship, and British Jumping Derby Programme (25-29 August 1999).

Websites:

The All England Jumping Course, Hickstead – http://hickstead.co.uk/

See also:

Showjumping

-John Crawford/Scott Crawford

Highland Games

The Highland Games incorporate feats of strength and agility that were practised throughout Scotland, but their formal organization and annual occurrence seems to have begun after about 1820. The Scottish Highland Games have not only been a traditional facet of Scotland's sporting history, but they have also evoked and presented to the rest of the world a particular image of Scotland – an image that is closely associated with the traditional organized Highland Gatherings such as those founded at Braemar (1817), St Fillans (1819), Lonach (1823), Ballater (1866), Aboyne (1867), Argyllshire (1871) and Cowal (1871); an image that is closely associated with kilted athletes and dancers, the skirl of the pipes, local and in some cases royal patronage, the distinct sub-culture of the heavies and a sense of bonhomie.

Just as important as the more glamorous Highland Games of the contemporary period are many of the less formal, local Highland Games (in both the Highlands and the Lowlands). Writing in 1923 in *Hebridean Memories*, Seton Gordon wrote that 'the greatest event in the lives of the Uist and Barra crofters takes place in July, when the annual Highland Gathering is held'. Just as the great feature of Uist Gathering is the piping, the component events of the different Highland Games were often secondary to the social function of meeting friends, and in this sense the actual contests were more a spectacle than the *raison d'être* of the games themselves. The atmosphere of these less formal events, such as those at Glenelg and Uist, are as equally traditional as those at Braemar and Lonach, and yet they are a world apart from the more formal, rationalized, commercial Highland Games circuit of the late 20th century.

Many of the folk origins of the Highland Games of today have a popular history that pre-dates the Victorian period. The alleged point of origin of the Braemar Gathering is often quoted as being an 11th-century hill-race to the summit of Craig Choinneach, organized by Malcolm Canmore, the function of the hill-race being to select the ablest athletes so that they could serve as postal runners for the King. Describing his childhood on Islay in the 1820s and 1830s, the land reformer John Murdoch talked of shinty, cock-fighting, athletic events and feats of strength as being those traditional Highland sports. One of the points of origin of 'tossing the caber' lies in the raising of the roof couples of the traditional Highland croft. The *hairst-kirn*, or gathering, after the harvest had been collected was often seen as a seasonal celebration at which dancing, throwing the putting stone and hurling the hammer all contributed to joyous celebrations of communal loyalty and friendly rivalry. Writing in the 1820s, one writer describes such a harvest-kirn celebration at which a party of Celts amused themselves by their extraordinary feats in putting the stane, hopping, leaping and running.

Queen Victoria's attachment to Balmoral, Braemar and Royal Deeside is often quoted as the single most important factor that contributed to the development of the Scottish Highland Games. Indeed, the predominant image of the modern Scottish Highland Games is one that, perhaps mistakenly, still owes much to the royal patronage bestowed by Queen Victoria upon the likes of the Braemar Royal Highland Society Gathering and the Gathering of the Lonach Highland and Friendly Society. The stamp of royal approval provided for by Queen Victoria attending the Braemar Gathering in 1848 contributed to a sense of respectability and royal approval but at the expense of some of the traditional content. The Braemar Gathering had its origins in a Friendly Society that, like the carters with their horse-racing, started annual games. As the traditional role of the monarchy declined during the 19th century, royal games became increasingly important. Events such as the Braemar Royal Highland Society Gathering contributed to a growing nucleus of activities that helped to define a British, Scottish and Highland sporting calendar which also included the Derby (Epsom), Ascot racing week (Gold Cup) and various shooting seasons.

The development of the Scottish Highland Games also contributed to an émigré culture overseas. One cannot divorce the development of Highland Games overseas from the diverse conditions that gave rise to emigration in the first place. Numerous Scottish societies emerged in order to facilitate the preservation, albeit in a particular form, of Scottish customs – including what the 1903 register of Scottish Societies called national athletic games. Highland Games were incorporated into the agenda of Scottish societies such as those formed in Philadelphia (1749), Savannah Georgia (1750), New York City (1756), Halifax Nova Scotia (1768), St John New Brunswick (1798), Albany (1803), Buffalo (1843), New York (1847), Detroit (1849) and San Francisco (1866). Thus, on a more critical note, while the attachment of Queen Victoria to Balmoral and Braemar might have contributed to the popularity of the Highland Games throughout Scotland, the policies of that same monarchy, most notably The Emigration Advances Act of 1851, also contributed to the process by which Highland Games developed in North America and overseas.

Finally, the period from about 1920 to the present has seen some Highland Games become increasingly professionalized and subject to the standardization of rules imposed by various governing bodies interested in promoting world records and commerce. The Scottish Games Association was founded in 1946 and charged with formally regulating the modern Highland Games circuit. Yet, the history of commerce readily shows that wherever commercialization emerges, with its attendant pressures of professionalism and associated problems such as the taking of performance-enhancing drugs, the law profession closely follows. Perhaps this has been the price to pay for the continuing survival of the Highland Gatherings and yet it is crucial to recognize that the Games are as similar as they are different. A different sense of community, place and function attached to Highland Games may exist in Braemar, Aberdeen, Edinburgh, Airth, Cowal, Lonach, Aboyne, Uist and Halkirk. They all provide insights into Scottish history and culture.

References:

Donaldson, E., *The Scottish Highland Games in America* (Gretna: Pelican, 1986).

Gordon, S., *Hebridean Memories* (Glasgow: New Wilson Publishing, 1923).

Jarvie, G., *Highland Games: the Making of the Myth* (Edinburgh: Edinburgh University Press, 1991).

Further reading:

Webster, D., *Scottish Highland Games* (Edinburgh: Reprographia, 1973).

Yorke, P., *Three Nights in Perthshire* (Glasgow: 1821).

-Grant Jarvie

Hill Climbing (Motor Car)

The first hill climb was held at Chanteloup in France in November 1898. In the following year, a similar event was staged on Petersham Hill near Richmond, attracting some forty entrants to a course 325 yards in length and with an average gradient of one in twelve. A Barrière tricycle emerged victorious with an electrically powered vehicle in second place. The first competitive hill climb not forming part of a general speed trial took place in January 1900; some six months later, the Catford Cycle Club sponsored a hill climb with a section reserved exclusively for motor cars. Hill climbs and sprints proved extremely popular with motoring enthusiasts and by 1924, some eighty events of this kind were held in Britain. As the number of clubs promoting hill climbs multiplied, the Royal Automobile Club (R.A.C.) became increasingly involved in regulating the sport, including, for example, the formulation in 1906 of a handicapping system. This, together with the limited inconvenience caused to non-motorists, helped hill climbing to escape prosecution, even though the speed limit could be exceeded. Even with the emergence of Brooklands and other closed circuits, the accessibility of hill climbing made it a central feature of British motor sport in the

inter-war years. Hill climbing at the major national venues, such as Shelsey Walsh, which had emerged by 1939, quickly resumed after the conclusion of hostilities in 1945. The sport was given further impetus in the post-war period by the growing popularity of four-wheel-drive vehicles designed to accommodate off-road motoring.

References:

Brendon, P., *The Motoring Century: the Story of the Royal Automobile Club* (London: Bloomsbury, 1997).

Mays, R., 'Hill Climbing', in E. Howe (ed.), *Motor Racing* (London: Seeley Service and Co., 1939).

Nicholson, T. R., *Sprint: Speed Hillclimbs and Speed Trials in Britain, 1899-1925* (Newton Abbott: David & Charles, 1969).

Nye, D., *Motor Racing in Colour* (Poole: Blandford Press, 1978).

See also:

Motor Racing

-David Thoms

History

In its simplest form, sports history consists of facts and, of course, statistics, whether it be football scores, racing results or cricket averages. Indeed, a large proportion of the material that is traditionally considered to make up 'sports history' consists of little more than lists of trophy winners and match results, and chronological accounts, often match-by-match, of club and team performances. Although there is nothing wrong with this *per se*, sports history could, and should, offer much more than this. One example of this is the 1883 F.A. Cup Final played at Kennington Oval, in which Blackburn Olympic beat the Old Etonians by two goals to one. Sports histories record the score, but much more significant is the fact that a public-school Old Boys team had been defeated by a side which included various tradesmen of different crafts: Blackburn's victory signalled that at the élite level, the game of soccer was being taken over by working-class players. The result also marked a geographical shift in the location of playing power, as the Cup came north for the first time in the history of the competition. Both of these factors were to lead to professionalism. Thus, simply recording a score of 2-1 ignores much of historical significance. Another example of sports history failing to record the real significance of sporting events is the result of the 1886 Cambridgeshire horse-race. Traditional accounts which show that St Mirin, ridden by Fred Archer, lost by a neck, hide the weight problems of the champion jockey which eventually led to his suicide.

This 'chronicle and numbers' approach typifies much traditional non-academic sports history – there is a long history of the (usually male) amateur enthusiast extolling the story of his favoured club or sport. That said, some amateurs have produced work that ranks alongside that of the best academic and professional writers. However, although these writers usually get their sports facts correct, they too often deal with their topic without reference to the wider issues. Despite this, their work can still aid more serious studies by providing the empirical evidence needed to test academic hypotheses.

Academic sports history itself was slow to develop in Britain. Most non-results-oriented sports history has traditionally focused on the cultural history of ordinary people. This is probably the reason why academics have avoided the subject, instead they have left the field to journalists and enthusiastic amateurs. Later, physical educators embraced the subject but again, as a general rule, they were not trained as historians and the works they produced tended to be narrative works rather than analytical. Despite this, and unlike the situation in continental Europe, the physical education sector has not come to the fore in British sports history. This is partly because of the British approach to sport, which has tended to look at sport in terms of competitive games rather than general physical culture.

In recent years the overall standard of sports history has risen significantly. This has been due to a number of factors, including the general move towards 'history from below', the boom in social history towards which most sports history gravitates, and the growth of the sports industry coupled with an increasing awareness of its relevance to society. In the academic sphere, British sports historians now have their own association, the British Society of Sports History, which each year holds conferences and publishes its associated journal, the *Sports Historian*. Research centres are beginning to flourish too, current examples including De Montfort University's International Centre for Sports History and Culture, the Institute of Football Studies at the University of Central Lancashire, the Sir Norman Chester Centre for Football Research at the University of Leicester, the Football Research Centre at the University of Liverpool and the Centre for Sports Studies at the University of Stirling.

More readable than most sports history has been a genre that has emerged in the past decade combining literature, history and personal reminiscence. Nick Hornby's *Fever Pitch* has spawned a host of imitators of varying quality. Although weak on authority, these works are strong on authenticity and bring in the passion and emotion of sport, something sadly lacking in most academic writing on the topic.

The past decade has also seen the development of a sports heritage industry, based around sports museums and sports tourism, which utilizes the historical sporting landscape. Although some of these ventures, especially those at club level, have been criticized for perpetuating historical myths and inaccuracies, they do demonstrate a public interest in sports history – or at least a belief by commercial interests that this is the case. This view has also been accepted by film and television producers, who have produced documentaries utilizing archival footage and often, at least on television, involving critical sports historians. In contrast, film has to date been far less mindful of academic credibility or historical accuracy, thus presenting the public with embroidered versions of actual sporting events. This difference in approach between the two media is unfortunate and perhaps confusing to the consumer of sports history, for as Polley notes, 'arguably these are the most important of all the genres, as more people watch television programmes and films than read history books or visit specialised museums'.

In Britain, like most nations, sport plays a significant role in the economic, social and political life of the country. It is therefore vital that historians attempt to discover the origins and development of links between sport and the wider community. In doing so, however, care must be taken to ensure that myths do not become established as historical facts; research should be undertaken into not just what happened, but why it happened; and, most importantly of all, sports historians should ensure that even when writing academic studies they do not eliminate the excitement and drama associated with sport, which are the elements that make it so special in the first place.

References:

Polley, M., *Moving the Goalposts: a History of Sport and Society Since 1945* (London: Routledge, 1998).

Further reading:

Vamplew, W., 'History', in D. Levinson and K. Christensen (eds.), *Encyclopedia of World Sport* (Santa Barbara: ABC-CLIO, 1996), vol. 2, pp. 414-418.

See also:

British Society of Sports History

-Wray Vamplew

Hockey (Field)

Modern hockey is a derivative of a wide variety of stick and ball games that were played in such diverse areas as the Nile Valley, Athens and ancient Rome. More recent research has indicated that the Aztecs played a stick and ball game, and comparisons between the modern sport of hockey and these ancient games are inevitable. Pope Gregory IX was seen as a patron of the emerging game in the 14th century, whilst the east windows in Gloucester Cathedral illustrate a player with a stick. In 1363, a statute of Edward III banned hockey, as it distracted people from archery. Evidence of games of hurling, shinty and bandy having been played over the centuries are common, and 'hockie' appears in Irish records as a banned game in 1527.

The modern game would appear to have originated from Eton College, and the school chronicle produced a set of rules in 1868. Other schools, such as Marlborough and Winchester, were also early participants. These rules formed the basis of the set of rules produced by the first Hockey Association when it was formed, though regional variations were still widespread. The most important early club, due to their pioneering work, was Blackheath, whose records date from 1861. Players from this club played with a solid rubber ball on a pitch that was 200 yards long and 70 yards wide. The rather rough game adopted by Blackheath did not meet with the approval of West London Clubs such as Teddington, who introduced the shooting circle to the sport in order to ensure a safer and more skilful game.

Due to the increased popularity of the sport a national association became necessary and on January 18th, 1886, the Hockey Association was formed. This Association was for men only and women developed their game separately from the men, starting the All England Women's Hockey Association (A.E.W.H.A.) in 1896. The two Associations eventually joined together in 1997 to form the English Hockey Association.

The first international matches were played by men in 1895 when England, Ireland and Wales all played matches. The following year, the ladies played their first international match when England beat Ireland 2-0 in Dublin.

The International Rules Board was instituted in 1900 to develop men's hockey and to standardize the rules throughout the growing number of countries that were playing the game. The prime result of this was to give the umpire status, for previously he had been able to give a decision only when an appeal had been made.

Men's hockey was included as an Olympic sport at the 1908 London Games, when England won the gold medal. The sport was not included in 1912 at the Stockholm Games, but reappeared in 1920 at Antwerp when England retained the gold medal. In 1924, the sport was again excluded, but it returned in 1928 and has remained an Olympic sport ever since. The 1920 gold medal was the last time that an individual home country appeared in the Olympic games and all subsequent entries have been as Great Britain. 1928 saw the start of India's domination of the game for five successive Olympic tournaments and they were only eventually beaten by Pakistan in 1960, whose players, in any case, were all of Indian origin. The British men's team won the gold medal at the Seoul Olympics in 1988 and this helped increase the sport's popularity over several years.

Women's hockey did not achieve Olympic status until 1980 and this tournament was hampered by withdrawals for political reasons. However, it has grown steadily and has become an accepted part of the Olympic tournament, and from 2004 will have the same number of competitors as the men's tournament.

The spread of hockey as a world game and its acceptance as an Olympic sport necessitated the formation of an international controlling authority. The founding father was a Frenchman, Mr. Paul Léautey, who called a meeting of hockey-playing countries and formed the International Hockey Federation (Fédération Internationale de Hockey – F.I.H.) on January 7th, 1924. The F.I.H. grew steadily from seven founding members to the present number of over ninety. England did not join until 1970, when the

International Rules Board also came under the auspices of the F.I.H.

The women's game paralleled that of the men and the International Federation of Women's Hockey Associations (I.F.W.H.A.) was founded in 1927. The women organized their own championships until 1982, when the two bodies amalgamated leaving the F.I.H. as the governing body for world hockey. This ensured that both men and women played to the same rules, removing some of the earlier differences that occurred through having separate rule books.

Leagues and cups were frowned upon in the early years and amateurism was promoted. The women's game allowed leagues far earlier than did its male counterpart. Today the structure is similar to most other sports with a pyramid formation, with international competition, national leagues, divisional leagues and finally local leagues at the base. The Federation of International Competition Hockey instituted a World Cup in 1971, whilst the European federation developed both club and international competitions in 1970. This pattern then spread to other continents from Europe. The women moved from I.F.W.H.A. tournaments to holding their first world cup in 1983, and continental tournaments for women were instituted in 1984.

The A.E.W.H.A. holds the record for the largest recorded attendance of a hockey match, when 60,707 attended the England versus Wales international at Wembley Stadium in 1969. This annual event was a major fixture in the hockey calendar until the 1980s, when the advent of Astroturf made the grass surface redundant. In the modern men's game, large crowds attend in India and Pakistan, whilst in Europe, Holland and Germany provide the largest numbers of spectators.

The stick has changed from the original 'English head', via the 'Indian head', to a variety of styles. Early sticks were made of maple, but were soon being made of ash with cloth handles. Ash was superseded by mulberry, which could withstand the greater compression needed for the short head. Sticks are now coated in fibre glass or Kevlar (a synthetic fibre), and manufacturers have introduced aluminium sticks and graphite composites, although the F.I.H. have decreed that only wood will be allowed at international level from 1999. The 1887 rule that the stick must be able to pass through a 2-inch ring still stands today, and a maximum weight of 28 ounces is permitted.

Early pitches varied in size but from the early rules of the Hockey Association a 100 yard by 60 yard rectangle became standard. The numbers actually playing in a team have remained at eleven, though substitutes and rolling substitutions have made squads of up to sixteen possible. Grass pitches have given way to synthetic pitches or 'Astroturf', upon which most club hockey and all regional and international hockey is now played. This has revolutionized the skills of the game with its even, true surface, particularly as the offside rule was abolished in 1997, allowing attackers to use all the available space.

Britain was to host the 1998 World Cup tournament, staging the final at the specially prepared Willesden Stadium (North London). A few years later, a new national stadium was constructed at Milton Keynes, where all international matches are now played.

Indoor hockey is a game adapted from field hockey and is a six-a-side game that originated in Germany. The pitch is 40 yards by 20 yards and the game lasts twenty minutes each way. Hitting is not allowed and the ball may only be pushed or dribbled, except for shooting at goal when flicking is permitted, and lighter sticks have been developed to suit the game. All corners are penalty corners, and this game first introduced the concept of a no offside rule, subsequently adapted by the outdoor game.

From early beginnings in Germany, the game spread and the International Hockey Federation took over the sport in 1966. The game grew in Britain during the 1970s, with Scotland being particularly successful at the amended game. The first official F.I.H. tournament took place in 1972 in Berlin and was won by Germany, the dominant force in the sport. A Home Countries Championship was introduced in 1976.

References:

Arlott, J. (ed.), *Oxford Companion to Sports and Games* (Oxford: Oxford University Press, 1975).

Miroy, N., *The History of Hockey* (Hemel Hempstead: Chiltern Books, 1989).

Scottish Hockey Union, *Handbook of the Scottish Hockey Union* (Edinburgh: Scottish Hockey Association, 1997).

Smith, B. (ed.), *Balsam Hockey Yearbook* (Manchester: Dabs, 1990).

Further reading:

McWhirter, N. and Greenberg, S., *The Guinness Book of Olympic Records* (Harmondsworth: Penguin, 1980).

Websites:

The English Hockey Association – http://www.hockeyonline.co.uk/

The International Hockey Federation – http://www.fihockey.org/

-Eugene Connolly

Holme Pierrepont

The first still-water, multi-lane 2000-metre rowing course in Britain was constructed at Holme Pierrepont, Nottingham, from reclaimed gravel pits and came into use in 1972.

The impetus for this important development came from the East Midlands division of the Amateur Rowing Association (A.R.A.) and their A.R.A. representative, Martin Brandon-Bravo, later to become President of the A.R.A. and M.P. for Nottingham South. Considerable support came from Nottinghamshire County Council under their Chairman, Alderman Mrs Yates, as well as the Sports Council.

The course was built to international specifications in consultation with the International Rowing Federation (F.I.S.A.), and the administration buildings and spectators' facilities received architectural awards. Today, it is a base for the highly successful Nottingham County Rowing Association.

Also at the Centre are a course for white-water canoeing (opened in September 1986) and a lake for water-ski jumping. The main course is also used for angling, canoeing, sailing and several other water sports.

In 1972, the A.R.A. introduced a National Championship at Holme Pierrepont, which became the venue the following year for the World Junior Championships and for the highly successful World Rowing Championships in 1975 and 1986.

For several years the Nottingham International Regatta took place at Holme Pierrepont, but obtaining entries from the Continent proved a problem and the regatta was abandoned after 1988. The National Schools Regatta, Nottingham City regatta and other regattas are held annually.

The British Canoe Union has held its National Sprint Championships at Holme Pierrepont since the mid-1970s, as well as a number of Long Distance/Marathon Championships and, following completion of the white-water course, a number of slalom championships. In 1989, it moved its headquarters to Holme Pierrepont from Surrey.

The regatta course hosted the World Canoe Sprint Championships in 1981. The first World Marathon Canoeing Championships were held on the regatta course and neighbouring River Trent in 1988 and in 1995 the white-water course was host to the World Slalom Championships. It has also been the venue for national and international angling and triathlon events.

In 1997, significant new facilities were added to the existing residential accommodation and boat storage facilities.

In common with all open-air 2000-metre courses, Holme Pierrepont can be seriously affected by wind conditions, which make the lanes unfair and unrowable on occasions. At its best, however, it can match any course in the world.

Websites:

The National Water Sports Centre – http://www.nationalwatersports.co.uk/

See also:

Angling; Canoeing; Rowing

-Geoffrey Page/Richard William Cox

Horse of the Year Show

For more than fifty years, the Horse of the Year Show has been the climax of the British equestrian season. Its unique blend of showjumping and show classes has proved enduringly popular with the equestrian community and the wider public.

The Horse of the Year Show's origins lay in the thinking of Captain Tony Collings who, in 1948, proposed that there should be a 'champion of champions' show to draw together the best of what could be seen in local and regional events. His idea was pursued by Colonel Mike Ansell of the British Show Jumping Association and Colonel V. D. S. Williams of the British Horse Society. Having witnessed the popularity and success of the famous Parisian indoor show, known as 'Le Jumping', they became convinced that Colling's proposal of an autumn event as the culmination of the home season would provide a viable and attractive sporting spectacle.

The first Horse of the Year Show took place in 1949 at the Harringay Arena under the joint sponsorship of the British Show Jumping Association and the Greyhound Racing Association, the latter being involved as the proprietors of the arena. After ten shows, the event had out-grown Harringay and it moved to its present home at the Wembley Arena in 1959. Since 1997, the event has been managed by Grandstand Media, who were responsible for the Golden Jubilee celebrations in 1998.

At its inception in 1948 there were 400 competitors. Over fifty years, participation levels have risen to the degree that in 1998, there were over 1,200 entries. There are now four main components that draw competitors and spectators alike to the Wembley Arena each year. The

National Classes, which are the finals of the top nine British Showjumping Championships, stand alongside a programme of thirteen International Showjumping classes, twenty Showing classes and pure equestrian entertainment, the latter including such traditional favourites as the 'Musical Drive of the Heavy Horses' and the 'Pony Club Mounted Games'.

To the wider public, however, the Horse of the Year Show is synonymous with showjumping. In 1948, the crowd were excited by the achievements of Colonel Harry Llewellyn on Foxhunter and Pat Smythe on Finality, and through the decades, many great riders and horses have participated in the Horse of the Year Show, to the extent that a 'Hall of Fame' for the ten greatest riders and horses has now been established.

The riders clearly have a special feeling for the Horse of the Year Show and this is highlighted by the present-day leading showjumper, John Whitaker, who has stated that 'Winning at Wembley is the pinnacle of every equestrian's career.'

References:

Horse of the Year Show: Golden Jubilee Brochure (London: Grand Media Ltd, 1998).

Websites:

The Horse of the Year Show – http://www.hoys.co.uk/

See also:

Showjumping; Wembley Stadium; White City

-Trevor James

Horse-racing – The American Invasion

In 1896, a solitary American jockey, W. Simms, rode in Britain and secured only four wins, but these were from a mere nineteen mounts, a winning percentage of 21.5, amongst the highest in the land. His visit was a precursor for an American invasion that was to significantly influence the domestic racing industry. The prime mover was Tod Sloan. On his first short sojourn in 1897 he had fifty-three mounts and won on twenty of them. He returned the following autumn, winning forty-three races from ninety-eight mounts – a phenomenal percentage of 43.9. In 1899, his strike rate fell to 31.3 per cent, but his 345 mounts yielded 108 victories, securing him the jockeys' championship. By 1900, four of the top ten riders were from the United States, including champion jockey, Lester Reiff.

Although their remarkable performances can be partly attributed to the riding of doped horses, the main reason was their different riding style. English jockeys rode erect with a comparatively straight knee and a good length of rein; in contrast the Americans pushed the saddle forward, shortened both stirrups and reins, and rode with knees bent, crouching along the horse's neck. By cutting wind resistance and giving a better weight distribution on the horse they gained a significant advantage. In order to compete, British jockeys had to follow suit and adopt the American methods. By 1902, the invasion was over, with only two Americans riding regularly in Britain; however, almost all British jockeys continued to race 'Americano'.

References:

Vamplew, W., The Turf: a Social and Economic History of Horse Racing (Harmondsworth: Allen Lane, 1976).

Further reading:

Watson, A. E. T., 'The American Jockey Invasion', Badminton Magazine, no. 24 (1907), pp. 422-433.

-Wray Vamplew

Horse-racing – Breeding

All the major racing nations of the world have imported the English thoroughbred and based their own breeding on the English model. Yet this itself was dependent upon foreign horses, for all thoroughbred horses in modern racing stem from three stallions imported into the country centuries ago – the Byerley Turk (born 1680), the Darley Arabian (born 1700) and the Godolphin Barb (born 1724). The Turk was captured at Buda in 1686 and ridden as a charger by Captain Byerley before being put to stud in England; Thomas Darley purchased his Arabian in Aleppo in 1704 and sent it to his Yorkshire estate; and the Barb, in reality a Yemeni stallion, was imported to stand at stud for the Earl of Godolphin. Paradoxically, given their influence on modern racing, none of these Arab horses were recorded as having ever raced. The value of this eastern blood lay in the toughness and stamina of these desert horses, which combined thorough selective breeding with the best of British stock, produced the modern thoroughbred. Subsequent controlled inbreeding and outcrossing has resulted in the present-day racehorse, that compound of power and elegance, strength and beauty, stamina and speed.

For many years, however, breeders attempted to produce outstanding horses without any theoretical backing behind their efforts; they merely appreciated that in some way qualities could be passed on from generation to generation. Whilst they showed an appreciation of racecourse performance and immediate family record, they were unaware that the female line was just as important as the male. Not until Mendel's work on heredity became better known did racehorse breeders begin to act on any explicit theoretical basis. In recent times, more scientifically-based genetic research has assisted breeders, but there is no magic formula. A judicious union of selected blood strains is more likely to produce good horses than random coupling, but still many great horses have produced some far from noteworthy offspring.

Breeding was mainly a private enterprise affair but during the 18th and 19th centuries the government intervened in the breeding market by offering prizes for winners of specific long-distance races – King's or Queen's Plates – which were designed to produce winners with stamina suitable for breeding cavalry remounts. These fell away as the commercial realities of racing offered larger prizes to sprint and handicap racing. In 1916, Colonel Hall Walker M.P. (later Lord Wavertree) presented the nation with his entire stud of valuable thoroughbred stock on condition that the government purchased his breeding and training establishments. Initially the use of the public purse to create a National Stud was justified on military grounds but the rationale later switched to the economic contribution made to exports. In 1967, the Stud moved to Newmarket and is now one of the most prestigious centres of the racehorse breeding industry.

Breeders rely extensively on the historical record of pedigrees. These are found in the *General Stud Book*, first compiled by James Weatherby in 1791 and updated ever since by the firm that bears his name.

References:

Magee, S., *The Channel Four Book of Racing* (London: Sidgwick & Jackson, 1989).

Vamplew, W., *The Turf: a Social and Economic History of Horse Racing* (London: Allen Lane, 1976).

Further reading:

De Moubray, J., *The Thoroughbred Business* (London: Hamish Hamilton, 1987).

Rasmussen, L. and Napier, M., *Treasures of The Bloodstock Breeders' Review* (London: J. A. Allen, 1990).

Websites:

The National Stud –
http://www.nationalstud.co.uk/

-Wray Vamplew

185

Horse-racing – Flat-racing

Horse-racing is of considerable antiquity, being recorded in Britain during Roman times and with references to its existence throughout the Middle Ages. Both Henry VIII and Elizabeth I established stud farms, and by the 16th century regular races for a prize of silver bells or a cup were being held at places such as Chester, Paisley and Carlisle. The enthusiasm of the Stuart kings for field sports led to the establishment of Newmarket as a major flat-racing centre, whilst Ascot owes its existence to the interest of Queen Anne.

The early 18th century saw the start of serious breeding of the racing thoroughbred, based on three stallions of Middle Eastern origin. Race meetings at this time normally consisted of matches between two horses and races between several horses running in heats, often over 3 or 4 miles, the winner being the first to win two heats. Such was the popularity of the sport and the spread of race meetings that in 1740, Parliament attempted to limit its growth by defining minimum prize levels. In 1752, the recently formed Jockey Club moved to Newmarket and over the next 120 years made the town the headquarters of flat-racing, gaining control of the sport throughout Britain.

Until the late 18th century, racehorses were brought into competitive running relatively late in life and carried quite heavyweight jockeys. Although there had been three-year-old races at York in the 1730s, it was not until the establishment of the first three 'classics' between 1776 and 1780 that races for young horses over 2 miles or less were considered important events. The potential of such races for gambling was soon realized and sweepstakes, handicap and weight-for-age races became popular. By the mid-19th century, lighter jockeys and young horses were the norm, and heats had vanished from all but minor meetings.

Horse-racing was Britain's main spectator sport well into the 19th century. For many towns the annual race meeting was the major social event of the year, bringing together all classes of society, though the gentry might also attend balls and the theatre while the lower classes had fairs, side-shows and some races of a less serious nature to amuse them. Until the opening of Sandown Park in 1875 there was at most courses no admission charge except for those in carriages, on horseback or seeking entry to a stand. Apart from rents from the proprietors of gaming booths and refreshment tents, the main sources of prize-money were entry fees and subscriptions and sponsorship from local notables and those such as innkeepers and other tradesmen who hoped to profit from the meeting. With the introduction of 'gatemoney' meetings and the greater commercialism of the sport in the last quarter of the 19th century, such support all but vanished. Even major courses such as Epsom and Doncaster were left behind the enclosed courses in terms of prize-money, and the Eclipse Stakes at Sandown reached £10,000 at a time when the 'classics' offered less than half this sum. In order to compete, most existing courses formed limited liability companies and adopted gatemoney status, though the process took years to complete. Other, minor courses had already fallen victim in the 1870s to Jockey Club regulations on minimum prizemoney, or secured their salvation by switching to National Hunt racing where such stringent financial rules did not apply.

The railways greatly improved the lot of racehorses which, with rare exceptions, had previously to walk between meetings. They also helped leading jockeys to become the first 'sporting superstars', by allowing them to take advantage of increased riding opportunities, particularly when the later London area courses held regular Saturday meetings. By the mid-19th century, the electric telegraph had greatly facilitated the transmission of horse-racing information and opened up betting opportunities to a wider public, even though off-course cash betting was illegal (and continued to be so until 1961).

Racing was one of the first sports to become international. The 1860s saw an invasion of French-bred horses which began to carry off the top prizes, but English jockeys rode regularly in both France and Belgium, taking advantage of the continental Sunday to increase their incomes. At the end of the century, American jockeys invaded the British turf and forced change in British racing habits and style.

A 19th-century visitor to a race meeting today would note that the basics of the sport remain the same – periods of calm interrupted by frenetic activity – but other things would be unrecognizable. Technology is now much more influential, with race cameras to assist the stewards, photo finishes to aid the judge, computers to help the handicappers, starting stalls to equalize opportunity at the start, all-weather courses to allow flat-racing to proceed all year round, and television commentary to provide information both to the stay-at-home spectator and the betting shop habitué. The bookmakers would still be there but in addition there is the totalizator – commonly referred to as the Tote – a form of pool betting introduced in 1928 to tap into the gambling revenue and put profits back into racing. Economic rationalization has reduced the number of courses, but Sunday and evening racing has been introduced in an attempt to increase attendances. The business world has become more involved via corporate entertaining, ownership of horses carrying company names, and sponsorship, reintroduced on a significant scale with the Whitbread Gold Cup in 1957. Overall, sponsorship is now responsible for around a quarter of prizemoney. Nevertheless, racing today is dependent upon the betting levy imposed on bookmakers and betting shops and the generosity of owners who continue to race mainly with their own money. Syndication has enabled ownership to become more diverse, socially and economically, but

wealth still counts and the past two decades have witnessed domination initially by pools millionaire, Robert Sangster, and latterly by the oil-rich Sheikhs of Dubai.

References:

Tyrrel, J., *Running Racing: the Jockey Club Years Since 1750* (London: Quiller, 1997).

Vamplew, W., *The Turf: a Social and Economic History of Horse Racing* (London: Allen Lane, 1976).

Further reading:

White, J., *The Racegoers' Encyclopedia* (London: CollinsWillow, 1997).

-Wray Vamplew/John Tolson

Horse-racing – Governance and Administration

For most of the past 200 years, British racing has been controlled by the Jockey Club, a self-elected body. Initially formed to arrange match races and settle gambling debts between members, over time it took more responsibility for organizing racing at Newmarket generally. From the early 19th century, other meetings that wished the Club to adjudicate on disputes were required to adopt the Jockey Club rules for their events. By 1900, the Club controlled flat-racing, though jump-racing remained outside its authority. Indeed, the Club had not wished to involve itself in that side of the sport, although Admiral Rous, senior Jockey Club steward at the time, had assisted the National Hunt Club in formulating its rules when it was established in 1866. In 1968, the two bodies were merged to provide racing with a unified controlling body, a precursor to incorporation by Royal Charter in 1970. Although this had the disadvantage that any change to its constitution, however trivial, required Privy Council permission, it did offer significant protection from political interference.

As public money – via a levy on bookmakers and from totalizator turnover – became increasingly important in the finance of racing, concern was expressed that control of the sport still lay in the hands of a private, self-perpetuating body. The Racecourse Betting Control Board had been set up in 1928 to distribute the profits of the totalizator but had never had much financial influence on the sport. In 1961, following the legalization of off-course betting, the Horserace Betting Levy Board was created to contribute to the costs of improving the breed of racehorses, advance veterinary science, and invest in on-course technical and security services, prizemoney and racecourse development. Nevertheless, the Jockey Club continued to have the dominant voice in determining the direction of British racing. In 1991, an inquiry into the industry's financial structure argued that it was in the sport's interest for the fragmented sectors to co-operate in a modernized power structure. Consequently, in 1993 the British Horseracing Board was set up to give owners, trainers and others in the industry more say. Only a minority of its members came from the Jockey Club. Its remit involves responsibility for negotiating racing's share of the betting levy, marketing the sport, and overseeing public relations policy for the industry.

Despite this, the Jockey Club still formulates, enforces and administers the rules of racing, investigates possible breaches of those rules and punishes offenders, appoints stewards to control individual meetings, supplies and licences officials, as well as authorizing fixtures and programmes. Administrative assistance comes from Weatherbys, a family firm working under contract to the Jockey Club. The relationship dates back to 1771, when James Weatherby was appointed Keeper of the Match Book, Stakeholder and Secretary to the Jockey Club. As well as producing the *Racing Calendar*, the official organ of the Jockey Club, and the *General Stud Book*, the official genealogical record of the English thoroughbred, they are responsible for recording entries to races and keeping accounts for many owners, trainers and jockeys.

References:

Hill, C. R., *Horse Power: the Politics of the Turf* (Manchester: Manchester University Press, 1988).

Tyrrel, J., *Running Racing: the Jockey Club Years Since 1750* (London: Quiller, 1997).

Further reading:

White, J., *The Racegoers' Encyclopedia* (London: CollinsWillow, 1997).

Websites:

The British Horseracing Board –
http://www.bhb.co.uk/
The Jockey Club –
http://www.thejockeyclub.co.uk/

-Wray Vamplew

Horse-racing – Jockeys

Jockeys are extraordinary sportspersons. They contrast with others uniquely in terms of their physique, age, gender and the danger of their occupation. In what other job are participants expected to peak mentally and physically up to six times a day, even more if there are evening meetings, for six and increasingly seven days a week; risk serious injury every time they go to work; and all the time restrict themselves to a diet designed to keep their weight well below the norm?

Jockeys were among the first sports professionals. They are also amongst the lightest. Indeed, the most obvious difference between jockeys and most other sportspersons is their size. Why jockeys have to be so small is not really clear but it can be speculated that the emergence of lighter weights owes something to gambling owners – and most of them were – realizing that lower weights gave an advantage in a race as well as lessening the risk of breakdown of valuable thoroughbred racing bloodstock, particularly as younger horses began to be raced. Whatever the reason, it forced all riders, apart from those blessed with natural lightness, to eat little and combat even that with a regimen of long walks in heavy clothes, Turkish baths and purgatives. Even riders with no apparent weight problems often found themselves trying to sweat off that additional pound, for an ability to ride at a lower weight increased the chances of employment in a competitive profession where there were always far more jockeys chasing mounts than there were rides available. Inevitably, such wasting weakened their constitutions: tuberculosis was almost an occupational disease. Over time, the Jockey Club has raised the minimum weight to its present level of 7 stone 10 pounds, in contrast to the 5 stone 7 pounds of 1860. Modern jockeys also have the benefit of access to scientific knowledge on nutrition, but theirs is still a life of fierce self-discipline. At the same time as existing on a starvation diet of tea and toast for breakfast, no lunch and a light supper, they have to keep fit and strong enough to control 1,000 pounds of horseflesh. For jump jockeys, poundage is less of a problem as most weights carried are above the 9 stone 7 pound mark, often the top weight in flat-racing.

The labour market situation is one of chronic oversupply. Fortunately, today, unlike in the 19th century, amateurs can only compete against professionals over jumps if they have been awarded a permit to do so and, apart from novelty events, there are no opportunities for amateurs to race against their paid counterparts on the flat. Competition, however, has had to be faced from foreign riders. In 1990, the list of the top ten jockeys in the British championship was literally a league of nations – it featured three Irishmen, two Scots, two Welshmen, an American, an Italian and a South African. Yet the regular international movement of jockeys is no modern phenomenon. It dates back well into the 19th century, coinciding with the development of the railways and steam shipping. No women could race in those days and the Jockey Club decision in 1972 to allow women to race at all, and in 1975 to allow them to participate as professionals, not unexpectedly caused some controversy and consternation in a male chauvinistic industry. To date, although women have ridden some winners, with the exception of Alex Greaves, they have not yet emerged as a major threat to their male counterparts.

All workers run the risk of industrial injury though for most the chances of being so injured are minimal. For jockeys, however, serious injury at work is not a possibility or even a probability; it is inevitable. Every leading jockey, whether flat or National Hunt, has suffered serious injury during their careers. For those who ride over hurdles and especially jumps, falls are an accepted part of the business. A rule of thumb is to expect a fall every fourteen rides and an injury every eighty. Falls are rarer on the flat but they occur unexpectedly. At least a jump jockey knows that most falls happen when his horse meets obstacles deliberately placed in its path and can be mentally prepared to take action. Flat-racing has no such advance warning system and when a horse slips over at high speed, often in the midst of other half-ton creatures, the consequences can be severe. Both forms of racing became more hazardous during the 19th century; flat-racing with the decline of long-distance staying events, and jumping as it became a faster-run affair.

The vocation of jockey is significantly different from 'normal' occupations in that the place of work varies daily. In the pre-railway era riders had to travel to meetings by coach, on horseback, or even walking with their racing saddles tied to their waist. Tommy Lye was said to have travelled over 6,000 miles in a season. The coming of the railway eased travel problems but most top jockeys took advantage of the new mode of transport not to relax but to increase their workload (and earnings). Nat Flatman, champion jockey in 1849, a year before there was any significant railway network, raced on only 75 days of the season, but by 1899, Sammy Loates, the leading rider in that season, was able to manage 179 days. Estimates of the respective distances travelled are 4,270 and 10,770 miles. Two major points can be made about workloads of the modern jockey. First, the vast majority of riders would prefer a heavier workload. The top few jockeys monopolize the mounts available, leaving the bulk of riders to join the demoralizing and stressful struggle for the few remaining opportunities. Second, to the initial travel convenience offered by the railway can be added that of the automobile, plane and helicopter, all of which have enabled the top riders to race more frequently than in the past; they are now able to include both afternoon and evening meetings on the same day within their itinerary. A professional jockey may have to cover between 50,000 and 60,000 miles annually in Britain alone.

References:

Tolson, J. and Vamplew, W., 'Derailed: Railways and Horse-Racing Revisited', *Sports Historian*, 18 (1998), pp. 34-49.

Vamplew, W., 'Riding For a Fall: the Health Hazards of Professional Jockeys in Nineteenth and Twentieth Century British Horseracing', in G. Pfister and T. Terry (eds.), *Sport and Health* (Proceedings of the 5th ISHPES Congress, Lyon, 1997).

Further reading:

Tanner, M. and Cranham, G., *The Guinness Book of Great Jockeys of the Flat: a Celebration of Two Centuries of Jockeyship* (Enfield: Guinness, 1992).

See also:

Memorable Events – Fred Archer's Suicide; Memorable Events – Frankie Dettori's Seven

-Wray Vamplew

Horse-racing – National Hunt

It is only relatively recently that people have been racing horses over obstacles. The modern sport of National Hunt racing includes steeplechasing over fences, and hurdle races over smaller and less substantial obstacles. Like flat-racing, the sport is administered by the British Horseracing Board under rules set by the Jockey Club. The racing season runs from August to June. Horses tend to be older than in flat-racing (at least three years old for a hurdler, five years old for a steeplechaser), carry bigger weights (the minimum is 10 stone, or 64 kilograms) and over longer distances (a minimum of 2 miles, or 3.2 kilometres). Regular race meetings are held at forty-two racecourses in Britain, of which twenty-three are confined to jump racing.

The first steeplechase was reputedly a match run between the churches of Buttevant and St Leger (hence the name) in Ireland in 1752, but the sport became really popular in the 1830s when some enterprising publicans began to organize races. Amongst the best known were Thomas Coleman, who operated a cross-country race in St Albans for several years from 1830, and William Lynn, who began a similar event a few years later near Liverpool. This became the Grand National, first run at Aintree in 1839. It was won by a horse called Lottery, whose exploits and achievements became so well known that he was often excluded from other races. The Grand National soon became the best-known race in the country, and has remained so ever since. Aintree was exceptional in having a grandstand on part of the course, even for the first Grand National. Most races were staged over open country, with no fixed or regular course as yet. Rules were determined locally and often poorly enforced.

Although popular, this form of racing had many critics. It had developed from both hunting and flat-racing, but many hunt supporters opposed the sport because it attracted crowds of undesirable spectators. Similarly, the Jockey Club had no truck with the sport at first. It was not until the need for some form of consistent governance was accepted that a ruling National Hunt Committee, a direct parallel to the Jockey Club, was set up, in 1866, to administer the sport throughout the country. Curiously, hurdle races, which seem to have originated in the 1830s using sheep hurdles as obstacles, were first included under the umbrella of flat-racing. In 1867, the National Hunt Committee became responsible for both steeplechases and hurdle races. The National Hunt Committee and Jockey Club were formally amalgamated in 1970.

By the last quarter of the 19th century, jump racing had developed the pattern recognizable today, with a distinct season and consistent rules and regulations. It was essentially a professional sport for specially trained horses, with races run over laid-out racecourses. Early races had been run across open country and even though part of the Grand National was run over farm land until 1885, this was by then unusual. Yet this very organization induced some enthusiasts to recall what they supposed to be the proper purpose of jump racing – a fair test for hunting horses and amateur riders. Fothergill (Fog) Rowlands was one of the first to take this view when he organized a 'Grand Annual' Steeplechase for hunting horses, first held in 1859. It did not become an annual event until some years later, but then found a permanent home at Cheltenham, where it now occupies a place in the famous festival meeting. Others of like mind set up hunt race meetings and point-to-point events. These came to be overseen by the National Hunt Committee as once-a-year meetings organized by local hunts to raise money (the first being that by the Atherstone Hunt in 1870) and were confined to horses that had been 'regularly and fairly hunted' in the preceding season.

By far the best known and most valuable race remained the Grand National, which since 1843 had been a handicap. However, in 1924, the Gold Cup, a level-weight race, was introduced at Cheltenham. Three years later, the Champion Hurdle was inaugurated. Both were to become the most prestigious races of their type in the calendar and form the centrepiece of the most prestigious meeting, the Cheltenham Festival, in March each year. Like nearly all major races, they are now commercially sponsored. The first horse-race to be so was a steeplechase, the Whitbread Gold Cup, in 1957. The sport has also received royal patronage, though not to the same extent as flat-racing. The Prince of Wales won the Grand National in 1900 with Ambush II; in the 1940s, the then Queen first took an interest in jump racing with a horse called Monaveen. As Queen Mother she became perhaps the best-known owner of all.

But it is the horses that have received particular adulation. As mature animals, steeplechasers and hurdlers can race year after year and become firmly imprinted in the public mind. The great Golden Miller won five Gold Cups in succession in the 1930s, as well as the Grand National; Reynoldstown won the Grand National twice. With mass exposure through television, public interest grew even more. The Irish horse, Arkle, was particularly popular and won three successive Gold Cups in the 1960s before injury forced retirement. Perhaps most famous of all was Red Rum, the only horse to have won three Grand Nationals (and finish second twice). He became so well known that he was constantly in demand in retirement for public appearances. Since that era, the great Desert Orchid, a Gold Cup winner, has similarly entered public affection.

There have also been problems. As long ago as the 1820s the famous sporting journalist 'Nimrod' (Charles Apperley) accused the sport of cruelty to horses. In recent years, the Grand National, in which there are frequent fallers and not infrequent deaths, has been the target of organized protests, which have often proved to be disruptive. Despite repeated measures to reduce the danger posed by steeplechase fences, especially at Aintree, the risks and danger can never be altogether eliminated.

References:

Blew, W. C. A., *A History of Steeplechasing* (London: John C. Nimmo, 1901).

Seth-Smith, M., Willett, P., Mortimer, R., Lawrence, J., *The History of Steeplechasing* (London: Michael Joseph, 1966).

Further reading:

Ayres, M. and Newbon, G., *Over the Sticks: the Sport of National Hunt Racing* (Newton Abbott: David & Charles, 1971).

Munting, R., *Hedges and Hurdles: a Social and Economic History of National Hunt Racing* (London: Allen, 1987).

Websites:

Aintree Racecourse – http://www.aintree.co.uk/
Cheltenham Racecourse – http://www.cheltenham.co.uk/

-Roger Munting

Horse-racing – Terminology

Like many other sports, there are a number of terms and phrases that are specifically peculiar to horse-racing.

For example, 'pattern races' are a series of prestigious events that test the merits of quality thoroughbreds of various ages over distances varying from 6-furlong sprints to the 20 furlongs of the Ascot Gold Cup. These races are graded into three 'groups', which are of similar standards throughout Europe.

At the other end of the quality spectrum are 'selling or claiming races', in which all losing horses can be claimed (for a specified sum) and the winner must be offered for sale by auction, though the owner receives only the sum specified in the race conditions, the surplus being shared equally between the owner of the second horse and the racecourse executive (or a charitable fund). If the owners pay to retain their winning animal they are said to have 'bought it in'.

Pattern races are non-handicap events in which the best horse should win, the only variations in weight being for gender, with fillies usually carrying lighter weights, and age, whereby differences in ability caused by maturative factors are allowed for. The 'weight-for-age' scale reflects the fact that as the season progresses, the edge enjoyed by an older horse over a younger one will diminish (though not disappear) and that it will be greater in longer distance stamina events than in the shorter sprint races, where speed is the key factor. In contrast, 'handicap races' are those in which

weights are allocated so as to take account of the varying abilities of the horses entered.

'Entries' to most races have to be made well in advance and indeed it is one of the arts of a trainer to plan a campaign for the horses in his care. If, at a stipulated date before a race, the horse's connections elect not to pay another sum to keep their animal in the race, then the original entry fee is declared 'forfeit'. Since 1992, owners have had to 'declare' the night before the race that their horse will or will not be running.

In deciding which jockey to employ, consideration will be given to any 'claiming allowance' which inexperienced riders are given. Those with less than twenty wins in their career are allowed to carry 7 pounds less than the horse's allotted weight, those with up to fifty wins get a 5-pound allowance, and those with up to ninety-five wins are given a 3-pound allowance. On the day of the race, it is vital to know the 'state of the going', which can range from heavy, soft, good to soft, good, good to firm, and firm or hard.

At the end of the race, jockeys must 'weigh in' to demonstrate that they have carried the weight with which they 'weighed out' before the race. The result as seen by the judge will then be official unless 'objections' have been raised. Objections give aggrieved parties the chance to complain that the rules of racing have been broken, though stewards can fine those who raise what they are feel are frivolous or vexatious objections.

References:

White, J., *The Racegoers' Encyclopedia* (London: CollinsWillow, 1997).

See also:

Ascot; Goodwood; Grand National

-Wray Vamplew

Hurling

The precise origins of the ancient Celtic sport of hurling, now played in Ireland and by Irish people across the world, are lost in the mists of time. The Old Irish Brehon Laws, dating to the 7th and 9th centuries CE, recognize the game. Hurling, 'the games which men call horlinges with big sticks of a ball on the ground' was forbidden by the Statutes of Kilkenny in 1366. The Statutes (composed in Norman French) were aimed at the English colonies of Northern Ireland, deterring them from succumbing to the Irish way of life. The Statutes of Galway (1527) and the Sunday Observance Act (1695) also mention the game. There were two homogenous versions of hurling – a winter game, adapted to a hard, frosty ground; and a summer variant, using a larger, softer ball, shorter and thicker clubs, and more aerial play. From the 17th century, hurling became the usual name in English for the summer game. Hurling remained popular in the 18th century, but the effects of the Famine in the 1840s, wholesale emigration and the erosion of a way of life which had ensured patronage for the game, led to its demise.

Hurling was resurrected in the second half of the 19th century. The Gaelic Athletic Association (G.A.A. – in Gaelic *Cumann Luthchleas Gael*) was formed in 1884 by Michael Cusack. The G.A.A. is a major part of Irish sporting and political life, administering Gaelic football and a wide range of other sporting and cultural activities from a multi-million pound, state-of-the-art stadium, Croke Park, in Dublin.

References:

Carbery, P., *History of Hurling* (Tralee: The Gaelic Athletic Association, 1946).

de Búrca, M., *The G.A.A. A History of the Gaelic Athletic Association* (Dublin: Cumann Lúthchleas Gael, 1980).

King, S. J., *A History of Hurling* (Dublin: Gill & Macmillan, 1996).

Further reading:

O'Maolfabhail, A., *Caman: Two Thousand Years of Hurling in Ireland* (Dundalk: Dundalgan Press, 1973).

Websites:

The Gaelic Athletic Association – http://www.gaa.ie/

-Hugh Dan MacLennan

I

Ice Hockey

Ice hockey is a sport played between two teams on ice, with up to six players of each team on the ice at any one time. Players propel a small round flat puck using sticks or their skates, with the object of placing the puck in the opposition net more times than the opposing side. The modern game is divided into three periods, each of twenty minutes. Origins of the game date back to stick and ball games played on ice in Northern Europe in the Middle Ages. The first match recognizable as modern ice hockey is attributed to British soldiers stationed in Ontario, Canada in around 1867, while the rules of the sport were first formulated at McGill University in Montreal, Canada in 1879, based upon those of British field hockey. At the beginning of the 20th century, the sport was championed in Britain by the then Governor-General of Canada, Lord Stanley of Preston, and his sons. The first organized ice-hockey match in Britain was played between the Universities of Oxford and Cambridge in 1895, with the first English League formed in 1903. This consisted of five teams from the South of England – Cambridge University, London Canadians, Princes and two teams from the London Henglers ice rink. In 1913-1914, the British Ice Hockey Association (B.I.H.A.) was formed by five teams from England – Princes, Cambridge and London Canadians being joined by the Royal Engineers and Manchester. In 1929, the Scottish Ice Hockey Association (S.I.H.A.) was founded, with the first Scottish League competition held that year. Ice hockey was particularly popular in Britain during the 1930s and 1950s, culminating in the Great British victory at the Olympic, World and European Championships in 1936 in Berlin. Though all but two of the British squad were born in Britain, most of the gold medal winning team had learnt the sport and trained in Canada. A British League was finally created in 1954, with the merging of the existing English and Scottish leagues, though increasing competition from other sources of leisure and entertainment, as well as rising wage demands of North American-dominated player rosters, saw the collapse of the British League in 1960. Ice hockey in Britain in the 1960s and 1970s was largely restricted to regional leagues and amateur teams and it was not until 1981-1982 that a British League was reinstated. 1996-1997 saw the first season of a new British Ice Hockey Superleague, with teams admitted on a franchise basis with no direct promotion or relegation. On February 23rd, 1997, a European ice hockey attendance record of 17,245 was set at the Nynex (now M.E.N.) Arena in Manchester for a game between the Manchester Storm and Sheffield Steelers. The British Superleague currently consists of eight teams, with a Belfast-based franchise planned for the 2000-2001 season and other franchises promised in the future. Below the Superleague, there is a league structure involving seasonal promotion and relegation that consists of a British national league and an English and a Scottish league, with a regional league structure below these.

References:

Drackett, P., *Flashing Blades: the Story of British Ice Hockey* (Marlborough: Crowood, 1987).

Drackett, P., *Vendetta on Ice* (Norwich: Ice Hockey World, 1992).

O'Brien, A., *Rinks to Arenas: Ten Years of British Ice Hockey* (Nottingham: Castle, 1998).

Sluyter, L., *A Game of Three Halves* (Edinburgh: Mainstream, 1998).

Sluyter, L., *Seasons To Be Cheerful* (Edinburgh: Mainstream, 1996).

Further reading:

Drackett, P., *Flashing Blades: the Story of British Ice Hockey* (Marlborough: Crowood, 1987).

Sluyter, L., *A Game of Three Halves* (Mainstream: London, 1998).

Websites:

The British Ice Hockey Superleague – http://www.iceweb.co.uk/

See also:

Roller Hockey

-Garry Crawford

Ice Skating (*see* Skating)

Industry (*see* Sports Industry)

Isle of Man T.T. Races

The Isle of Man, set in the Irish Sea between England, Ireland, Scotland and Wales, is at first glance an unlikely Mecca for motorcycle racing. The island measures just 33 miles by 13 (50 by 20 kilometres) and is known for its own currency, stamps, native tongue and the world's oldest continuous parliament, the Tynwald. However, the Isle is also world famous because of its Tourist Trophy (known as T.T.) series of motor races, which have been held on the island's roads ever since 1904. Originally these races were restricted to automobiles. In 1907, however, motorcycles were admitted and the torturous, undulating terrain made the T.T. race series arguably the most significant motor-cycle competition in the world.

The Oxford Companion to World Sports and Games notes, 'The oldest motor-cycle racing circuit still in use is the Snaefell mountain course over which the Isle of Man Tourist Trophy races are run. Starting at the town of Douglas on the south-east coast, the course takes a wide sweep to the west and north to enter the town of Ramsey on the north-east coast and thence return to the starting point, each lap measuring 37 3/4 miles (60.6 km) and taking in over 200 bends while climbing from sea level to an altitude of over 1,300 ft. (396 m). This circuit is the epitome of the natural road course, all the roads used being ordinary public highways closed for the racing and practice sessions.'

The first T.T. race over the Snaefell course took place in 1911. In 1957, the T.T. races were headlined by McIntyre, riding an Italian-made Gilera, who accomplished the first lap at over 100 miles per hour (161 kilometres per hour). Two years later, a new racing team, Honda of Japan, participated in the 125 cc race. Today, the premier T.T. racing bikes are streamlined technological wonders that carry riders around the Snaefell course at an average speed of 120 miles per hour (approximately 200 kilometres per hour).

During the T.T. Festival and the Manx Grand Prix it is difficult to travel across or around the island because of the road closures. There is a T.T. access road in Douglas that gives access to the centre of the mountain course during the event.

The T.T. races, traditionally held in the last week of May and the first week of June, create a carnival atmosphere that is extraordinary and unique. The picnicking crowds which celebrate the racers by flanking the 37-mile circuit are reminiscent of the community festivals that are part and parcel of another form of cycle racing in a different country – The Tour de France.

References:

Arlott, J. (ed.), *The Oxford Companion to World Sports and Games* (London: Oxford University Press, 1975), p. 669.

Further reading:

Bonini, G., 'Motorcycle Racing', in D. Levinson and C. Christensen (eds.), *Encyclopedia of World Sport* (Santa Barbara, California: ABC-CLIO, 1996), pp. 653-657.

Websites:

Isle of Man T.T. Races – http://www.iomtt.com/

See also:

Motorcycle Racing

-Scott Crawford

197

Jordanhill College

Jordanhill College was the location of the Scottish School of Physical Education, the centre for the training of male specialist physical education teachers in Scotland from 1931 to 1987. It was set up at Jordanhill Training College in Glasgow under the Directorship of F. N. Punchard, who had been appointed to the staff of Dunfermline College in 1919 and had established successful courses for men. This move was contemporaneous with the founding in England of one-year training courses for men who were already qualified teachers, by the Carnegie Trust at Leeds in 1933. Punchard, who had been a member of the first civilian specialist course in Physical Education in England in 1908, adhered to the Swedish system of gymnastics, and the gymnastic skill and adventure elements of physical education characterized the programmes.

In 1966, Jordanhill College first offered an undergraduate degree in Physical Education via the B.Ed. of the University of Glasgow, but the programme was not well suited to the subject. A degree validated by the Council of National Academic Awards was launched in 1974 and in 1978, the Scottish School started the first in-service B.Ed. degree of any Scottish College of Education.

The contraction of the college system advocated by the Scottish Tertiary Education Advisory Council led to a centralization of Physical Education training in Edinburgh and a merger into Moray House College. However, Jordanhill College retained its diversified undergraduate courses in Sport in the Community and Outdoor Education. It now forms the Faculty of Education of Strathclyde University.

References:
Cruickshank, M., *A History of the Training of Teachers in Scotland* (London: University of London Press, 1970).
'F. N. P.', *Scottish Journal of Physical Education*, vol. 5, no. 3 (October, 1977), p. 38.
Scotland, J., *The History of Scottish Education* (London: University of London Press, 1969).

Further reading:
Cruickshank, M., *A History of the Training of Teachers in Scotland* (London: University of London Press, 1970).

See also:
Carnegie Collge; Education – Teacher Training; Loughborough University

-Lorna Jackson

Journalism

Sports journalism, the reporting of sports news in press and broadcasting, developed in tandem with organized sport. Organized sport developed because people were willing to pay to watch events; sports journalism developed from their parallel willingness to pay to read about them.

Michael Harris notes that many early sports reports were supplied by readers rather than journalists. Racing results were a staple of the London press by the 1730s, accompanied by a 'steady upward curve' in cricket coverage.

The first 'name' sports reporter was Irish-born boxing writer, Pierce Egan, whose five-volume *Boxiana* (1813-1828), built on years of writing for the *Weekly Dispatch*, is the main source for the early history of the sport.

The 19th century saw the development of a specialized sporting press. *Bell's Life*, founded in 1822, evolved from origins as a society weekly. It was joined in 1859 by the daily *Sporting Life*, which was to swallow it in 1885. The *Sporting Life*, which survived until the 1990s, focused on horse-racing, whose almost daily meetings and large following of gamblers provided the ideal reader base. It was soon joined by two other dailies, the *Sportsman* (1865-1924) and the Manchester-based *Sporting Chronicle* (1871).

Weekly papers devoted to a particular sport, or group of sports, also grew in number. The *Field* (1852) survives as chronicler of country sports while *Cricket* (1882-1914) is described by Tony Mason as 'the most comprehensive account of the game's development before 1914, an essential source for any historian of the game'. *Athletic News* (1875-1931) covered a range of sports but was chiefly known for its detailed coverage of football. Its rise to mass circulation accompanied football's growth into Britain's most popular sport.

Football's growth helped stimulate the change that killed most of the specialized sporting press – extensive local and national press coverage. The first Saturday night editions carrying results and reports appeared in the 1880s, and still survive in the larger regional centres. This growth helped make sports-reporting agencies a worthwhile proposition. The Press Association, which serves the regional press, started a sports service in 1883 while the

Cricket Reporting Agency, famed for its connection with *Wisden Cricketers' Almanack*, started in 1880. Designated press seats and boxes were provided more systematically – the first Lords press box opened in 1867.

There had been comparatively little sports coverage in the mid-19th century national press. However, this changed towards the end of the century, with Sunday papers taking advantage of growing interest in Saturday games. Names such as the *Referee* and the *Umpire* reflected a focus on sport, although with a full news service. The *Daily Mail*, whose launch in 1896 is regarded as the foundation date of the modern popular press, provided a full daily page from the start.

Football and racing provided most copy for popular papers, with betting tips providing a bone of contention for the left-wing press. The Labour *Daily Citizen* (1912-1915) suffered resignations from its board when tips were introduced and *Daily Herald* (1912-1964) editor-proprietor George Lansbury fought a long and finally unavailing battle against them. Much of the sale of the Communist *Daily Worker* (1930) was attributed anecdotally to the excellence of tipster Cayton.

Extensive national press coverage destroyed much of the specialist press – *Athletic News* closed in 1931 and the *Sportsman* in 1924, with the *Sporting Life* and *Sporting Chronicle* surviving as papers devoted almost exclusively to racing. This helps to account for the absence of any British counterpart to Spain's *Marca* and *As*, France's *L'Equipe*, Italy's *Gazetta* or even a weekly all-sports magazine such as the American *Sports Illustrated*.

Sportsweek, an attempt to create a British *Sports Illustrated*, failed after a few months in 1986. Plans to re-launch the *Sporting Life* as an all-round sports daily foundered in 1998. *Sport First*, a Sunday paper devoted almost exclusively to sport, was launched in 1998.

National press coverage has grown steadily in the 20th century, but with significant changes of emphasis. Broadcasting usurped its role as the first provider of basic information, particularly results. This led to a greater emphasis on off-field events – much football news in the popular press is informed transfer speculation – and more comment. The star columnist was a mid-century novelty, epitomized by Peter Wilson of the *Daily Mirror* and Desmond Hackett of the *Daily Express*, the most successful popular papers of the period.

The 'quality' press has also played increasing attention. In the first half of the century, writers like Bernard Darwin of *The Times* (golf) and Neville Cardus of the *Manchester Guardian* (cricket) brought individual distinction to their papers, but comprehensive coverage took longer, led by the *Daily Telegraph*, whose huge circulation by broadsheet standards was partly attributable to the breadth of its coverage.

The use of sportsmen as writers, regarded warily by professional journalists, attracted condemnatory resolutions at the National Union of Journalists Annual Delegate Meeting as early as the 1920s. In recent years, the ghosted column – ostensibly by a player, but almost always written by a journalist on the basis of an interview – has spread from the tabloids to the broadsheets.

In the 1980s and 1990s, sport was increasingly perceived as a serious circulation builder. Coverage expanded rapidly, with dedicated sports pull-outs becoming a standard part of Monday papers as they sectionalized. It also began to permeate the news pages, both in the form of celebrity gossip and coverage of the political and economic issues arising from sport. Sports correspondents attached to news rather than sports desks became common in the 1990s. Sports journalism's rising status within the profession was reflected in 1998 by the appointment of Simon Kelner, a former sports editor, as editor of the broadsheet *Independent*.

Women writers, previously almost entirely confined to 'women's sports', began to appear in football and Rugby press boxes from the 1970s and 1980s, but there was no corresponding shift towards serious coverage of sport played by women. Sport continues to be the section of newspapers most read by men and least by women.

Magazines also proliferated, with football's 1980s fanzine movement triggering a response from mainstream commercial publishers.

References:

Harris, M., 'Sport in the Newspapers before 1750: Representations of Cricket, Class and Commerce in the London Press', *Media History*, vol. 4, no. 1 (1998), pp. 19-27.

Holt, R., *Sport and the British* (Oxford: Oxford University Press, 1989).

Mason, T., *Sport in Britain* (London: Faber & Faber, 1988).

Mason, T., 'Sporting News 1860-1914', in M. Harris and A. Lee (eds.), *The Press in English Society from the Seventeenth to Nineteenth Centuries* (London: Associated University Presses, 1986).

Further reading:

Glanville, B., 'Looking for an Idiom', New York Times (18th July, 1965), reprinted in Glanville, *People in Sport* (London: Sportsmans Book Club, 1968).

MacAdam, J., *The MacAdam Road* (London: Sportsmans Book Club, 1957).

Wilson, P., *The Man They Couldn't Gag* (London: Stanley Paul, 1977).

See also:

Media

-Huw Richards

Judo

Judu was developed by Professor Jigoro Kano in 1882 as a combat sport that uses unarmed techniques such as leverage, throws and holds. Kano based judo upon the martial art of *ju jitsu*. He introduced the sport into Britain in 1885, although it was Gunji Koizumi who established the sport in Britain. He opened the Budokwai Club in London in 1918 and appointed a professional wrestler, Yukio Tani, as the club's first instructor.

The sport was given a European dimension in 1926 following a match between the Budokwai Club and the German national team. The match proved to be popular and helped to promote judo throughout Europe. British and European governing bodies were established in 1948 and were followed by the formation of the International Judo Federation in 1951. The first European Championships were held in 1951 and the first world championships in 1956. Britain was successful at the 1957 European Championships, beating Holland 2-1 in the final. The first world championships for women were held in 1980. Judo became an Olympic sport for men in 1964 and for women in 1992. Britain's Kate Howey was the 1997 Senior World Champion. Other British successes include the winning of silver and bronze medals at the 1992 Olympics by Nicola Fairbrother and Kate Howey respectively.

References:

The British Judo Association website – http://www.britishjudo.org.uk/

Lewis, P., *The Martial Arts: Origins, Philosophy, Practice* (London: Prion 1996).

Websites:

The British Judo Association – http://www.britishjudo.org.uk/

-Ray Physick

Karate

The origins of karate can be traced back to Okinawa, an island situated between China and Japan. Upon being invaded by the Japanese in 1609 the Okinawans were disarmed, leaving them at the mercy of their conquerors. The islanders, keen to expel the Japanese from the island, consulted local monks about unarmed fighting techniques. The monks duly obliged, showing them how to strengthen and toughen their knuckles and elbows using straw pads and sand. The Okinawans also practised pounding their fists into tree trunks until they developed huge callouses on their hands.

The islanders were now ready to fight the Japanese unarmed, using their karate combat techinques – the word 'karate' actually means 'empty hand'. Japanese armour was made of bamboo and leather thongs, material that was easily penetrated by the hardened hands of the Okinawans. In fact, their hands were so hard that many Japanese were killed by Okinawans using the karate combat style. Even the Japanese cavalry could not cope, as the islanders used lethal kicks to frighten and disperse the horses.

Modern karate was introduced into Japan by Gichin Funakoshi in 1921. The sport spread from Japan to Europe and America after the Second World War. It remained a fragmented sport, however, until the Federation of All Japan Karate-do Organisations (F.A.J.K.O.) was formed in 1964. World championships, organized by F.A.J.K.O., were held in Tokyo in 1970. Soon after the championships, the World Union of Karate-do Organisations was formed and is now the international governing body of the sport (it was renamed the World Karate Federation in 1993). At the 1972 world championships, an all-British team became the first team ever to defeat Japan in international competition.

An organization similar to the F.A.J.K.O. was established in Britain in 1967. In 1991, the English Karate Governing Body (E.K.G.B.) was formed through the amalgamation of two bodies, the English Karate Council and the English Karate Board. The E.K.G.B. is recognized and supported by Sport England. The most popular form of karate in Britain today is *Shotokan*.

References:

Lewis, P., *The Martial Arts: Origins, Philosophy, Practice* (London: Prion 1996).

The English Karate Governing Body website – http://www.ekgb.org.uk/

The World Karate Federation website – http://www.wkf.net/

Websites:

The English Karate Governing Body – http://www.ekgb.org.uk/

The World Karate Federation – http://www.wkf.net/

-Ray Physick

Kick Boxing

Not dissimilar from karate, kick boxing involves the use of boxing techniques combined with kicking, in an attempt to win by either scoring points from a judge, or else preventing the opponent from continuing.

Kick boxing, however, is a sport diverse in its organization and content. Several styles of kick boxing exist, participants fighting under different rules, depending upon which association they are affiliated to.

Kick boxing has struggled to be officially recognized in Britain, as the Sports Council fails to recognize any of the different governing bodies. At present there are five different bodies that control the different versions of kick boxing in Britain.

The actual fights, at the amateur level, are based around three two-minute rounds. Opponents are chosen on the basis of weight and fighting experience. In professional bouts the fights last for ten rounds. There are a plethora of different titles on offer to those taking part. These are a product of the range of organizing bodies, regional and inter-club titles. For professional and amateur fighters there are British, European and World titles to pursue.

In Britain, the growing professional scene attracts only moderate prize-money, when compared to that available in Europe and the Far East. Since its arrival in Britain, kick boxing has steadily grown in popularity, especially during the 1990s, with clubs now to be found in most towns. While the majority of participants are men, the number of women taking part has also steadily increased. The 2000 World Championships were staged in Salford.

References:

Jackson, J., 'Kick Boxing: Lord of the Ring', *Nautlius Magazine*, vol. 4, no. 4 (August 1982), pp. 70-72.

Lane, D., 'High Kicking Profits: a Clean-Cut Hero and a New Wave of Martial Arts Films has Spawned the Contact Sport of the '90s', *Bulletin*, no. 114 (15 December 1992), pp. 93-94.

See also:

Boxing; Kung Fu

-Donna Musgrove

Knur and Spell

Knur and Spell is a game traditionally associated with the industrial areas of the West Riding of Yorkshire and Lancashire. Although there are many variations in the rules of the game and the equipment used, the basic principle is straightforward. It is to strike a small hard ball (the knur), which is either thrown up or suspended in a loop of cord, with a specially constructed stick (the bat). The aim is simply to drive the ball as far as possible, and shots of between 200 and 300 yards have frequently been recorded. Principally a pastime for working people, Knur and Spell was also commonly referred to as 'poor man's golf'.

In medieval times, matches were often played on Shrove Tuesday and Good Friday, and were occasions of strong inter-village rivalry. The earliest method of tossing up the ball seems to have involved placing it on one end of a flat piece of wood, which was itself balanced on a small round peg. The other end of the wood was struck smartly with the bat, causing the knur to spring up ready for striking.

The name 'Knur and Spell' derives from the Old Norse 'Nurspel', meaning 'ball game', which suggests that the sport has Viking origins. However, over the centuries, the Norse word 'spel' has been confused with the North Country 'spell', meaning a piece of wood. Thus the word 'spell' has come to be used for the trap from which the ball was hurled into the air.

In the 19th century and the years before the First World War, the game attracted an enormous following. In 1859, a match at Wibsey, Bradford, between Jackie Jagger and 'Bill at

Mount' is said to have been watched by a crowd of more than 10,000. Nearly all such contests were occasions for heavy betting, and matches were often played for stakes of £50 or £100, representing perhaps one or two years of wages to most people. During the 1920s, the Burnley F.C. goalkeeper, Gerry Dawson, played for £250 on the moors above the town. During recent years, however, the number of people with the skill to play the game and to make the specialized equipment has declined rapidly, and Knur and Spell has fallen into comparative obscurity.

References:

Spen Valley Local History Survey, *Pennine Pastimes: Knur and Spell* (Hebden Bridge: Pennine Heritage Network, 1984).

-Richard William Cox

Kung Fu

The martial art of kung fu has its origins in ancient China during the Chou dynasty, *c.* 1111-255 BC. Its modern form, however, was introduced to the monks at Shaolin Monastery in around 520 AD by an Indian monk called Bodhidharma. Kung fu is based upon exercises that are supposed to condition the body physically and the mind spiritually. The methodology of kung fu is said to come from the natural world, religion and cosmology. Fighting techniques have been adapted following the observation of mammals, birds and insects. Bodhidharma introduced 18 exercises to the monks of Shaolin, however, these were later increased to 170 by Kwok Yuen in 1589.

Kung fu was popularized by Bruce Lee in the 1970s, although his style of kung fu was an amalgam of kung fu plus western and Thai boxing techniques. This brand of kung fu became known as *jeet kune-do*, or 'way of intercepting the fist'. The sport is widely practised in the United Kingdom and is especially popular amongst students within many of Britain's universities.

References:

Lewis, P., *The Martial Arts: Origins, Philosophy, Practice* (London: Prion 1996).

See also:

Kick Boxing

-Ray Physick

Land and Water Speed Records

On October 4th, 1983, at Gerlach, Nevada, in the United States, Richard Noble catapulted his *Thrust 2* car, powered by a Rolls Royce RG 146 Avon MK. 302C engine from an R.A.F. F6 Lightning jet fighter, back across the sun-baked surface of the Black Forest desert. The timing computers calculated his average speed across the measured mile on this return run as 642.971 miles per hour. When combined with 624.241 miles per hour from the first run, this gave him an overall average of 633.468 miles per hour and Britain again held the Land Speed Record. The same desert location saw Briton Andy Green become the first driver to exceed the speed of sound when, in October 1997, in *Thrust SSC*, designed by Noble and powered by twin Rolls-Royce jet engines, he reached a phenomenal 763.035 miles per hour. In less than a century the record had reached a level never dreamed of by the early pioneers.

The first British holder was Charles S. Rolls, who held the record for two brief periods in 1903, the second time at 84.732 miles per hour. He was followed by Arthur E. Macdonald in 1905 (104.651 miles per hour), L. G. 'Cupid' Hornsted in 1914 (124.095 miles per hour) and Kenelm Lee Guinness in 1922 (129.171 miles per hour).

Onward and upward went the record, with many milestones reached by British drivers during the golden age of the Land Speed Record, the 1920s. Captain (later Sir) Malcolm Campbell, on Pendine Sands in South Wales, broke the 150-miles-per-hour barrier when he achieved 150.766 miles per hour in his Sunbeam *Bluebird* in 1925. This was Campbell's fourth of an amazing eleven records, the last of which he set at Bonneville Salt Flats, Utah, in 1935 when he became the first man to exceed 300 miles per hour, his latest *Bluebird* averaging 301.129 miles per hour. He had earlier become the first past the 250-miles-per-hour mark, reaching 253.968 miles per hour at Daytona Beach, Florida in yet another *Bluebird* in 1932. The last British holder before Noble was Sir Malcolm's son, Donald, who reached 403.135 miles per hour at Lake Eyre in Australia in the Campbell-Norris Bluebird-Proteus CN7. The 200-miles-per-hour hurdle had fallen to Sir Henry Segrave in 1927. Also in a Sunbeam, with twin V12 Matabele engines, he reached 203.793 miles per hour in Daytona. This was the second of Segrave's three records. He was knighted in 1929. John Godfrey Parry Thomas held the record briefly in 1926 but was soon eclipsed by Campbell, whose 1935 record in turn fell first to Captain George E. T. Eyston and then to John Rhodes Cobb, who between them raised the record six times at Bonneville between 1937 and 1947. Cobb's last effort, 394.196 miles per hour in the Railton Mobil Special, was to stand for thirteen years.

Not content with pursuing the record on land, Segrave also held the water speed record, becoming the first man to hold both records simultaneously, a feat later matched by both Campbells. Tragically, Segrave, Cobb and Donald Campbell were all to die in attempts on the water speed record. Segrave died in 1930 on Lake Windermere when his *Miss England II* hit a submerged log. Cobb was killed in 1952 on Loch Ness when the jet-powered *Crusader* left the water at over 240 miles per hour after hitting the wake of a spectator boat. Cambell had already broken the record seven times before he perished on Coniston Water in 1967, when the inevitably-named *Bluebird* arced out of the water at over 300 miles per hour. His body was never found.

References:

Harding, A. (ed.), *The Guinness Book of Car Facts and Feats* (Enfield: Guinness, 1980).

Holthusen, P. J. R., *The Land Speed Record* (Yeovil: Book Club Associates, 1986).

Matthews, P., Buchanan, I. and Mallon, B., *The Guinness International Who's Who of Sport* (Enfield: Guinness, 1993).

-Tony Rennick

Landyachting

The exhilarating sport of landyachting (or sandyachting) involves the sailing of 'wheeled yachts' on sand. The sport is cheap in that there are no running costs – all you need is a hard flat beach, a breeze, a sandyacht and a few hours in which to play.

The desire to harness the power of the wind and use it as a means of propulsion can be traced back some 3,800 years to the tomb walls of an Egyptian king. If, in your youth, you had tremendous fun using an old pram chassis, or something similar, as a go-kart, and tried to get the wind to blow it along by hoisting an old bedsheet as a sail, then you have already tried sandyachting.

There are numerous beaches around the country, but remarkably few of them are suitable for sandyachting, as it is not possible to sail on soft sand – the wheels dig in and the yacht will not move, even if a gale is blowing. If a beach is capable of being sailed on, then you can be certain that there is a history of people sailing sandyachts on it.

The sport was first drawn to the attention of the public in 1951, when footage of sailing on Saunton Sands, Devon, and on Southport Sands, was broadcast on the television. The Fylde International Sand Yacht Club was formed in August 1951, based at Lytham St Annes, near Blackpool, and remains the 'home' of the sport to this day.

Early sandyachts were generally very large, of heavy steel construction, and could only sail in strong winds. Howver, the imagination of the yacht-building engineers soon ran riot, and yachts of every possible shape and configuration were built. Some had four wheels, in a square, rectangular or diamond shape layout, and some had three, some with a single steerable wheel at the front, or at the rear, or even, in the case of the 'Crabber', independent steering to all three wheels.

The arrival of iceyachting technology on British beaches in 1963 revolutionized the sport and proved that sandyachts did not need to be huge to go fast. Sandyachts have shrunk in size over the years and two classes of sandyacht are raced in Britain today – Class 3 (large wing-rigged yachts of timber construction, capable of speeds up to 80 miles per hour) and Class 5 (smaller tubular-steel yachts with 5 square metres of sail, capable of speeds up to 65 miles per hour.

The sport is governed by the British Federation of Sand and Land Yacht Clubs (B.F.S.L.Y.C.), formed in 1965, and the competitive sport enjoys minority status with less than 100 active participants nationwide.

The informal sport of sandyachting, the enjoyment of the simple pleasure of sailing silently along sandy beaches on bright sunny days propelled only by the wind and leaving nothing but tyre marks, is enjoyed by nearly 350 people between the ages of seven and seventy.

References:

Parr, A., *Sandyachting: a History of the Sport and its Development in Britain* (Haverfordwest: The Author, 1993).

Websites:

The British Federation of Sand and Land Yacht Clubs – http://www.landyachting.org/

-Andrew Parr

Language

If the draft entries to this encyclopedia do not 'come up to scratch' (prizefighting), then the editors may have to 'take a different tack' (yachting), though they would certainly not 'throw in the towel' (boxing). Over the years, sporting terminology has infiltrated the nation's language so that most of us are now conversant with such English expressions of fair play as 'it's not cricket', 'a level playing field' and not 'moving the goalposts'. One sport alone, horse-racing, has given us 'first past the post' (though a pedant would note that in actuality races are won by first at the post), a 'two-horse race', 'under starter's orders', 'shouting the odds', 'coming down the home straight', and, a direct consequence of English racing conditions, 'horses for courses'. Historically, we have 'Archer's Up' meaning 'a near certainty', although this did not survive; and 'on one's tod' to mean 'alone', an expression which originated via the tactics of American jockey Tod Sloan, who revolutionized British jockeyship by racing from the front rather than waiting in the pack. Others which spring readily to mind include golf's 'stymied', 'bunkered', 'par for the course' and the 'rub of the green'; cricket's 'playing with a straight bat'; 'game, set and match' from tennis; 'snookered' and caught 'behind the eight ball' from the green baize games; as well as 'jumping the gun' from athletics.

More historically, and often with their original meaning forgotten, come 'crestfallen' when a fighting cock disappoints and playing 'fast and loose', as dangerous in one's love life as in unregulated archery. Semantic historians are also required to explain the origins of some sporting terminologies. Were 'heats' a derivation from a form of 'warm up' prior to the main event? Did tournament seeding emerge from the best horticultural practice of keeping seeds well apart so as to stimulate their development?

Some sporting terms, however, are incomprehensible to all but the cognoscenti. Although some cricket fielding positions such as wicket-keeper are obvious, the vast majority, including gully, silly mid-on, and fly slip require specialist knowledge. And what of the confusion between a wicket masquerading as a pitch, a set of stumps and a verdict against the batting side? Also confusing is that some words change their meaning from sport to sport. The stroke in rowing is the individual crew member who dictates the pace for the team, but in cricket and tennis it describes a shot, which also has two meanings within shooting, that of the ammunition used and also its actual firing. And, of course, the full nelson of wrestling is not to be mistaken with the less complete Nelson, which is a cricket reference to a score of 111. Even the habitués of the betting shop do not always appreciate the nuances of the bookmaking subculture –'carpet' for odds of 3 to 1, bottle for a point less – though they would be more at home decoding a race card than those who had never seen the inside of a Ladbrokes or William Hill office. Language impenetrable except to those within the sporting fraternity acts as a barrier to keep out the uninitiated (and unwanted), but, in this, sport is no different from law, academe and other areas where language is used to enhance the mystique of the profession.

209

Language is not fixed and neither is sport. Returning to fielding positions in cricket, 'long stop' has long gone but the one-day game has taken 'sweeper' from soccer, while the latter now features strikers, mid-fielders and wing-backs, playing positions unknown before the 1970s. In Rugby Union, the second row transformed themselves into locks and what was the lock forward became the number eight. Tennis has introduced the tie-break and lawn bowls the set. Golf technology has changed bogey, derived from the imaginary bogeyman opponent who shot the standard score, to being one over par. Perhaps the greatest changes are noticeable in sporting journalism: one only has to compare Pierce Egan's pugilistic reports of the early 19th century with Sky Television's hype for their pay-per-view boxing contests.

Indeed, commentary has developed its own use of language with the speech syntax of television differing significantly from that of radio, and with neither reflecting normal conversation, even that between sports fans. Moreover, an insistence on interviewing the uninterviewable has produced a plethora of clichés of the 'taking one game at a time' and 'a game of two halves' variety. Nevertheless, commentators and journalists have made their own contributions to the development of sporting language from the commonplace 'all over him like a rash' of man-for-man marking to the more erudite 'much ado about nothing nothing' of a scoreless fixture. There is a fashion: at the time of writing this entry, for example, 'up for it' was about to replace 'keeping their shape' as the 'in phrase' in football critiques. Yet manufactured phrases do not always catch on: 'pyjamaed clowns' as a protest against the uniforms of one-day cricket never reached the literary stature of the 'flannelled fools' of an earlier era. That said, 'sick as a parrot' has achieved colloquial cult status, as has Kenneth Wolstenholme's famous 1966 World Cup comment that 'they think it's all over'. It is the media that popularized the alliterative 'Hurricane Higgins', but attempts to impose nicknames on teams may founder: the Gunners and the Blades evolved out of the local economic environment, unlike the Rhinos, Bulls and other commercially manufactured inmates of the bestiary.

Britain exported not just its sport but often its sporting language. There were few takers for language courses to assist fans going to the 1998 World Cup Finals when it was realized that the French already had 'le football', 'le free kick' and 'le kickoff'. Indeed, most nations have a version of the word 'football', except the Italians, who prefer 'calcio', from their traditional Florentine game. Nevertheless, Britain has imported 'southpaw', devised by a Chicago baseball writer to describe the direction faced by a left-handed batter in his local stadium and 'pole position' taken from the markers around the inside of race tracks in America. Furthermore, it was an Australian journalist who coined the term 'bodyline' for the infamous test series of 1932/33.

Of course, sporting language is not just written or spoken. There are also visual forms of communication, for example the tic-tac men sending betting odds from ring to ring, umpires passing information on the cricket scorers, and the hand and body signals of Rugby referees which inform both crowd and players of the offence committed. Let us hope that as the final whistle sounds, this entry is not redcarded by the editors.

References:
Beard, A., *The Language of Sport* (London: Routledge, 1998).

Further reading:
Andrews, B., 'Tugging Four Bits Off the Deck at the WACA: Australian Sport and Australian English', in R. Cashman and M. McKernan (eds.), *Sport: Money, Morality and the Media* (Sydney: New South Wales University Press, 1980), pp. 136-161.

-Wray Vamplew

Law

The law, both civil and criminal, has intervened within sport in a number of ways. Whether the law *should* intervene within sport is a far more problematic area, as many would argue that sports should be permitted to regulate themselves without recourse to the courts. Historically, the law was often used to outlaw participation in sports when it was felt that this participation might result in a threat to public order or might detract from war effort. If people were indulging in less directed pastimes, they would not be spending as long practising archery for example. Recent years have witnessed a far more interventionist role for law in sport. For example, in the area of contract law players have sought legal review of their contractual arrangements and, in certain situations, to free themselves from their contracts so as to allow them to ply their trade elsewhere. In addition, there have been legal challenges against the governing bodies of individual sports questioning both how far the powers of such bodies extend and the legitimacy of their decision-making processes (see, for example, *Law v National Greyhound Racing Club Ltd* [1983] 3 All ER 300). This latter area has become particularly pronounced with respect to the granting of licences by bodies such as the Jockey Club and the British Boxing Board of Control (B.B.B.C.). For example, Jane Couch, otherwise known as the 'Fleetwood Assassin', brought a discrimination action against the B.B.B.C. after it consistently refused to grant her a boxing licence on the grounds that she was female. She was ultimately successful and became the first woman to be granted a professional boxing license in Britain. A woman trainer had successfully brought a similar action against The Jockey Club, *Nagle v Feilden* 1966 1 All ER 689.

The governing bodies will, through their rulebooks, attempt to exert some control over the activities and behaviour of the players. A common charge is of 'bringing the game into disrepute', which may cover a multitude of sins; similarly, there may be rules relating to the use of drugs. The administrators will need to ensure that any penalties handed out are consistent with respect to both the rulebook and past practice. As many sports have moved from amateur to professional status there is more at stake than reputation and bans may result in a serious loss of income and potential legal challenges.

The law has begun to intervene in sport in other ways, especially where players have been injured whilst playing. Technically, physical contact between players could result in legal action, however, due to the nature of sport, some element of contact is inevitable and a defence has developed on the basis that participants in sport consent to some element of contact. The issue of consent, however, is not as clear as it seems and much legal debate has centred on the issue of what a player can consent to, and how far such consent can extend. This has created problems of definition, especially where there is a conflict between the sports' own rules or laws, the working cultures of individual sports and 'the law', and some criminal actions have been brought against sports persons who have transgressed on the sports field. In addition, whereas once a career-threatening, or ending, injury would have been seen as being merely a 'fact of life', there have been a number of civil cases that have sought, and sometimes succeeded, in establishing liability where, for example, a negligent tackle has cut short a promising career. There have been a number of legal cases (such as *Eliot v Saunders*) that have looked at potential civil liability of players and clubs for injuries suffered during on-field play. In a wider sense, the law has confronted the issue of violence in sport. Whilst individual sports may have their own rules that deal with disciplinary maters and matters of violence and violent conduct, the law has also become involved in the sense of looking at the legitimacy of certain sports and sporting practices, such as boxing and shooting.

Apart from the sports themselves, and participants in those sports, being controlled by the law, there has been an increasing trend for consumers of sport to be regulated by the law. This has largely concentrated on public order and safety issues that became marked after a series of tragedies at football grounds in the 1980s (Bradford, Heysel and Hillsborough). There were a series of Government-led responses, such as the Popplewell Reports and the Taylor Reports. These led to a series of laws being enacted including the *Football Spectators Act* 1989, which sought to introduce membership cards and instigate a Football Licensing Authority, and the *Football (Offences) Act* 1991, which sought to regulate fan behaviour in terms of racist chanting, throwing missiles and encroaching onto the pitch.

A further area where law can be seen to be playing an active role in sport legal intervention has been in the area of company law, where commercial law has been utilized to evaluate the legitimacy of the take-over of football clubs. This has become more pronounced as sports have become increasingly commercialized and business oriented – one noteworthy example is the multi-million pound business that is Manchester United and the projected take-over by BSkyB (and the potential problems that ensued from this). Fan groups were mobilized to tackle this commodification of sport, although many fan groups conceded that the soul of football was sold long ago – the removal of the word 'football club' from the badge worn on the chests of the footballing arm of the business operation being seen by some as emblematic of this shift. It is, however, inevitable that as sport becomes more and more economically successful, the law, and lawyers, are sure to follow in its slipstream.

References:
Greenfield, S. and Osborn, G., *Contract and Control in the Entertainment Industry* (Aldershot: Dartmouth, 1998).

Further reading:
Grayson, E., *Sport and the Law* (London: Butterworths, 1994).

-Steve Greenfield/Guy Osborn

Law – Game Laws (*see* Game Laws)

Law – The Kerry Packer Trial

In 1977, Australian television magnate, Kerry Packer, frustrated in attempts to buy exclusive rights to Australian test cricket, signed thirty-five top cricketers to play a series of fixtures entitled World Series Cricket (W.S.C.).

The International Cricket Council (I.C.C.) and Test and County Cricket Board (T.C.C.B.) believed World Series Cricket would be in direct competition with 'official' test cricket and banned W.S.C. players from international and county cricket. Packer applied for a High Court injunction and a hearing was held, with the I.C.C. and T.C.C.B. facing charges of restraint of trade and inducement to breaches of contract. The plaintiffs were W.S.C. Pty Ltd and three individual players, Tony Greig, John Snow and Mike Procter. Robert Alexander, QC stood for the prosecution, Michael Kempster, QC for the defence.

The Judge, Mr Justice Slade, found overwhelmingly in favour of the plaintiffs – the rule changes made by the I.C.C. and T.C.C.B. were in restraint of trade. The T.C.C.B. had never entered into any commitment guaranteeing players future employment. Neither had the players signed any contract precluding them from playing for a private promoter. The defendants had done what they considered to be in the best interests of cricket but this did not justify their actions in law. The I.C.C. and T.C.C.B. did not appeal.

World Series Cricket was not a success. Packer sued for peace with the Australian Cricket Board and got his television rights. In addition, new sponsors were attracted to the game and players were awarded better pay and conditions. Cricket thus benefited from its enforced move towards commercialism.

References:

Blofeld, P., *The Packer Affair* (London: Collins, 1978).

Wisden Cricketers' Almanac, 115th edition (London: Sporting Handbooks Ltd, 1978).

Wynne-Thomas, P. and Arnold, P., *Cricket in Conflict* (London: Newnes, 1984).

Further reading:

Haigh, G., *The Cricket War: the Inside Story of Kerry Packer's World Series Cricket* (Melbourne: The Text Publishing Company, 1993).

Marqusee, M., *Anyone But England: Cricket and the National Malaise* (London: Verso, 1994).

Townley, S. and Grayson, E., *Sponsorship of Sport, Arts and Leisure* (London: Sweet & Maxwell, 1984).

See also:

Cricket; Test Matches

-Glenys Williams

Law – Overseas Players

The import of overseas players coming to practice their sport in the United Kingdom, either as professionals or amateurs, is a controversial issue. There are different problems depending on whether the player is a professional or not and on the player's nationality. Within the European Union, freedom of movement is prescribed by the Treaty of Rome and any regulations that prevent players from European Union countries moving between countries will be struck out by the European Court of Justice. Whilst within football the presence of overseas players in the Premier League became widespread in the 1990s, there are, in fact, many earlier examples of sportsmen coming to the United Kingdom. Cricket, in particular, has a long tradition of the participation of overseas players and in 1968, restrictions upon players entering County Cricket were eased. As a consequence, some of the world's greatest players, such as Imran Khan and Vivian Richards, have played for English counties. In addition, there have been many players who came to gain experience of English conditions by agreeing to play for amateur sides. Historically within football, the number of overseas players that any club could field was limited by a U.E.F.A.-prescribed rule that allowed three overseas players plus two assimilated ones (players that were treated as 'domestic' by reason of residence). This created a particular problem for English clubs engaged in European competition as for these purposes, Scottish, Irish and Welsh players were deemed to be 'overseas'. This anomaly has been removed as a bi-product of the Bosman case, although some have commented that the influx of foreign players into the Premier and Nationwide Leagues has deprived home-grown players of the chance to develop and that this may have repercussions for the international side.

References:

Greenfield, S. and Osborn, G., 'Oh to be in England? Mythology and Identity in English Cricket', *Social Identities*, 2 (1996), pp. 271-291.

Further reading:

McLellan, A., *The Enemy Within* (London: Blandford, 1994).

-Steve Greenfield/Guy Osborn

References:

Greenfield, S. and Osborn, G., *Contract and Control in the Entertainment Industry* (Aldershot: Dartmouth, 1998).

-Steve Greenfield/Guy Osborn

Law – Restraint of Trade

The doctrine of restraint of trade is a legal concept that deals with the enforceability of restrictions that may be placed upon performers under the terms of their contracts. Historically, this doctrine only applied to a very narrow compass of cases but in recent years has developed to embrace sports and other areas of popular culture.

All contracts that a professional sports person signs are, to a certain degree, in restraint of trade, the legal question that is asked of such contracts is whether their terms are reasonable and whether they can be enforced. The doctrine of restraint of trade has been used to successfully challenge restrictions imposed on professional cricketers during the Kerry Packer affair (*Grieg v Insole*) and the enforceability of boxer/management contracts (*Watson v Praeger*). Legal action has also been used to alter the terms and conditions of employment of professional footballers. The European case of Bosman attracted widespread publicity and has certainly allowed footballers throughout the European Union to ply their trade with a greater degree of freedom of movement. However, an earlier domestic example concerned George Eastham, who had a contractual dispute with Newcastle United F. C. in the early 1960s. Eastham's case was taken up by the Professional Footballers Association and, after a legal verdict in his favour, changes were eventually made in the way that players were bought and sold. The courts have recognized that a career in professional sport may often be of a limited duration and accordingly have sought to provide greater contractual freedom.

Lawn Tennis

Origins and Development

Lawn tennis owes its existence to the ingenuity and entrepreneurship of Walter Clopton Wingfield (1833-1912), a retired English major who had served in India and China. In the spring of 1874 he brought out his patented portable tennis set, which included net, net-posts, rackets and balls. The boxed sets were distributed by a London firm, French and Company, and, from the beginning, specimens were shipped to the European continent and the United States, soon making the game known there. It is true that a similar game called *pelota* had been played earlier, in the 1860s in Birmingham and in Leamington Spa, by another major, Harry Gem, and his Spanish friend Augurio Pereira, but this game presumably never became popular outside the inner circle of Gem's and Pereira's friends.

For patent reasons, Wingfield named his invention 'Sphairistikè or Lawn Tennis'. The latter name was designed to distinguish it from the game of tennis proper, inherited from the Middle Ages, but certainly on the decline in England at the time of Wingfield's 'invention'. (In a clearly defensive move, the adepts of the ancient game of tennis started to refer to their variety as *Real* Tennis from the 1890s.)

From its forerunner, tennis, lawn tennis took over the principle of striking a ball over a net; of only allowing strokes on the volley or after the first bounce of the ball; and the curious scoring system by fifteens. Unlike

214

real tennis, however, lawn tennis introduced standardized courts (78 feet by 27 feet) as early as 1877; in 1878, the height of the net was set at 4 feet 9 inches at the posts (this was lowered to four feet in 1880 and now stands at 3 feet 6 inches), and 3 feet in the middle, and the distance of the service line was set at 21 feet from the net. Standardization of the tennis ball, the flannel cover of which was an invention of J. M. Heathcote (1874), was also considered indispensable from the beginning.

Apart from discarding the complicated rules of real tennis, lawn tennis was also able to dispense with the expensive roofed facilities needed by the older game, on which many of these rules depended. The invention of the lawn mower had made it possible to trim sufficiently the lawns of the English manor, which led to the creation of smooth playing surfaces. These first served the popular game of croquet, then, after the mania for croquet had abated, they were usurped by the new game of lawn tennis. The discovery of vulcanization by Charles Goodyear resulted in the production of rubber balls filled with air, which bounced sufficiently high even on grass. This made superfluous the hard surface of the real tennis court, a prerequisite for the stuffed real tennis ball. As early as the 19th century, lawn tennis began to be played on other surfaces as well – on the asphalt of disused roller-skating rinks (as in the case of the famous Maida Vale Lawn Tennis Club) and on wood (a characteristic of the lawn tennis scene of Paris, later of the Scandinavian countries), and on clay (an invention of the Germans, who have played their championships on this surface since 1892, the final touch, a red top layer consisting of flower pots ground in a mill, being added to the courts by the Bad Homburg groundsman, Friedrich Becker, in 1898). From Germany, it seems, the clay court was, albeit reluctantly, introduced in England after the turn of the century.

Carpet surfaces and surfaces made of synthetic material belong to the modern era.

Originally, lawn tennis was intended as a five o'clock tea pastime, catering for the well-to-do and the landed gentry. In addition, it offered the Victorian matron an opportunity to engineer the marriage of a daughter with a promising young man from the neighbourhood. As a consequence, it was scoffed at by the real athletes of the time, university students who derisively referred to it as pat-ball and considered it a girls' game. However, after the first All England Championships of Wimbledon, for which a committee consisting of Henry Jones (a member of the All England Croquet and Lawn Tennis Club, the oldest in the country, founded in 1868), Julian Marshall and J. M. Heathcote (both members of M.C.C.) had laid down the rules, lawn tennis gradually began to be regarded – alongside cricket – as a serious élite sport. From cricket, too, lawn tennis adopted its sportswear – white linen shirts and flannels and, not infrequently, cricket caps. The credit for having worn shorts on Wimbledon's Centre Court (1933) must be given to an English player, Bunny Austin. The ladies for a long time continued to wear their everyday dresses, tightly laced corsets, petticoats and long skirts, with heeled shoes and broad-brimmed hats into the bargain. Until the turn of the century, this latter item prevented most of them from delivering an overhead service. Only the example of the young American, May Sutton, at the Championships of 1905, and the appearance at Wimbledon of Suzanne Lenglen (known as the 'Divine') after the First World War, eventually persuaded female tennis players to wear short skirts.

The basic strokes and tactics of the game had become established by the end of the 1880s. Since, in the early days, the majority of players consisted of adepts of real tennis, they used the familiar undercut stroke characteristic of that game. In the course of the 1880s, H. F. Lawford, singles champion in 1887, perfected the fast top-spin drive, which landed inside the court despite the absence of walls (a feature of real tennis), and the twin brothers William and Ernest Renshaw greatly improved volleying standards and introduced, with devastating effect, the smash and the overhead service. The Renshaw twins also revolutionized the doubles game in that they heavily relied on the volleying game, having advanced to a position near the service line immediately after the service. Before this, both doubles players had occupied a position near the baseline, the result being endless rallies. After the retirement of the Renshaws, doubles tactics were perfected by another pair of twins, the brothers Herbert and Wilfred Baddeley, oft-time doubles champions in the 1890s. The Baddeleys volleyed from close to the net.

In much the same way as other 19th-century sports, lawn tennis was dominated by men, but at an early date allowed women active participation. Although the first championship honours were awarded to them in Ireland (1879) rather than in England (first championships in 1884), the lawn tennis event of the Paris world exhibition in 1900 (later raised to the rank of Olympic games) featured a singles competition for women and a mixed doubles. Alongside golf, the sport therefore helped women to secure a place in future Olympics. England's Charlotte Cooper, the first Olympic ladies' champion, became the first internationally acknowledged sportswoman in the process.

According to 19th-century ideology, lawn tennis was, from the beginning, the preserve of the so-called amateur. As a consequence, the first All England Championships (1877) were open to amateurs only. The amateur (as a rule, a man of means who could well afford it) played a game for the game's sake only, and scorned any profit, monetary or in kind, that might arise or accrue from it. Increasingly, however, clubs and tournament managers heaped favours on prominent players, either by paying their travel expenses and footing their bills, or by awarding coupons which might be turned into cash money later. Attempts made by the Lawn Tennis Association (L.T.A.) in 1911, and by the International Lawn Tennis Federation in 1913 and 1933, to deal effectively with the evil of 'shamateurism' (as it was called) were doomed to failure. As time went on, it became an open secret that top amateurs were paid under the table. On the other hand, from the beginning of the 1930s (when the American Bill Tilden started signing the best amateurs for his professional tour in 1931), major amateur events such as the grand slam tournaments tended to be won by second-rate athletes, and crowds were deprived of the performances of the very best players, who had all joined the ranks of the professionals. Against a background of dwindling attendances, the L.T.A. and the B.B.C. in a joint effort spearheaded the first 'open' Championships in 1968, rallying for the first time amateurs and professionals alike.

England's supremacy in the sport remained unbroken until after the turn of the century, when it was first rumoured that it was not going to last. The yardsticks by which international success was measured were the Championships and the Davis Cup. The victory of a veteran at Wimbledon in 1909 (the forty-year-old A. W. Gore, in the absence of Australian and American players) and the Davis Cup triumph over Australasia of 1913 were, so to speak, the swansongs of English tennis for a long time. Only during the 1930s did a long-awaited messiah appear in the person of Fred Perry, who not only scored three successive wins at Wimbledon but, teamed with Bunny Austin, helped England to capture the Davis

216

Cup four times in a row (1933-1936). In addition, two Wimbledon singles titles were won by England's Dorothy Round. Apart from a single success by an Englishwoman, Virginia Wade, in 1977 at the centenary of the Wimbledon Championships, English lawn tennis has been waiting for another messiah ever since.

Governance and Administration

Despite the activities of Harry Gem and his friends, the All England Lawn Tennis and Croquet Club is, conceivably, the oldest lawn tennis club. Founded in 1868 as the All England Croquet Club, the club added the words 'lawn tennis' to its name before its first championships in the spring of 1877, and afterwards took over responsibilities for the governance of the game. Before that date, administration of the sport had been carried out by the M.C.C. Annual meetings of club secretaries took place from 1883, and the meeting of 1888 resulted in the foundation of the Lawn Tennis Association (L.T.A.), which was so named despite the fact that the United States National Lawn Tennis Association had been established as early as 1881. In the course of the inaugural meeting, it was decided that the All England Club would enjoy the privilege of perpetually holding the Championships, whereas to the L.T.A. would be entrusted the guardianship of the rules. In the following decades, the L.T.A. was considered to be the supreme body of the sport all over Europe. Important continental organizations, such as the Hamburg Lawn Tennis Guild (under the auspices of which the German championships were held from 1892), the Berlin Lawn-Tennis-Turnier-Club 'Rot-Weiss' and even countries such as Belgium, were among its members. The influence of the L.T.A. began to weaken only after the turn of the century, when national organizations came into being on the continent. The L.T.A. lost its unquestioned authority in 1913, when the International Lawn Tennis Federation (I.L.T.F.) was founded in Paris.

Nevertheless, English representation in the I.L.T.F remained strong. Its inaugural meeting was attended by no fewer than four Englishmen, R. J. McNair, H. H. Monckton, B. Sabelli and A. E. M. Taylor, and the I.L.T.F., acknowledging England's pioneering role in the evolution of the sport, conferred upon the L.T.A. a maximum of six votes and the exclusive right to hold lawn tennis world championships (synonymous with the Championships of Wimbledon). The L.T.A., in turn, transferred the rules inherited from the All England Club to the custody of the I.L.T.F., after stipulating that they should be always be printed in the English language. England lost its sixth vote in 1923, when a compromise was worked out in order to persuade the United States to become a member of the I.L.T.F. In the process, the Championships of Wimbledon lost the privilege of being called world championships, and had to be satisfied with being ranked as official championships of the I.L.T.F., together with the championships of Australia, France and the United States.

Backed by the big profits of the Wimbledon Championships (over £31 million in 1997), the L.T.A., located at The Queen's Club, West Kensington, London, W14 9EG, is now trying to raise standards of lawn tennis in Britain. In so doing, it has recently been given a boost by the success of two promising players, Montreal-born Greg Rusedski, number four in the world rankings in 1998, and Tim Henman, born and bred in Oxfordshire and a Wimbledon semi-finalist in the same year. In an attempt to gain more strength in depth at a professional level, the Association has responded to the 'Greg and Tim Factor' with a number of initiatives, such as community tennis partnerships, a five-year development plan, a coach licensing scheme, and programmes designed to attract youngsters such as Junior Aces, Love Tennis, Play Tennis 98, Nestlé Starter Tennis and the Midland Bank/L.T.A. schools coaching programme. Since the shortage of indoor courts has always been considered a hindrance to progress in a

217

country with Britain's climate, the L.T.A. launched the Indoor Tennis Initiative (I.T.I.) in 1986. As a result, forty-four I.T.I. centres have since been established, with six more to open in the near future. The number of indoor facilities has been raised from 320 in 1988 to more than 800. Membership of the L.T.A. has grown from 41,000 in 1990 to over 67,000 in 1997. 3.7 million people play tennis, it is estimated, and half of these are under twenty-five years of age.

The Scottish Lawn Tennis Association and Tennis Wales are affiliated to the L.T.A. The Scottish Lawn Tennis Association was founded in Edinburgh in 1895, some seventeen years after the first Championships (1878), which had been won by James Patten (later Sir James Patten MacDougall), a young advocate who had experimented with Wingfield's invention outdoors on the Grange Cricket Field as early as 1874. The control of lawn tennis in Northern Ireland is not in the hands of the British L.T.A., but is exerted by the Irish Tennis Association in Dublin.

In 1970 and 1971 respectively, two circuits for professionals were initiated by the I.L.T.F. and by the U.S.-based World Championship Tennis. This eventually led to an administrational restructuring of world tennis, with the formation of a Grand Prix Committee by the I.L.T.F. It consisted of three members of the I.L.T.F. and three members representing professional players. In 1974, the Grand Prix Committee was superseded by the Men's International Professional Tennis Council (renamed the Men's Tennis Council in 1988), which originally comprised six members, three of which were elected by the I.L.T.F., another three by the players. In 1976, another three members were added to this board, delegated by the North American, European and Rest of the World tournaments respectively. In 1990, the Men's Tennis Council was replaced by the A.T.P. Council, the executive board of the A.T.P. Tour. This was named after the Association of Tennis Professionals (A.T.P.), a

players' union founded in 1972. (There is an analogous organization for women, the Women's Tennis Association [W.T.A.], founded in 1970.) The A.T.P. Tour inherited from the original World Championship Tennis circuit the so-called 'masters', a tournament in which the most successful players of the Tour compete in a round robin (a tournament in which each player competes in turn against every other). This is the culmination of the tennis year. The International Tennis Federation, which dropped the word 'lawn' from its title in 1977 and moved to new head-quarters in London in 1998, has in recent years tried to reassert itself. Traditionally governing amateur and recreational tennis, the grand slam tournaments, the Davis Cup and the Federation Cup (women), it has seen to the reinstatement of lawn tennis in the Olympic programme (since 1988; open to professionals) and, in order to counterbalance the extremely attractive masters of the A.T.P. Tour, created the so-called Grand Slam Cup, which has, since its introduction in 1990, offered prize moneys little short of obscene (6 million dollars at the inaugural event in Munich, for example). Qualification for this event depends on a player's overall performance in the four grand slam tournaments.

Famous Venues

Although there are some well-known venues apart from Wimbledon, such as Bournemouth (British Hard Court Championships), Manchester (Northern Championships), Eastbourne and Nottingham (various events), the one that has achieved international fame is that of the London suburb of Wimbledon. The original site of the cradle of lawn tennis was on the three-terraced croquet lawns of the All England Croquet Club between Worple Road and the track of the London and Southampton Railway, close to Wimbledon Station. That is why special features of the venue were a wicket gate from the 'railway path', and the so-called railway stand of the Centre Court (the one with the railway to its rear only a few yards away), where the noise of passing trains was, not unlike that of the planes at Flushing Meadows in the United States, felt to be a real nuisance, especially during the Olympic tennis tournament of 1908. The Centre Court nevertheless deserved its name, since it was surrounded by the other courts. After the First World War, in order to meet the ever-growing demand of the public, the present new ground in Church Street was opened by King George V in 1922. A memorable event took place during the opening match on the new ground. After Leslie Godfree had served the first ball and his opponent had netted the return, Godfree rushed to the net and put the ball into his pocket for posterity. The new venue retained the age-honoured institution of the Centre Court, irrespective of the fact that it no longer did justice to its name in a literal sense. In 1993, the Committee for Management of the Championships resolved on a long-term plan to take Wimbledon into the 21st century. The objective of the plan was to improve all facilities in order to secure for the Championships its status as the world's supreme annual lawn tennis event. The first step in this direction, a new No. 1 Court seating a capacity crowd of 11,429 spectators, was completed in 1997. The new court, in order to be by its very architecture clearly recognizable as the younger brother of the Centre Court, has been counter sunk into the hillside. It also comprises a new largely underground Broadcast Centre. A final stage of the plan envisages the erection of a new No. 2 Court at the other extremity of the grounds, so as to create an architectural balance between the Centre Court (capacity 13,120 seats), which would, once again, occupy the centre of the grounds, and the new No. 1 and No. 2 Courts on either side of it. Wimbledon, apart from hosting the Championships, has been the stage for other major events as well – the Wightman Cup, the Olympic tennis event of 1908, the Wimbledon Professional Championships in 1967, and,

most important, many Davis Cup matches that not only involved teams of the British Isles against their opponents, but until 1937 tied other nations as well in the then customary Final and Interzone Final Rounds. Thus, for instance, what has been called 'the match of the century' between the German Gottfried von Cramm and the American Donald Budge was part of the 1937 Interzone Final Round between Germany and the United States, which followed the Championships of that year.

Famous Competitions and Memorable Events
The most prestigious competition is, of course, the Championships of Wimbledon.

These were contended for the first time in 1877, following a suggestion by Henry Jones, a 19th-century authority on games who, under the pen-name of Cavendish, contributed to the society journal *The Field*. According to a popular anecdote, the pony roller of the All England Croquet Club was in need of repair, and Cavendish hoped that the revenues of the tournament would cover the expenses. The championship trophy, a silver cup presented by *The Field*, was captured by a certain Spencer Gore, a rackets player, who, by adopting rather unusual volleying tactics from a position close to the middle of the net, already played a game that was going to be essentially different from real tennis, the sport played by most of the other competitors. In the course of the 1880s, the new game took shape in that its main characteristics, powerful topped forehand and backhand drives from the baseline, volleying, overhead service and the smash were perfected by the Renshaw twins who, naturally, dominated the game at the time. Gentlemen's Doubles and Ladies' Singles with championships status were introduced at Wimbledon in 1884, while Ladies' Doubles and Mixed Doubles were only introduced in 1913.

England was represented at the first Olympic lawn tennis event (Athens 1896) by the Oxonian George Stuart Robertson, the Australian Edwin Flack and the Irishman John Pius Boland, another Oxford student and later an M.P. for Ireland. Boland was victorious both in the singles and, partnered by a German from Hamburg, Friedrich Adolf Traun, in the doubles. After the games, Flack's competing for England gave rise to a controversy between Robertson and Boland in *The Oxford Magazine*. In 1900, England, whose team included the invincible Doherty brothers and the Wimbledon heroine Chatty Cooper, virtually swept the board, as did Cooper at the London Olympic games of 1908. More moderate success in the Olympics continued after the First World War at the Antwerp (1920) and Paris (1924) games, albeit through the efforts of England's ladies only. However, British hopes were noticeably absent when lawn tennis was readopted into the Olympic canon in 1988 after a lapse of sixty-four years. A reminder of the dark cloud hanging over England's tennis was the melancholy which made itself felt at the appearance in Seoul of one of England's all-time greats, ninety-two-year-old Kathleen ('Kitty') Godfree, née McKane, winner of a gold medal in the women's doubles in 1920 and a silver and a bronze medal in 1924. Kitty Godfree did not live to see another Olympic event, but died on June 19th, 1992. An indicator of recent progress was the reaching of the doubles final at the Centenary Games of Atlanta in 1996 by the English pair Neil Broad and Tim Henman.

Another competition in which England wrote lawn tennis history was the Davis Cup, the men's world championships for teams representing their country. The cup has been claimed to be his own invention by the man after whom it is named, Dwight Filley Davis, a millionaire's son from St. Louis. In the summer of 1899, Davis and other outstanding American players undertook a journey to California where the matches they played caused great enthusiasm. This, according to Davis, inspired him to present a challenge cup

for international matches after the model of the then popular America's Cup, contended by sailing crews. In all likelihood, however, the idea of the cup goes back to the year 1896 when an American, Charles Adolph Voigt, made a similar suggestion in the presence of Davis at a tournament in Niagara-on-the-Lake, on the Canadian border. The format of the Davis Cup tie is four singles matches and one doubles match played over a period of three days, each match being a best-of-five sets meeting. Each team consists of four players, two of which are nominated as singles players and who play their opponents on the first day and, in reverse order, on the third day. The doubles is contended on the second day. The first two Davis Cup nations were the United States and the United Kingdom in 1900. The two initial matches in 1900 and 1902 (the 1901 event was skipped) were contended on American soil and national feelings ran high when England lost both ties because of the absence, for health reasons, of their outstanding players, the brothers Reggie and Laurie Doherty. In 1903, however, in a memorable match the Doherty's struck back, captured the cup and took it home. It remained in England, mainly thanks to the excellence of the younger Doherty brother, until 1907, when Anglo-American hegemony was broken by a new power, Australasia (Australia and New Zealand combined). It was not until 1933, when England's Bunny Austin and Fred Perry ended a long uninterrupted series of wins by the famous Musketeers of France, that England asserted itself again. England's three-year winning streak, however, was destined to be its last Davis Cup achievement of the 20th century.

In an attempt to enhance interest in women's tennis, one of America's all-time women's champions, Hazel Hotchkiss Wightman of Boston, donated a silver vase to the U.S. Tennis Association as a prize for a team competition similar to the Davis Cup. The format of the Wightman Cup, which started in 1923 at the new Forest Hills Stadium at the West Side

Tennis Club in New York and involved the teams of America and Great Britain, was a best-of-seven competition, consisting of a surprising five singles and two doubles. Three players on each side were nominated as Nos. 1, 2 and 3, of which the first two had to play against each other in reverse singles (four matches as in the Davis Cup), and the Nos. 3 against one another only once. Unlike the Davis Cup, the Wightman Cup was restricted to the teams of the United States and Great Britain, to the exclusion of other nations. It was dominated by the United States because of their greater depth in first-class players. The Wightman Cup, played in Britain in even years and in the United States in odd years, lost its prestige after the introduction of open tennis because leading American players preferred to play in prize-money tournaments. It was discontinued in 1989. Another important women's team competition is the Federation Cup, inaugurated in 1963 to mark the fiftieth anniversary of the foundation of the I.L.T.F. In this competition, a team consists of at least two players and a maximum of four who play two singles and one doubles (best of three matches). As England in the decades since its inception has never even been able to field two top players, let alone four, no success has been achieved in this competition.

Terms and Concepts

Lawn tennis has inherited the core of its terminology from the medieval French ball game *jeu de la paume*, from which real tennis is descended and which was played, as the name implies, with the palm of the hand. The very name of 'tennis' goes back to a cry *tenez!*, meaning 'hold!', with which the serving party was obliged to initiate a rally, and to which the answer was either *oui* ('yes') or *s'il vous plaît* ('if you please'), which signalled readiness for play. (In a similar way, the words 'ready?' and 'play!' were in the early days used in lawn tennis.) The term 'deuce' goes back to the French numeral *deux* ('two'), in the phrase *être à deux points du jeu* ('to be two points from winning the game').

The curious counting by fifteens seems to mirror the fact that medieval tennis matches were invariably played for money. The coin with which gains or losses were assessed was the *gros denier tournois*, the 'great penny of Tours'. It was worth fifteen *deniers* ('pence') and the sum total that might be staked in a match was apparently limited to sixty by the medieval authorities, hence the four times fifteen for each game (the original score of forty-five was shortened to forty in the 16th century). Among the basically French counting terms, the term 'love' is an exception. Contrary to popular belief, its origins lie in the misconceived Dutch word *lof* ('praise'), used euphemistically for utterly unsuccessful play – the player who had gained nothing at all claimed to have played *omme lof*, meaning something like 'for the honour', rather than for filthy lucre. The term *service* is French, as is *racket*, the word for the implement with which the service was executed. Underlying the latter is the French term *la chasse*, which in ball games denoted the driving of the ball, or rather *rachasse*, 'driving the ball back' or 'returning the ball'. Via a Flemish loan word, *raketse*, the French term found its way into the English language, where it became *racket* (having lost the final *s*, which was, albeit wrongly, considered a plural). In much the same way as the leading role played by the French in medieval and Renaissance tennis led to the adoption of French terms in the English language, the pre-eminence of England and the United States in the sport in modern times has left its traces in other languages as well. Good examples of this are two terms now universally used, namely the compounds 'grand slam' and 'tie-break'. The first (ultimately from the card game of bridge) refers to the greatest success in the game, the winning in the course of a single year of the championships of Australia, France, Great Britain (Wimbledon) and the United States. It is said to have been applied to lawn tennis for the first time by the American journalist Allison Danzig in 1933, when the Australian

'Gentleman' Jack Crawford was on the point of winning all four, but then lost the U.S. championship to Fred Perry. The term 'tie-break', a 'means of deciding a winner [..] out of two who have tied' (*The Oxford English Dictionary*) came into being around the year 1970, when it became an expedient in indoor tournaments confined to one court. In a tie-breaker, a player wins the set, not in the usual manner by being two games ahead after 5-5 in games, but by being the first to reach seven points, after a score of six games all, provided there is a two-point advantage. In more recent times, the coinage 'grand slam' has proved productive when the German player Steffi Graf, after winning her only grand slam (1988), topped her performance by adding to the four titles an Olympic gold medal. This yielded the expression 'golden slam'. Only very rarely do dictionaries keep abreast of such innovations in sporting terminology.

Leaders and Personalities

The man to whom we owe the game of lawn tennis was an Englishman, Walter Clopton Wingfield, the son of a captain serving in Canada. The inventor was born on October 16th, 1833 in the house of his grandfather, the vicar of Ruabon (in Welsh, Rhiwabon) in the county of Denbigh, Wales. After attending Sandhurst, he served in India and China, returning to England in 1861. Having settled in London, he obtained a patent for a game he called *sphairistikè*, or 'lawn tennis', in 1874, the equipment for which he later sold in boxed sets distributed by a London-based firm, French and Co. Wingfield took an active part in the initial stages of the game's development, but by 1877, the year of the first Wimbledon tournament, he had lost interest in it. Wingfield died on April 18th, 1912, and is buried at Kensal Green Cemetery, near Harrow Road in the Northwest of London. A 'Wingfield Cafeteria', fittingly so called because the Major was also the founder of a Culinary Society, now adorns the new Court No. 1 complex in Wimbledon.

Lawn tennis was made popular in the first decades of its existence by two pairs of brothers, the twins William and Ernest Renshaw, and Reginald and Laurence Doherty. The Renshaws were born in Leamington Spa on January 23rd, 1861, and educated at Cheltenham together with Endicott Peabody, the founder of the famous Groton School in America. The brothers, sons of well-to-do parents, put an end to the approach which had been taken to the new game by former real tennis players by introducing the strokes characteristic of modern tennis – the overhead service and the smash. Both men of means, they could afford to play tennis even during the winter on the French Riviera, thus making the game a sport of all seasons. Their scientific method secured Ernest one (1888) and William seven singles Championships at Wimbledon (1881-1886; 1889), a record to date. The Renshaws died young, Ernest on September 2nd, 1899, William on August 12th, 1904.

The brothers Reginald Frank Doherty (October 14th, 1872-December 29th, 1910) and Hugh Laurence Doherty (October 8th, 1875-August 21st, 1919), sons of a London printer and educated at Westminster and Cambridge, in the years before and after the turn of the century were the outstanding representatives of the game. Both accomplished all-court players, Reginald, arguably the best British player of all time, was believed to be a cut above his brother, although the latter, owing to his more robust constitution, was to achieve the better record. Reginald won four Wimbledon singles Championships and, partnered by his brother, in a team considered invincible, eight doubles titles, whereas Laurence captured five singles Championships. In addition, each brother won two gold medals at the Paris Olympics in 1900, and Laurence was the first non-American to win a U.S. singles National Championship in 1903. Owing to their efforts, English supremacy in the Davis Cup lasted from 1903 to 1906. More than for their sporting prowess, the Dohertys, despite their dying so young, are remembered for their sportsmanship, especially on the European continent, where sports writers extolled them as the epitome of the English national character. In 1931, wrought iron Doherty gates were erected at Wimbledon's South-East Entrance to pay tribute to the brothers' achievements.

The first woman to make her mark in the history of lawn tennis was Dorothea Katherine Douglass Chambers (September 3rd, 1878-January 7th, 1960), the daughter of a vicar from Ealing, Middlesex. Her career was characterized by the fierce antagonism between her and the Californian May Sutton before the First World War, and the French tennis heroine Suzanne Lenglen after the First World War. Her defeat by the latter in 1919, after a memorable match, marked the end of one tennis era, and the beginning of another. Her seven Wimbledon Championships, with an unbroken series of wins between 1910-1914 (she did not play in 1912), constituted a record that has only been broken twice – in the 1930s by the American, Helen Wills Moody (eight wins); and, more recently, by Martina Navratilova (nine wins).

Not a record holder herself, Kathleen Godfree, née McKane (May 7th, 1896-June 19th, 1992) was the only woman ever to beat, in 1924, the future record holder Helen Wills at the Championships. In addition, in 1926 she and her husband Leslie Godfree were the only married couple ever to win the Wimbledon mixed doubles title. Successful in both the Olympic tennis events of 1920 and 1924 (doubles gold and mixed silver in 1920, and doubles silver and mixed bronze in 1924), she was (besides the French Musketeer Jean Borotra) the only competitor in the 1924 Olympic event to see the revival of Olympic tennis in Seoul after an interval of sixty-four years. Not least because of her longevity, and the charm and simplicity the old lady exhibited on that occasion, she became a tennis legend.

When Frederick 'Fred' John Perry (May 18th, 1909-February 2nd, 1995) in 1933 won the U.S. National, and in the year following the Wimbledon singles, it was thirty and twenty-five years respectively since an Englishman had done so. However, despite these triumphs, two additional Wimbledon singles titles (1935 and 1936) and his major contribution to four successive years of English Davis Cup victories (1933-1936), the son of a cotton spinner's relations with the top representatives of the sport in the posh All England Club were problematic. In 1935, when amateurism still reigned supreme and after his turning professional, the club even annulled his membership. During the Second World War, Perry became an American citizen and served in the U.S. forces. After the War he founded a well-known sportswear company bearing his name (1949). Having returned to his British roots and embarked upon a media career, the prodigal son became reconciled with the All England Club after the introduction of Open tennis, in token of which the Fred Perry statue opposite the entrance of its members' enclosure was unveiled in 1984. It was meant to commemorate the fiftieth anniversary of his victory in the Gentlemen's singles.

Virginia Sarah Wade was born on July 10th, 1945 in Bournemouth. Graduating from Sussex University with a B.Sc. degree in Mathematics and Physics, she stirred up the emotions of the whole nation when, on July 1st, 1977, Wimbledon's centenary year and shortly before her thirty-second birthday, she won the women's singles Championship. She had been the first and only female British winner of the U.S. Open as early as 1968 and had been Australian Open champion in 1972, but with this victory she crowned her long career, which lasted until 1987. She was the first woman to be elected to the committee of the All England Club, and worked as a commentator for C.B.S. Sports.

Off the tennis court, two personalities of English extraction made a name for themselves in the game, Lance Tingay and Ted Tinling. Lance Tingay (July 14th, 1915-March 10th, 1990), in his capacity as tennis correspondent of the *Daily Telegraph* for almost thirty years (1952-1981), brought to bear on his writing his literary expertise (he was an adept researcher into the life and work of Anthony Trollope), thus giving it a rare quality most conspicuous in his history book *100 Years of Wimbledon*, the official volume to mark the centenary of the Championships in 1977. He greatly contributed to the sport's high prestige, and was justly made an honorary member of the All England Club. Cuthbert Terrance, latterly 'Ted' Tinling (June 23rd, 1910-May 23rd, 1992) was born in Eastbourne but spent much of his youth in France for health reasons, where he fell under the spell of tennis not least through the influence of the 'Divine' Suzanne Lenglen, whom he frequently umpired. The experience doubtless prepared the way for his lifelong championing of the cause of women's tennis, not least as the first and greatest tennis couturier, who dressed most of the leading women tennis players. In 1982, he received the Women's Tennis Association (W.T.A.) Special Services Award. As a writer (author of *White Ladies* and *Love and Faults*) and broadcaster equipped with a sharp and sometimes wicked wit, he did much to popularize the game. He, and all the others here mentioned, are enshrined in the International Tennis Hall of Fame at the Newport Casino, Rhode Island.

References:

Atkins, R., 'Spotlight on Great Britain. Courting Hope and Glory', in *ITF World. The International Tennis Federation's Quarterly Magazine*, Issue 3 (September 1998), p. 10f.

Barrett, J., *100 Wimbledon Championships: a Celebration* (London: Willow Books, 1986).

Cook, J. (ed.), *International Who's Who in Tennis* (Dallas, Texas: World Championship Tennis Inc. 1983).

Evans, R., *Open Tennis: the First Twenty Years* (London: Bloomsbury Publishing Ltd, 1988).

Gillmeister, H., *Olympisches Tennis: die Geschichte der olympischen Tennisturniere (1896-1992)* (St. Augustin: Academia Verlag Richarz, 1993).

Gillmeister, H., *Tennis: a Cultural History* (London: Cassell/Leicester University Press, 1998).

Heathcote, C. G. et al, 'Lawn Tennis', in J. M. Heathcote et al., *Tennis, Lawn Tennis, Rackets, Fives* (London: Longmans, Green & Co., 1903. rev. ed.), pp. 127-349.

Little, A. and Tingay, L., *Wimbledon Ladies – a Centenary Record. 1884-1984. The Singles Champions* (Wimbledon: The Wimbledon Lawn Tennis Museum, 1984).

Little, A. and Tingay, L., *Wimbledon Men – A Hundred Championships. 1877-1986. The Singles Champions* (Wimbledon: The Wimbledon Lawn Tennis Museum, 1986).

Parsons, J., *The Ultimate Encyclopedia of Tennis* (London: Carlton/Hodder & Stoughton Ltd, 1998).

Robertson, G., *Tennis in Scotland: 100 Years of the Scottish Lawn Tennis Association, 1895-1995* (Edinburgh: Scottish Lawn Tennis Association, 1995).

Websites:

The Lawn Tennis Association –
http://www.lta.org.uk/lta.htm
Wimbledon – http://www.wimbledon.org/

See also:

Museums and Halls of Fame – Wimbledon Lawn Tennis Museum; Real Tennis; Wightman Cup; Wimbledon

-Heiner Gillmeister

League Against Cruel Sports

The League Against Cruel Sports, established in 1924 by Henry Amos and Ernest Bell, pursues a dual approach to animal protection that combines campaigning with conservation. It has ensured that the press, politicians and public are well informed of the cruelty involved in field sports. League investigators have made strenuous efforts to expose the reality behind the respectable façade of hunting. They remain vigilant and, if possible, bring to justice those involved in illegal bloodsports such as badger baiting, dog-fighting and cock-fighting. The organization has been instrumental in promoting legal protection for the badger, including the protection of their setts. The League-sponsored *Wild Mammals (Protection) Act*, introduced in 1996, provides basic protection for all wild mammals, although hunting remains legal. In the same year, the League joined forces with the Royal Society for the Prevention of Cruelty to Animals and the International Fund for Animal Welfare to promote a Campaign for the Protection of Hunted Animals. The League has also successfully mobilized cross-party support in Parliament for the campaign to abolish hunting with dogs and live hare coursing.

Since 1959, the League has purchased land of special benefit to wildlife, mainly in Somerset and Devon. Their practical conservation sanctuaries include an array of natural meadow habitats, home to a variety of animal species. In order to enhance respect for wildlife, the League organizes school talks and educational visits to its wildlife sanctuaries. It has a small permanent group of staff based at its headquarters in London. Subscriptions provide the League's main source of funding, and members receive its *Wildlife Guardian* journal, outlining its work at national level, and have the opportunity to join one of the many Local League Support Groups.

References:

Directory of British Political Organisations (Harlow: Longman, 1994).

Shipley, P., *The 'Guardian' Directory of Pressure Groups* (London: Wilton House Publications, 1976).

Websites:

The League Against Cruel Sports – http://www.lacs.org.uk/

See also:

Field Sports; Game Shooting; Wildfowling

-John Martin

League Cup

The Football League Cup was first competed for in 1960, but clubs were not compelled to enter the competition until the beginning of the following decade. The competition consists of a knockout tournament between all ninety-two members of the Football League in England. The trophy itself dates back to the late 19th century, when it was competed for by teams representing Tyneside shipyards. The first few years of the competition saw many teams decline to enter the fray, as they believed it to be of little significance in an already overcrowded season. This attitude changed, however, when the Football League announced that the winner would gain automatic entry into European competition.

The League Cup's early history is notable for the disdain shown by the bigger clubs within the Football League, with many of their supporters dubbing the trophy the 'Mickey Mouse Cup'. One of the biggest, Liverpool, went on to win the competition four times in a row (1981-1984), a record that is unbeaten. Nottingham Forest join Liverpool in having the most wins in the competition.

The League Cup became the first major knockout tournament to be sponsored, and has been known variously as the Milk Cup (1982-1986), the Littlewoods Cup (1987-1989), the Rumbelows Cup (1990-1992), the Coca-Cola Cup (1993-1998) and the Worthington Cup (1999-).

The interest in the competition has now come full circle, with many of the Premiership's top clubs regarding the competition as meaningless. This has coincided with the loss of an automatic European place to the winners.

References:

Brown, T., *The Ultimate Football League Cup Statistics Book* (Basildon: Association of Football Statisticians, 1992).

See also:

Association Football

-Sam Johnstone

Lilleshall

Lilleshall Hall in Shropshire was originally built in 1829 as a hunting lodge for the Duke of Sutherland, and the architect was Sir Jeffry Wyatville. Situated near to Newport, in 1951 it became a National Sports Centre. The funds for its acquisition and initial development became available after a fund-raising effort in South Africa, which was undertaken in appreciation of the United Kingdom's assistance during the Second World War.

During the 1950s and 1960s, facilities were developed that fully enabled Lilleshall to fulfil its role as a National Sports Centre. With 30 acres of playing fields, a variety of artificial surfaces, tennis courts and extensive indoor facilities, it became synonymous with sporting excellence. Equipped with these facilities and a residential capacity of 180, the Centre provided a supportive environment for an extensive range of sports. These included archery, athletics, cricket, football, golf, gymnastics and hockey. In particular it became the Football Association's main training centre and the headquarters of the British Amateur Gymnastics Association.

In 1984, Lilleshall became associated with a major attempt to promote excellence in football coaching and education. The Football Association National School was established at the Centre so as to provide teenage boys with the opportunity to develop their footballing skills whilst still continuing their more conventional education at the nearby Idsall School in Shifnal. This pioneering residential initiative was significant in two ways – first, boys attending the school were able to develop in readiness for a professional playing career; and second, the initiative also contributed to the thinking behind the funding of specialist sports colleges within the state education sector. Its very success in terms of promoting excellence brought about the closure of this specialist school in 1999, because its example had led to the estab-lishment of various club-based academies that fulfilled the same role at a local level.

The decision to develop a National Academy of Sport with a number of specialist centres has meant that Lilleshall's future as a centre of sporting excellence has been assured, with football, gymnastics and squash being its specialist areas.

References:
Pickering, D., *The Cassell Soccer Companion: History, Facts, Anecdotes* (London: Cassell, 1995).

Websites:
Lilleshall – http://www.lilleshall.co.uk/

See also:
Association Football; Gymnastics

-Trevor James

Literature

British literary tradition and sport have been related as cultural phenomena since before the development of modern sport – witness, for example, Hazlitt on prize boxing and fives; Dickens and Lewis Carroll on cricket; Betjemen on tennis; Hemmingway on fishing; Joyce on the horrors of school sports; and Sillitoe on running and football. Today there are two distinct types of literature relating to sport; the first consists of writing about sport and its related activities, the second features depictions of sport in imaginative literature. There has been an enormous growth in both kinds of writing in accordance with a growing interest in sport in society in general. It has yet to be seen whether this represents an increased involvement in sporting life by those who read such literature or is simply a substitute for more direct involvement in the activity.

Writing about sport is by no means a coherent genre as it covers such a wide range of material. Sports writing includes specialist academic, coaching, medical, legal and administrative texts; newspaper, sports specific and general magazine articles; programmes, fanzines and team guides; and biographies, autobiographies and histories of teams and individuals. Hagiography is the norm in sporting biography, especially those recent 'autobiographies' in which well-known professional sportspersons have used less well-known writers, usually journalists, to ghost-write their work. Interestingly, when writing feature articles or technical texts the same device is often deemed not to be necessary.

The proliferation of writing about sport has led to a significant degree of specialization within the field. In a recent editorial for *F.I.F.A. Magazine*, Keith Cooper reflected upon the phenomenon in writing, 'it is in some way encouraging that even in this age of increasing dependence upon the electronic media as a source of information, the written word and the accompanying photograph retain a fascination'. He then moved on to justify a F.I.F.A. World Cup Edition on the grounds that, 'of course, F.I.F.A. bears a weight of authority which places it apart from even the very best of the private magazines'. This encapsulates the relationship of sport and writing. Sport's essentially transitory nature and the partiality of the experience of those who participate means that those who are specialists have both an expertise and a brand name with which to distinguish their observations. Indeed, this fascination with verisimilitude might be said to be the feature which links the disparate kinds of writing about sport and which prompts the special relationship between two abstract sets of rules and symbols.

However, writing about sport is also linked with the notion of amateur involvement, from the school sports day programme and the match reports of local village teams to the increasingly sophisticated cult of the fanzine. The vigour of this kind of writing derives from the partisan, often parochial, sentiments expressed, which, on a larger scale could be seen to be xenophobic. In some senses, sports writing may be seen to be democratic in that,

in an era of post-compulsory education, so many are willing to try an interpretation, or make a conjecture from something imprecise or incomplete, either in written or oral form. However, the literal sense of such writing is not only the meaning of the words but also the meaning of the utterance. It is noticeable that the number of black writers and women writers who specialize in sports writing is still relatively small and the token inclusion of those who are not able-bodied white males in sporting literature in recent years serves mainly as exceptions to prove a very slowly changing rule. However, the subject matter of sporting pursuits of all kinds goes far beyond the major sports covered in the newspapers (football, Rugby, cricket, motor racing, horse-racing, golf and boxing). Children's fiction also provides useful comparisons with other kinds of literature that deploy sport as symbol or metaphor because of the fairly overt ideology that usually informs the story line in a range of material from textbooks to comics.

The pleasure of reading about sport may derive from a combination of escapism and recognition of reality in a parallel form which takes us out of our own world whilst reflecting our concerns. To a large extent, the escapist element has as its main source of reference nostalgia. This is particularly evident in L. P. Hartley's *The Go-Between*, which uses the metaphor of a cricket match to communicate social tensions. Aristocratic Trimingham plays handsome drives off the front foot because biology and social conditioning have made him tall and taught him to hold his head high. The peasant farmer, Ted, plays off the back foot across the line with pulls and hooks because he is self-taught and does not know that such play is a sin in the coaching manual. However, he has a good eye and has the strength to play the shots because of his muscular physique. Maudsley, the banker, reveals his cowardice by nudging out miserly singles but he plays the winning inning because time is on his side. Whilst the protag-

227

onist, Leo, reveals his difficulty in shaping a social identity in his ambivalence over which side he wants to win, he catches out Ted in a reflex action that foreshadows the later scene in the outhouse. Similar difficulties in negotiating a social identity can be seen in *The Football and Sports Library* short stories concerning female footballers, in which the eponymous heroine (Ray of the Rovers, Bess of Blacktown, Meg Foster Footballer, Nell O' Newcastle) must deal with class, gender and race ideologies whilst retaining her essential femininity. Another way of examining the relationship between sport in literature and social identity is to take a particular kind of sport and to examine the variety of its treatment in literature. In the case of equestrianism, for example, it is mentioned in as diverse texts as the cartoons of Thelwell, the romances of Jilly Cooper, the thrillers of Dick Francis, in the novels of Lawrence and in children's comics such as *Horse and Pony*. Though some sports have well-defined sub-genres of literature devoted to them (the poetry of cricket for example), others have little coverage so a future line of enquiry could examine why certain types of writing about certain sports flourish and others have yet to develop.

Whilst recent American novelists (De Lillo, *Underworld*; Roth, *American Pastoral*; and Ford, *Independence Day*) use baseball as metaphors for a golden age of childhood, fairplay, pre-nuclear weapons, summer, regional loyalty and a life of leisurely pace, English novelists have increasingly written about urban contemporary concerns in recent years. The question of authority has been addressed, especially in writing about football but also now in many other sports, by the adoption of authorial devices developed by writers keen to 'give voice' to experiences hitherto marginalized by the mainstream. Thomas Healy's use of dialect in his non-fiction account of boxing, *A Hurting Business*, is a notable contribution to this body of work.

References:

Cooper, K., 'The Value of the Written Word', *F.I.F.A. Magazine* (June 1998). Also available online at http://www.fifa.com

Hartley, L. P., *The Go-Between* (London: Penguin, 1997).

Healy, T., *A Hurting Business* (London: Picador, 1996).

Melling, A., 'The Working-Class Heroine in Popular Football Fiction, 1915-25', *The International Journal of the History of Sport*, vol. 15, no. 1 (1988), pp. 97-122

Further reading:

Coleman, N. and Hornby, N. (eds.), *The Picador Book of Sportswriting* (London: Picador, 1996).

Scannell, V., *Sporting Literature: an Anthology* (Oxford: Oxford University Press, 1987).

See also:

Drama; Film

-Jean Williams

Liverpool Gymnasium

The Liverpool Gymnasium in Myrtle Street was officially opened on November 6th, 1865. It was the brainchild of Liverpool gymnasts John Hulley and Charles Mealey, no doubt influenced by the setting up of similar facilities in Birmingham, Leeds, London and Oxford.

The gymnasium soon became acknowledged as one of the centres of sporting life in England. Many of Liverpool's leading families of the day patronized the gym and pupils from far and wide came to study there. Amongst the well-known personalities of the day to visit the centre in its early years were Charles Kingsley (then a canon of Chester Cathedral), Thomas Hughes (then an M.P.) and Prince Alfred (Duke of Edinburgh).

Membership reached a peak in 1869 but declined throughout the 1870s. Dwindling receipts and a disappearing act by its first Director, John Hulley (said to have eloped with the daughter of a Liverpool shipping magnate), led to the gym being sold to the Y.M.C.A. in 1881.

Under the directorship of Alexander Alexander (1882-1896), the gymnasium began to regain some of its former splendour and become famous as a proponent of the British system of physical training. Some of its gymnasts gained international reputations and its display team was much in demand. Among its students and later staff in this period was Irene Marsh, who later founded the Ladies Physical Training College in Southport (today a part of Liverpool John Moores University).

Growing concerns of the Y.M.C.A. that individuals were increasingly being attracted to the gym by feats of strength and circus rather than to become followers of Christ helped lead to the resignation of Alexander in 1896.

Under its third and, as it turned out, final Director, Mr Wareing, the gymnasium underwent numerous changes as it attempted to counteract its declining popularity. Boxing, rifle shooting and then roller-skating were all introduced at different times to capitalize on popular trends in society at large, and in the 1930s fitness classes were organized for the unemployed. Eventually it became too heavy a financial burden on the Y.M.C.A. and, rather timely, the building was requisitioned in 1937 by the Secretary of State to be used for issuing gas masks and ration cards.

When, after the Second World War, the building was de-requisitioned, the gym was sold to the local hospital board, finally being demolished in the 1970s to make way for car parking.

References:

Parry, N. A., *The Liverpool Gymnasium*, M.Ed. thesis, University of Manchester, 1974.

Parry, N. A., 'Pioneers of Physical Education in the Nineteenth Century', *Physical Education Review*, vol. 2, no. 1 (1979), pp. 11-24.

See also:

Birmingham Athletic Institute

-Richard William Cox

Liverpool Olympics

In 1862, Charles P. Melly, president of the Liverpool Athletic Club, and his friend, John Hulley started a series of five or six 'Grand Olympic Festivals' which, when taken together, covered all the sports played at the first Olympic Games in Athens in 1896 apart from shooting, cycling, lawn tennis and the marathon. In 1862 only, 'Gentlemen Amateurs' were admitted to Mount Vernon Parade Ground where twenty-two sports were contended for, such as broadsword, boxing, 330 yards flat-race, Indian club exercises, sabre versus bayonet, 1,200 yards steeplechase, 4 miles walking, pole-leaping, throwing the cricket ball, and an essay competition. Five gold, twenty-two silver, and twenty-three bronze medals were awarded. Between 7,000 and 10,000 spectators watched the scene. The 'Olympic Festival' of 1863 was enriched by a 2.5 mile swim. In addition, a large stage for combat sports was erected and a circular track of 440 yards built. In 1864, the third Festival was staged in the Zoological Gardens. There were two stages, many entries for the essay competition, and a running and standing long jump. The fourth 'Olympic Festival' must have taken place at the same time as the inauguration of the 'National Olympian Association' in Hulley's grand Liverpool Gymnasium in 1865. The fifth 'Olympic Festival' of 1866 was staged in Llandudno, Wales and lasted for four days; four aquatic sports and a sailing competition from Liverpool to Llandudno completed a programme in which seventy-seven medals were awarded. The sixth and last international 'Olympic Festival' of 1867 needed three sites: Hulley's Gymnasium, the Sheil Park Athletic Grounds and the Birkenhead Great Float. In 1871, Hulley went bankrupt.

References:

Bell's Life in London, August-October, 1862, 1866

Daily Post (Liverpool) August-October, 1863-1864

Liverpool Mercury, August-October, 1863-1864, 1867.

Rühl, J. K. and Keuser, A., 'Olympic Games in 19th-century England with Special Consideration of the Liverpool Olympics', in R. Naul (ed.), *Contemporary Studies in the National Olympic Games Movement* (Frankfurt: Peter Lang, 1997), pp. 55-70.

Further reading:

Rees, R., *The Development of Sport and Recreation in Liverpool in the 19th Century*, M.Ed. dissertation, University of Liverpool, 1968, pp. 60-75.

Rees, R., 'The Olympic Festivals of Mid-Victorian England', *Olympic Review*, no. 111 (1977), pp. 21-23.

See also:

Cotswold Games; Morpeth Olympics Games; Much Wenlock Games

-Joachim Ruhl

London Marathon

The London Marathon is run over the traditional distance of 26 miles and 385 yards, but it is not a conventional marathon. It was intended to be, and has become, a huge sporting festival and celebration.

Its architect and founder was Chris Brasher, a former Olympic steeplechase champion and a celebrated sports journalist. He wanted to establish a marathon that was different, in effect a 'people's marathon'. Certainly the response of the competing and spectating public has fulfilled this dream. Applications for entries always heavily exceed the places available, with the numbers actually being permitted to run now exceeding 40,000, making it the largest marathon field in the world. Equally, the preparedness of spectators to line the route all the way from Charlton Park, past the Cutty Sark and over Tower Bridge, through the Docklands and East End, and back through the Tower of London to Buckingham Palace and the finish in The Mall is ever-increasing.

Since its inception in 1981, the formula for the race has remained much the same, although the picturesque finish on Westminster Bridge has been replaced by the grandeur of The Mall, and the scale of entries has meant that separate starts are required for élite men, élite women, wheel-chaired competitors and the general running enthusiast. The all-inclusive nature of the London Marathon is reflected by the deliberate inclusion of every type of athlete from the wheel-chaired to the élite to the veteran, some of whom have exceeded eighty years of age. However, it is also a marathon with a wider mission because it actively encourages the participation of sponsored runners who represent good causes, such as Terry Kavanagh of Havering, who has raised £14,000 for the Parkinson's Disease Society, whilst being himself a sufferer of that condition. Literally millions of pounds have been raised by individuals and surpluses from the Marathon's own fee, and

A fun runner passes Big Ben during the 2000 London Marathon (Action Images/John Sibley)

sponsorship income is distributed to recreational schemes through the London Marathon Charitable Trust. This is how Chris Brasher's aim of a 'people's marathon' is being fulfilled.

Nevertheless, the London Marathon is a serious race for most and its record times – 2:06:36 for men, set by Antonio Pinto of Portugal in 2000, and 2:21:06 for women, set by Ingrid Kristiansen of Norway in 1985 – show that it is highly competitive and a potentially fast course. The best British times are by Steve Jones (2:08:16 in 1985) and Veronique Marot (2:25:56 in 1989).

References:

Athletics Today, vol. 6, no. 16 (16 April 1992), pp. 11-23.

Athletics Weekly, (16 April 1997), pp. 4-14.

Athletics Weekly, (22 April 1998), pp. 23-30.

Athletics Weekly, (29 April 1998), pp. 2-13, 38-42.

The Flora London Marathon Magazine, Issue 2 (1997).

Further reading:

Winter, A. E. H., *From the Legend to the Living: Being the Story of the Marathon Race from its Inception in Ancient Greece BC 470 and the History of the Polytechnic Marathon Race from 1909 to its Diamond Jubilee in 1969* (private publication, 1969).

Websites:

The London Marathon –
http://www.london-marathon.co.uk/

See also:

Athletics; Road Running

-Trevor James

London Polytechnic

There had been an attempt to establish a 'polytechnic' in Regent Street in 1838, but the Regent Street Polytechnic that became such a formative influence in English education and sport was founded in 1881.

The founder was Quintin Hogg, later Lord Hailsham, who is described in a memorial plaque in the rebuilt Polytechnic building (1911) as an 'Education and Christian Benefactor' who 'expanded his work by founding the Polytechnic in 1881-2'. In Portland Place, amidst the traffic, is a statue of Quintin Hogg (1845-1903) which is a memorial to him, but also to those from the nearby Polytechnic who died during the First World War. The imagery of Hogg's statue conveys the values and priorities of his Polytechnic, because he is depicted giving equal value to book learning and sporting activity. In essence, it reflects the ethos of 'Muscular Christianity', which was part of his education. Inside the Polytechnic building, now the Fyvie Hall of Westminster University, another plaque explains that the reconstruction in 1911 was a memorial to the late Edward VII and it refers to the commitment of the Polytechnic to the 'physical and moral development of youthful subjects'.

This twin commitment is further revealed by a double set of honours boards which reveal that, from 1898 until the establishment of what was to become the University of Westminster, it awarded an annual trophy for the best educational achievement and the best 'athletic' performance, thereby confirming the message of the nearby statue. The latter was the Studd Trophy. Over the years, the award has been given to sportsmen from various disciplines, such as swimming, boxing and cycling, but it is clear that the majority of awards have been given to athletes. Six names stand out: Willie Applegarth (1912/13), Olympic medallist and the greatest of the pre-First World War sprinters; Albert Hill (1919/20/21), Olympic gold medallist and the greatest middle-distance runner of his time; H. F. V. Edward (1922), Olympic sprint bronze medallist; E. MacDonald Bailey (1950), the greatest sprinter of the immediate post-Second World War years; Colin Campbell (1968 and 1970), a great quarter miler; and Alan Pascoe (1971/72/73/74/75), one of the greatest hurdlers of all time.

This roll of honour explains why, of the many sports clubs that arose from the Regent's Street Polytechnic, the Polytechnic Harriers were the most remembered and celebrated. The

231

'*Marylebone Cricket Club – The New Pavilion at Lord's*', *taken from* The Architect, *Nov 1st 1889* (M.C.C.)

Polytechnic Harriers became associated with the Chiswick track, but their name confirmed that they were connected to this most important educational and sporting institution. However, the Polytechnic's Kinnaird and Sward Trophies are now no more, and the Polytechnic Marathon, founded after the London Olympic Marathon of 1908, has also ceased. Indeed, even the Polytechnic Harriers have been subsumed into another club. Nevertheless, the achievements of this unique establishment, especially in athletics, still stand the test of comparison with modern activities and clubs.

The other two sports with which the Polytechnic has a strong association are cycling and water polo, producing many internationals over a number of years.

References:

Winter, A. E. H., *Polytechnic Heritage: They Made Today; A History of the 100 years of the Polytechnic Sports Clubs and Societies* (private publication, 1976-1978. 4 vols.).

Further reading:

Barrington, D., *Polytechnic Harriers, 1933-1983* (Private publication, 1983).

Clynes, E. H. L., *Polytechnic Harriers, 1883-1933* (London: Polytechnic Harriers, 1933).

Winter, A. E. H., *From the Legend to the Living: Being the Story of the Marathon Race from its Inception in Ancient Greece BC 470 and the History of the Polytechnic Marathon Race from 1909 to its Diamond Jubilee in 1969* (private publication, 1969).

See also:
Water Polo

-Trevor James

Lord's Cricket Ground

Lord's Cricket Ground, a 13-acre site in St John's Wood, London, has been the home of Marylebone Cricket Club (M.C.C.) since 1814. Middlesex County Cricket Club played its first match at Lord's in 1877 and has been based at the ground ever since. Test matches have been played at Lord's since 1884.

The oldest building at Lord's is the Members' Pavilion (architect, Thomas Verity) built in 1890. It contains the famous Long Room, through which cricketers make their way to and from the wicket. Its Victorian elegance is complemented by the striking lines of the Mound Stand (architect, Michael Hopkins and Partners), opened in 1987 to celebrate M.C.C.'s bicentenary. Other recent developments include the new Grandstand (architect, Nicholas Grimshaw, 1998), and the futuristic NatWest Media Centre (architect, Future Systems, 1999).

A famous Lord's figure is the Father Time weather vane, a gift from Sir Herbert Baker, architect of the second grandstand.

The 3.5-acre Nursery End, purchased by M.C.C. in 1887, houses the Indoor School (architect, David Morley), whose coaching facilities are available to all cricketers.

At the pavilion end, the Harris Memorial and Coronation Gardens are both popular picnic sites on big match days. There is a real tennis court (a game played at Lord's since 1838) and the M.C.C. Museum, which houses the world's finest collection of cricketing art and memorabilia.

Very much the administrative centre of cricket, Lord's is also the home of the England and Wales Cricket Board and the International Cricket Council.

References:

Kerr, D. R. and Peebles, I. A. R., *Lord's, 1946-1970* (London: Harrap, 1971).

Lewis, A. R., *Double Century: the Story of MCC and Cricket* (London: Hodder & Stoughton, 1987).

Warner, Sir P., *Lord's, 1787-1945* (London: Harrap, 1946).

Websites:

Lord's – http://www.lords.org/

See also:

Cricket; M.C.C.; Museums and Halls of Fame – Lord's Cricket Museum

-Glenys Williams

Loughborough University

Although Loughborough University did not receive the Royal Charter conferring university status until 1966, the history of the institutions that now comprise the university goes back to 1909, when Loughborough Technical Institute was opened. The Institute, which became Loughborough College in 1918, offered day and evening courses ranging from mechanical, aeronautical, automobile, electrical and civil engineering, to art, commercial and domestic subjects and teacher education. After the First World War, playing fields and sports pavilions were developed, and the College, though not itself a university, was admitted to the Universities' Athletic Union in 1929. Physical training was included in the programmes of the various departments, and a department of Physical Education was formed in 1931. It was 1936, however, before specialist teachers' courses in the subject were started, when a one-year post certificate course was established. The College School of Athletics, Games and Physical Training followed in 1937, and three-year courses for teachers and other professionals ensued. The students (entirely male) were eligible for the award of Diploma of Loughborough College (dating from 1918).

Specialist courses in physical education (and handicraft, as it was then called) became the hallmark of Loughborough College, achieving national acclaim.

Following the Second World War, in 1952, the institutions comprising Loughborough College were separated into four distinct colleges – Loughborough College of Technology, under the Ministry of Education; and Loughborough Colleges of Art, Further Education and Teacher Training, financed by Leicestershire Education Committee.

Physical Education continued to flourish, first as a two-year teaching certificate course with a further Diploma (of Loughborough College) year for the better students, then as a three-year combined course from 1960. Loughborough Training College became Loughborough College of Education in 1963.

In 1965, women were admitted for training as primary school teachers, and later, for the one-year post graduate certificate of education in 1971, but the three-year secondary school physical education course remained for men only until 1977. By then, the College of Technology had been re-designated, first as a College of Advanced Technology (1957), then as Loughborough University of Technology (1966). In the College of Education, the four-year bachelor of education course, including physical education, which had started in 1965, lasted until the amalgamation of the College of Education and the University in 1977. At this point, physical education was transferred to the Department of Physical Education and Sports Science (Recreation Management was added to this title in the early 1990s), in the School of Human and Environmental Science (which itself became the Faculty of Social Sciences and Humanities in 1997, after the final change of institutional name to Loughborough University in 1996). The academic base of the department broadened considerably, and Bachelors, Masters and Doctoral programmes in all three areas developed the work beyond the original courses in teacher training.

Throughout the years, Loughborough's prowess in the sporting field, through the Student Union, links with outside sports clubs and national organizations, has remained paramount. Loughborough students have long been dominant in inter-university sport, and students past and present have achieved Olympic and international honours in almost every sport.

References:

Cantor, L., *Loughborough University of Technology: Past and Present* (Loughborough: Loughborough University of Technology, 1990).

Loughborough College Calendar 1935-1936 (Loughborough: John Corah and Sons Ltd, 1935).

Further reading:

Cantor, L. and Matthews, G., *Loughborough: From College to University, A History of Higher Education at Loughborough, 1909-1966* (Loughborough: University of Technology, 1977).

Websites:

Loughborough University – http://www.loughborough.ac.uk/

See also:

Carnegie College; Education – Teacher Training; Jordanhill College

-Rob Jones

Management

Traditionally, sport in Britain has been delivered by a vast network of voluntary, public and private sector organizations. Over the past two decades the management of these organizations has changed considerably and the traditional demarcations between the three sectors have become blurred. While voluntary clubs and the governing bodies which represent them internationally still form the central means of delivering 'amateur' sport in Britain, the structure and management of these organizations has become increasingly more sophisticated. Typically, clubs and governing bodies were run by enthusiastic and dedicated volunteers who filled coaching and administrative positions. These people operated relatively informally with minimal policies and procedures to guide their operations. Their main responsibilities were to ensure the enforcement of the amateur code, run national championships and, where appropriate, send representative teams to international competitions.

In recent years, these organizations have become increasingly commercial and hence have had to be more 'business like' in their operations and management. Many are no longer solely voluntary but employ paid professional coaches and administrators to help oversee their operations. The informal ways of running clubs and national governing bodies have been reduced as funding bodies such as Sport England and the growing number of commercial sponsors involved in sport have demanded more financial and operating accountability, something that has resulted in an increase in formal policies and procedures. In addition, the volunteer managers, who traditionally required only enthusiasm and a knowledge of the sport to do their job, are now having to possess a more sophisticated set of management skills as clubs and governing bodies engage in such complex activities as applying for lottery funding, creating partnerships with local authorities, and brokering television and sponsorship agreements.

The role of the public sector organizations has also changed over the last two decades. The initial involvement of the public sector in sport, in the form of both central and local government, was a product of the post-war creation of a welfare state. There was an assumption that the government had a responsibility to improve the lives of individuals and that sport and related recreational activities had a role to play. The structure and management of the welfare state was guided by principles of hierarchy, planning, direct control and centralization. The major role of government was the provision of sport facilities and the facilitation of participation opportunities. In the late 1980s, the public sector was transformed from a bureaucratic hierarchically structured set of organizations to a more differentiated network of independent or quasi-autonomous internal units operating with devolved control. The 'new public management', as the operational mode of these organizations become known, involved the introduction of 'market mechanisms', that is to say pri-

235

vate sector operating principles, into the public sector. In regard to the operation and management of publicly provided sport, the principle changes involved an increase in user charges for involvement in sport, the opening up of local authority sport provision and related services to competitive tendering, the creation of internal markets in local authorities, and the devolution of control in which the providers of sport services operate as independent units and compete with each other.

A significant cultural change at the turn of the century has been the Labour Government's introduction of 'Best Value' to replace the shortcomings of the compulsory competitive tendering process introduced by the Conservative Government in 1998. From April 2000, all local governments are obliged by law to ensure that continuous improvements are made in the way their leisure (and other) services are run. Best Value Performance plans indicate what the council's targets and objectives are, how well they are performing and how they compare with others.

Changes have also come about in the private sector provision of sport. For many years, private sector operators have seen sport and related activities as a profitable market. However, the growth of private sector involvement in the sport has, in the last two decades, been unprecedented. Spending on sport is forecast to grow faster than any other area of the leisure industry, with estimates of £11 billion in 1998. Fitness clubs, racquet clubs, sporting goods stores, sport equipment companies, sport sponsorship agencies and companies promoting recreational sporting opportunities have all grown at an unparalleled rate. Even firms whose main interests are not sport related have seized on the popularity of sporting events and sports personalities to market their products, and as a consequence spending on sport sponsorship by such entities as soft drink producers, financial institutions, car manufacturers, and tobacco companies has grown rapidly. A number of successful business people have seen the potentially lucrative market that sport offers and have sought to diversify their business portfolios by buying interests in

sport organizations such as football or Rugby clubs.

The growth of private sector involvement in sport has meant that there has been an increased demand for managers with business expertise and a knowledge of the sport industry. As a result, several universities have, in recent years, established sport management courses. In the Midlands alone, De Montfort University offers an M.A. and a B.A. degree in sport and leisure management, Loughborough University offers an M.A. in sport and recreation management, and Coventry University offers an M.B.A. in sport management. London University offers an M.Sc. and M.B.A. in sports management. The interest in managerial issues related to sport has also led to the creation of a number of sport management related organizations. One of the main British organizations is the Institute of Leisure and Amenity Managers. I.L.A.M., as it is known, is a professional organization with members from both the public and private sectors. Its mandate is more broadly concerned with leisure than sport and its principle objectives involve lobbying whenever legislation is likely to influence the leisure industry, education and training within the leisure industry, career counselling, and the professional development of its membership. The European Association for Sport Management (E.A.S.M.) is more specifically concerned with sport and has those who are interested in the academic study of sport, rather than those professionally involved, as it main members. Many British academics interested in sport management are members of E.A.S.M. and it holds an annual conference and also has a journal. More established than E.A.S.M. is its North American equivalent, the North American Society for Sport Management (N.A.S.S.M.). Like E.A.S.M., N.A.S.S.M. runs an annual conference and produces an academic journal which appears quarterly. A number of British academics interested in sport management regularly attend the N.A.S.S.M. conference and contribute to its journal, *The Journal of Sport Management*.

References:

Houlihan, B., *Sport, Policy and Politics: a Comparative Analysis* (London: Routledge, 1997).

Slack, T., 'Changing Boundaries and New Management Implications for Leisure Organizations', in E. Jackson and T. L. Burton (eds.), *Leisure Studies: Prospects for the Twenty-First Century* (College Station, Pennsylvania: Venture Publishing Inc., 1999).

Further reading:

Slack, T., *Understanding Sport Organizations: the Application of Organization Theory* (Champaign, Illinois: Human Kinetics, 1996).

See also:

Economics of Sport; Marketing; Sports Sponsorship

-Trevor Slack

Manx Grand Prix

International motorcycling is controlled by the Fédération Internationale de Motorcyclisme (F.I.M. – International Motorcycling Federation), and this organization supervises the most important international races, known as Grand Prixs. Austria, Belgium, France, Germany, Italy, the Netherlands and Spain all have a long tradition of hosting national Grand Prix races. One of the world's most famous Grand Prix races, however, is the Manx Grand Prix, held on the Isle of Man over the last two weeks of August. As with all Grand Prix events, the Manx one has a variety of racing engine cubic capacity (i.e. horsepower) categories. In the 1960s, the arrival of Japanese manufacturers such as Yamaha, Honda, Suzuki and Kawasaki rearranged the map of racing success, although Gherado Bonini makes the point that 'From 1960 to 1995 Japan won 90 world titles for building motorcycles, but only 4 for racers.'

Bill Moore, in his biographical reminiscences *Many Memories* (formerly available on the internet), recalls visits to the Isle of Man in 1947 and 1948, when he watched riders 'hurtle' down inclines. He writes, 'I can still smell the Castrol R as the first bikes flashed by.' On a return visit to the island in 1996 he 'discovered that... [a] sec-

ond cousin, Tony Duncan had won a rare double victory, in the lightweight and junior events of the 1995 Manx Grand Prix'.

One of the most useful narratives on the Manx Grand Prix is an essay by Paul Vale entitled 'Diary of a Manx Grand Prix Rider' (formerly available on the internet). This is an account of preparation, practising and racing by a competitor, David Vale, who finished number forty in the 1997 Manx Grand Prix Junior Race and number eleven in the Lightweight division. A sample entry reads, 'August 24 1997 – The practice was good and dry, but the quick time that he [David Vale] wanted to put in had gone to pot. The bike had needed new tyres for this practice and the decision was made to try Michelin. This caused major handling problems for the bike. The bike was wandering, drifting and generally not steering at all well. Dave was fighting from keeping it mounting curbs and bouncing off verges.'

In both his 1997 Manx races, Vale's average speed, in a race of approximately one-and-a-half hours, was over 100 miles per hour.

References:

Bonini, G., 'Motorcycle Racing', in D. Levinson and K. Christensen (eds.), *Encyclopedia of World Sport* (Santa Barbara, California: ABC-CLIO, 1996), vol. II, pp. 653-657.

Websites:

The Manx Grand Prix –
http://www.motorsport.co.im/mgp/

See also:

Motorcycle Racing

-Scott Crawford

Marathon Racing

The mythological stories surrounding the marathon provided the impetus for Michel Breal, a friend of Pierre de Coubertin (the founder of the modern Olympics), to propose that it should form the highlight of the first revived modern Olympics in 1896.

The first Olympic marathon to be organized outside Europe was at the 1904 St Louis Olympics in the United States. Four years later, the Games came to London. On May 9th, 1908, a trial race was organized in Coventry by Birchfield Harriers Athletic Club. Although there were several trials held, this was held over a distance near to that in the Olympics and has therefore been recognized as the first marathon to be held in Britain.

The following year, the Polytechnic Harriers event was launched and this remained the only British marathon to be held annually until 1923. In 1925, the Polytechnic hosted the first A.A.A. Championship, which was won by Sam Ferris of the Royal Air Force. Ferris subsequently won eight Polytechnic events, competed in three Olympics and the Empire Games of 1930 and 1934.

The first marathon in Ireland was held in Dublin on May 16th, 1909, and the inaugural national championships were held in 1925.

British women had to wait until 1978 for the inaugural Women's Amateur Athletic Association Championship, which was incorporated into an established marathon race in the Isle of Wight. Margaret Lockley was the first champion, followed by Joyce Smith in 1979 and 1980. Internationally, the first women's marathon was held at the 1982 European Championships in Athens. It is worth noting that this was four years before the women's 10 kilometres was introduced. The following year, the marathon was added to the women's programme at the Helsinki World Championships, and in 1984, at the Los Angeles Games, it was added to the Olympic programme. This was followed by the inaugural Commonwealth Games women's marathon at the Edinburgh Games of 1986.

Probably the most important race in recent years for British marathon running has been the London Marathon. The inaugural race was held in 1981 and it remains the most prestigious race for athletes of all levels.

References:

Gynn, R., *The Guinness Book of the Marathon* (Enfield: Guinness Superlatives Ltd, 1984).

Lovesey, P., *The Official Centenary History of the Amateur Athletic Association* (Enfield: Guinness Superlatives Limited, 1979).

Martin, D. E. and Gynn, R. W. H., *The Marathon Footrace: Performers and Performances* (Springfield, Illinois: Charles C. Thomas, 1979).

Further reading:

Quercetani, R. L., *Athletics: a History of Modern Track and Field Athletics (1860-1990) Men and Women* (Milan: Vallardi & Associati, 1990).

Watman, H., *History of British Athletics* (London: Robert Hale, 1968).

See also:

London Marathon; London Polytechnic

-Lynne Duval

Marketing

Any examination of the role of marketing in sport needs to be preceded by a definition of marketing. The frequently quoted definition of marketing in many text books is the one drawn from the British Chartered Institute of Marketing that defines marketing as 'the management process responsible for identifying, anticipating and satisfying customer requirements profitably'. The word 'profitably' can be replaced by the word 'efficiently' when used in the context of not-for-profit organizations.

Marketing can, and should, be considered both a function within, and a philosophy of, the business. The marketing philosophy or concept is a belief that the whole organization needs to be market focused in order to satisfy customer needs better than the competition. The marketing function is basically responsible for the management of the marketing mix elements, which in their simplest form consist of market research and the four 'p's of product, price, promotion and place. The principles of marketing can apply to all sports individuals or organizations, whether they be professional or amateur, profit making or non-profit making.

There are two distinct but complementary elements to any definition of sport marketing.

Firstly there is the marketing of sport, which involves sports leagues, associations, clubs and individuals marketing their events, products and services directly to sport consumers. Secondly there is marketing through sport, which involves the activities of consumer and industrial organizations that use sport as a vehicle to market their products and services to sport consumers. Sports marketers therefore need to be concerned with the marketing of their sport to both the sport consumer and to those who use sport as a marketing vehicle, i.e. sponsors and advertisers.

Increased competition in the leisure and entertainment industry has increased the need for professional marketing approaches in the sports industry. Historically, sports organizations in Britain have been slow to adopt marketing principles and practices and have suffered from marketing myopia, that is seeing itself as being in the sports industry rather than being in the entertainments and leisure industry. For example, attendances for professional football in England declined to 16 million in 1986 from 30 million in 1966. This decline was mirrored by a fall in television viewers, with only 12 million people watching the F.A. Cup final in 1988 as compared to 30 million in 1970. This long-term decline was, in part, the result of the changing leisure demands of a more affluent society. More alternative attractions had eroded the customer base, ranging from D.I.Y., shopping and in-home entertainment to other domestic sports and foreign imports such as Italian soccer. However, the decline was also the result of the industry's failure to adapt to these changes. By the late 1980s, the football industry was characterized by financial and business mismanagement, dilapidated stadia, hooliganism, poor quality leagues and international footballing failure. Since the early 1990s, the football clubs have been adopting a more market-focused approach to their operations, implementing strategies that have been commonplace in the United States for some years.

Marketing of sport as a specific component within sport management has been particularly evident in the United States since the early 1980s. American sports franchises have taken the lead in adopting traditional marketing principles and practices commonplace in other leisure and service industries to make the sports experience more 'customer friendly'. This has involved the hiring of professional marketers, the introduction of customer research programmes, development of ancillary products and services such as merchandise and the provision of ticket booking facilities, flexible pricing packages, all-seater stadia, quality catering facilities, pre-match entertainment and high levels of customer service. They have also placed considerable emphasis on promotion, branding and public relations.

The sports industry is just one part of the service sector and, as a result, marketing a sports event or club is in many ways similar to marketing other leisure utilities and services such as the theatre, cinema and concerts. However, the unique characteristics of the sport product and the unusual market conditions have required marketing personnel to adopt different marketing strategies from those used in other service sectors.

Unlike other industries, the sports market is characterized by joint interdependence in that the clubs together provide the core product, i.e. the game. The relationship which exists between one sports club and its rivals is characterized by mutual dependency, without each other there is no product. Sports organizations therefore simultaneously compete and co-operate. It is therefore not possible to consider the marketing of individual sports clubs in isolation from the marketing of the sport as a whole, as marketing plays an important role at the league/association level of the sport. It is the league authorities who decide on the nature of the core product offered, i.e. league structure, rules and regulations, match scheduling, television and sponsorship contracts and income distribution.

At club level, the sports marketer traditionally has no control over the core sports product and its outcome. The nature of the core product is determined by the league/association, who decide on the rules and level of competition, and the club coaches, who pick the team/individuals and decide on the tactics and style of play. As the sports result and performance cannot be guaranteed, marketers need to make the overall offering attractive enough so that the sport performance is not the overriding factor. Therefore, marketing managers in sports clubs or associations are often responsible for developing ancillary product and service extensions that complement the sport spectacle and contribute more to a sport consumer's overall satisfaction.

The sports consumer is often considered to be different from consumers in other industry sectors in that they have an emotional attachment to the sport or club and see themselves as 'fans' rather than customers. Because of this emotional attachment, they do not have the opportunity to switch to a competing 'brand' if their team is not performing. This unique characteristic can be a double-edged sword for sports marketers. On the one hand this fan loyalty provides commercial opportunities for product and service extensions in areas such as merchandising. However, it can also leave sports marketers open to accusations of exploitation if not handled with care and sensitivity. British sports clubs also hold an important position within their respective communities, which again has important implications for sports marketers in terms of their public relations activities.

As pointed out above, sport is both a consumer and an industrial product. Corporate customers have become increasingly important for sports clubs and leagues in terms of sponsorship, advertising and corporate hospitality revenues. With the ever-growing media coverage of sport, sports sponsorship provides businesses with a wide range of opportunities to promote their products and services. Sponsors are attracted by the popularity of the sport and the resulting media exposure. Sponsorship allows companies to target specific market seg-

ments and provides them with an alternative to more traditional communications tools, such as advertising, which has become increasingly expensive and prone to 'clutter'.

References:

Gavron, J., 'Association Football. A Battered Sport and a Troubled Business', *The Economist* (May 31st 1986), pp. 45-53.

Mullin, B. J., Hardy, S., and Sutton, W. A., *Sport Marketing* (Champaign, Illinois: Human Kinetics, 1993).

Shilbury, D., 'Characteristics of Sport Marketing: Developing Trends', *ACHPER National Journal*, (Autumn 1989), pp. 21-24.

Further reading:

Shank, M., *Sports Marketing: a Strategic Perspective* (Upper Saddle River, New Jersey: Prentice Hall, 1999).

Vamplew, W., *Pay Up and Play the Game: Professional Sport in Britain, 1875-1914* (Cambridge: Cambridge University Press, 1988).

See also:

Commercialism; Management

-Dave Hudson

Martial Arts (*see* Aikido, Judo, Karate)

Mascots

A mascot is a person, animal or thing supposed to bring good luck. Although the use of mascots goes back to antiquity, they were not always called mascots. The word originally entered the English language thanks to a popular operetta called 'La Mascotte', which ran for over 1000 performances and was translated from French into English and performed in Britain and the United States between 1880 and 1882. The plot of this operetta involved a farm girl who brought good luck to whoever possessed her. The trans-

The Birmingham City mascot on the ball
(Action Images/David Slater)

lated title became 'The Mascot' and the concept of a mascot as a person, animal or object as a source of luck was therefore established.

Many clubs and teams have recognized the entertainment and marketing value of establishing their own mascot character. It can have an identity and may also be a selling tool, a source of entertainment and amusement for children, or a rallying point.

Mascots have also been used in recent years in the Soccer World Cup, from World Cup Willie (a lion playing football) in England in 1966 to Footix (a smiling cockerel) in France in 1998. The Olympic Games have also used mascots to help promote the spirit of the Games, beginning in Munich (1972) with Waldi the Dachshund. The mascots are designed to add personality to the competitions, capturing styles, traditions and cultures all mixed together in an animated form. Many other host countries have used an animal to represent their culture, most notably Misha the Bear at the 1980 Moscow Games, and Sam the Eagle at the 1984 Los Angeles Games.

See also:

Rituals and Superstition

-Kyle Phillpots

M.C.C. (Marylebone Cricket Club)

The Marylebone Cricket Club (M.C.C.) was founded in 1787 when cricket was emerging from its pastoral roots into an era of aristocratic patronage. Its ground, Lord's, was named after its original owner, Thomas Lord. Its present site in St John's Wood, London has been the home of M.C.C. since 1814.

M.C.C. became cricket's leading authority, producing in 1788 its first code of Laws. Sir Pelham Warner (1946) wrote that throughout its history, M.C.C. has reigned but not ruled. In 1898, M.C.C. formed the Advisory County Cricket Committee and the Board of Control for Test Matches at Home, forerunners of today's governing body. In 1903-1904, M.C.C. sent its first official England side overseas, a role it continued until 1977. In 1968, aware that the national game should not be administered by a private club, M.C.C. instituted the Test and County Cricket Board, the National Cricket Association and the Cricket Council, who amalgamated in 1997 to form the England and Wales Cricket Board, British cricket's governing body. Until 1993, M.C.C. also administered the International Cricket Council (I.C.C.).

M.C.C.'s current role contains five stated aims:

(1) Maintaining Lord's as a leading cricket venue.

(2) Guardianship of the Laws of Cricket.

(3) Promoting cricket to young people in the United Kingdom (including the M.C.C. Young Cricketers Scheme).

241

(4) Assisting the I.C.C. with the development of cricket overseas.

(5) Providing services and facilities for members.

In 1998, M.C.C. voted to admit women to the Club, a move that will enable it to continue its pioneering role into the 21st century.

References:

Warner, Sir P., *Lord's, 1787-1945* (London: Harrap, 1946).

Further reading:

Kerr, D. R. and Peebles, I. A. R., *Lord's, 1946-1970* (London: Harrap, 1971).

Lewis, A. R., *Double Century: the Story of MCC and Cricket* (London: Hodder & Stoughton, 1987).

Warner, Sir P., *Lord's, 1787-1945* (London: Harrap, 1946).

Websites:

Lords and Marylebone Cricket Club – http://www.lords.org/

See also:

Cricket; Lord's Cricket Ground; Museums and Halls of Fame – Lord's Cricket Museum

-Glenys Williams

Media

The cultural, commercial and global impact of sport has been intrinsically related to the rise and expansion of media practices, institutions and technologies in the 20th century. In Britain, the media has advanced the commodification of sport in the contemporary era, and furthermore, generated myths, metaphors and meanings that articulate aspects of British culture and national identity. Arguably, the media has not merely recorded and analysed sport, but has informed its development and conduct, often impacting upon its execution and regulation.

British sporting newspapers in the late Victorian era, such as *Bell's Life in London*, *Sporting Magazine* and *Athletic News*, adopted an informative but sometimes euphoric style that promoted the 'visualization' of events, and anticipated the often emphatic commentary practices in both press and broadcasting which serve to 'spectacularize' even the most mundane of contests. Circulation of sports-orientated publications was vigorous, and specialist football papers proliferated. As early as 1906, the press provided a 'same-day' results service, often wiring bullet-point match summaries to typesetters throughout the game in order that as soon as it was finished, the paper could go to press. Sports coverage increased in the popular press, and emphasis was placed upon football reporting in order to attract a working-class readership. The quality broadsheets' middle-class orientation led to concentration on cricket, Rugby Union and horse-racing.

The impact of photography in the early 1920s was crucial in the development of sports reporting. Caricatures, portraits and sketches of players and events were replaced by action pictures, and later, in the *Sunday Graphic* during the 1940s, these were often annotated with extracts of radio commentary by Raymond Glendenning. However, as reporting changed its character, responding more to a perceived market rather than an established public interest, information and lyrical exposition were replaced by increased 'gossip' and feature material about the culture surrounding sport. Increasingly, investigative reporting took place, resulting most notably in *The People's* 1964 revelations of bribery and match-fixing in soccer. Tabloid sensationalism, by the 1960s, saw the rise of the sporting cliché and a focus on 'celebrity', arousing concern about matters of representation and fairness.

Though film newsreels helped to popularize sport further, this was accentuated with the rise of television. Ten years after the first radio broadcasts of the England versus Wales Rugby Union clash at Twickenham and the Arsenal versus Sheffield United match in 1927 came the first televised soccer. Early matches often featured Arsenal, or fixtures at Wembley, as the

Alexandra Palace transmitter was conveniently close. The first live match covered fully was the 1938 Cup Final between Preston North End and Huddersfield Town, which was watched by approximately 10,000 people, significantly fewer than those at the ground itself. Only *The Daily Herald* was prescient enough to recognize the potential of television, which grew rapidly with the vast numbers of televisions purchased to watch the Coronation in 1953. Now it is rare that a viewing audience on television does not massively outnumber spectators at an event. Unsurprisingly, revenue from broadcast rights to television coverage has become increasingly important in the political economy of sport, and has become the focus for key debates concerning matters of media ownership and control, and its effect on the conduct of sport itself.

By 1950, sports administrators and broadcasters had recognized that the televising of sports had potentially contradictory outcomes. On the one hand, attendances might reduce; on the other, broadcasts could promote an interest in the sport and an awareness by sponsors and advertisers. The Association for the Protection of Copyright in Sport articulated these issues, provoking the Postmaster General to establish the Sports Television Advisory Committee to facilitate research into the matter, to take advice from sports associations, and to evaluate the broadcasting model established in the United States. Results were inconclusive, but the B.B.C. were fully aware of the implications of the emergence of commercial television in 1955, and competitive tendering for rights. Recognizing the importance of football coverage, the independent companies bid for live broadcast rights, but the general scepticism of the Football League about televised soccer, the pedigree of B.B.C. sports broadcasting (*Sportsview*, its flagship magazine programme, was first broadcast in 1954) and limited broadcasting infrastructure prevented I.T.V. from fully establishing itself.

Though *World of Sport* was to temporarily challenge *Grandstand* for the sports audience on Saturday afternoons, I.T.V. remained perpetually at a disadvantage until it secured exclusive rights to soccer highlights in 1978, effectively removing the B.B.C. institution, *Match of the Day*, from the schedules. Pressured by government, sports administrators and broadcasters themselves, the B.B.C. and I.T.V. agreed on ten 'listed events' of 'national interest' – the English and Scottish F.A. Cup finals, test cricket, Wimbledon, the Boat Race, the Grand National, the Derby, the World Cup soccer finals, the Commonwealth Games and the Olympics – which would not be subject to exclusive rights agreements. Though the 1981 and 1984 Broadcasting Acts safeguarded this agreement, the 1989 bill allowed bidding for rights, and with the increasing impact of satellite broadcasting, and the on-going success of Rupert Murdoch's BSkyB Sky Sports in securing rights to key British events, most notably Premiership football, Rugby League and England's Rugby Union matches, the media landscape has considerably changed. As mass audiences watch less live sport, radio reporting and press coverage has once more become crucial to a sporting public. It is clear that pay-per-view broadcasting compromises the 'national memory', and that major achievements in British sport may soon only be known to fragmented broadcast audiences and back-page affiliates. The proliferation of multi-media and cross-media coverage, however, has stimulated increased awareness of sport's importance in British society overall, particularly in relation to its commercial worth and cultural value. Anxiety may prevail that British sport is now merely another branch of show business, with attendant fears of vulgarization and intrusive broadcast 'gimmickry' on the actual conduct of games, but arguably, the media itself merely articulates and amplifies sport's intrinsic qualities and traditions; sometimes rejuvenating individual sports, and furthering the cause of sport in the personal, social and political contexts of local, regional, and national identity.

Further reading:

Conn, D., *The Football Business: Fair Game in the 90s?* (London: Mainstream, 1998).

Ford, J., *This Sporting Land* (London: New English Library, 1977).

Holt, R., *Sport and the British: a Modern History* (Oxford: Clarendon Press, 1990).

Kelly, S., *Back Page Football: a Century of Newspaper Coverage* (Harpenden: Queen Anne Press, 1995).

See also:

Journalism; Television

-Paul Wells

Media – *Athletic News*

The *Athletic News* first appeared in 1875, the product of the same partnership of Edward Bleackley and Edward Hulton that had published the *Sporting Chronicle* from their Manchester offices since 1873. The two papers were complementary, the *Chronicle* concentrating on horse-racing while the *Athletic News* promised its readers that it would soon be the leading journal covering amateur sport in the United Kingdom. However, it quickly accepted that professionals could not be ignored and opened its columns to all sporting subjects, so long as they were discussed in 'the tone and temper characteristic of gentlemen'.

It was first published on Saturdays, had moved to Wednesdays by 1880, then Tuesdays and finally became a Monday paper, costing one penny, from December 1888. This was three months after the beginning of the inaugural season of the Football League and it was for its extensive coverage and championing of professional football that the *Athletic News* became noted. Indeed, the editor between 1895 and 1900 was John J. Bentley, who was the President of the League from 1894 to 1910. The circulation of the *News* grew with the popularity of football from 20,000 a week in the mid-1880s to 180,000 during the football season a decade later.

Although it started out as a provincial paper, it gradually took on a national coverage with special correspondents in London and Scotland. Apart from racing, few sports went unnoticed but it was its wide-ranging and stylish football coverage, from 1900-1921 supervised by J. A. H. Catton as editor, which set it apart. It was amalgamated with the *Sporting Chronicle* in 1931.

References:

Inglis, S., *League Football and the Men Who Made It* (London: Collins, 1988).

Mason, A., *Association Football and English Society, 1863-1915* (Brighton: Harvester, 1980).

-Tony Mason

Media – Fanzines

One of the most interesting developments in British football in the 1980s, fanzines are magazines produced by fans for fans, usually totally independent of clubs. Fanzines have become a key arena for fans to express themselves in modern football (and, more recently, other sports), and one of the main ways during the 1980s in which supporters convinced a hostile British public that they were not just violent hooligans. With origins in the 1970s (the much vaunted *Foul*), fanzines were essentially a product of the 1980s, a response to the treatment of supporters, violence, the decline of football, and the attempts of Margaret Thatcher's governments to introduce new legislation affecting the game.

Fanzines have many common characteristics, using humour, sarcasm and abuse to get their points across. Most revolve around individual clubs (with nearly every club having a fanzine by 1991) and often offer alternative viewpoints on the game. Their politics vary – some (like at Leeds) have been very active in anti-racism, while others (Celtic and Rangers) celebrate identities that may be less commendable or progressive. However, most support anti-racism (though sexism is a problem) and anti-hooliganism, and all start from the premise that fans are more than simply consumers of football, and have the right to criticize the players and the clubs they love.

Clubs have often been hostile to fanzines, with some banned from stadia, but in an age of massive cultural change in football, fanzines remain important in offering fans one of the few ways to express themselves that remains free from media or club censorship or control.

References:

Giulianotti, R., 'Enlightening the North: Aberdeen Fanzines and Local Football Identity', in R. Giulianotti and Armstrong, G. (eds.), *Entering the Field: New Perspectives on World Football* (Oxford: Berg, 1997), pp. 211-237.

Haynes, R., *The Football Imagination: the Rise of Football Fanzine Culture* (Aldershot: Arena, 1995).

Jary, D., Horne, J., and Bucke T., 'Football "Fanzines" and Football Culture', *Sociological Review*, 38, 3 (1991).

Further reading:

Haynes, R., 'Vanguard or Vagabond? A History of When Saturday Comes', in S. Redhead (ed.), *The Passion and the Fashion: Football Fandom in the New Europe* (Aldershot: Avebury, 1993).

Moorhouse, H. F., 'From Zines like these: Fanzines, Tradition and Identity in Scottish Football', in G. Jarvie and G. Walker (eds.), *Scottish Sport in the Making of the Nation* (London: Leicester University Press, 1994), pp. 173-194.

-Rex Nash

Media – Radio 5

Radio Five Live was launched in March 1994 as the national B.B.C. radio station to cover live news and sport. Until then, B.B.C. radio sports output had been carried by Radio 2 and subsequently by Radio 5 until that network was axed. Despite initial misgivings about the balance between sport and news, and the possible sidelining of sport, these fears have proved to be unfounded and the station has become a major success, winning the Sony Radio Station of the Year Award in 1996 and 1998.

In its new home, far more airtime has been devoted to sport. Although coverage had increased in the move from Radio 2 to Radio 5, there is now room for live commentary and discussion on a far wider range of sports. As well as football, Rugby Union and tennis, sports such as ice hockey, Rugby League and basketball have been covered. There are also sports bulletins every half-hour and Radio Five Live has become the home of the long-running Saturday afternoon programme *Sports Report*, which celebrated its fiftieth birthday in 1998. Sporting personalities such as Gary Lineker, David Gower and Will Carling have all presented sports programmes, as have Michael Parkinson and former M.P. David Mellor.

With advances in digital radio, the amount of sports coverage on the network is likely to increase further. However, growing competition from independent radio suggests that Radio Five Live will face a challenge if it is to maintain its pre-eminent position in the sports-radio field.

Websites:

Radio Five Live –
http://www.bbc.co.uk/radio5live/index.html

-Graham McMillan

Media – Sky Sports

In 1992, British Sky Broadcasting (BSkyB), owned by Rupert Murdoch's News International group, paid £304 million to secure the exclusive rights to broadcast live Premiership football. In doing so, Sky Sports became a significant player in British sports coverage for the first time, challenging all the previous orthodoxies and traditional models of terrestrial broadcasting.

Other exclusive rights deals followed. BSkyB created the 'Super League' in Rugby League, playing the sport in summer to parallel the season played during the winter in Australia and New Zealand, for enhanced global audiences and cross-hemisphere competitive opportunities. The company also secured the rights to England internationals in Rugby Union, effectively breaking the B.B.C. monopoly of Five Nations coverage, and splitting the home unions politically and commercially. Further deals secured exclusive coverage of triumphant British Ryder Cup wins; Frank Bruno's World Heavyweight Championship victory over Oliver McCall; coverage of overseas test cricket and key one-day matches; and a range of other significant events in racing, tennis and basketball.

Rupert Murdoch suggests that live sports coverage is the 'battering ram' with which he seeks to secure pay-per-view subscription audiences. It is crucial both for the political economy and the cultural kudos of its broadcasters. Sky Sports has challenged the dominance of the B.B.C. and provoked other broadcasters into the sports broadcast marketplace. Arguably, Sky Sports have compromised the national memory by fragmenting the 'common experience' of watching major sporting events, but equally, sports authorities will benefit from higher television revenues in order to fund grass-roots development and maintenance of facilities.

References:

Horsman, M., *Sky High: the Inside Story of BskyB* (London : Orion Business, 1997).

-Paul Wells

Media – *Sporting Chronicle*

The *Sporting Chronicle* might never have been started at all in 1871 had not the existing Manchester papers decided to exclude all betting and racing news. The idea and the money for the new paper came from a former local cotton man-

ufacturer, E. O. Bleackley, but it was the printer whom the enterprise was to launch into the ranks of millionaires. Edward Hulton had worked as a compositor for the *Manchester Guardian* before setting up his own printing business. The first edition of his new racing paper appeared on February 14th, 1871. Entitled the *Tissue*, it was bought mainly by publicans. The name was soon changed to the *Prophetic Bell* and was retitled again in 1873 as the *Sporting Chronicle*. By then it was already expanding its sporting coverage, but at a time when the existing specialist sporting press was all London-based, the *Chronicle* was aimed at the northern punter. It soon established itself as part of the developing sub-culture of modern northern sport and went daily in 1880.

Horse-racing was to remain its core content and, apart from the occasional anti-puritan editorial, there was little deviation from sporting news. The main writers used pseudonyms, giving them a semblance of continuity and consistency that appealed to readers looking for authoritative judgements. The paper incorporated the *Athletic News* in 1931 and continued to be an all-purpose sports paper after the Second World War. However, in August 1953 it reverted to being solely a racing paper and with the competition of press, radio and television becoming ever more fierce, the *Sporting Chronicle* finally closed in July 1983.

References:

Mason, N., 'Sporting News 1860-1914', in M. Harris and A. Lee (eds.), *The Press in English Society from the Seventeenth to the Nineteenth Centuries* (London: Associated University Press, 1986), pp. 168-188.

-Tony Mason

Media – *Sporting Life*

There was no sports page in the daily press of the 1850s, when *Bell's Life* and *The Field* monopolized the production of the national sporting news. However, in March 1859, a twice weekly penny paper which steered clear of politics and confined its news largely to horse-racing, coursing, hunting, cricket, athletics 'and all minor sports' entered the lists. This was the *Sporting Life*, which became so successful a business that it bought the title *Bell's Life* from the Hulton Press when it was put up for sale in 1886.

By then, the *Sporting Life* had become a penny daily, publishing results and reports of most sports but concentrating on horse-racing, where its accuracy and completeness, especially in its recording of the starting prices, gave it an important advantage over the competition. Three steam rotary presses enabled it to produce 18,000 copies per hour and it claimed a circulation of 300,000 a day. Like the other major sporting papers, the *Sporting Life* also promoted and sponsored sports, holding the stakes, providing referees, presenting trophies and publishing sporting annuals.

In 1920, it was bought by Odhams Press and in 1924, it took over the *Sportsman*. It also began to publish the first summary of probable runners and riders and a betting forecast aimed at the non-race-going punter. Racing came to monopolize its columns. It appeared to be as much a part of horse-racing as the Jockey Club, but in 1986 it began to face competition from the Sheikh Mohammed-owned *Racing Post*. By this time, *The Life* was owned by the Mirror Group, and when they bought the *Racing Post* for £1.00 in 1997, it was the *Sporting Life* which was closed after 139 years.

References:

Mason, T., 'Sporting News 1860-1914', in M. Harris and A. Lee (eds.), *The Press in English Society from the Seventeenth to the Nineteenth Centuries* (London: Associated University Press, 1986), pp. 168-188.

Further reading:

Vamplew, W., *The Turf: a Social and Economic History of Horse Racing* (London: Allen Lane, 1976).

-Tony Mason

Media – Sports Personality of the Year

The title of B.B.C. Sports Personality has been awarded every year since 1954 to the sportsperson whose achievements have most impressed television sports fans. The trophy, modelled on the first post-war television camera, is presented at a ceremony each December to the person who has received the highest number of votes in a B.B.C. viewers' poll and concludes a televised review of the sporting highlights of the year.

Chosen by the general public, the winner tends to reflect the level of media exposure of himself and his sport (women and minority sports are underrepresented, as are participants in team sport, for which there is a separate award).

Of the forty-four winners up to 1999, fifteen have come from athletics, a further seven from motor sports and the remainder largely from tennis, golf, boxing, ice skating, swimming and cricket. Three sports stars have won the award twice, boxer Henry Cooper and racing drivers Nigel Mansell and Damon Hill, while the ice skating duo of Torvill and Dean were joint winners in 1984 and H.R.H. Princess Anne was winner in 1971. Of the nine female Sports Personalities, only three have won since 1973 – athletes Liz McColgan and Fatima Whitbread and tennis player Virginia Wade – which suggests that women have failed to make much impact on the minds of television viewers in the recent past.

The final winner of the 20th century was Lennox Lewis, the new undisputed Heavyweight Champion of the World. 'Sports Person of the Century', awarded in December 1999, was the former three-times Heavyweight Boxing Champion of the World, Mohammed Ali.

References:

Gearing, B. and McNeill, P., *Seventy Years of BBC Sport* (London: André Deutsch, 1998).

-Joyce Kay

Media – *Sportsman*

When the *Sportsman* was first issued in August 1865, it was able to claim that racing had always formed, 'and must continue to form, the most prominent feature in an English sporting newspaper'. When it closed in 1924, its columns reflected a much more complex sporting world.

The founders of the paper were particularly keen to offer inside knowledge of betting markets and reports from the training quarters. The paper first appeared twice a week, then three and four times, before becoming what it claimed was the world's first sporting daily in March 1876. It was to provide a record of a growing range of sports in long, closely packed columns of print for almost half a century. It was produced by gentlemen rather than players, many of the contributors being public school and university educated, often freelancers or part-timers who got their chance through the old-boy network. It increasingly sponsored several sports, including billiards, boxing and professional sculling and by 1914 was the leading football paper in London, though in 1889 it had allocated five columns to the Boat Race and only one to the Cup final.

It opposed the activities of the Anti-Gambling League early in the 20th century and the Sporting League was established through the medium of its columns. Candidates for office in Parliament and county councils were asked to support the rights of the people to the free enjoyment of all sports, pastimes and recreations.

The expansion of sporting news in the dailies and weeklies after 1918 put pressure on specialist sporting papers and the *Sportsman* was the most distinguished victim, being bought and closed by Odhams Press in 1924.

References:

Mason, T., 'Sporting News 1860-1914', in M. Harris and A. Lee (eds.), *The Press in English Society from the Seventeenth to the Nineteenth Centuries* (London: Associated University Press, 1986), pp. 168-188.

-Tony Mason

Memorable Events – Death of Tommy Simpson

The demise of cyclist Tommy Simpson during the 1967 Tour de France was the first known drugs-related death of a British sportsperson. On the thirteenth stage, 133 miles from Marseilles to Carpentras, Simpson collapsed in high temperatures half a mile from the summit of the virtually shadeless Mont Ventoux. Although the official cause of death was given as dehydration and exhaustion, it was later acknowledged that Simpson, like many other cyclists, had been using amphetamines. The taking of such drugs was a well-established practice among long-distance racing cyclists in the days when there were no dope controls. Indeed, attempts to introduce drug tests in 1966 had been fiercely opposed by leading cyclists, including five-times Tour winner Jacques Anquetil, who argued that professionals could not cope with their long season without resort to stimulants.

Simpson had been world professional road-race champion in 1965, but an injured leg, broken on a family skiing holiday, meant that he missed most of the following season and was unable to exploit his title commercially. Aged twenty-nine, he saw the 1967 Tour de France, the world's greatest cycle race, as his last remaining chance to make big money out of his sport. As a mark of respect, the fourteenth stage from Carpentras to Sète was a slow procession with Barry Hoban, a member of Simpson's team, the pre-determined winner. A memorial stone was erected near the Ventoux summit where, each year, cycling fans still leave mementoes in tribute to a fallen champion.

References:

Rendall, J., 'Death of a Cyclist', *Sunday Telegraph Magazine*, 13 July 1997.

-Wray Vamplew

Memorable Events – Frankie Dettori's Seven

With his fractured English, trademark leap from his winning mounts in the unsaddling enclosure and unbridled enthusiasm for the sport, Anglicized Italian jockey Frankie Dettori had already established himself as a firm favourite with the racing public prior to events at the Ascot Festival Day meeting on September 28th, 1996.

Dettori's six races produced six winners: Wall Street (2-1), Diffident (12-1), Mark of Esteem (100-30), Decorated Hero (7-1), Fatefully (7-4) and Lochangel (5-4). The record for one day's riding was the six wins and a dead heat secured by George Fordham from eight rides at Stockbridge in 1867. In modern times, both Gordon Richards at Chepstow in 1933 and Alec Russell at Bogside in 1957 had gone through a six-race card. At Ascot, there was one race still to come. Fujiyama Crest was Dettori's final mount. Its recent form justified an opening price of 12-1, but bookmakers quickly slashed that to make it the favourite at 2-1, as the betting public followed their saviour. Dettori justified their support by securing victory by a neck after leading throughout, thereby galloping into turf history as the first jockey to win all seven races on the card. It was estimated that bookmakers on and off the course lost several million pounds. A bookmaker's cheque to a fortunate punter and racing plates from several of the winners are on display at York Racing Museum.

References:

Daily Telegraph (30 September 1996).

Further reading:

Dettori, F., *A Year in the Life of Frankie Dettori* (London: Mandarin, 1996).

See also:

Horse-racing

-Wray Vamplew

Memorable Events – Fred Archer's Suicide

A head, only a head. So short was the winning margin of Sailor Prince in the 1886 Cambridgeshire that jockey, Fred Archer, rider of second-placed St Mirin, blamed himself for the defeat as his mount carried a pound overweight.

Archer was champion jockey for thirteen consecutive seasons but had never won a Cambridgeshire, a major non-classic race. So keen was he to end this drought that he undertook to ride at 8 stone 6 pounds, a reduction of 12 pounds in less than a week. This left him so weak that he contracted first a chill and subsequently typhoid, and was unable to fight it off. On the anniversary of his wife's death he shot himself, a victim of illness, melancholy and wasting.

Archer was not unusual in having weight problems – almost all riders had to eat little and combat even that with sweating and purgatives. Yet even naturally lightweight riders often tried to lose an additional pound or two, as this increased their chances of employment – there were always far more jockeys than rides available.

Over time, the Jockey Club has raised the minimum weight to its present level of 7 stone 10 pounds, in contrast to the 5 stone 7 pounds of 1860. Modern jockeys also have the benefit of access to scientific knowledge on nutrition, but theirs is still a life of fierce self-discipline. At the same time as existing on a starvation diet, they also have to keep fit and strong enough to control 1,000 pounds of horseflesh.

References:

Welcome, J., *Fred Archer: a Complete Study* (London: Lambourn Publications, 1990).

Further reading:

Humphris, E. M., *The Life of Fred Archer* (London: Hutchinson, 1923).

See also:

Horse-racing – Governance and Administration; Horse-racing – Jockeys

-Wray Vamplew

Milk Race

Until 1993, the Milk Race was Britain's premier cycling event. It owed its existence to the British League of Racing Cyclists (B.L.R.C.), which was formed during the Second World War by enthusiasts who yearned for a British version of such continental massed-start classics as the Tour de France, the Giro d'Italia and the Vuelta a España. They met with stiff opposition, not only from motoring magazines but also from government; indeed, in 1947, a Ministry of Transport committee threatened to outlaw such races on public roads. Alone among the cycling organizations of the time, the B.L.R.C. refused to be intimidated and continued to stage races that they were convinced the public wanted to see. They were proved right with the success of the first tour of Britain in 1951; five years later, the Road Traffic Act of 1956 legalized road racing.

The first tours were sponsored by the *Daily Express*, but by 1958 the Milk Marketing Board had taken over and the event, now one of the sport's premier amateur races, became known as the Milk Race. Its amateur status lasted until 1983 when it became open. The last race was held in 1993, after which the Milk Marketing Board withdrew its sponsorship.

Four riders managed two Milk Race victories – the Dutchman Fedor den Hertog (1969 and 1971), Yuri Kashurin of the Soviet Union

(1979 and 1982) and Britons Bill Bradley (1959 and 1960) and Reg West (1965 and 1967). The closest finish was that of 1976, when Bill Nickson beat fellow Briton, Joe Waugh, by the margin of only five seconds, this after 1,035 miles and fourteen days of racing.

References:

Evans, J., *The Guinness Book of Cycling Facts and Feats* (Enfield: Guinness Superlatives, 1996).

See also:

Cycling

-Tony Rennick

Morpeth Olympic Games

The 'Morpeth Wrestling and Athletic Games', founded by Edmund Dobson in 1873 under the patronage of Lord Decies of Bolam, had, until 1881, consisted of wrestling, 120-yard and 440-yard handicap races, the high jump, the pole leap and 440-yard hurdles. In 1882, their name was changed to the 'Morpeth Olympic Games'.

Originally held in Brewery Field, all handicap races were for professionals and organized in heats, ties and finals. In 1883, there were 73 entries for the 120-yard race, with handicaps from scratch ranging from 2 to 25 yards. Gate-money and entrance-stakes guaranteed high cash prizes. In 1890, there were 224 entries for the 130-yard race and 130 for wrestling, while in 1891 there were 294 entries for the 120-yard race. In 1896, the Games moved to a new site at Grange House Field. Apart from stone-lifting in 1890, the three-legged race and egg-and-spoon race in 1892, and the 300 yards in 1902, the events hardly changed. Two afternoons were needed in 1912, when further athletic disciplines were added.

The Games were discontinued during the First World War, but were re-instituted by George Jackson in 1919, and staged on Mount Haggs Field from 1921 to 1939. In 1922, 280

250

starters enlisted for the 120 yards, while in 1935, boxing was introduced. The Games were interrupted one more during the Second World War, and then returned to Grange House Field in 1946. There were thirty-six heats in the 80 yards in 1952. After the death of John Nicholson, the main handicapper from 1920 to 1939, in 1957, the Games were staged for the last time in 1958. All the records of the local 'Olympic Committee' have been lost.

References:

Moffatt, F. C., *Turnpike Road to Tartan Track. The Story of Northern Foot Races* (Morpeth: privately printed, 1979).

Newcastle Daily Chronicle, Newcastle (1873-1929).

Newcastle Daily Journal, Newcastle (1873-1958).

Newcastle Evening Chronicle, Newcastle (1885-1910, 1912-1958).

Newcastle Weekly Chronicle, Newcastle (1873-1940, July 1946-1952).

Further reading:

Morpeth Herald (1873-1920, 1925).

Thielgen, J., *Entstehung und Entwicklung der 'Morpeth Olympic Games' von 1873-1958*, Hausarbeit 1. Staatsexamen, Deutsche Sporthochschule Köln, 1996.

See also:

Cotswold Games; Liverpool Olympics

-Joachim Ruhl

Motor Boat Racing

Motor boat racing, often referred to as powerboat or speedboat racing, started soon after the invention of the internal combustion engine in 1887.

The earliest reference to a powerboat race in Britain is one across the English Channel in the early 1900s, which was at an average speed of sixteen knots. However, the early development of the sport in Britain took place on inland waters. The circuit races were of limited length and duration. Although inland circuit racing is more of a spectator event, off-shore long-distance racing is the one which generates most publicity. One of the first major events to attract public attention was the *Daily Express*-sponsored race from Cowes to Torquay in 1961 (from 1968 this was extended to Torquay and back). Others followed, such as the *Daily Express* Putney (on the River Thames) to Calais and back race the year after, and the Round Britain Race in 1969. Both types of racing fall under the aegis of the Royal Yachting Association.

More recently, power/speed boating has been banned in some areas because of environmental concerns about problems such as noise and water pollution, bank erosion and the destruction of natural habitats.

Websites:

The Royal Yachting Association – http://www.rya.org.uk/

-Richard William Cox

Motor Cross (*see* Hill Climbing; Scrambling)

Motor Racing

The history of the motor car begins with the Daimler-Benz vehicle of 1895, and the birth of motor sport soon followed. Even in this early period, British cars and drivers raced on the Continent. In 1907, the first Grand Prix race was held in France. Motor racing on the Continent took place on public roads, but from the beginning road racing was banned in Britain. Consequently, the first purpose-built racing circuit in the world was at Brooklands in Surrey. It had steeply inclined banking on its long, fast corners and was used from 1907 to 1939. The first two British Grands Prix were held at Brooklands in 1926 and 1927.

Donington Park, near Derby, was used for Grand Prix racing between 1935 and 1938.

Between the two world wars, British success in international motor racing, unlike motorcycle racing, was limited. Two manufacturers held a place at the top level, Sunbeam and Bentley. The Le Mans twenty-four-hour race for sports cars was inaugurated in 1923, and Bentley won it in 1924 and between 1927 and 1930. However, the firm was then bought by Rolls Royce, who had no interest in racing. The most conspicuous British driver was Henry Seagrave (1896-1930), who was killed breaking the world water-speed record. The sport was dominated by the French, Germans and Italians – between 1924 and 1955 there were no British Grand Prix victories. The highest levels of motor racing were conducted in Europe and the United States, although each was independent of the other: Grand Prix racing is still quite different from American Indycar racing.

After the Second World War, disused airfields with tarmac surfaces provided the starting point for developing new circuits, most notably at Silverstone in Northamptonshire (1948) and at Brands Hatch in Kent (1949). Brands Hatch held its first Grand Prix in 1964, and for two decades the British Grand Prix alternated between the two circuits. Since 1987, Silverstone has been the sole venue for the event. Five Grands Prix were held at Aintree between 1955 and 1962. Donington reopened in 1977 and the European Grand Prix was held there in 1993.

In the 1950s, greatly increased car ownership brought the creation of other forms of racing on dozens of other airfields from Davidstow in Cornwall to Crimond, north of Aberdeen. Crowds of 20,000 to 30,000 were common at these events. Formula 3, first held in 1951, was for cars with engines up to 500 cc and encouraged broader participation. With rapidly changing relationships between performance and price, other events were devised. For example, the British Touring Car Championship was started in 1958, although it remained a comparatively minor attraction for thirty years, only beginning to regularly draw crowds of over 20,000 in the 1990s.

During the 1950s, British drivers won individual Grands Prix driving for foreign teams, Stirling Moss (born 1929) for Mercedes-Benz and Maserati, Peter Collins (1931-1958) with Ferrari. Moss, who won sixteen Grands Prix, was never a Drivers' Champion. This prize was not won by a British driver until Mike Hawthorn (1929-1958) in 1958. Then Britain had a series of champions – Graham Hill (1929-1975) in 1962 and 1968, Jim Clark (1936-1968) in 1963 and 1965, John Surtees (born 1934) in 1964, and Jackie Stewart (born 1939) in 1969, 1971 and 1973. Later came James Hunt (1947-1993) in 1976, Nigel Mansell (born 1953) in 1992, and Damon Hill (born 1960), son of Graham, in 1996.

The consistent success of British teams and drivers after 1960 had its roots in developments immediately after the Second World War. In 1946, John and Charles Cooper built their first car with a 500 cc single-cylinder engine. Nine years later, they won a Grand Prix using a Bristol engine, and later used Coventry-Climax, Maserati, B.R.M. and Chevrolet engines. They were the first to use an engine built using light alloys, placed in the middle of the chassis, rather than the then-customary heavy engine in front. Thus they had a lighter car which had better braking and a better power-to-weight ratio. With Moss and the Australian Jack Brabham driving for them, Cooper won the Constructors' Championship in 1959-1960. British Racing Motors (B.R.M.), who first raced in Formula 1 in 1951, were set up to use the support of British industry to challenge continental domination. Their V16 engine was an outstanding design, but the undercapitalized B.R.M. were unable to build it reliably. They won the Constructors' Championship in 1962 and survived in Formula 1 until 1977. The third British team to emerge was Vanwall, funded by Tony

Vandervell, which only took part in Formula 1 from 1955 to 1960, but were Champions in 1958. Their success was partly due to the chassis that Colin Chapman designed for them in 1956.

Then came Chapman's Lotus. Chapman built his first car in 1948 and in 1960 his Lotus 18 won its first Grand Prix. It owed much to developments copied from Cooper, and had a glass-fibre body and a very low centre of gravity. In 1962, the Lotus 25 became the first monocoque: this was the car with which Jim Clark became Drivers' Champion in 1963. Lotus had a number of barren years after 1973, but in 1978 were again Constructors' Champions when their cars used the 'ground effect principle' to improve their road holding.

Chapman also played a major part in the reshaping of the commercial side of motor racing, when in 1968 he accepted sponsorship from the Gold Leaf tobacco company. The John Player Special (1974) was named after another sponsor. At the same time, television revenues were forced upwards and Bernie Ecclestone, President of the Formula 1 Constructors' Association, emerged as the central figure in the financing of Formula 1. After 1980, the numerous engineering talents needed for the continuous development of racing machines were joined by specialists in raising finance – Frank Williams built his team on Saudi Arabian money as well as the design genius of Patrick Head.

Formula 1 is now an international business, but it has as strong links with Britain as with any other country. In the first forty years (1958-1997) of the Constructors' Championship, the title was won thirty times by teams based in England: Vanwall (once), Cooper (twice), BRM (once), Lotus (seven times), Brabham (twice), Tyrrell (once), McLaren (seven times) and Williams (nine times).

In the 1950s, sports-car racing was almost as important as Formula 1. The Le Mans twenty-four-hour race was the most important event, and it was won by Jaguar's XJ-120 C-types in 1951 and 1953, and by D-types between 1955 and 1957. In the last two of these years, the winners were not a Jaguar works team but the private Ecurie Ecosse, based in Edinburgh and perpetually short of money. Of the many figures associated with Le Mans, the one truly outstanding individual was 'Wilkie' Wilkinson, a master mechanic of great experience. Three decades later, Jaguar had further success with the XJR-9LM in 1988 and the XJR-12 in 1990.

Further reading:

Haskell, H., *Colin Chapman: Lotus Engineering* (London: Osprey Automotive, 1993).

Higham, P., *The Guinness Guide to International Motor Racing* (Enfield: Guinness Superlatives, 1995).

Jenkinson, D., *Vanwall: the Story of Tony Vandervell and his Racing Cars* (Cambridge: Stephens, 1975).

See also:

Aintree; Brands Hatch; Brooklands Circuit; Donington Park; Hill Climbing; Oulton Park; Rallying; Scrambling; Silverstone; Stock-car Racing

-John Burnett

Motorcycle Racing

Motorcycle racing takes place on a variety of different types of racetrack and using a number of different types of machine. However, the most popular form is known as road racing, a name that is somewhat misleading as the majority of road races are actually run on specially prepared closed circuits. The Auto-Cycle Union, founded in 1903 as the Auto-Cycle Club but renamed in 1907, governs most forms of motorcycle racing in Britain, including off-road racing, drag racing and hill climbing. Internationally, the sport is governed by the Fédération Internationale de Motocyclisme (F.I.M. – International Motorcycling Federation), which was established in 1904. Motorcycle races are usually divided into classes based upon engine capacity,

British motocycle racing superstar Carl Fogarty takes a corner at the 1999 Superbike World Championship, Donington Park (Action Images/Mick Walker)

the most typical being the 250 cc, 350 cc, 500 cc and 750 cc classes.

Initially, motor races took place on public roads, often alongside car races. However, during the Paris to Madrid road race for cars and motorcycles in 1903, a series of accidents occurred which led to injuries to both competitors and spectators alike. This forced the French authorities to ban such races (they had already been banned in Britain for a number of years), and henceforth motorcycle racing became confined to specialist tracks.

The sport is heavily promoted by the Isle of Man Government, which introduced its Tourist Trophy (T.T.) races in 1907. The race circuit for the T.T. remains the oldest in the world, the races taking place over the island's mountainous roads. The famous Snaefell climb was added in 1911, providing a stern test of any rider's racing skills. Unfortunately, over the years the difficulty of the course has been responsible for taking the lives of many riders.

Another famous motorcycle-racing circuit, renowned because of its oval banks, was Brooklands, which was built in 1907.

During the First World War, motorcycles were used by the military. This served to increase the popularity of motorcycling in the postwar period. Within six months of the war ending, Auto-Cycle Union membership had increased by 18,000. Britain dominated the sport during the 1920s both in the manufacture of racing bikes and on the racing circuit. This dominance was challenged during the 1930s by the fascist regimes of Italy and Germany. Car and motorcycle manufacturing were regarded as key modern industries and as modernization was a crucial factor in underpinning nationalist ideology, these industries were of vital importance to the right-wing governments. Indeed, Germany's BMW and Italy's Guzzi became symbols of national prestige. Initially, Germany's dominance was prevalent in the lighter class of bikes such as 250 cc, whereas the Nortons of Britain still reigned supreme in the 350 cc and 500 cc classes.

In the post-Second World War period, however, Britain's motorcycle industry was eventually eclipsed by the Italian Gilera motorbikes and then by the Japanese motorcycle industry. British riders, on the other hand, were still in great demand. Due to the increased foreign competition, the famous Norton company was forced to withdraw from racing in 1955. However, even the highly modernized Japanese motorcycle industry was forced to withdraw from racing in the late 1960s. Ironically, this marked a return to the early ideals of motorcycle racing, with small firms and private owners building racing bikes that were more akin to ordinary road bikes. Their reign was short, however, as the European-dominated Fédération Internationale de Motocyclisme and the American Motorcycle Association established a new international race for 750-cc-class machines. The sport had been languishing for a number of years but with the introduction of 750 cc races, spectator interest revived once again and was followed by the re-entry of the big manufacturers into competitive racing. This has once again led to motorcycle racing bikes, like Formula 1 racing cars, bearing little resemblance to those used on the road by ordinary motorcyclists.

Over the years, Britain has had many World Champions in all the different classes, with household names including Geoff Duke, Mike Hailwood, Phil Read, Barry Sheene, John Surtees and, more recently, Carl Fogarty.

References:

ACU Handbook 1999
The Auto-cycle Union website – http://www.acu.org.uk/

Websites:

The Auto-cycle Union – http://www.acu.org.uk/

See also:

Isle of Man T.T. Races; Manx Grand Prix

-Ray Physick

Mountain Biking

Mountain biking is a thriving and accessible sport in Britain with a multitude of local races graded according to age and ability. Mountain bike orienteering offers opportunities for solo riders and teams to test their map reading and survival skills against speed across country. The mountain bike has become the machine par excellence of tourists and long-distance riders and offers stability and smooth handling on a variety of surfaces as a result of a frame design featuring thicker tubes, a longer wheelbase, distinctive knobbly tyres and, more recently, front and rear suspension.

In Britain, off-road cycling has long been popular. The British Cyclo-Cross Association was formed in 1954 and the Rough-Stuff Fellowship in 1955 to organize touring and racing across the countryside on adapted touring bikes. Marin County, California provided the setting for the emergence of contemporary mountain biking – during the mid-1970s cyclists discovered the delights of racing down mountainsides at top speed on heavy, single-speed Schwinn bikes. Former racing cyclists, Gary Fisher, Joe Breeze and Charlie Kelly competed in the early races and were influential in the technical development and marketing of the all-terrain bike.

Professional mountain bike racing takes a variety of styles – cross-country, which was included in the Olympics for the first time in 1996; downhill; hillclimb; slalom; trials; enduro and path-finding events. There are British regional and national championships as well as an annual World Cup series of events for men and women decided on points awarded throughout the season. Since 1990, there has been a unified world championship featuring cross-country and downhill events held in Europe and the United States. Britain forms an increasingly strong presence in the sport and sent a team of thirty-four riders to the 2000

World Mountain Bike Championships. The team included Caroline Alexander, a former European champion and winner of a round of the World Cup series and Barry Clarke, former British champion. Yorkshireman Steve Peat and Scot Carrick Crawford Anderson are both top class competitors in the World Cup series.

References:

Crowther, N., *The Ultimate Mountain Bike Book* (London: Aurum, 1996).

Evans, J., *The Guinness Book of Cycling Facts and Feats* (Enfield: Guinness, 1996).

Hughes, T. and Hughes R., *Pedal Power! A Guide to Cycling and Bikes* (London: Blandford, 1995).

Skilbeck, P., *Mountain Biking* (Marlborough: Crowood, 1996).

Further reading:

Berto, F. J., *The Birth of Dirt: Origins of Mountain Biking* (San Francisco: Van der Plas, 1999).

Websites:

Cycling UK (The Cycling Information Point) – www.cycling.uk.com

The Rough-Stuff Fellowship – http://www.rsf.org.uk/

The Trail Cyclists Association – http://www.trailquest.co.uk/

See also:

Cycling; Cyclo-Cross

-Ann Furtado

Mountaineering

Men have been climbing mountains or crossing passes for military or commercial purposes since Ancient Roman times, and although some summits were places of worship, high mountains were long considered as inconvenient barriers or ugly places of horror.

This began to change towards the end of the 18th century, when the Romantic movement's interest in wild nature began to develop. This brought many people who were doing the 'Grand Tour' along alpine paths on their way to Italy. Windham and Pockoke's visit to the glaciers of Chamonix and the 'Mer de Glace' in 1741, and the account they made of it, ascertained that high mountain regions were accessible.

The desire to conquer Mont Blanc was initiated by De Saussure, a Swiss scientist in 1760, and the first successful attempt to climb the mountain was completed by Jacques Balmat and Michel Paccard in 1786.

The French Revolution and Napoleonic wars interrupted the flow of British tourists to the Alps, but it resumed after 1815.

The glaciers of the Alps began to excite a specific interest in the scientific community (for example, J. D. Forbes) when Albert Smith's ascent of Mont Blanc and the diorama he made of it attracted a wide audience amongst the English public.

However, these visits remained examples of scientific pursuits or adventurous tourism and it was not until the mid-1850s that a small body of British professional men, such as Alfred Wills, Francis Fox Tuckett and E. S. Kennedy, started climbing alpine peaks for pleasure's sake.

The foundation in 1857 of the Alpine Club, with John Ball as its President, led to what was to be called 'the golden age of mountaineering', during which all the major peaks of the Alps were conquered (most of them by Britons). The Alpine Club also acted as a model for all the great continental mountaineering clubs.

The Matterhorn accident in 1865 aroused considerable controversy about mountaineering – the mountain was ascended by Edward Whymper, although unfortunately four of his companions were killed. Subsequently, approaches and techniques started to change, with guideless climbing and a more daring generation of rock climbers, like A. F. Mummery, emerging.

New playgrounds began to be explored – the Caucasus by A. W. Moore, the Andes by Edward Whymper, and the Himalayas by forerunners such as Douglas Freshfield, Martin Conway and Francis Younghusband, while the British Isles acted as a new field for rock-climbing for a widened class of hill-lovers.

Scores of daring women had been climbing mountains for decades when the Ladies' Alpine Club was eventually founded in 1907. The same year, Tom Longstaff and two guides were the first to climb a peak above 23,000 feet in the Himalayas.

In 1922, Mallory, who was to disappear in 1924 together with Irvine, while trying to climb Mount Everest, was the first to reach 27,000 feet without oxygen.

As could be expected, no new feats were recorded during the two world wars, and the next feat to come was in 1953, when Edmund Hillary and Tenzing, members of the British party led by John Hunt, reached the summit of Mount Everest.

Since then, men like Chris Bonington, Doug Scott, Joe Tasker and Peter Boardman have led successful expeditions in the Himalayas, thus proving that British mountaineers have remained amongst the most accomplished in the world.

Further reading:

Engel, C. E., *A History of Mountaineering* (London: Allen & Unwin, 1950).

Irving, R. L. G., *A History of British Mountaineering* (London: Batsford, 1955).

Mason, K., *Abode of Snow: a History of Himalayan Exploration and Mountaineering From the Earliest Times to the Ascent of Everest* (London: Diadem, 1987).

Websites:

The Alpine Club – http://www.alpine-club.org.uk/

See also:

Rock Climbing

-Michel Tailland

Much Wenlock Games

The Wenlock Olympian Games were the brainchild of Dr William Penny Brookes (1809-1895), son of the local practitioner William Brookes in Much Wenlock/Salop. Dr Brookes had studied medicine in London (Guy's and St Thomas's Hospitals), Padua and Paris before he returned to Much Wenlock in 1831 to take over his father's surgery. Through his various functions and offices he became the benefactor of his village – he was Commissioner for Roads and Taxes, improved the water-supply system, helped in renovating the Guildhall and Church, and helped to build the Corn Exchange and a Hospital. He was also chairman of the Wenlock Gas Company (which provided street-lamps) and succeeded in supplying his village with its own siding of the Much Wenlock and Severn Valley Railway. In 1841, he became a Justice of the Peace and founded the Wenlock Agricultural Reading Society (W.A.R.S.), with its lending library, reading-room, museum and classes for arts, music and botany to improve the intellectual standard of the rural population, especially of the working classes. However, for the promotion of their moral, intellectual and physical improvement, Brookes instituted a 'Wenlock Olympian Class' (W.O.C.) under the auspices of the W.A.R.S. in 1850, which staged eleven 'Annual Meetings' locally from 1850 to 1860.

Its aims were to encourage outdoor recreation and to award prizes for 'skill in athletic exercises and proficiency in intellectual and industrial attainments'. During the decade in question, an array of forty-four diverse and colourful events were included in the programme, which was staged on the local race-course (and later on Windmill and Linden Fields). These events were: cricket, foot-races (all ages), football, quoits, the standing high leap, the standing long leap, hopping (50 yards on one leg), the foot-race (old women), the 200 yards, the 880 yards, hurdling (one round), archery, hammer-throwing, stone-throwing (15 pounds), the wheelbarrow race, the jingling match, sewing (girls), knitting (women), the running high leap, the running long leap, knitting (girls), arithmetics (boys), writing (boys), walking (880 yards), recitation (boys/girls), 110 yards (boys), the prison base, the sack race, the donkey-race, reading/spelling (boys/girls), bible history (boys/girls), English history (boys/girls), drawing (boys/girls), pole-climbing, tilting at the ring, the pigrace, the javelin (distance), the spear (ring), essays on physical education, poems on M.W.G., solo singing (girls), glee singing, the ode on victor in tilting, and rifle shooting. Not all the events were staged each year, however. Some events were restricted to inhabitants but others were signed up for by athletes from as far afield as London and Liverpool. The fine for drunkenness, profane language and misbehaviour was five pennies.

After Brookes heard of E. Zappas's impending Olympic Games in Athens he corresponded with the Greek organizers in 1858, was sent the programme and donated the 'Wenlock Prize', worth £10, for the winner of the tilting event in 1859. In November 1860, he became president of the 'Wenlock Olympian Society' (W.O.S.), which had emerged from the W.O.C., separated from the W.A.R.S., and become independent. After consultations with members of the W.O.C. in March 1860, he formally inaugurated the 'Shropshire Olympian Society' (S.O.S.) in 1861, which staged four 'Shropshire Olympian Games' in rotation at county-level in Much Wenlock (1860), Wellington (1861), Much Wenlock (1862) and Shrewsbury (1864). After having studied the Athens programme of 1859, Brookes resumed his Greek correspondence with Queen Amalia in October 1860 and adorned his 'Wenlock Olympian Games' (W.O.G.) with a pseudo-hellenic varnish in the years to come. They were staged on the 'Olympian' Field, Greek inscriptions decorated

the ribbons, victors were crowned with laurel and olive wreaths, and bronze, silver, and gold medals were coined, the latter with the effigy of Nike, Greek goddess of victory, encircled by a Greek passage taken from Pindar. The javelin (in 1859) and three pentathlons (in 1868 and 1869) were added to the programme.

Between 1861 and 1895, twenty-six new events were added to the Wenlock Olympian Games: tilting with ponies (1861); singlestick (1862); water-color drawing and throwing the cricket ball (1865); distance quoits (1866); pentathlon (in gymnastics), pole leaping, steeple chase with water leap and three-legged race (1867); sword exercise and amateur pentathlon (1868); 32 pound right/left shot-putting, pentathlon (children), 440-yard handicap hurdling and boxing (1869); 1 to 3 mile bicycle races (1876-1878); the Zulu-contest (1879); tug-of-war (1880); brass band contest (1882); 1-mile tricycle race (1885); obstacle race (1891); tent pegging (1892); Victoria cross race and Balaclava melee (1893); the umbrella/cigar race (1894); and the gimcrack race (1895). Initially, these events were open to amateurs only, although professionals appeared from 1868 onward, and handicapping began in 1869.

In 1865, Brookes co-founded the 'National Olympian Association' (N.O.A.), which was inaugurated in John Hulley's Gymnasium in Liverpool and which staged six National Olympian Games in London (1866), Birmingham (1867), Wellington (1868), Much Wenloch (1874), Shrewsbury (1877) and Hadley (1883). However, one of its usurping objectives to 'form a centre of union for the different Olympian, Athletic, Gymnastic, Boating, Swimming, Cricket, and other similar Societies' met the wrath of the Amateur Athletic Association and led to its end soon after. Nevertheless, in 1877, Brookes renewed his contacts with Greece and, with the help of J. Gennadius, the Greek Chargé d'Affaires in London, persuaded King George I to donate a silver cup with a Greek inscription for the winner of the pentathlon at the fifth National Olympian Games in Shrewsbury, which the Greek King called 'the modern Olympia of the British'. Brookes's final endeavours in the autumn of 1880 to organize an 'International Olympian Festival, to be held in Athens', at international level, met with no support and failed.

In October 1890, the eighty-one-year-old Brookes staged an autumn meeting in honor of the twenty-seven-year-old Pierre de Coubertin, who had come to England to learn more about athletics, physical education and school sports, and who was still an 'Olympic greenhorn' at that time. Two months later, Coubertin wrote that it had been thanks to Brookes that the Olympic Games had survived. Both corresponded and Brookes was invited to the 1894 Congress in Paris but had to decline because of failing health. In 1894, he even wrote to the Greek Prime Minister to support Coubertin. Brookes died in 1895, four months before Athens 1896. In 1908, writing of Brookes, Coubertin reported that 'this romantic English practitioner of another age had turned his little village into a metropolis of popular sports'. The Wenlock Olympian Games were discontinued during the two world wars but were revived once more in 1950 and 1977. Today, the Games offer a large programme of modern events and have recently welcomed eminent visitors from the Olympic community.

References:

Mullins, S., *British Olympians: William Penny Brookes and the Wenlock Games* (London: British Olympic Association, 1986).

Neumüller, B., *Die Geschichte der Much Wenlock Games (1850-1895)*, Diplomarbeit, Deutsche Sporthochschule Köln, 1985.

Rühl, J. K., 'Moderne Olympische Spiele vor Coubertin – Die englische Szene', in I. Diekmann and H. J. Teichler (eds.), *Körper, Kultur und Ideologie. Sport und Zeitgeist im 19. und 20. Jahrhundert* (Bodenheim: Philo Verlagsgesellschaft, 1997), pp. 48-78.

Wenlock Olympian Society Minute Book I (1850-1876), *Book II* (1877-1895).

Young, D. C., *The Modern Olympics. A Struggle for Revival* (London: Johns Hopkins University Press, 1996).

Further reading:

Furbank, M., Cromarty, H. and McDonald, G., *William Penny Brookes and the Olympic Connection* (Much Wenlock: Wenlock Olympian Society, 1996).

Rühl, J. K., 'Das Amateurideal und der Einfluß Griechenlands auf die Olympischen Spiele in Much Wenlock. Ein Beitrag zum Verhältnis von Pierre de Coubertin und William Penny Brookes', in A. Luh and E. Beckers (eds.), *Umbruch und Kontinuität im Sport. Reflexionen im Umfeld der Sportgeschichte. Festschrift für Horst Ueberhorst* (Bochum: N. Brockmeyer, 1991), pp. 201-216.

Young, D. C., 'The Origins of the Modern Olympics. A New Version', *International Journal of the History of Sport*, no. 4 (1987), pp. 271-300.

See also:

Cotswold Games; Liverpool Olympics; Morpeth Olympic Games

-Joachim Ruhl

Munich Disaster (*see* Disasters: Munich, 1958)

Murrayfield

Murrayfield is the headquarters of the Scottish Rugby Union (S.R.U.), the governing body for Rugby Union in Scotland. The first development on the site came in 1922, when 19 acres were purchased from Edinburgh Polo Club, previous international matches having been played at Inverleith. The new ground and stand were officially opened with a Scotland versus England match in March 1925; an extension to the West stand in 1936 raised the capacity to 15,228 seats.

Murrayfield had the first 'electric blanket' under-soil heating installed in 1959, and a new East stand was added in time for the 1983 international matches. The largest attendance recorded at an international match was in 1975, when the gates were closed on a crowd of around 105,000 spectators. Following publication of the Taylor Report in 1989, the S.R.U. launched a debenture scheme to transform the ground into an all-seater stadium (capacity 67,500 spectators), thus removing the famous terraces. The clock that had stood behind the south end terrace ('the Clock end') was repositioned. At the same time, the under-soil heating was replaced by gas-heated piping running 10 inches beneath the turf.

Since completion of the new oval stadium in 1993, Murrayfield has become a venue for such assorted events as a visit by the Pope, the staging of rock and pop concerts, and as the summer home of the Scottish Claymores American football team. It hosted the first Rugby World Cup Sevens in 1993 as well as Rugby World Cup matches in 1991 and 1999.

References:

Scottish Rugby Union, *The Murrayfield Debenture* (Edinburgh: Scottish Rugby Union, 1991).

Thorburn, S., *The History of Scottish Rugby* (London: Cassell, 1980).

Websites:

The Scottish Rugby Union Murrayfield page – http://www.sru.org.uk/murrayfield.cfm

See also:

Rugby Union

-Lorna Jackson

Muscular Christianity

The 'Muscular Christianity' movement originated in the public schools of the mid-Victorian era, as the sons of the traditional landed gentry and those of the newly affluent industrialist middle classes first came into contact. What better place for these two groups to forge an alliance than in the sports arena? The

Duke of Wellington himself had claimed that Waterloo had been won on the playing fields of Eton and it was this concept of games as manly and character building that was behind the rise of the 'Muscular Christians'.

Thomas Arnold, headmaster of Rugby, was determined to turn out of his establishment a new breed of 'Christian Gentlemen' not only educated in the arts and sciences but well equipped to serve the Empire, having absorbed on the playing field those Victorian virtues of morality, leadership, sportsmanship and patriotism. The new cult of athleticism was intended to develop a sense of discipline and duty as an example to the lower orders. The new officer class was to be chivalrous and a champion of the weak.

To this end, team games were encouraged over individual sports and this, together with the whole ethos of the new movement, was reflected in the literature of the time. The hero of Thomas Hughes' *Tom Brown's Schooldays* is a devotee of football and cricket; the odious bully, Flashman, is not. Another writer to capture the spirit of the age was Sir Henry Newbolt, with his immortal line 'Play up! play up! and play the game!'

References:

Birley, D., *Sport and the Making of Britain* (Manchester: Manchester University Press, 1993).

Hughes, T., *Tom Brown's Schooldays* (London: J. M. Dent & Sons, 1975).

Partington, A. (ed.), *The Oxford Dictionary of Quotations* (Oxford: Oxford University Press, 1992).

See also:

Fair Play; Ethics

-Tony Rennick

Museums and Halls of Fame

Sports museums are vital for the preservation of Britain's sporting heritage. It is in their collections of photographs, archives and memorabilia that the history of sport can be documented and illustrated, but it is here too that the drama, romance, passion and emotion of sport can be replicated. They are also sport history's public face and their curators are in a position to influence the community's perception of the subject.

Unfortunately, too many of the smaller museums are run by enthusiastic collectors trained neither in curatorial skills nor as sports historians, which results in the presentation of artefacts without adequate explanation and a failure to set them in their appropriate social, economic or political setting. Sports museums inhabit that part of the sporting world obsessed with winning, and generally give insufficient recognition to either participation or that most typical of sports experiences – losing. Club museums in particular have a 'glory, glory' mindset and fail to present some of the downside of sports history. Almost without exception they cater for the nostalgia market and have institutionalized the concept of a 'golden age' in virtually every sport. They eschew the controversial and deliberately present history with omissions by emphasizing the game-oriented side of sports history to the exclusion of the social or political.

Britain does not possess a national sports museum covering a range of sporting activities invented and pursued in this country. Perhaps it never will, given the emergence of national museums for football, Rugby Union, horse-racing, cricket and rowing, and the presumed reluctance of their curators to pass on their artefacts to another body. Nor has Britain ventured far along the American track of halls of fame with annual, much publicized inductions of stars from a particular sport. Indeed, Britain has only two named halls of sporting fame, that at Cheltenham for National Hunt racing, for which there are no formal voting procedures, and that for Rugby League at Rothwell near Leeds, which has not inducted anyone for several years and, as it is in a public house, bears more resemblance to a sports bar than a shrine of honour. What has emerged in Britain in

recent years is the club museum, mostly small-scale and often with amateur curators, but with a scattering of much larger enterprises, such as that of Manchester United Football Club. All of them reflect pride in the achievements of their parent club, though a few have a more commercial edge to their activities.

One of the major problems facing sports museums is that of finance, needed both to acquire artefacts in a market in which the wealthy private collector is now venturing, and to fund the day-to-day educational activities, exhibition development, and administrative operations. A survey undertaken in the early 1990s revealed a strong dependence on subsidies from fund holders such as sports governing bodies, prestigious independent sports clubs, local authorities and regional tourist boards. This may be lessened by the availability of lottery funds, which have already provided several million pounds to the football museums being developed at Hampden Park (Glasgow) and Preston.

References:

McCormack, P. A. C., *A Consideration of the Development of British Sports Museums*, Master of Social Sciences thesis, Ironbridge Institute / University of Birmingham, 1993.

Vamplew, W., 'Facts and Artefacts: Sports Historians and Sports Museums', *Journal of Sport History*, vol. 24, no. 2 (Summer 1998), pp. 268-282.

Further reading:

Cox, R. W., 'Sports Archives, Libraries and Museums in the U.K. – What Should be the Policy?', *The Sports Historian*, 16 (May 1996), pp. 156-159.

Websites:

The British Society of Sports History's Sports Museums Webpage –
http://www.umist.ac.uk/sport/mus.html

See also:

Old Trafford

-Wray Vamplew

Museums and Halls of Fame – British Golf Museum

The British Golf Museum is located in St Andrews and contains a diverse and unique collection of golfing memorabilia, making it perhaps the finest of its kind in Britain. After two introductory galleries, the Museum is set out chronologically, telling the story of the history of golf in Britain and British influence abroad. This is done through thematic displays within the different time periods that combine objects, vivid text panels and interactive displays.

Since it opened in 1990, the Museum staff have done much original research, which is reflected in the quality of the displays. These not only explore the basic elements of the game, such as equipment development and the history of the major championships, but go beyond this. They look at how golf relates to the development of other sports and of society in general. The items on display range from the expected clubs, balls, medals and trophies to unexpected fine art, decorative art, architecture and literature.

These all combine to bring the history of the game alive. They tell many stories. Some deal with long forgotten early heroes of the game and others with today's household names. Some highlight the very slow growth of the game in the 18th and 19th centuries and others tell the stories of the early golfing societies and how their competitions shaped the future course of the sport. Some bring dramatic moments to life and others show how golf is not just about champions.

References:

Lewis, P. N., Clark, E. R. and Grieve, F. C., *A Round of History at the British Golf Museum* (St Andrews: Royal and Ancient Golf Club Trust, 1998).

Websites:

The British Golf Museum –
http://www.britishgolfmuseum.co.uk/

See also:

Golf

-Peter Lewis

Museums and Halls of Fame – Cheltenham Hall of Fame

Cheltenham racecourse is universally renowned as 'the home of National Hunt racing'. The Hall of Fame there is a celebration of steeplechasing and its history. Honoured within the Hall are National Hunt legends such as Golden Miller, Cottage Rake, Arkle and Desert Orchid. The Hall of Fame contains sixteen different panels, covering all the vastly different aspects of National Hunt racing. Racegoers, riders and trainers, masters at Cheltenham, and the influence of the Irish are all illustrated via a triumvirate of artefacts, photographs and words. Cheltenham is the first racecourse to implement the American notion of a Hall of Fame. Members are elected when appropriate and are synonymous with recognized greats within the sport.

The Hall of Fame opened in 1994 and is updated when necessary. The aim is for the entire display to be constantly relevant to steeplechasing today and also to give an accurate insight into the heritage and nostalgia so prevalent in the sport. Permanently playing videos depict classic Champion Hurdle and Gold Cup winners as well as winners of other major races. Combine this with the colours Pat Taaffe wore when Arkle won the Gold Cup, Dawn Run's Gold Cup winning bridle and Simon Sherwood's saddle when victorious on the nation's favourite, Desert Orchid, and the significance of the Hall of Fame as a focal point for steeplechasing becomes evident. The Hall is open to the public from Monday to Saturday as well as on racedays.

Websites:

The Cheltenham Hall of Fame –
http://www.cheltenham.co.uk/ahallhome.htm

See also:

Horse-racing

-Edward Gillespie

Museums and Halls of Fame – The Football Museum, Preston

Despite England's unique contribution to 'the people's game', there has been no national museum to celebrate this history. This was to change in the year 2000 with the opening of The Football Museum, which aims to collect, preserve and interpret the rich heritage of football for the public benefit. The Museum's collections of football memorabilia include the F.I.F.A. Museum Collection, widely recognized as the finest collection of its kind in the world. Over 1,000 objects of historical significance have also been donated to the Museum by members of the public.

There could be no more appropriate location for the Museum than Deepdale Stadium, the home of Preston North End Football Club, the first winners of the world's oldest professional football league in 1888-1889. Initially to be housed in two of the new stands of the refurbished stadium, the Sir Tom Finney Stand and the Bill Shankly Kop, the Museum will, in time, extend around all four sides of the ground.

The Football Museum has been made possible by a grant of over £7.5 million from the Heritage Lottery Fund, and aims to be recognized as the national museum of football for England. There is a comparable project in Scotland. The Museum, which is operated entirely separately from the football club, is a registered charity, governed by a board of independent trustees.

The Football Museum has received the full support of major national and international football bodies, including F.I.F.A., the Football Association, the Football League and the Professional Footballers Association.

References:

Pratten, R., *Towards Full Time for Football in Museums*, M.A. Dissertation, University of Leicester, 1997.

Websites:

The Football Museum –
http://www.uclan.ac.uk/footmus/footmus.htm

See also:

Association Football

-Kevin Moore

Museums and Halls of Fame – Lord's Cricket Museum

The M.C.C. Museum at Lord's Cricket Ground contains a unique collection of cricketing art and memorabilia. It opened in 1953 as a memorial to all cricketers who died during the two world wars. The first Curator, Diana Rait Kerr (1945-1968), was succeeded by Stephen Green. He remains Curator after thirty years.

The Museum's most famous exhibit is the Ashes urn, the trophy for which England and Australia have competed since 1882. Also on display are the Wisden Trophy, the I.C.C. Cricket World Cup, the Gillette Cup and the Benson and Hedges Cup. Valued items of cricket kit worn by famous players lie alongside numerous bats and balls. These include the bat Denis Compton used to score 3,816 runs in 1947, and that with which Graham Gooch made 333 runs for England against India at Lord's in 1990. The balls with which Jim Laker took a record nineteen test match wickets against Australia in 1956 are given pride of place. The Museum also houses a gallery displaying a fine assembly of cricket paintings of all periods. Two more unusual exhibits are the sparrow killed by a ball in

263

1936 and a Chinese Punch Bowl (*c.* 1786) that was probably commissioned by Thomas Lord himself.

Recent developments include an exhibition gallery (opened 1997), the Brian Johnston Film Theatre (opened 1998) and a new display (opened 1999) that places the development of world cricket in its historical and social context.

The M.C.C. Museum is open to visitors on all match days and at other times via guided tours.

References:

Rice, T. M. B., *Treasures of Lord's* (London: CollinsWillow, 1989).

See also:

Lord's Cricket Ground

-Glenys Williams

Museums and Halls of Fame – National Horseracing Museum, Newmarket

Opened by the Queen in 1983, the Museum occupies the former Subscription Rooms next to the Jockey Club on Newmarket High Street. Here, 400 years of racing history are imaginatively represented by paintings and photographs, trophies and other memorabilia, which are complemented by videos and computer displays.

The visitor can trace the development of the thoroughbred from the original three Arabian stallions through to Mill Reef and Brigadier Gerard, and famous steeplechasers like Arkle and Red Rum. The careers of many great jockeys from Robinson to Piggott are recalled, together with the achievements of the most successful trainers. The development of racing as an institution is not neglected, and influential figures in its formative years, such as Sir Charles Bunbury and Admiral Rous, are given due recognition.

Two recent additions are the 'Hall of Fame', which focuses on the 20th century and its personalities – equine as well as human – and the 'Practical Gallery', where the visitor can ride the horse simulator and discover the daily routine in a trainer's yard. This is effectively complemented by tours to training grounds, yards and studs, operated by the Museum with former jockeys and other racing professionals as guides.

The British Sporting Art Trust collection of paintings is housed in two galleries within the Museum, where there is also an extensive archive, on which research can be undertaken.

Although not part of the Museum, Newmarket Library houses a major collection of racing books, including a complete set of the *Racing Calendar* from 1774.

References:

Onslow, R., *Guide to the National Horseracing Museum* (Newmarket: National Horseracing Museum, no date).

Further reading:

Vamplew, W., *The Turf: a Social and Economic History of Horseracing* (London: Allen Lane, 1976).

See also:

Newmarket

-John Tolson

Museums and Halls of Fame – River and Rowing Museum

The River and Rowing Museum opened in Henley-on-Thames in a new building by the architect David Chipperfield in 1998. It was set up by the River and Rowing Museum Foundation to cover three linked themes – the international sport of rowing, the River Thames and the town of Henley-on-Thames.

The centre-piece of the rowing gallery is a unique collection of racing boats, augmented by displays which track design changes from the early 1800s to the present day. The boat that won the first Oxford versus Cambridge Boat Race, held in Henley in 1829, is at the museum, as well as some spectacular failures and boats that have won at the Olympic Games.

The main theme of the gallery is the quest for speed, beginning with exhibits on the Athenian trireme and such work boats as the Venetian gondola, the whaleboat, the lifeboat and the Thames wherry. The technique of rowing and its social history are also covered, the latter by a Rowing Hall of Fame which acknowledges the movers and shakers of the sport and outlines its history and that of its institutions. The growing boat collection includes traditional Thames craft, and the Henley Gallery has displays on the Henley Royal Regatta.

The museum also contains the Thomas Keller library and study centre, which covers all the subject areas. There is an education centre and programmes for all ages. The museum won many awards in its first year, including the Best Building in England and the Museum of the Year awards.

References:
The River and Rowing Museum website – http://www.rrm.co.uk/

See also:
Henley Royal Regatta; Rowing

-Chris Dodd

Museums and Halls of Fame – Rugby Museum, Twickenham

The Museum of Rugby, located at Twickenham Stadium, displays and preserves the world's largest and most comprehensive collection of Rugby Union memorabilia. The collection includes artefacts of every conceivable type,

The Rowing Gallery in the River and Rowing Museum, Henley-on-Thames (photograph by Jaap Oepkes)

spans the game's entire history and covers every playing nation. In the display cases, the famous, such as 'The Calcutta Cup, England versus Scotland since 1877' – line up with the obscure and bizarre (1970s Polish pin badges).

Owned and financed by the Rugby Football Union (R.F.U.) – the sport's governing body in England – the Museum is seen as a promotional tool for the development of the sport, but has a secondary role (as with other Museums based in sports stadia) in helping to increase stadium usage on non-match days.

The R.F.U.'s collection came together over many years through presentations made to England teams, books collected by individuals, match programmes retained, and so forth. In 1982, the collection was put on display in Twickenham's South Stand. No proactive collection policy followed, except for occasional requests for donations.

The 1990s saw major rebuilding at the stadium and a purpose-built, multimedia Museum of Rugby was constructed in the new, three-tier East Stand. To boost the existing collection of artefacts, the R.F.U. purchased the Rugby-related items from Harry Langton's famous football collection, and supplemented the static display cases with audio-visual and interactive displays and touch-screen computers.

Unveiled in January 1996, the Museum of Rugby is a superb example of how the history of a sport can be successfully interpreted within the confines of a museum.

See also:

Twickenham

-Jed Smith

Museums and Halls of Fame – Scottish Football Association Museum

The Scottish Football Association Museum is the world's first national museum of football,

and is housed in the new South Stand at Hampden Park in Glasgow. The museum is operated by the Scottish Football Association Museum Trust (S.F.A.M.T.), which was established as a result of co-operation between the Scottish Football Association and Glasgow City Council. The S.F.A.M.T. is a limited company and a registered charity. As a result, all profits are used to fund research, new exhibitions, and improving the museum's many services. The Museum occupies a site of 4,250 square metres at Hampden, but also has access to many other areas of the 33-acre site.

Its objective is to collect, preserve and display the history of the game in its widest form. History galleries explore the history of the game in Scotland and the contribution Scots have made to the world game. Other significant galleries will look at the development of tactics, training, health and fitness, and the relationship between football and the growth of the mass media. Alongside the galleries will sit the museum's sound archive and library, containing the holdings of all the national associations, regional leagues and bodies in Scotland.

Websites:

Scottish Football Museum –
http://www.scottishfa.co.uk/museum/index.htm

See also:

Hampden Park

-Ged O'Brien

Museums and Halls of Fame – Wembley Experience

Each day between 10 a.m. and 4 p.m., tours of Wembley stadium are available to visitors. The tours depart from the Banqueting Suite every thirty minutes in groups of around fifty and last for ninety minutes. Beginning with a review of Geoff Hurst's controversial goal in the 1966 World Cup Final, the tour then offers a comprehensive, well-organized trip around the stadium. The places visited are: the Control Room, showing how events are supervised on the day; the Olympic Gallery, where the most expensive seats in the stadium are located; the television studio; the cinema (including a ten-minute video film of the history of the stadium); the hospital; the south side team changing room and bathing area, which is now used permanently by the England team; the players' tunnel and pitch entrance; and the royal box and retiring room. The Wembley Land Train transports visitors around the perimeter of the stadium to view major features. The name of Coca Cola, the company which sponsors the stadium and the tour, is ubiquitous. Each tour is led by a guide, whose commentary is supplemented at intervals by video and recorded details presented by television personality Desmond Lynam. The information is tailored for a general audience, and those seeking specialist knowledge on either the sporting or architectural history of the stadium will find little to satisfy them. Visitors may avail themselves of a small cafe and shop, but there is no museum.

References:

Wembley Stadium Tours leaflet

Further reading:

Inglis, S., *The Football Grounds of Britain* (London: Willow Books, 1996).

Low, A. R., *Wonderful Wembley* (London: Stanley Paul, 1983).

See also:

Wembley Stadium

-Jeff Hill

Museums and Halls of Fame – Wimbledon Lawn Tennis Museum

The Wimbledon Lawn Tennis Museum (W.L.T.M.) is magnificently sited, as its twelve adjacent exhibition areas are housed in a wing of Wimbledon's Centre Court. This allows visitors to look down on one of the world's most famous playing areas. A visit to the museum is incomplete unless tied in with a conducted tour of the Wimbledon complex, which is a marvellous mosaic of 'known' major courts and miscellaneous outer courts.

The W.L.T.M. spotlights major themes in the historical development of tennis. There are displays on the origins of tennis; the birth of the new game; the popularization of tennis; the Victorians; the Edwardians; the development of the tennis racket; the move to Church Road; the significant tennis happenings between the First World War and the Second World War; the creation of open tennis and the game's professionalization; and the evolution of modern 'power' tennis. As with most major sporting museums, new exhibits are constantly being developed. A databank is also available so that visitors can find answers to their questions about Wimbledon and tennis.

For those who wish to study or research any aspect of tennis, there is the Kenneth Ritchie Wimbledon Library, which contains a collection of British and foreign lawn tennis books, annuals, periodicals, programmes, postcards and video cassettes from over sixty countries. There is no charge for admittance to the library.

The W.L.T.M. is located at Church Road, Wimbledon, London SW19 5AE, and is easily accessible from Southfields Station on the District Line of the London Underground.

References:

Little, A., *This is Wimbledon: the Official Guide to the Championships* (London: All England Lawn Tennis and Croquet Club, 1996. 16th ed.).

The Kenneth Ritchie Wimbledon Library – Catalogue 1995 (London: All England Lawn Tennis and Croquet Club, 1995. 6th ed.).

Further reading:

Crawford, S. A. G. M., 'Wimbledon Lawn Tennis Museum', *Journal of Sport History*, 25 (Spring 1998), 160-162.

See also:
Lawn Tennis

-Scott Crawford

Museums and Halls of Fame – York Racing Museum

York Racing Museum is at present housed on the fourth floor of the five-storey Tattersall's Grandstand at York Racecourse, itself based on the Knavesmire, to which local racing was transferred in 1731 following the too frequent flooding of the Clifton Ings course. When the Tattersall's stand was being constructed in 1965, the racecourse executive decided to incorporate a museum as 'a celebration of racing history'. Advice was sought from turf antiquarian, Major Fairfax-Blakeborough, and a public appeal for racing memorabilia produced many donations and other items on loan. The collection is continually being added to, thanks mainly to the generosity of the racing world. Of particular interest are the racing silks of Fred Archer, champion jockey from 1874 to 1886, and the tail of Voltiguer, the losing horse in the famous match race against The Flying Dutchman on the Knavesmire in 1851. Recent exhibits have commemorated Phil Bull, founder of the betting guide Timeform, and Frankie Dettori's seven-in-a-row at Ascot, which includes racing plates from the winners and a photocopied cheque from a lucky punter on the day.

A major feature of the museum is the associated racing library, which contains not only several hundred volumes of modern material but also *Racing Calendars* dating back to the earliest issues and almost complete runs of *Ruff's Guide to the Turf, The General Stud Book* and other bloodstock literature. Although the museum is normally only open to the public on racedays, the library can be made available to researchers at other times for a small fee by prior arrangement.

References:
York Racing Museum pamphlet

See also:
Horse-racing

-Wray Vamplew

Music

Music is linked with sport in the late 20th century in a variety of ways – as entertainment, a statement of national identity, a commercial gimmick, an integral element of performance, a leitmotif or a vehicle for crowd participation. The opening extravaganzas of Olympic and World Cup competitions, the ritual of national anthems, the arrival of the gladiators at major fights and the pre-match entertainment at Rugby League or American football are all built around music. While some sports fans could not name them, Puccini's *Nessun Dorma* will forever be associated with the 1990 Football World Cup, Ravel's *Bolero* with Torvill and Dean's championship ice dance performances and Fleetwood Mac's *The Chain* with the B.B.C. television coverage of Grand Prix motor racing. Some sports still contrive to be mainly music-free zones – particularly more individual, middle-class games such as tennis or golf – but few can avoid becoming themed by the media or subject to the intrusion of commercial music and advertising.

Although there are a number of traditional songs depicting sporting activities, such as *The Blaydon Races* or *John Peel*, and, historically, music and sport may have intermingled on fair days and local holidays, these two leisure activities only became more closely connected after the rise of music hall and gate-money football in the last decades of the 19th century. Brass bands certainly provided entertainment for Victorian football crowds while Edwardians not only listened but sang along to a mixture of hymn tunes and music hall favourites, sometimes providing their own musical accompaniment on bugles, piccolos and concertinas. It has even been suggested that Saturday afternoon football had a detrimental effect on the popular music making of the times by offering a more exciting alternative to band and choir practice.

While military bands and massed choirs still feature at show-piece Rugby and football matches, community singing belongs to an era when crowds of 70,000, largely male, frequently cloth-capped, packed the terraces of major grounds. Changes in culture and society, particularly the arrival of 'pop' music, have seen the adoption by football fans of chart-topping songs such as *You'll Never Walk Alone* and *We Are The Champions* as crowd anthems. And although certain chants have attained notoriety, especially the irreverent and frequently offensive Protestant and Catholic songs of Glasgow Rangers and Celtic, football crowds have sometimes shown considerable inventiveness in their choice of tune and lyric. Numerous versions of *Que Sera Sera* have supported the quixotic adventures of the Scottish national team, rhyming 'what will be' with 'Wem-bel-ee' or 'Gay Paree' as the occasion demanded, and the ubiquitous 'one…, there's only one…' (to the tune of the 1960s hit *Guantanamera*) has been adapted by fans throughout Britain in praise of their favourites. These crowd-led songs are in contrast to the commercial recordings inspired by occasional cult figures such as George Best (*Belfast Boy*), Cyril Knowles (*Nice One Cyril*) and Eric Cantona (*Ooh Aah Cantona*), while footballing references featured increasingly in the music of the 1980s independent bands (for example, *All I Want For Christmas Is The Dukla Prague Away Kit*). And, lest it be thought that commemorating sportspersons in music is a quirk of the late 20th century, the Highland Games athlete A. A. Cameron (1875-1951) had a piece of bagpipe music named after him.

The association between sport and music has been extended during the 20th century

from football to a variety of other events. There are some sports in which music plays an integral part – ice skating, ice dancing, synchronized swimming and gymnastic floor exercises – and others, such as one-day cricket and boxing, in which it has been introduced as a gimmick, with individual sportsmen entering the sporting arena to their own personal choice of music. The heavyweight boxer, Frank Bruno, even called his autobiography *Eye of the Tiger* after his own pop anthem. Instrumentalists are known to have played at skating rinks in the early years of this century and short sound bites of music greet ice hockey goals and touchdowns in American football, famed for its marching bands and dancing cheerleaders. 20th-century Rugby has supplied opportunities for both stirring Welsh part-singing and the sexually explicit song, fortunately reserved largely for the team bus and perhaps an anachronism in an age of increasing political correctness and female participation in sport. Rugby, like football, has its own anthems and has been responsible for raising *Flower of Scotland* from obscurity to potent symbol of national identity. But the formal playing and singing of national anthems at prestigious sporting occasions and orchestrated set-piece celebrations and military-style parades are in sharp contrast to the less structured musical background provided by crowd participation or by jazz groups at racecourses and cricket grounds. Club recognition of vocal support has led to suggestions of 'singing stands' at football grounds; conversely, the 'boring brass band', whose rendering of *The Great Escape* followed the 1998 England World Cup Team around France, has subsequently been banned by at least one club.

The inter-relationship of popular music and sport can be seen in numerous ways – the staging of rock concerts at sport stadia, the involvement of rock stars such as Elton John in the financial management of clubs and the high profile liaisons of female pop stars and top footballers ('Posh Spice' and David Beckham,

Louise and Jamie Redknapp). And although music has tended to impinge on sport, there are also examples of sport intruding into the realm of music. There have been occasional forays into recording studios by football stars either individually or as teams – top 20 hits such as *Fog On The Tyne* and *Diamond Lights* are one-off examples of the musical talents of Messrs Gascoigne, Hoddle and Waddle, and cup finals and league championships have provided excuses for entire teams to crowd round a microphone to extol the triumphs of the season. These warblings are often colour-coded (*Come On You Reds, Blue Is The Colour*), mascotted (*Ossie's Dream*) or, in the case of World Cup squads, blatantly optimistic (*This Time [We'll Get It Right], Easy, Easy*).

The adoption of pop music by crowds and sports personalities since the 1960s has more recently been varied by the use of popular classics. Although the *Grand March* from *Aida* is unlikely to become the favourite in British football grounds which it is in Europe, television coverage of sport has brought the football-loving 'Three Tenors' to a far wider audience than is usual for opera singers and the televising of successive football and Rugby World Cup competitions in the 1990s has made hits of the serious music used to introduce the programmes. Classical themes may be increasingly employed as leitmotif since they do not require royalty payments. Many individual sports have become closely associated with their television theme music (for example, cricket, snooker and tennis), as have many sports programmes, from radio's *Sports Report* to television's *Match of the Day*. The increasingly sophisticated use of music to market and identify sport and sports stars is far removed from the traditional *Abide With Me*.

References:

Russell, D., *Popular Music in England, 1840-1914: a Social History* (Manchester: Manchester University Press, 1997).

-Joyce Kay

Myths

Some myths are tied in with sporting superstition. For example, there is no hard evidence that a batsman in cricket is more likely to be out on a score of 111 than on 110 or 112, yet Nelson is continually referred to when that individual or team score lights up the scoreboard (see p. 324).

Other sporting myths develop as nostalgia clouds memory. Indeed, all sports appear to have a 'golden age', usually beyond living memory. Many sports commentators allude to a previous era in particular sports, or sport generally, in which money played a less prominent role than now and in which genuine amateurism prevailed; drugs, violence and corruption were non-existent; and everyone, both on and off the pitch, 'played the game'. Sports historians have shown that this was never really the case and that in the days of pre-commercialized sport, violence towards animals and fellow players featured strongly and corruption was not uncommon because of the gambling which underwrote many sports. Research has also suggested that the rhetoric of public school sport was not always matched by behaviour on the field of play. Sport became commercialized during the so-called 'Golden Age' of late Victorian Britain – another myth pricked – and shamateurism (the making of money through sport despite one's amateur status), foul play, drug use, gamesmanship and crowd trouble followed. It should also be noted that the 'Golden Age' was one of class discrimination and sexism. Certainly the definitions of 'amateur' and 'professional' were social not economic concepts. You were not labelled as a professional if you were a gentleman who rode (or rowed) against other gentlemen for high-stake wagers. Wages were another matter, and the Amateur Rowing Association did not mince its words when it defined an amateur as not including anyone 'who was or ever had been by trade or employment for wages a mechanic, artisan or labourer'. And, of course, half the population of Britain was excluded from participation simply by reason of their gender.

A lack of a sense of history thus can result in myths emanating from inadequate knowledge. Other myths are deliberately created. Although British sport has not gone to the lengths of American baseball, which set up a special commission to establish (wrongly) that the game owed nothing to English rounders, it almost matches it with the enquiry of the Old Rugbeian Society in 1895, which concluded that in 1823 William Webb Ellis 'with a fine disregard for the rules of football as played in his time, first took the ball in his arms and ran with it thus originating the distinctive feature of the Rugby game'. Yet research has shown that this story did not emerge until 1877, some fifty-four years after his alleged innovation occurred. There were no eye-witnesses, merely octogenarian recall. It was advanced because an old boy was keen to disassociate his school's game from plebeian folk football in which ball-carrying had been common. Almost twenty-five years later still, a commemorative plaque was erected at Rugby School in an attempt by Rugby to re-assert its position in the public school hierarchy by demonstrating that it originated the game. The invention of this sporting tradition has succeeded: the average British sports fan now almost inevitably associates Webb Ellis with the invention of Rugby.

References:

Baker, W. J., 'William Webb Ellis and the Origins of Rugby Football: the Life and Death of a Victorian Myth', *Albion*, 13 (1981).

Vamplew, W., *Pay Up and Play the Game: Professional Sport in Britain* (Cambridge: Cambridge University Press, 1988).

Further reading:

Morgan, P., 'Comment on 'Myth and Reality in the 1895 Rugby Split' by Tony Collins', *Sports Historian*, 17 (1997), pp. 112-113.

-Wray Vamplew

National Coaching Foundation

Since 1983, the National Coaching Foundation (N.C.F.), the only organization dedicated to the development of coaching and coaches in the United Kingdom, has provided educational and developmental opportunities for 130,000 sports coaches. Presently, 15,000 coaches and 12,000 schoolteachers participate annually in N.C.F. programmes.

The N.C.F. was founded as the coaching arm of the (then) Sports Council and was based at Beckett Park in Leeds, on the site of the Carnegie School of Physical Education. Dr Nick Whitehead was the N.C.F.'s first director and there was a complement of five staff. Sue Campbell succeeded as director in 1985 and the first national network of offices was established at fourteen institutes of higher education in 1987.

In 1990, the N.C.F. became an independent charity and established Coachwise as a wholly owned trading subsidiary. The Diploma in Professional Studies (Sports Coaching) was launched in the same year.

In 1993, the N.C.F. merged with the British Institute of Sports Coaches and the headquarters were relocated to Cardigan Road, in the Leeds suburb of Headingley, where they remain to this day. Two years later, Geoff Cooke became the N.C.F.'s new chief executive until he, in turn, was succeeded by John Stevens in 1997. In 1999, the N.C.F. launched 110 new premier coaching centres throughout England. Each centre delivers a core programme of N.C.F. workshops providing the best possible facilities and amenities.

By 1998/9, the N.C.F. had an annual turnover of approximately £3.4 million (not including Coachwise). The main sources of this turnover were grant aid from U.K. Sport and Sport England (72.7 per cent), earned income (22.2 per cent) and subscriptions (5.1 per cent). By 1999, the number of staff employed had risen to fifty-five at the N.C.F. and a further twenty-nine at Coachwise. The staff is organized in six teams – Coach Education (Services, Standards and Structures), Communications, High Performance Coaching, Local Coaching Development, Management Services, and Research and Design. The N.C.F. network in Britain includes ten coaching development officers, based at Sport England's Regional Training Units for Sport, and partnerships with the coaching units of Northern Ireland, Scotland and Wales.

The N.C.F. provides sports coaches with a wide range of practical workshops, at a number of different levels, in three areas – fitness and training, sports psychology, and coaching principles and management. The N.C.F. offers three qualifications. The N.C.F. Award in Coaching Studies develops a basic knowledge and understanding of the principles of sports coaching. The N.C.F. Certificate in Coaching Studies is for practising coaches wishing to enhance their professional development through a nationally recognized qualification. The N.C.F. B.Sc. (Hons) Degree in Applied Sports Coaching, validated by De Montfort University, Leicester, is aimed at experienced coaches aspiring to excellence in their coaching. In addition, N.C.F. membership services, on payment of an annual subscription, provide a comprehensive package of benefits, including insurance, to over 10,500 sports coaches.

Websites:

The National Coaching Foundation – http://www.ncf.org.uk/

See also:

Coaching

-The National Coaching Foundation

National Equestrian Centre

The National Equestrian Centre (N.E.C.) was a national equestrian events venue for many years. It was built on Stoneleigh show ground, Kenilworth, Warwickshire in 1965. Three hundred founder members of the N.E.C., a group that included Her Majesty the Queen, were asked to donate 100 guineas each. This sum of £30,000 was brought up to the final £70,000 by loans, which were needed to build the riding school and office block. By June 1967, the offices of the British Horse Society (B.H.S.) and the British Show Jumping Association (B.S.J.A.) had moved to Stoneleigh, and phase one of the formation of the N.E.C. had been completed. The most up-to-date Riding School in the world was completed in July 1968.

Its purpose was to raise the standard of instruction throughout the country by training instructors. It offered groups and societies a site at which to further their own specialist interests, and provided a central location at which to school their horses under the eyes of the experts. Within a year the Centre had proved its value. 'Its value can only be assessed by whether or not horsemen believe this Centre is necessary for the well being of horsemen and horses; this I am glad to say has been achieved', commented Colonel Sir Michael Ansell, C.B.E., in the first National Equestrian Centre Official Review in 1969.

Since then, the N.E.C. has seen numerous conferences, competitions, courses, and lessons with both the local riding and pony clubs and some of the worlds equestrian élite. When the National Exhibition Centre, Birmingham was opened in 1976, confusion with the names meant that the National Equestrian Centre was renamed the British Equestrian Centre (B.E.C.).

In July 1999, the B.E.C. saw the last of its active days. Health and safety laws had increased over the years and the B.E.C. no longer met the stringent requirements. It no longer answered the real needs of a national training centre and the cost of upgrading it was astronomical. As the show ground expanded around the B.E.C., the area available for parking B.E.C. lorries and cars became totally unacceptable. It was not used enough to be able to foresee how the costs would be recuperated.

The indoor riding school, and with it the 'British Equestrian Centre', was taken down in the late summer of 1999. The offices remain at the National Agricultural Centre, Stoneleigh, with the B.S.J.A., British Dressage, British Endurance, the Joint Measurement Board and the British Horse Trials Association also located there. The British Horse Society has relocated to Stoneleigh Deer Park. The Royal Agricultural Society of England (R.A.S.E.) plans to build a new exhibition hall on the B.E.C. site, to be completed by May 2000. The British Equestrian Federation, British Horse Society and R.A.S.E. are working closely together on a major new initiative to attract funding in order to develop a new National Equestrian Centre at the northern end of the show ground.

See also:

Badminton House; Eventing; Showjumping

-Michaela Baxendale

National Lottery

The National Lottery has had possibly more impact on sports development than any other single factor in the 20th century. It was the brainchild of the Conservative Prime Minister, John Major, a sports enthusiast with a personal mission to increase participation in sport, both nationally and at an individual level. Lotteries had existed in other countries for some time, but nowhere had this form of voluntary taxation been used to fund sport to such an extent.

The first National Lottery draw was held in 1994 and in the year that followed, an estimated £180 million of 'lottery money' was invested in sport. Distribution of this money was handed to the Sports Council. The Lottery Act of 1997 permitted the Sports Council to direct lottery funds towards target groups as opposed to being simply reactive.

During 1995, most National Lottery applications came from relatively small voluntary clubs, particularly for football, cricket and bowls facilities – 65 per cent were for under £100,000 and 40 per cent were for less than £40,000. Before long, however, a number of multi-million pound grants were being awarded to fund nationally and internationally significant facilities, such as those for the 2002 Commonwealth Games in Manchester.

As attention was increasingly drawn to the limited amount of capital funding available for assisting élite athletes prepare and compete on the international stage, the Government began to grant aid to the governing bodies of sport to fund coaches, sports science and medicine support services and the expenses of individual athletes. Further pressure came from local authorities, charities and other organizations struggling to maintain existing facilities and, in 1996, the Government also agreed to fund on-going costs associated with projects closely related to their strategic goals, such as increased participation in inner city areas, amongst ethnic minority groups, youths and women.

By the turn of the century, almost 2 billion pounds had been invested in, or committed to, sport from the National Lottery. Over 3,000 awards, amounting to a total value of £959 million, have been spent or committed to capital programmes and £80.5 million has been allocated to the 'World Class Performance Programme'. Unfortunately for sport, the popularity of the National Lottery started to decline during the late 1990s and income was also being used to fund heritage and other non-sporting projects. There is speculation that National Lottery money will eventually be spread even further afield to fund education and health.

The popularity of the National Lottery severely impacted on other funding agencies. The consequential slump in the football pools industry caused a massive reduction in the money the Football Trust and the Foundation for Sport and the Arts had to distribute and, despite the Government's promise not to reduce its spending on sport, it did start to reduce the grant it gave to Sport England.

Websites:

The National Lottery –
http://www.nationallottery.co.uk/

See also:

Sports Sponsorship

-Richard William Cox

National Playing Fields Association

The National Playing Fields Association (NPFA) was founded in 1925 as a charity to protect playing fields, recreation grounds, sports fields and public open spaces throughout the United Kingdom, and was granted a Royal Charter eight years later.

It was given responsibility for nearly 500 fields, which were presented to the nation by George V to mark his Silver Jubilee in 1935, and their upkeep and administration remain part of its duties.

The Duke of Edinburgh became NPFA President in 1948, and spent several years working daily at the Association's offices in London. He has maintained a close and active interest in its work ever since. Her Majesty The Queen graciously accepted the position of Patron on her accession in 1952.

The NPFA is now the country's leading charity dealing with the promotion of active leisure and the protection of playing fields, recreation grounds and sports fields, although its area of interest has widened considerably since its establishment.

Apart from managing its own fields, it campaigns for the protection of greenfield sites and fields that can be used for leisure by children and families. It also offers help and advice on the day-to-day management and maintenance of fields.

It often works in co-operation with building firms, offering specialist advice on the preparation and design of play areas in new housing developments.

The Association has been responsible for the design and construction of more than forty Multigames Walls in fields across the country. The Multigames Wall offers children the chance to play tennis, football, basketball and cricket without adult supervision.

In schools, the NPFA runs the National School Sports Awards in England and the SportsMarc Cymru certificates in Wales, to promote play, sport and physical education programmes.

Recent developments have been the promotion of Midnight Basketball at several inner city sites, and the opening of a chain of nine Millennium Centres, 'village halls for the inner city'.

NPFA Cymru was launched in early 1999 to advance the NPFA's work in Wales.

References:

National Playing Fields Association website – http://www.npfa.co.uk/

Websites:

National Playing Fields Association – http://www.npfa.co.uk/

See also:

Central Council of Physical Recreation

-Elsa Davies

National Sports Centres (*see* Crystal Palace; Glenmore Lodge; Holme Pierrepont; Plas Menai; Plays Y Brenin; Strathclyde Water Park; U.K. Sailing Academy, Cowes)

Nationalism

Nationalism has played a key role in sport over the centuries. It has taken many different forms, but is undoubtedly an important ingredient within the popular success of modern organized sport. Whether at the Olympics or in the World Cup, élite global sporting events use the nation state as the standard form of identity and recognition.

In the British Isles, the situation is highly complex, as there is more than one form of the nation state. At some events, such as the Olympic Games, there is one team that represents Britain. This team marches into the stadium under the Union flag and, if successful, stands on the podium for the national anthem, *God Save the Queen*. In other events, however, such as the Commonwealth Games or in football, Britain is broken down into its constituent parts of England, Scotland, Wales and Northern Ireland, each of which have their own flags and anthems. In Rugby Union, an Irish team which represents all thirty-two counties of the island of Ireland and which is based in Dublin further confuses the situation. In professional golf, the idea of a British nation has ceased to exist as golfers from the home nations play in the Ryder Cup as part of a European team.

The nation state has historically been the main unit of international sporting competition. This situation emerged in the 19th century as a result of the codification of sport into its modern forms, and because of the ongoing internationalization of European and global politics. As sport became organized, with a clear set of rules, competitive leagues and agreed organizational structures, so each sport became 'national'. This meant that there was a defined and common national ruling body. In cricket, the Marylebone Cricket Club revised the rules of the game and took national control from 1835. Other examples of this process include the Football Association established in 1863, the Rugby Football Union in 1871, the Amateur Boxing Association in 1880, the Gaelic Athletic Association in 1884 and the Hockey Association in 1886. The emergence of national sporting bodies took place during a period of intense empire building, colonial competition and European wars. It was perhaps inevitable that the competition between nations in the military, colonial and economic spheres would find an outlet in sport.

With the advent of national organizing bodies in different sports, so the first international competitions took place. These events were clearly a test of national pride and were accompanied by all the jingoism of nationalism. The first international match in football took place in 1872 between Scotland and England. This was followed by regular encounters between the 'home' nations. In 1904, the Fédération Internationale de Football Association (F.I.F.A.) was formed in Paris, and by 1905 all the home nations had joined. F.I.F.A. allowed for the development of intense

international competition on the football field and such matches became conduits for nationalism. The first World Cup took place in 1930 and the tournament has been seen as the pinnacle of footballing success ever since. Accompanying the establishment of world football was the setting up of the modern Olympics. Baron Pierre de Coubertin brought together the representatives of thirteen nations in Paris in 1894 to discuss the possibility of an international sporting competition. The meeting resolved that a competition be held every fourth year and that every nation be invited to compete. The first Olympics were held in 1896, and the first games of the 21st century will be held in Sydney in 2000. The Sydney Olympics will use, as did the first games in Athens, the nation state as its method of organization. Competitors do not compete for individual glory, but for that of their nation. The direct nature of the competition between nations is given a further nationalistic edge by the use of excessive national symbolism – flags, anthems, national uniforms and the medal table that places successful nations in rank order.

The nationalism that has been attached to all sporting events and organizations that use the nation state as its unit of competition has been exacerbated by other accompanying factors. Since the advent of modern sport, there has been a great media interest in the different competitions that take place. It is international competitions that receive most media attention, and whether through the press, radio or television, the audience at home is invited to cheer on 'our' boys and girls. At the extreme level, the nationalism attached to international sporting encounters has taken on the vestiges of xenophobia and racism. This has led, in football especially, to scenes of hooliganism that have attached themselves to the different national representatives in club competitions and national teams in international matches.

As nationalism and its accompanying fervour are so readily created by sport, it is perhaps unsurprising that governments have been keen to make the most of sport. Throughout the 1930s, the extreme European regimes manipulated sport and the success of the nation's athletes as a way of sustaining nationalist feeling. In 1938, the English football team travelled to Berlin to play Germany, a match they won. The English team effectively recognized the nationalist and supremacist agenda of the Hitler regime by giving the Nazi salute. It was important for the nationalism of Germany that a visiting team recognized their regime, but equally important for English sporting nationalism that the visitors won. Sport, especially the Olympics, was dogged by the politics of nationalism during the Cold War era. Athletes became the representatives of the nation, national pride and of ideologically based political systems when they took part in competition. The effect of this process reached its hiatus with the 1980 and 1984 Olympic boycotts. The need to win has driven British governments to spend large sums of money, primarily through the U.K. and regional Sports Councils and, more recently, with huge investment in the U.K. Sports Institute. The money is being spent to produce world-beating sportspeople who will produce morale-boosting victories for the nation.

In addition to the explicit political nationalism that has accompanied sport, there is a more benign and idealized civic nationalism that sport has produced. Such nationalism depends on imagery, tradition, idealization and myth making. The B.B.C. has been foremost in the creation of such a nationalism. Prior to the incursion of satellite television into sports coverage, the B.B.C. mapped out the sporting year that was common to Britain and the British. This year began with the Rugby Union Five Nations, progressed through the Boat Race and the Grand National to the Cup Finals in England and Scotland, before moving on to a summer of Wimbledon, the British Open, the Derby, Glorious Goodwood and the

cricket test series. Such a year offered a common denominator that brought the British together.

The idealism of the sporting year is reinforced by a nationalism that depicts certain games and sports as 'ours'. For the English, these games may be cricket and football, for the Welsh, Rugby Union, the Scots have Shinty, while the Irish maintain their affection for Gaelic games.

How the process of political devolution will affect the nationalism attached to sport in Britain is unclear. With the emergence of political structures that clearly identify the Scottish, Welsh or Northern Irish nation as existing, one wonders if there will be such a great need for the romantic pull of sport and the ninety minute patriot.

Further reading:

Jarvie, G. and Walker, G. (eds.), *Scottish Sport in the Making of the Nation. Ninety Minute Patriots?* (Leicester: Leicester University Press, 1994).

Sugden, J. and Bairner, A., *Sport, Sectarianism and Society in a Divided Ireland* (Leicester: Leicester University Press, 1993).

Wigglesworth, N., *The Evolution of English Sport* (London: Frank Cass, 1996).

See also:

Politics

-Mike Cronin

Netball

Netball is the most widely played 'female' sport in Britain. The sport's governing body, the All England Netball Association, lists approximately 60,000 registered participants and 3,000 schools with over 1 million schoolgirl players.

A sport deemed appropriately feminine, netball was not a 'male' sport copied by women, nor was it ever played by men, and thus it was a sport for women that was never opposed to the extent that other team games were. Women's football, for example, had its support from the F.A. withdrawn in 1921, despite huge popularity.

Developed at the end of the 19th century, netball was devised by female students of physical education at Madame Bergman Österberg's Physical Training College in Hampstead, in rejection of the American sport of basketball, which was introduced to England in the early 1890s but was considered to be too physical for young women. The modified game was played in the gymnasium with two baskets hung on the walls at each end.

By 1901, the first set of netball rules were published by the Ling Association, an association of gymnastics teachers from Österberg's College. Various changes resulted – the posts were raised in height and the baskets replaced by rings and nets. Hence the sport of netball was born. A historic meeting of February 12th, 1926, resulted in the formation of the All England Women's Netball Association, which later became the All England Netball Association.

The game was established as the major team sport for working-class girls largely because the sport could take place in the limited spaces of the playgrounds of urban schools.

In 1929, playing territories were devised, the first of which was the South East. Nine territories later developed and despite geographical alterations, nine regions remain to this day.

The first annual competition, the 'Inter-County Tournament', was staged in 1932 and the first international between England and Scotland took place in 1938. Such matches resumed after the Second World War, with England defeating Scotland and Wales in May 1949.

An English touring side was invited to South Africa in 1956 and to the West Indies in 1962. Thus the game of netball, once firmly established in Britain, was introduced to several Commonwealth countries.

As the game spread, the International Netball Federation was instituted and international rules were drawn up in 1960. The first World Tournament was hosted by England in 1963 and eleven countries took part. Australia were victorious, New Zealand a close second and England third.

England were the hosts once again for the World Championships in 1995. Once again Australia were the victors, with South Africa second, New Zealand third and England fourth.

The All England Netball Association is striving to raise the profile of the English game despite limited funding, sponsorship and publicity. In contrast, Australian and New Zealander netball enjoy good television exposure and sponsorship.

However, things are improving and in August 1997, 'England Netball' received approximately £1 million from the English Sports Council to activate its plans 'to be the best in the world by 2003'. At the 1999 World Championships in New Zealand, England came third.

References:

Baggallay, J., *Netball for Schools* (London: Pelham, 1967).

Netball (The official publication of the All England Netball Association, 1933-1998).

Websites:

The All England Netball Association – http://www.england-netball.co.uk/

-Nicky Fossey

Newmarket

Newmarket owes its pre-eminence in British flat-racing in large measure to the interest of the Stuart Kings in field sports. Its fortunes declined during the early Georgian period, but in 1752 the incipient Jockey Club established itself in the town, and thereafter the reputation and influence of both spread gradually throughout the sport.

For the past 250 years, Newmarket has enjoyed twenty-five to thirty days of racing a year, but for much of that time remained remote and exclusive, its use of widely different starts and finishes in successive races discouraging all but the most hardy racegoers. There are two courses at Newmarket, the Rowley Mile and the July Course. The former is used for the two Classics, the 2000 Guineas (1809) and the 1000 Guineas (1814) in the spring, and for the Cambridgeshire (1839) and Caesarewich (1839) in the autumn. The July Course is reserved for the summer meetings, when its tree-shaded paddock and informal atmosphere provide an ideal setting. Major improvements have been made in the last thirty years to the somewhat spartan facilities, particularly at the Rowley Mile Course, to provide a greater level of spectator comfort. The more modern outlook of recent management was underlined when the first sponsorship of Classic Races in Britain took place at Newmarket in 1984.

The transfer of the National Stud to the town in 1967 confirmed its status as the premier training ground in Britain, while its bloodstock sales also underline the wide range of facilities available to the racing industry and to supporters at the headquarters of British flat-racing.

References:

Gill, J., *Racecourses of Great Britain* (London: Barrie & Jenkins, 1975).

Magee, S. (ed.), *The Channel Four Book of the Racing Year* (London: Sidgwick & Jackson, 1990).

Wright, H., *The Encyclopaedia of Flat Racing* (London: Robert Hale Ltd, 1986).

Websites:

Newmarket Racecourses – http://www.newmarketracecourses.co.uk/

See also:

Aintree; Ascot; Horse-racing

-John Tolson

Odsal Stadium

Home of Bradford Bulls Rugby League Club (formerly Bradford Northern) since its opening in September 1934, Odsal stadium has hosted some of the biggest sports crowds in Britain, including until 1999 a Rugby League world record 102,569 at the replay of the 1954 Challenge Cup Final between Halifax and Warrington.

Odsal was the brainchild of Bradford Council's Director of Cleansing, Ernest Call, who oversaw the conversion of the former quarry into a stadium using the controlled tipping of household waste. On completion, it was claimed that Odsal would never put up 'stadium full' notices because it had a capacity of 150,000.

The 1954 cup final attendance was one of Odsal's many huge crowds during the attendance boom following the Second World War. By way of contrast, its lowest attendance occurred in 1964, when only 324 people turned up to see Bradford play Barrow, just four years after 83,190 people had watched the 1960 Rugby League championship final.

As well as Rugby League, including twenty-five international matches, Odsal has also staged speedway, including the 1985 and 1990 World Speedway Finals, cricket, the Harlem Globetrotters basketball team, Kabaddi, showjumping, stock-car racing, trotting and wrestling. In the 1985-1986 season, Bradford City played twenty-one games there following the fire disaster at their Valley Parade ground.

Odsal's vast crowds earned it the title 'the Wembley of the North'. Over the years, many schemes for developing the stadium, including turning it into a covered superdome, have been proposed but none, as yet, have come to fruition.

References:

Delaney, T., *The Grounds of Rugby League* (Keighley: The Author, 1991).

Gate, R., *There Were A Lot More Than That: Odsal 1954* (Ripponden: The Author, 1994).

See also:

Rugby League

-Tony Collins

Offside

Offside generally denotes an area of play beyond a real or imaginary (and movable) line which players from a team may not venture into or interfere with play within. It is a concept and rule of play that is unique to invasion games. Offside is a law that is often adapted in order to make a sport more attractive to its spectators.

The main purpose of the offside rule is to equalize the balance between the defending and attacking sides. In soccer, for example, the rule was designed to stop the game from degenerating into a free-for-all, with teams simply lobbing the ball from one end of the pitch to the other.

The offside rule differs from sport to sport. In some sports, for example Association Football, the line is drawn very much in favour of the defending side and is relatively simple to understand. In other sports, such as Rugby Union and Rugby League, the line is generally drawn to favour the team in possession and is far more complex. In all cases, the offside line restricts the movements of players from one or both teams. In 1925, the governing body of Association Football changed its offside law in favour of the attacking side in order to encourage more goals.

Because of the difficulty in judging whether a player is offside, a decision that relies on the interpretation of an official or officials, it is a law that provokes much controversy, particularly since the advent of the television action reply.

References:

Pocock, T., *The Official Rules of Sports and Games* (London: Hamlyn, 1995. 19th ed.).

-Kyle Phillpots

Old Trafford Cricket Ground

Old Trafford has been the home of Lancashire cricket since 1857, when the ground was opened. Lancashire have always played most of their matches there and in 1884 it became the second venue after the Oval to stage test cricket in England.

The 18-acre ground was owned by the de Trafford family (who gave the Manchester suburb its name) until 1898, when it was purchased for £24,000. The pavilion was built in 1894 by Frank Muirhead, who also designed the one at the Oval. The pavilion was used as a hospital during the First World War and bombed during a blitz in the Second World War.

Many historic matches have been played on the ground, notably Jim Laker taking 19 wickets against Australia in 1956. In 1902, Victor Trumper scored a century before lunch for Australia. In 1984, Viv Richards scored 189 for the West Indies in a one-day international against England. One of the most remarkable one-day matches ever played took place on the ground in 1971 when, in the Gillette Cup semi-final, David Hughes scored 24 in an over at 8.55 p.m., in dismal light, with 24,000 spectators roaring Lancashire on.

In 1989, the Lancashire members overturned more than 100 years of tradition by allowing women full membership rights and access to the pavilion for the first time.

Old Trafford was one of the first grounds in England to stage floodlit cricket in 1998 and for the start of the 1999 season, an ambitious seventy-bedroom hotel will open, giving panoramic views of the ground.

References:

Lorimer, M. G. and Ambrose, D., *Cricket Grounds of Lancashire* (West Bridgford: Association Of Cricket Statisticians, 1992).

Marshall, J., *Old Trafford* (London: Pelham Books, 1971).

Websites:

Lancashire County Cricket Club –
http://www.lccc.co.uk/

See also:

Cricket

-Malcolm Lorimer

Old Trafford Football Stadium

Old Trafford, Manchester United Football Club's magnificent stadium, dates from 1909-1910 when it replaced the Clayton ground. The enormous sum of £60,000 for the site was donated by the club's greatest early benefactor, J. H. Davies. This relatively palatial ground had a solitary stand with various facilities and a capacity of 80,000. It saw United's largest ever Football League attendance of 70,504 for the visit of Aston Villa in 1920, and the lowest attendance for a League match ever when only thirteen people turned up to watch Stockport County play Leicester City in 1921.

By the inter-war period, the ground had aged and needed redeveloping. Bombed during the Second World War, it had to be closed, the club returning to a modestly restored Old Trafford in 1949.

Only in the 1960s and 1970s was the ground further developed, largely financed by the club's football pools. The 10,000 capacity United Road Stand (1964) contained the first private boxes in Britain. The rest of the ground was eventually covered to match, and by 1985, it stood comparison with modern continental stadia. It had a unity that many British grounds lacked, but some supporters claim that it has lost atmosphere since the demise of standing areas.

The new North Stand prefigures the future development of the 'Theatre of Dreams'. The current capacity is around 60,000, but this will no doubt be increased. Old Trafford has a high level of business activity with conference facilities, a megastore, a Red Cafe and a museum, which is well worth a visit. The ground has paid host to F.A. Cup finals, World Cup and Euro 96 matches.

References:

Crick, M. and Smith, D., *Manchester United: the Betrayal of a Legend* (London: Pelham, 1989), Chapter 10.

Inglis, S., *The Football Grounds of Great Britain* (London: Willow, 1995).

Further reading:

Young, P. M., *Manchester United* (London: Heinemann, 1960).

Websites:

Manchester United Football Club – http://www.manutd.com/

-Robert Lewis

Olympic Games

The modern Olympic phenomenon was a late 19th-century revival of an ancient Greek festival. A French aristocrat, Baron Pierre de Coubertin, acted as the driving force and provided the vision. He amalgamated the 'Muscular Christian' teachings from English public schools and American universities with the ancient Greek tradition of Olympian festivals, and also the experience of 'olympick' gatherings seen across Europe from the 17th century. At a conference in Paris in 1894 to examine the issue of amateurism, Baron de Coubertin polled delegates regarding his proposal to revive the ancient Olympic Games. Following a favourable response, he established the International Olympic Committee (I.O.C.) as the executive authority within the Olympic Movement, a very significant step in the future development of the Olympic Games. The I.O.C. members proposed a quadrennial festival according to Greek tradition. This resulted in inaugural celebrations in Athens in 1896. Despite the intrusion of two world wars, there have been regular celebrations of the Olympic Games ever since.

The initial Olympic festivals were haphazard affairs. Indeed, it was the unofficial 'Intercalary' games of 1906 in Athens that repositioned the games within the Greek context of antiquity and tradition. By 1912, both the Olympic Movement and potential hosts had learned valuable lessons from the experiences of previous festivals. Subsequently, preparations and organization began to improve significantly. This period saw the I.O.C. President's role begin to develop in terms of influence and importance. The Los Angeles Games of 1932 were the next significant developmental stage for the Olympic Movement, as they were the first to clear a profit, despite a global depression.

283

Change within the Olympic movement became increasingly rapid. With the Nazi party hosting the 1936 Olympic Games in Berlin, the festival provided a vehicle where political and propaganda issues were accentuated. Such political intrusion plagued many future Olympic festivals. Numerous issues have challenged the Olympic Movement, fuelling this process of ongoing organizational adaptation and change.

Although the media was slow to recognize the potential of the Olympic Games, once they became involved, further organizational shifts were inevitable. After the Rome Olympics in 1960 and as new technology changed the structure of broadcasting, revenues from this source escalated dramatically. Tensions associated with organizational commercialism and the impracticalities of amateurism have also affected diverse aspects of Olympic festivals. This process was completed following the marketing and sponsorship associated with the 1984 Los Angeles Olympics, and the introduction of The Olympic Programme (T.O.P.), also in 1984.

Since 1945, every Olympic Games has been affected to some degree by prevailing political tensions. Furthermore, certain contemporary issues have the potential to threaten both the moral authority of the Olympic movement and the viability of the games themselves. Drug and substance misuse directly conflicts with traditional Olympic ideals. The issue of gigantism, or the unchecked over-expansion of the Olympics, also potentially threatens their future. However, if the Olympic Movement can continue to incorporate external influences and adapt as a pragmatic organization, the Olympic Games will continue to prosper.

References:

Guttmann, A., *The Olympics: a History of the Modern Games* (Urbana, Illinois: University of Illinois Press, 1994).

Hill, C. R., *Olympic Politics: Athens to Atlanta (1896-1996)* (Manchester: Manchester University Press, 1996).

Young D. C., *The Modern Olympics: a Struggle for Revival* (London: Johns Hopkins University Press, 1996).

Further reading:

Guttmann, A., *The Games Must Go On: Avery Brundage and the Olympic Movement* (New York: Columbia University Press, 1984).

Mandell R., *The Nazi Olympics* (Urbana, Illinois: University of Illinois Press, 1987).

Websites:

The International Olympic Committee – http://www.olympics.org/

The British Olympic Association – http://www.olympics.org.uk/

See also:

British Olympic Association; Cotswold Games; Liverpool Olympics; Morpeth Olympic Games

-Jonathan Thomas

Olympic Games – London 1908

London hosted the fourth modern Olympic Games in 1908 when Rome, the original host, could not stage the Games due to financial problems exacerbated by the volcanic eruption of Mount Vesuvius in 1906. Held in conjunction with the English-Franco Exposition from April 22nd to October 31st, 1908, the Games welcomed teams from twenty-two nations, composed of 1,999 men and 36 women, who competed for 327 medals in 109 events. The host nation dominated the medal count, taking 45 per cent of those awarded.

As a benchmark in preparation, organization and administration of the Olympic Games, London left a lasting impression upon the modern Olympic movement. A new 70,000-seat stadium was constructed for the event. Additionally, the British Olympic Association (B.O.A.) established a limitation of three entries per event from each nation. More importantly, the B.O.A. stipulated that all participants had to be amateurs in the purest sense of the term – that they could not have derived income from any type of sportive endeavour. Furthermore, the B.O.A. expected each national Olympic association, as well as national and international sports federations, to enforce this amateur code.

Political tension between England and Ireland marred the Games. Great Britain required Irish athletes to compete as part of the British team rather than as a separate team under their own flag. The most dramatic protest to the British subjugation of the Irish came from the United States, whose team was composed of many athletes of Irish ancestry or birth. During the opening ceremony's parade of nations, Ralph Rose, world record holder in the shotput, refused to dip the flag before the English King.

Tensions between the British and the United States spilled over into the competition, particularly in the 400 metres run, in which track officials, all British, disqualified American John Carpenter for running wide to prevent Briton Wyndham Halswelle from passing him on the homestretch. In addition to the disqualification of Carpenter, officials ruled that the race would be run again two days later. Only Halswelle competed in the rerun, as the only other contestants, Americans William Robbins and John Taylor, boycotted the event in protest over Carpenter's disqualification. In response to what was perceived by the I.O.C. as biased officiating, the Olympic governing body ruled that Olympic officiating would become international in 1912.

References:

Findling, J. and Pelle, K. (eds.), *Historical Dictionary of the Modern Olympic Movement* (Westport, Connecticut: Greenwood Press, 1996).

Matthews, G. M., 'The Controversial Olympic Games of 1908 as Viewed by the New York Times and the Times of London', *Journal of Sport History*, no. 7 (Summer 1980), pp. 40-53.

-Adam Hornbuckle

Olympic Games – London 1948

London staged the first post-Second World War Summer Olympic Games in 1948, the first Olympic gathering since the 1936 Olympiad in Berlin, Germany. Encumbered by the reconstruction following the war, London nevertheless hosted successfully what then ranked as history's largest Olympic assembly, as 4,099 athletes from fifty-nine nations participated in the Games. As the first Olympic Games of the Cold War era, London anticipated many of the issues that would confront the Olympics over the next fifty years.

The International Olympic Committee (I.O.C.) selected London as the site of the 1948 Olympic Games so as to limit the travel costs for European nations, whose economies had been devastated by the Second World War. Although some Britons opposed London hosting the Olympics because of the financial strain it would put on the frail British economy, most enthusiastically supported the Olympics for the prestige it would bestow upon the former world power. Although the Games ultimately cost £750,000, the event garnered a modest profit between £10,000 and £20,000.

Cold War politics chilled the 1948 Olympic Games. Although London welcomed athletes from Eastern European nations whose governments had fallen under the influence of Soviet communism after the Second World War, the Soviet Union itself did not participate in the Games, since it did not have a national Olympic committee nor membership in any amateur sports federations. The Soviets did, however, send observers to the Games, in anticipation of competing in 1952. So as to avert a boycott by Arab nations, the I.O.C. declined to invite the newly formed nation of Israel. Finally, the I.O.C. did not allow Germany and Japan, the chief belligerents of

The opening ceremony of the 1948 Olympic Games at Wembley Stadium (Popperfoto)

286

the Second World War, to participate in the Games.

Despite the chilly political overtones, many sterling athletic performances offered Britain, if not the entire globe, a feeling of physical and spiritual renewal. Much of that sentiment came from the exploits of Holland's Fanny Blankers-Koen who, after finishing sixth in the high jump in the 1936 Olympic Games, won gold medals in the 100 and 200 metres, 80 metre hurdles and 400 metre relay twelve years later in London.

References:

Findling, F. and Pelle, K. (eds.), *Historical Dictionary of the Modern Olympic Movement* (Westport, Connecticut: Greenwood Press, 1996).

Guttmann, Allen, *The Olympics: a History of the Modern Games* (Urbana, Illinois: University of Illinois Press, 1992).

Wallechinsky, D., *The Complete Book of the Summer Olympics* (Boston, Massachusetts: Little, Brown & Company, 1996).

-Adam Hornbuckle

Olympic Games – Olympic Bids

The term 'Olympic bid' refers to the process undertaken by potential Olympic host cities, where proposals for staging the games are extensively analysed by the bid evaluation committee established by the International Olympic Committee (I.O.C.).

Even though Britain has both appeared, and won medals, at every modern Olympics, as well as having hosted the Olympic Games twice, it has never actually won a bid to host the Olympics. Prior to the Second World War, there was no bidding process as such. In both 1908 and 1948, London stepped in at short notice, to host the games during a difficult period for the Olympic movement.

More recently, British cities have begun to bid for the right to host the Olympic Games. Following the unparalleled success of the Los Angeles Olympic Games of 1984, the right to host the festival became increasingly appealing to prospective host cities worldwide – directly reflecting the growing popularity of the Olympic Games as an international event. A delegation from Birmingham attended the Los Angeles Games to examine the best way to launch and manage a bid for the 1992 Olympics. London also sought the nomination of the British Olympic Association (B.O.A.) as official British bid city for 1992. However, as the Birmingham bid was far more advanced than that of London, Birmingham was officially accepted by the B.O.A. Although ultimately unsuccessful, the Birmingham bid paved the way for later British bids.

The battle for the 1996 centenary Olympic Games was even harder fought. This time, however, Birmingham was beaten in the race for the British nomination by Manchester. Although the bid committee for Manchester had been established to launch a bid for the 1992 games, they realized that Birmingham was significantly advanced in its planning and therefore their proposal was simply more organized and attractive. However, when the B.O.A. did announce the British host city for 1996, Manchester had supplanted Birmingham as the favourite. Their high-profile bid was a mix of excellent transportation links, extensive sporting infrastructure, exhaustive planning and widespread governmental support. Ultimately, Manchester too was to be disappointed when Atlanta impressed the I.O.C. evaluation committee sufficiently to be granted the right to host the centennial games. Interestingly, one of the other cities bidding for the 1996 centenary games was Athens. Greece was widely viewed as the spiritual home of the Olympic movement, yet it was subsequently overlooked by the I.O.C. in favour of the home of the Coca-Cola company, a major Olympic sponsor.

Most recently, in the bidding for the Summer Olympic Games in 2000, Manchester, the official British bid, was beaten once more. The team that secured the Olympic Games of

2000 for Sydney acknowledged that the experience which they were able to draw upon from previous Australian Olympic bids turned out to be invaluable to their bid. It is clear that any successful bid needs to be adaptable throughout the period between being awarded and hosting the Games. The wider issues associated with the development of the Olympic movement are reflected in the emphasis and dynamics of a particular Olympic bid.

References:

De Lange, C. P., *The Games Cities Play: the Olympic Games from Athens 1896 to Athens 2004* (Pretoria: C. P. de Lange, 1998).

McGeoch, R. and Korporaal, G., *The Bid: How Australia Won the 2000 Games* (Victoria: Heinemann Australia, 1994).

Manchester and Birmingham Olympic bid documents (British Olympic Association Library, 1 Wandsworth Plain, London).

-Jonathan Thomas

Open Championship

Golf's Open Championship, which began in 1860, was started by the Prestwick Golf Club. The original trophy was an ornate 'Challenge Belt', presented by the Earl of Eglinton, who had already presented a similar type of belt to be competed for by the Irvine Archers.

The first Open was not, in fact, an open competition – it was for professionals only and it was by invitation. What is now recognized as the first Open Championship was played on October 17th, 1860, at Prestwick at the end of their Autumn Meeting. A total of eight players played three rounds of the 12-hole course. The rules were changed in 1861 so that amateur players could compete and there was no prize for the Open until 1863; the winner simply received the Belt for a year. In 1863, it was decided to give money prizes to those finishing second, third and fourth but the winner still only received the Belt. The next year, 1864, the

winner received £6. The average field in the 1860s was twelve players.

The original rules of the competition in 1860 had stated that the Belt 'becomes the property of the winner by being won three years in succession'. In 1870, Tom Morris Junior won the Belt for the third year in a row and took possession of it. He won £6 for his efforts out of a total prize fund of £12. No championship was held in 1871 whilst the Prestwick Club entered into discussions with the Royal and Ancient Golf Club and the Honourable Company of Edinburgh Golfers over the future direction of the event.

One of the key turning points in the history of the Open took place at the Spring Meeting of the Prestwick Club in April 1871. At that meeting, it was proposed that 'in contemplation of St Andrews, Musselburgh and other clubs joining in the purchase of a Belt to be played for over four or more greens, it is not expedient for the Club to provide a Belt to be played solely for at Prestwick'. This was countered with an amendment that Prestwick should provide a new Belt and continue to be the host of the event. The amendment was defeated and from that date onwards, the Open ceased to be under the sole control of the Prestwick Golf Club.

The Championship was played again under this new agreement in 1872 and the new trophy was the now world famous 'Claret Jug'. Until 1891, the host club remained responsible for all arrangements regarding the championship, which was played over 36 holes in one day. The average number of entrants in this period was thirty-six.

In 1892, the Honourable Company of Edinburgh Golfers took four radical steps to transform the Open Championship. It expanded the championship to 72 holes over two days instead of 36 in a single day; imposed an entrance charge for all competitors; moved the Championship to a new green at Muirfield; and increased the total prize fund from £28.50 to an advertised £100. These actions were all taken unilaterally by the club, with the increased purse to counter a rival tournament held at Musselburgh.

A meeting was held between the three host clubs on June 9th, 1893, for the purpose of 'placing the competition for the Open Championship on a basis more commensurate with its importance than had hitherto existed'. Three resolutions were agreed. Two English clubs, St George's, Sandwich and Royal Liverpool, would be invited to stage the Championship and join the rota, now of five clubs. Four rounds of 18 holes would be played over two days. The second resolution was that each of the five clubs would contribute £15 annually to the cost of staging the Championship, and the balance of expenses would come from an entry fee for all competitors. The prize money would total £100, with £30 for the winner, plus £10 for the cost of the medal and decreasing prizes down to twelfth place. The third resolution was that the date of each year's Championship would be set by the host club, which would also bear any additional necessary expenses. The representatives of the five clubs became known as the Delegates of the Associated Clubs. The 1893 Championship was played under these conditions.

The increasing number of entrants caused a cut to be introduced after two rounds in 1898 and the event was played over three days between 1904 and 1906, before it reverted to two days in 1907 with the introduction of qualifying rounds. The average number of entrants from 1892 to 1914 was 141. The total prize money was raised to £125 in 1900 and £135 in 1910.

On January 24th, 1920, the Delegates of the Associated Clubs for the Open asked the Royal and Ancient Golf Club to take over 'the management of the (Open) Championship and the custody of the Challenge Cup' and this was agreed by the club on February 21st, 1920. The new Championship Committee was responsible for running both the Open and Amateur Championships.

The Open was played regularly over three days starting in 1926 and the total prize money had reached £500 by 1939. The prize money was increased to £1,000 in 1946, reached £5,000 in 1959 and £10,000 in 1965. Over the following years it increased dramatically to £50,000 in 1972 and to £100,000 in 1977. The £250,000 barrier was broken in 1982, the £500,000 one in 1985 and the £1,000,000 one in 1993. In 2000, the total prize money was £2,750,000, with £500,000 going to the winner, Tiger Woods of the United States.

The Open was first televised live in 1955 and changes were made to the format, reflecting the success of the Championship and the influence of television. From 1957, the leaders went out last after 36 holes to facilitate television coverage. In 1963, exemptions from pre-qualifying were introduced for the leading players and due to the increasing number of competitors, in 1966 the Championship was played over four days, with the final day moved from Friday to Saturday. Since 1980, the Championship has been scheduled to end on a Sunday instead of a Saturday.

Further reading:

Alliss, P., *The Open* (London: Collins, 1984).

Mackie, K., *Open Championship Golf Courses of Britain* (London: Aurum Press, 1997).

Websites:

The Open Championship – http://www.opengolf.com/

See:

Golf

-Peter Lewis

Orienteering

Orienteering is said to combine the qualities of the mind and body. This is because athletes need to match their fitness as cross-country runners with map-reading skills.

As early as 1917, the Army Sports programme included a race involving the use of a map and compass for its officers, however, it is generally accepted that the origins of the sport are to be found in Scandinavia. Certainly it was the Finns, Swedes and Norwegians who developed the sport and who were instrumental in forming the International Orienteering Federation in 1964.

The sport of orienteering first took a hold in Britain in Scotland, where the terrain was similar to that in parts of Scandinavia. Olympic steeplechaser, John Disley, organized an event in England in 1964 and by 1967 a British Orienteering Federation had been formed, staging its first national championship in that year.

After a significant period of growth in the late 1960s and early 1970s, when it was said to be the fastest growing sport in Britain, the rise in popularity has plateaued.

Today, orienteering takes place over different terrain (including canoe orienteering on inland water) throughout Britain. However, it is perhaps best known by many in Britain as an effective way of teaching map-reading in primary and secondary schools.

Further reading:

Seiler, R. and Hartmann, W., 'Orienteering: an Annotated Bibliography', *Scientific Journal of Orienteering*, 10 (Autumn 1994), 1-78.

Websites:

The British Orienteering Federation – http://www.cix.co.uk/~bof/whatbof.html

-Richard William Cox

Oulton Park

Oulton Park, which is located close to Tarporley in Cheshire, was opened in 1953 under the auspices of the Mid-Cheshire Motor Club. Together with a number of other motor sport venues, it now forms part of the Brands Hatch Leisure Group. The circuit, which runs through the grounds of the former Oulton Hall with its trees and lakes, had an initial lap distance of 1.504 miles, but two extensions opened in 1954 increased this to 2.761 miles. These modifications, including a banked turn, were designed to promote high-speed racing. The Park's natural features also proved popular with drivers by helping them to identify corners and by serving as a guide to judgement. Yet the course has proved challenging for novice drivers and has even produced some anxious moments for experienced competitors such as the Lotus team's Reg Bicknell, who suffered a locked brake at the Cascades during the 1956 Gold Cup race and went over the bank and into the lake. He managed to escape without injury.

Oulton has hosted a number of relatively minor international events as well as the more prestigious International Gold Cup race. Stirling Moss won the first Gold Cup at Oulton in 1954, covering the circuit in his Maserati at an average speed of 83.48 miles per hour. He secured a total of five victories in this event, attracting large numbers of spectators. Club meetings at the Park have also been well supported. Oulton continues to offer a broad range of events, including Formula 3 and motorcycle racing, and the British Touring Car Championship.

References:

Davis, S. C. H. (ed.), *Motor Racing* (London: Seeley Service and Co., 1959).

Georgano, G. N., *The Encyclopaedia of Motor Sport* (London: Michael Joseph, 1971).

Pritchard, A., *Lotus: the Sports Racing Cars* (Wellingborough: Stephens, 1987).

Further reading:

Rendall, I., *The Chequered Flag: 100 Years of Motor Racing* (London: Weidenfeld & Nicolson, 1993).

Websites:

Brands Hatch Leisure Group – http://www.brands-hatch.co.uk/

See also:

Motor Racing

-David Thoms

Oxford University

Sport has played an important role within the University of Oxford since its establishment during the 12th century, through the achievements of students, contests between its constituent colleges and annual 'varsity matches' with the University of Cambridge.

By 1600, the gentleman-scholar was expected to attend commercial establishments in Oxford to acquire dancing, fencing, horse riding and vaulting skills. The Laudian Code of 1636 governed the University and its members' conduct. Scholars had to refrain from swordplay, hunting, dice, cards, 'ball-play in the private yards and greens of the townsmen', and any sport or exercise causing 'danger or inconvenience' to others. Thereafter, bowls, fives and tennis were played inside college property. The Code was increasingly flouted after 1800 (hunting and cricket flourished beyond the traditional University precinct) and was superseded in 1854.

Improved transport led to competition with more distant teams, including Cambridge. The first varsity match against Cambridge was the 1827 cricket match, with the Boat Race starting in 1829, contests which became annual events from 1838 and 1856 respectively. A growing number of sports clubs became involved in varsity matches, for example athletics from 1864 and Rugby Union from 1872. A student playing in the varsity match of a major sport is awarded a 'Blue' and in other sports a 'Half Blue'.

From the 1860s, the encouragement of sport by senior University members mirrored developments in public schools, helping to establish college sports grounds, cricket in the University Parks (1880) and the Iffley Road Sports Ground for Rugby and athletics (1899).

After women's colleges were founded in 1878, female students participated in badminton, lawn tennis, croquet and rowing, initially with a social, non-competitive purpose. The Women's Boat Club started in 1926 and the female Boat Race in 1927.

The ideals of the gifted amateur and fair play embodied in Oxford sport by 1870 were exemplified through the involvement of Oxonians in establishing national sporting bodies and codifying their rules – for example, the formation of the Amateur Athletic Association in 1880 by Clement Jackson, Montague Sherman and Bernard Wise. Such ideals were unsustainable and the zenith of Oxford sport was over by the 1930s, when academic life became more demanding. However, the Boat Race on the Thames and the Rugby Union Varsity Match retain their appeal to television audiences of millions. The apex of Oxford's social and sporting year is Eights Week, the college rowing championships held during the summer term.

A University review in 1998 recommended merging the separate women's and men's clubs in individual sports, redeveloping Iffley Road to include a swimming pool, improving facilities in the Parks and establishing an Athletic Union to oversee University sport.

Among University members who have enjoyed international sporting success are Charles Burgess Fry (world's best long jump record, 1894, and England cricketer), Ronald Poulton Palmer (captain of the England Rugby Union side, 1914), Roger Bannister (first runner of a sub-four-minute mile, at Iffley Road, 1954), David Hemery (Olympic 400 metre hurdles gold medallist, 1968), and Imran Khan (captain of Pakistan's cricket team in the 1980s).

References:

Case, T., 'Oxford University Cricket', in Ranajitsimhaji, Maharaja Jam Sahib of Nawanagar (ed.), *The Jubilee Book of Cricket* (Edinburgh: William Blackwood & Sons, 1897), pp. 306-337.

Hibbert, C. and Hibbert, E. (eds.), *The Encyclopaedia of Oxford* (London: Macmillan, 1988).

Manning, P., 'Sport and Pastime in Stuart Oxford', *Oxford Historical Society*, LXXV (1920), pp. 83-135.

Oxford University Gazette, (22 October 1998).

Selwyn, N., 'Social and Cultural Activities', in A. Crossley (ed.), *A History of the County of Oxford, Vol. IV, The City of Oxford* (Oxford: Oxford University Press, 1979), pp. 425-430.

Further reading:

Chesterton, G. and Doggart, H., *Oxford and Cambridge Cricket* (London: Willow Books, 1989).

Dodd, C., *The Oxford and Cambridge Boat Race* (London: Stanley Paul, 1983).

Frost, D., *The Bowring Story of the Varsity Match* (London: Macdonald/Queen Anne Press, 1988).

Websites:

Oxford University Sports Federation – http://www.sport.ox.ac.uk/index.htm

See also:

University Boat Race

-Mark Hathaway

P

Parachuting

One of the first documented descents by parachute took place in 1802 over London. The successful drop was performed by Frenchman Andre Jacques Garnerin (1769-1823). According to J. A. Cuddon, Garnerin made his descent from a height of 8000 feet (2,438 metres) in an umbrella-shaped parachute constructed out of white canvas and with a diameter of 23 feet (7 metres).

Parachuting contests, although they originated in the United States in 1926, developed most rapidly in the Soviet Union. By 1936, that country had 115 parachuting schools. The first world parachuting championships were held in Lesce-Bled, Yugoslavia in 1951. The organizing body, the Fédération Aéronautique Internationale (F.A.I.), oversaw five countries in competition. Three years later, Yan in France hosted the next world championships with the inaugural team title as the premier competition. Since 1956 (Moscow, USSR) the world championships have been a biennial event. For many years the Soviets dominated men's and women's competitions. They won the men's team title in 1954, 1958, 1960, 1966, 1972 and 1976; and the women's team championship in 1956, 1958, 1966, 1968, 1972 and 1976.

One of the most informative narratives on the origins, development and growth of parachuting is a chapter entitled 'Parachuting Down Through the Ages' by Dan Poynter in his *Parachuting: the Skydiver's Handbook* (1992). While parachuting is not an Olympic sport, skydivers did participate in the opening ceremonies of the 1998 Olympics in Seoul, Korea.

Parachuting embraces a variety of events such as free-fall relative work, paragliding and para-ascending. In recent years, with the advent of both new technologies and new techniques, parachuting has become more akin to the balletic grace and flow of such sports as surfing, trampolining, springboard diving, snowboarding and aerial gymnastics. In contemporary free-fall training, some of the basic moves include a figure eight, a barrel roll, forward and backward loops, style tuck, backslide, T, daffy, layout backloop, twist through, knee turn, boxman and delta position. As Poynter admits, 'Skydiving is evolving so rapidly that there is always something new to learn.'

Skydivers are propelled solely by the 32-feet-per-second (9.8-metres-per-second) force of gravity, and the wide range of free-fall speeds that can be reached by a free-falling parachutist highlights the importance of the relationship between varying body positions and air resistance.

The most important parachuting organization in Britain is the British Parachute Association (B.P.A.) Safety and Training Committee. While clearly a high-risk extreme sport, the statistics for parachuting indicate that the B.P.A. enforce rigid safety parameters for the sport. The B.P.A. have a national map of Great Britain and Northern Ireland that lists all affiliated drop zones. This means that these centres (they may be military or civilian ones) are run under the rules and regulations of the B.P.A. Operations Manual. The centres include St. Merryn, Cornwall (the most southern site), Londonderry, Northern Ireland (the most western), Strathallan Airfield, Perthshire (the most northern), and Headcorn, Kent (the most eastern).

The B.P.A. was founded in 1962. Today there are approximately thirty-five parachute clubs with a membership of more than 25,000. Fifteen elected council members control and supervise all aspects of skydiving on behalf of the Civil Aviation Authority. The B.P.A. has full-time officers and they include a National Coach and Safety Officer, a Technical Officer and administrative staff. The B.P.A. is represented on the Council of the Royal Aero Club, the Fédération Aéronautique Internationale (F.A.I.) and the Commission Internationale de Parachutisme (C.I.P.). A recent B.P.A. survey noted that 85 per cent of members were aged eighteen to thirty-five years, with a high number actively involved in other sports.

Over 85 per cent of British parachuting clubs share the use of their site with other recreational or commercial activities. Approximately half of all parachute clubs share their space with recreational flyers or a flying club. About forty percent of parachuting clubs face restrictions on when or where they can fly/drop.

To join a parachuting club, applicants must be physically fit and have a reasonable weight to height ratio. Applicants aged forty or over require a doctor's certificate/medical certificate.

U.K. Parachuting, a commercial company operating out of Old Buckenham Airfield, Norfolk advertises a Tandem Skydiving course (£170), a Static Line Round Course (£95), a Static Line Ram-Air Progression course (£180) and an Accelerated Freefall course (£1200). The latter is described on the U.K. Parachuting website as 'The ultimate course for those want-ing the fast track to becoming a skydiver. Your first jump is from 12,000 feet accompanied by two instructors, whose in air assistance allows you to progress quickly through the eight learning levels necessary to qualify as a solo sky-diver.'

In 1990, the 20th World Parachuting Championships returned to Yugoslavia. Today, parachuting forms the largest internationally represented aeronautical sport within the F.A.I. There are hopes that skydiving will eventually become an Olympic sport.

References:

Arlott, J. (ed.), *Oxford Companion to World Sports and Games* (London: Oxford University Press, 1975).

Cuddon, J. A., *International Dictionary of Sports and Games* (New York: Schocken, 1979).

Earle, M. and Coombe, C., 'Air Sports', in *Handbook of Sports and Recreational Building Design – Outdoor Sports* (Oxford: Butterworth Heinemann, 1993), vol. 1, pp. 128-129.

Freedom of the Skies – Skydiving (Leicester: British Parachute Association, Leicester, [n.d.]).

U.K. Parachuting official website – http://www.keme.co.uk/~ukps/

Zumerchik, J. (ed.), *Encyclopedia of Sports Science* (New York: Simon & Schuster/Macmillan, 1997), vol. 1.

Further reading:

Poynter, D., *Parachuting: the Skydivers Handbook* (Santa Barbara, California: Para Publishing, 1992).

Websites:

U.K. Parachuting – http://www.keme.co.uk/~ukps/

See also:

Gliding Sports

-Scott Crawford

Para-gliding (*see* Gliding Sports)

Pedestrianism

An early form of professional athletics, pedestrianism was at its most popular during the early to mid-19th century, although 'running footmen' were perhaps the earliest versions of pedestrians. Essentially walking or running for wagers either against other competitors or in a race against time, the early pedestrians were drawn from all sections of society and included women.

Challenges were issued both privately and publicly and some of the great exhibitions were often terminated for fear of public riot. Exhibitions were staged for entertainment as well as the opportunity for the competitors to side wager and thus add to their earnings. These demonstrations of feats of endurance continued well into the 19th century and there are recorded matches between British 'Peds' and those of the United States, specifically the legendary Deerfoot. Such matches often spawned great press interest as well as social comment in the form of 'essays' on the subject and books on training.

Arguably the best known 'Ped' was Captain Barclay Allardice, whose feat of walking 1,000 miles in 1,000 hours on the heath at Newmarket in 1809 for 1,000 guineas is the most recorded, although Foster Powell was also very well known. George Wilson's attempted walk of 1,000 miles in twenty days in 1813 was terminated after 750 miles when police arrested him on public order charges.

Training manuals proliferated and usually included illustrations of the foremost pedestrians such as Charles Westhall, Levett, Lang and Mills and the Americans, Weston and Kennovan. These publications reached their zenith around the 1860s to 1890s and were used to publicize training methods as well as record times, distances and wagers.

Women also attempted records, with E. M. Freeman attempting walks for wagers of up to £100. Kelynack, Anderson, Dunn and Mary Marshall were other well-known women 'Peds', as were two Americans, Cushman and Irvine. Anderson surpassed Barclay's record in 1878 at Kings Lynn by walking 1.5 miles every hour for 672 hours, recording a total of 1,008 miles.

Pedestrianism died out with the advent of organized cross-country running and the formation of the amateur governing body. Pedestrianism is seen by some as the forerunner of current professional athletics and is still associated with betting.

References:

Anderson, E., 'The Running Footmen of 19th Century England', Running Times, (March 1981), pp. 17-20.

Chambers, R., The Book of Days. A Miscellany of Popular Antiquities in Connection with the Calendar. Vols. 1 and 2 (republished, Detroit: Gale Research, 1967).

Egan, P., Sporting Anecdotes. A Complete Panorama of the Sporting World (London: Neeley & Jones, 1807. 2nd ed.).

Jamieson, D. A., Powderhall and Pedestrianism: the History of a Famous Sports Enclosure 1870-1943 (Edinburgh: W. & A. K. Johnston, 1943).

Lupton, J. I. and Lupton, J. M. K., The Pedestrian's Record (London: W. H. Allen, 1890).

McCausland, H., Old Sporting Characters and Occasions from Sporting and Road History (London: Batchworth Press, 1948).

Race Walking Association, The Sport of Race Walking (Middlesex: Race Walking Association, 1962).

Radford, P. F., 'The Art and Science of Training and Coaching Athletics in Late 18th and Early 19th Century Britain', in Proceedings of the XI HISPA Congress (Glasgow: HISPA, 1985, pp. 80-82).

Further reading:

Thorn, W., Pedestrianism: or, an Account of the Performances of Celebrated Pedestrians During the Last and Present Century (Aberdeen: Brown & Frost, 1813).

Westhall, C., Training for Pedestrianism (London: Ward, Locke, 1868).

Wilson, G., Memoirs of the Life and Exploits of G. Wilson, the Celebrated Pedestrian (London: Dean & Munday, 1815).

See also:

Athletics

-Hamish Telfer

Physical Education Association of the United Kingdom

The Physical Education Association was founded on January 9th, 1899, as the Association of Swedish Physical Educationists. Mary Hankinson (Bedford Österberg Physical Training College, 1896-1898) invited thirty women physical educationists, trained by Madame Bergman Österberg, to form an association exclusively for trained teachers of Swedish Gymnastics. Madame Bergman Österberg, out of the country at the time, was invited to become President – an honour she declined because of the ridiculous title. She refused the Presidency throughout her life, even after the title was changed in April 1899 to the Ling Association. Five further changes in title occurred with 'Ling' retained for fifty-seven years before the name Physical Education Association was adopted in 1956.

The original objectives of the Association were to band together teachers of Swedish Gymnastics in the British Isles, ultimately obtain a registered list of those duly qualified to teach Swedish Gymnastics and give massage scientifically, arrange meetings and holiday courses at different times, and publish a list of vacant posts. The motto *Mens Sana Incorpore Sano* was adopted.

Today, the Association, a professional lead body and national consultee, in implementing its Mission Statement, promotes and develops high standards of subject knowledge and understanding; and represents and supports teachers, students and personnel working in physical education.

A President, Vice-President, Secretary, Treasurer and Committee of nine were appointed in 1899 to run the Association. Today, a President, Vice-President, Past-President, Treasurer and three paid staff, together with twenty-nine members, several of whom serve on more than one of ten commit-tees, manage the affairs of the Association. Innumerable members serve on ad hoc groups.

Membership has changed from being exclusive to inclusive, from 30 to in excess of 4,500, from being open only to women holding a Madame Bergman Österberg certificate or anyone trained at the Royal Central Gymnastic Institute, Stockholm to anyone falling into one of nine categories. These categories are – members (holding an approved professional qualification); fellows (elected); licentiates (probationers); associates; joint; retired; students; corporate; and primary schools.

From inception, annual courses and meetings were organized and subsequently extended to embrace conferences, seminars, symposiums and Fellows' Days. Services have included demonstrations, advice, awards, resources for research, merchandise and publications. Publications have included the *Annual Report*, detailing the work of the past year; the *Monthly Supplement* (1900), providing current information; the *Journal of School Hygiene and Physical Education* (1909), containing articles of interest; and, today, the *British Journal of Physical Education* and *Primary P.E. Focus*, keeping members abreast of current issues, ideas and knowledge.

The Association has always been actively involved in the establishment of allied associations – for example, the Association of Organisers of Physical Education (1919); the Central Council of Recreative Physical Training (1935); the Federation of Societies of Teachers in Physical Education (1933); and the British Council of Physical Education (1973). Specific campaigns have included Women Teachers for Women (1902); the appointment of the first Woman Inspector of Physical Training (1907); and no further cuts in allocation of time for Physical Education (1979).

The first offices were located in Mary Hankinson's home until two rooms could be rented at 10 Mecklenburg Square, London. Other venues have included Ling House, London (three sites) and Birmingham; Francis

House, London; and, today, Ling House, Building 25, London Road, Reading RG1 5AQ.

References:

Archival material held by the Physical Education Association of the United Kingdom.

Webb, I. M., '75 Years On', in G. F. Curl (ed.), *Man and His Movement: Proceedings of the 75th Anniversary Conference of the Physical Education Association of Great Britain and Northern Ireland* (London: Physical Education Association, 1974), pp. 15-44.

Webb, I. M., *Women's Physical Education in Great Britain 1800-1966 (With Special Reference to Teacher Training)*, M.Ed. thesis, University of Leicester, 1967.

Further reading:

Bailey, S. and Vamplew, W., *The History of the Physical Education Association, 1899-1999* (Forthcoming).

Websites:

The Physical Education Association of the United Kingdom – http://www.pea.uk.com/

-Ida Webb

Pigeon Racing

Pigeon racing is one of those ambiguous sports that continues to see itself marginalized. While the activity is profiled in John Arlott's *Oxford Companion to World Sports and Games* (1975) and J. A. Cuddon's *International Dictionary of Sports and Games* (1979), it was not included in Mark Young's *Guinness Book of Sports Records* (1997), a volume noted for listing exotic and modern activities such as ultra lighting, bungee jumping and street luge.

The term 'pigeon racing' is inaccurate – the sport should be defined as 'the racing of homing pigeons'. A major feature of the sport is the transporting of the pigeons, usually in specially constructed transporters, to a release point that is hundreds of miles away from the birds' home loft. The pigeons are released at a prearranged time. As the pigeons gradually return to their home lofts, the times are recorded and logged in. The pigeon covering the distance in the quickest time is the winner. Because of the tenor of the race and the sometimes relatively leisurely pace of the pigeons – long distance races, for example, take days and hours, not minutes and seconds – some observers remain unconvinced that the activity is a sport. Smaller competitions can seem old fashioned in the sense that the race owners return the data sheet of the elapsed time to race officials by mail. The verified results of a regional or provincial race may take more than a week to be fully circulated.

In the 19th century, Belgium was the pioneer of promoting pigeon races and breeding quality racing birds, and the country continues to be the world's foremost pigeon racing nation. In second place is Great Britain. J. A. Cuddon notes the popularity of pigeon racing in Belgium, with 2 million rings issued annually. Champion birds are highly prized. In 1975, the racing pigeon *De Blicksem* was sold for £10,500.

The exploits of premier racing pigeons should, however, emphatically erase the notion of pigeon racing as an inferior sport. J. A. Cuddon describes the feat of one pigeon that was released in West Africa on April 8th, 1845 and was found, albeit dead, 1 mile away from its loft at Nine Elms, Wandsworth, London on June 1st. The fifty-four-day odyssey entailed a minimum air mileage of 5,400 miles (8,700 kilometres). The first officially recorded 500-mile (804-kilometre) performance within twenty-four hours was achieved by *Motor* and its owner, G. P. Pointer. The bird was released at Thurso in the North of Scotland on June 30th, 1896. *Motor's* average speed was an extraordinary 49.5 miles per hour (79.6 kilometres per hour).

The Oxford Companion to World Sports and Games comments on the major problem facing the sport's expansion within Britain, noting the '...increasing human population ... [and] the rising cost of land. The back garden, the traditional site for the pigeon loft, is fast disappearing ... and the time may come when those with this facility will be the fortunate few.'

Richard Holt, in his *Sport and the British* (1990), has the tension between the forces of continuity and the cultural landscape of modern sport as a central theme – in other words, the inter-relationship between the old and the new. Holt writes, 'Working men, who bred pigeons ... were obscurely celebrating another aspect of traditional country sports.' *Sport and the British* paints a memorable canvas of pigeon racing in a vignette of only 600 words. Miners were the backbone of British pigeon racing. Holt writes, 'Often living in industrial villages close to the countryside ... miners seem to have had a particular feeling for the natural warmth and graceful speed of ... birds.'

Pigeon racing has a marvellously rich vocabulary all of its own. A 'squab' is a young pigeon aged one to thirty days, a 'pumper' is a foster parent, and 'tripping' is a term used for young birds when they leave the immediate area of the loft and fly for long periods before returning.

British pigeon racing relies heavily upon a grass roots movement of hundreds of small local clubs. For example, the (East Anglia) Norwich Premier club, founded in 1948, has twenty members and a computer programmed to calculate velocities and itemize race results, and a printer for the rapid reproduction of a race result for each of the competing members. Their website speaks of a 'club [that] is not for the faint hearted, competition is fierce with no quarter asked and no quarter given'.

Military pigeons in many respects epitomize the stamina and persistence of racing birds. The Smithsonian Institute, Washington, D.C. has in its collection a mounted exhibit to commemorate the *Kaiser*, a German carrier pigeon captured by American forces at the Battle of the Meuse in 1918. *Kaiser* lived until he was thirty-two. One of England's best-known military pigeons was *Mary*, who was wounded twenty-two times during the Second World War before being killed in action.

In 1997, *Champion Dabber* won the Tony Cornwell Memorial Trophy, presented by the Royal Pigeon Racing Association, for the best all-round performance of a single pigeon during the United Kingdom racing season. Pigeon-racing columnist Frank Tasker noted that 'Champion Dabber', bred and raced by Terry Sherratt, had defeated a record entry of 5,628 birds and collected total prize money of £5,108.

Frank Tasker described Geoff Kirkland of Coalport, Shropshire as the 'Miracle Man' of British pigeon racing. In his career to date, this fancier has won twenty Royal Pigeon Racing Association awards and nine first places in the Open National Race.

References:
Arlott, J. A. (ed.), *Oxford Companion to World Sports and Games* (London: Oxford University Press, 1975).

Cuddon, J. A., *International Dictionary of Sports and Games* (New York: Schocken Books, 1979).

Holt, R., *Sport and the British: a Modern History* (Oxford: Oxford University Press, 1990).

Frank Tasker's web pages – http://www.cevi.be/pp/freddy/frank.htm

Racing Pigeon Support Web – http://www.comonco.com/

Further reading:
Trevithick, A., 'Pigeon Racing', in D. Levinson and K. Christensen (eds.), *Encyclopedia of World Sport* (Santa Barbara, California: ABC-CLIO, 1996), vol. II, pp. 750-752.

Websites:
British Homing World – http://www.pigeonracing.com/

-Scott Crawford

Plas Menai

Plas Menai is the National Watersports Centre for Wales, offering facilities for sailing, canoeing, rock climbing and mountain leadership courses. Situated on the Menai Strait between

Bangor and Caernarfon, it was purpose-built in 1980. Originally named Plas y Deri, it took its present name on its formal opening after completion in 1983.

The centre is owned by the Sports Council for Wales and, as the only sea-based centre in the United Kingdom, it is not surprising that it has established a national reputation for sailing. It has become the headquarters of the Welsh Yachting Association and many of the national squads use it as a training base, particularly the Optimist Class. Negotiations are presently taking place to establish a joint national sailing academy with Pwllheli.

In addition, it has developed major courses in windsurfing and water-skiing, whilst the Welsh and British governing bodies for canoeing are also regular users of the centre. Its location on the fringe of Snowdonia was a key factor in the formation of the Mountain Leader Training Board for Wales, and though there was initial concern that its programme may conflict with the activities organized at the English-owned National Mountain Centre at nearby Plas y Brenin, those fears were allayed by a system of cross-representation on the respective management committees.

Plas Menai is scheduled to play an integral part in the strategy for the creation of the U.K. Sports Institute Wales – a role which has been enhanced by the recent link-up with University of Wales, Bangor.

References:

Sports Council for Wales, *Annual Reports* (1981-).

Websites:

Plas Menai – http://www.sports-council-wales.co.uk/plasmenai/welcomeplas.htm

-Alun Evans

Plas Y Brenin

Despite its Welsh name (it translates as 'The King's House' and commemorates the grant from the King George VI Memorial Fund which ensured its purchase) and its location at Capel Curig in the heart of Snowdonia, Plas y Brenin is owned by Sport England.

The National Mountain Centre owed the impetus behind its creation to the National Parks and Countryside Act 1948, which sought to restore levels of health and fitness to a community still recovering from the hardships of the war years, and it was opened in 1955. Unlike the contemporary National Sports Centres at Lilleshall and Bisham, it has always remained dependent on the generosity of others for the provision of training facilities – the neighbouring farmers and landowners of North Wales.

While kayaking and canoeing courses are based on the nearby Treweryn River and regular orienteering programmes take place, the centre plays its most significant role in the development of mountaineering and maintains a close relationship with the British Mountaineering Council. Plas y Brenin and Glenmore Lodge are the only centres offering courses leading to the Mountain Instructor's Award or the top canoe coach award, and the establishment of the Mountain Leader Training Board office at the centre has placed it at the forefront of the development of equipment and training. Most national sports centres are measured by their provision for medal-winning sports; Plas y Brenin is remarkable for the high level of technical competence instilled in those who participate in mountain pursuits.

References:

Evans, H. J., *Service to Sport: the History of the CCPR, 1935 to 1972* (London: Pelham Books, 1974).

The Sports Council (Sport England since 1997), *Annual Reports* (London: Sport England).

Websites:

Plas y Brenin – http://www.pyb.co.uk/

-Alun Evans

Player Violence

Coaching journals condemn violence, sports authorities punish those who commit it and fair play advocates abhor it, so why does violence still occur on the sports field? Any discussion is bedevilled by two problems of definition. One is whether verbal abuse, particularly racial, should be classed as player violence. The other is the grey area between legitimate aggression and illegitimate assault, as denoted by the rules of various sports and the perceived motivation of the transgressor. That said, essentially the arguments against sports violence focus on economic costs or moral turpitude.

The economic argument against sports violence centres on the risk of injury caused by foul play. However, the available evidence suggests that the proportion of sports injuries attributable to violent play is very small. Nevertheless, even if on-field violence does not significantly raise the nation's health bill, those individuals who are hospitalized or incapacitated by foul play certainly suffer economic disadvantage. Sport, particularly body contact games, is hazardous enough without adding to the risks by tolerating violent on-field behaviour. A second strand of the economic argument is that violence by players could incite crowd disorder with resultant personal injury and property damage.

The moral stance against sports violence has both a micro sport and a macro societal aspect. Within sport, the use of violence to secure an advantage is cheating: allowing the race to go to the brutal rather than the swift or skilled undermines the basic principles of fair play. Much sports violence is not only against the rules of sport but it also breaks the law of the land. Many players, and indeed most sports fans, do not see violence on the field in the same light as an assault off the field. Partly this is because, historically, sport has enjoyed immunity from prosecution where the rules of the game have sanctioned certain activities. Those playing sport have, in effect, agreed to accept the risks of hard tackles and short-pitched bowling, and the law has concurred, or at least turned a blind eye. Yet players do not consent to being punched on the football field or being kicked in Rugby – these actions are illegitimate in sport and illegal in law. Nevertheless, most sports associations would prefer to handle these matters themselves without the intervention of the courts. However, the fact that significant numbers within the sports sector do not accept that the law should be applied to violent players is not an overwhelming argument for non-intervention.

Although the media focuses on violence in élite sport, there is no doubt that it is prevalent at all levels. Many people are to blame for this, including those coaches whose careers depend – or whose egos thrive – on the right result and so instruct their players to take out opponents; selectors who continue to choose known enforcers in their teams; match officials who allow verbal and physical abuse to go on unchecked; and administrators who pay only lip service to the enforcement of codes of conduct in their sports. Ultimately, however, players must take responsibility for their own actions. Those who do not conform to acceptable standards of on-field behaviour are liable to punishments ranging from cautions to sendings-off and disqualification, with ensuing suspensions from the sport, the length dependent upon the severity of the offence and the past record of the offender. Interestingly, rehabilitation via educative means does not feature in the rulebook of any sports association. In recent years the sin-bin has become more common as a means of introducing consistency into on-field punishment in that, unlike a sending-off, a player serves the same length of sentence whether the offence was committed early or late in the game. Occasionally, clubs whose players have a poor disciplinary record are punished by fines and deductions of league points.

Sports violence, like most forms of violence, is generally learned behaviour and as such should be susceptible to modification. Moreover, the level and type of sports violence which society finds acceptable can change – with its specified number of limited-time rounds, weight divisions, and, above all, gloves, modern professional boxing, possibly the most brutal of today's sports, appears almost wimpish alongside its bareknuckle prizefighting predecessor. Violence is part of many sports but the rules do distinguish between the hard tackle and the stamping in the maul, the use of the elbow and the head-butt. Physical hardness need not be removed from the playing of games – for this is central to many sports – but illegitimate violence should be eliminated. The challenge for players is to play their sport within its rules and for sports associations and clubs to take action to lessen the extent of illegal violence. The club is the basic reference point for most players and it is here that an environment conducive to fair play can be engendered. If this does not occur, then it is likely that a stricter interpretation of the law could lead to more players being charged with criminal assault – injured sportspersons, more aware of their legal rights, increasingly might sue not only their violent opponents, but also match officials and even selectors for failing in their duty of care. Perhaps of even more concern, participant levels in some sports could be reduced as players and parents opt for alternative, less violent recreational pursuits.

Finally it should be noted that boxing is a special case of sanctioned violence in which the protagonists have consented to physical injury being inflicted by their opponents. However, this is within specified rules that outlaw certain target areas, allow referees and doctors to stop a contest, limit the number of rounds, and use scientifically designed gloves which limit the damage both to hands and the opponent. The law has also distinguished between boxing in which an element of skill is exercised and fighting in which brute force and butchery predominate. Boxing is a traditional sport and this, along with a willingness to modify its brutality, may have helped its legal survival. In view of the overwhelming medical opposition, however, it is unlikely that any new human blood-sport could be established in Britain today.

References:
Smith, M. D., *Violence and Sport* (Toronto: Butterworths, 1983).

Further reading:
Vamplew, W., Sports Violence in Australia: its Extent and Control (Canberra: Australian Sports Commission, 1991).

–Wray Vamplew

Politics and Government

Political and governmental intervention in British sport can be divided into two types – the reactive, where the government is forced by what it perceives as crisis situations to intervene in sport; and the more pro-active, where attempts are made to use sport for a variety of political objectives. But however governments have intervened in sport, the popular notion that politics and sport are separate in Britain is a fallacy.

The history of crisis interventions in British sport covers a range of situations, but the most common has been football violence, where successive governments since the 1960s have increasingly sought to deal directly with the spiralling trouble associated with the professional game. Often part of a wider law and order agenda, Margaret Thatcher's administrations challenged football's governing bodies to address the issue and then intervened in football in particular once they felt that the sport's authorities were unable to deal with the problem. Measures included the Public Order Act of 1986; changes to the law on the sale of alcohol on trains; increased powers for police, and, most famously, the Membership Card Scheme of the late 1980s (derided by opponents as the 'Identity Card Scheme'), through which supporters would have had to buy membership cards to attend matches. Intended to prevent known hooligans from getting into stadia, it was universally opposed by football, the governing bodies even joining forces with fan groups to challenge it. The history of football since the 1970s has seen many such interventions by government, and hence is extremely politicized, as witnessed once more during the trouble in France during the 1998 World Cup.

Other famous interventions include attempts (again by Margaret Thatcher) to prevent British athletes from competing in the 1980 Moscow Olympics, after the Soviet invasion of Afghanistan. This particular episode clearly demonstrated how the government had come to view sport as part of its own legitimate sphere of operations, and was prepared to subordinate athletes and their interests to the interests of British diplomacy, Cold War power politics and domestic political motivations.

While such episodes grab the headlines, the history of governmental involvement stretches back much further, to 1935 and the creation, within the Ministry of Education, of the Central Council for Recreative Physical Training (later the Central Council of Physical Recreation), which sought to bring governing bodies together in a spirit of collective co-operation. Both the Council and the Sports Council (created in 1965) set about reshaping the face of British sport, channelling and advising on the increasing state funding for recreation facilities to sports bodies (over £400,000 in 1963), and creating the seven National Recreation Centres (including Bisham Abbey, Lilleshall and Crystal Palace). The creation of the Sports Council and its subsequent establishment under Royal Charter in 1972 sealed government's role in sports provision and funding, which from the mid-1960s had come to include funding for British participants in élite

international competition. Equally, the appointment of Lord Hailsham as the first Minister for Sport signalled the arrival of a new attitude towards sport, and the elimination of the notion that sport and physical recreation were not the province of the State and were essentially private matters.

The government-funded Sports Council particularly sought to increase participation in sport across the community, with programmes like 'Sport For All' (launched in 1972) and a host of other schemes aimed at getting specific sections of the community into sport and physical recreation (notably women and minority groups). The success of these schemes has been patchy and certain groups still have low participatory levels, but nonetheless, government-backed organizations clearly saw the social significance of sport and physical recreation. Other motivations included health, but more obliquely, social control. The provision of sport has often been used as a form of safety valve for inner-city areas, which increasingly have been beset by economic problems and decline since the late 1970s. Sport has been employed as part of attempts to alleviate the worst of those conditions, and distract alienated working-class youth from violence, vandalism and trouble. This approach has not worked and rests upon a misunderstanding of the nature of life in inner-city areas. There are also those who argue that sport was simply being used by capitalist society to seek to maintain control over the working classes, but whatever the motivation, the notion that the provision of sports facilities could deviate working-class, male youth from behaviour the State disapproved of has clearly failed. This strategy of using sport as a safety valve was also particularly applied to Ulster, where provision of sports facilities was the highest in the country in the early 1980s, once more in an attempt to pacify working-class communities and youth, and steer them away from political struggles. Once again, the strategy failed, serving only to reinforce the religious divide in Northern Ireland. By the 1980s, however, the Thatcher

Government had moved the focus of Sports Council work more towards provision of facilities and funds for élite competitors rather than mass participation, in line with Conservative notions of patriotism and élite competitors as representatives of the country.

Other important interventions include the introduction of Compulsory Competitive Tendering for local authority facilities from the late 1980s, which critics have claimed has led to sports centres adopting a more business-oriented approach, with consequent effects on prices and community access. Equally significant has been the sale of sporting facilities by local councils and schools, after an order from the Department for Education and Science in 1981 that laid down a minimum size of fields for each school, leading to huge sales of 'excess' fields for shopping and housing developments.

All these diverse interventions highlight quite clearly both the politicized nature of British sport, and the central role of government in many of these situations, and how, therefore, it is impossible to speak of sport in Britain without some considerations of the role of government.

References:

Coghlan, J., *Sport and British Politics since 1960* (London: Falmer Press, 1990).

Further reading:

Allison, L. (ed.), *The Changing Politics of Sport* (Manchester: Manchester University Press, 1993).

Houlihan, B., *The Government and Politics of Sport* (London: Routledge, 1991).

-Rex Nash

Politics and Government – The Suffragette Movement and Sport

In 1913, the suffragette movement targeted sports venues as part of its increasingly violent campaign in support of votes for women. Sport, as a bastion of male power and privilege, was an obvious choice for militant action and a variety

of destructive tactics were employed at diverse places of sport – golf clubs, bowling greens, cricket clubs, race courses, lawn tennis clubs, football grounds and billiard rooms. Grandstands at Ayr, Birmingham and Hurst Park racecourses were destroyed by fire, causing damage estimated at several thousand pounds. Perth cricket pavilion was burnt down and unsuccessful arson attempts were also made at Dundee lawn tennis club and Kelso and Cardiff racecourses. Holes were cut in the turf of bowling greens in Glasgow, greens were damaged at Kilspindie golf links and a bomb was discovered in a billiard room in Dundee. Although few arrests were made in connection with these incidents, suffragettes were sentenced to nine months and three years imprisonment for the attacks at Kelso and Hurst Park.

One of the most famous episodes in suffragette history, however, occurred at the Epsom Derby meeting of 1913. As the runners approached Tattenham Corner, Emily Davison ran on to the track, was knocked down and died several days later. It has never been established if this was a political protest – it is said that she tried to bring down the horse belonging to King George V – or simply a tragic accident as she tried to cross the course.

References:

Leneman, L., *A Guid Cause – The Women's Suffrage Movement in Scotland* (Edinburgh: Mercat Press, 1995).

Rosen, A., *Rise Up Women! The Militant Campaign of the Women's Social and Political Union, 1903-14* (London: Routledge & Kegan Paul, 1974).

See also:

Gender

-Joyce Kay

Polo

Polo is a team sport in which equestrian players attempt to propel a ball into opposing goals, using long-handled mallets. Its historical ori-

303

gins lie in various ancient and medieval Asian team games, which were adapted by British army officers serving in northern India in the mid-19th century. It was first played in the United Kingdom, under the name of 'hockey on horseback', by eight-a-side teams from the 10th Hussars and the 9th Lancers at Hounslow in 1896, and was quickly taken up by officers of other regiments. In a very short space of time, regimental matches were being played at various venues in and around London, including Richmond Park, Lillie Bridge and Woolwich Common. Outside London, it was adopted by army officers, university students and others, and in 1873 a set of rules was produced by the Monmouthshire Polo Club. In the mid-1870s, the game became organized around the Hurlingham Club, which published its first rules in May 1875. Updated annually until 1939, these became accepted as binding for all games in England, and the club-based Hurlingham Polo Association became the sport's national ruling body. Polo's accessibility has always been limited by the resources needed to play the game, and its early spread in relatively élite circles can be seen by the institution of the Championship Cup in 1876, the Oxford versus Cambridge university fixture and the Inter-Regimental competition in 1878, the County Cup in 1885, the Westchester Cup between England and the United States in 1886, and the formation of the County Polo Association in 1895. In the 1890s, polo spread to Scotland, based around regiments in Aberdeen and Edinburgh. It also spread overseas in this period, particularly in Argentina (a major source of polo ponies), India, southern Africa, Spain, and the United States.

Polo was badly affected by the First World War, but it was revived and experienced various rule changes and administrative developments in the inter-war period. During and after the Second World War it also declined, due to the loss of playing spaces to agricultural use and to increases in taxation undercutting some enthusiasts' resources. It was revived through the efforts of some landed supporters in the late 1940s, notably the Duke of Edinburgh and Lord Cowdray. Its survival was ensured by a shift towards professionalism, with teams bringing in numbers of overseas players, by sponsorship from high status companies (such as Pimms and Rolex), and by corporate entertainment being hosted at high-profile events. These aspects have all heavily relied upon what polo writer John Watson has called the sport's 'socially symbolic cachet that is second to none in the sporting world'. Both the upsurge in interest and the exclusive nature of the sport can be seen from the increases in the number of registered players, from 467 in 1965 to 1,200 in 1990, and in the number of clubs, from twenty-three to thirty in the same period. The clubs are concentrated in southern England and East Anglia, including Ascot Park, Guards (at Windsor), Cowdray Park, Cirencester, Cambridge and Newmarket, but the sport is also played elsewhere in the U.K. and Ireland, including Edinburgh, Kildare and Wicklow.

References:
Watson, J. N. P., *A Concise Guide to Polo* (London: Sportsman's Press, 1989).

Further reading:
'Marco' (Earl Mountbatten), *An Introduction to Polo* (London: J. A. Allen, 1976. 6th ed.).
Spencer, H., *A Century of Polo* (Cirencester: World Polo Associates, 1994).
Watson, J. N. P., *The World of Polo: Past and Present* (London: Sportsman's Press, 1986).

Websites:
The Hurlingham Polo Association – http://www.hpa-polo.co.uk/

-Martin Polley

Pools (*see* Gambling; Foundation for Sport and the Arts)

Professional Footballers' Association

The Professional Footballers' Association (P.F.A.) evolved from the struggle by Association Football players to control their legal and financial destinies.

In 1885, when professionalism was first recognized, players enjoyed complete freedom to negotiate individual contracts and wages but, by 1900, football's governing bodies had severely curtailed that freedom. The retain-and-transfer system tied a player to his club for life, while the maximum wage capped his earnings regardless of skill or achievement.

The first player's union, formed in 1897 to challenge the transfer system, collapsed in 1900. Re-constituted in Manchester in 1907 to fight for wage reform, and led by prominent players such as Billy Meredith and Charlie Roberts, it achieved little but survival.

During the inter-war period it struggled to establish a players' accident insurance scheme and to defend its members' legal rights as workmen. After the Second World War, however, led by Secretary Cliff Lloyd and backed by a membership willing to strike, the union succeeded in removing the maximum wage restriction (1961) and successfully challenged the retain-and-transfer system in the High Court (1963).

In the 1980s and 1990s, the P.F.A. utilized its share of television revenues to considerably expand its role in the education and vocational training of professional players. It now offers members comprehensive legal and financial advice, fights to maintain employment opportunities for players at all levels of the game and, through its Football In The Community schemes, helps to promote and develop the game at the grassroots level.

References:

Harding, J., *For the Good of the Game: the Official History of the Professional Footballers' Association* (London: Robson Books, 1991).

Further reading:

Dougan, D. and Young, P., *On The Spot: Football as a Profession* (London: Stanley Paul, 1975).

Guthrie, J., *Soccer Rebel: The Evolution of the Professional Footballer* (Pinner: Pentagon, 1976).

Harding, J., *Football Wizard: the Billy Meredith Story* (London: Robson Books, 1998).

Websites:

The Professional Footballers Association – http://www.thepfa.co.uk/

See also:

Association Football; Unions and Strikes

-John Harding

Professional Golfers' Association

In 1901, the main source of income for the vast majority of golf professionals came from their club, for looking after the course and for teaching the members, making them clubs and selling them balls. Increasingly, however, clubs began letting the shop out to tender, thus undermining the economic position of the resident professional.

Leading tournament professionals such as Andrew Taylor and James Braid had less need of the shop earnings as they secured a good living from prize money and exhibition matches. Nevertheless, they were aware of the plight of many of their fellow professionals and supported their attempt to rectify matters. Indeed, on September 9th, 1901, Taylor was elected Chairman and Braid Captain of the newly formed London and Counties Golf Professionals' Association. On December 2nd, 1901, the name was changed to the Professional Golfers' Association and its membership extended to all professional golfers, club-makers and their assistants throughout Britain. Although it had been preceded by a Midlands Golf Association, the P.G.A. was the first nationwide trade union in British sport. Its primary objective was to look after the welfare of the professional golfer and, to this end, it quickly established a benevolent fund and an employment agency.

It has survived 100 years serving its members, despite a major split in 1971 between the tournament professionals and those who earned their living at the club level. One consequence of the dispute was that the headquarters of the Association were moved to Apollo House at the Belfry course, where young professional golfers are now taught their trade at a high tech 'golf academy'.

References:

Lewis, P. N., *The Dawn of Professional Golf: the Genesis of the European Tour, 1894-1914* (New Ridley: Hobbs & McEwan, 1995).

Websites:

The Professional Golfers' Association – http://www.pga.org.uk/

See also:

Golf; Unions and Strikes

-Wray Vamplew

Psychology

In the United States and the former Soviet Union, it is possible to trace the development of sport psychology back at least 70 years, and possibly even 100 years. However, in Britain, it can be traced back only as far as the 1960s and the work of John Whiting at Leeds University, Barbara Knapp at the University of Birmingham, and John Kane at St Mary's College. Early research was dominated by questions relating to skill acquisition and visual-motor co-ordination, and in this area the quality of John Whiting's research has been recognized worldwide. Nearer home, Whiting's work did not seem to receive the recognition that it deserved, probably because physical education was not generally recognized as an academic discipline, and he eventually left Britain to do his best research at the Free University of Amsterdam. Other early research focused upon personality in sport, but this area did not really 'take off' in the way that motor control and learning research did. One of the main reasons for this was probably the fairly crude theoretical basis on which the research was founded.

During the 1970s, sports science began to emerge from the parent discipline of physical education, and a number of new departments were established in previously unheard of institutions. Perhaps understandably, the study of physiology and biomechanics was a higher early priority for these departments than was sport psychology. However, gradually, sport psychology established a toehold in most departments and, by the middle of the decade, the British Society of Sport Psychology had been established with a membership of about fifty people. Almost all of the psychologists who had an interest in sport were, at this time, academics and, until the very end of the decade, there were virtually no applied sport psychologists working with performers.

The early 1980s saw the beginnings of sport psychology as we think of it today. The British Society of Sports Psychology became integrated into the British Association of Sports Sciences; the National Coaching Foundation included various aspects of sport psychology in its programme of coach education courses; and applied consultants began to work with high-level performers in a number of forward-thinking sports. However, there was still considerable suspicion amongst many coaches that there was nothing anyone could do about performers' psychology and that 'messing with their minds' would cause more harm than good. The vast majority of practising sport psychologists still worked in academic institutions, so research interests started to reflect the issues that arose from their applied work. This period saw the emergence of research in motivation, stress and performance, and the use of psychological skills to enhance performance (for example, imagery, goal-setting, relaxation, and self-talk). Indeed, as the decade progressed, this sort of social psychology research gradually

306

came to dominate the experimental motor skills research that had been the early 'flagship' for sport psychology. It is also worthy of note that around this time the study of health-related exercise as an area distinct from sport led to the establishment of exercise psychology as another area of study and practice. Early research had been performed in this area by Leo Hendry, who was a professor of education at Aberdeen University. More recently, Stuart Biddle and Ken Fox, both formerly of Exeter University, but now at Bristol and Loughborough respectively, have been major players in this area.

During the 1990s, sport and exercise psychology 'came of age'. Lew Hardy was appointed as the first professor of sport psychology at the University of Wales, Bangor and similar chairs followed at the Universities of Birmingham, Manchester Metropolitan, Loughborough, Brunel, Sheffield Hallam, Edinburgh and Bristol. Applied work became 'flavour of the month' with most national teams and squads, and a number of British researchers established worldwide reputations for their research, particularly in stress and performance, motivation, the use of psychological skills in sport, and motor skills (which is steadily re-establishing itself as a major research area). Many sport psychologists thought that Lottery funding would create new career opportunities in sport psychology outside of academia. However, Lottery support for sports science work with national teams and squads has been very 'stop-go' in nature so that, although a number of sport psychologists do now work as full-time consultants to teams and individuals, most of them also work in areas other than sport to supplement their income and stability.

Current issues in sport and exercise psychology include the professional accreditation of sport psychologists, the lack of a funding agent for performance-focused research in sport psychology, the lack of clear career structures outside of academia, and the 'loss' of potential sport psychologists to exercise and health psychology because of the higher levels of funding and clearer career paths that exist in this area.

-Lew Hardy

Public Schools (*see* Education - Public School Sport)

Pugilism

Origins and Rules

Fighting with the fists (pugilism) emerged as a recognizable sport in 1743, when seven rules 'for the better regulation' of fights in Jack Broughton's New Amphitheatre in London were agreed and subsequently published. Prior to that, fistfights were only one of several forms of 'Prize Fighting'. Others included fighting with cudgels, quarterstaffs and backswords. From the mid-18th century, the organization of competitive fights at specialized venues, and the teaching of pugilism as a system of self-defence, developed together.

Pugilistic fights were at first somewhat static, toe-to-toe affairs as the fighters stood and exchanged blows. Throws were also allowed. It was considered 'unmanly' to 'shift', so blows were parried and blocked and not avoided with footwork. A 'round' continued until one of the fighters went down from a blow. Thirty seconds were permitted between rounds as each fighter's second and bottle-holder prepared him for the next round. The fight ended when a fighter could not be brought to the scratch line in the centre of the ring. Broughton's Rules specified how a round would begin and end, and outlined the activities of the seconds and bottle-holders, the appointment of umpires, and how the money should be divided. They gave very little detail on the technicality of fighting. What was allowed or prohibited was established primarily by reference to precedents, and not written down. The New Rules of The London Prize Ring were agreed in 1838 and were revised in 1853. By this time there were twenty-nine rules.

Governance

Pugilism reached its first pinnacle of popularity between 1785 and 1795, when Tom Johnson, Richard Humphries and Daniel Mendoza were the stars of Pugilism's Prize Ring, and its second between 1801 and 1811, when Jem Belcher, Hen Pearce (the Game Chicken), John Gulley and Tom Cribb held the title of 'Champion'. The centre for pugilism was London, but a large number of its stars came from the Bristol area. Its stars also included Jewish, Black and Gypsy fighters. Patronage by the Prince of Wales and his circle was an important factor in the popularity of pugilism in the 1780s, and the growing importance of the title 'Champion' was a driving force later. Pugilism was against the law, and, before 1814, it probably only survived as a sport through the presence of wealthy patrons and the force of personality of some long-serving members of the pugilistic community. Paramount among these were John 'Gentleman' Jackson (fighter, teacher, stakeholder and organizer), Joe Ward (second), Bill Gibbons (who kept and set up the ring), Captain Barclay (gentleman patron and trainer) and Pierce Egan (journalist).

In 1814, the Pugilistic Club was set up to assume a more formal organization of the sport. By this time, however, the sport was in decline. Disputes over 'fixed' fights and prize-money increased and patronage slipped away. It survived in a diminished form, nevertheless, through the 1830s with Jem Ward, Jem Burke and William Thompson (Bendigo), through the 1840s with Ben Caunt and Nick Ward, and the 1850s with Bill Perry (the Tipton Slasher), Tom Sayers and Harry Broome, all of whom were successful fighters. The end of pugilism

can be marked by the fight between Heenan and Sayers in 1860.

Personalities

The most important single figure in the history of pugilism was John Jackson. He became Champion of the Prize Ring when he defeated Daniel Mendoza in 1795, but never fought again. Shortly after winning the title, he joined Harry Angelo in rooms on Bond Street in London where Angelo taught fencing, and Jackson boxing. These rooms became known as 'Jackson's Rooms' and Jackson was so popular it was said that one third of the nobility, including the Prince of Wales and Lord Byron, took lessons from him. Jackson was strong, well built and developed a reputation for good manners and good management, and he became the trusted link between the wealthy gentlemen of the aristocracy who supported pugilism financially, and the fighters, seconds and bottleholders who were the practical side of the sport. He became known as 'Gentleman Jackson', and he remained the linchpin of pugilism until he retired from his Rooms in 1821.

In the 1780s, Richard Humphries was also known as 'Gentleman', and it was the series of fights between him and Daniel Mendoza (1787-1790) that launched pugilism into its first Golden Age. Mendoza took the sport to new heights through his skill and 'science'. Jem Belcher (1799-1803) brought youth and unprecedented speed, and Tom Cribb brought 'bottom' or competitive toughness (1809-1811). Other stars of pugilism were Hen Pearce (the Game Chicken), who was never beaten (1803-1805), and John Gulley, who was Champion between 1807 and 1808 and later became an M.P. in the 1832 Reform Parliament.

In the 1840s, Ben Caunt brought huge physical size into the ring, and in the 1850s Tom Sayers brought youth, activity and resilience, and showed that relatively small men could also be successful. In the 1850s, it was age and experience that were often decisive. Bill Perry (the Tipton Slasher) held the title of the

A 19th-century painting of a pugilism contest. The caption reads 'The Interior of the Fives Court, With Randall and Turner Sparring.' (© Copyright The British Museum)

Champion for four years and until he was thirty-eight years old. William Thompson (Bendigo) had a fighting career that lasted eighteen years, and Tom Sayers, whose fight with John Heenan (the Benicia Boy) marks the effective end of pugilism, fought competitively for eleven years, despite being one of the smallest fighters of his era.

Incidents

At its best, pugilism attracted the attention of royalty, drew large crowds and even brought new expressions into the English language – for example, 'throwing one's hat into the ring' and 'not coming up to scratch'. It was also an arena in which fighters from all parts of the country and of different ethnic backgrounds came together. They acted as seconds and bottle-holders for each other, showing little long-term hostility to each other and even less malice. In the rough and ready environment of prize fights, where significant sums of money were often at stake, the pugilists also pioneered a code of conduct between themselves that was eventually to lead to the concept of 'fair play'.

For example, in 1790, during their fourth and final fight, Daniel Mendoza had Richard Humphries in such a helpless condition that, at one stage, he could have hit him at will, but chose instead to 'lay him on the ground without the least injury'. In 1805, Jem Belcher, who by this date had lost the use of one eye, was fighting Hen Pearce when, in round twelve, Pearce forced Belcher against the ropes and into a position where he could not defend himself. At that point, Pearce pulled out of a punch and said 'I'll take no advantage of thee Jem, I'll not hit thee, no, lest I hurt thine other eye'. He repeated this behaviour in round sixteen, and the crowd was said to be 'lost in admiration'.

Two fights for the Championship in 1810 and 1811 between Tom Cribb, the ex-

Champion and Tom Molineux, an ex-slave from Virginia, stimulated enormous interest nationally. In 1810, the crowd broke the ring and prevented an almost certain victory for Molineux. For the re-match, the most common estimate of the crowd was 20,000, and yet, because prize fights were against the law, the venue was semi-secret and 100 miles out of London. Cribb won, but only after eleven weeks of specialized training in Scotland with Captain Barclay, an advantage not shared by Tom Molineux.

There was similar national interest in 1860 in another title fight between an American and English fighter, the fight between Tom Sayers and John Carmel Heenan (the Benicia Boy). Once again, the crowd was huge, and once again the ring was broken during the fight. The referee was forced out of position and his view obscured. Several scrappy rounds were fought without a referee, and the fight ended in chaos. Both fighters were badly hurt and the fight was stopped, with no decision reached. Little wonder that pugilism never recovered its earlier popular following.

At its worst, pugilism was subject to crowd disorder and indifferent officiating. There were disputes about 'fixed' fights, fighters failed to turn up, and there were arguments about the distribution of prize-money. There were deaths in the ring and as a consequence of the punishment received. It was a hard, physically bruising sport that often seemed to pander to the worst excesses of the crowd. Many of the fighters drank to excess. It was a hard way to earn money and respect. For the gentlemen of the aristocracy and the public at large, however, pugilism produced great excitement and nationally known stars. During the long Napoleonic wars it seems to have inspired many to develop and demonstrate their valour and 'manliness' under a recognized code of rules.

References:

Brailsford, D., *Barenuckles: a Social History of Prize Fighting* (Cambridge: Lutterworth Press, 1988).

Egan, P., *Boxiana; or Sketches of Modern Pugilism* (London: G. Smeeton, 1812) (Facsimile edition, Leicester: Vance Harvey Publishing, 1971).

Ford, P., *Prizefighting: the Age of Regency Boximania* (Newton Abbot: David & Charles, 1971).

Henning, F., *Fights for the Championship* (London: Licensed Victuallers Gazette Offices, 1902. 2 vols.).

Further reading:

Hazlitt, W., 'The Fight', *The New Monthly Magazine* (December 1821).

Lloyd, A., *The Great Prize Fight* (London: Cassell & Co., 1977).

See also:

Boxing

-Peter Radford

Punting

A punt is a shallow, flat-bottomed, square-ended craft, customarily used on the River Thames for transport and fishing – distinctive pleasure and racing punts were unknown before 1860. Fishing punts were about 25 feet long and 3.5 feet wide and race-punts are up to 35 feet long and 2 feet wide, singles and doubles races covering distances of three eighths of a mile to one mile. Today, punt-racing is held only on the shallower lower Thames. Initially, pleasure and working punts were 'run' or 'walked', the pole (up to 16 feet long) going in at the bow and the punter walking to the stern, pushing the craft along. The saloon style of lighter-weight pleasure punts developed after 1880, four inwards-facing passengers being punted ('pricked') bow first by a punter standing on the stern, or vice versa.

Punt races started at Eton College in 1830, however they were banned in 1852 as the school authorities felt that punting facilitated covert smoking and drinking. The period 1840-60 saw the start of river-based sporting and leisure activities, with the larger towns on the River Thames instituting regattas. Punt-racing between professional watermen featured at the first Henley Regatta of 1839 and the Oxford City regattas of 1841 and 1842. Following the decline of work-punts when net fishing was prohibited (1857) and West London's rapid population growth with the arrival of the railway (1864), boating on the Thames increased significantly.

In 1877, Henry Tagg of Molesey advertised in *Sporting Life* for entrants to a two-mile challenge punt-race (prize £15), which was won by Edward Andrews over the Maidenhead Mile course. Abel Beesley of Oxford beat Andrews in 1878, was unchallenged until 1886, when the Thames Punting Club (T.P.C.) instigated the Professional Championship, and retired undefeated (1890). The championship was held at Maidenhead until 1953, W. Haines winning nine times between 1891-1908.

The Thames Punting Club was formed at Sunbury in 1885 to encourage punting among amateurs and professionals, albeit separately, adopting the same socially exclusive definition of amateur as the Amateur Rowing Association. It was reorganized in 1890 by William Grenfell (1855-1945), later Lord Desborough, who won the T.P.C. Amateur Punting Championship (instigated 1886) between 1888 and 1890. Other leading amateurs have been J. H. Secker (champion 1904-1907, 1909) and P. Chuter, winner of the Ladies' Amateur Championship 1957-1966. Clubs affiliated to the T.P.C. include Dittons, Thames Valley, Wargrave, and Wraysbury. There were no championships between 1970 and 1981. In 1999, Mark Hawes was amateur champion and Judy Graham the ladies' champion.

With rowing predominant, only one punt championship has been held at the University of Oxford, in 1905, and punts arrived at Cambridge later than in Oxford (*c.* 1902). The popularity of pleasure punting lasted from the early 20th century to the 1950s, particularly on the Thames, Cam, Severn, Avon, Trent, Dee, Great Ouse, and Wear. In the 1950s, however, it was over-taken by a new enthusiasm for motor boats, except at Cambridge and Oxford, where it remained popular. In 1953, the Cambridge University Dampers Club and Oxford University Charon Club formed to contest an annual relay race employing punts. After 1973, however, commercial punt-hirers tired of the damage caused and the relays ceased.

References:

Prior, M., *Fisher Row: Fishermen, Bargemen, and Canal Boatmen in Oxford, 1500-1900* (Oxford: Oxford University Press, 1982).

Rivington, R. T., *Punting: Its History and Techniques* (Oxford: R. T. Rivington, 1983).

Squire, P. W., 'Punting', in R. P. P. Rowe and C. M. Pitman (eds.), *Rowing* (London: Longmans, Green & Co., 1903. 2nd ed.), pp. 233-289.

Thames Valley Skiff Club, Results: Punt Championships 1999 (http://www.tvsc.co.uk, 1999).

Further reading:

Rivington, R. T., 'Punting', in C. Hibbert and E. Hibbert (eds.), *The Encyclopaedia of Oxford* (London: Macmillan, 1988), pp. 342-343.

-Mark Hathaway

311

Quoits

The sport of quoiting dates back to at least late medieval times and in a variety of forms was still widely practised in many parts of Britain at the start of the 19th century.

Beginning in the 1820s and 1830s, however, its popularity increased dramatically. At its peak during the Victorian era, quoiting was one of the most popular working-class participant and spectator sports, supporting numerous professional players and a widespread gambling culture. Casual, relatively unorganized forms of play were increasingly replaced by formal club structures, national and regional governing bodies, organized competitions and more standardized codes of practice. As played in the later years of the 19th century, the game typically involved throwing a metal ring, weighing from 6 pounds to 14 pounds or

Miners playing quoits, Wark on Tyne, 1860 (Northumberland Record Office ref. NRO 878/8)

more, at an iron or steel pin driven into a circle of stiff clay, usually 18 or 21 yards from the thrower. Two points were awarded for each quoit that ringed the pin and one point for each quoit landing nearer to the pin than that of one's opponent. The first player or rink (team) to reach a pre-determined total of points won the match.

Since the First World War, the popularity of the sport has steadily declined, partly as a result of the demise of the coal-mining industry, which had come to provide its main body of support, but chiefly because of its inability to compete with the attractions of soccer for working-class males. Today, apart from a handful of clubs in Scotland, Wales and northern England, and the occasional international fix-ture, there is little to remind us of its halcyon days during the Victorian era.

References:

Tranter, N. L., 'Organised Sport and the Working Classes of Central Scotland, 1820-1900: the Neglected Sport of Quoiting', in R. J. Holt (ed.), *Sport and the Working Class in Modern Britain* (Manchester: Manchester University Press, 1990), pp. 45-66.

Tranter, N. L., 'Quoiting in Central Scotland: the Demise of a Traditional Sport', in *The Forth Naturalist and Historian*, no. 15 (1992), pp. 99-116.

Further reading:

Tranter, N. L., 'Quoiting', in G. Jarvie and J. Burnett (eds.), *Sport, Scotland and the Scots* (Edinburgh: Tuckwell Press, 1999), pp. 11-22.

-Neil Tranter

R

R.A.C. Rally (*see* Rallying)

R.A.C. Rally (*see* Rallying)

Racism and Ethnicity

The growth of racism and ethnic diversity in British sport has tended to revolve around the issues of discrimination, prejudice, hostility and exclusion from British sport that have been experienced by sportsmen and women from different racial and ethnic backgrounds. The success and failure of Britain's black athletes has tended to dominate both the historical and press coverage of these developments. However, the presence of various Irish, Polish, Chinese and other immigrant groups is also an important but under researched aspect of British sporting history.

It is important to point out that racism itself comes in different forms. It is wrong, for example, to equate the racism that is experienced by black footballers in Britain with that experienced by English-born cricketers from within the Asian community in Yorkshire or Bradford. For a fuller account of the rise to prominence of sportsmen and women from different racial and ethnic backgrounds, read *Black Sportsmen* by Ernest Cashmore and *Heroines of Sport: the Politics of Difference and Identity* by Jennifer Hargreaves. Another interesting read is Phil Vasili's *The First Black Footballer*, which accounts for the life of Arthur Wharton (1865-1930). Arthur Wharton played for Preston North End from 1886, almost eighty years before Albert Johanneson signed for Leeds United in the 1960s and more than 100 years before Liverpool Football Club signed John Barnes from Watford Football Club in 1987.

The 1998 Task Force report into racism in English football pointed out that Black and Asian people make up 1 per cent of the crowds at Premier League football matches but 7.3 per cent of the population in England. The Asian community in 1997 accounted for 1.7 million people in England and yet no Asian footballer played with a Premier League club or had broken through into the international team. This does not hold true for the game of cricket, in which several players from Asian communities have played for England.

Racism in British sport varies from sport to sport and takes on different forms. It affects both men and women. Yet in general terms it is possible to identify at least three forms of racism that have historically affected British sport – structural racism, individual racism and overt racism. Structural racism implies that forms of racism are embedded within the structures of society, employment, housing, education and sport. In Britain, the Stephen Lawrence report into the activities of the police force suggested that institutional racism was endemic within the British police. Institutional racism refers to the sets of rules and procedures that discriminate against sportsmen and

315

women from different racial and ethnic backgrounds. Individual racism refers to the actions and attitudes of individuals to people from racial and ethnic backgrounds that support or reproduce discrimination on the basis of racism or ethnic prejudice. Overt racism can take many forms and is deep rooted in some aspects of British sporting culture. Examples include cases of 'paki-bashing' and the adoption of false assumptions about certain sporting attributes and abilities of people of colour. Many racist ideologies about the sporting abilities of people from different racial and ethnic backgrounds have influenced these groups' sporting experience.

While many black women athletes have broken through in the athletics arena, there is still a vast under-representation of women from ethnic minority backgrounds in positions of power and influence in British sport. As with gender, the inherent use of the body in sport has meant that sportswomen from ethnic minority backgrounds have been subject historically to myths involving stereotypic notions of ability, prejudices, politics and pressures of integration.

The Race Relations Act of 1976 states that by law, local authorities and organizations, sporting or otherwise, have to address issues of race and racism. This means that sporting bodies and people in positions of power and influence in British sport have to address issues of racial stereotyping, issues of access, special provision, and promotion and funding of minority sports for racial or ethnic minority groups.

The term 'ethnicity' draws its point of origin from the Greek term 'ethnos', meaning tribe or nation, and in reality the meaning of the term lies somewhere between the two. Many ethnic groups experience forms of racism through sport but this is not the same form of racism as that experienced overtly by black Afro-Caribbean or Asian Britons. The Welsh, the Scottish, the Irish and the English all carry with them different meanings of ethnicity as do Protestants and Catholics, Muslims and Arabs,

Serbs and Croats. All of these ethnic groups have communities in Britain who identify and experience sport through various ethnic gazes. The Glasgow Rangers versus Glasgow Celtic Football game has historically been more than just a game but a display of ethnic identity between Irish Catholic Scots and Scottish Protestant culture. Regardless of the cosmopolitan composition of the modern teams, the terraces tend to reproduce die-hard notions of ethnic football rivalry in the West of Scotland. Sectarianism is but a further specific form of ethnic tension.

References:

Cashmore, E., *Black Sportsmen* (London: Routledge, 1982).

Hargreaves, J., *Heroines of Sport: the Politics of Difference and Identity* (London: Routledge, 2000).

Vasili, P., *The First Black Footballer: Arthur Wharton, 1865-1930* (London: Frank Cass, 1998).

Further reading:

Polley, M., *Moving the Goalposts: a History of Sport and Society Since 1945* (London: Routledge, 1998).

-Grant Jarvie

Rackets

Rackets (also spelt 'racquets') originated during the 18th century in the Fleet and King's Bench debtors' prisons, when real tennis players who had fallen on hard times hit balls against the high prison walls. Later, closed and open (unroofed) courts were built, often in association with taverns, but the game expanded rapidly when the services and some leading public schools adopted it. Courts survive at Sandhurst, Dartmouth, Gibraltar and thirteen schools, but not one of some seventy courts built in India is now in active use. Interest is growing in North America, where there are ten courts, and at the four clubs in England at Queen's (London), Manchester, Seacourt (Hayling Island) and Newcastle, whilst St

Paul's School is in the process of building a court. The Jesters Club has a substantial fixture list, but no permanent home.

A standard court has floor dimensions of 60 feet by 30 feet, a front wall height of 32 feet, and a back wall height of 12.5 feet, the walls having a surface of very hard black plaster. Balls were made of compressed cloth, covered with white sheepskin, until a polythene core was developed in the 1950s, giving a more consistent pace and bounce. The covering is now made of surgical plaster. A serious threat to the survival of rackets was the rapid expansion, between the wars, of squash rackets, first played at Harrow. With a court area only a little more than one-third the size, and a rubber ball which did not break rackets, it was a cheaper alternative. Rackets survived because it is such an exhilarating game to play, particularly doubles, and because the speed of the ball and its true flight and bounce appeal to talented games players. Each game is scored up to 15, with singles usually the best of five games, and doubles the best of seven.

Rackets continues to have close links with real tennis and is governed by the Tennis and Rackets Association, founded in 1907, with headquarters at the Queen's Club, Palliser Road, London W14 9EQ. Here most of the major tournaments are held, the best attended being the public schools singles for the HK Foster Cup at Christmas, and the doubles at Easter. These are organized by the schools' professionals, who have a vital role in coaching players from the age of thirteen, and encouraging the use of school courts in the evenings by local adults, including some ladies. These evening clubs play in a National League. The most successful teams in the schools doubles championship, begun in 1868, have been Harrow, winners on twenty-nine occasions, Eton on twenty-two occasions, Winchester on fourteen occasions, Rugby on thirteen occasions and Malvern on ten occasions. In the Old Boys' competition for the Noel-Bruce Cup, begun in 1929, the leading schools are Eton (winners twenty-one times), Rugby (seventeen times), Tonbridge

(thirteen times) and Harrow (nine times). The first match between Oxford and Cambridge universities was in 1855; since then, Oxford have won sixty-nine matches, Cambridge forty-three, and nineteen have been drawn.

The first world champion was Robert Mackay in 1820. The longest reigning world champion was Geoffrey Atkins (1954-1972). James Male (1988-1999) is the only completely ambidextrous player to have reached the top flight in this most demanding of games, and is unique in serving with either hand. He lost the title to the professional, Neil Smith, and has challenged him.

References:
Aberdare, Lord, *The Willis Faber Book of Tennis and Rackets* (London: Stanley Paul, 1980).

McKelvie, R, *The Queen's Club Story, 1886-1986* (London: Stanley Paul, 1986).

Websites:
U.K. Rackets – http://www.rackets.co.uk/

-Norman Rosser

R.A.F. Cosford

The relatively remote Royal Air Force station at Cosford in Shropshire would seem to be an unlikely location for a major athletics venue and facility, but for over twenty-five years it was the focus of Britain's national and international indoor athletics programme.

Indoor athletics originally began at R.A.F. Cosford in November 1955, when the Midland Counties Athletic Association held a meeting in a hangar at the airbase. In those early days, races were run on the concrete floor of the hangar, and athletic events at Cosford were rather overshadowed by indoor athletics at R.A.F. Stanmore, which had a wooden sprint track and was regularly visited by B.B.C. television cameras.

In March 1962, the Midland Counties Athletic Association was informed that an

317

indoor track could be provided through joint funding from the Department of Education and Science and the Amateur Athletic Supporters Association. The potential grantors stipulated that a permanent site would have to be found, and the authorities at R.A.F. Cosford readily agreed to provide such a site. The installation of the banked 220-yard track, later modified to 200 metres, at R.A.F. Cosford led to a period of over twenty-five years during which the indoor arena became a centre of excellence in British athletics. Ironically, this period coincided quite markedly with the 'Troubles' in Northern Ireland and athletes and spectators frequently had to endure protracted security checks, but the attendances were nonetheless buoyant, with the local railway halt becoming very busy when major meetings were taking place.

From the first A.A.A. Championships in 1965, when Derek Ibbotson set a new British 2-mile record, through countless international encounters with the United States and Russia and other spectaculars, it was also a centre of local competition for vast numbers of club athletes, with over 1,400 entries being recorded for open meetings. In addition, it acted as a major coaching centre during the winter months for sprinters, hurdlers, throwers and jumpers, thus contributing to the important improvements in standards that occurred during the 1970s and 1980s.

When Peter Lovesey wrote his *History of the Amateur Athletic Association* in 1979, he commented that 'regrettably Cosford is still the only banked board track in this country'. About twelve years later, the authorities at R.A.F. Cosford decided that they needed the hangar for other purposes and, in 1992, indoor athletics at Cosford ceased. Nothing permanent has replaced it, although excellent temporary facilities exist at such venues as the National Indoor Arena and the Kelvin Hall.

The emergence of indoor athletics at Cosford reflected the optimism of its times, but its demise was, in part, a product of another form of optimism, reductions in military spending arising from the 'peace dividend' at the end of the Cold War.

References:

Lovesey, P., *The Official Centenary of the Amateur Athletic Association* (Enfield: Guinness Superlatives Limited, 1979).

Mitchell, R., *Midland Counties Amateur Athletic Association 1880-1980* (Birmingham: Midland Counties Amateur Athletic Association, 1980).

See also:

Athletics – Indoor Athletics; R.A.F. Sports Board

-Trevor James

R.A.F. Sports Board

The Royal Air Force Sports Board currently supports thirty-three different sports, each with its own association, ranging from athletics to waveriders. Its main aim is to use its resources to best effect so as to promote and develop sport within the R.A.F., thereby contributing to the operational effectiveness of the R.A.F. Sport is encouraged and is accessible to all servicemen/women.

R.A.F. sport dates from the First World War when officers of the Royal Flying Corps subscribed to a central fund to support sport. The R.A.F. Sports Board, formed in 1921 with a secretary, has grown into a five-man secretariat as a focus for sport within the R.A.F. Funding for sport is provided partially from the public purse and partially from servicemen themselves. The R.A.F. Sports Lottery commenced in 1993 and provides individual ticket holders with the opportunity to win cash prizes and fund grants to assist R.A.F. stations, sports associations and individual sportsmen/women in their sporting activities.

The R.A.F. Sports Board supports three main competitions in the Royal Air Force – namely, the inter-station, the inter-command and the inter-services. Players competing against the Royal Navy or the Army in inter-service events are awarded their R.A.F. colours for the sport at which they have represented their service.

During national service, hundreds of outstanding sportsmen represented the R.A.F., including the whole Davis Cup squad. R.A.F. sportsmen and women continue to compete in sport at the highest levels and some are national champions or have represented their country. Over recent years, the R.A.F. has set out to provide centres of excellence for its various sports and R.A.F. representative teams play their home fixtures at these centres. R.A.F. servicemen/women need to be fit to fight; by investing in sport, the R.A.F. Sports Board helps to achieve that aim and make a career in the R.A.F. more enjoyable.

Websites:

The R.A.F. Sports Board –
http://www.raf.mod.uk/life/sportbrd.html

See also:

Army Sport Control Board; R.A.F. Cosford; Services Sport

-Nigel Quincey

Rallying

Motor car rallying in its modern form incorporating long-distance timed trials and tests of driving skill developed in Britain from the introduction of the R.A.C. Rally in 1932.

The origins of the sport, however, are to be found in the reliability trials that proliferated at the beginning of the century, including the most ambitious of them all, the One Thousand Mile Trial, staged by the Automobile Club (later the R.A.C.) in 1900 to help defuse public opposition to motor vehicles. Although the Trial was a public relations success, concerns over safety in particular limited use of the highway to reliability and short-distance sprint events. However, rallying as a branch of motor

sport did develop elsewhere, which eventually promoted a more positive approach in the United Kingdom. A long-distance rally from Peking to Paris was held in 1907, while in 1911 the Monte Carlo Rally had its inaugural run. The Monte Carlo Rally, and the glamour surrounding it, attracted great interest in Britain, particularly after the first home success in 1926 by the Hon. Victor Bruce and W. J. Brunell, driving an AC Bristol.

The removal of the universal 20-miles-per-hour speed limit in 1930 helped to promote rallies organized by a number of local motor clubs. This was followed by the introduction of the R.A.C.'s own event in 1932, which attracted 341 entrants. The R.A.C. Rally quickly became a major part of the motor sport calendar, receiving formal recognition as an event of international status in 1951. The Lombard R.A.C. Rally, as it became known, was characterized from the early 1960s by the success achieved by Scandinavian drivers, particularly Erik Carlsson (Sweden) and Hannu Mikkola (Finland). Rallying attracted much public interest in the post-war decades, partly due to its exposure on television. In addition, finance has been injected into the sport as many leading car manufacturers came to regard it as a more cost-effective way of promoting their products than Grand Prix racing.

References:

Brendon, P., *The Motoring Century: the Story of the Royal Automobile Club* (London: Bloomsbury, 1997).

Hamilton, M., *RAC Rally* (Haywards Heath: Partridge Press, 1987).

Matthews, P., *The Guinness Encyclopedia of International Sports Records and Results* (Enfield: Guinness, 1995. 4th ed.).

Nye, D., *Motor Racing in Colour* (Poole: Blandford Press, 1978).

See also:

Motor Racing

-David Thoms

319

Real Tennis

Also known as 'royal tennis' or just 'tennis' in Great Britain, real tennis is the predecessor of most other popular racket games – squash, badminton and lawn tennis. It is played with lopsided rackets and solid balls in an elaborate enclosed court. Like lawn tennis, the court is divided by a net, although in real tennis the net is higher at the sides and droops down low at the middle. Probably developed in France and originally played with the hands, hence the French name *jeu de paume*, the game is currently played in only five countries. With twenty-seven courts, England has by far the largest number of the forty-six or so courts in use worldwide. The Tennis and Rackets Association, founded in 1907 at The Queen's Club, is the governing body of the sport. The game receives royal patronage from H.R.H. The Earl of Wessex.

There are no standard dimensions for the court, but the following are recommended by the Tennis and Rackets Association – overall length 110 feet and overall width 39 feet. The width of the penthouses (lean-tos) to be found on three sides of the court is 7 feet 6 inches, and these are positioned 7 feet from the floor at their lower edges and 10 feet 6 inches from the floor at their higher edges. The height of the playline is 18 feet and the height of the building at the eaves 30 feet. The net is 5 feet high at the sides and 3 feet high at the middle. Scoring proceeds as love, 15, 30, 40 and game, probably derived from a sexagesimal monetary system that was convenient for betting purposes. A set is won by the first to reach six games. Although there are numerous constituents (rules and features of the court), the complexity of the game is often exaggerated. However, the system of *chases* is an essential difference from other modern games and is often quite difficult to grasp. A key element of the game, which it shares with squash (but not lawn tennis), is playing the ball to good 'length' – that is, so that the ball's second bounce would/does occur near the end (penthouse) or back wall of the court. Applying cut to the ball also helps to achieve this. Good length relates to *chases*, which primarily occur when the ball bounces a second time. A good *chase* is made on an opponent's side if it is near the end wall, while a poorer *chase* is near the net – the lines on the floor acting as a means to mark and remember the *chases* made (e.g. '*chase* 1 yard' or '*chase* 6 yards'). The areas where *chases* can be made are different on the two sides of the court, and *chases* also occur when the ball enters the side galleries (except for the 'winning' gallery). When two *chases* are made, or if there is one *chase* and game point is reached, then players change ends and the *chase(s)* are played off. Since service is made from one end of the court, the playing off of *chases* is the only mechanism by which change of service occurs – giving *chases* great tactical importance.

The Royal Tennis Court at Hampton Court Palace, where tennis has been played almost uninterrupted since King Henry VIII first built a court there, is regarded as the centre of real tennis, if not its 'home'. This reputation is despite more matches of significance being played at The Queen's Club, and despite the fact that Falkland Palace in Scotland has the oldest court still in use. There was a revival of the game in the late 19th century and again in the late 20th century through to the present. The current revival (since 1990) has resulted in full memberships at clubs, the building of six new courts and the restoration of at least three others. The balls continue to be handmade, with covers stitched on by club professionals in a manner little different from the 15th century, although there have been recent attempts to mass produce a standard ball.

There are numerous important British championship events, such as the Amateur Singles (Queen's Club Cup), the M.C.C. Gold and Silver Racquet Cups, and the British Open. A number of important international events, such as the Bathurst Cup, are also sometimes held in England. Notable English players of recent times are Howard Angus (World Champion 1976-1981), Chris Ronaldson (World Champion 1981-1987) and Julian Snow (Amateur Champion 1987-1989 and 1991 to the present). Wayne Davies (Australia) has been either World Champion (1987-1994) or contender each year from 1983 to 2000, except for 1998.

References:

Aberdare, Lord, *Willis Faber Book of Tennis & Rackets* (London: Quiller Press, 1998).

Cox, J. C., *Strutt's Sports and Pastimes of the People of England* (London: Methuen & Co., 1903).

Gillmeister, H., *Tennis: a Cultural History* (London: Leicester University Press, 1997).

Ronaldson, C., *Tennis: a Cut Above the Rest* (Oxford: Ronaldson Publications, 1999. 4th ed.).

Websites:

The Real Tennis website – http://www.real-tennis.com/

See also:

Lawn Tennis

- Peter M. B. Cahusac

Religion

Throughout history, religion has had significant influence on the way sports have been organized, diffused, ameliorated or suppressed. At particularly important turning points in the evolution of sport, religious beliefs and persuasions have led to transformations of traditional games, contests and sports. Roughly four such paradigmatic crises can be identified during which religious intervention and controversy triggered major shifts in the make-up and constitution of sport: the emergence and establishment of sacrificial blood sports in antiquity (c. 3000 BC – 500 AD); the abolition of pagan blood sports by early Christianity (6th century AD); the Puritan Revolution and the birth of

modern sports in Britain (16th-18th century); and the religious promotion of competitive and mass sports in reaction to the Industrial Revolution.

With the gradual termination of the Neolithic period and the emergence of Bronze Age civilizations, all sports and ritual contests became an essential constituent of pagan religions. All pagan sports were fundamental components of sacred rites. For more than 3000 years, ancient sports and sport cults (such as the religious festivals of Olympia, Delphi and Athens) were integral to Greek, Roman and Near Eastern religions. Similar contests were part of sacred cults of ancient cultures in the British Isles. The use of sports and contests in purification rites and athletic festivals was a common feature of all Bronze Age civilizations throughout the world. The level of sanctioned violence against humans and animals was remarkably high in ancient sports.

One of the most important transformations in the relationship between religion and sport occurred between the 4th and 6th century AD. As Christianity gradually became the officially sanctioned state religion of the Roman Empire, most traditional sports were radically suppressed on religious grounds. The violent nature of many of these contests contradicted the basis of Judaeo-Christian ethics. Jews and Christians were uncompromising in their attitude towards pagan contests and spectacles. Eventually, the Greek athletic festivals and Roman gladiator shows were abolished. By the middle of the 6th century AD, after a life span of more than 3,000 years, ancient sports had been practically wiped out throughout the Roman world. Yet some of the most popular of ancient blood sports survived the repeated church bans throughout the Middle Ages. Many of these surviving games and contests were absorbed and refashioned by the Roman Catholic Church and eventually reappeared in Shrovetide and Easter ceremonies from the 12th century onwards. Until the Puritan Revolution, mob football and blood sports

321

remained the most popular forms of collective recreation in medieval Britain.

As a result of the Protestant Reformation in the 16th and 17th centuries, traditional sports and games were perceived by many reformers as profane, cruel and immoral. The Puritans, in particular, preached about the importance of hard work and the moral corruption of idle play and violent games. Whilst recreation that reinvigorated and 're-created' mind and body was regarded as legitimate by the Puritans, diversions that were considered wasteful and irreverent became prime targets of their denunciation. Consequently, many traditional pastimes were either suppressed or radically adapted, whilst sports on Sundays were generally banned. When the Puritan hegemony came to an end after the Restoration in the 1660s, traditional sports and festivals were revived and actively promoted again. Yet the ethical ideals of the Puritans had a permanent influence that led to significant changes in the general attitude to sport, pastimes and games. In many respects, the Puritan revolution paved the way for the civilizing and modernizing process of Western sports in general, and British sport in particular. It took another century before the struggle against cruel sports, initiated by the Puritans, was completed with the outlawing of the most notorious blood sports in the 1830s. Ever since the Puritans began their religious challenge of medieval sports, the ethical problem of sport violence and, to a lesser extent, the question of Sunday sports have remained amongst the most tenacious controversies in English culture and history. Even today, the continuous controversies in Britain and the Western world about the ethical predicaments of violent sports and animal contests are often stirred by religious convictions.

During the early period of the Industrial Revolution, church leaders actively discouraged workers from any participation in sports and games. Emphasizing the Puritan work ethos, most clerics continued to preach the importance of hard work in contrast to the corruption of sport and idleness. The church's disapproving attitude towards general sports participation only changed when Britain's ruling class became worried about the physical health of factory workers. When these concerns became prevalent in the middle of the 19th century, religious arguments were applied, for the first time, to justify the participation in sport. The rapid development and promotion of mass sports and physical education can be attributed to the detrimental effects industrialization had on the health and, by consequence, diminished productivity of the work force. In contrast to their traditional condemnation of sports, church leaders now became vociferous advocates of physical exercise in the interest of good health, higher productivity and subservient manners. The promotion of competitive sports and healthy leisure activities also underlined the church's growing concern about effective strategies for integrating an increasingly radicalized and socially alienated working class. As a result of these concerns, a new religious tenet emerged in Britain during the 19th century. Generally known as 'Muscular Christianity', it asserted the positive connotation of bodily strength and power. It maintained that a strong and healthy body had religious significance since physical fitness was required to meet the demands of godly work and obedient behaviour. Physical weakness, according to this new doctrine, was associated with moral and spiritual deficiency. By contrast, physical activities and team sports were promoted as a means to foster moral character, good health, gentlemanly behaviour and patriotism. By the late 19th century, the combined impetus of the Industrial and Darwinian revolutions had produced widespread urbanization and secularization in Britain. From this time on, the seemingly perpetual culture clash between religion and sport receded, giving way to mutually supportive forms of co-existence. Indeed, spectator sports increasingly appeared to replace religion as the most popular mass activity.

Today, all that remains of the long-lasting conflict between religion and sport in Britain is the occasional participation of clerics in debates about contemporary sport ethics which address distinct problems such as sport violence, fox hunting and drug abuse in sport.

References:

Hoffman, S. J., *Sport and Religion* (Champaign, Illinois: Human Kinetics, 1992).

Mechikoff, R. A. and Estes, S. G., *A History and Philosophy of Sport and Physical Education* (Boston: McGraw-Hill, 1998).

Further reading:

Sport and Religion – Proceedings of the 9th HISPA Congress (Lisbon: Instituto Nacional Dos Desportos, 1982).

-Benny Peiser

Rhythmic Gymnastics

The sport of rhythmic gymnastics began in the former Soviet Union during the 1940s and was recognized by the International Gymnastic Federation (F.I.G.) in 1961. It is a female only discipline in which the gymnast performs her exercises whilst using various pieces of hand apparatus. Each movement should interpret the accompanying music and should be choreographed according to a strict code of difficulty.

The sport involves a combination of dance, gymnastic movements and apparatus handling. There are five apparatus items – the rope, hoop, ball, clubs and ribbon, but only four of these are used in competition at one time. Routines are performed to music and last between sixty and ninety seconds. The music should contain changes in mood and tempo, but only one piece can be used in each routine.

All routines must show fundamental body movements including leaps and jumps, balances, pivots, and flexibility movements. Acrobatic elements, such as cartwheels and walkovers, are now permitted and the gymnast is required to demonstrate amplitude, flexibility and skill.

Another aspect of rhythmic gymnastics is the multiples competition. At the élite level, a group of five gymnasts perform two routines – one routine uses five similar apparatus, while the other routine involves two different apparatus. They perform the same elements as the individual gymnasts, but add in difficult exchanges and formations. At the grassroots level of the sport, multiples competitions also include pairs and trios routines.

World championships have been conducted since 1963 and group exercises were first included in 1967. The dominating nations in the 1980s were the U.S.S.R. and Bulgaria, but many more nations have improved their performances in recent years. In 1984, rhythmic gymnastics was first included in the Olympic programme, while the Atlanta Games of 1996 saw the first inclusion of group exercises. London hosted the World Rhythmic Gymnastics Championships in 1979, whilst Telford staged the European Rhythmic Gymnastics Cup in 1995.

The current British champion is Rebecca Jose (Spelthorn), with Natasha Hibbit (South Essex) and Laura Mackie (Craigswood) finishing second and third respectively in the 1999 National Championships. Jose and Hibbit were joined by Joanne Beattie (Phoenix) at the World Championships in Osaka, Japan in September 1999, but although they managed scores in excess of nine (out of ten) consistently, the standard was so high that thirty-second was the highest placing they achieved either individually or collectively.

References:

Bott, J., *Rhythmic Gymnastics* (Marlborough: Crowood Press, 1995).

Websites:

The British Amateur Gymnastics Association – http://www.baga.co.uk/

See also:

Gymnastics

-Frank Galligan

323

Ritual and Superstition

Many British sports traditions are still steeped in ritual and superstition. For example, George Orwell called sport 'war without the shooting'. Certainly several sports can be considered as having warlike origins. Modern football is traced back by some historians to the ancient game of 'Daneshead', when the Anglo-Saxons celebrated victory over Viking invaders without need of a ball. Archery is another modern sport with obvious warlike connotations, but even apparently peaceful pursuits such as golf and bowls can be included – the object is still to hit a target. Boxing, the 'noble art', is the sport that comes nearer than any to ritualized violence; despite its rules and safety regulations it can still bring out the atavistic arousal of the crowd at the sight of blood.

Nor is the actual performance of sport the only outlet for ritual and ceremony. A boxer enters the ring wearing a flamboyant cloak and to the fanfare of trumpets. A golfer is assisted in his club selection by his caddie, much as a medieval knight would be accompanied into battle by his faithful squire. Cricket captains walk to the middle to toss a coin in full view of the crowd, who have no chance of seeing which way up the coin lands. Major tournaments spend fortunes on elaborate opening and closing ceremonies. When the F.A. Cup Final moved to Wembley in 1923, community singing became an established part of the proceedings and in 1928, *Abide with me*, Queen Mary's favourite hymn, evolved into an essential part of what was then the season's climax.

Over the years, the sporting world has also seen numerous imaginative and arcane attempts by participants to tip the balance of success and failure in the right direction. Some of these superstitious beliefs are truly bizarre. For years, cricketers have considered 'Nelson', the score of 111 runs or its multiples, as unlucky, in the erroneous assumption that Lord Nelson had only one eye, one arm and one leg. The good admiral, in reality, held on to both legs. Statistical analysis has proved that 111 is no more likely than other adjacent numbers to bring about a dismissal or the end of a side's innings, but cricketers remain unconvinced. Golfers maintain that it is unlucky to have a black cat sleep on their golf bags or to approach a hole only to have a robin alight on the iron marker. Borrowing a pencil from an opponent will bring bad luck, as will stumbling on the steps leading from the fourth tee (presumably because this equates to the thirteenth on a nine-hole course).

Footballers are among the most superstitious. Manager Jack Tinn guided Portsmouth to a 1939 F.A. Cup Final victory over Wolves and attributed his success to his lucky spats, tied before each game by winger Fred Worrall, who himself carried a lucky sixpence and miniature horseshoe. In more recent times, Don Revie always wore the same 'lucky suit' for big matches and Leicester City striker Steve Claridge took his own sheets to the team's hotel. International footballer and less successful manager, Alan Ball, summed it up: 'I'm not a believer in luck … but I do believe you need it.'

References:

Morrison, I., *Golf Facts* (London: Stanley Paul, 1993).

Pickering, D., *The Cassell Soccer Companion* (London: Cassell, 1997).

Rundell, M., *The Dictionary of Cricket* (Oxford: Oxford University Press, 1995).

See also:

Mascots; Myths

-Tony Rennick

Road Running

The history of marathon racing dates back to the Ancient Greeks and road races were an established part of 19th-century sport, with long-distance running and walking races (pedestrianism) regularly being held. The father of modern British road racing has been recognized as Arthur

Manchester and District Business Houses two-mile team race in Fallowfield, 1930
(Documentary Photography Archive, Manchester. Ref.: 107/1 G18/27)

Newton, who won the Comrades Marathon in South Africa three times and published four books and numerous magazine articles. On his return to England, he held Sunday afternoon sessions with enthusiasts and from these discussions they developed the idea of establishing a long-distance race over a similar distance to the Comrades Marathon. The London to Brighton road race (51.75 miles) was subsequently established, with sponsorship from the *News Chronicle*. Forty-seven runners started the first race, which was held in August 1951 as part of the Festival of Britain celebrations. One of the organizers, Ernest Neville, recognized that enthusiasm for road running was increasing and decided, in 1952, to inaugurate a new organizational body, the Road Runners Club (R.R.C.). This body is credited with having a significant impact on the development of road running in Britain.

During the 1960s, the growing interest that was being shown in road running was noticed by the Amateur Athletic Association (A.A.A.). As a result, the Road Race Advisory Committee was set up and this worked closely with the R.R.C. In response to the greater numbers participating, the A.A.A. National Road Relay Championship was introduced in 1967. The 1980s witnessed a further surge of interest and, in 1983, the British Association of Road Runners (B.A.R.R.) was established. Whereas individual runners affiliated to the R.R.C., the aim of the B.A.R.R. was to improve the promotion and organization of road races, and it was the events themselves that were affiliated to the association.

Under the current administrative structure, U.K. Athletics is responsible for British road running, from 1-mile races to ultra-distance events. A Performance Service Team administers each athletic discipline and road running is one section of the Endurance Team. There are several championships organized by U.K. Athletics but these have recently been rationalized so that championship medals are only awarded in events that lead to representative honours. As a result, there is an annual U.K. half-marathon and marathon championship. The Amateur Athletic Association of England

(A.A.A.) organizes an annual championship six-stage and twelve-stage relay for the men and a four-stage relay for the women. The leading clubs from the rest of Britain are also invited to participate. In addition to the U.K. championships, there is an A.A.A. of England 10 kilometre and marathon championship each year and either a 10-mile or a half marathon. As the distances are so similar, it is felt that it is unnecessary to have both these distances in any given season. Apart from the relays, all these events are incorporated into existing races. In addition, the Athletic Associations of Scotland, Wales and Northern Ireland organize similar championship events in their own territories.

There are many international road events, including a Commonwealth, European, World and Olympic marathon, a World half marathon and the Eikedin relays.

References:

Temple, C., *Cross Country and Road Running* (London: Stanley Paul & Co. Ltd, 1980).

Temple, C., *Marathon, Cross Country and Road Running* (London: Stanley Paul & Co. Ltd, 1990).

Websites:

The Road Runners Club –
http://www.roadrunnersclub.org.uk/index.html

See also:

Athletics

-Lynne Duval

Robert Dover's Games (*see* Cotswold Games)

Rock Climbing

Rock climbing, so often seen as the poorer relation of mountaineering, is a skilful sport, which, although highly regionalized in Britain, is widely popular.

Rock climbing has a long history. Although a skill which was developed on the sea cliffs around the country by those taking the eggs of nesting sea birds, it moved inland in the wake of industrialization. With the development of large urban areas in the north of England in the 19th century, people looked to the countryside as a way of escape. Be it on foot, by bike or on the new railway network, those that explored rural areas such as the Pennines or the Lake District saw the peaks and cliffs as a challenge to be conquered. Whereas mountaineering was the preserve of upper-class adventurers who could afford overseas travel, rock climbing belonged to the urban working classes. Rock climbing was a product of a number of different demands. In the face of industrialization, the strenuous physical exertion of rock climbing coupled with the risks of such a dangerous sport provided an arena for the pursuit of a masculine-defined pastime that promoted a rugged moral fibre.

The class division led to a degree of snobbery that still exists. In 1953, a pro-mountaineering writer condemned rock climbers as mere rock gymnasts who did not posses the ability to cope with the real challenges that face the mountaineer. Rock climbers were viewed as lightweights who were climbing short routes. These routes required quick problem solving and only short bursts of physical activity. Such physical effort was very different to that demanded by mountaineering. However, the brevity of rock climbing, and the immediacy of the technical challenge, remains its very attraction.

Rock climbing takes place outdoors in Britain in four key areas – Wales, Cumbria, the Pennines and Scotland. The climbs in these areas are supplemented by the sea climbs of Cornwall. Rock climbing has four main varieties – bouldering, buildering, rock climbing and artificial climbing.

Bouldering is the most basic form of rock climbing, and viewed by many as the purest type. It involves climbing solo without ropes on rock and boulders up to 30 feet in height. Bouldering offers climbers a safe environment, in addition to technically difficult and strenuous challenges. Bouldering is especially popular in the Pennines.

Buildering uses the same skills as bouldering, but takes place not on natural outdoor stone, but on the sides of buildings or purpose-built climbing walls. Buildering was a development of the 1970s. Climbers began building their own climbing walls on the sides of garages and houses using cement and bolts. The French developed these basic walls by using fibreglass and sand to build the modern climbing walls which are a feature of most major cities. There are now fifty-two purpose-built climbing walls in London and the South East alone. Indoor climbing is currently seen as a major part of the leisure industry, as well as an accompaniment to, and practice for, outdoor climbing.

Rock climbing, as well as a generic title, is also a specific type of climbing. It consists of climbing rock for its own sake as either a free climb or in competition. This type of climbing involves no artificial aids other than those that ensure the climbers safety.

Artificial climbing involves moving up a rock face by artificial means. This can involve the use of bolts that have been placed in the rock, or the insertion of nuts into cracks in the rock face. This type of climbing is usually done on those types of rock that could not be free-climbed, such as rock overhangs.

Artificial climbing specifically, but all types of rock climbing generally, have benefited hugely from the impact of technology. Whereas the early years of climbing were dominated by heavy-soled boots, thick ropes and oily all-weather outfits, recent decades have witnessed the development of a whole host of materials and devices to improve the life of the climber. Ropes have got stronger and lighter and there has been the development of various slings, crabs, harnesses, nuts, rocks, friends and bolts that secure the climber and make the whole process much safer. While such devices do not remove the need for skill and agility from the climber, they do ensure that climbs can be attempted without such a great element of risk. The heavy boots have, especially on indoor walls, been replaced by rubber-soled friction boots that provide greater grip for the climber. Clothing is now lightweight, warm and waterproof, and since the 1980s climbers have been great advocates of lycra clothing as a way of ensuring maximum mobility.

The British Mountaineering Council (B.M.C.) governs British rock climbing. Based in Manchester, the B.M.C. produces guidebooks for rock climbers, provides information and publishes its own magazine, *High*. The need for information is vital in rock climbing, and has a long history. Since the late 19th century, all climbs, or routes, have been graded. There are presently guidebooks that cover all the climbs in the different areas of Britain. In Britain, there are two grading systems for rock climbing, which stretch from a grading of moderate, the easiest climb, to E7, the most technically difficult. The first climbs graded very severe were laid out by Owen Glynne in the 1890s, while Jim Birkett pioneered E1 in the 1940s. Some modern climbers, such as Ben Moon, are currently pioneering routes that are graded E8 and E9, although these have yet to be included in any guidebooks. The history of the grading system is an excellent vehicle for understanding the popularity and competitiveness of rock climbing as a sport, and the effect that increased fitness and improved technology have had on the ability of climbers to tackle the hardest of climbs.

There are no written rules for rock climbing apart from those that govern indoor climbing wall competitions. As a result, there is an intense debate amongst modern climbers. Is the sport about free climbing without assistance, or is it acceptable to use artificial aids? While such intense discussions continue, rock climbing will remain a fascinating sport, full of contradictions, but still a true test of skill.

327

References:

Birkett, B., *Lakeland's Greatest Pioneers: a Hundred Years of Rock Climbing* (London: Hale, 1983).

Birkett, B., *Modern Rock and Ice Climbing* (London: A. & C. Black, 1988).

Griffin, A. H., 'A Century of Rock Climbing', *Climber and Rambler*, 21, 10 (October 1982), 45-46.

Further reading:

Brunning, C., *Rock Climbing and Mountaineering* (London: Faber & Faber, 1953).

Websites:

The British Mountaineering Council – http://www.thebmc.co.uk/

See also:

Mountaineering

-Mike Cronin

Roller Hockey

Roller hockey, while having similarities to field and ice hockey, has its own distinctive rules and equipment (for example the roller hockey stick and ball). A game is played between two teams of five players. Roller hockey first appeared in London during the 1880s and has been played on an organized basis since the 1890s. Charlie Chaplin and Stan Laurel, the famous silent movie pioneers, were keen players of the sport.

Roller hockey was originally called rink hockey. Its first national organization, the National Rink Hockey Association, was formed in 1912. It was this body that formulated the first uniform rules. In 1949, when the sport changed its name to roller hockey, the governing body also changed its name accordingly. The game has always been played on an amateur basis.

The British governing body played a key role in promoting the sport internationally and was a founder member of the international federation in 1924. The 1926 European Championships were held in England at Herne Bay, Kent – England emerged as European champions. The first world championships, held in Stuttgart in 1936, were also won by England.

Today the sport is played worldwide in over sixty countries and is particularly popular in Spain, Portugal and much of Latin America. At the 1992 Barcelona Olympic Games, roller hockey was a demonstration sport.

References:

National Roller Hockey Association website – http://www.nrha.demon.co.uk/

Rules of the Game: the Complete Illustrated Encyclopaedia of All the Sports of the World (London: CollinsWillow 1990).

Websites:

The National Roller Hockey Association – http://www.nrha.demon.co.uk/

See also:

Roller-skating

-Ray Physick

Roller-skating

Rolling-skating techniques evolved out of ice skating. Following the development of roller skates by Joseph Merlin in 1760, ice skaters took the opportunity to practice their skating when there was no natural ice to skate on. Hence, many roller-skating disciplines were adapted from ice skating. Merlin's skates were rather primitive and allowed the skater little control, while actually stopping was often a major problem. Following design changes by James Plymton in 1863, rubber cushions were fitted on the axles thereby making it easier for skaters to use their body weight to control their movements. Skates were further improved in 1884, following the introduction of ball-bearing wheels by Richardson.

Initially skates had wheels made of wood or metal, but with the development of highly durable plastics, these were replaced with light-weight polyurethane plastic wheels, which gave the skater greater mobility and better grip on the skating surface. The development of roller-blade skates in the late 20th century ushered in another significant design change. Instead of the standard four-wheeled rectangular configuration, roller-blade skates have a single row of wheels, giving skaters even greater mobility.

Ice skaters formed the National Skating Association (N.S.A.) of Great Britain in 1879, and the Association incorporated roller-skating into its ranks in 1893. Aldwych Skating Club, formed in 1908, is Britain's oldest skating club. In 1909, at the instigation of C. Wilson, the British one-mile championship was established, with Wilson winning the inaugural race. National roller figure-skating championships were introduced the following year. This event was won by W. Station of London. Until 1939, men and women competed in the same singles events at the national championships. In 1922, a national roller-dance competition was introduced. The event was dominated by Blazer, who won the event each year until 1927. On three occasions his dance partner was Miss Hogg.

The Fédération Internationale de Roller Skating (F.I.R.S. – International Roller Skating Federation) was founded in 1923 and organized the first world championships for speed skating at Monza in 1937. World championships for roller figure and dance skating were first held in 1947 in Washington D.C., although it was 1953 before world championships for women were held. During the 1950s and 1960s, Britain was regarded as one of the world's top skating nations, but has since slipped back.

In the early 1990s, the N.S.A. split into separate organizations for roller and ice skating. Following the split, roller-skating was organized by the Federation of Roller Skating (F.R.S.), which later added the title British to its name. This body survived for only a few years before further splits took place. This time,

speed skating split away from the other disciplines and formed the Federation of Inline Speed Skating (F.I.S.S.), while artistic roller skating was placed under the umbrella of the Federation of Artistic Roller Skating (F.A.R.S.). Both federations are recognized by F.I.R.S., the international governing body.

References:

Arlott, J. (ed.), *Oxford Companion to World Sports and Games* (London: Oxford University Press, 1975).

The Federation of Inline Speed Skating website – http://www.inlinespeed.co.uk/

Rules of the Game: the Complete Illustrated Encyclopaedia of All the Sports of the World (London: CollinsWillow 1990).

Websites:

The Federation of Artistic Roller Skating – http://www.british-roller-skating.org.uk/

The Federation of Inline Speed Skating – http://www.inlinespeed.co.uk/

See also:

Roller Hockey; Skating

-Ray Physick

Roses Matches

The phrase 'Roses match' is most often used to describe a game of cricket between Yorkshire and Lancashire County Cricket Clubs. The name refers to the county symbols of Yorkshire and Lancashire, white and red roses respectively. Football matches, Rugby matches and other sporting encounters between teams from the two counties have also been described as Roses matches, but the phrase remains centrally a cricket term.

Yorkshire and Lancashire County Cricket Clubs were formed in 1863 and 1864 respectively. The first official match between the two took place in 1867 at Whalley. Yorkshire won that and the next five Roses matches, with Lancashire having to wait until 1871 for their first triumph. Yorkshire are historically the more successful county, having won a greater number of county championships and the majority of Roses matches.

In the 'folklore' of Roses cricket, the rivalry between Yorkshire and Lancashire is said to be based on the long history of general competition between the two counties, dating back to the War of the Roses in the 15th century. It is doubtful whether Roses matches were initially seen in this context, but by the 1890s they had certainly developed into fiercely competitive occasions.

In addition to an intense rivalry, cricket matches between Yorkshire and Lancashire are also said to be based on mutual respect and a shared set of 'northern' values. Both sides believe that Roses matches typify tough and competitive cricket, and claim that they have historically represented the game at its professional best.

References:

Hodgson, D., *The Official History of Yorkshire County Cricket Club* (Marlborough: Crowood, 1989).

Midwinter, E., *Red Roses Crest the Caps: the Story of Lancashire County Cricket Club* (London: The Kingswood Press, 1989).

Further reading:

Cardus, N., *The Roses Matches 1919-1939* (London: Souvenir, 1982).

Russell, D., 'Amateurs, Professionals and the Construction of Social Identity', *The Sports Historian*, 16 (May 1996), 64-80.

Websites:

Lancashire County Cricket Club – http://www.lccc.co.uk/

Yorkshire County Cricket Club – http://www.yorkshireccc.org.uk/

See also:

Derby Matches

-Gavin Mellor

Rounders

Rounders is a bat and ball game played between two teams. The size of the teams can be flexible although there must be a minimum of six and a maximum of fifteen players in a team and no more than nine players from each team may be on the field of play at any one time. Matches are often played between mixed-sex teams – when this occurs a maximum of five male players per side is allowed. The rounders pitch is made up of a bowling square and four vertical posts, known as bases, which are set at equal distances around the pitch.

Rounders has a long tradition in England, where it has been played since Tudor times. References to the game can be found in the 1744 publication *A Little Pretty Pocketbook*, while the *Boys' Own Book* of 1828 devotes a chapter to the sport. Jane Austen was certainly aware of the game, for she mentions it in her classic novel *Northanger Abbey*.

The game gained in popularity towards the end of the 19th century and was particularly popular in the working class areas of Liverpool and Scotland. One result of this popularity was the establishment of the Liverpool and Scottish Rounders Association in 1899. This would seem to indicate that local leagues, as well as matches, between the two areas were organized. Rounders also became a popular sport in schools, with many areas organizing leagues between local schools. In addition, it became well established in many workplace sports clubs in areas such as Merseyside and Sheffield; many of these teams were also members of local leagues. Eventually, as the sport developed, it became necessary to have uniform rules, which in turn required a central governing body. Hence, the National Rounders Association (N.R.A.), which emerged out of the Womens' Teams Games Board, was established in 1943.

It was 1976, however, before the N.R.A. organized a national tournament, the hosts being Rhyl. Significantly, most teams that entered were mixed sex, confirming that rounders remains one of the few sports where men and women compete on equal terms. Indeed, the tournament was won by Atlas, a mixed-sex team from Sheffield. International matches take place between the countries of the British Isles, the first international being between England and Wales in 1977. Since then, regular international matches, both at senior and under-twenty-one level, have taken place on a home and away basis. Rounders teams from England attended the celebrations to mark Dublin's millennium in 1988 and played against teams from Ireland. There are currently adult leagues established in the West Midlands, East Midlands, Wales, South West England, North West England, Yorkshire and Humberside, South England and South East England. There are also county associations in Leicestershire, South Yorkshire, Northamptonshire and Dorset, while Lancashire is discussing the formation of a similar association. Many school leagues also still exist. There is no worldwide organization for rounders, although the game is played in various parts of the world by the Womens' Army Rounders Team.

References:

The National Rounders Association website – http://rounders.punters.co.uk/

Websites:

The National Rounders Association – http://rounders.punters.co.uk/

-Ray Physick

Rowing

Origins and Development

The first known rowers were the Egyptians, in around 4000 BC. For thousands of years, trading communities depended on rowing or paddling for their livelihood. People and goods were moved by oar, fish and whales were pursued by oar, war was waged and peace was kept by oar, mail delivered and lives saved by oar. A boat's shape depended upon the materials available, where it was to be used, and the task it would be used to perform.

In rowing, the oar is attached to the boat, whereas a canoe's paddle is an extension of the paddler's arm. The oar is a secondary lever, which enables greater bulk to be moved or greater speed to be achieved, or both, from a 170-oar trireme of 400 BC to a modern racing shell. The paddle has the advantage of nimbleness and silence in shallow, narrow waterways, kayaks and birch-bark canoes being perfect for hunting the lakes, rivers and forests of North America.

Regattas began in Venice in the 1200s. Competitive rowing in Britain was developed in the 1700s by the men who worked rivers and ports, encouraged by the betting instinct of the growing urban population. Amateurs, at first chiefly from Eton and Westminster schools and the universities of Oxford and Cambridge, were shown the way by professionals in the early 1800s. Regattas and clubs started wherever suitable water was found. Every Victorian town had a boating lake and every great house had boats on its lake. The governing body for England and British international rowing, the Amateur Rowing Association (A.R.A.), was founded in 1882.

Governance and Administration

England, Scotland and Wales each have their own governing body for rowing, but England's Amateur Rowing Association's affiliation to the International Rowing Federation (Fédération Internationale des Sociétés d'Aviron – F.I.S.A.) makes it responsible for the Great Britain international team. The Irish Rowing Union is the governing body for the island of Ireland.

The A.R.A. grew out of the Metropolitan Rowing Association, which was set up by clubs, mostly on the tidal Thames, to promote strong crews at Henley Royal Regatta. Before this, both the Oxford and Cambridge Boat Race and the Henley Stewards operated a rigorous amateur definition, which banned professional coaching and barred 'menial and manual workers' from rowing at Henley. Suspicion that artisans, particularly those who worked 'in and about' boats, had a physical advantage over professional men and landed gentry led to their isolation between truly professional oarsmen and amateurs who became synonymous with 'gentlemen'. Manual workers who did not compete for money were thus neither professionals nor amateurs.

The A.R.A.'s early failure to move away from this led to the split of the Muscular Christian-led National Amateur Rowing Association (N.A.R.A.) in 1890. The N.A.R.A. distinguished only between rowing for money or no material reward. Henley's ban on the Australian Olympic eight in 1936 because they were policemen eventually brought all to their senses. The A.R.A. dropped the manual labour bar in 1938. The merger of the A.R.A. and the N.A.R.A. was agreed in 1955, the A.R.A. having joined F.I.S.A. (founded 1892) before the 1948 Olympics rowing events were held in Henley.

The A.R.A. and Henley now follow F.I.S.A.'s definition, which makes rowing open in keeping with the International Olympic Committee, which dropped its amateur pretence in 1976. The A.R.A. employs national and regional coaches, sets the rules of racing for most English regattas, and operates a safety code.

Personalities and Leaders

Steven Redgrave is British rowing's leading competitor, having won four gold medals in consecutive Olympic Games up to 1996, a record unsurpassed in an endurance sport. By 1998, he also had eight world and seventeen Henley titles. Between winning Olympic golds in 1992 and 1996, Redgrave and his partner, Matthew Pinsent, remained undefeated in fifty-nine major races in their coxless pair. Their medal in 1996 was Britain's only Olympic title. The British rowing team delivered four world titles in 1997 and three in 1998, including the women's double sculls with Gillian Lindsay and Miriam Batten. Assisted by high performance awards from the Sports Lottery Fund, rowing's record remains at the top of British amateur

sport (references to 'amateur' have been dropped by the international federation F.I.S.A., the A.R.A. and the Henley Stewards since 1996).

Notables in the 1990s include the Searle brothers, Greg and Jonny, who won the Olympic coxed pairs title in 1992 in the last three strokes of their final, with Garry Herbert coxing. The Scot, Peter Haining, won the world lightweight single sculling titles from 1993 to 1995, the first to achieve three consecutive wins.

Redgrave began his career with a junior medal in 1980 and has been a career oarsman ever since. Pinsent and the other members of the coxless four who are aiming at the Olympics of 2000, Tim Foster and James Cracknell, all began as world junior medal winners. The coaches currently responsible for the successes are Jürgen Grobler (senior men), Mike Spracklen (senior women) and Mark Banks (juniors).

Competitions

Hundreds of regattas and time trials cater for more than 500 rowing clubs in Britain. The largest multi-lane regattas are the National Schools for juniors, held at Nottingham, and the National Championships, held at Nottingham or Strathclyde Park, while the 420-entry Head of River Race for men's eights from Putney to Mortlake is the largest time trial. British indoor championships conducted on rowing machines are an annual fixture. The burgeoning of rowing for women from the 1970s has brought with it a huge increase in women's events, including Henley Women's Regatta (1988). Henley Royal Regatta attracts entries of over 500 crews and now includes some events for women.

British crews compete in the Olympic Games, the annual senior and junior world championships, the Nations Cup for under-twenty-three year-olds and the annual Rowing World Cup series.

The oldest continuous sporting event in Britain is Doggett's Coat and Badge, first run in 1715, a sculling race from London Bridge to Chelsea for watermen – and now women – who have recently completed their apprenticeship. Sculling and rowing for money prizes, boats or badges, like Doggett's, which signified that the bearer was a champion as well as a licensed waterman, was hugely popular in the 1800s and led to a world professional sculling championship that lasted until the 1930s. The significant milestones in amateur rowing were the Boat Race (1829), the Wingfield Sculls (1830) and Henley Regatta (1839), all of which required rules of racing. Chester regatta dates from 1733 and Durham from 1834.

Memorable Events

The unfortunate nature of rowing is its inaccessibility for spectators. However, there have been three races in recent times that should remain memorable for many years.

The victory of the brothers Greg and Jonny Searle over Giuseppe and Carmine Abbagnale was the race of the 1992 Olympics. The Searles were more than two lengths down on the Italian 1988 champions at half way. The Abbagnales were traditionally quick in the first half, while the Searles were known sprinters. And sprint they did, leaving it so late that their snatched victory in the last three strokes was breathtaking. Cox Garry Herbert was quite justified in bursting into tears during the national anthem.

Peter Haining's long career as a tenacious competitor threatened something sensational as the seasons rolled. It came in the Czech Republic in 1993 when, leading the lightweight single sculls final about 300 metres from home, the Scot's scull caught a buoy and stopped him dead. Haining restarted like a man possessed and overhauled the three men who had slipped past. That night a friend liberated the offending buoy and gave it to Haining for his birthday. He won the next two world titles.

In the final of the Ladies' Plate at Henley in 1989, the lightweights of Nottinghamshire County routed the heavyweight and thus far undefeated Harvard crew, setting a new course record. A re-row was awarded when it was revealed that driftwood impaled on the Harvard boat's fin had impeded them. Later, in the gloaming, the lightweights trounced Harvard again and lowered their previous record. County's victory was as much psychological as physical. David's first slaying of Goliath caused perhaps 10,000 spectators to stay late and roar support for their second.

References:

Cleaver, H. R., *A History of Rowing* (London: Herbert Jenkins, 1957).

Dodd, C. *The Story of World Rowing* (London: Stanley Paul, 1992).

Halladay, E., *Rowing in England: a Social History* (Manchester: Manchester University Press, 1990).

Wigglesworth, N., *Ths Social History of English Rowing* (London: Frank Cass, 1992).

Further reading:

Rowing Almanac (London: A.R.A.)

Regatta Magazine (London: A.R.A., 1987-).

Websites:

The Amateur Rowing Association – http://www.ara-rowing.org/

The International Rowing Federation – http://www.fisa.org/

Henley Royal Regatta – http://www.hrr.co.uk/

See also:

Doggett's Coat and Badge; Henley Royal Regatta; Holme Pierrepont; Strathclyde Water Park; University Boat Race

-Chris Dodd

Royal International Horse Show

The inaugural Royal International Horse Show took place in 1907. It opened at Olympia with the title of the 'International Horse Show'. It added the word 'Royal' four years later with the advent of the King George V Gold Cup showjumping competition. The Olympia era was, in the words of sport historian Sir Derek Birley, a mixture of traditions with 'end-of-hunting-season frolicking' and 'military eventing'. While the show survived the social and economic vagaries of the First World War, it was suspended in 1939 with the onset of the Second

World War. In 1945, the show resurfaced at the White City, and for 1945 and 1946 it was re-titled the Victory Show. In 1947, it was rein-stated as the Royal International Horse Show and, according to Peter Jeffery, 'became the Mecca for anyone connected with horses, attracting vast audiences for showjumping and showing classes as well as competitions for the then-new riding club movement'.

In 1968, the show shifted from the White City to Wembley Stadium's soccer pitch, a venue better known for international soccer games and championship Rugby League fixtures. Unlike Wimbledon or the Boat Race – with very much fixed and permanent locations – the Royal International Horse Show is the quintessential peripatetic sporting event. In 1970, it moved to the indoor Wembley arena. In 1983, it returned to the White City, but when the White City closed it moved to the National Exhibition Centre at Birmingham. In 1992, it moved to Hickstead (10 miles north of Brighton) and was welcomed there by showjumping icon, entrepre-neur and Hickstead owner, Douglas Bunn.

The show is administered by the British Horse Society and is its annual flagship for members and the public. The current commer-cial sponsor is Traxdata, a computer media company.

Hickstead, set in the green Sussex countryside, is considered one of the greatest showjumping venues in the world. Over 150 trade exhibitors attend the Royal International Horse Show and the trade-stand village covers a major portion of the showground. Commercial sponsorship is a key element in contemporary equestrian sport, as can be seen from the 1999 programme. The pre-mier events were the Samsung Nations Cup, the Hasseroder Queen Elizabeth II Cup, and the Traxdata King George V Gold Cup.

During the 1950s, television transformed showjumping into an everyman's at-home drama. The British Broadcasting Corporation drew several million peak-time viewers and Dorian Williams, described by Steven Barnett as the 'voice of B.B.C. showjumping', used his upper-class accent and nuanced expressions of gentility to describe riders of all classes – from blue-collar Harvey Smith to 'blue blood' Ann Moore – and present an élitist sport as egalitar-ian fare.

References:

Barnett, S., *Games and Sets: the Changing Face of Sport on Television* (London: British Film Institute, 1990).

Birley, D., *Playing the Game: Sport and British Society, 1910-1945* (Manchester: Manchester University Press, 1995).

Laird, D., *Royal Ascot* (London: Hodder & Stoughton, 1976), pp. 14-18.

Official Traxdata Royal International Horse Show Programme (7-11 July 1999).

Websites:

The Royal International Horse Show – http://www.hickstead.co.uk/RIhs.htm

See also:

Horse of the Year Show; Showjumping

-John Crawford/Scott Crawford

Royal Navy Sports Control Board

The Royal Navy and Royal Marines Sports Control Board was set up in 1919 in response to demand from the Fleet. Its activities were more or less restricted to providing advice to, and general supervision of, recognized recre-ational organizations, so as to enable them to become self-supporting. Capital was raised ini-tially by charging gate money at selected events.

Over the years, the sphere of influence of the Sports Control Board and its composition have changed and expanded. Today, as well as providing general encouragement and guidance to sport at all levels, it is responsible for co-ordinating, financially and otherwise, the activi-ties of the thirty-three recognized Royal Navy and Royal Marines sports associations, as com-pared to a total of thirteen which existed in 1922. The Board also provides financial assis-tance for coaching, kitting out newly commissioned ships and to individual sportsmen and sportswomen of international potential. However, it is the various associations themselves that actually provide direct professional and administrative support to Navy sportspersons, for example by defining coaching policies or supplying officials.

The execution of the policy for sport and recreation throughout the Royal Navy is the responsibility of the Director of Navy Physical Training and Sport, who is also the head of the Physical Training Branch. He is based at H.M.S. Temeraire in Portsmouth. The support and facilities provided by the Royal Navy for its personnel are second to none and, throughout the country from Cornwall to Scotland, there are sports centres that provide sailors with every kind of sporting opportunity.

-Brian Davies

Royal Patronage

Having royal patronage in the titular sense is quite widespread amongst sporting bodies, but royal patronage which takes the form of both active participation and enthusiastic support occurs in a much narrower range of sports.

Queen Elizabeth II has inherited a royal enthusiasm for horse-racing which can be traced back beyond Queen Anne's decision to create the Royal Ascot racecourse in 1711 to the era of Henry VIII and Queen Elizabeth I. An owner of racehorses, like her mother, her regular arrivals at Royal Ascot on Ladies Day and at the Epsom Derby are eagerly awaited and enthusiastically greeted by the crowds.

The Queen with her horse Hopeful Venture after it had won the Hardwicke Stakes on the last day of the Royal Ascot Meeting, 1968 (Hulton Getty Picture Collection)

335

In modern times, the Queen's elder children, the Princess Royal and the Prince of Wales, have shown themselves, like their father, the Duke of Edinburgh, to be actively engaged in horsemanship. The Princess Royal's career as a three-day eventer reached a climax when she represented Great Britain at the Moscow Olympics in 1980. Although now ruled out by injury, the Prince of Wales had a long career as a polo player. In recent times, the Duke of Edinburgh has been at the forefront of the developing sport of carriage racing.

No Wimbledon All-England Tennis Final is complete without the presence of the Duke and Duchess of Kent, who have given their active support to the event for many years. This support was inherited from the Duke's mother, Princess Marina, and the present Duchess's individual interest in the players is always apparent and greatly appreciated.

Horsemanship and tennis are the principal sporting preoccupations of the Royal Family in modern times, but the regular royal presences at all the great modern sporting occasions, such as the F.A. Cup Final, the Calcutta Cup Rugby matches, Rugby League Challenge Cup Finals and the Braemar Highland Games, all show the natural affinity the Royal Family have with the sporting enthusiasms of the nation.

References:

Laird, D., *Royal Ascot* (London: Hodder & Stoughton, 1976), pp. 14-18.

See also:

Ascot; Horse-racing; Sailing; U.K. Sailing Academy, Cowes

-Trevor James

Rugby League

Origins and Development

Rugby League was born on August 29th, 1895, when representatives of the twenty-one leading Rugby Union clubs in the North of England met at the George Hotel in Huddersfield to found the Northern Rugby Football Union (N.R.F.U.).

The immediate cause of the split was the refusal of the Rugby Football Union (R.F.U.) to allow clubs to pay players compensation for time lost at work due to playing the game, otherwise known as 'broken time'. The George Hotel meeting agreed to sanction the payment of six shillings per day for 'broken time'.

The origins of the break date back to the 1880s, when Rugby became a mass spectator sport throughout Yorkshire and most of Lancashire, bringing an influx of working-class players to the fore. Fearing a loss of control of its sport, the R.F.U. refused to modify its opposition to payments for play and forced the northern clubs to split.

Confined to its northern strongholds, Rugby League developed into a distinct sport. In 1898, the line-out was abolished and in 1906, the number of players per side was reduced to thirteen. The ruck and maul were also abolished and replaced with an orderly play-the-ball after a tackle. Goals were reduced in value to place the emphasis on open play and the scoring of tries. This philosophy continues to animate the sport, as was seen in 1966 when the 'limited tackle' rule was introduced.

The game spread to Australia and New Zealand in 1907, regular tours to and from these countries becoming an essential feature of the game, to France in 1934 and a host of other countries in the late 1980s. Despite this, the professional wing of the sport has largely remained locked in the North of England, with the partial exception of London.

Governance and Administration

Since its inception, the Rugby Football League (R.F.L.), as the N.R.F.U. became in 1922, has governed the sport. The R.F.L. is answerable to the Rugby League Council, which comprises the member professional clubs. Internationally, Rugby League is governed by the Rugby League International Federation, a successor to the Ruby League International Board, which was founded in 1948.

The amateur game, which is played by around 1,500 clubs throughout Britain and Ireland, is administered separately by the British Amateur Rugby League Association, which was founded in 1973.

At every level, the game is organized on a league basis, the very top professional flight being the Super League. In 1995, following a deal with British Sky Broadcasting (BSkyB), the professional season was switched from winter to summer.

Knockout cup competitions are also a feature of the game, the most famous being the Challenge Cup, the final of which is played at Wembley each year. In this combination of league and knockout tournaments, the structure of the sport closely resembles that of soccer.

Leaders and Personalities

Many of the sport's most influential personalities are enshrined in its Hall of Fame.

Harold Wagstaff, captain of Huddersfield and Great Britain in the years immediately preceding and following the First World War, was instrumental in shaping a 'scientific' mode of play in which both backs and forwards were expected to run, handle and pass the ball.

Gus Risman, Great Britain captain in the pre- and post-Second World War eras, was the first man to captain two separate sides, Salford and Workington Town, to league and Challenge Cup triumphs. Roy Francis, who began his coaching career with Hull in 1951 and was probably the first black man ever to coach a British professional sports team, was a pioneer in the use of sports science and psychology.

Off the field, the position of secretary, later known as the chief executive, of the R.F.L. has historically wielded great influence in the sport. Joseph Platt oversaw the distinctive changes to the game following its birth in 1895. He was succeeded in 1920 by Scotsman John Wilson,

who was instrumental in France's adoption of the game and the decision to take the Challenge Cup final to Wembley. Bill Fallowfield's reign lasted from 1946 to 1974 and encompassed both the post-war attendance boom and the rapid retraction of the game's support in the 1960s. Under David Oxley, the game consolidated its base and took limited steps to expand its appeal. Appointed in 1992, Maurice Lindsay signed the historic and highly controversial 1995 deal with BSkyB that established the Super League and summer Rugby, yet his regime was the most short-lived of all, Lindsay being succeeded in 1998 by Neil Tunnicliffe.

Famous Venues

Unlike Rugby Union, Rugby League has never felt the need to build a national stadium of its own. Probably the most prominent British Rugby League venue is Wembley, which stages the Challenge Cup final every year and test matches with Australia and, in 1993, New Zealand.

The first cup final was played in 1929, when Wigan defeated Dewsbury, and the first Rugby League international was staged there the following year when Wales lost 10-26 to Australia.

The annual trip of tens of thousands of Rugby League supporters to London to see the cup final has acquired a quasi-pilgrimage status, so much so that it became the basis for playwright Alan Plater's play and a television series, *Trinity Tales*, in the 1970s.

Headingley, the host of the first Challenge Cup final in 1897, and Bradford's Odsal Stadium, for many years home of the world record Rugby League crowd, are still among the sport's most prominent grounds.

Wigan's Central Park, opened in 1902, was the game's most historic ground in Lancashire, having staged almost fifty international matches, three Challenge Cup and five Championship finals. Wigan moved from Central Park to the JJB Stadium in Wigan in 1999.

The lack of investment in stadia and the increased safety requirements following the publication of the Taylor Report in 1990 led to a number of other clubs abandoning their traditional homes and either building new grounds or sharing with local soccer clubs, for example, Huddersfield, who in 1994 took up shared residence with Huddersfield Town at the new £16 million, state-of-the-art Alfred McAlpine Stadium.

Famous Competitions

The league championship has always been the most important tournament in Rugby League. Indeed, part of the reason for the formation of the Northern Union was the desire for a structured league competition for the best clubs.

The sport's first champions were Manningham, later to transform themselves into Bradford City A.F.C. With the exception of a handful of seasons, all professional clubs played in the same division until 1973, when a two division structure was introduced.

Until the advent of the two division system, the champions were decided by a play-off system composed of the leading teams in the league. In 1960, the Championship Final between Wakefield Trinity and Wigan attracted over 83,000 spectators. This concept was revived in 1998 to decide the Super League champions.

However, first above all other Rugby League competitions for romance and spectacle is the Rugby League Challenge Cup. Batley beat St Helens at Headingley in the inaugural 1897 competition. Before moving to Wembley on a permanent basis in 1929, the final was played at a number of different league grounds across the North of England.

Modelled on the F.A. Cup, the early stages of the competition are played by amateur teams, the most successful of which win the right to play against the professional teams in the later rounds.

The most successful Challenge Cup side are Wigan, who by 1998 had won the trophy six-teen times and had a run of forty-three unbeaten matches in the competition between 1988 and 1996.

Memorable Events

Rugby League is unusual among sports in that it has a precise date and place of formation. Consequently, the 1895 meeting at Huddersfield's George Hotel is probably the most famous event in the history of the sport. The 1954 Challenge Cup Final replay at Odsal, which attracted an official gate of 102,569, is also one of its key moments.

On the field, the July 1914 match between Britain and Australia in Sydney has gone down in history as the 'Rorke's Drift' Test Match, after the British army's defence in the face of overwhelming odds of Rorke's Drift in the 1879 Zulu War. Down to nine men at one stage, an injury-hit British team led by Harold Wagstaff beat a full-strength Australian side 14-6 to win the series.

The second test match of the 1958 Anglo-Australian series in Brisbane rivals the 1914 test for heroism. Great Britain levelled the series despite having only twelve men, four of those suffering from serious injuries, including captain Alan Prescott who played all but three minutes with a broken arm.

In the 1968 Challenge Cup Final, a last minute try left Wakefield Trinity 11-10 behind Leeds. With the final kick of the match, Don Fox, one of the most reliable kickers in the game, only had to convert the try from in front of the goalposts to win the Cup. In torrential rain and on national television, he missed. Rarely has the thin line between sporting success and failure been so cruelly highlighted.

Concepts and Terminology

Although its origins are in Rugby Union, Rugby League has developed a distinct terminology of its own and has also imported concepts and terms from both Australian Rugby League and American football.

The 'play-the-ball' is its most distinct feature. Also known as a ruck in Australia, the play-the-ball takes place after a tackle has been completed. The tackled player gets to his feet, puts the ball down in front of him and, with his foot, rolls it back to the player standing behind him, known as the 'dummy half'.

As with the scrimmage in American football, the play-the-ball was introduced to speed the game up and remove from the game the disorderly and violent rucks and mauls of Rugby Union.

Each side has six tackles, or play-the-balls, in which to score. If they do not, the ball is handed over to their opponents for six tackles. The concept of 'limited tackle' Rugby League was introduced at the start of the 1966-1967 season. Possession of the ball was initially restricted to four tackles, as in American football, but was increased to six in 1972.

The need to make the sport more attractive to spectators, and also to increase the involvement of players, has underpinned the evolution of League into a distinct sport.

Tries are therefore worth four points, double the value of goals, while a drop-goal, known as a 'field-goal' in Australia – goals scored from a kick when the ball is dropped and kicked at the moment it hits the ground – are worth only one point.

References:

Collins, T., *Rugby's Great Split: Class, Culture and the Origins of Rugby League Football* (London: Frank Cass, 1998).

Delaney, T., *The Grounds of Rugby League* (Keighley: The Author, 1991).

Gate, R., *The Struggle for the Ashes: the History of Anglo-Australian Rugby League Test Matches* (Ripponden: The Author, 1986).

Further reading:

Moorhouse, G., *A People's Game: the Centenary History of Rugby League Football, 1895-1995* (London: Hodder & Stoughton, 1995).

Websites:

The British Amateur Rugby League Association – http://www.barla.org.uk/

The Rugby Football League – http://www.rfl.uk.com/

See also:

Headingley; Odsal Stadium; Wembley Stadium; World Cup Rugby League

-Tony Collins

Rugby Union

Origins and Development

Although there are many claims as to the folk origins of the game of Rugby Union, the most popular originates in England, where in 1823 a young eighteen-year-old student from Rugby School named William Webb Ellis is alleged to have picked up the ball during an intra-school game and grounded it at the far end of the opposing sides' area. The plaque at Rugby School reads 'This stone commemorates the exploit of William Webb Ellis who with fine disregard for the rules of football as played in his time first took the ball in his arms and ran with it, thus originating the distinctive feature of the Rugby game.' His fellow students and school officials censured the boy but he had planted the idea of running with the ball.

The acceptance of the game unintentionally founded at Rugby School was slow, gradual and fragmented. In 1846, a meeting of school representatives was called at Cambridge in an attempt to unify the game of football. Concurrently, the handling game also began to take shape. The Rugby School rules of 1846 provided a code of play, albeit diffuse and somewhat confusing, that nonetheless constituted a definitive moment in that the practice of Rugby became legalized and encoded. Allegedly the first Rugby club was formed at Cambridge in 1839, with Edinburgh Academy (1857), Merchiston Castle (1858), Blackheath (1858) and Richmond (1861)

W. L. Thomas. 'Football at Rugby', signed and dated 1870. Pen and ink sketch (Hulton Getty Picture Collection)

amongst the earliest clubs to be formed. The first Edinburgh Academy match against a team from the University of Edinburgh was an extraordinary affair, with the match being played over four Saturdays starting on December 26th, 1857, and finishing on January 16th, 1858. When football was introduced as a sport at Oxford University, the Rugby game was favoured and the Oxford University Club was formed in 1869, with Cambridge University following in 1872. The Rugby Football Union was formed in 1871, with the Scottish Football Union emerging in 1873. In 1874, the Irish Rugby Union was formed in Dublin, while the Welsh Rugby Union was founded in Neath in 1881.

One of the oldest international fixtures is that of the Calcutta Cup match played annually between Scotland and England. The inscription upon the original cup reads 'The Calcutta Cup presented to the Rugby Football Union by the Calcutta Football Club as an international challenge cup to be played for annually by England and Scotland-1878.' The first Calcutta Cup match was played at Raeburn Place in Edinburgh in 1879. The records on the base of the original cup carry an anomaly, however, for although the cup was first competed for in 1879, an inspection of the plinth shows records extending back to the first international in 1871, eight years before the Calcutta Cup came into being.

In England, during the early 1870s, Rugby football was played and watched by a relatively homogenous upper-middle-class clientele and confined mainly to the clubs and schools of the South. Already by the end of that decade, it had begun to permeate downward through this class hierarchy, particularly in the North. According to *Barbarians, Gentlemen and Players* (1979), the period from about 1850 to 1900 was but a stage in the development of the game when football in its public-school forms spread into society at large and when independent clubs came to form the principal base for the game. It was also during this period (in 1895) that the game of Rugby 'split' into the then amateur game of Rugby Union and the professional game of Rugby League. Rugby Union became a professional sport when the International Rugby Football Board (I.R.F.B., founded in 1886) declared in 1995 that the amateur principles upon which the game had been founded should no longer constitute the basis for its organization and that it should become an open game.

Although uneven, by the end of the 19th century the Rugby Union game had also been subject to a process of diffusion throughout the colonies and dominions of the British Empire. This might be viewed as an early stage of the globalization of Rugby associated with the modern Rugby World Cup. By the end of the 20th century, the 1999 Rugby World Cup, which was won by Australia, involved teams from South Africa, Scotland, Spain, Uruguay, New Zealand, England, Tonga, Italy, France, Fiji, Canada, Namibia, Wales, Argentina, Samoa, Japan, Argentina, Australia, Ireland, the United States and Romania.

Famous Venues

The four home countries' international grounds are the best known British and Irish Rugby venues, Dublin's Lansdowne Road being the oldest. It was first used for a provincial game in 1876 and for an international match in 1878, when England were the visitors. The ground has undergone several facelifts since then, with stands being added and rebuilt on the east and west sides in 1908, 1927, 1955 and 1983, though its capacity is still only 50,000. Unusually for a major sporting arena, there remain open terraces for standing spectators at each end. Belfast's Ravenhill ground, which held only 30,000, was also an international venue until 1954.

Cardiff Arms Park has been the citadel of Welsh Rugby since the first international played

there in 1884. It was so named because the ground adjoined the Cardiff Arms Inn, where for many years players changed and walked to the ground, even for internationals. Its first stand to accommodate seated spectators was built in 1881; several additions followed until a major double-decker stand was erected in 1934. Further extensive rebuilding occurred between 1968 and 1984, and again between 1997 and 1999, to provide a 72,500-seater state-of-the-art Millennium Stadium to host the 1999 Rugby World Cup. Cardiff R.F.C. played on the Arms Park from their formation in 1875 until 1970; they now have their own ground, which has retained the name Cardiff Arms Park, adjoining the Millennium Stadium. No other international ground in the world is located so centrally in the heart of its capital city.

The Twickenham ground which staged the Rugby World Cup in England in 1991 was by then unrecognizable from 'Billy Williams' cabbage patch', the 10-acre market-garden site bought by the R.F.U. in 1907. The first game played there was between Harlequins and Richmond in October 1909, and the first international match the one between England and Wales in January 1910. The ground, cavernous but cold, has been further developed since 1991 and now boasts a 75,000 capacity stadium.

Inverleith in Edinburgh was Scotland's main international ground until 1925. In 1922, the Scottish Rugby Union bought land at Murrayfield, on the city's western outskirts, that had been used by the Edinburgh Polo Club, and development was completed in time to stage the final international match of the 1924-1925 season. A peculiar feature of Murrayfield was the installation in 1959 of an underground heating system, the famous 'electric blanket'. Murrayfield originally had three large uncovered terraces for standing spectators and a capacity of 80,000 (exceeded by the world record 104,000 who watched Scotland versus Wales in 1975). Since then, the ground has been converted into a 70,000 all-seater covered stadium.

341

England's Lawrence Dallaglio wins a line out against Wales in the Five Nations at Twickenham, February 21st 1998 (Action Images)

There are several famous club venues with historic associations, like Llanelli's Stradey Park, Swansea's St Helens and Leicester's Welford Road, all of which have, in their time, hosted international matches.

Famous Competitions

Rugby Union was one of the last major sports to establish a world championship when pressure from the Southern Hemisphere countries persuaded the more cautious Europeans to agree to the introduction of a Rugby World Cup tournament in New Zealand in 1987. It has been held every four years ever since; of the home countries England has the best record, reaching the final in 1991, when they were beaten 12-6 by Australia.

The four home countries began playing each other in the 1880s, and by 1910 they also included France, thus creating the 'Five Nations' championship, though the phrase only came into common usage in the 1960s. It became the 'Six Nations' with the inclusion of Italy in 1999-2000.

Seven-a-side Rugby is a Scottish invention, its beginnings attributed to a Melrose butcher in 1883. It established itself permanently in the Scottish Borders, and spread southwards. The Middlesex Sevens, established in 1926, remain an end-of-season high point in the social calendar of English Rugby, while the major international showpiece, the Hong Kong Sevens, began in 1976, followed by the Rugby World Cup Sevens in 1993.

At the full fifteen-a-side level, local as opposed to international competitions were seen as inimical to the amateur ideal, and for more than eighty years the only all-England competition was the County Championship, first won by Yorkshire in 1888-1889. It still exerts an appeal in areas of strong county identity like Cornwall, but its significance has been eroded by the creation of an English club cup competition, first sponsored by the John Player tobacco company in 1971-1972. Between 1984 and 1996, the competition was dominated by Bath, who were also virtually undefeated in the English national league structure set up in 1987. Wales followed a similar pattern, with a Cup competition established in 1971-1972 (won by Llanelli eleven times by 2000) and a national league structure in 1990. The Irish Provincial Championship was first played in 1946-1947, with an All-Ireland club championship established in 1990, while the innovators in this sphere, surprisingly given their traditional conservatism in Rugby matters, were Scotland, where leagues had been introduced in 1973-1974, and a club cup competition in 1995-1996.

The (Heineken) European Cup was launched in 1955-1956, and was expanded by the introduction of a second tier of competition, a European Conference containing twenty-four sides from the home countries, France, Italy and Romania, the following season.

Famous Sides

The Welsh XV of 1905 ranks as one of the most celebrated in the annals of the game, as Wales were the only side to defeat the New Zealand All Blacks on their first tour of the British Isles. Captained by E. Gwyn Nicholls, this was a Wales side whose nucleus won six Triple Crowns between 1900 and 1911. The inter-war period (1919-1939), however, was dominated by the mostly public-school educated sides of England and Scotland. The English side of the 1920s, when England won four Grand Slams, were notable for the polished halfback play of W. J. A. Davies and C. A. Kershaw, in concert with the robust and technically advanced backrow of A. F. Blakiston, A. T. Voyce and W. W. Wakefield, who captained the side between 1924 and 1927.

Scotland won the Triple Crown on three occasions between the wars, but their only Grand Slam (until 1984) was won in 1925, when the entire threequarter line consisted of the speedy and high-scoring Oxford University quartet of A. C. Wallace, G. G. Aitken, G. P. S. Macpherson (captain) and I. S. Smith.

Ireland, captained by hooker Karl Mullen and inspired by the genius of Jack Kyle at outside-half, enjoyed a golden era in the late 1940s, winning consecutive Triple Slams (1948, 1949) and their one and only Grand Slam to date in 1948.

For sheer consistency (unbeaten at home in the Five Nations between 1969 and 1982) and the brilliance of their backs (Gareth Edwards, Barry John, J. P. R. Williams, Gerald Davies, Phil Bennett), the Welsh sides of the 1970s that won six Triple Crowns and three Grand Slams between 1969 and 1979 stand out above all the others. The 1971 side was arguably the finest of them all; after clinching the Grand Slam with a magnificent win against a rampant French side in Paris, this team, captained by John Dawes, provided the majority of the first ever British Lions team to win a test series in New Zealand later that year.

At the collective level, the most successful British and Irish Lions teams have been, in addition to those of 1971, Willie John McBride's undefeated 1974 side and Martin Johnson's 1997 Lions, both of which won test series in South Africa.

Memorable Matches

A number of memorable matches might be mentioned and the following are but a selection from the history of the game of Rugby Union in Britain.

Academy Ground, Edinburgh, March 27th, 1871 – Scotland versus England – this was the first Rugby international ever played. Each side consisted of twenty players and the game was played for fifty minutes each half. Watched by 4000 spectators, Scotland won by a goal and a try to a try. This fixture became the Calcutta

Cup match when, on closing down, the Calcutta Football Club converted its funds into silver to produce the trophy first played for in 1879.

Cardiff Arms Park, December 16th, 1905 – Wales 3 New Zealand 0 – a game hailed at the time as being for 'the world championship' and still regarded in both countries as the most famous ever. The All Blacks were making their first visit to the British Isles, and by the time they reached Wales on the final leg of their tour, they were unbeaten, having amassed over 800 points and conceded only 27 in twenty-seven games. After thirty minutes play a well-rehearsed decoy move to the right saw Welsh wing Teddy Morgan race over in the left hand corner to break the stalemate in a closely contested struggle and secure the only score of the game. Controversy subsequently surrounded the non-award by referee John Dallas of Scotland of a try claimed by Bob Deans of New Zealand.

Twickenham, January 3rd, 1925 – England 11 New Zealand 17 – the Second All Blacks team of 1924-1925 were undefeated when they arrived at 'H.Q.' for the final game of the tour. England were riding high, having won the Grand Slam in 1921, 1923 and 1924. The game was notable not so much for the All Blacks' confirmation of their invincibility as for the first sending off in international Rugby, when referee Albert Freethy (Wales), frustrated from the kick-off by continuous mayhem among two vigorous sets of forwards, issued a warning that the next offender would be dismissed. In the tenth minute this proved to be the All Blacks' second row forward, Cyril Brownlie, who left the field amidst the hushed silence of 60,000 spectators including the Prince of Wales (later Edward VIII), whose presence was deemed to have made the incident more regrettable.

Murrayfield, March 21st, 1925 – Scotland 14 England 11 – this game saw the opening of the home of Scottish Rugby. England had been champions in 1924 but Scotland, who had already beaten France, Wales and Ireland, posed a potent threat through their brilliant old Oxford University threequarter line. 70,000 were admitted, the largest crowd to watch a Rugby match to that date, and thousands were locked outside. Those inside saw canny outside half Herbert Waddell guide a young Scotland team to victory over a veteran England side, some of whose senior members collapsed in relief and exhaustion at the final whistle.

Twickenham, January 4th, 1936 – England 13 New Zealand 0 – this game etched itself on the public memory after cinema newsreels of the time showed the two spectacular first-half tries by the dashing Russian prince, Alexander Obolensky, the second of which was a magnificent diagonal sweep across the defence from right to left culminating in a glorious 40-yard sprint for the line. A further try by the other wing, Hal Sever, and a Peter Cranmer dropped goal, sealed victory over the third All Blacks, whose only other defeats on their 1934-1935 tour were by Swansea and Wales.

Ravenhill, Belfast, March 12th, 1948 – Ireland 6 Wales 3 – this was the year of Ireland's Grand Slam; to clinch it they needed to beat a Welsh side blessed with the talents of the likes of Bleddyn Williams and Haydn Tanner. Ireland dominated through the intensive spoiling tactics of their magnificent back row of Jim McCarthy, Des O'Brien and Bill McKay. Winning try scorer Chris Daly was mobbed by the 30,000 capacity crowd at the end of the match, which brought the Irish their first Triple Crown since 1899, and their only Grand Slam to date.

Cardiff Arms Park, April 15th, 1967 – Wales 34 England 21 – the classic 'Boys' Own Paper' story. This fixture had been dogged by tight marking and low scoring for many years. Wales had already lost the season's previous three matches, while England were hoping for the Triple Crown. Eighteen-year-old Keith Jarrett of Newport, chosen out of position at full back, scored a phenomenal 19 points; as well as kicking all his goals, he raced on to an English punt upfield to dash 50 yards along the touchline for one of Wales's five tries to England's three in a game that presaged the high-scoring internationals of the future.

Murrayfield, February 6th, 1971 – Scotland 18 Wales 19 – a match of the highest drama as two attacking sides exchanged the lead continuously throughout the match until Wales seized it with five minutes left and Scotland had insufficient time to regain it. The crucial score came from a Gerald Davies try, which required a conversion from near the touch-line to win the match. London Welsh flanker, John Taylor, duly obliged with a superb left-footed kick, dubbed 'the greatest conversion since St Paul'.

Murrayfield, March 17th, 1990 – Scotland 13 England 7 – Scottish Rugby's greatest moment. At stake for both sides were not only the Calcutta Cup, but the Triple Crown and Grand Slam as well. The most dramatic moment preceded the game itself. England took the field first, and there was a long pause when, in an atmosphere choking with tension, powerful loose-head prop and captain David Sole led Scotland out with measured tread at a solemn walking pace.

Wembley, April 11th, 1999 – Wales 32 England 31 – a hair-raising cliff-hanger, the final Five Nations match of the century. England, captained by Lawrence Dallaglio, were once again lined up for the Triple Crown; Wales had already lost to Scotland and Ireland but against all expectations had snatched a magnificent 34-33 victory in Paris. Superb place kicking by Neil Jenkins, powerful scrum-maging and tenacious defence kept Wales in touch with England until a dramatic last-minute try by Scott Gibbs, converted by the unerring Jenkins, gave Wembley (Wales' temporary home during the building of Cardiff's Millennium Stadium) one of the most spine-tingling moments in its history.

References:

Davidson, J. Mcl., *The International Rugby Union: a Compendium of Scotland's Matches* (Edinburgh: Polygon, 1994).

Dunning, E. and Sheard, K., *Barbarians, Gentlemen and Players* (Oxford: Martin Robertson, 1979).

Griffiths, J., *The Book of English International Rugby 1871-1982* (London: Willow, 1982).

Smith, D. and Williams, G., *Fields of Praise, the Official History of the Welsh Rugby Union 1881-1981* (Cardiff: University of Wales Press, 1980).

Van Esbeck, E., *One Hundred Years of Irish Rugby: the Official History of the Irish Rugby Football Union* (Dublin: Gill and Macmillan, 1974).

Further reading:

Macrory, J., *Running with the Ball: the Birth of Rugby Football* (London: Harper, 1991).

Money, T., *Manly and Muscular Diversions: Public Schools and the Nineteenth-Century Sporting Revival* (London: Duckworth, 1997).

Reason, J. and James, C., *The World of Rugby: a History of Rugby Union Football* (London: B.B.C., 1979).

Websites:

The Irish Rugby Union website – http://www.irfu.ie/

The Rugby Football Union website – http://www.rfu.com/

The Scottish Rugby Union website – http://www.sru.org.uk/

The Welsh Rugby Union website – http://www.wru.co.uk/

See also:

Cardiff Arms Park; Murrayfield; Myths; Twickenham; World Cup Rugby Union

-Gareth Williams/Grant Jarvie

Ryder Cup

The Ryder Cup was donated for play between teams of American and British professionals by Samuel Ryder, seed merchant and enthusiastic golfer, in 1927. Impressed by an unofficial match at Wentworth in 1926, won convincingly by the British team, he was inspired to present the Cup. The first match was played in 1927 in Worcester, Massachusetts and since then, barring wartime, it has been played every second year. It was alternately held in the United States and Britain until 1997, when continental Europe staged the event for the first time.

The first five events went to the home teams, but after that the Cup was dominated by the Americans until well into the 1980s, with only one post-war British victory, in 1957, and one tie in 1969. The balance began to change when, in 1979, continental players were made eligible. In 1985, Europe won at the Belfry and followed this with their first victory on American soil, in 1987. Since then, a series of closely fought battles have ended in a draw in 1989, American victories in 1991, 1993 and 1999 and European triumphs in 1995 and 1997.

Selection methods and format have changed frequently, but the friendly rivalry between the two teams has not. Professionals play not for money or even for personal glory, but for their country or continent and their team-mates, and offer their best in the battle to win the Ryder Cup.

References:

Laidlaw, R. (ed.), *The Royal and Ancient Golfer's Handbook 1998* (London: Macmillan Press, 1998).

Lewis, P. N., Clark, E. R. and Grieve, F. C., *A Round of History at the British Golf Museum* (St Andrews: Royal and Ancient Golf Club Trust, 1998).

Viney, L., *The Royal and Ancient Book of Golf Records* (London: Macmillan Press, 1991).

Williams, M., *The Official History of the Ryder Cup 1927-1989* (London: Stanley Paul & Co., 1989).

Websites:

The Ryder Cup – http://www.rydercup.com/

See also:

Golf

-Peter Lewis

S

Sailing

Sailing large yachts competitively has always been the preserve of the rich, due to the costs entailed in building, maintaining and crewing a competitive boat. As noted in *The Game*, the spread of wealth and desire for ostentation in the 19th century gave an impetus to the nouveaux rich who started to take to the water.

The racing of large yachts with fixed keels usually takes place on coastal waters and is referred to as 'Ocean Racing'. The most notable race on the British calendar is the Fastnet Race, which was first run in the 1920s. Races can, of course, be much shorter or longer – for example, the *America's Cup* or *Whitbread Round the World Challenge*. Some fixed-keel boats also race on large expanses of inland waters and estuaries. The Lake District and the Solent are popular British venues.

Dinghy racing is by far the most popular type of sailing in Britain. Although dinghies have been around for many years, there were only two classes of note before the Second World War – the International 12 class and 11 class. The real impetus to the development and spread of the sport came after the Second World War with the popularity of do-it-yourself and the availability of kits. Designer Jack Holt published the plans for making numerous types of dinghy in *Yachting World*, and these were taken up by D.I.Y. enthusiasts, many of whom eventually took to the water and learned to sail. Many new classes evolved, catering for different ages, abilities and purses. These range from the Optimist (child's trainer boat), through the highly popular Mirror (small crew boat) and Laser (single-handed) to the Finn class (an Olympic class). New technologies, such as glass-reinforced plastic hulls and dacron sails, have helped improve performance, reduce cost and also often make them easier to construct.

A major feature of racing is the handicap system, which was introduced in the late 19th century to facilitate racing boats of different sizes on level terms. In handicapped racing, boats start together but the last over the finishing line could still feasibly be the winner.

Britain can boast many world champions over the years, covering just about every class. It has often been said that the close proximity of all Britons to water has helped it to produce so many talented sailors.

The sport has also enjoyed considerable royal patronage over the years. Small boat racing benefited from the Prince of Wales Trophy for the International 14 class, first awarded in 1927. Even today, the Duke of Edinburgh and the Prince of Wales are regulars at Cowes during race week.

References:

The Game: the Marshall Cavendish Encyclopedia of World Sport (London: Marshall Cavendish Ltd, published weekly 1969-72).

Websites:

The Royal Yachting Association – http://www.rya.org.uk/

See also:

Admiral's Cup; Fastnet Race; U.K. Sailing Academy, Cowes

-Richard William Cox

St Andrews

Golf is known to have been played at St Andrews since before 1552, when Archbishop Hamilton reserved the rights of the townspeople to use the links 'for golff, futball, schuteing and all gamis'. As early as 1691, the town was known as the 'metropolis of golfing'.

The golf courses at St Andrews are public courses, run today by the St Andrews Links Trust and Management Committee. There are five 18-hole courses, the Old Course, the New Course (1895), the Jubilee (1897), the Eden (1914), the Strathtyrum (1993) and a 9-hole course, the Balgove (1972). There is also a driving range, practice area and clubhouse.

A round on the Old Course was originally 22 holes, 11 holes out and the same 11 back. In 1764, the first four holes were combined into two to give a round of 18 holes. The shared greens were converted to double ones in the winter of 1856-1857.

A number of St Andrews golf clubs use the links, the most celebrated of these being the Royal and Ancient Golf Club of St Andrews (the R.&A.).

In 1754, twenty-two noblemen and gentlemen of Fife presented a Silver Club to be played for annually over the links of St Andrews. The Society of St Andrews Golfers was to develop from this annual competition, with the winner of the Silver Club becoming Captain. The members met regularly to play golf, but also to dine and drink at local taverns.

From the early 19th century, the Club began to grow dramatically in size and the Captain came to be chosen by election. William IV agreed to be the Club's patron in 1834 and it became the Royal and Ancient Golf Club of St Andrews. In 1854, the Club opened its first permanent base, a clubhouse built adjacent to the course. As the century progressed, the number of golf clubs in Britain increased greatly and the R.&A. developed a position of influence. By 1897, there were around 1,153 golf clubs in Britain, many following the R.&A.'s Rules. There was a feeling that regulation was required and the R.&A., spurred on by outside pressure, set up the Rules of Golf Committee. In 1920, they also took over responsibility for the Open and Amateur Championships, and since 1922, they have organized the Walker Cup with the United States Golf Association.

St Andrewans who made their living from the sport have played an important part in its history. Hugh Philp, acknowledged as one of the greatest clubmakers, was based in St Andrews. Allan Robertson, feather ball maker, and Tom Morris, club and ball maker and greenkeeper at St Andrews, were also among the finest golfers of all time, as was Tom Morris Junior. These are only a few of the great club and ball makers and players who have been based in St Andrews.

References:

Lewis, P. N., Clark, E. R. and Grieve, F. C., *A Round of History at the British Golf Museum* (St Andrews: Royal & Ancient Golf Club Trust, 1998).

Websites:

The St Andrews Links – http://www.standrews.org.uk/main.html

See also:

Golf

-Peter Lewis

Sandyachting (*see* Landyachting)

Scrambling

Scrambling, or moto-cross, is a motorcycle race conducted over natural terrain. Riders as young as six are allowed to race, but riders this young are permitted to use only bikes with automatic transmission and a maximum engine size of 60 cc. Engine capacity for riders up to the age of seventeen is 125 cc, while for adults the maximum bike size is 1300 cc.

The sport has its origins in the south of England where, in 1927, various motorcycle clubs organized a cross-country trail that they thought would be 'a rare old scramble'. The sport henceforth became known as 'scrambling' in Britain. Following the Second World War, the sport became increasingly commercialized, particularly in France. There, a French businessman by the name of Poirer organized commercial meetings in and around Paris. In Europe, the sport adopted the name 'moto-cross', and such was its popularity that an international tournament for national teams, the Moto-Cross des Nations, was formed in 1947.

During its formative years, the top riders came from Britain and Belgium, but during the 1950s their supremacy was increasingly challenged by Swedish riders. In 1952, the Fédération Internationale de Motocyclisme (F.I.M. – International Motorcycling Federation) organized the first European Championships for machines up to 500 cc. The first champion was the Belgian rider V. Leloup.

Though the sport has a strong spectator base in France, Belgium and Britain, it has resisted over-commercialization. It has, however, enjoyed significant television exposure, particularly during the 1960s when it was a regular feature on the B.B.C.'s Saturday *Grandstand* programme. More recently, support for the sport has remained strong in the north of England, particularly in the Pennine region of West Yorkshire, home of the current world indoor and outdoor champion Duggie Lampkin.

References:
The Auto-Cycle Union Handbook (London: Maurice Spalding Publicity, 1975-1988).

Websites:
The Auto-cycle Union – http://www.acu.org.uk/
The International Motorcycling Federation – http://www.fim.ch/en/

See also:
Motorcycle Racing

-Ray Physick

Services Sport

In the mid-19th century, when Muscular Christianity was influencing the preoccupations and focus of English public schools and universities, and thereby creating a strong enthusiasm for purposeful sporting involvement, this enthusiasm was mirrored in the attitudes and behaviour of the Army and the Police. The latter had already recognized the utilitarian benefits of sport, especially the fact that fitness was a key to effectiveness.

Sports days can be traced at all the principal military academies during the mid-19th century – the Royal Military College, Sandhurst; the Royal Military Academy, Woolwich; and the East India Company College, Addiscombe. Woolwich held a sports day of a pattern to be adopted by the public schools as early as 1848, and the College at Addiscombe held similar events twice yearly from 1850 until its closure after the Indian Mutiny.

The East India Company College was an institution that placed a high premium on physical fitness, to the degree that in 1851 the first purpose-built gymnasium in Britain was constructed for its students. Almost alone of the various features of the college, this structure, although wholly modified inside, has survived behind the houses in Havelock Road, East Croydon, until the present day.

The police recognized the inherent value of sport, both in terms of fixtures and in terms of teamwork. As early as 1886, the City of London constabulary had its own athletics club and the Metropolitan Police provided a massive sports ground for its officers at Imber Court, near Thames Ditton. It was said of the Metropolitan Police that they specifically encouraged cross-country running amongst their officers because a fit officer who could pursue a suspect for some distance at a measured pace would be more easily able to make an arrest without resistance from a panicking criminal who did not have that same sense of pace.

As time developed, the Royal Navy and the Royal Air Force also came to be active promoters of sporting excellence, with the Royal Air Force, for example, providing indoor athletics venues at R.A.F. stations such as Stanmore and Cosford. Combined Service teams have been a regular feature of sporting competitions in recent times in such areas as the first-class cricket and Rugby programmes and also in athletics and cross-country running. A number of the most prominent sportsmen and sportswomen have emerged from, and with the active encouragement of, the services, with the former world 1-mile record holder Derek Ibbotson (R.A.F.), hurdler Kriss Akabusi (Army) and middle-distance runner Kelly Holmes (Army) being typical examples.

Although not a disciplined service like the services mentioned above, the emerging fire brigades in the late 19th century also recognized the value of fitness for their staff. Until the White City Stadium closed in 1970, the high point of the regional athletics programme was the London Fire Brigades Sports, an event which was highly competitive, if unconventional with its mixture of handicap and unusual events, such as sack races and obstacle courses for Brigade members, which occurred alongside the A.A.A. Relay Championships that were an established feature of the meeting. The accent on fitness for purpose continues into the present time with very few fire brigade depots being without basketball nets and football goalposts for the use of officers in the monotony between emergency calls.

References:

Cardwell, J., *City of London Police Athletic Club: 100 Years of Heroes, 1886-1986* (London: London Police, 1986).

'Foot Racing at Woolwich', *Bell's Life in London* (14 October 1849).

See also:

Army Physical Training Corps; Army Sport Control Board; R.A.F. Sports Board

-Trevor James

Shinty

The word 'shinty', in Gaelic *iomain* (the older of the two) or *camanachd*, may derive from the Gaelic *sinteag* – to skip, bound, hop, leap – although there may also be a link to the word *shinny* (sometimes *shinnie*), which described a stick and ball game. *Jamieson's Dictionary* refers to shinty play throughout Scotland, on one occasion as 'an inferior species of golf'. Its provenance in England (particularly the north) is detailed in the *English Dialect Dictionary*.

Shinty is played with a stick (called the *caman*, originally made of willow, hazel, oak, elder, elm or birch; now of laminated manufacture) and a ball (originally made from fungus, then wood, wound in twine, or cork with horse hair. The modern ball is approximately the size of a tennis ball and has a cork and worsted interior, and an outer cover made of leather or another approved material.

Shinty was introduced to Scotland, along with Christianity and the Gaelic language, 2,000 years ago by Irish missionaries. Throughout time, versions of stick and ball games have been played in virtually every area of Britain, from wind-swept St Kilda to the Scottish Borders; from Yorkshire's moors to Blackheath in London. Shinty is linked (not always with complete accuracy) to golf and ice hockey, and is played across four continents by Highland exiles. The game also made its mark on the war-ravaged wastes of Europe during the two world wars.

In strictly Scottish terms, the earliest written reference to shinty (or *schynnie*) is in 1589, in an edict in the Kirk Session Records of Glasgow banning the game in the churchyard. Shinty has been the subject of bye-laws and litigation on the streets of Edinburgh, Paisley and Oban and the roads of rural Argyll. However, shinty has never been outlawed in the way that the Irish game of hurling was by the Statutes of Kilkenny and Galway, not even in the aftermath of Culloden, when Highland dress was proscribed and the Gaelic language subjected to a war of attrition.

It was usual in the Highlands to have the principal games of shinty at New Year or Old New Year (January 1st or January 12th/13th), although other festivals were also marked in other areas of the country. Games were often played between two districts or parishes, with no limit to the numbers taking part or the time taken. Usually the stakes were simply the honour of either half of the district. Occasionally a hogshead of whisky was given to the winners by the organizer.

In many areas, shinty died out towards the middle of the 19th century, but continued in places such as Badenoch, Lochaber and Strathglass, where interest never waned and the annual *cluidh-ball*, or ball-play, was maintained. The modern, organized form of shinty dates from October 1893, when the Camanachd Association, the game's ruling body, was formed at Kingussie. Rules and regulations were agreed and a competitive structure established.

Shinty is currently played by teams of twelve with substitutes. There are approximately forty teams in the Association, with games played at all levels, from primary school to international, where Ireland are the regular opponents.

Scotland's record, against overwhelming numerical odds, has been remarkable. A developing women's game is a modern addition.

References:

Etymological Dictionary of the Scottish Language (Paisley: John Jamieson, 1879).

MacLennan, H. D., *Shinty* (Nairn: Balnain Books, 1993).

MacLennan, H. D., *Not an Orchid* (Inverness: Kessock Communications, 1995).

Further reading:

Hutchinson, R., *Camanachd!: the Story of Shinty* (Edinburgh: Mainstream, 1989).

Macdonald, Rev. J. N., *Shinty: a Short History of the Ancient Highland Game*, (Inverness: R. Carruthers, 1932).

Websites:

The Camanachd Association – http://www.shinty.com/main.htm

-Hugh Dan MacLennan

Shooting (*see* Game Shooting; Target Shooting; Wild Pigeon Shooting)

Showjumping

The origins of showjumping can be found in many ancient civilizations, which trained horses to race and to do gymnastics. During the Renaissance period, many of the pastimes practised in ancient Greece were revived, among them gymnastic horse-riding exercises. Indeed, it is from the Renaissance period that modern horse-riding competitions can be traced. Militaristic use of horses during wartime also required a high level of riding skill, and such skill was adapted for sporting use during peacetime. Moreover, during the medieval period, agricultural fairs began to

351

hold exhibitions of horses and horsemanship and this led to the further development of gymnastic and jumping exercises for horses.

Although horse riding was commonplace in historical times, there was considered to be an 'art of horse riding', and present-day showjumping is a modern interpretation of, and development from, this traditional art. The exact date of the first showjumping competition in Britain is unknown, but the sport gained in popularity during the 19th century. The first competitive event was held at the Agricultural Hall Society horse show in 1869. It proved such a popular attraction that other agricultural shows followed suit and began to include showjumping events during the 1870s. However, during this formative period, rules were ad hoc, which led to allegations of unfairness amongst competitors. This eventually led to the adoption of standardized rules at agricultural shows.

Although showjumping made its first Olympic appearance at the 1900 Games, it was 1912 before it became an established Olympic sport. Meanwhile, in 1907, the first International Horse Show was held in Britain, with seven countries competing. With the establishment of the Fédération Équestre Internationale (F.E.I. – International Equestrian Federation) in 1921, international competition and rules became standardized. The F.E.I. governs all international shows, the most important of which are the Nations Cup and the President's Cup. The former is an international team event, each team having four riders, while the latter, established in 1965, constitutes the sport's world championship.

In modern society, just as in the ancient and medieval societies, gymnastic horse riding has strong roots among army officers in the cavalry. This led to showjumping being dominated by men from a military background, particularly during the interwar years. The first post-war Olympic Games in 1948 saw all the competitors for the forty-four showjumping events come from military backgrounds. Since then, however, the influence of the military has declined.

Even before being exposed to extensive television coverage in the 1960s, the sport's spectator base was beginning to grow. Simplification of competition rules and more attractive courses helped prepare the way for this. This also made the sport more telegenic, which in turn increased attendances at events still further. Another factor in the growing popularity of the sport was greater commercial sponsorship, which served to give the sport even more exposure.

The sport obtained its first genuine national governing body in Britain with the establishment of the British Show Jumping Association in 1923. Riding education, on the other hand, is regulated by the British Horse Society. Regional competitions for adults and young people – the Pony Club class – provide a sporting season that reaches its climax in the Horse of the Year Show at the Wembley Arena each year.

References:

Arlott, J. (ed.), *Oxford Companion to Sports and Games* (London: Oxford University Press, 1976).

Podhajsky, A., *The Complete Training of Horse and Rider* (London: Harrap, 1982), pp. 17-20.

Richards, L., *Dressage: Begin the Right Way* (Newton Abbot: David & Charles, 1975).

Websites:

The British Show Jumping Association – http://www.bsja.co.uk/

See also:

Hickstead; Horse of the Year Show

-Trevor James/Ray Physick

Silverstone

The Silverstone Circuit was constructed on a former Royal Air Force Second World War airfield. When it opened in 1948 it was really no more than a sprawling area of tarmac fringed by straw bales. Today it is home to the British Grand Prix, one of the showcase events of Formula 1 Grand Prix motor racing. The British Grand Prix, thanks to national, European and world television satellite coverage, reaches a global audience of 300 million.

Silverstone is located in Northamptonshire, near Towcester. The original race circuit was 3.67 miles (5.9 kilometres) long. The current length is 3.194 miles (5.140 kilometres) and the Silverstone racing compound covers 324 hectares (800 acres). The average width of the track is 15 metres, while the track surface is made out of 'Prixmat' (a stone mastic asphalt). The lengths of the main straights are: Hangar straight (738 metres), Abbey straight (479 metres), Pit straight (421 metres) and Farm straight (200 metres). For the 1998 British Grand Prix, the total seated capacity was 50,389. The cost of a four-day all-admission ticket was $315. The inaugural Silverstone British Grand Prix in 1948 was won by Luigi Villoresi in a Maserati. His average speed was 72.28 miles per hour (116.32 kilometres per hour).

Silverstone has been a dramatic stage for a series of closely contested racing match-ups. The decade of the 1950s saw an Argentinian, an Italian and an Englishman (Juan Manual Fangio, Alberto Ascari and Stirling Moss) driving Italian (Ferraris or Maseratis) or British (Vanwalls) race cars battle one another for World Championship honours. In the 1960s, two Scots, Jackie Stewart and Jim Clark, took on Englishman Graham Hill in new mid-engined machines that had replaced the old front-engined automobiles.

In 1977, England's James Hunt won the British Grand Prix at Silverstone and went on to win the World Championship. In 1998, there was considerable controversy when Michael Schumacher of Germany was awarded the victory as a result of the race commissioners' decision to cancel a ten-second penalty awarded against him during the race.

At the 1998 Silverstone British Grand Prix, racing teams entered were: TWR Arrows, Benetton, Ferrari, Ferrari/Shell, Stewart Grand Prix, Jordan Mugen Honda, Prost, McLaren Mercedes, Minardi, Red Bull Sauber Petronas, Williams and Tyrrell. The Silverstone racing season runs from February to November and features national and international races as well as rally sprints.

The opening rituals and pageantry of the British Grand Prix at Silverstone rivals the atmosphere at the Indianapolis 500 in the United States. As the racing cars line up, there is a 'Red Devils' display (parachuting), a march past by the Band of the Scots Guards, and a fly-over from the 'Red Arrows' (an R.A.F. aerobatics group).

Silverstone is known as the home of British motor racing. On October 3rd, 1998, Silverstone celebrated its 50th anniversary with a Golden Jubilee Party.

References:
Georgano, G. N. (ed.), *The Encyclopedia of Motor Sport* (New York: Viking Press, 1971).

Further reading:
Chick, G., 'Formula 1 Auto Racing', in D. Levinson and K. Christensen (eds.), *The Encyclopedia of World Sport* (Santa Barbara, California: ABC-CLIO, 1996), vol. I, pp. 354-358.

Websites:
Silverstone Circuits Ltd –
http://www.silverstone-circuit.co.uk/

-Scott Crawford

Skating – Figure

Figure skating is distinct from speed skating in that it involves a series of movements, jumps and spins, whereas speed skating is centred on racing. Britain has a long and successful history of figure skating. Originally, figure skating was more popular amongst wealthier city dwellers. Many members of the Royal family were keen on the sport. Queen Victoria's husband, Prince Albert, almost drowned when he fell through the ice while skating. Coupled with danger, there were other problems associated with ice-skating. Previously, skaters had to wait until winter to enjoy their sport, but by 1896 London had three indoor skating rinks.

In competition, there are mens' and womens' individual events and a pairs' event. The competition consists of a long freestyle and short compulsory programme, judged on technical merit and artistic impression. Each judge can award a maximum of six points. Ice dancing is performed in pairs, and is more a form of dance, unlike the pairs event, which has many more jumps and spins.

Figure skating is the oldest Olympic winter sport. The first winner of an individual Olympic event was British woman Florence Syers in 1908. Britain continued to perform well in Olympic skating events. Britain won back-to-back gold medals in the Mens' individual event in 1976 and 1980 with John Curry and Robin Cousins respectively. In 1976, ice dancing was included on the Olympic schedule. In 1984, British ice dance pair Jayne Torvill and Christopher Dean became gold medal winners. They reappeared ten years later to win a bronze medal in 1994, in Lillehammer, Norway.

References:
Bird, D. L., *Our Skating Heritage: a Centenary History of The National Skating Association of Great Britain, 1879-1979* (London: National Skating Association of Great Britain, 1979).

Further reading:
Heller, M. (ed.), *The Illustrated Encyclopedia of Ice Skating* (New York: Paddington Press, 1979).

Websites:
The National Ice Skating Association – http://www.iceskating.org.uk/

See also:
Roller-skating

-Julie Anderson

Skating – Speed

Speed skating originated in the Netherlands and was imported by Frieslanders who worked on the building of canals in Britain. It was adopted first as a means of transport and later as a sport. The first recorded race in Britain was held on the Fens in eastern England in 1763. Every town in the north and east of England had its own champion. There was a good deal of betting on these races throughout the 18th and 19th century.

Speed skating has changed in the 20th century. There are now two types of speed skating – long and short track. Long track has been part of the mens' Olympic programme since Chamonix in 1924 and the womens' since 1960. Long-track skating consists of two skaters racing against the clock on a two-lane 400-metre track. Both men and women compete in a 500, 1000 and 5000 metre race. Men also race in the 10,000 metres, and women have a 3000 metres competition.

The first official short-track meet was in Ayr, Scotland in 1948. The first internationally recognized meet was in Solihull, England in 1978. Short-track speed skating made its official Olympic debut in 1992 at Albertville, France. There is a relay raced in a *peloton*, or group, and an individual event on a track measuring 111 metres in length.

Although a long history of speed skating exists in Britain, no British athlete has won Olympic gold in the sport. Changing climatic conditions have prevented outdoor championships from taking place on a regular basis, especially in the Fens, home of the sport in Britain.

References:
Bird, D. L., *Our Skating Heritage: a Centenary History of the National Skating Association of Great Britain, 1879-1979* (London: National Skating Association, 1979).

Heller, M. (ed.), *The Illustrated Encyclopedia of Ice Skating* (New York: Paddington Press, 1979).

Websites:

The National Ice Skating Association – http://www.iceskating.org.uk/

Further reading:

Liebers, A., *The Complete Book of Winter Sports* (New York: Coward McCann and Geoghegan, 1971).

-Julie Anderson

Skiing

It has always been a little mystifying to the European skiing nations that the British should have had such an influence on the beginnings of modern alpine skiing. After all, northern folk had been skiing for four to five thousand years before the British began lobbying for 'downhill' and 'slalom'. In fact, although there is a monk on skis on Hereford Cathedral's *Mappa Mundi*, and it is clear that some of the Norwegian conquerors used skis during the Viking period, the English did not start skiing until the 19th century.

When the wealthy journeyed to Switzerland in the late 19th century, they found a few Norwegians and Swiss trying skis. The delights of repeating their summer mountain excursions on skis in winter developed into modern alpine skiing.

The Public Schools Alpine Sports Club – in fact an economic venture by the travel promoter, Henry Lunn – organized winter holidays for the upper classses. Lunn's son, Arnold, proselytized for downhill racing as early as 1913, and in the 1920s developed slalom. Both these 'disciplines' had their genesis in winter mountain touring. Once the peak had been reached, the view imbibed and the pipe smoked, the accomplished ski runner tracked the snow as straight down as possible. Early races were often called 'straight races', and 'taking it straight', redolent of the fox-hunt, was a sign of dash and verve. However, once the skier reached the woods, he had to dodge and swerve among the trees. Slalom simulated 'tree running'. Lunn first stuck sticks in the snow, then flags and finally poles, now called gates. He badgered the world ski community, then much under the domination of Norwegian styles, for a decade or more before the Fédération Internationale de Ski (International Ski Federation) finally admitted alpine skiing to the program in 1930. It made its Olympic debut in the Games of 1936.

Until the Second World War, skiing was a sport of the wealthy. Only after the war, and more especially in the 1960s and 1970s, did a vast new clientele with disposable money begin to enjoy the increasing number of packaged vacations in the many new ski centres which mushroomed in the Alps.

The Ski Club of Great Britain, founded in 1903, remains the main source of information for all matters to do with skiing. The Club estimated that 800,000 people would ski in the 1998-1999 season, and the Scottish skiing grounds at Aviemore have faithful clientele. The beginner can learn on artificial slopes – there were twenty-seven in 1980, while the expert can get a packaged helicopter skiing week in Canada's Bugaboos. Cross-country addicts can journey north of the Arctic Circle in Lapland, and all can ski in the summer in New Zealand – leisure time and finances permitting.

British racing had a distinguished history in the 1930s, especially in the women's events. The one British record holder was Graham Wilkie, who briefly held the world speed-skiing title at 212.514 kilometres per hour in 1987.

Although the British do not shine among the array of continentals on the racing circuit, all who enjoy alpine skiing should thank Arnold Lunn, for it was he who 'opened up a new epoch in skiing, and it bore his personal stamp'.

References:

The annual volumes of what came to be titled *The British Ski Year Book*, 1905-1914, 1920-1971; *Ski Survey*, 1972 (Jan.-Feb.) and 1997; and *Ski and Board* (Oct. 1997-).

The billiard room of the Garrick Club in 1869, by H.N. O'Neil (1817-1880) (The Garrick Club; Theartarchive Ltd)

Allen, E. J. B., 'The British Moment in Ski History', Paper read to the Committee on European Sport History seminar, Katowice, Poland, September 1997.

Caulfield, V., *How To Ski and How Not To* (London: Nisbet, 1912).

Lunn, A., *A History of Ski-ing* (Oxford: Oxford University Press, 1927).

Richardson, E. C., *The Ski-Runner* (London: The Author, 1909).

Websites:

The Ski Club of Great Britain – http://www.skiclub.co.uk/

-John Allen

Snooker

Snooker uses a billiards table and twenty-two balls (fifteen red balls, six coloured balls and a white cue ball). According to Garry Chick, 'Snooker was developed in British colonial India in the mid-1870s and is extremely popular in Great Britain and former British colonies, including Canada.'

Neville Chamberlain, the British army officer credited with creating the game, showed a wonderfully inventive streak by linking colours and numbers, thus making the challenge of snooker not just to 'pot' the ball (and so score points), but to set up the cue ball so as to facilitate scoring on subsequent shots. In 1891, in England, the following scoring system was adopted: red ball – 1 point, yellow – 2 points, green – 3 points, brown – 4 points, blue – 5 points, pink – 6 points, and black – 7 points. The game has a marvellous built-in sense of theatre and drama as rival players attempt to gain a rhythmic momentum and ascendancy, by achieving a sequence of shots called a break. The maximum possible number of points in a break is 147. Despite the fact that World Professional Championships commenced in 1927, it was not until April 23rd, 1988, that Cliff Thorburn of Canada achieved a maximum break in world championship competition.

The derivation of the word 'snooker' is intriguing. Originally the word was applied to first-year incoming cadets at the Woolwich Military Academy, England. Chamberlain took the term and used it as his moniker for anyone who lost at the game. To be 'snookered' during the game is when a scoring shot is effectively stymied and obstructed by a ball that the player must not hit with the cue ball.

One of the main factors behind snooker's modern popularity, both as a recreational tap-room amusement and a professional sport, is the remarkable way in which it became an absorbing facet of television entertainment. In 1969, a British survey of top-ten sports most enjoyed on television placed Association Football in first place with support of 52 per cent. Snooker was unranked. Twenty years later, in 1989, the survey returned snooker in first place with a following of 43 per cent. Steven Barnett, in his *The Changing Face of Sports on Television* (1990), has twenty indexed references on snooker. Nevertheless, Barnett was cautious about the permanent nature of snooker's popularity and commented on a sport that had 'almost certainly passed its heyday' and was 'starting to slide'. Richard Holt saw things differently. In *Sport and the British*, he spoke of a sport's renaissance thanks to colour television and noted that B.B.C. 2's television coverage of snooker had transformed the game 'into an extraordinary national obsession'. The game attracts enormous levels of corporate sponsorship, most notably from tobacco and alcohol business interests.

Snooker is no longer exclusively an English sport. Although the 1998-1999 Embassy World Rankings (containing sixteen players) included eight Englishmen, it also included three Scots and other players from Ireland, Wales, Malta, Canada and Thailand.

Nicknames are part and parcel of snooker. James Wattana is 'Thai-Phoon', Alain Robidoux is 'Scoobie', Steve Davis is 'The Nugget', Jimmy White is 'Whirlwind' and John Higgins is 'The Wizard of Wishaw'. In 1998, the 'Wishaw Wizard' won the £220,000 Embassy World Professional Open Championship with an 18-12 victory over Ken Doherty of Ireland, the 1997 winner. Ranked number one in the world in September 1998, Higgins' career earnings had reached £1,383,632.

The contemporary sport in Britain is not without its critics. The 1998 World Championships were shown on B.B.C. television, but late night scheduling and a plethora of 'recorded', as opposed to live, coverage caused much negative comment. 1998 was also the year of the Ronnie O'Sullivan scandal. He was stripped of his Benson and Hedges Irish Masters title and the £61,130 first prize after failing a drug test. The test showed traces of cannabis.

On April 16th, 1998, Fred Davis O.B.E. (born 1913) died at his home in North Wales. While not as good as his legendary elder brother, Joe Davis, who won fifteen world championships, Fred Davis played in the post-Second World War era that saw snooker decline and then re-emerge in the 1970s. Davis won eight world titles and even when the first world rankings appeared in 1976, as a sixty-six year old, he was ranked fourth. When arthritis forced Davis to retire in 1992, he was recognized as the oldest active professional sportsman in the world.

References:
Chick G., 'Billiards', in D. Levinson and K. Christensen (eds.), *Encyclopedia of World Sport* (Santa Barbara, California: ABC-CLIO, 1996), vol. 1, pp. 109-119.

'WWW Snooker', compiled by Hermund Ardalen – http://www.stud.ifi.uio.no/~hermunar/Snooker/

Further reading:
Barnett, S., *Games and Sets: the Changing Face of Sport on Television* (London: British Film Institute, 1990).

Holt, R., *Sport and the British: a Modern History* (Oxford: Oxford University Press, 1990).

-Scott Crawford

Sociology of Sport

Analytically speaking, there has been a debate about the sociology of sport in Britain for at least the past forty years, maybe longer. Indeed, long before sociological thought (Comte,

Spencer and Marx) sought to define the social, Adam Ferguson talked about sport and games as a necessary component of civic life. Writing in the 18th century, Ferguson saw sport as a type of collective ceremony through which community solidarity could be demonstrated.

Numerous factors have contributed to the development of the sociology of sport in Britain but at least three sets of considerations are worth mentioning: (i) the recognition that sport was an important facet of life and could contribute to many of the core sociological debates about structure, agency and social change; (ii) the recognition that sport was not autonomous from the rest of society and that the structure, meaning and organization of sport reflected broader changes in terms of social relations and social conditions in a changing British society; and (iii) the growth of organizations, university modules, courses and specialist journals. Each of these influences helped to support a distinct British contribution to the sociology of sport field.

The sociology of sport has at least two main traditions. The first, which might be called the formal or official approach, has consisted of empirical studies into a range of problems, developments and specific types of sport. The second, by contrast, has involved a more historical and theoretical approach that asks questions about the changing nature of sport and its varying role in terms of social change and social action. The value of the latter approach is that it helps individuals to understand that the social and political dimensions of sporting activity can often reveal answers and questions to broader social concerns. Such concerns might include areas of research such as violence in society, unemployment, sexism, racism, nationalism and poverty, to name but a few central concerns that pervade both sociology and the sociology of sport.

It has generally been accepted that the sociology of sport has historically demanded two sorts of inter-dependent work. First, the development of concepts or ideas that help to reveal how particular cultures or institutions in British society operate; and second, the testing of these ideas against research data. During the 1970s and 1980s, the sociology of sport identified with a number of grand theoretical debates and paradigms that characterized much of what was developing in sociology. A vast amount of literature could easily be associated with different sets of values in terms of Marxist, figurational, functionalist and feminist approaches to sport, to name but a few. Different centres throughout Britain became associated with different schools of thought. Throughout the 1990s, the sociology of sport has become much more eclectic and open and has deliberately moved towards debates with different bodies of knowledge such as history, cultural studies, media studies, organizational studies and feminist studies.

Distinctive topics of sociological research have included such areas as football hooliganism; social inequality through sport; sport and nationalism; sport and labour migration; sporting organizations; sport and youth; global sport; sport and religion; sport and the media; sport, education and society; sport and body culture; sporting cultures; sport and violence; sport and community; sport and racism; and sports policy.

A significant overlap between history and sociology has given rise to different forms of a historical sociology of sport, which has been a focus for much research. Leading figures in the field of sociology have always argued that sociology itself emerged as an attempt to make sense of the profound social transformations between traditional and modern societies, and as these transformations continue to gather pace, so does the attempt to understand the place of sport in these changes.

Different centres throughout Britain have provided an academic base for much of the sociological research that has developed in Britain, notably Leicester University, Stirling University, Loughborough University and Brighton University, amongst others. Among sociology's leading proponents have been Anthony Giddens, Eric Dunning, Jenny Hargreaves, Grant Jarvie, Joe Maguire, Alan Tomkinson and Garry Whannel. Sociology in the future is likely to remain both attractive and an internally divided discipline that attracts criticism from those who are, for whatever reason, resistant to social change. The sociology of sport will continue to develop as a specialist discipline and attract those who are interested in both contemporary and historical aspects of social change, social action and the interdependence of theory and data.

References:

Hargreaves, J., *Sporting Females: Critical Issues in the History and Sociology of Women's Sports* (London: Routledge, 1994).

Jarvie, G. and Maguire, J., *Sport and Leisure in Social Thought* (London: Routledge, 1994).

Kew, F., *Sport: Social Problems and Social Issues* (London: Heinemann, 1997).

Further reading:

Cashmore, E., *Making Sense of Sports* (London: Routledge, 1990).

Dunning, E., *Sport Matters* (London: Routledge, 1999).

Maguire, J., *Global Sport: Identities, Societies, Civilizations* (Cambridge: Polity Press, 1999).

See also:

Geography

-Grant Jarvie

Softball

The game of softball was developed from baseball during the latter part of the 19th century. It is claimed by some that the Farragut Boat Club in Chicago was responsible for the birth of the game in 1887, following an improvised game of baseball. Members of the club used a broom handle for a bat and a boxing glove for a ball, hence the name softball. There are two versions of softball – fast pitch and slow pitch.

In the past, the game has been called kitten ball, mush ball, indoor baseball, playground baseball and diamond ball. The first rules for the sport were formulated by the National Amateur Playground Ball Association of the United States, founded in 1908. This Association was the forerunner of the Amateur Softball Association of America, which was established in 1933.

Following the Second World War, softball developed internationally, becoming a worldwide sport – by the 1960s, it was played in over fifty countries. Inaugural world championships for women were held in 1965 and for men in 1966. The 1965 women's final was won by Australia, who beat the United States 1-0 in Melbourne, while the 1966 men's final, held in Mexico City, was won by the United States.

Softball came to Britain somewhat later, although it is now well organized following the establishment of the British Softball Federation (B.S.F.) in 1984. In the same year, the first leagues were formed. The game has spread rapidly since – in 1984 there were only twenty teams, but today there are 500 clubs in Britain, 250 within the London area alone.

Britain hosted the inaugural slow-pitch European Championships in 1998, a tournament held under the auspices of the European Softball Federation. Due to the success of these championships, the International Softball Federation decided to resurrect the world championships in 2001. Britain, who beat the Czech Republic in the European Championships, was to represent Europe.

References:

Arlott, J. (ed.), *Oxford Companion to Sports and Games* (London: Oxford University Press, 1976).

Personal conversation with Bob Fromer of B.S.F. National Development.

Websites:

The British Softball Federation – http://www.baseballsoftballuk.com/

-Ray Physick

Sophia Gardens

The Sophia Gardens complex lies a mile from the heart of Cardiff and has become a recreational centre for the population of the Welsh capital and the Principality, with the riverside complex containing the Welsh Institute of Sport and the headquarters of Glamorgan County Cricket Club.

The Gardens take their name from Sophia, the wife of the second Marquess of Bute. Her husband owned much of the land upon which Cardiff rapidly grew. This resulted in over-crowding, so in 1854 Sophia decided to provide the townsfolk with an area of secluded walks and a field for healthy recreation.

A bowling green was opened in 1877-1878 and by 1900, the Sophia Gardens Field (or Gala Field) was used for cricket, Association Football, athletics, cycling, fêtes and other civic gatherings. In 1947, the Butes gave the Gardens (and their whole estate) to Cardiff Corporation, on the understanding that they would be preserved for recreation.

In 1951, a single storey pavilion was built and in 1958 it hosted the boxing and wrestling bouts of the Commonwealth Games. During the 1960s, Cardiff Athletic Club transferred some of their hockey, cricket and Rugby activities from the Arms Park to the Gardens, and in 1967 Glamorgan made the ground their Cardiff home.

In 1971, the Sports Council for Wales acquired land for the National Sports Centre for Wales (now the Welsh Institute of Sport), and in 1996 Glamorgan bought the cricket ground, and built an indoor school, which was also used by Australia in the 1999 Cricket World Cup.

References:

Hignell, A. K., *Cricket Grounds of Glamorgan* (Nottingham: Association of Cricket Statisticians and Historians, 1986).

Further reading:

Hignell, A. K., *The History of Glamorgan County Cricket Club* (London: Christopher Helm, 1988).

Plumptre, G., *Homes of Cricket: the First-Class Grounds of England and Wales* (London: Queen Anne Press, 1988), pp. 113-118.

Powell, W. A., *The Wisden Guide to Cricket Grounds* (London: Stanley Paul, 1992), pp. 132-139.

Powell, W. A. (ed.), *Cricket Grounds* (Surrey: Dial House, 1995), pp. 36-37.

Wooller, W., *Glamorgan* (London: Arthur Barker, 1971).

-Andrew Hignell

Spectators, Fans and Crowd Disorder

Sport has been watched by groups of spectators from its early beginnings. Crowds gathered at the Roman chariot races, as they did for games in many other ancient societies. Generally, we can define spectators as the crowd en masse, fans as committed supporters, and crowd disorders as the occasional result of accompanying over-enthusiasm.

The role of the spectator in Britain grew as sport became more specialized and fewer were able to participate. Recreation became increasingly important in a work-intensive society, and local communities indulged vicariously in supporting their favourites. Some older sports, like hunting, were not suited to this, whereas others such as prizefighting, cockfighting, cricket and traditional football were, given their oppositional nature. Certain sports involved violence, and spectators could, and did, become involved. Until the early 19th century, crowds could be partly mixed socially, with the more raffish elements of the aristocracy and squirearchy mingling with the lower classes. Women participated in the less violent games, and formed part of the communal audience.

Industrialization meant that some of these pursuits declined in popularity as fewer workers had the leisure time to watch. However, shorter working hours and increased holidays and wages from around 1850 in parts of the country such as Lancashire meant a renewal of the audience for popular leisure. Fairs, bonfire celebrations and wakes were more subdued, controlled by the increased powers of local authorities and police. 'Rational recreation' such as bands, choirs, walks and museum trips attracted some workers; however, more popular were new forms of commercialized spectator sports. These included athletics, rowing, cricket, horse-racing and, especially, football. Despite this, many women were tied to domestic and work routines and could not attend.

Reformed football spread from the public schools by 1880, especially to Scotland, Sheffield, Birmingham and Lancashire. Large crowds attended in urban areas, and were charged admission to increase club funds. Initially, crowds included sizeable proportions of the middle classes and women, which declined as the number of working men increased. The excitement of the game, fed by competitions and local rivalries, increased its attraction. Association Football and the northern variant of Rugby, later called Rugby League, were obsessions with many workers who became fans. They remained loyal to one club, usually local. Such loyalties and identities were less evident in cricket, professional rowing, pedestrianism or athletics, although individual heroes could be idolized.

Enclosed racecourses were essential from the 1880s, as competition meant that they needed to attract paying spectators. Cricket attendances and rivalries were stimulated by the County Championship and local leagues in the North and Midlands, but crowds generally never reached the level of football. Cricket and racing tended to attract a larger element of middle-class spectators, and the latter a significant proportion of women. The founding of the Football League in 1888 produced a great increase in attendances, which only reached its peak in the late 1940s. In Scotland, football attendances have always been dominated by Glasgow Rangers and Celtic, partly because of sectarian rivalries.

The development of Rugby cup competitions and leagues in Lancashire and Yorkshire encouraged enthusiasts to support their local team. Rugby League supporters were predominantly working class, as in football. In Wales, Rugby Union became a popular working-class sport in the south, although there was significant football support in that area and parts of the north.

Most spectators of popular team sports such as Rugby, cricket or football came to see their team win, and such partisanship remains self-reinforcing even today. Local loyalties and family ties influenced the choice of club to support, until the recent 'globalization' of sport eroded loyalties to some extent. Supporters bask in the glory of their team's victories and suffer in defeat. Spectator enthusiasms in various sports have always been expressed as forms of carnival celebration, via colours, songs, chants, banners, ribbons etc., although these have varied over time. Since the influence of the *Taylor Report*, money from BSkyB television, the advent of the Premiership and football club investment, the composition of the football crowd has become more middle class and less local.

Enthusiasm sometimes provoked crowd disturbances, and these continue to be a problem, especially in football. Sports like tennis and motor racing, whilst attracting large crowds, seem to have few disturbances. Such sports are less oppositional, support tending to be for individuals like Nigel Mansell rather than clubs as symbolic identities. 'Barracking' of rival teams or fans was deemed unsporting by amateur enthusiasts, particularly in the early days, but was often indulged in by partisan working-class fans. It is very frequent today, even in more 'refined' sports such as cricket or tennis.

Hooliganism, as evidenced in crowd disturbances, has become a major concern recently, although it was prevalent in early organized sport as well. Gambling was certainly a cause in horse-racing, boxing and football, and alcohol has played a part in exacerbating such behaviour. Hooliganism has most commonly been associated with football, and some researchers have indicated that it declined in the inter-war period, and resurfaced in a serious form in the late 1960s.

Various causes have been suggested – the violent norms of working-class males, 'frustration disorders' over results, poor facilities, bad refereeing decisions and the like, or the social psychology of individuals and crowds, amongst others. Clashes between rival groups were not common in the early period, but became larger and more frequent from the 1970s. Disturbances have also recently accompanied the England team, where links with right-wing political groups have been suspected. There is some evidence that behaviour has improved at football matches and race meetings because of better facilities and organization, and stricter crowd control. In recent years, hooliganism has declined but not disappeared. Some have suggested that the disaffected youth have been diverted into alternatives such as the 'rave' scene or drug and dance culture. What remains to be fully explained is why such hooliganism is not significantly attached to other sports with similar working-class audiences, such as Rugby League, league cricket, dog racing, speedway or basketball.

References:

Dunning, E., Murphy, P., and Williams, J. *The Roots of Football Hooliganism: an Historical and Sociological Study* (London: Routledge, 1988).

Guttmann, A., *Sports Spectators* (New York: Columbia University Press, 1986).

Holt, R., *Sport and the British: a Modern History* (Oxford: Oxford University Press, 1989).

Vamplew, W., *Pay up and Play the Game: Professional Sport in Britain, 1875-1914* (Cambridge: Cambridge University Press, 1988).

See also:

Taylor Reports

-Robert Lewis

Spectators, Fans and Crowd Disorder – Hampden Park Riot 1909

The Hampden Park riot of April 1909 took place at a Scottish F.A. Cup Final replay between the Glasgow clubs, Celtic and Rangers. A crowd of 61,000 wanted a result on this occasion, and apparently the press had given the impression that extra time would be played. When there was no result after ninety minutes, supporters refused to leave as confused players of both teams remained on the field. Some felt that the clubs and authorities wanted another replay to raise revenues. The removal of a corner flag by an official as the players left the field sparked off the trouble. Goalposts, nets and pay-boxes were destroyed and burnt, and fire-hoses were cut, amongst other damage.

Around 200 police were involved. Mounted police, after being pelted with stones and bottles, drew batons and forced spectators back into the enclosures. Disturbances continued until around 7 p.m. Approximately 100 people were injured, including policemen and firemen. Dozens of spectators were taken into custody, although only three were charged.

Various causes were suggested, including professional criminals, 'undisciplined' youths, or 'a few dozen ruffians' venting their feelings. The riot appears not to have been confrontational or sectarian, in the sense of Orangemen versus Fenians or Protestants against Catholics, as clashes between Celtic and Rangers have traditionally been, but a classic case of a 'frustration disorder' that escalated in scale, possibly because of resentments against the police and authorities, into one of the most serious incidents ever seen inside a British football stadium.

References:

Murray, B., *The Old Firm: Sectarianism, Sport and Society in Scotland* (Edinburgh: John Donald, 1985).

Athletic News (19, 26 April 1909).
Sporting Chronicle (19, 20 April 1909).
Times (19, 20 April 1909).

Further reading:

Bradley, J. M., 'Football in Scotland: a History of Political and Ethnic Identity', *International Journal of the History of Sport*, vol. 12, no. 1 (April 1995), pp. 81-98.

Finn, G., 'Racism, Religion and Social Prejudice: Irish Catholic Clubs, Soccer and Scottish Identity I', *International Journal of the History of Sport*, vol. 8, no. 1 (May 1991), pp. 72-95.

See also:

Hampden Park

-Robert Lewis

Spectators, Fans and Crowd Disorder – Record Crowds

Within the sport of football there is a tendency to revise history, particularly following the introduction of the Premier League. A 'year zero' is given as 1992, as the F.A. have marketed the game to a new generation of supporters, many with different demographic characteristics from the traditional fan. This is particularly true when it comes to gauging records within football, none more so than record crowds. In reality, the vast majority of club crowd records date back to the time of terraces and unrestricted entry into grounds. Historians and fans alike have called this period the 'Golden Era' and, depending on whom you read, it is acknowledged that the period is essentially the years just before the Second World War, and the seven years following it. Most crowd records stand for one-off cup games, or for local 'derbies', particularly those played in Glasgow and Liverpool. The F.A. Cup Final of 1923, the first to be held at Wembley Stadium, holds the unofficial record for highest attendance at a football match in the United Kingdom, with an estimated 210,000 spectators. This match gave rise to fears about crowd safety at football matches, and an inquiry into the match found that procedures for the entry of spectators were not adequate. The fear of overcrowding, together with the escalation of hooligan activity, lead to a more thorough system of entrance to grounds.

Following the publication of the Taylor Report into the Hillsborough Disaster of 1989, the implementation of all-seater stadia meant that crowds at games became smaller. Most of the élite clubs in England and Scotland are now beginning to reach their old legal terrace capacities in their redeveloped stadia, with notable examples being Old Trafford, Celtic Park and Anfield. It is unlikely that the record crowds of the 1940s and 1950s will ever be safely reached again in Britain but, as we are continuously told, records are being broken weekly in the Premier League.

References:

Rothman's Football Yearbook (London: various publishers, annual).

-Sam Johnstone

Speedway

Speedway is a form of professional organized motorcycle racing originating in the early decades of the 20th century, where riders on specially adapted motorcycles race clockwise on a suitably approved loose surface circuit over four laps. It is a sport that requires unique riding skills, nerve and respect for other riders, as bikes can reach speeds of 70 miles per hour and have no brakes. Speedway riders must master a skidding or broadsiding manoeuvre that involves putting the rear wheel into a sideways skid in order to negotiate the bends at high speed. It is a sister sport to grass track racing, long track racing and ice speedway racing.

Speedway riders have traditionally been contracted to teams but are also able to compete in individual events. They have always been paid according to results, in team racing at a rate per point gained. In the early days, star riders commanded huge prize money, as their name could add thousands to the attendance. It was common for top riders then to earn £100 a meeting.

Speedway bikes have changed remarkably little in the seventy years of the sport – they still consist of a 500 cc engine mounted on a frame of varying rigidity. They have no brakes because the speed of racing, together with the close proximity of riders on narrow circuits, means that any sudden reduction in speed could result in collisions. Bikes also use a single gear based on a fixed but changeable gear sprocket. Fuel for speedway bikes has developed from petrol-based mixtures to the pure methanol demanded by today's high-performance engines. Stripped down road-bikes were originally used until the advent of the specialized Douglas, Rudge, JAP, Weslake and the currently used Jawa and GM engines.

The origins of speedway are thought to have developed from dirt track and board racing in the United States and grass track racing in Australia in the 1910s and 1920s. The perceived wisdom is that showman Johnnie Hoskins ran the first speedway meeting at West Maitland, New South Wales, Australia in 1923 as a showground attraction that took off immediately.

Introduced to Britain in 1927, a meeting at Droylsden, Manchester preceded the first major event at the High Beech, Essex, in February 1928, where although 3,000 spectators were expected, 30,000 turned up. The success of that meeting attracted businessmen who could see a profit to be made from the sport and tracks opened all over the country, usually sharing existing greyhound stadiums. Britain has continued to be the major world centre of the sport.

The establishment of league speedway in 1929 saw the first in a series of boom periods for the sport. The Southern League and English Dirt Track League (Northern League) heralded the start of league and knockout cup

racing, which has continued to the present day. Famous teams such as Belle Vue (Manchester), Wembley, West Ham, Wimbledon, New Cross, Birmingham, Coventry and Crystal Palace drew in five-figure crowds on a regular basis in the late 1920s and into the 1930s.

Speedway has always attracted a predominantly working-class support, as tracks were generally set up in industrial areas. An admission charge of one shilling was normal in the early 1930s yet despite five-figure crowds, the prize money demanded by the star riders and the job losses of that era led to many promoting companies going broke. Twenty-seven league teams in 1929 were reduced to a National League of nine teams by 1932. League racing continued at several London tracks throughout the 1930s, right up to the advent of the Second World War. Surprisingly, several tracks ran during the War, most notably at Belle Vue.

The re-emergence of speedway in 1946 saw a startling growth in teams, tracks and riders over the ensuing ten years. Leagues expanded to three divisions and the public, desperate for entertainment in peacetime, flooded in their thousands to tracks from Exeter to Edinburgh and Norwich to Cardiff. In the early 1950s, over 12 million spectators watched speedway in Britain, making it second only to football in terms of attendances. The World Championship Final, traditionally held at Wembley Stadium, attracted crowds of 90,000.

By the mid-1950s, the shortage of money and increasing cost of living led to a sharp drop in attendances and the decade saw a repetition of the 1930s decline, with again only a handful of teams in the big cities competing in league speedway.

The establishment of the Provincial League in 1960 saw promoters reopening tracks and new sites being developed. The success of the new league led to tensions between the National League and the Provincial League until the sport decided a compromise had to be reached. Lord Shawcross led an inquiry into the future of the sport in 1964 and the outcome was the formation of a single British League, run by the British Speedway Promoters' Association. The governing body of speedway remained the Speedway Control Board, a division of the Auto-Cycle Union.

From the 1970s to the Present

Speedway has, over the past thirty years, seen periods of boom and near bust. The 1970s saw growth in support that declined again in the 1980s. The sport has always had its share of star riders and names like Ove Funden, Barry Briggs, Ivan Mauger, Ole Olsen and Bruce Penhall achieved superstar status in the 1960s and 1970s. Television coverage of speedway's big events, like World Championship Finals, kept the sport's profile high until this ceased in the 1980s.

Currently (2000), there are three leagues – the British Élite League (ten teams), which attracts the world's best riders; the British Premier League (thirteen teams), which uses predominantly British riders; and the British Conference League (seven teams), an amateur league aimed at bringing younger riders into the higher levels of the sport. The resumption of televised speedway on Sky Television is attracting new spectators. Speedway in Britain is aware that competition for people's leisure time is greater now that at any time in the past and it must adapt to the demands of the 21st-century spectator to survive.

References:

May, C., *Ride It: the Complete Book of Speedway* (Yeovil: Haynes Publishing Group, 1976).

Rogers, M., *The Illustrated History of Speedway* (Ipswich: Studio Publications Ltd, 1978).

Further reading:

Fraser, G. and Henry, J. (eds.), *The Speedway Researcher Magazine* (Stirling and Edinburgh: Editors, 1998-).

Speedway News Magazine (London: Various, 1928-1954).

Speedway Star Magazine (Surbiton: Pinegen Ltd, 1952-).

Websites:

The British Speedway Promoters' Association – http://www.british-speedway.co.uk/

See also:

Motorcycle Racing

-Graham Fraser

Sporting Art

Traditionally characterized as the depiction of equestrian and field sports in paintings and prints, sporting art flourished between 1700 and 1850. A more inclusive definition would now encompass other media, such as photography and contemporary art that represents more popular activities, such as soccer.

Conventional sporting art is an unusually British taste and practice, although its attractions are not restricted to sports enthusiasts. Fishing, deer and fox-hunting, shooting, horse-racing, coaching scenes and farm animals are the normal subjects. Unlike continental art, these works often display a preference for unceremonious and outdoor scenes.

There were Flemish exponents of the genre before the emergence of Francis Barlow (1626?-1702), whom, as the premier native-born practitioner, is considered the 'Father' of British sporting art. He illustrated and published *Severall Wayes of Hunting, Hawking and Fishing According to the English Manner* (1671). He also etched one of the first racing prints of quality, *The Last Horse Race Run Before Charles II* (1687).

The relationship between landscape, hunting, equestrianism and pastoral romanticism has formed a strong focus for sporting artists. There has been a steady market for their artistic output, continuing in an unbroken and fairly unremarkable fashion from 1660 to the present. The popularity of sporting art was assisted, after 1700, by sports becoming better organized and less the preserve of an aristocratic élite, as with horse-racing post-1735.

365

Newmarket was the setting for John Wootton's (1682?-1764) racehorse paintings from *c.* 1715. Other commercially successful early exponents were Pieter Tillemans (1684-1734) and James Seymour (1702-1752). Patrons increasingly employed accomplished specialized artists to accurately depict their animals and the sporting events they participated in, rather than reflecting majestic and heroic ideals. Studies of fox-hunting and shooting proliferated after 1750, whilst the practice and artistic representation of deer hunting and hare coursing declined. These factors help explain sporting art's lowly status among the wider artistic community by 1800 and why George Stubbs' (1724-1806) talents were largely unrecognized by peers. Stubbs' brilliant draughtsmanship and superb anatomical studies of animals are reflected in (and seemingly influenced) the work of others, like Sawrey Gilpin (1733-1807) and Jacques-Laurent Agasse (1767-1849).

The demand for sporting pictures between 1775 and 1850 produced many prints, frequently humorous, notably by Henry Alken (1785-1851), James Pollard (1792-1867) and the cartoonist Thomas Rowlandson (1756-1827). These often satirical views (e.g. Alken's *Qualified Horses and Unqualified Riders*) mirrored changing attitudes that, after 1820, perceived certain animal sports as cruel and sportsmen as arrogant, such behaviour conflicting with an emergent society of manners. Traditional sporting scenes continued to provide a profitable niche for many artists, including John Nost Sartorius (1759-1828), Benjamin Marshall (1768-1835), his student John Fernerley (1782-1860) and John Frederick Herring Senior (1795-1865), a prolific painter of Classic horse-race winners.

Established artists, like James Ward (1769-1859), created superlative sporting art as part of a wider repertoire of subjects. The work of Sir Edwin Landseer (1802-1873), the best known British animal painter, often analogized the characters of man and beast, as with his portrait of a Scottish stag, *The Monarch of the Glen* (1850). Sir Francis Grant (1803-1878), President of the Royal Academy (1866), was principally a portraitist but, as a keen huntsman, painted many fox-hunting pieces.

Sports, in particular cricket, could still provide art with an important stimulus after 1850. Influenced by French Impressionism and challenged by the emerging preference for photography, Joseph Crawhall (1861-1913) and Robert Bevan (1865-1925) enlivened their animal and sporting paintings with a fluidity of movement and invigorating colours. Sir Alfred Munnings (1878-1959) was one of the few painters to follow in similar vein, contesting the restrictions of conventional style. Contemporaneously, Lionel Edwards' (1878-1966) work followed the traditional pattern. William Powell Frith's painting *Derby Day* (1858) marked a departure from the documentary approach, with the sport becoming emblematic and the spectators the subject. With this painting of a contemporary event, Frith (1819-1909) discarded his earlier emphasis on historical tableaux. All these changes find expression in, for example, John Robertson Reid's *A Country Cricket Match* (1878), Camille Pissaro's *Cricket at Bedford Park* (1897) and Spencer Gore's *The Cricket Match* (1909).

Individual portraits of famous sporting personalities have been another way of using art as a means of record, particularly since the advent of photo-journalism after 1900. The more recent prominence of team sports has also been captured, as with Peter Blake's *Tottenham Hotspur* (1962) – the stars of popular sport being painted by the star of pop art.

The use of photography in sport reflects aesthetic, technological and scientific developments. The earliest photographs (1850-*c.*1900) are static and posed, due to unwieldy cameras and plate-film formats. Innovations such as George Eastman's celluloid roll film (1888), cartridge roll film (1895) and Brownie box camera (1900) allowed more intimate and immediate photographs to be taken, thereby popularizing photography. The lightweight Leica camera developed by Oscar Barnack (1924) increased the speed and spontaneity of portraying sporting events. Photographs allow clarity, realism, reveal emotions and every element of the action, and can be used creatively or to document. Recent prominent sports photographers include Tony Duffy, Gerry Cranham, Patrick Eager, Chris Smith, Eamonn McCabe and Tim O'Sullivan.

Sporting competitions are often combined with cultural events, for example at the Olympics and the World Cup. For the Football Association's ninetieth anniversary (1953) the Arts Council sponsored figurative paintings by British artists of leading footballers and matches in progress. *Offside!*, a Manchester exhibition of contemporary paintings, photographs and video art, exploring the relationship between soccer and society, took place during the 1996 European Football Championships.

Compared to painting, photography and prints, the decorative arts and sculpture are used infrequently in sporting art. There has been little mass production of commemorative statues, pottery, plates or figurines, although individual presentation pieces of riders, horses and their owners are not uncommon – the bronzes of the racehorses *Favonius* by Sir Joseph Boehm (Jockey Club, 1871) and *Aureole* by Herbert Heseltine (Royal Collection, 1957), for instance. James Butler's bronze of the cyclist Reg Harris (1920-1992) is an exceptionally fine example of sporting statuary, which was unveiled at the Manchester Velodrome in 1995.

References:

Deuchar, S., *Sporting Art in Eighteenth-Century England: a Social and Political History* (New Haven: Yale University Press, 1988).

Huntington-Whiteley, J. (ed.), *The Book of British Sporting Heroes* (London: National Portrait Gallery, 1998).

Simon, R. and Smart, A., *The Art of Cricket* (London: Secker & Warburg, 1983).

Walker, S. A., *Sporting Art: England 1700-1900* (London: Studio Vista, 1972).

Wingfield, M., *A Dictionary of Sporting Artists, 1650-1990* (Woodbridge: Antique Collectors Club, 1992).

Further reading:

Connor, P. and Lambourne, L., *Derby Day 200* (London: The Royal Academy of Arts/Westerham Press, 1979).

Egerton, J. and Snelgrove, D., *British Sporting and Animal Paintings, 1655-1867* (London: The Tate Gallery for the Yale Center for British Art, 1978).

Wingfield, M., *Sport and the Artist, Vol. I, Ball Games* (Woodbridge: Antique Collectors Club, 1988).

Websites:

Works by many of the artists mentioned above can be viewed online at the website of the Tate Gallery – http://www.tate.org.uk/

See also:

British Sporting Art Trust

-Mark Hathaway

Sporting Eccentrics

When Jamie Redknapp's innocuous long-range shot looped high towards the Peruvian goal during a friendly international at Wembley on September 6th, 1995, goalkeeper Rene Higuita, rather than making an easy catch, decided to dive forward and take the ball above his head with the studs of both boots, sending it back into midfield with his trademark 'scorpion kick'. The crowd and the British sporting press delighted in the antics of 'El Loco' – typical Latin temperament, they agreed. However, the common sentiment was that British players do not behave like this – British players are supposed to take sport far more seriously. But do they?

It was, after all, Britain who gave the world Eddie 'the Eagle' Edwards, a Cheltenham plasterer and the world's worst ski-jumper, who confessed that his jam-jar glasses invariably steamed up when he jumped. Finishing last in the 1988 Calgary Winter Olympics, Eddie became a national hero, earning life membership of the Monster Raving Loony Party. He was following in illustrious footsteps. Six years earlier, Scottish priest Father John Archie MacMillan had water-skied up and down the Sound of Eriskay while playing the bagpipes. In 1971, Nicolette Milnes-Walker, a University of Wales research psychologist, had sailed across the Atlantic single-handed – in the nude. And whatever possessed Leicester Swimming Club in the 1960s to appoint a chairman named Ivor Finn? There must be something in the water!

Nor have Britain's oddballs confined themselves to pursuits aerial and aquatic. Max Faulkner, one of golf's most eccentric characters, won the British Open in the austere days of 1951 after playing the final round wearing a blue and white striped shirt atop an amazing ensemble of canary-yellow plus-twos with matching shoes and socks. Mad Max was, appropriately enough, partnered by the equally batty caddy, Mad Mac, who would scan the fairways for hazards using binoculars without lenses. Rain or shine, Mac would wear a raincoat but not bother with a shirt. His most famous advice to Max on a tricky green was the helpful 'Hit it slightly straight, sir.' Mac's words of wisdom would have been welcome back in 1890, when the unfortunate but determined A. J. Lewis, playing in a Peacehaven, Sussex competition, took 156 putts on one green before stumbling off into obscurity.

Cricket has produced a number of strange characters over the years, including the legendary W. G. Grace. The good doctor once denied a fielder stationed on the boundary the chance of catching him out from a lofted shot by declaring the innings closed while the ball was in mid-air. On another occasion, when some unfortunate umpire had the temerity to give him out, the great man coolly replaced the bails and thundered, 'They've come to see me bat, not you umpiring.' A batsman of lesser

renown but equal enthusiasm was Sir Julien Cahn, furniture magnate and cricket nut who, between 1923 and 1941, led his country-house side on tours to such hotbeds of the summer game as South America, Canada and Denmark. The admirable Sir Julien batted in inflatable pads, which his chauffeur blew up with a bicycle-pump before each innings. These cumbersome accessories made walking somewhat hazardous, so Sir Julien would often make his way to the wicket in a bath chair.

Considering the shenanigans of these and other British sporting crackpots, El Loco's performance seems pale in comparison. What's a scorpion kick between loonies?

References:
Randall, D., *Great Sporting Eccentrics* (London: W. H. Allen, 1985.)
Sutherland, D., *The Mad Hatters: Great Sporting Eccentrics of the Nineteenth Century* (London: Robert Hale, 1987).
Tibballs, G., *Great Sporting Eccentrics* (London: Robson Books, 1997).

-Tony Rennick

Sporting Heroes

Britain has played a major part in the development of modern sport and with it the sporting hero. Although national heroes have tended to be soldiers, explorers or inventors, those who excelled in sport have also achieved growing public fame in modern times. Journalists, writers and broadcasters have all had a major role in the making of heroes whose achievements have been presented as representing different aspects of British identity.

The first sporting heroes were often the servants of noblemen – 'running footmen' or 'pedestrians', grooms who became jockeys or cricketing tenant farmers. They were often in the employ of the nobility, who gambled on the talents of jockeys like Sam Chifney or 'pugilists' (boxers) like Jack Broughton (1705-1789), perhaps the first English sporting hero. Cricket emerged as the most popular team sport, moving from southern villages like Hambledon, which had a famous team of aristocrats and farmers, to the northern counties. The coming of the railway in the early Victorian years led to the first all-star England touring team, whose players included figures of national renown like the large and genial Kentish farmer, Alfred Mynn.

With the emergence of amateurism in the second half of the 19th century, a new standard of sporting heroism was established. Excellence of performance was not enough. The amateur hero was supposed to combine natural talent and personal virtue. This 'manly' ideal was shared by new middle-class sporting heroines like the tennis players Lottie Dod and Dorothea Chambers. They were followed between the wars by Kitty Godfree and Dorothy Round, whilst Fred Perry became the supreme hero of the men's game with three Wimbledon titles, though his fame suffered after he moved to the United States and turned professional.

The first heroes of football were gentlemen amateurs like G. O. Smith of Charterhouse and the Corinthians. However, the professionals soon took over and the new working-class heroes were men like Steve Bloomer of Derby or Billy Meredith, a lanky Welshman, who played until he was fifty for Manchester City and Manchester United, between 1894 and 1924. The inter-war years saw a host of stars, notably Dixie Dean of Everton, followed by Tommy Lawton and the younger Stanley Matthews, though the southern middle classes were reluctant to endorse northern working men as national heroes.

Similarly, the class and regional split in Rugby made it impossible for English Rugby stars to achieve full public recognition. Cricket was the English national game and it was here that the English sporting hero was most fully developed, from the founding father of modern cricket, W. G. Grace, the large and bearded Gloucestershire doctor, to the clean-shaven public school boys in their 'immaculate whites' like C. B. Fry, the great batsman who also played football and Rugby for England and broke the world long jump record. Beating Australia came to be seen as a true test of English sporting manhood. The great professional batsmen of the inter-war years – the openers Jack Hobbs and Herbert Sutcliffe, Frank Woolley, Wally Hammond and the young Len Hutton – all played some of their best cricket against Australia.

The modern Olympic Games was another heroic arena. Between the wars, Britain produced some outstanding gold medallists such as the modest railwayman, Albert Hill, who won the 800 and 1500 metres in 1920. More widely known and celebrated, however, were university students like Harold Abrahams, Eric Liddell and Douglas Lowe. Their success in the Paris Olympics of 1924 was later selectively celebrated in the hugely successful sporting film of the 1980s, *Chariots of Fire*, which coincided with the remarkable triumphs of British middle-distance runners Coe, Ovett and Cram.

Britain was, of course, three nations in one state. Wales had its own remarkable string of Rugby heroes, whose exploits seemed to stand for the spirit of the nation, from Arthur Gould in the early years to Gareth Edwards and the great team of 1970s. Industrial Wales had a great boxing tradition, too, with Jimmy Wilde and Tommy Farr, who narrowly lost to Joe Louis in 1937. Scotland had its fighting legends like Benny Lynch from the Gorbals but it was football that created the real Scottish popular heroes, who were watched by some of the biggest crowds in the world, nearly 150,000 in the great games at Hampden Park: men like Patsy Gallacher and Jimmy McGrory of Celtic, or Alan Morton of Rangers, who played in the 'Wembley Wizards' side that beat England 5-1. Beating England was the true mark of the Scottish hero, a test Denis Law and Jim Baxter passed magnificently at Wembley in 1967 when Scotland beat an English team that had just won the World Cup.

Television brought a new dimension to sport in the 1950s. The B.B.C. showed the 1953 Cup Final where Matthews finally got his Cup winner's medal and became an English icon. In the same year, Dennis Compton, the 'Brylcream Boy', scored the winning runs as England regained the Ashes. There was a last flourish of amateur heroics, too, with Peter May and Colin Cowdrey batting for England and a group of Oxford undergraduates led by Roger Bannister breaking the four-minute mile in 1954.

The social position and the public image of the British sporting hero changed dramatically in the 1960s with the decline of amateurism, the rise of female sport and the new impact of the tabloid press. Television had brought the Olympics to the British public live and promoted a new generation of sporting heroines like the swimmer Anita Lonsbrough and athletes, Mary Rand, Anne Packer and Lillian Board (the 'golden girls'). The B.B.C. also covered Wimbledon and the triumphs of Angela Mortimer, Ann Jones and Virginia Wade. Women's sport had come of age. In the 1980s, the javelin produced national figures like Tessa Sanderson and Fatima Whitbred while ice dancing had Jayne Torvill and Christopher Dean, whose Olympic *Bolero* drew record television viewing figures.

The new tabloid press met the challenge of television by sensationalizing the lives of the stars. It was becoming harder to be a hero and easier to be an anti-hero, as George Best and Paul Gascoigne ('Gazza') discovered. As Britain's place in the world diminished, sporting success seemed to become more important and the public demanded heroes who were entertaining both on and off the field. Satellite television has brought an unprecedented amount of live sport into the home. More than ever sporting heroes are expected to be 'personalities', appearing on chat shows and panel games. Black sportsmen and women have become ever more important, from boxers like Frank Bruno to athletes such as Daley Thompson and Linford Christie and football's John Barnes and Ian Wright. Older kinds of hero, like the Olympic oarsman Steve Redgrave, co-exist in the public mind with the instant super-rich young stars like Liverpool's Michael Owen, reflecting both a residual British admiration for the amateur tradition and an increasing worship of glamour, money and media exposure.

References:

Duncanson, N. and Collins, P., *Tales of Gold* (London, Queen Anne Press, 1992).

Holt, R., Lanfranchi, P. and Mangan, J. A., *European Heroes: Myth, Sport, Identity* (London: Frank Cass, 1996).

Huntington-Whiteley, J., *The Book of British Sporting Heroes* (London: National Portrait Gallery, 1998).

-Richard Holt

Sports Acrobatics

The International Federation of Sports Acrobatics (I.F.S.A.) was founded in 1973 with Great Britain amongst its founder members and in 1998 became part of the International Gymnastic Federation (F.I.G.). Its history is rooted in the ancient fairs and festivals of the Middle Ages and the travelling fairs and circuses of the 18th and 19th centuries. There are aspects of acrobatic activity to be found in many sports, but particularly in circus activities. Many of these activities are both traditional and popular, which ironically may have served to considerably delay their acceptance as bona fide sporting activities until relatively recently. There are now hopes that the activity may eventually become part of the Olympic programme.

The sport is often referred to as 'Sports Acro' and is considered by many to be the most exciting form of gymnastics. There are two aspects of competition – tumbling, and pairs or group. Tumbling by both men and women is performed on a 25-metre-long sprung track. There are three tumbling runs, namely somersaults, twisting somersaults and a combination series.

The pair/group competition consists of partner exercises requiring both balance and tempo and focuses on agility and flexibility. These exercises are performed with, or on, a partner and embrace both synchronous and dynamic movement.

There are five divisions included in the pair/group category – Men's Four (men's group), Men's Pair, Mixed Pair, Women's Pair, and Women's Trio (women's group). The floor area for this aspect of competition is 12 metres square and routines normally last between 2.5 and 3 minutes. The routines are performed to music, and this serves to enhance both the nature of the performance and the culture of the performers.

In 1982, the World Sports Acrobatics Championships were held at Wembley in London, whilst 1997 saw the success of British sports acrobats at the World Championships in Manchester. Great Britain has a reputation as one of the strongest nations in the world and in 1997, Kathryn Peberdy of the West Kirby Gymnastic Club became the first ever Western European to win the World All-around title. In 1998, British competitors won five gold and two silver medals at the World Championships in Minsk, coming third behind the Ukraine and Russia in the overall medals table. The sport in Britain is governed by the British Amateur Gymnastics Association.

References:

British Amateur Gymnastics Association website – http://www.baga.co.uk/

Encyclopaedia Britannica website – http://www.britannica.com/

Smith, M., *An Introduction to Sports Acrobatics* (London: Stanley Paul, 1982).

Websites:

British Amateur Gymnastics Association – http://www.baga.co.uk/

See also:

Gymnastics

-Frank Galligan/Ray Physick

Sports Announcing and Commentating

Sports announcing and commentating is the act of providing a spoken description of a live sporting event, or insight and analysis after a sporting event. Announcing and commentating can be done in person to enlighten live spectators, or via television or radio, known as sportscasting.

In person at an event, an announcer's responsibilities include introducing the competitors, announcing officials' calls, and filling in the live spectators on match developments they might have missed. The development of audio technology in the early part of the 20th century made it possible for sport announcers to get the information across to larger and larger crowds. In 1912, Lee de Forest invented the 'Audion' vacuum tube amplifier, an important step on the road to electronic amplification. The first loudspeaker with the basic design of modern loudspeakers, composed of a voice coil and cone, was created in 1924. Woofer and tweeter technology was added to loudspeakers in 1935, significantly reducing distortion.

While many crossovers exist among television and radio sportscasting roles, radio sportscasters hold the responsibility for describing the event in detail for listeners who do not have the benefit of visual observation. Television sportscasters focus on supplementing the visual information with statistics, player identification and updates on the score and time remaining. The play-by-play announcer and the

371

colour commentator work in conjunction to tell what is happening in the match and to provide insight and 'colour' in the form of statistics, history, anecdotes about players, and other interesting facts. Sideline reporting, which developed in the 1970s, includes interviewing players and coaches and providing information gleaned from the sidelines, such as injury updates and reasons for personnel moves. Additional types of sportscasters are studio hosts, who report from a studio during breaks in the action, rather than from the stadium, and provide analysis and updates on other sporting events; news show sport anchors; and sport talk show hosts.

Due to the effects of the Broadcasting Acts of 1990 and 1996, many new stations sprang up, providing a nearly limitless supply of airtime for live sporting events. This development affected the style of television sportscasting in several ways. First, a number of commentators from years past, such as Wilson and Moore, were able to revive their careers, bringing with them the intense patriotism more popular in earlier days. Second, some obscure sports were made more popular by their media coverage on the new all-sports stations. Third, the wide availability of live matches on television diluted the need for weekly sport-in-review programmes, leaving the content of such programmes largely redundant. Sport coverage moved out of its more subdued, thoughtful style to favour energy, wit and entertainment.

See also:
Media

-Jennifer Crabb

Sports Council (now Sport England)

The organization that is now known as Sport England has had a number of names and guises. The Sports Council was first established as an advisory body in January 1965 under the chairmanship of the Minister for Sport, Denis Howell M.P. The organization was given the task of advising the Government on matters relating to the development of amateur sport and physical recreation services and of fostering co-operation among statutory authorities and voluntary organizations.

The executive Sports Council was formally constituted by Royal Charter on February 4th, 1972, and the first chairman was Dr (later Sir) Roger Bannister. Separate sports councils for Scotland and Wales were also established in 1972 dealing with domestic affairs and grants in those countries, while the Sports Council had overall responsibility for British sports matters and grants in England. The Sports Council for Northern Ireland was established in 1974.

In 1972, the Sports Council, Scottish Sports Council and Sports Council for Wales launched the 'Sport for All' campaign to create wider public awareness of the value of sport and physical recreation in society and to call for action throughout Britain in extending and improving facilities and increasing participation. Throughout the 1970s and 1980s there were a series of campaigns aimed at various target groups. Some groups were identified because of their relatively low participation (the over fifties), others because of equal opportunities considerations (people with disabilities) and others still because of social considerations (unemployed people). As well as campaigning for increased participation in sport, the Sports Council was heavily involved in the increasing development of sports facilities, both through the use of grants and through providing technical advice.

The National Lottery commenced operation in November 1994 and the Sports Council became the distributing body for sport in England. In its first year of operation, 901 projects shared Lottery funding of £150 million towards total project costs of £355 million.

In 1995, after extensive consultation, a more streamlined structure for the organization of sport in the United Kingdom was adopted, following the publication of a Government policy paper *Sport: raising the game*. Under the revised system, the old G.B. Sports Council disappeared and a newly established English Sports Council assumed responsibility for the development of sport in England. The sports councils in Scotland and Wales remained virtually unchanged, while another new organization, the U.K. Sports Council, took responsibility for issues that needed to be dealt with at U.K. level. The English Sports Council continued to be the Lottery distributing body for sport in England and, in 1999, the U.K. Sports Council also became a distributor.

In March 1999, the English Sports Council's public profile was strengthened and simplified under the brand name of 'Sport England'. The objective of Sport England is to lead the development of sport in England by influencing and serving the public, private and voluntary sectors. It aims to get more people involved in sport, provide more places to play sport, and encourage the winning of more medals through higher standards of performance in sport.

Through the Active Schools, Active Communities and Active Sports programmes, together with its services to the governing bodies of sport, the development of the Sport England institutes as part of the U.K. Sports Institute, its continuing sports facility development and advice, and its information and research programmes, Sport England continues to underpin the development of sport.

References:
Sports Council, *The Sports Council, a Report* (London: Central Office of Information, 1966).

Sports Council, *The Sports Council, a Review 1966-69* (London: Central Council for Physical Recreation, 1969).

Sports Council, *Annual Report 1972-73* (London: Sports Council, 1973).

Further reading:
Sports Council and English Sports Council annual reports.

Websites:
Sport England –
http://www.english.sports.gov.uk

See also:
Central Council of Physical Recreation; Wolfenden Report

-Sally Hall

Sports Industry

As the commercialization of sport has developed, so too has the idea of sport as an industry. The sports industry contributes to the British economy in five areas – employment, consumer spending, tourism, economic regeneration and the creation of 'value-added' (the difference between total revenue and the cost of bought-in raw materials). Much of the revenue sport generates, such as advertising, transport provision and media work, is indirect and therefore difficult to quantify. However, the Sports Council has been prominent in attempting such exercises in order to argue for sport's wider importance and needs.

It is estimated that in 1990, sport-related economic activity created a value-added of £8.27 billion, or 1.7 per cent of Britain's Gross Domestic Product. Sport's value-added contribution to the economy is of a similar magnitude to the food manufacturing industry and greater than motor vehicle manufacturing.

Sport's contribution to economic regeneration is less clear. The presence of a successful professional sports club has long been regarded as being of benefit to the local economy and profile of its region, but again such assertions are difficult to quantify. The provision of participatory sporting facilities, such as swimming pools and gymnasiums, undoubtedly attracts significant numbers of visitors to an area. In 1996, for example, the most popular tourist attraction in Wales was Swansea Leisure Centre. In 1995, the sports tourism market was worth £1.5 billion.

The sport industry is undoubtedly a significant and growing business. In 1995, it accounted for £10.4 billion worth of consumer spending (2.24 per cent of the national total) and over 500,000 jobs. Consumer spending, including gambling, on sport and related items rose by over 14 per cent in real terms between 1985 and 1990, compared with 3 per cent for the whole economy. With fashions in sports clothing and footwear changing rapidly and the growth in subscription charges and fees for participatory sports, spending continues to increase significantly.

Sport is an industry that spans the voluntary, commercial and public sectors and, like any industry, both central and local government subsidize, regulate and tax it. Unlike more obviously commercial activities, public funding is given to sport for personal, health and social benefits. The economic benefits are of secondary importance and not a justification of policy.

Central government subsidies of sport in Britain are not as significant as in other Western nations since the state has been slow to recognize the economic and prestige benefits of the sports industry. Local government subsidies of sport too are falling as a proportion of their total expenditure. However, since 1994, the National Lottery has boosted the subsidies received by sport significantly.

Non-profit-making sports organizations in Britain also suffer from a significant tax burden in contrast to practices elsewhere. The Sports Council believed in 1993 that the United Kingdom was the only country in the world to tax its Olympic competitors. Overall, for every pound of local and government support sport receives, it gives back £5 to the taxpayer. It is such figures that make sport an important national industry.

References:

A Digest of Sports Statistics for the UK (London: Sports Council, 1991).

Sport in the Nineties: New Horizons (London: Sports Council, 1993).

The Sport England Website Information Sheets: Basic Facts about Sport – http://www.english.sports. gov.uk/resources/info/basic.htm

'Tourism in Wales', *Western Mail*, 3 July 1997.

Further reading:

Industry Trends and Forecasts: U.K. Sports Market (London: Key Note Market Review, 1994).

Sport England, *Policy Briefing 2: the Economic Impact of Sport in England* (London: English Sports Council, 1997).

See also:

Sports Sponsorship

-Martin Johnes

Sports Management (*see* Management)

Sports Medicine

Some writers have suggested that the origins of sports medicine can be traced back to the Ancient Greeks and Romans. However, the development of sports medicine as we know it today – that is, the more or less systematic application of the principles of medicine and science to the study of sporting performance, and the institutionalization of this practice in professional associations, research establishments, scientific conferences and journals – is more properly seen as a development of the late 19th and 20th centuries.

A. J. Ryan suggests that the first use of the term 'sports medicine' to describe an area of research and clinical practice centred around the performances of athletes appears to have been in February, 1928, when two doctors attending the Second Winter Olympic Games at St Moritz in Switzerland convened a meeting of physicians who were attending the Games with the teams of competing nations. It was at this meeting that the Association Internationale

Medico-Sportive was founded. In 1934, the Association changed its name to the Fédération Internationale de Médicine Sportive (F.I.M.S. – International Federation of Sports Medicine), a name that it has retained ever since.

In Britain, the development of modern sports medicine can be traced back to the late 19th century. In 1892, the British medical journal *The Lancet* reported on the dangers of the 'long and sleepless' bicycle rides that were then coming into fashion. Ryan has suggested that the section on first aid in sport, written by J. B. Byles and Samuel Osborn for *The Encyclopedia of Sport*, which was published in England in 1898, 'may have been the first writing in English that can be characterized as sportsmedicine in terms of relating to the medical problems encountered by sports participants'.

One of the most prominent British pioneers of sports medicine was the physiologist A. V. Hill who, in 1922, won the Nobel Prize for Physiology or Medicine for his work on the production of heat in muscle fibres. He later worked at Cornell University where he studied athletes, and sprinters in particular, in order to analyse athletic performance as a larger-scale scientific problem; Hill wrote that 'matters of very great scientific interest can be found in the performances of that extraordinary machine, the human athlete'.

One of the earliest English textbooks on sports medicine was Charles Heald's *Injuries and Sport, A General Guide for the Practitioner*, which was published in 1931. In his book, Dr Heald, who rowed for King's College, Cambridge, when they won the Thames Cup at the Henley Regatta in 1904, described characteristic injuries for thirty-six different sports. In the book's preface, he explained that many sports injuries 'are exceedingly obscure and troublesome, and the practitioner who is confronted with them will consult standard textbooks in vain. It is to assist those who have to deal with such injuries that this book has been compiled'. The first book in English to use the term 'sports medicine' in its title was J. R. P. Williams's *Sports Medicine*, published in 1962.

The institutional development of sports medicine has been particularly rapid since the early 1950s. In Great Britain, the British Association of Sport and Exercise Medicine (formerly the British Association of Sports Medicine) was established in 1953 by Sir Adolphe Abrahams and Sir Arthur (later Lord) Porritt. The Association now works closely with the National Sports Medicine Institute of the United Kingdom (N.S.M.I.), which is based in the Medical College of St Bartholomew's Hospital in London. In 1999, the N.S.M.I. announced the development of the Register of Exercise and Sports Care: U.K. (RESCUE), which is expected to become the primary information resource in the United Kingdom for those requiring access to sports medicine and sports science support providers.

References:

Hoberman, J., *Mortal Engines: the Science of Performance and the Dehumanization of Sport* (New York: The Free Press, 1992).

Ryan, A. J., 'Sportsmedicine History', *The Physician and Sports Medicine*, (October 1978), pp. 77-82.

Ryan, A. J., 'Sports Medicine in the World Today', in A. J. Ryan and F. L. Allman, Jr (eds.), *Sports Medicine* (San Diego, California: Academic Press, 1989. 2nd ed.), pp. 3-21.

Further reading:

Waddington, I., 'The Development of Sports Medicine', *Sociology of Sport Journal*, vol. 13 no. 2 (1996), pp. 176-196.

Websites:

The International Federation of Sports Medicine – http://www.fims.org/

The National Sports Medicine Institute of the United Kingdom – http://www.nsmi.org.uk/

The Register of Exercise and Sports Care: U.K. – http://www.rescu.org.uk/

See also:

British Association of Sport and Exercise Medicine

-Ivan Waddington

Sports Science

Sports science refers to the application of scientific methods to the study of phenomena and events in the fields of sport and exercise. It is an interdisciplinary subject area in the sense that it employs scientific approaches of both the behavioural (psychology, sociology) and human (anatomy, biochemistry, biomechanics, physiology) sciences in an integrated manner. It can also be considered to be multidisciplinary in that the various scientific methods can be applied separately to study particular aspects of sport and exercise.

Sports science is nowadays a highly respected subject for study at undergraduate or postgraduate level in universities in the United Kingdom. It is also an applied area for professional work, for example in the provision of scientific support for élite athletes. Sport can be liberally defined to include leisure and recreation as well as competitive sport and formal exercise training. Consequently sports science has relevance in health and exercise fields as well as laboratory-based work.

In the United Kingdom, sports science emerged as a hybrid, having origins in both physical education and sports medicine. Its growth in this country paralleled its development elsewhere. In European countries, notably Germany and the Scandinavian nations, sports science grew out of physical education with its established tradition of a systematic theoretical base for sports training and the physical education curriculum. In the United States, sports science was integrated with both physical education and sports medicine professions, without attaining its own identity separate from the pedagogic on the one hand and the clinical world on the other, as it has in the United Kingdom.

Formal recognition of sports science as a valid area of academic work was established with the first B.Sc. (Hons) degrees in Sports Science at the Liverpool Polytechnic (later known as Liverpool John Moores University) and at the University of Loughborough in 1975. In subsequent years a number of institutions of physical education diversified to initiate undergraduate degree programmes in related areas of sports studies, movement science/studies and so on. In recent years, specialization or modularization of degree programmes has enabled students to choose between concentrating on particular disciplines, for example, biomechanics, psychology or physiology, and maintaining a balanced and integrated sports scientific training. The study of sports science has become progressively more attractive, places on degree courses are at a premium and the market for graduate employment has continued to expand. The burgeoning exercise and fitness industry is a major source of employment but personnel engaged in work with élite sports performers tend now to include many with sports science backgrounds. Practically all of the 'project assistants' working on sports science support programmes of national governing bodies gained their intellectual training on sports science degree programmes.

The acceptance of sports science in the academic world is reflected also in the recent increase in institutions offering masters courses and research posts in sports science. It is enhanced by the appointment of chairs in sports science, closely related specialisms (for example, movement science and movement studies) and in specific disciplines (for example, sports psychology and applied physiology). It is manifest also in the incorporation of sports science in the title of university departments or sections.

A number of institutions with sports science courses have developed strong research emphases, offering post-graduate qualifications (M.Phil. and PhD) by research. Some impetus to this programme of research was given through the research studentships awarded by the Sports Council. The awards were dispersed across the sports science disciplines and have included applications in leisure, recreation management, fitness and sports injuries as well as sport and excellence. The breakdown of these indicates that the majority of submissions were in the field of exercise physiology. These programmes were open to competition and did not necessarily form a coherent overall thrust or follow an overall goal. They were concerned with fundamental areas of investigation, for example to establish more reliable and rigorous tests of physiological fitness; to test innovative types of equipment; to understand better social and psychological processes underlying sports participation and performance; and to investigate human biological systems and their responses to exercise. The scheme was confined to the award of two scholarships per annum designed to lead to doctoral theses. Altogether, twenty-five scholarships were awarded in the period 1980-1992, these being selected from a total of 268 submissions. Five of the projects were directly related to high-level competitive sport, three were concerned with leisure and physical education, two were purely theoretical and one was an animal study. Of the remainder, nine were studies of training and five could be described as experimental physiology. These scholarships were complemented by major initiatives where funding was directed towards: the establishment of physiological studies of muscle metabolism at Loughborough University (metabolic and hormonal responses to brief high intensity exercise); drug detection techniques at King's College, University of London; and the Training of Young Athletes (T.O.Y.A.) project at the Institute of Child Health, University of London.

In 1992, the Sports Council commissioned a review of sports science in order to establish priorities for the funding of sports science research in the United Kingdom. The report, prepared by Professor Tom Reilly and entitled *Strategic Directions for Sports Science Research in the United Kingdom*, was published by the Sports Council in 1992. Subsequently, two major research projects were funded, focusing on the areas that were deemed to be most in need of fundamental research. These were concerned with 'overtraining' and 'anxiety' in competitive sport. Originally, it was intended that these programmes would be complemented by the addition of new projects each year. With the establishment of the United Kingdom's Sports Institute in 1998, the research programme was reconfigured to sit alongside the sports science support work for the high-priority sports. Meanwhile, the vast majority of research in sports science continues to be subsidized by universities' own resources.

Side by side with the growth in maturity of sports science as an academic entity was the establishment of a professional body representative of the field. The Society of Sports Science was inaugurated at Milton Keynes in April 1977 and held its first scientific meeting in September of that year at Loughborough. A British Society of Sports Psychology had already existed and a Sports Biomechanics Study Group was active in the early 1980s. These were integrated into a British Association of Sport Sciences in 1984. The new organization settled into a structure with specialist sections in biomechanics, physiology and psychology. An Open Section provided an opportunity for new interest groups to become formalized but has assumed responsibility for interdisciplinary work and research that straddles the other disciplines, particularly notation and computerized match analysis. This section was renamed 'Interdisciplinary' after the Association as a whole amended its name to the British Association of Sport and Exercise Sciences (B.A.S.E.S.) in 1992. This reflected the interest of a large body of the membership in 'exercise for health' rather than in competitive sport and the alliance with health professional associations (for example, the Health Education Authority).

The Association as a whole has gained status by: publishing its own *Journal of Sports Sciences* since 1983, which has an international reputation and is published monthly in association with the International Society for Advancement of Kinanthropometry; holding a prestigious annual Sport and Science conference, as well as section conferences, seminars and workshops throughout the year and co-sponsoring international conferences; establishing codes of practice and accreditation procedures for its consultants in physiology, psychology and biomechanics, and guidelines for testing of athletes; and representing sports science in discussions with government agencies, through formal links with the health promotion agencies and with the European College of Sports Science (established in 1995).

In 1988, the Sports Council delegated responsibility for sports science support for governing bodies to the Sports Science Education Programme, administered by the National Coaching Foundation. The British Association of Sport and Exercise Sciences is heavily involved in, and deeply committed to, this process of providing sports science support to British sport. Responsibility for co-ordinating the programme, which was funded by the Sports Council, was initially placed in the hands of the Sports Science Support Officer, who would meet with a national governing body representative to identify the requirements of the sport. An appropriate accredited sports scientist was then identified and involved in the planning and carrying out of the scientific support for that sport. Quality control was assured through the accreditation processes of B.A.S.E.S. and through its formulation of codes of conduct and procedural guidelines. Sports science support included, for example, physiological monitoring of top performers and guidance of training programmes; biomechanical analysis and dissemination of educational material through technical reports, videos or computer graphics; and psychological preparation for competition.

The Sports Council's Sports Science Education Programme was effective by ensuring that: the sports science support provided addressed problems appropriate to the athletes' needs as perceived by coaches; quality control was assured through allocating projects only to accredited sports scientists and laboratories; a mutual trust was developed between sports scientists, coaches and athletes and lay and professional administrators; and a co-ordinated structure existed to enable national governing bodies to access sports science expertise.

The programme was terminated in 1998 to make way for support through the newly established U.K. Sports Institute. Sports science support was then accessed by means of National Lottery funding of the national governing bodies, being built into the 'world class performance plans' for the respective sports. This type of sports science support work was not solely for the sports that operated within the U.K. Sports Institute, which catered for sports on the Olympic Games programme. As Association Football, Rugby League and Rugby Union became more systematic in their preparation for match-play, more opportunities for sports science work opened up in the professional clubs. Such a change in attitude toward sports science within these sports confirmed the acceptance of the sports science professional in an applied setting.

Nowadays, sports science in the United Kingdom offers a wide range of attractive posts to those with appropriate qualifications. There is no indication that the market is likely to be saturated with sports science graduates, particularly as the curricula are altered to meet sport industry's demands. The professional areas of sports science are increasingly systematized so that there is effective quality control of services. The consequences are a high standard of practice and a rewarding experience.

Websites:
The British Association of Sport and Exercise Sciences – http://www.bases.co.uk/

See also:
Sports Medicine

-Tom Reilly

Sports Sponsorship

Sponsorship involves the investment of cash or in kind, in return for commercial benefits. The Institute of Sports Sponsorship states that 'Sports sponsorship is a partnership between business and sporting organisations and individuals that seeks to achieve benefits for both parties. By entering into a sponsorship agreement both sport and business seek to influence and motivate third party groups who are spectators, participants or consumers.'

Sponsors now play an integral part in financing British sport and an activity which may have amounted to £2.5 million in 1971 is currently reckoned to be worth over £300 million a year.

There are occasional examples of sponsorship before 1945. A few railway companies funded horse-races in the 19th century but donations from local tradesmen and the patronage of the aristocracy or town council were more significant. Professional golf received support from the *News of the World*, *The Tatler* and Perrier before 1914 and in the first half of the 20th century, athletics also benefited from limited commercial involvement with the *News of the World* and Oxo. However, sports sponsorship has largely developed in the post-war period, expanding rapidly, often controversially, and in a variety of ways. The spread of sponsorship agreements across a range of sports took place against the background of commercial television and the growth of advertising in the 1950s, and the decline in spectators and gate-money receipts in the 1960s and 1970s. The first beneficiaries were National Hunt racing, which saw Whitbread and Hennessy-promoted steeplechases in 1957, and cricket, whose flagging fortunes were revived and traditional image irrevocably altered by the introduction of one-day, limited-over cup competitions sponsored by Gillette and Benson and Hedges. By the 1980s, football league sponsorship was commonplace and the flat-racing Classics had all attracted major endorsements. By the closing years of the 20th century, there was a visible commercial presence in all major and many minor sports, from Rugby to croquet, from the Olympic Games to the Oxford and Cambridge Boat Race.

Sports sponsorship at the élite level has tended to feature two specific fields of business, the tobacco and drink trades (Embassy World Snooker Championship, Johnnie Walker P.G.A. tournament) and the financial sector (Britannic Assurance County Cricket Championship, Nationwide Football League, Lloyds TSB Five Nations Rugby). Nevertheless, sponsoring companies in the 1990s have ranged from multinational giants such as Coca Cola to local businesses such as Gosforth Decorating Services, and the sponsorship of individual athletes and lowlier teams and events has brought forth a wider group of advertisers. However, although most local primary school football teams now seek a sponsor for their kit, it has sometimes been difficult to attract and retain sponsorship deals for minority sports tournaments and women's sport.

The reasons for the growth of sponsorship are varied and complex. Initially, it has been suggested that the ban on tobacco and alcohol advertisements, together with the rising costs of more traditional forms of advertising, may have led to an increase in sponsorship agreements. Companies not only sought maximum publicity for their name and products but frequently chose sporting areas which associated those products with positive images. The drink and tobacco trades in particular have attempted, hypocritically some would say, to improve public perception of their products by association with seemingly healthy outdoor pursuits. Early involvement with less respectable events, such as snooker and darts tournaments or race meetings, has expanded to include sponsorship of golf and Formula 1 motor racing (Dunhill, BAT) and equestrian events, yacht racing and cricket (Whitbread, Fosters). The ways in

379

which advertisers have chosen to market their goods have also developed over time, from perimeter fence hoardings and competitors' clothing to attaching the sponsor's name to a competition or league, which ensures maximum repetition on sports and news programmes, for example Carling Premiership, Cornhill Insurance Test Matches. This particular ploy not only raises brand awareness but gets round the problem of B.B.C. coverage, which technically excludes advertising.

From the sports perspective, clubs and organizations in the second half of the 20th century have not only had to wrestle with the problems of antiquated facilities but also compete with an expanding number of leisure opportunities and a vastly increased coverage of sport on television. In order to pay for improved amenities and a general level of entertainment that might halt the decline in numbers of spectators, sport has embraced sponsorship as a way of funding necessary changes and bringing additional revenue. With the endorsement of sports clothing and equipment and the ubiquitous replica football strips, the marketing of sportspersons and brands has advanced in tandem to the point where athletes are used as walking or running billboards.

Among the more controversial sponsorship deals are logos painted on cricket pitches for maximum televisual impact and the renaming of sports stadia to include that of the sponsor, such as Huddersfield's Alfred McAlpine Stadium, Bolton's Reebok Stadium, Wigan's JJB Stadium, and the Fosters Oval. The importance of television coverage to sponsored events has been a factor in alterations to both the rules of several sports and the timing of matches, neither of which have met with universal approval. There are increasing conflicts over sponsorship clashes – in horse-racing, the trainers, jockeys and races may each be sponsored by different companies; in football codes, players and clubs may have contracts with rival brands of footwear. However, there are also examples of sponsorship co-operation, such as the attempts by Glasgow Rangers and Celtic football clubs to secure joint shirt sponsors.

Sponsoring firms have encountered different problems. The popularity of this form of advertising has seen a considerable hike in the amounts demanded by clubs and organizations in recent years, and some potential backers may have been deterred by increased costs and the uncertainties of the global economy in the late 1990s. Some forms of publicity may even be detrimental to the advertiser – a sponsorship agreement with Paul Gascoigne was cancelled following the intense media coverage of his domestic and alcohol-related difficulties, while BAT was the focus of adverse press comment in relation to its proposed sponsorship of Formula 1 motor racing.

Sports sponsorship can be controversial. It is also big business. In the 21st century, it is likely to get even bigger.

Further reading:

Polley, M., *Moving the Goalposts: a History of Sport and Society Since 1945* (London: Routledge, 1998).

Websites:

The Institute of Sports Sponsorship website – http://www.sports-sponsorship.co.uk/

See also:

Alcohol; Commericalism; Marketing; Television

-Joyce Kay

Sprinting (Motor Car)

Motor car sprinting, effectively speed trials over relatively short distances, developed rapidly in Britain during the early years of the 20th century, becoming a key feature of British motor sport; some eighty sprint events, including hill climbs, were held in 1924.

Apart from its general appeal to motoring enthusiasts, sprinting's popularity derived from the fact that, unlike in many other European countries and the United States, long-distance races were not allowed on public roads. Short-distance events, usually no longer than a mile, were tolerated, even though the speed limit was commonly ignored. Sprints were also held on private land and on suitable seaside beaches and promenades. They were easily organized by the motoring clubs that sprang up during this period and were supported by the motor manufacturers who used them to test their products. Some sprints developed into formal race meetings, with the Bexhill Speed Trials, held for the first time in 1902, becoming something of a model. Here, part of Bexhill promenade, Sussex, was sealed off to allow motor cars to compete over a flying kilometre.

Motor car sprinting was undermined in the mid-1920s by the R.A.C.'s decision to prohibit speed trials on public roads, and by the more hostile stance taken by the Board of Trade towards the use of the foreshore for racing. The growing popularity of circuit racing, rallies and eventually drag racing helped to lessen the appeal of speed trials during the inter-war period and beyond.

References:

Brendon, P., *The Motoring Century: the Story of the Royal Automobile Club* (London: Bloomsbury, 1997).

Nicholson, T. R., *Sprint: Speed Hillclimbs and Speed Trials in Britain, 1899-1925* (Newton Abbot: David & Charles, 1969).

Nye, D., *Motor Racing in Colour* (Poole: Blandford Press, 1978).

Richardson, K. E., *The British Motor Industry, 1896-1939* (London: Macmillan, 1976).

See also:

Motor Racing

-David Thoms

Squash

Squash is a racket game played in a wall-enclosed court with a small soft rubber ball. It was developed from the game of rackets at Harrow School from about 1860, and the first set of rules was described in 1886. Using a smaller court with a wooden floor and a softer 'squash' ball, it may have been introduced for schoolboys as a preparation for the faster, more demanding (and more expensive) parent game. A similar game was developed in the United States but using a hard ball. British squash was first regulated by a sub-committee of the Tennis & Rackets Association and then by the Squash Rackets Association from 1928. Regional associations for Northern Ireland, Scotland and Wales were formed later. The World Squash Federation is the international governing body of the sport.

The standard court measures 21 feet wide by 32 feet long, with out-of-court lines 15 feet high at the front and 7 feet high at the back, connected by straight lines down the sides. There is a 19-inch high strip (known as the tin) along the bottom of the front wall, above which the ball must be hit. Generally played as a singles game, the scoring is up to 9 points with points won only by the hand-in (serving) player. If the score in a game reaches 8 points all, the player who scored 8 first can choose to 'set one' or 'set two'. In the case of 'set one', the game ends when a player reaches 9 points. In the case of 'set two', the game ends when a player reaches ten points. The ball is hit alternately by the two players, and each time the ball must be returned before the second bounce (either volleyed or taken after the first bounce) and must hit the front wall before the floor at some time in its trajectory. The configuration of the court and the slow bounce of the ball encourage the use of a great variety of shots, including the drive, lob, kill, nick, boast and drop shots. The general tactic of the game is to play the ball away from the opponent to make its return as difficult as possible. This primarily involves playing shots to good 'length' (where the second bounce would land as near to the back wall as possible) and 'tight' (close) to the side walls.

Interest in the game grew slowly at first, from about 1900. The first championships for men and women were played in England in 1922, and inter-varsity matches started in 1925. Interest grew more rapidly with the widely publicized performances of players such as the Egyptian diplomat F. D. Amr Bey (Amateur Champion 1931-1933 and 1935-1937, Open Champion 1932-1937) and Hashim Khan (Pakistan, Open Champion 1950-1955, 1957). Popularity reached a peak in Great Britain in the 1970s, this largely due to the remarkable achievements of Jonah Barrington (Republic of Ireland, Open Champion 1966-1967, 1969-1972). Barrington's efforts to further popularize the game through tours and 'clinics' continue to influence the game. However, since the 1980s there has been some decline in interest in squash, partly attributable to its failure to capture mass television audiences (compared with other sports like lawn tennis and golf) and a consequent inability to attract big money sponsorship. There are now nearly 50,000 courts in over 130 countries; England, with some 8,660 courts, has the largest number.

A recent notable player was Jahangir Khan (Pakistan) who won ten Open Championships. The greatest woman player was Heather McKay (Australia), who from 1962 until 1977 won every World Championship until she retired unbeaten. The major international events are the biannual World Open Championships and the World Team Championships. The British Open Championship remains the most important annual event.

References:

McKenzie, I., *The Squash Workshop: a Complete Game Guide* (Marlborough: Crowood, 1993).
Wallbutton, T., 'History of Squash' (http://www.squash.org/wsf/history.phtml)

Websites:

The Squash Rackets Association – http://www.squash.co.uk/
The World Squash Federation – http://www.squash.worldsport.com/

-Peter M. B. Cahusac

Stock-car Racing

The sport of stock-car racing emerged during the prohibition years (1919-1933) in the United States. In an attempt to evade the authorities, illicit distillers, located in the mountains, used charged-up passenger cars to transport their illegal cargo. Mountainous roads and fast cars required specialized driving techniques – techniques that were eventually utilized for stock-car racing.

During the 1930s, these charged-up cars were used in races on beaches, mostly in the southern states. Daytona beach became something of a centre for the sport and it was here that the National Association for Stock Car Auto Racing (N.A.S.C.A.R.) was founded in 1947. The professional sport soon became very popular in the United States, attracting crowds in excess of 100,000 for Grand National events, which vary in length but are usually between 250 and 600 miles. Cars, though superficially like passenger cars, are completely modified to racing-car standard.

Stock-car racing was introduced to Britain in 1954 by the newly created British Stock Car Racing Association, at the time a consortium of promoters with twenty franchises. The Association ran two classes – Senior (with an unrestricted engine size) and Formula 2 (with an engine size limited to a maximum of 1172 cc). Additional organizations and classes also came into being, such as Speedworth International, which introduced Supertox, Hot Rod and Midget classes. One of the attractions of the sport was its cheapness compared to other forms of motor sport. Another interesting feature is that the stock-car promoter pays the driver 'start money' to race and does not collect an entry fee off the owner or driver.

After a period of popularity in the 1960s and 1970s, interest in the sport amongst the public at large started to decline, to the extent that today racing takes place on only a few tracks around the country.

References:

Arlott, J. (ed.), *Oxford Companion to Sports and Games* (London: Oxford University Press, 1976).

See also:

Motor Racing

-Richard W. Cox/Ray Physick

Stoke Mandeville

Stoke Mandeville is synonymous with disabled sport in Britain and around the world. In 1944, the Stoke Mandeville Hospital for the Spinal Injured was opened in Aylesbury, Buckinghamshire. The hospital's original function was to provide rehabilitation for the thousands injured during the Second World War. Stoke Mandeville's founder, Sir Ludwig Guttmann, believed that sport, as a vehicle for the rehabilitation of the spinal injured, was of the utmost importance and vital to their recovery and adapted lifestyle.

In 1948, the first Stoke Mandeville Games were held in the grounds of the Hospital, with sixteen ex-servicemen and women competing in an archery competition. The Games became international in 1952, when a team from the Netherlands arrived in England to compete. The first sports stadium for the disabled, the Stoke Mandeville Sports Stadium for the Paralysed and Other Disabled, was opened by Queen Elizabeth in 1969. The Stoke Mandeville World Wheelchair Games are held every year in Aylesbury during the summer, except in Olympic years when the Paralympics are staged.

In 1949, Sir Ludwig Guttmann predicted that one day there would be an Olympic Games for the disabled held alongside the able-bodied Games. This earned him the title of 'Father of the Paralympics'. In 1960, Sir Ludwig's vision became a reality when 400 disabled athletes from twenty-one countries competed in their own International Stoke Mandeville Games for the Paralysed at the Olympic site in Rome.

Sir Ludwig Guttmann died in 1980, but his vision for Stoke Mandeville as a location for providing disabled people with a chance to participate in sport still lives on today.

References:

Guttmann, L., *A Textbook of Sport for the Disabled* (Aylesbury: HM+M, 1976).

Scruton, J., *Stoke Mandeville: Road to the Paralympics. Fifty Years of History* (Aylesbury: Peterhouse Press, 1998).

See also:

Disability Sports

-Julie Anderson

Stoolball

Stoolball emerged as a loosely structured spring and summer pastime in Tudor England, played largely in woodland areas, and has often been claimed as a precursor of cricket. The 'stool' may have been used as either wicket or bat.

In its modern form, two teams, normally of eleven a side, play with two wickets (1 foot [30 centimetres] square boards) mounted on poles 4 feet 6 inches (1.37 metres) tall and 16 yards (5 metres) apart, using any convenient grass surface. Soft balls, derived from real tennis, are bowled underarm from one wicket to a bat holder standing at the other. The bat is normally wooden, and is shaped like a rather heavy table tennis bat. After striking the ball, the bat holder runs between the two wickets unless bowled or caught out. The winning team is the one that has scored the highest number of runs. There are two umpires, who are normally male, whilst the players are predominantly female. The rest of the bowler's team are spread out as fielders.

It was revived in south-eastern England in the 1840s to fill the spare time of rural girls.

Small county organizations emerged, but most games took place between neighbouring villages. It was eventually given wider exposure by an eccentric lawyer, country landowner and part-time soldier, William W. Grantham of Sussex, who exploited it to revive 'Merrie England' and help wounded soldiers recuperate before returning to the First World War trenches. A tireless publicist, he used the game to raise charitable funds and promote international understanding between the wars. However, he alienated those who regarded it as essentially a women's game and who provided its main support. By the 1930s, there were around 1,000 clubs scattered throughout England, but the battle for control was fought in the south-east between Grantham's Stoolball Association of Great Britain (founded 1923) and various women's groups. Grantham's association died with him in 1942.

After 1945 there was a quiet revival. In the late 1970s, a new National Stoolball Association emerged, dealing largely with the south-east and some 200 clubs – although many more are not affiliated. However, the Association allows mixed teams, a practice that some older players deplore, insisting on all-female teams. Stoolball remains as a much-loved amateur game primarily for women, as important a symbol of the south-eastern English summer as cricket is for men.

References:

Lowerson, J., 'Stoolball and the Manufacture of Englishness', in G. Pfister et al. (eds.), *Spiele der Welt im Spannungsfeld von Tradition und Moderne* (Sankt Augustin, Germany: Academia Verlag, 1996).

Lowerson, J., 'Stoolball, Conflicting Values in the Revivals of a Traditional Sussex Game', *Sussex Archaeological Collections*, 133 (Lewes: Sussex Archaeological Society, 1995).

Websites:

The National Stoolball Association – http://www.nsa.dircon.co.uk/

-John Lowerson

Strathclyde Water Park

Strathclyde Country Park was developed in the 1970s by completely revivifying an area of industrial and mining waste in Lanarkshire. This was one of the most ambitious regeneration projects ever carried out in Scotland, and has provided one of the country's biggest leisure facilities.

At the heart of the Country Park lies Strathclyde Loch, a man-made lake that has as its main feature an Olympic-standard rowing course, one of the very few sporting facilities in Great Britain that is consistently maintained at the technical standards required to host world-level events.

As well as the water-based sports facility provided by the rowing course, Strathclyde Park also has an eighteen-hole golf course, a number of all-weather football and hockey pitches, a unique set of Roman ruins, a bird sanctuary and Scotland's largest 'fun' theme park.

Strathclyde Park's rowing course was first used for domestic-level competition in 1979, and made its international debut when it hosted the rowing and canoe (demonstration sport only) events of the thirteenth Commonwealth Games in 1986. For this event, new start and finish towers were added to the existing rowing course facilities as well as the first electronic timing equipment. With these additions, the Strathclyde Country Park rowing course came up to the required top-level standards. This has allowed the Scottish Amateur Rowing Association to successfully host a number of top-class international events, culminating in the largest-ever World Rowing Championships that took place in August 1996.

See also:

Rowing

-Mike Haggerty

Superstition (*see* Ritual and Superstition)

Surfing

Surfing, the riding of waves on a board, originates in Polynesia. The Polynesians used a type of surfboard to get ashore and their activities were recorded by Captain Cook in 1777 in Hawaii and Tahiti. Cook also observed that the islanders surfed for pleasure. Following European colonization, however, missionaries banned the practice in 1821, regarding it as an immoral pastime.

It was almost a century before surfing re-emerged. The Hawaiian, Duke Kahanamoku, successfully introduced the sport into Australia in 1915 before officially resurrecting surfing in Hawaii in 1921. He was also responsible for establishing the first surfers' club at Waikiki.

Technological developments have transformed the sport in the last few decades. Using technology developed during the Second World War, manufacturers have been able to produce ever lighter boards using polyurethane foam and fibreglass.

Surfing arrived on British shores in 1955, when Australian surfing experts taught lifeguards in Devon and Cornwall how to surf. Subsequently, the Surf Life Saving Association of Great Britain was formed in Cornwall and Devon. During the 1960s, the sport boomed both in Britain and internationally, and the sport remains popular to this day. Over 100,000 people regularly surf in Britain. It is also a major industry, generating over £86 million of business in 1997. Body surfing and canoe surfing are popular alternatives to the more commonly known board surfing.

Since 1966, the British Surfing Association (B.S.A.) has been the governing body of the sport. The B.S.A. is affiliated to the International Surfing Association and the Central Council of Physical Recreation.

References:
Arlott, J. (ed.), *Oxford Companion to Sports and Games* (London: Oxford University Press, 1976).
British Surfing Association, *An Introduction to Surfing* (Penzance: British Surfing Association, [n.d.]).

Websites:
The British Surfing Association – http://www.britsurf.co.uk/
The Surf Life Saving Association of Great Britain – http://www.lifeguards.org.uk/

See also:
Canoeing

-Ray Physick

Swimming

Competition

Swimming is a method of propulsion through water. There are four competitive swimming strokes. The fastest is front crawl, more often referred to as freestyle, and the others are backstroke, breaststroke and butterfly. There are also events in which all four strokes are combined in one race known as individual medley.

Casual swimming in rivers and the sea during the summer months was a popular recreational activity during the late 18th century and throughout most of the 19th century. There were no financial constraints, no specialist equipment was required and it was extremely refreshing. There were recognized 'safe spots' in rivers, estuaries and bays for beginners and experts alike.

Various groups of recreational swimmers gathered together to formalize their activities during the second quarter of the 19th century. Huddersfield and Lockwood Swimming Club is known to have organized races in 1825, and in 1828 the St George Swimming Club in Liverpool was using Britain's first municipally owned baths. Initially, at these and other clubs, members spent time learning to swim and improving their stroke technique. They also raced against each other as they became increasingly proficient and annual programmes of races emerged in various parts of

The Y.W.C.A. Swimming Club Team at the High Street Baths, Hathersage, Manchester in c. 1909 (Documentary Photography Archive, Manchester, Ref.: 617/1 L14/38)

the country. Crowds enjoyed watching and betting on exciting and potentially dangerous open-water swimming races.

From the early 1860s, clubs organized 'all-comers' events for impressive trophies and often money, to encourage contact with 'racers' from other clubs. Some clubs thought that their particular open races were sufficiently national in character to be labelled 'national championships'. A handful of clubs in London attempted to clear up the confusion by establishing an organization to regulate championships. The Associated Metropolitan Swimming Clubs was established in 1869, becoming the London Swimming Association later in the same year and the Metropolitan Swimming Association by 1870. Within three years, a dozen provincial clubs had also become involved in its activities and so its title was changed to the Swimming Association of Great Britain. During the next fifteen years, there were numerous attempts to separate amateurs from professionals in all contests but without success. Matters came to ahead in 1884 when

the 'better class clubs' resigned to establish a solely amateur body, the Amateur Swimming Union. After two years of almost continuous feuding, the two sides set up the Amateur Swimming Association, agreeing on a suitable 'amateur' definition.

Racing at traditional open water sites lost much of its attraction at the end of the century as scores of private and public indoor 'baths' provided more attractive alternatives. These arose largely from national and local initiatives to improve public health and middle-class demands for exclusive, well-appointed recreational and social facilities. Permissive Public Baths and Wash-houses Acts in 1846, 1847 and 1872 enabled local authorities to borrow money to build individual baths, wash-houses and, later, swimming pools for the 'labouring classes'. Private baths clubs, in common with golf, tennis and cricket clubs, were recreational, sporting and social centres where professional groups could meet in pleasant, informal surroundings. By 1914, there were 270 public and private indoor establishments in England and Wales, 30 in Scotland and 5 in Ireland.

Indoor facilities stimulated the development of swimming clubs. Members were taught to swim and coaching was provided for skilled swimmers. Various intra-club and handicap competitions were also introduced to maintain and raise standards. The annual club gala was the highlight of the season. By the 1890s, a set of aquatic activities had emerged which formed the basis for clubs' swimming programmes until the 1940s. The main features were numerous intra-club and several open races, a 'scientific swimming' display and a game of water polo. Clubs issued annual fixture cards and an annual swimming season was established which began in April and ended in October.

During the final quarter of the 19th century, the Amateur Swimming Association set about controlling, organizing and promoting all aspects of swimming. Initially, it brought order to a number of diffuse practices by formalizing and disseminating rules for competitions. Later, it planned national calendars that included inter-city and home international representative fixtures, trials and national championships.

International swimming on a global scale began in 1896 at the first Olympic Games of the modern era. Six of the thirteen nations involved entered eighteen swimmers in three freestyle events held in open water. A different swimming programme was organized at the second Olympiad, in Paris in 1900. It took place on the River Seine. Further changes were made at St Louis in 1904 and London in 1908. By this time, the Olympic Games Committee recognized that uniformity was required and the Amateur Swimming Association suggested that its rules used at the London Olympiad, amended if necessary, be adopted. During the Games, the Amateur Swimming Association's Honorary Secretary, George Hearn, successfully led competing nations to establish a worldwide swimming association, the Fédération Internationale de Natation Amateur (F.I.N.A. – International Amateur Swimming Federation).

It created a uniform set of rules for swimming, diving and water polo, applicable to all international competitions, and assumed responsibility for the verification of world records and the compilation of world lists. This marked the start of a growing interest from national governing bodies in international competition and the Olympic Games provided the stage on which international comparisons were made.

Britain enjoyed some success at the second Olympiad in Paris – John Jarvis winning the 1,000 metres and 4,000 metres freestyle – but it has never surpassed its achievements at the Olympic Games in 1908. Henry Taylor won gold in the 400 metres and 1,500 metres freestyle and Fred Holman won a gold in the 200 metres breaststroke. A fourth gold was gained in the 4 x 200 metres freestyle relay. Only three British men have won gold medals since this time – David Wilkie (200 metres breaststroke) in Montreal in 1976, Duncan Goodhew (100 metres breaststroke) in Moscow in 1980 and Adrian Moorhouse (100 metres breaststroke) in Seoul in 1988. British women have recorded even fewer successes. Relay teams won gold medals in 1908 (4 x 200 metres freestyle) and 1912 (4 x 100 metres freestyle) and there have been three individual golds – Lucy Morton (200 metre breaststroke in 1924), Judy Grinham (100 metres backstroke in 1956) and Anita Lonsbrough (200 metres breaststroke in 1960).

Life-Saving and Survival

The Royal Humane Society, founded in London in 1774 with the object of making awards to people who performed acts of bravery in saving, or trying to save, human life, was the first of numerous humane societies in the late 18th and throughout the 19th century that campaigned, developed rescue and resuscitation methods and provided rescue services to prevent drownings by recreational swimmers in open water. At the same time, some of the many swimming clubs that emerged in the third and final quarters of the 19th century practised rescue techniques and organized competitions, but they were carried out unsystematically and at a local level.

A rising annual toll of over 2,000 deaths by drowning by 1890 led some prominent swimming administrators of the period to ask the Royal Humane Society to undertake instruction using its own organization and staff. It declined due to a lack of resources. Undeterred, the administrators established the Swimmers' Life Saving Society in 1891 and within twelve months it had published a rescue and resuscitation handbook and organized a national competition, sponsored by Lever Brothers, in which twenty-four teams competed. Soon after, branches were established throughout the country and a graded proficiency scheme and systematic training structure were introduced.

The Royal Life Saving Society, as it is now known, has been very successful in preventing needless drownings through raising public awareness of safety in and on water, providing instruction to the public and training lifesavers and lifeguards. It is the recognized leader in lifesaving education. Its water safety, rescue and resuscitation programmes are taught in over fifty Commonwealth countries.

Long-Distance

For most of the 19th century, long-distance endurance feats or races for money across estuaries and bays or along rivers were relatively popular seasonal spectacles. For the most part, unique, local rules were formulated by patrons and entrepreneurs, advertisements were placed in the local press and gambling was common. They declined in the last quarter of the century with the emergence of racing over much shorter distances in indoor swimming pools, organized by local clubs according to a set of nationally agreed amateur rules. Nevertheless, activity continued as amateur clubs near to suitable open-water racing sites emerged as organizers of existing and new events during the late 19th century and the first half of the 20th century.

Increased interest after around 1950 eventually led to the establishment of the British Long Distance Swimming Association (B.L.D.S.A.) in 1956, and by the 1960s it had revived or introduced annual and periodic British championships over distances ranging from 3 to 22 miles at nationally recognized sea and inland racing locations such as Torbay, Kings Lynn, Lake Windermere and Loch Lomond. At the same time, its affiliated clubs and associations have continued to stage dozens of open championships throughout Britain over distances between 2 and 20 miles. In addition, some clubs, such as the Morecambe Cross Bay Swimming Association and the Solent Swimming Club, observe (or investigate), ratify and issue certificates for all successful swims in their locality. The B.L.D.S.A. also awards certificates for legitimately observed and timed swims over 5 miles where no local club or association exists.

A strong competitive element thrives alongside camaraderie and friendship in this challenging sport. Winning is important for some, while others find considerable satisfaction in completing the course or achieving a personal best time.

Synchronized

Floating and underwater displays were novelty items at clubs' swimming galas in the late 19th century. They were entertaining interludes between swimming races. Graceful or ornamental swimming was performed mainly by men, but women became involved at the turn of the century. In the 1920s, female 'floatation teams' from North America developed aspects of life-saving and graceful swimming into artistic activities. Figures and strokes were arranged into routines and performed at shows and galas. Initially there was no music. Changes to swimming patterns were notified by whistles. Music was added in the early 1930s as an accompaniment and then some groups began to swim to the beat. The idea spread to Europe and Britain's first water pageant took place in

1936 in London as part of the first swimming gala of the Women's League of Health and Beauty.

This marked the beginning of synchronized swimming and within a few years a competitive structure had emerged, consisting largely of rather mechanical compulsory figures and strokes. These had been replaced by free, expressive musical routines by the 1950s. The Metropolitan Diving School in London established a synchronized swimming group and in 1958 it competed in the first European Championships in Amsterdam. The country's first synchronized swimming club was established at the Seymour Hall Baths in London in 1961 and by 1964, the Amateur Swimming Association had assumed responsibility for the organization and promotion of the sport in England. The first national championships were held in 1969. Great Britain won the European Championships in 1977 and 1983 but lost ground after this time.

References:

Besford, P., *Encyclopaedia of Swimming* (London: Robert Hale & Co., 1971).

Bilsborough, P., *One Hundred Years of Scottish Swimming* (Stirling: Scottish Amateur Swimming Association, 1988).

Keil, I. and Wix, D., *In the Swim: the Amateur Swimming Association from 1869 to 1994* (Loughborough: Swimming Times Ltd, 1996).

Pearsall, R., *Lifesaving: the Story of the Royal Life Saving Society – The First 100 Years* (Newton Abbot: David & Charles, 1991).

Sinclair, A. and Henry, W., *Swimming* (London: Longmans, Green & Co., 1900).

Further reading:

Amateur Swimming Association, *A.S.A. Handbook of Synchronised Swimming* (Loughborough: A.S.A. Swimming Enterprises, 1991).

Forsberg, G., *Modern Long Distance Swimming* (London: Routledge & Kegan Paul, 1963).

Oppenheim, F., *The History of Swimming* (New York: Swimming World, 1970).

Terret, T., 'Professional Swimming in England before the Rise of Amateurism, 1837-75', *International Journal of the History of Sport*, vol. 12, no. 1 (1995), pp. 18-32.

Thomas, R., *Swimming* (London: Sampson Low, Marston, 1904).

Websites:

The British Long Distance Swimming Association – http://www.bldsa.org.uk/

The International Amateur Swimming Federation – http://www.fina.org/

The Royal Life Saving Society – http://www.lifesavers.org.uk/

See also:

Channel Swimming

-Peter Bilsborough

T

Table Tennis

Table tennis – like all sports – was not invented, but evolved over a long period, and there is no certainty as to when balls were first struck to and fro over a net on a table.

However, in 1890, a Mr David Foster patented his Parlour Lawn Tennis (no. 11037) with the optimistic injunction 'No Family should be without one'; in fact, only one example is known to have survived. This was certainly tennis-on-a-table, in keeping with the Victorian liking for miniaturization, but with the severe restriction that it was played on a court with tennis lines inside a 'fence', suggesting a family pastime rather than a sport. Moreover, the ball gave a very unsatisfactory bounce.

In 1891, John Jaques and Son, the company most associated, over many years, with table tennis, produced their Gossima; this was closer to table tennis today, but it did not catch the imagination of the public until it was relaunched as Ping-Pong in 1900, with the introduction of a celluloid (or parkesine) ball, brought over, it is said, from the United States. Gossima was followed, in the same year, by Slazenger's Whiff-Waff and a host of imitations, all claiming to be 'new'.

From 1900 to about 1904, there was a huge craze for table tennis – the first table tennis magazine, *Table Tennis and Pastimes Pioneer*, listed 113 English clubs in 1902 and claimed 20,000 readers; the Xylonite Works at Brantham in Essex produced six tons of balls per week; and Crystal Palace Club boasted of 500 members. The *Sheffield Independent* gave six reasons for the popularity of table tennis: 'It is inexpensive and it is adaptable to the family table, it only requires two players, both sexes meet on fairly equal terms, first experiences are usually encouraging, and it offers the widest scope for real skill.'

The craze manifested itself at two levels – the domestic scene and the tournament scene; table tennis was immensely popular as an after-dinner recreation for the genteel, but tournaments at such venues as the Queen's Hall and the Royal Aquarium, Westminster, attracted large entries. It is clear from the dozen manuals published around 1901-1902 that the play was far more sophisticated than is generally appreciated today.

The Table Tennis Association and the rival Ping-Pong Association were set up, within four days of each other, in December 1901, with the only important difference being that ping-pong favoured the double-bounce service, but within two years both versions were in serious decline; the craze simply burnt itself out, not to be revived until 1922, when the Table Tennis Association (later English Table Tennis Association) was re-formed under the chairmanship of the Honourable Ivor Montagu. Table tennis is therefore unique as a sport in having two histories.

The laws as published in the new handbook were accepted as authoritative not only in Great Britain, but, eventually, all around the world. The International Table Tennis Federation (I.T.T.F.) followed in 1926. Eight countries, including England and Wales, were represented at the first congress and world championships; Scotland have taken part since 1947 and Northern Ireland since 1935.

From the very beginning of table tennis, right up to the mid-1950s, there was no limitation on the material, size, shape or weight of the bat (strictly racket), but the almost universal use of a rubber sponge covering led to a stringent definition of the law relating to the materials which could be used.

Post-war table tennis, like all racket sports, has been dominated by technical developments with equipment. Bats covered with thick sponge or crepe rubber, as opposed to the traditional pimpled rubber, came into prominence in the early 1950s, but because of their extra spin and speed, which was said to baffle opponents and spoil table tennis as a spectacle, these surfaces were banned in England for the season 1956-1957, and then throughout the world from 1959, when racket standardization restricted thickness of bat coverings each side to 4 millimetres of pimpled rubber, or a sandwich of pimpled rubber (pimples either inwards or outwards) on sponge.

The 'sandwich' bat became the most popular bat amongst serious players following standardization. In England, in 1960, a little-known player, Stan Jacobson, perfected a high trajectory, relatively slow, excessive topspin or 'loop' stroke. This technique was emulated and developed to the extent that spin serves followed by fast, heavy topspins or 'loop-drives', are now the basis of the modern sport.

In order to counter the effectiveness of 'combination bat twiddling' (the turning over in the hand of a bat covered with two totally different surfaces), a new regulation was implemented in 1984 forcing players to use two different coloured rubbers. Regulations have also been passed to restrict the length of 'long pimples' (which produced unpredictable effects) and to ban 'fast' liquid adhesives (for applying bat rubbers) that contained unacceptable levels of toxic substances.

Between 1926 and the mid-1950s, mainly Eastern European players, such as Victor Barna (Hungary) and Richard Bergmann (Austria), dominated world table tennis, although England, too, produced world singles champions in Fred Perry (1929), who went on to greater fame in lawn tennis, and Johnny Leach (1949 and 1951). England won the Swaythling Cup world men's team event for the only time in 1953. The Rowe twins, Diane and Rosalind, were the best known of England's world doubles champions (1951 and 1954). Scotland's greatest ever player, Helen Elliot, twice won the world women's doubles title (1949 and 1950).

Since the mid-1950s, Japanese and then Chinese players have gained world ascendancy, using mainly penholder grips in contrast to the traditional European shakehands grip. The only notable successes of English players during this period came at a European level – Jill Hammersley (Parker) was women's champion in 1976; John Hilton was men's champion in 1980; and Desmond Douglas was Top Twelve men's champion in 1987.

Largely through the work of the then President of the International Table Tennis Federation, Welshman H. Roy Evans, and to a lesser extent the contacts of the Chairman of the English Table Tennis Association, Charles Wyles, the American, English and other Western national teams toured China in April 1971, heralding a breakthrough in international relations between China and the West in a process coined 'Ping Pong Diplomacy'. Olympic recognition, owing much to Roy Evans, came at Seoul in 1988. Table Tennis had led the sporting world in removing distinctions between 'amateurs' and 'professionals' in 1935. The limit in prize-money was removed in 1985, during Roy Evans's term in office.

The sport has continued to expand internationally, from 8 affiliations to the I.T.T.F. in 1926, to 47 in 1950, and 184 in December 1999. In Britain, participation continued to rise until just after the 1977 World Championships in Birmingham, at which time it was at the same level as lawn tennis.

References:

Crayden, R., *The Story of Table Tennis: the First 100 Years* (Hastings: The English Table Tennis Association, 1995).

Gurney. G. N., *Table Tennis: the Early Years* (St Leonards-on-Sea: The International Table Tennis Federation, 1989).

Websites:

The English Table Tennis Association – http://www.etta.co.uk/

The International Table Tennis Federation – http://www.ittf.com/

-Gerald Gurney

Target Shooting

Firearms have been used for competitive shooting since around the 15th century as a natural progression from target shooting with the longbow.

Early firearms were relatively inaccurate and at first could only be used for target shooting at very close range. The sport was perfected on the Continent and only became officially recognized in Britain with the foundation of the National Rifle Association in 1860.

The Association was born within the framework of national defence and because it sprang from largely patriotic motives, it had the blessing of Queen Victoria, who founded the Queen's Prize Contest in 1860 with prize money of £250. Other lucrative prize monies followed in competitions confined in most instances to military personnel. Many clubs were formed throughout Britain, although after the Second World War the sport lost most of its military characteristics.

Today, target shooting is practised in many forms and with a variety of weapons, ranging from full-bore service rifles to pistols.

Full-bore target shooting can be divided into three classes: target rifle, service rifle and match rifle. Target rifle competitions are conducted entirely from the prone position at distances from 200 to 1000 yards. Service rifle competitions include standing, kneeling and firing with movement. Match rifle competitions allow the use of any type of rifle with any magnifying or telescopic sight, provided it is restricted to a 7.62 mm barrel.

Small-bore target shooting is the more popular in Britain. It is confined to rifles of 5.6-mm calibre with targets at 50 and 100 yards outdoors, 15 and 25 yards indoors.

Pistol shooting dates back to Tudor times and was also confined largely to the armed forces until recent times. Events include rapid-fire pistol at 25 metres, free pistol at 50 metres and centre-fire pistol and standard pistol at 25 metres. Pistol shooting is one of the events included in the modern pentathlon.

Most of the prestigious British events were held at a range in Wimbledon until a National Centre for Shooting was created at Bisley (in Surrey) in 1889. This has been the venue for all major competitions since and will be the venue for the 2002 'Manchester' Commonwealth Games.

References:

Antal, L., *Pistol Shooting* (East Ardsley, Wakefield: E. P. Publishing, 1980).

Websites:

The National Rifle Association – http://www.nra.org.uk/

See also:

Wild Pigeon Shooting

-Richard William Cox

Taylor Reports

Seen by many as a watershed in British football, the Taylor Reports of 1989 and 1990 signalled the end of an era. Appointed by the Government to enquire into the Hillsborough Disaster, Lord Justice Taylor produced two damning reports that shook the game, and led to its total reconstruction in the 1990s.

The *Interim Report* considered the specific events at Hillsborough in April 1989, and found that the worst disaster in British football was caused by a total failure of police control and management, exacerbated by a badly maintained and managed ground at Sheffield Wednesday. Taylor rejected tabloid allegations that Liverpool fans were responsible for the disaster, and instead condemned the whole mentality of police and clubs towards supporters, arguing that an obsession with cost-cutting, profit and the threat of hooliganism led to serious failures in crowd control, maintenance of facilities and attitude towards supporters.

In the *Final Report* published in January 1990, Taylor rejected the ID card membership schemes favoured by the Conservative government, and instead recommended a fundamental rethink of the safety and maintenance of British grounds, the introduction of all-seater stadia, and a new relationship between fan and club based on respect. Some of his better ideas were rejected, notably on ticket prices and the creation of a stadium design council, but Taylor's reports remain the cornerstone of British football in the 1990s, and are probably far more important than even he could have hoped for.

References:

Taylor, Lord Justice, *The Hillsborough Stadium Disaster: Interim Report* (London: HMSO, 1989).

Taylor, Lord Justice, *The Hillsborough Stadium Disaster: Final Report* (London: HMSO, 1990).

Further reading:

Williams, J., and Wagg, S. (eds.), *British Football and Social Change: Getting into Europe* (London: Leicester University Press, 1991).

See also:

Association Football; Disasters; Spectators, Fans, and Crowd Disorder

-Rex Nash

Technology

Technology in sport is the use of man-made objects or materials in order to change or enhance sporting performance. Some sports rely more on technological advances than others, but throughout the latter part of the 20th century, there have been few sports that have not been influenced in some way by technology.

Technology has been beneficial to sport in many ways. Timing in racing has moved from a hand-held stopwatch to apparatus that can time to within thousandths of seconds. The photo-finish camera, first used at the 1932 Olympic Games, has ensured that the margin for misjudgement in a race is reduced to a minimum. The use of light-sensitive equipment has been extended, for example in tennis, where 'Cyclops' assists officials to make the correct line call. Moreover, thanks to computers, officials do not need to spend endless hours adding up scores in order for spectators to learn the results. Technology has provided computers to do this job.

Training methods have changed with the advent of improvements in technology. Athletes have access to more equipment that allows them to watch themselves on video, test their fitness in a laboratory, and adjust their diet in order to gain peak performance. Problems of climate can be solved using technology. Training apparatus can be used to provide constant training for the athlete, regardless of inclement weather. Technological advances in material such as Lycra has had an impact on sports clothing such as swimsuits. The athlete in the water or on the track is now more aerodynamic.

Safety equipment has undergone vast improvements owing to technology. The rather precarious position of the jockey has been improved by equipment such as hard hats and body padding. The starting gates first used in flat-racing provided a safer and fairer way of getting several nervous and large animals racing. Motorsport has been made safer with fire-resistant suits, helmets and body reinforcement in cars. Even recreational sport has been influenced by technology. Mouthguards, shinguards, heavy padding and batting helmets in cricket are all designed to protect the safety of the sportsperson.

As well as safety, technology has also influenced sporting equipment. During the 19th century, the process for 'vulcanizing' rubber changed the design of many balls used for sport. The graphite and Kevlar composites favoured by contemporary British players like Tim Henman have replaced tennis racquets originally made out of wood, used by players such as Fred Perry. Golf is another sport in which technology has had a significant effect with carbon shafts, titanium heads and stainless steel inserts all common in golf clubs today. Surfaces used in sporting venues, such as the tartan track or artificial turf are all advances in technology. For the disabled sportsperson, improvements in technology have allowed disabled athletes to reach a new level of performance with improved design of artificial limbs and wheelchairs.

For those who choose to watch sport as opposed to participate in games, technology has also had a significant effect. The advent of radio, followed by television in the 1950s, allowed those who wanted to sit in the comfort of their own home and watch sport to do so. Advances in cameras and their use have enabled the viewer to take advantage of the close-up and slow-motion replay. The camera mounted on the top of the Formula 1 car or the camera in the centre of the stumps in cricket are all advances that enable the viewer to feel part of the game. Satellites have made it possible for sporting events all over the world to be beamed into living rooms and now there are several channels devoted solely to sport, allowing the sports lover at home to watch sport from all four corners of the globe. Even if a spectator is at the sporting venue, large video screens

ensure that the sports fan sees every detail of the action.

As well as improving sport, technology has been accused of influencing sport in an adverse way. With increased knowledge of the body, certain drugs can be used to affect performance in both humans and animals. Horses and greyhounds can be given drugs in order that their performance is affected to cause them to either win or lose a race. Some snooker and darts players have been accused of taking beta-blockers, which slow the heart rate in order that the athlete is more relaxed and therefore less likely to miss a shot. Although technology is used in order to catch these athletes who may have an unfair advantage through drug taking, that type of technology is slower to develop than the one used to boost performance. Technological hardware has been held responsible for affecting sporting results. Those from the 1991 World Athletics Championships in Tokyo were called into question as the tartan track had not been designed to the correct specifications, and was deemed to have given athletes an unfair advantage. Technology has been accused of taking the excitement out of sporting competition. For example, the improvements to the McLaren cars on the 1998 Formula 1 Grand Prix circuit at the beginning of the season were far superior to the others teams, with the result that McLaren won consistently. Many followers of Formula 1 became disenchanted, knowing that one particular team would probably win every race.

Sport is a multimillion-pound business, which has become reliant on technology as a selling point. The notion that technology will improve athletic performance produced, especially through the 1980s and early 1990s, a multimillion-pound shoe industry, as companies fought for global dominance of the market. Shoes were not the only sporting equipment that technology was used to sell. Clothing, racquets and balls were all products used to profit from the consumer notion of improved technology equalling improved performance.

Technology is always changing. The most revolutionary development twenty years ago is virtually obsolete today. Technology's impact on sport and society should not be underestimated.

References:

Dyreson, M., 'Technology', in Levinson, D. and Christensen, K. (eds.), *Encyclopedia of World Sport*, vol. 3 (Santa Barbara, California: ABC-CLIO, 1997), pp. 1014-1017.

Hoberman, J., *Mortal Engines: the Science of Performance and the Dehumanization of Sport* (New York: The Free Press, 1992).

Jones, E., *Sport in Space: the Implications for Sport of Cable and Satellite Television. Report to the Sports Council and the Central Council of Physical Recreation* (London: The Sports Council, February, 1985).

Nawrat, C., Hutchings, S. and Struthers, G. (eds.), *The Sunday Times Illustrated History of Twentieth Century Sport* (London: Hamlyn, 1995).

Further reading:

McNeil, I., *An Encyclopaedia of the History of Technology* (Suffolk: Routledge, 1996).

Potts, R., *The Social Construction of a Sporting Technology*, M.Sc. thesis, Imperial College, 1995.

Rintala, J., 'Sport and Technology: Human Questions in a World of Machines', *Journal of Sport and Social Issues*, vol. 19, no. 1 (February 1995).

-Julie Anderson

Television

Between 1922 and 1955, the British Broadcasting Corporation (B.B.C.) had a monopoly of broadcasting in Britain, and consequently played a dominant role in the development of British television sport. The B.B.C. launched the world's first public broadcast television service in 1936, but although pioneering broadcasts of Wimbledon, the Derby and the Cup Final were made, television sets were expensive, transmissions only reached those within 20 miles of Alexandra Palace and the maximum audience was around 20,000.

Television broadcasting, suspended at the start of the Second World War, was re-launched in 1946 as part of post-war reconstruction and the 1948 Olympics were broadcast. By 1950, only 2 per cent of British households had a television license, but by 1960 the figure was 82 per cent. The B.B.C. resisted the idea of paying for the right to broadcast sport, maintaining that it only paid 'facility fees'. Sport governing bodies, concerned at their own position, organized an Association for the Protection of Copyright in Sport. However, the imminent launch of a rival commercial channel prompted the B.B.C. to acknowledge that it was, in effect, buying rights, and payments began to rise.

In 1955, when I.T.V. (Independent Television) was founded, the B.B.C. had many in-built advantages in the ensuing competition for sport coverage. It was a more prestigious institution and it already had national coverage, facilities and technical resources, production and technical expertise, contacts in the sport world and long-term exclusive contracts with major sports. Major sport events had become national events, and the B.B.C. benefited from the authority and prestige of association with major state, royal and sporting occasions. I.T.V.'s federal structure and the relative lack of interest in sport by many of its companies was a handicap. The new channel had some success with Wimbledon tennis, which it abandoned at the end of the 1960s, horse-racing and professional wrestling, which the B.B.C. did not regard as a suitable sport.

Key programmes established in this period included *Sportsview* (B.B.C., 1954), *Grandstand* (B.B.C., 1958), *Match of the Day* (B.B.C., 1964) and *World of Sport* (I.T.V., 1964). Anglia TV introduced the first video highlights of football in 1962. The launch of B.B.C. 2 in 1964 led to an increase in the amount (although not the percentage) of sport on television, gave the B.B.C. the means to increase the range of sports coverage, led to the spread of Sunday cricket, and enabled extended coverage of cricket, tennis and golf.

In the 1960s, the Independent Television Authority insisted that the I.T.V. network should provide good sports coverage as part of its public service remit. This led to the establishment of *World of Sport* in 1964 and a central sports unit in 1967. From 1968, a new company, L.W.T. (London Weekend Television), assumed responsibility for *World of Sport*, and launched the football highlights programme, *The Big Match*, on Sunday afternoons. In the United States, A.B.C. launched *Wide World of Sport* and *Monday Night Football*, and competition between the three major networks, A.B.C., N.B.C. and C.B.S., triggered off a dramatic rise in the amounts paid for the television rights to major events.

The 1960s were a period of rapid technical advance. Video recording was introduced at the start of the decade, and video editing became possible soon after. The action replay was introduced in time for the 1966 World Cup, followed by the development of slow motion replays. Colour was fully launched in Britain in 1968, and new light-weight mobile cameras enhanced the range of shots available. Television was at first slow to spread; by 1950 there were 5 million television sets worldwide but still only Great Britain, the United States and the Soviet Union had television. By 1970, there were 250 million sets in 130 countries and, during the 1970s, television grew rapidly in Africa, Asia and Latin America. The spread of communication satellites gave television live access to international events around the world. Telstar, launched in 1962, bridged the Atlantic; in 1964, the Tokyo Olympics were broadcast live to 39 countries, and the 1968 Mexico Olympics were the first to be seen in colour in Britain.

In the United Kingdom, concern that television organizations might acquire exclusive contracts for major occasions had led the Government to reserve the right to make non-exclusive rules by statutory order. A clause in the Television Act of 1954 allowed the Government to designate 'listed events', for which exclusive television rights were not allowed. Listed events included the F.A. Cup

Final, the Boat Race, Wimbledon Tennis, test match cricket, the Grand National and the Derby. Public antagonism over duplication of coverage of major events, such as the Olympic Games and the World Cup on both major channels, was identified as an issue in the *Annual Report* (1977). The report proposed greater co-operation between the channels and alternation between them. B.B.C. reluctance to adopt this strategy helped push I.T.V. towards the strategy of opting out of some major event coverage, whilst trying to secure others exclusively.

The growth of television sport and the banning of cigarette advertising on television in 1965 helped trigger a sport sponsorship boom. Sport sponsorship in Britain grew from less than £1 million in 1966 to £16 million in 1976. By 1980 it was around £46 million, in 1989 it was estimated at £200 million and in 1996 it was thought to be over £300 million. In 1986, five of the top six events (measured by amount of television hours) were tobacco sponsored, but since this date progressive restrictions are gradually removing tobacco sponsorship.

The introduction of Channel Four in 1982 ushered in a new era for British television sport, stimulating growth in independent production, building an audience for American football, cycling and Sumo, and fostering a fresh approach to the conventions of production. The deregulation of broadcasting and the introduction of new channels and new modes of delivery, such as satellite and cable, have given a further boost to the competition to acquire television rights to major events. The public service concept of broadcasting has yielded to commercialization and commodification. Television sport has become a key element in the globalization of culture. Football has been colonizing new markets in the United States and Japan. American football, baseball, Australian rules football, Rugby Union, sumo, and even cricket and snooker, have all been targeting new potential markets.

397

In the 1990s, the dramatic rise of BskyB satellite broadcasting and its pay-per-channel sports coverage has transformed television sport. Huge rights payments for football have contributed to the financial strength of the Premier League, enabling importation of foreign players and large pay rises for top footballers. The B.B.C. and the other terrestrial channels have lost rights to many top events, but the expansion of European football competitions has resulted in an increase in the amount of live football on terrestrial television. We are now on the threshold of a digital revolution, in which a growth in pay-per-view for major events and a dramatic growth in the amount of television sport will be key features.

References:

Barnett, S. *Games and Sets: the Changing Face of Sport on Television* (London: British Film Institute, 1990).

Gearing, B. and McNeil, P., *Seventy Years of BBC Sport* (London: Andre Deutch, 1999).

Whannel, G., *Fields in Vision: Television Sport and Cultural Transformation* (London: Routledge, 1992).

See also:

Media – Sky Sports; Media – Sports Personality of the Year; Sports Announcing and Commentating

-Garry Whannel

Test Matches

According to the *The Wisden Book of Test Cricket*, the phrase 'test match' was coined during the very first cricket tour to Australia when, in 1861-1862, games between H. H. Stephenson's team and each of the Australian colonies were described as 'test matches'. However, whilst this may provide the first description of an international match in this form, statisticians do not consider this to be the first legitimate 'test match', as the teams during these tours were often mismatched. The tourists might field the traditional eleven players, but the home side opposition would have a greater number of players. Thus, the first official test match is taken from the time when the sides fielded equal numbers, which occurred during the fourth tour to Australia in 1876-1877. The date of the first 'test match' is therefore generally taken to be March 15th-19th, 1876. The game was played at Melbourne Cricket Ground and was won by Australia by a margin of 45 runs. Quite astonishingly, the Centenary Test played 100 years later finished with the same result by the exact same margin. In the intervening period there had been experiments with the length of test matches, including the 'timeless test' in South Africa (1938-1939). Here, after ten days play with the game nearing its denouement, the boat to take the English side home could wait no longer and the game ended lamely as a draw. This experiment was not repeated and test matches in cricket are now scheduled for five days. In England, test matches have historically always begun on a Thursday and until the early 1980s, play was never scheduled for Sundays. However, television and other requirements altered this and Sunday play now occurs in all test matches with the final day, Monday, often offering unreserved tickets for spectators at lower prices.

During the development of Kerry Packer's World Series Cricket in 1977, a project that arose in competition to the 'official' matches, a legal dispute arose over the use of the word 'tests' and whether it was contrary to the Australian Trade Practices Act. Eventually World Series Cricket was permitted to use the word 'SuperTests' to describe the matches. The International Cricket Council determines which matches are sanctioned as official tests and disputes have arisen particularly with respect to rebel tour matches against the then isolated South African side.

Whilst the term 'test' is most readily associated with cricket, it is also applied to sports aside from cricket. For example, both Rugby League and Rugby Union use the term to describe a series of international matches.

References:

Frindall, W., *The Wisden Book of Test Cricket*, Volumes I and II (London: Headline, 1995).

Haigh, G., *The Cricket War: the Inside Story of Kerry Packer's World Series Cricket* (Melbourne: The Text Publishing Company, 1993).

See also:

Cricket

-Steve Greenfield/Guy Osborn

Trampolining

The British Trampoline Federation (B.T.F.) was formed in 1965, but the sports of trampolining and tumbling actually go back for many centuries. Indeed, many cultures have used outstretched animal skins to propel upwards and safely catch descending performers. For hundreds of years there have been rebound acts in circuses, with others involving floor and aerial somersaults.

Modern trampolining emerged during the second half of the 20th century and uses equipment based on the early trampolines built by George Nissen in the United States in 1936. Today's trampolines are capable of projecting an athlete to heights of almost 10 metres, allowing repetition triple somersaults with comparative ease.

Competitive activity commenced in the United States after the Second World War and spread to Europe and the United Kingdom during the 1950s and early 1960s, with display teams involved in its promotion. In 1964, the International Trampoline Federation (F.I.T.) was formed by seven founder member federations; however, by the end of the 20th century, membership had been extended to forty-two national federations. Championship activity has developed and grown continuously since the first World Championships were held in 1964. They are now held every two years, with European Championships being held since 1969. European Youth Championships have been held since 1972, and the introduction of the World Cup event in 1993 has seen a growing interest in the sport, with television companies broadcasting live coverage of some major events.

There are both individual and pairs events for men and women, as well as team competitions for teams of three or four members. At the end of the first two competitive rounds a team result is obtained, with the top ten competitors in each category proceeding to a further optional routine to decide the individual and pairs competitions. Routines are marked for style as well as difficulty, but style is weighted far more heavily, encouraging aesthetic rather than dangerous performance.

The disciplines of double-mini trampoline and tumbling have featured in the F.I.T. World Championships since 1976, and the number of participating nations is slowly growing. However, tumbling is also part of sports acrobatics, which in Britain is now under the aegis of British Gymnastics. It was briefly an Olympic sport in 1932 but was not embraced by the F.I.T. until 1976.

In double-mini trampoline, athletes perform three passes with a maximum of two skills in each, and a further two passes in the final. A pass includes the run-up, mounting the bed, a maximum of two moves and dismounting onto a soft landing area. The best ten athletes proceed to the final, where the competitor with the highest score is the winner. Double-mini trampoline has also emerged as a branch of trampolining since the mid-1970s.

As the millennium closes, the sport of trampolining is about to be embraced within British Gymnastics as the result of a vote within its membership and was due to become an Olympic sport in the Games of 2000 in Sydney.

Britain has enjoyed some success at the international level. In the 1999 Word Age-Group championships, held at Sun City in South Africa, Britons Kirsty Ward, Lauren Allen and Stacy Dunn finished first, second and third in the individual event for eleven and twelve-year-old girls, whilst Kirsty Ward and Lauren Allen also finished first in the synchronized event. Colleen Stopforth finished first in the individual event for fifteen and sixteen-year-old girls. Simon Milnes finished second in the individual event for seventeen and eighteen-year-old youths and also won the synchronized event with Glen Rate (who came fourth in the individual event). In the senior championships held a month earlier at the same venue, Jamie Moore finished ninth in the Ladies individual event whilst Britain's team finished fifth overall. For the men, Lee Brearley finished fourteenth in the individual event and with Paul Smyth finished eleventh in the synchronized event. Britain had both men's and women's teams qualified to take part in the World Games to be held in Akita, Japan in August 2001.

References:

Phelps, E. and Phelps, B., *Trampolining: the Skills of the Game* (Marlborough: Crowood Press, 1990).

Walker, R., *Trampolining for Coaches and Performers* (London: A. & C. Black, 1988).

Websites:

The British Amateur Gymnastics Association – http://www.baga.co.uk/

See also:

Sports Acrobatics

-Frank Galligan

Triathlon

Triathlon is an endurance race that combines competition in three very different disciplines – swimming, cycling and running. Over twenty-five years, triathlon grew from being an informal activity to an Olympic Sport. It began in California in 1974, when a friendship group of sports enthusiasts, including athletes, swimmers and cyclists, who trained together began to look for ways of competing together as well.

Out of this arose, in stages, competitions that incorporated running, swimming and cycling. This form of multidisciplinary competition became increasingly popular in California, although the experimental nature of its approach meant that some practised competitions with just running and swimming whilst others included canoeing as well. Sometimes the races were relays and at other times, two-person teams had to complete a course together. Nonetheless, by 1977 it was generally recognized as a highly individual sport involving three disciplines and had become known as triathlon.

In 1977, John Collins of the United States Navy initiated an endurance competition that was to influence the future direction of the sport. On the Hawaiian island of Oahu, he proposed that a single competition should embrace the Waikiki rough-water swim of 2.4 miles, the round-the-island cycle race of 112 miles and the Honolulu marathon, in what would become an 'ironman race'. In February 1978, fifteen people embarked on this three-stage challenge and eleven hours and forty-six minutes later, Gordon Haller was the first winner, with eleven further competitors finishing.

By 1980, triathlon was attracting television coverage in the United States, and by 1982, it had become an international spectacular, with women as well as men competing. The sport soon reached Europe and the British Triathlon Association was formed in 1983.

Since that time, the sport has continued to grow in popularity. Competitions are contested at three levels of intensity – Ironman, half-Ironman and sprint. The sprint version is standardized for championship purposes at 750 metres swimming, 20 kilometres cycling and 5 kilometres running.

The most successful figures in British triathlon are Simon Lessing, who has been World Champion five times; Sarah Springman, who has been European Champion at the Ironman distance; and Sarah Coope, who has been European Champion at the half-Ironman distance.

Such is the status of triathlon, achieved over such a short time span, that it is to be contested for the first time at Olympic level at Sydney in 2000.

Websites:

The British Triathlon Association – http://www.britishtriathlon.co.uk/

-Trevor James

Triple Crown

In British sport, the term 'Triple Crown' generally refers to one of the four British Isles Rugby teams (Scotland, England, Ireland and Wales) beating each of the other three in the same season. It is a symbolic title with no designated trophy.

Keith Quinn notes that the first Triple Crown winner was England in 1883, but Terry Godwin makes the point that the first mention of the term 'Triple Crown' was not made until a report on March 20th, 1899 in the *South Wales Daily News*.

While the professionalization of the game has had a considerable impact on who wins and dominates Triple Crown Rugby in the late 1990s, until 1990 there had been a surprising level of equality. At the end of the 1990-1991 season, Wales had seventeen Triple Crowns, England sixteen, Scotland ten and Ireland six. Nevertheless, for some countries there were long waits for the 'unofficial' British championship. For example, Ireland had a near half-century gap between triumphs in 1899 and 1948.

Although Rugby is the national game of Wales, the same does not apply for either Scotland or Ireland, where the player numbers are between one-tenth and one-twentieth of those that England can draw upon. In the late 1990s, England was the dominant Triple Crown force. Their winning the Triple Crown five times in the 1990s indicated a clear superiority over the other three home nations. The engine that now drives English Rugby is the vast club network, which is well funded and strongly supported by both spectators and sponsors.

References:

Godwin, T., *The International Rugby Championship, 1883-1983* (London: Willow Books/Collins, 1984).

Quinn, K., *The Encyclopedia of World Rugby* (Moffat, Scotland: Lochar Publishing, 1991).

Further reading:

Sommerville, D., *The Encyclopedia of Rugby Union* (London: Aurum Press, 1997).

See also:

Rugby Union

-Scott Crawford

Tug Of War

Tug of war is a sport in which two teams of competitors pull against each other at opposite ends of a thick rope. It has its origins in the English tradition of vigorous country pursuits and to this day is more likely to be a feature of a country show or school sports day than a more formal sports meeting. This small sport is famous for its vociferous participants and supporters. Passions run high when sixteen people are exerting brute strength through a single rope. In 1958, at the Amateur Athletic Association (A.A.A.) Championship catchweight final between New Haw and Woodham and Ford Sports, one spectacular pull lasted an extraordinary five minutes and ten seconds.

Tug of war is part of a wider family of activities regulated by the English A.A.A. Under their guidance, the Tug-of-War Association was founded in 1958 by twelve clubs in order to lead the sport more effectively, and by the 1990s its membership had grown to 156 clubs with 2,000 members. There have been A.A.A. Championships since 1910 and between 1927 and 1970, the 100 stone and catchweight championships were actually part of the main championship programme. Since 1970, the A.A.A. Tug-of-war Championships have been held at other locations, a by-product of concerns about the effect that tug-of-war contests were having on stadium in-fields. Tug of war did, however, return as a demonstration event in the main programme of the A.A.A. Championships in 1999, albeit being held on the out-field of the Alexander Stadium in Birmingham.

The 1999 A.A.A. Tug-of-war Championships were held at the Bolea Sports Ground, Middleton, Manchester with a 640 kilogram category (in which the combined weight of each team of eight pullers must not exceed 640 kilograms) and a catchweight category (in which there are no weight restrictions). An indoor A.A.A. Tug-of-war Championship is also held annually and there is an inter-counties championship. In 1996, the Tug-of-War Association introduced a national School Competition for fifteen and sixteen year olds, with a final that year being held at the Northampton Town Show. World Championships are also regularly held.

Tug of war was an Olympic event from 1900 to 1920. When Great Britain took the gold in 1908, there were American allegations, rejected by the judges, that the British competitors had illegal prongs and heel-plates on their boots. It is expected that tug of war will return to the Olympic programme in 2004.

Rules for tug of war first appeared in 1879, when a set was drawn up for the New York Athletic Club. The A.A.A. introduced its first rules in 1887.

The most well-known team in tug of war is Wood Treatment Bosley, who won fifteen successive A.A.A. Championships at catchweight between 1959 and 1974. It was also Wood Treatment Bosley who won the demonstra-

tion event at the A.A.A. Championships in 1999.

References:
Amateur Athletic Association of England, *Annual Report* (1993), p. 24; (1994), p. 14.
Athletics Weekly, (6 October 1999), p. 4.
Lovesey, P., *The Official Centenary History of the Amateur Athletic Association* (Enfield: Guinness Superlatives, 1979).

Websites:
The Tug-of-War Association – http://www.tugofwar.co.uk/

-Trevor James

Tumbling (*see* Gymnastics; Sports Acrobatics; Trampolining

Turnhalle

The Turnhalle was the gym of the German Gymnastic Society and was founded on August 6th, 1861, at 26 St Pancras Road, London. It was designed by Ed Grüning, built by Messrs Piper & Wheeler and inaugurated on January 28th, 1865. Intended for thirty squads of ten men, its dimensions are 120 feet in length, 80 feet in width and 57 feet in height. It also housed a smaller gym, additional reception rooms and a library.

The Society soon began to expand its activities. On November 6th, 1868, E. R. Ravenstein, the speaker, became co-founder of the National Olympian Association. In 1866, his wife Ada supervised the first section of female gymnasts in England. Annual gymnastics displays were staged between 1867 and 1885, and in 1868 a Choral Section was established. On January 7th, 1869, the Metropolitan Swimming Association was founded in the Turnhalle, and in 1871 the Literary Department was set up. The Society became a founding member of the Amateur Athletic Association in 1880, and its gymnastics championships were the model for the Amateur Gymnastics Association established in 1888, whose secretary, E. L. Levy, was a major delegate in 1905 when the British Olympic Association was formed.

The Turnhalle became the centre of German cultural life in London, and its members attended the German Turnfeste on the Continent (1863 to 1913). In 1908, however, the premises were sold to the Great Northern Railway, and in 1914 all Germans were interned. Finally, the Society was liquidated in 1916. Ironically, the Turnhalle itself was damaged during a German air raid on July 7th, 1917. It was later restored and used as a sorting office for parcels before being leased to private companies. Today, its leaking roof is a listed structure.

References:

Anthony, W. D., 'Rural Roots of the Modern Olympics. A German Foundation for British Sport', *Sports International*, no. 6 (Spring 1982), pp. 36-37.

Bernett, H., 'Vom Schwarz-Rot-Gold zum Schwarz-Weiß-Rot. Die Geschichte des Deutschen Turnvereins in London 1861-1916', in A. Luh and E. Beckers (eds.), *Umbruch und Kontinuität im Sport. Reflexionen im Umfeld der Sportgeschichte. Festschrift für Horst Ueberhorst* (Bochum: N. Brockmeyer, 1991), pp. 298-309.

Ravenstein, E. G., 'Jahresbericht des deutschen Turnvereins in London für 1865', *Deutsche Turnzeitung – Blätter für die Angelegenheiten des gesammten Turnwesens*, vol. 11 (6 April 1866), no. 14, pp. 109-111.

Further reading:

'Der Deutsche Turnverein in London', in Anglo-German Publishing Co. (eds.), *Die Deutsche Kolonie in England* (Hagen, Westfalia: Bald & Krüger, 1913), pp. 61-63.

Wildt, K. C., *Auswanderer und Emigranten in der Geschichte der Leibesübungen* (Schorndorf: Hofmann, 1964).

See also:
Gymnastics

-Joachim Ruhl

Twickenham

The site for the current Twickenham Rugby football ground was picked in 1907 by Billy Williams. The land parcel of 10.25 acres was bought by the English Rugby Union for £5,572. The first match took place in October 1909 between Harlequins and Richmond.

Twickenham Rugby Club, however, and its playing fields close by Twickenham Stadium, had been in existence since 1867. Simon Weathers mentions that, in 1873, 'Twickenham Football' was the newspaper advertisement slogan used to attract players – no older than seventeen, and only the sons of gentlemen – to join a 'lightweights' team, a 'proper' team and a 'seconds' team.

The first international Rugby match at Twickenham took place in 1910 between England and Wales. Since 1921, Twickenham has been the home venue for inter-services championships, the London Counties region team and the Middlesex Sevens, arguably the unofficial world championship of club seven-a-side Rugby.

Twickenham Stadium, which opened in 1909, witnessed, in its early years, a number of England victories. An omen of things to come was England's first defeat at the hands of the South African team on their 1912-1913 tour of Great Britain, Ireland and France.

Apart from being the home of the English Rugby Union, Twickenham has become the administrative hub of the International Rugby Board. While there are those who would argue that Ellis Park, South Africa or Cardiff Arms Park, Wales are more potent secular Meccas of Rugby, Twickenham is still invested with a remarkable degree of spiritual symbolism and cultural resonance. J. A. Mangan, in an essay entitled 'Games Field and Battlefield', describes a Dulwich schoolboy, Paul Jones, who was killed in France in 1917. In a letter to his father before his death Jones wrote, 'I remember seeing those two [already killed in action] as captains of England and Ireland respectively, shaking hands with each other and with the King at the Great Rugby Football match at Twickenham.'

In the 1920s, domestic British Rugby was so popular, according to Sir Derek Birley, that 43,000 watched a 1924 Calcutta Cup game at Twickenham, and this resulted in the building of a new stand and extensions to enclosures and terraces one year later. The crowd capacity for Twickenham thus rose to 56,000.

Twickenham has witnessed many innovations. Player numbers and a live B.B.C. radio broadcast attracted much comment at the 1927 England-Wales game. A decade later, a still further enlarged Twickenham saw a crowd of almost 70,000 watch the All Blacks play England. The gate receipts were such that the English Rugby Union made a donation of £1,000 to the King George V Jubilee Trust.

In modern Rugby, Twickenham hosted the final of the 1991 World Cup Final, which was a monumentally hard-fought defensive battle with Australia defeating England by twelve penalty points to six penalty points.

References:

Cuddon, J. A., *International Dictionary of Sports and Games* (New York: Schocken Books, 1979).

Weathers, S., *Twickenham R. F. C. Website* (http://www.users.dircon.co.uk/~weathers/)

Further reading:

Birley, D., *Playing the Game: Sport and British Society, 1910-45* (Manchester: Manchester University Press, 1995), pp. 172-173.

Mangan, J. A., 'Games Field and Battle', in J. Nauright and T. J. L. Chandler (eds.), *Making Men: Rugby and Masculine Identity* (London: Frank Cass, 1996), p. 150.

Websites:

The Rugby Football Union – http://www.rfu.com/

See also:

Rugby Union

-Scott Crawford

U.K. Sailing Academy, Cowes

The U.K. Sailing Academy was built in 1969 for the Sports Council. Operating seasonally under the name of the National Sailing Centre (N.S.C.), it catered for adults undertaking intermediate to advanced dinghy sailing and yachting courses on a site of approximately 3 acres.

In 1988, the National Sailing Centre was purchased by the Lister Trust, a charitable organization founded by Noel Lister, formerly the Chief Executive of M.F.I. (the national furniture superstore) and a keen yachtsman in his own right. The name was changed to Club U.K. and the emphasis shifted from adults to youngsters. In 1990, the Centre received patronage from H.R.H. the Princess Royal and since that time has received Her Royal Highness and other members of the Royal

Sailing during Cowes Week, July 31st 1999 (Action Images/Peter Jay)

405

Family on numerous occasions, including Cowes Week, the international yachting festival. Within five years of reopening as Club U.K. (subsequently the National Youth Watersports Centre), the occupancy rate rose from 6,000 visitors to over 27,000 per year. Later renamed the U.K. Sailing Centre and open all year round, the Centre began to offer professional training and qualifications to those seeking watersports as their career.

Taking its current name of the U.K. Sailing Academy in 1996, and converted to allow full disabled access, it now receives funding from the Lister Trust to the tune of £200,000 per annum, which is channelled into a capital development programme, bursary and sponsorship activities. The U.K. Sailing Academy is now recognized as the largest professional watersports training establishment in Europe, and a primary centre for introducing youngsters to the great outdoors via a watersports medium.

Websites:

The U.K. Sailing Academy –
http://www.uk-sail.org.uk/

See also:

Sailing

-Toby Beardsall

Unions and Strikes

The issues of both the formation of, and participation in, organized trade unions, and the related issue of taking industrial action, obtained much greater relevance as sports began to become more professionalized towards the end of the 19th century. In Association Football, the first attempt to form a players' union was that instigated by 'Billy' Rose of Wolverhampton Wanderers, who wrote to all Football League clubs in 1893 suggesting that leading players should get together to have a voice in the issues that were pertinent to

them. Whilst this was unsuccessful, by February 1898 the Association Footballers' Union had been formed and by 1907, the players union as we know it today had come into being, with the formation of the Professional Footballers' Association (P.F.A.) at the Imperial Hotel in Manchester in December of that year.

There is a long history of disputes between the P.F.A. and the football authorities. This tension became particularly marked in the late 1950s and early 1960s. At this time, the twin elements of the maximum wage and the retain-and-transfer system were still staunchly supported by the League and the dispute over terms and conditions was subsequently brought to a head by the players in 1960. At the annual general meeting of the P.F.A. that year, the refusal of the authorities to discuss what had been the two main bones of contention since the players' organization started so enraged the delegates that they empowered the Committee to take any steps they thought necessary to bring about the removal of these restrictive and unjust rules. Four fundamental issues were isolated for negotiation – the abolition of the maximum wage provisions; the right of a player to retain a slice of his transfer fee; a new system of player retention; and the drawing up of a new contract that was more in line with the needs of modern players. The League's response was to offer certain concessions such as a rise in the minimum wage, an increased television fee and a sum to be paid to players on the transfer list. This, however, failed to deal with the root of the P.F.A.'s discontent – the maximum wage and the transfer system. The response of the P.F.A. was to organize three players' meetings in London, Birmingham and Manchester that virtually unanimously supported taking further action in support of their original demands. Accordingly, the League's offer was rejected and the P.F.A. issued a strike notice that would expire on January 21st, 1961. With the threat of a strike causing the League some disquiet, significant concessions were offered, the abolition of the maximum wage and the promise of longer contracts being the centrepiece. The offer still, however, failed to tackle the main bone of contention, the retain and transfer provisions, and the P.F.A. rejected the offer as it stood, having consulted their members. On January 18th, three days before the strike was due to begin, the two sides met in an attempt to forge a resolution of the dispute, with Labour Conciliation Officer Tom Claro as 'referee'. Ultimately, agreement appeared to have been reached and the strike was averted. However, when the agreement was analysed in detail, the retain and transfer situation remained unclear. Rather than threaten another strike, the P.F.A. was given the chance to confront the League provisions through the courts when George Eastham began his attempt to free himself from his contract with Newcastle United. Subsequently, there have been a number of instances of threatened strike action, often concerning the apportionment of broadcasting monies.

The development of player power following the financial success of the Premier League gave strikes a different dimension. At the start of the 1998-1999 season, Pierre Van Hooijdonk refused to return from the summer break to play for his club, Nottingham Forest F.C., in protest at his perception that the newly promoted club lacked ambition. The impasse lasted for over three months before an agreement was reached, largely on economic grounds, that saw him return to the Club, although he remained on the transfer list. The club clearly wanted to sell him but had been unable to find a buyer at the right price. The difficulty for the club involved is that the player represents a substantial investment and whilst it is possible to keep the player's registration and prevent him from playing elsewhere, this principled stand may not ultimately benefit the club either financially or on the pitch. Players are not always concerned with questions of ambition or money, for example Lars Bohinen of Norway refused to play for his country against France over the question of nuclear testing.

Professional cricketers were some way behind their footballing colleagues with regard to union organization. Until the setting up of the Professional Cricketers Association in 1967, there was no body to represent the rights and interests of the players. Membership was limited at first but gradually reached 100 per cent of first-class players in 1976. By the late 1970s, the Association had obtained a role within cricket's hierarchy, being represented on the Registration Tribunal and the discipline committee and also having the right to sit in on Chairmen's Advisory meetings. If hostility still lurked in some backwaters of the Establishment, it was no longer overt.

Cricket is not the only sport that has seen players organized into a professional association fairly late on in the game's history. For example, in professional boxing a significant development, although one that has not as yet perhaps achieved as much as it would have wished, has been the formation in February 1993 of the Professional Boxers' Association. This is a members' organization funded through an annual subscription. Prior to the formation of the P.B.A., there were no bodies designed specifically to cater for the needs of professional boxers. The P.B.A. has as its objectives the promotion and protection of its members' interests (including contractual rights) and the provision of a variety of forms of assistance in any matter arising out of a member's involvement in professional boxing. It also seeks to administer benefit funds for members and former members. Whilst there had been a perceived recognition that boxers needed protection in a medical sense, the formation of the P.B.A. was a reaction to wider concerns of a fiscal nature. There was also the added advantage that the P.B.A. could act efficiently on behalf of the individual boxers within the administrative machinery of professional boxing.

The recently professionalized Rugby Union has also seen the emergence of a players' union. Ironically though, the major dispute that existed after professionalization was between

407

The University Boat Race on the River Thames, 1994 (Action Images)

the clubs and the Rugby Football Union, which led to the players being withdrawn from England training sessions by their employers, the clubs.

References:

Greenfield, S. and Osborn, G., *Contract and Control in the Entertainment Industry* (Aldershot: Dartmouth, 1998).

Harding, J., *For the Good of the Game: the Official History of the Professional Footballers' Association* (London: Robson Books, 1991).

Websites:

The Professional Cricketers Association – http://www.thepca.co.uk/

The Professional Footballers' Association – http://www.thepfa.co.uk/

See also:

Association Football; Professional Footballers' Association

-Steve Greenfield/Guy Osborn

University Boat Race

The Oxford and Cambridge University Boat Race began in 1829 when students at Oxford responded to a challenge from Cambridge to row a match at or near London in eight-oared boats. The race took place at Henley-on-Thames on June 10th, Oxford winning easily.

Cambridge students formed their University Boat Club in 1828, while Oxford followed suit after the third race in 1839. The university boat clubs exist solely to produce a crew to challenge one another for their private match. Participants must be full-time students, and to be awarded a Blue, an oarsman must pass the end of the Fulham Wall in the race.

Five races were held from Westminster to Putney before the present Putney to Mortlake course of 4 miles 374 yards was first used in 1845. The race became annual (except for during the two world wars) in 1856, and is normally run close to the top of the tide in late March or early April, the crews tossing for stations.

On the face of it, the Boat Race is a simple two-boat race, which may explain the partisan popularity which extended far beyond the rowing world in the 1800s and which continues, particularly on television, today. For those taking part over the huge tidal S-bend, it is a long and complex race, and has maintained a very high standard of preparation. The Boat Race has nurtured beginners and has been a nursery for internationals. Recently it has been popular among postgraduates approaching the end of their international careers.

A few notable personalities include Boris Rankov, who is the only person to have won five consecutive races, and Susan Brown (Oxford), who was the first woman to cox the race. Notable events include the sinking of the Oxford boat in 1957 and the Cambridge Boat in 1978 due to adverse weather conditions.

References:

Burnell, R., *One Hundred and Fifty Years of the Oxford and Cambridge Boat Race* (London: Precision Press, 1979, with supplement, 1980).

Burnell, R., *The Oxford and Cambridge Boat Race, 1829-1953* (Oxford: Oxford University Press, 1954).

Dodd, C., *The Oxford and Cambridge Boat Race* (London: Stanley Paul, 1983).

Halladay, E., *Rowing in England: a Social History* (Manchester: Manchester University Press, 1990).

Further reading:

Regatta Magazine (London: Amateur Rowing Association, 1987-).

See also:

Rowing

-Chris Dodd

University Sport (*see* Birmingham University; British Universities Sports Association; Cambridge University; Loughborough University; Oxford University, University Boat Race)

V

Violence (*see* Player Violence)

Volleyball

Volleyball was invented by William Morgan in Holyoke, Massachusetts in 1895, and spread gradually via the Y.M.C.A. movement and the U.S. armed forces. The modern sport, introduced to the Olympic Games in 1964, has become one of the world's most popular games, with over 210 national associations in the international body, the Fédération Internationale de Volleyball (F.I.V.B. – International Volleyball Federation), which was established in 1947, and over 800 million players worldwide. Volleyball was introduced to Britain by U.S. servicemen, with the game's post-war expansion aided by émigré Europeans and the fire service. The Amateur Volleyball Association (A.V.A.) of Great Britain and Northern Ireland was established in 1955. Don Anthony, who was instrumental in this, remains the Honorary President of the English Volleyball Association, which replaced the A.V.A. in 1972. Scottish Volleyball became affiliated to the F.I.V.B. in 1970, followed by Northern Ireland in 1982 and Wales in 1989. Volleyball is administered, regulated and developed by associations in each of the home countries – together they form the British Volleyball Federation.

The sport grew significantly in the 1970s and 1980s with the proliferation of indoor sports halls and the broadening of the schools P.E. curriculum. The first Commonwealth Volleyball Tournament was held in England in 1981. There are national, regional and district leagues and cup competitions throughout Britain. The sport is very popular in schools and is a widespread recreational activity, with over 2 million adults playing volleyball occasionally. English and Scottish teams take an active part in European Volleyball Confederation tournaments. Great Britain also takes part in the Paralympics, and a flourishing Beach Volleyball circuit was established in the 1990s. Volleyball is a young sport in the United Kingdom but has already become a well-established amateur sport.

Websites:

The International Volleyball Federation – http://www.fivb.org/

The English Volleyball Association – http://members.netscapeonline.co.uk/chasvolleyball/index.htm

-John Lyle

Water Polo

Water polo is a ball game that has something in common with both basketball and football. It is played by two teams of seven players, one of whom must act as goalkeeper, and four reserves, who may be used as substitutes. The object is to throw the ball into the opponent's goal.

Water polo was pioneered in Britain in the 1870s. Initially, it was played as a novelty item at club galas to relieve spectators from the monotony of watching programmes of competitive swimming. Unique rules were used. Some of these were collated and written down in London, the Midlands and Scotland in the late 1870s and early 1880s. Eventually a universal set of rules was formulated and adopted in England by the Swimming Association of Great Britain in 1885 and these were used for the first international match, which took place in 1890 between England and Scotland. The Scots won 4-0, despite their unfamiliarity with some of the English rules. The match revealed the lack of standardization within the game and so it was agreed to establish an International Board of the Amateur Swimming Association, which included Scottish representatives, to standardize further the rules and these were adopted in 1892. Soon after, Ireland entered the fray, losing 12-0 to England in 1895, and Wales played international water polo for the first time in 1897, losing 3-2 to Scotland.

Britain, the game's pioneers, dominated the early Olympic tournaments. A British team won gold at the first competition in 1900 in Paris. They did not enter the 1904 Olympiad in St Louis but they were successful again in 1908 (London), 1912 (Stockholm) and 1920 (Antwerp). Hungary (who knocked out Britain in 1924 in Paris), Italy, and the former Yugoslavia and Soviet Union have generally dominated the sport since this time. British teams worthy of special mention because of their distinguished history include in Scotland, Motherwell and England, Polytechnic (London).

References:

Besford, P., *Encyclopaedia of Swimming* (London: Robert Hale & Co., 1971).

Keil, I. and Wix, D., *In the Swim: the Amateur Swimming Association from 1869 to 1994* (Loughborough: Swimming Times Ltd, 1996).

Sinclair, A. and Henry, W., *Swimming* (London: Longmans, Green & Co., 1900).

Further reading:

Arlott, J. (ed.), *The Oxford Companion to Sports* (London: Oxford University Press, 1985).

Bilsborough, P., *One Hundred Years of Scottish Swimming* (Stirling: Scottish Amateur Swimming Association, 1988).

Juba, K., *All About Water Polo* (London: Pelham, 1972).

-Peter Bilsborough

Water-skiing

The British Water Ski Federation was formed in 1951 with its first club being Ruislip Lido. However, there are references to forms of recreational water-skiing taking place in Britain much earlier, especially off the Yorkshire coast.

Water-skiing is the art of travelling on water with the aid of one or two skis, in the wake of, and while holding a rope from, a towing motor launch. The skier holds on to a bar handle attached to a tow-rope measuring no more than 75 feet.

The three disciplines of competitive water-skiing are slalom, jumping and figures (or tricks). Although the sport is said to have originated on the West Coast of the United States, where climatic conditions are more favourable than in the United Kingdom, Britain has had its share of world champions, especially in the 1980s with Mike Hazelwood and Elizabeth 'Liz' Hobbs.

A National Centre for Water Skiing was built at Holme Pierrepont in the mid-1970s.

Further reading:

The British Water Ski Federation – http://www.bwsf.co.uk/

-Richard William Cox

Waterloo Cup

Initiated in 1836 by William Lynn, the Waterloo Cup remains the most popular, prestigious and controversial hare-coursing event in Britain. Taking place at Altcar in Lancashire, initially alongside the Grand National steeplechase, the competition was the catalyst for the immense popularity of coursing during the 19th century. By 1838, the eight-dog stake had quadrupled and was attracting entries of the best dogs by well-known owners throughout the country. Success in the Cup became the acme for every courser.

Prior to the 1830s, coursing was a country gentleman's sport, either informally for exercising dogs, or through clubs such as Swaffham (1776) or Newmarket (1805). The coming of the railways and the popularity of the Waterloo Cup enabled the sport to lose its élitist image. During the 1850s, there were 383 Coursing Clubs in existence, which, together with the public interest generated by the Waterloo Cup, necessitated a national representative body. Organizers of the 1857 Waterloo Cup reiterated the need for 'one uniform set of rules' and for a 'tribunal formed on the principles of the Jockey Club for all matters relating to Coursing'. The National Coursing Club was duly formed one year later, with the rules adopted by coursing clubs throughout Britain and Ireland. By this time, the Cup was raised to a sixty-four-dog stake, requiring of the winner success in six gruelling courses against the strongest possible entry, a format retained to the present day. Despite the introduction of greyhound racing in the 1920s, the Waterloo Cup has maintained its widespread appeal for coursers. This is also despite the fact that for the past twenty years or more it has been heavily lobbied and repeatedly interupted by anti-blood sport protesters.

References:

Ash, E., *The Book of the Greyhound* (London: Hutchinson & Co., 1933).

Cox, H., *Coursing and Falconry* (London: Longmans, Green & Co., 1892).

Personal communication with Sir Mark Prescott, the Countryside Alliance.

See also:

Hare Hunting and Coursing; League Against Cruel Sports

-Callum Mackenzie

Weightlifting

British tradition in weightlifting goes back as far as the 18th century. In the early years, Britain was a major force in the sport, but apart from successes achieved during the post-Second World War period, it has since suffered a decline.

Many popular festivals, particularly in Scotland, traditionally included tests of strength. The élite loved to admire muscled men and King William III is said to have enjoyed the performances of Richard Joy, who was capable of lifting up to 2,254 pounds. The physicist Desgoulieres, a student of Sir Isaac Newton and member of the Royal Society, was sceptical of the giant Thomas Topham until he watched with his own eyes this Hercules lift a barrel of water weighing 1,836 pounds. Desgoulieres included Topham's exercises in his academic physics courses.

In the last two decades of the 19th century, weightlifting began to undergo a process of standardization. It was at this time that the term 'weightlifting' first entered into English and, after a short time lapse, into other European languages also. The first international championship took place in London in March 1891, and included two separate competitions. The first involved the use of dumbbells while in the second competitors lifted modern barbells. In the first decade of the 20th century, international competitions switched to barbell-only exercises. The Indian-born British weightlifter, Launceston Elliot, won a gold medal at the first Olympic Games in Athens in 1896. His triumph remains the only British gold medal to date (2000) in modern Olympic weightlifting.

Following an unsuccessful attempt to establish a governing body in 1898, the British Amateur Weight Lifters' Association (B.A.W.L.A.) was founded in 1911. The most renowned British weightlifter of this period was W. A. Pullum, the first man capable of raising double his bodyweight overhead with two hands. British and continental European weightlifting followed different rules until after the First World War, with Britain organizing its Amateur Championships using even-stone bodyweights. This was to change after

1920 when the International Weightlifting Federation was established to regulate international competition. In 1928, the Federation established three official standard lift categories – the snatch, the clean and jerk, and the press. In 1948, a British Empire and Commonwealth Council was founded, which still exists today as the Commonwealth Weightlifting Federation, based in Wales. The B.A.W.L.A. abolished the use of even-stone bodyweights in its Amateur Championships in 1955.

Britain enjoyed its most successful era in international weightlifting in the decades following the end of the Second World War, winning two silver and two bronze Olympic medals during this period. Louis Martin, the most successful British lifter ever, took four world titles in the Middle Heavyweight class in the late 1950s and early 1960s. In total, seven Olympic medals for weightlifting have been won since 1896.

Since the mid-1960s, when Eastern European and Asian weightlifters began their long dominance of international competitions, British weightlifting has fallen into a decline. The most successful British athletes of recent years have been women, who were allowed to compete in an official championship for the first time in 1986, more than a century after the men's sport first began to take off. In the 1990s, Myrtle Augee twice won the European Union Championship and once the European Championship.

References:

Kirkley, G., *Modern Weightlifting* (London: Faber & Faber Limited, 1957).

Young, D., 'Weightlifting', in Karen Christensen and David Levinson (eds.), *Encyclopedia of World Sport* (Santa Barbara, California: ABC-CLIO, 1996), vol. 3, pp. 1154-1158.

Further reading:

Bonini, G. 'London as the Cradle of Modern Weight Lifting', *The Sports Historian*, 20, 2 (2000).

Desbonnet, E., *La force physique. Traité d'athletisme* (Paris: Berger Levrault & Compagnie, 1901).

Matthews, P. and Buchanan, I., *The All-time Greats of British and Irish Sport* (Enfield: Guinness Publishing Limited, 1995).

Websites:

The British Amateur Weight Lifters' Association – http://www.bawla.com/

The International Weightlifting Federation – http://www.iwf.net/

-Gherardo Bonini

Welsh Handball

Handball, or '*Pel-law*' in Welsh, has probably been played throughout Wales in one form or another since the 17th century. Sometimes known as 'tennis' or 'fives', the game evolved from churchyard ball-playing onto purpose-built ball courts associated with public houses (for example, the Tennis Court Inn, Cardiff, 1777; the Ball Court Inn, Merthyr Tydfil, 1802). This folk sport was popular in 19th-century Glamorgan, although venues were also to be found in Carmarthen, Wrexham and along the border towns.

Points were scored only on service, until an agreed total was reached, and the hand-made ball was struck with the bare hand. Games were played at singles or doubles and on a home and away basis, as there were slight differences in courts and rules. These matches, in particular, created great local rivalries and attracted large crowds, purses and wagers.

Handball produced many folk heroes and characters. William 'Wil o'r Wern' Griffiths was a prominent 19th-century Rhondda Champion worthy of his own financial 'backers'. The late 1870s saw Dr Ifor Ajax-Lewis, of Llantrisant, throw the world a challenge, stating that he and Richard 'Dick Ted' Andrews, of Nelson, would play any other pair for £1,000. A similar challenge had been announced by the men of Brecon ninety years earlier.

The famous Old Ball Court on the Square, Nelson 1906 (Welsh Handball Association)

416

The Ball Court at Nelson remains the only playable venue in Wales. Dated 1860, the court is a unique sporting arena, of interest to historians, tourists and handballers worldwide. Its champions include John 'Shoni Hugh' Griffiths (1860s), Tom Phillips (1890s), Bert Morgan (1910s), Ken Lockier (1920s), Tommy 'Champ' Jones (1930s/40s), Cliff 'Sprinter' Lewis (1930s/40s) and Kerry Wilde (1980s).

Founded in 1987, the Welsh Handball Association preserves traditional three-wall handball and in 1995 adopted United States Handball Association one-wall rules, enabling international competition. Lee Davies became the first Welsh World Champion in 1997. Justin 'Sheepy' Evans won an All Ireland one-wall title in 1999.

References:

Dicks, K., *Irish Handball Yearbook 98 and 99* (Kilkenny: People Printing Ltd, 1997, 1998).

Jones, H. J., *Nelson Handball Court – History of the Court and its Players 1860-1940* (1994).

Jones, T. V., 'Medel, I Handball and Fives', *St Fagans Folk Museum Magazine*, (1985).

Owen, T. M., *The Customs and Traditions of Wales* (Cardiff: University of Wales Press, 1991).

Thomas, W. S. K., *Georgian and Victorian Brecon: Portrait of a Welsh County Town* (Llandysull: Gomer Press, 1993).

See also:

Handball

-Kevin Dicks

Wembley Stadium

Wembley stadium in north London has staged many different sports and been the focus of a variety of allegiances, from the international to the local. Though never formally designated a 'national' stadium, Wembley has acquired such all-embracing appeal that its pre-eminent stature among British sports grounds has long been assured. The stadium was built during 1922-1923 as part of the 225-acre site of the British Empire Exhibition (1924-1925), much of which had disappeared by the end of the decade. Wembley's distinctive appearance was achieved by the use of the new material of reinforced concrete, its unusual elliptical configuration, and a Romanesque architectural style, typified in rounded arches and the twin towers that frame the main entrance. On big occasions such as the F.A. Cup Final, Wembley has an impressive appearance that befits a stadium whose aesthetic inspiration is the Colosseum in Rome. The oval shape also suited greyhound racing, which became for many years the principal source of the stadium's income.

Wembley's place in English national culture was established at the stadium's inauguration. April 28th, 1923, saw the first staging there of the Cup Final, when some 200,000 spectators found their way into a stadium that had been designed to hold two-thirds that number. That the match went ahead after a short delay was accounted a triumph of English good sense and discipline. The events quickly passed into national legend as the 'white horse' final, so named because of the policeman and his mount who had taken a leading part in restoring order. Since then, Wembley has produced many other memorable moments. Several have been associated with football (the 'Matthews Cup Final' of 1953 and England's victory in the 1966 World Cup stand out), but boxing, showjumping, Rugby League, hockey and speedway (the stadium having been the home of Wembley Lions) have also contributed to Wembley's fame. The stadium housed the track and field events of the 1948 Olympics, which are remembered for the achievements of the Dutch sprinter Fanny Blankers-Koen, and the introduction to world athletics of the illustrious Emil Zatopek. In more recent years, the stadium company, anxious to increase revenue, has diversified. Since 1972, rock concerts have been regular events and have featured, among others, the Rolling Stones and Madonna. John Paul II celebrated mass there during his papal visit of 1982. By this time, Wembley's age raised doubts over its ability to compete with modern multi-purpose stadiums for the staging of global sporting events. Though for safety reasons the capacity has been reduced from the longstanding 100,000 to just below 80,000, little modernization had taken place beyond the extension of the roof (1963) and the building of the Olympic Gallery (1989).

In 1995, the Sports Council initiated an open competition for the construction of a new national stadium with money from the National Lottery. Wembley was chosen as the site in preference to others including Birmingham and Manchester. The outcome will be the complete replacement by 2002 of the existing stadium, with not even the twin towers remaining as a physical reminder of Wembley's past.

References:

Hill, J. and Varrasi, F., 'Creating Wembley: the Construction of a National Monument', *The Sports Historian*, 17 (November 1997), pp. 28-43.

Inglis, S., *The Football Grounds of Britain* (London: Willow Books, 1996).

Low, A. R., *Wonderful Wembley* (London: Stanley Paul, 1983).

Further reading:

Pawson, T., *100 Years of the F.A. Cup: the Official Centenary History* (London: Heinemann, 1972).

Websites:

Wembley Stadium –
http://www.wembleynationalstadium.co.uk/

See also:

Association Football; Rugby League

-Jeff Hill

White City

The White City was a 60,000-seater stadium specially constructed for the 1908 Olympic Games in London. When completed it had a concrete cycle track, cinder running track and, within the circumference of these, a sunken swimming bath for diving and water polo. The stadium was dedicated on the May 14th, 1908, as the 'Great Stadium'. Olympic events were held there for athletics, archery, cycling, diving, football, gymnastics, hockey, lacrosse, Rugby, swimming, water polo and wrestling.

From 1908 until 1914, Imre Kiralfy, the Hungarian owner of the facility, hired out the stadium for athletic, cycling, swimming and wrestling events. There is also evidence of the venue being used for fly-casting. During the two world wars it was used for military purposes.

In 1926, Brigadier-General Critchley leased the stadium for greyhound racing, which proved so popular that at one time it drew crowds of up to 90,000 spectators. The sport continued to take place at the White City right up to its closure, although by that time the Greyhound Racing Association was experiencing financial difficulties. In 1937, the stadium witnessed Britain's largest betting tote to date.

A new athletics track was built in 1932, upon which the British Empire Games were held in 1934. It was the venue for the Amateur Athletic Association Championships until 1971. Altogether, over 100 world records were set on the White City track.

Speedway was held at the White City in 1928-1929, 1977-1979 and 1981. Queens Park Rangers Football Club played their home matches at the White City in the 1930s and 1960s. One of the first floodlight Rugby matches took place at the White City in 1932. Records reveal evidence of clay pigeon shooting in 1933 and cheetah racing in 1937.

U.S. forces brought American football (1944-1945) and baseball (1953) to the City. Between 1932-1955 a number of major boxing bouts were staged.

The International Horse Show was held at the White City in 1947, 1957 (then the International Horse Show) and again in 1983 before it was demolished in September of that year.

See also:

Athletics; Olympic Games

-Dave Terry

Wightman Cup

The Wightman Cup was an Anglo-American tennis competition which was intended to promote international tennis among women in much the same way as the Davis Cup did for men. The cup owed its name to Hazel Hotchkiss Wightman, daughter of a landed family from Healdsburg, California, who as Hazel Hotchkiss had been a most successful player herself (she was the winner of a record forty-five U.S. national singles and doubles titles) and the rival of another famous Californian, May Sutton. She had donated the cup as early as 1920, after marrying George Wightman, an excellent real tennis player who, in 1924, became president of the United States Lawn Tennis Association, and settling in Boston. The only nation to challenge was England in 1923. In the following years, the cup was contended annually between the United States and England, and was captured by the winner of a best-of-seven rubbers match, which comprised five singles and two doubles. The first match was won 7-0 by the American team. Over the years, every leading American and British female player took part. As time went on, and with America's superiority ever increasing, interest in the competition declined dramatically and it became difficult if not impossible to attract sponsorship. With a score of 51-10 victories in favour of the United States in 1989, the event was eventually discontinued. Nevertheless, an under twenty-ones version of it named after Maureen Connolly has been instituted in its place, for which teams of the United States and Great Britain are once again competing. This seems to be the most sensible continuation of an old tradition.

References:

Digby-Baltzell, E., *Sporting Gentlemen: Men's Tennis from the Age of Honor to the Cult of the Superstar* (New York: The Free Press, 1995).

Parsons, J., *The Ultimate Encyclopedia of Tennis* (London: Carlton/Hodder & Stoughton Ltd, 1998).

See also:
Lawn Tennis

-Heiner Gillmeister

Wild Pigeon Shooting

Wild pigeon shooting preceded clay pigeon shooting, the common term for inanimate shotgun shooting at moving disc-shaped targets or 'clays'. In wild pigeon shooting, live pigeons were released from specially constructed box traps. Pigeons were either caught in the wild or provided by specialist pigeon breeders. As the direction of the birds' flight was unpredictable, they posed a challenge to the skill of the shooter.

By the mid-19th century, it was a popular and internationally recognized pastime for the wealthier sections of the shooting fraternity. The leading centres of the sport were Monte Carlo, the Cercle des Patineurs in Paris and Hurlingham, under the jurisdiction of the London Gun Club. The organizing bodies were responsible for ensuring the rules of fair play. At this time, the London Gun Club fulfilled the same role for its members as the Jockey Club did for the racing community. During the heyday of the officially organized side of the sport, elaborate sweepstake competitions were organized for wealthy patrons. Periodically, they were also organized unofficially on an ad hoc basis.

Concern for the welfare of the birds led to live trap shooting finally being banned in 1921. Even prior to this, the increase in its popularity, and difficulties in securing the necessary supply of live birds, led to substitutes being found. Initially this took the form of shooting at glass balls, projected by spring-loaded devices. The clay target is said to have originated in 1880, when George Ligowoski observed boys skimming flat stones across a lake. This gave him the idea for saucer-shaped objects, which could be launched into the air from a trap and provide challenging targets for the shooter. By the end of the 19th century, these had evolved into the disc-type clay targets called clay pigeons.

The Inanimate Bird Shooting Association (I.B.S.A.) was formed in 1892, holding its first championships at Wimbledon Park, London the following year. Clay Pigeon Shooting appeared at the 1900 and 1908 Olympic games, with Britain winning the team competition on both occasions. The sport still retains its Olympic status, and is a sport in which British athletes have traditionally performed well. The I.B.S.A. became the Clay Bird Shooting Association in 1903, a name it retained until 1928 when a central body named the Amateur United Clay Pigeon Association of Great Britain came into existence. The following year, this changed its name to the Clay Pigeon Shooting Association (C.P.S.A.), the name it retains to this day. The C.P.S.A. is the governing body for the sport in Britain and organizes championships at county, regional and national level.

The sport has been transformed by the development of automatic clay traps, which can throw clays in a multitude of different ways, imitating a variety of quarry. There are various disciplines, such as down the line, skeet and trap, each with their own special techniques, rules and regulations.

There are two specialist methods of shooting where the quarry is still primarily made up of wild pigeons, namely decoying and roost shooting. In the former, pigeons are attracted to a specific area of their feeding ground by artificial decoys and then shot from a hide. This method can provide an effective way of securing a large bag. In the latter, pigeons are shot in the evening by waiting for them to return to their roosting areas near woods at dusk. In the aftermath of the Second World War, when pigeons were a serious agricultural pest, the government organized roost shoots on

designated evenings in order to maximize the number of birds shot as they moved from one roost to another.

The terminology used by shooters still harks back to the days of shooting live birds. A target is called a bird, a hit is a kill, while the machines which propel the targets are still called traps.

References:

Clay Pigeon Shooting Association, *Booklet No. 1*.

Croft, P., *Clay Shooting* (London: Ward Lock, 1998).

Hammond, B., 'Glass Ball and Feathers', *Pull!* (March 1988).

Humphries, J., *Clay Pigeon Shooting* (London: Blandford, 1995).

Further reading:

Murton, R. K., *The Wood-Pigeon* (London: Collins, 1965).

Walsingham, T. (et al.), *Shooting: Field and Covert* (First published 1900, reprinted Southampton: Ashford Press Publishing, 1987).

Websites:

The Clay Pigeon Shooting Association – http://www.cpsa.co.uk/home.shtml

See also:

Game Shooting

-John Martin

Wildfowling

Wildfowling is a specialist branch of shooting, which traditionally involved the pursuit of wild ducks and geese on marshes and foreshores. The birds were shot on their flight lines at dawn and dusk, or on their feeding grounds using decoys to attract them. Unlike other forms of shooting, success at wildfowling depends more on the wildfowlers' understanding of the habits and habitat of their quarry rather than their marksmanship. It is a physically demanding sport, requiring significant skill to identify the quarry and to appreciate the importance of tides and weather conditions. The success rate in securing quarry is very uncertain, hence the term 'wild goose chase'. The increase in the artificial rearing and stocking of inland waters with ducks since the 1970s has lead to an expansion of the sport.

Puntgunning was a traditional form of wildfowling. Sportsmen crept up on the birds by lying in a flat-bottomed shallow canoe-type boat before shooting at them with specially designed large-bore, muzzle-loading guns. Before the Second World War, it provided a precarious way of earning a living for a select band of professional shooters willing to brave the crawling tides of winter dawns and moonlit nights. The decline in the number of wildfowl and the prohibition of the sale of dead wild geese in the 1960s undermined the sport as a commercial activity and led to it becoming the preserve of enthusiastic amateurs.

Whilst not technically classified as game, ducks and geese are also protected during close seasons and by legislation which proscribes the killing of certain species. The government has the power to impose a ban on the shooting of all types of wildfowl during periods of exceptionally bad weather. Most participants in the sport belong to wildfowling clubs, which are affiliated to the British Association for Shooting and Conservation, which deals exclusively with this branch of shooting.

References:

Willock, C., *The ABC of Shooting* (London: André Deutsch, 1975).

See also:

Field Sports

-John Martin

Wimbledon

Lawn tennis was first played at Wimbledon in 1875, after the All England Croquet Club (founded 1868) rented a ground of 4 acres there between Worple Road and the London and South Western Railway. The first Lawn Tennis Championship was held in 1877, for which a new code of laws was introduced. As a consequence, the Club was renamed the All England Croquet and Lawn Tennis Club, dropping the word croquet altogether in 1882. (It was retitled the All England Lawn Tennis and Croquet Club in 1899, its title to date, which emphasizes the predominance of the first-named sport.) The Club colours of dark green and purple were introduced in 1909.

The first Championship was a Gentlemen's Singles event, the Ladies' Singles and Gentlemen's Doubles Championships were to follow in 1884, the Ladies' Doubles and Mixed Doubles being raised to Championship status only in 1913. In that year, all Wimbledon Championships were given the title 'World Championships on Grass' by the newly created International Lawn Tennis Federation (I.L.T.F.), a practice abandoned after 1923, when the Federation initiated the four 'Grand Slam' tournaments (the championships of Great Britain [Wimbledon], France, Australia and the United States) to do justice to the other great tennis nations. The term 'Grand Slam' is said to have been coined by the *New York Times* correspondent Allison Danzig in 1933 when the Australian, Jack Crawford, was on the point of winning all four championships.

The old grounds, built during the 1880s and comprising of nine courts encircling a Centre Court, were replaced by a new complex at Church Road (formerly Wimbledon Park Road) in 1922, owing to the spectator boom occasioned by the appearance of Suzanne Lenglen. Since then, Wimbledon has seen major restructuring and improvements on an almost annual basis. Only once, in 1940 when the Championships were suspended, were these changes forced by circumstances not in the power of the All England committee – on that occasion, the Club's tool house and the roof of the Centre Court were struck by German bombs. A bomb scare in 1990 caused only the temporary suspension of play. In more recent times, major operations have included the construction of a new Centre Court roof in 1992, through which a perfect view from all seats was achieved; and the erection, in the course of a Long Term Development Plan, of the new No. 1 Court, which now dominates the ground. It was opened in 1997 by the Duke of Kent, whose family has been associated with the Club since 1929 when Prince George (later Duke of Kent) became its president.

In the course of its long history, attendances at Wimbledon have grown steadily, although figures of daily totals and championship aggregates are not available for the early years. In the last decade at Worple Road, the ground was said to be 'packed to suffocation' when the attendance reached 7,500; overall attendances at the time have been estimated between 60,000 and 70,000. The record attendance for a meeting was 436,531 in 1997, almost double that of 1932, the first year on record, when 219,000 people attended.

The steady increase in attendance ran parallel to the ever-growing participation of foreign competitors. In the days of the American May Sutton and the Australian N. E. Brookes, who in 1905 and 1907 became the first non-British champions, foreigners were at liberty to enter. After 1919, entries became so numerous that only foreign players nominated by their national associations were accepted without question, all others being subjected to evaluation by a subcommittee, which in recent years has made its decisions on the basis of computer rankings. The present draw of 128 for the men's singles was first instanced in 1922, with qualifying competitions of various forms beginning in 1925. The same number of entries, 128, was conceded to the ladies' singles not earlier than 1983, a fact which mirrors the conservative attitude of the Club.

Conservatism has long been a feature of Wimbledon, conspicuous in well-known regulations such as the stipulation that the colour of tennis wear should be 'predominantly in white'

(1963; modified to 'almost entirely in white' in 1995). On the other hand, innovations such as the introduction of the yellow ball (1986), once sanctioned by the All England Club, are sure to afterwards become established in the sport as a whole. Generally speaking, Wimbledon continues to be the mainstay of British tennis, not least because of the fact that the surplus arising from the Championships – not less than £30,000,000 in 2000 – is allotted to the Lawn Tennis Association for the purpose of developing tennis in Great Britain.

References:

Barrett, J., *100 Wimbledon Championships: a Celebration* (London: Willow Books 1986).

Little, A., *Wimbledon Compendium 1998* (Wimbledon: The All England Lawn Tennis and Croquet Club, 1998).

Websites:

Wimbledon – http://www.wimbledon.org/

See also:

Lawn Tennis

-Heiner Gillmeister

Windsurfing

Windsurfing as a sport began in 1964, although it was 1969 before it became an established competitive sport. The question of who was responsible for designing the first windsurfing board is a matter of controversy, but what is clear is that modern board design has revolutionized the activity, making it one of the most popular water sports.

Newman Darby, from the United States, is one man commonly credited with the invention of the windsurfing board, although his craft had more in common with small boats than windsurfing boards. His vessel was made up of a square sail that was attached to the mast by a gaff stay. Sailors stood in front of the rig and used their body and wind assistance to move the craft, while steering was achieved by moving the rig fore and aft.

Another designer who laid claim to being the first board designer was Peter Chilvers of Britain. Chilvers' craft was made of plywood, upon which he attached the mast via a universal joint, a two-piece wishbone boom (or wishboom) and a Bermudan rig. His design, however, suffered from serious technical problems, which were overcome by an American, Hoyle Scwheitzer. Scwheitzer incorporated a fully articulated universal joint for the mast and a double-sided wishbone boom to support the sail. He patented his design in 1968, calling it a 'windsurf'. However, this patent was successfully challenged by Chilvers who, supported by the French plastics company Bic, was able to have Scwheitzer's patent annulled in English law in 1984. Bic were keen to exploit the growing windsurf market and saw the support of Chilvers as crucial to this strategy.

The sport has grown rapidly in the last twenty-five years, its popularity seemingly increasing with every new board design. Better board design has enabled windsurfers to increase speed and introduce jumps, making it a very attractive spectator sport. Modern boards are lightweight and durable and have excellent safety features, such as foot straps and body harnesses, making it a very safe sport both for the weekend water-sports enthusiast and the professional.

During the 1990s, a professional scene developed which attracted large crowds, particularly in Europe where crowds in excess of 100,000 are not uncommon. Crowds are attracted by the fast speeds, over 50 knots, that a professional can achieve and the complicated jumps over waves, which give the sport great excitement. Several world speed records have been broken at the Marine Lake in West Kirby on the Wirral Peninsula. The introduction of the World Cup professional circuit in the 1990s also enhanced spectator appeal. Promoters, ever ready to cash in on a sport's popularity, have developed indoor windsurfing, using wind generating fans in an attempt to simulate outdoor conditions.

Windsurfing became a full Olympic sport at the 1984 Los Angeles Games. In 1992, separate disciplines for men and women were introduced by the International Olympic Committee. The governing body for windsurfing in Britain is the Royal Yachting Association.

References:
O'Shea, F., *Learn to Windsurf* (London: Ward Lock 1997).
Royal Yachting Association Website – http://www.rya.org.uk/

Websites:
The Royal Yachting Association – http://www.rya.org.uk/

See also:
Sailing

-Ray Physick

Wisden Cricketers' Almanack

Wisden Cricketers' Almanack's sobriquet as 'the Cricketers' bible' reflects its fame and importance to students of the game, and underlines its claim as the most eminent work of sporting reference.

First published in 1864 by John Wisden, a notable professional cricketer of the day, the slim volume of 112 pages was a true almanack, containing much information on a wide range of sports and historical events. By 2000, *Wisden* contained over 1,500 pages and had reached 137 not out.

This feat of publishing longevity was fortuitous. Although *Wisden* saw off many competitors in the late 19th century, it had itself only just survived a period of severe crisis in the mid-1880s. Today, the volumes covering these early years are prized and valuable collectors' items.

By the 'Golden Age' of cricket in Edwardian years, *Wisden* had established itself as the eminent cricket publication. The

423

decision to publish in 1916, despite the First World War and the lack of normal cricket, was due to the desire to pay tribute to the great W. G. Grace, who had died in 1915. This slim volume set the precedent for unbroken publication during both world wars.

Wisden was published in paper covers between 1864 and 1937. From 1938 to date, the softback version has had linen covers. In 1896, the first hardback volume was produced, but this did not receive the familiar yellow dust-jacket until the 1965 volume.

The first illustration appeared in 1889 when the editor included a photographic plate of 'Six Great Bowlers' of the previous season. This was the forerunner of *Wisden*'s 'Five Cricketers of the Year', an important annual accolade and an award a player can receive only once in his career.

The *Almanack*'s reputation has been based on its detailed coverage of cricket throughout the world, although it has never claimed infallibility. It has had a comparatively small number of editors during its existence, their comments on the cricketing issues of the day always being very influential.

Owned by millionaire cricket enthusiast John Paul Getty since 1994, *Wisden* looks to the future with confidence.

Further reading:

Gutteridge, L. E. S., 'A History of Wisden', *Wisden Cricketers' Almanack* (London: Sporting Handbooks for Wisden & Co., 1963), pp. 74-88.

Williams, M. and Phillips, G., *The Wisden Book of Cricket Memorabilia* (Oxford: Lennard Publishing 1990).

Websites:

Wisden – http://www.wisden.co.uk/

See also:

Cricket; Media

-Barrie Watkins

Wolfenden Report

Sport and the Community: the Report of the Wolfenden Committee on Sport was published in 1960 at the end of a sporting decade that had witnessed the decline of Britain's sporting prowess, symptomatic of her decline as a world power.

Under the Chairmanship of Sir John Wolfenden, the Committee launched a debate on the role of sport in the community, examining factors affecting the development of sport and making recommendations on practical measures to be taken against the background of the growing power of communist sport and increased state support in capitalist democracies, exemplified by West Germany's Golden Plan.

Beginning with a factual account of the current position, Wolfenden examined problems confronting British sport, discovering the dropout of young people from sport after leaving school; the potential of sport to divert young people from crime; the need for a coaching structure; anomalies in attitudes to amateurism; and the position of Sunday sport. The Committee made fifty-seven recommendations, including that an annual sum of £5 million be distributed by a Sports Development Council. Whilst recognizing that facilities compared unfavourably with other countries, arguments supporting a Ministry of Sport responsible for finance and policy were rejected as alien to national attitudes.

In 1962, the ruling Conservative Party gave Lord Hailsham, an Education Minister, responsibility for sport and in 1965, the newly elected Labour Party created an Advisory Sports Council, which was granted a Royal Charter in 1972 and operates at arms length from government policy.

References:

Sport and the Community: the Report of the Wolfenden Committee on Sport (London: Central Council of Physical Recreation 1960).

See also:
Central Council of Physical Recreation; Sports Council

-Charles Jenkins

Women's Sports Foundation

The Women's Sports Foundation (W.S.F.) is a registered charity, recognized by Sport England as the only organization in Britain that is solely committed to improving and promoting opportunities for women and girls in sport at every level. Established in 1984, the W.S.F. is an organization run by a small team of full-time staff, with the support of national and regional volunteers. Its vision statement, 'Equity for Women in and through Sport', contains five key aims – to increase awareness of issues surrounding women's involvement in sport; to support the involvement of women and girls in sport at all levels and in all capacities; to encourage improved access to sporting opportunities for women and girls; to challenge inequality in sport and seek to bring about change; and to raise the visibility of all British sportswomen.

The W.S.F. implements a wide range of initiatives to achieve these aims, including educational and training initiatives; working in partnership with key agencies; lobbying key decision-makers; providing advice and comment on key issues; encouraging research into areas of relevance to women's and girls' sport; raising the awareness of career opportunities in sport for girls and women; working to equip sportswomen to deal with the media, gain a high profile and attract funding and sponsorship; and answering enquiries on sport and providing a range of resources.

Membership benefits include networking opportunities, the W.S.F. quarterly newsletter and regular fact and information sheets on matters of relevance to women's sport. There is also a quarterly calendar showing the top women's sports events in the United Kingdom and access to the full range of W.S.F. resources and displays at discounted prices. There is a W.S.F. annual conference and other regional and national events.

Websites:
The Womens' Sports Foundation – http://www.wsf.org.uk/

See also:
Gender

-Elizabeth Taplin

World Cup Cricket

The Cricket World Cup has become the premier international one-day competition since its inauguration in England in 1975 with the pioneering sponsorship of the Prudential Assurance Company. The basic format has been two equal groups of teams, with the top two teams in each contesting the semi-final and then the final. For the 1975 World Cup, this comprised the six test-playing nations (England, Australia, India, New Zealand, Pakistan and the West Indies) plus Sri Lanka and East Africa. Subsequent competitions have been held every four years, with the winners of the International Cricket Council Trophy being added to the test sides, thereby encouraging cricket worldwide.

The West Indies won the first two World Cups, and both finals followed a similar pattern. Having lost early wickets, the Caribbean side recovered through the strokeplay of Clive Lloyd and Viv Richards. On both occasions, their genius saw the West Indies to a formidable total, which was beyond the Australian batsmen in 1975 and their English counterparts in 1979.

India's accurate medium-pacers turned the tables on the West Indies in the 1983 Final, and four years later they co-hosted the Reliance World Cup with Pakistan, where Australia narrowly defeated England in the final by 7 runs. The 1992 event, staged in Australia and New

Zealand, was the largest in the event's history, and saw a change to the format with floodlit matches, coloured clothing and the eight test-playing sides (now including South Africa and Sri Lanka), plus Zimbabwe. After a round robin of eight games each, the final was played under lights at Melbourne, where Pakistan beat England by 22 runs.

The 1996 Wills World Cup, staged in India, Pakistan and Sri Lanka, saw a return to the group format, with the United Arab Emirates, Holland and Kenya joining the nine test nations (Zimbabwe having been added to the list of test nations in 1992). Sri Lanka, thanks to the audacious pinch-hitting of Sanath Jayasuriya and the cultured batting of Aravinda de Silva, duly became World Champions with a 7-wicket defeat of Australia in the final. The 1999 World Cup saw a return of the competition to Britain, with Australia beating Pakistan in the final.

References:

Frindall, B., *NatWest Playfair Cricket World Cup, 1999* (London: Headline, 1999).

Lemmon, D., *One Day Cricket* (London: Century Benham, 1988).

See also:

Cricket

-Andrew Hignell

World Cup Rugby League

The idea of a Rugby League world cup competition was first mooted in the 1930s. The French Rugby League proposed holding a world cup in 1948 and 1951, but it was not until 1954 that the project came to fruition.

Held in France, the inaugural competition was contested by Australia, France, Great Britain and New Zealand. Over 30,000 gathered for the final at the Parc de Princes stadium in Paris to see an under-strength Great Britain side overcome France 16-12.

The 1957 world cup was played on a league basis and won by the hosts Australia. The league format was also used in 1960 when Great Britain won in England.

The tournament then took on a somewhat erratic schedule, taking place in 1968, 1970, 1972, 1975 and 1977, with Australia winning each time, apart from Great Britain's 1972 triumph in France.

In 1985, the tournament was resurrected and played over a three-year period, being notable for the participation of Papua New Guinea and the first appearance of New Zealand in the final, which Australia won 25-12.

The same format was used for the 1989-1992 tournament, won by Australia, who beat Great Britain 10-6 in front of a record 73,631 at Wembley.

The 1995 tournament was held in Britain to coincide with the sport's centenary and attracted seventeen participating nations, divided into the World Cup proper and an emerging nations competition. Over a quarter of a million people watched the tournament, which was, yet again, won by Australia, who defeated England 16-8 at Wembley. The final of the year 2000 tournament will be held at Old Trafford football stadium in Manchester.

References:

Andrews, M., *The ABC of Rugby League* (Sydney: ABC, 1992).

Fletcher, R. and Howes, D., *Rothman's Rugby League Yearbook 1993-94* (London: Hodder Headline, 1993).

Fletcher, R. and Howes, D., *Rothman's Rugby League Yearbook 1996* (London: Hodder Headline, 1996).

See also:

Rugby League

-Tony Collins

World Cup Rugby Union

Unlike soccer and track and field, Rugby has been slow to establish a 'world championship'. A major factor in inhibiting the development of a 'Rugby Olympics' was a 1958 resolution passed by the International Rugby Board forbidding its member nations from organizing such a competition. The fear was that a World Cup would lead the way to the global professionalization of Rugby.

The inaugural World Cup (1987) was staged in New Zealand and Australia. Despite some early one-sided matches (for example, Italy were walloped 70-6 by New Zealand, who then trounced Fiji 74-13), most games were closely contested. At Eden Park, Auckland, the New Zealand All-Blacks defeated France 29-9 in the final.

The second World Cup (1991) used a number of venues around the United Kingdom. Lesser-known countries such as Canada and Western Samoa made it through to the quarter-finals. The final was a hard fought battle between England and Australia. The Australians won 12-6.

The highlight of the third World Cup (1995) was the return to the Rugby world stage of South Africa, following the dismantling of apartheid. The games were played at a number of grounds around South Africa, with Rustenberg, Pretoria, Johannesburg, Bloemfontein, Durban, East London, and Port Elizabeth all hosting matches. A titanic final between South Africa and New Zealand saw the South Africans narrowly win, by a score of 15-12. The game was given a remarkable degree of political impetus, with a leavening of racial reconciliation, by the presence of Premier Nelson Mandela. He presented white Afrikaner captain Francois Pienaar with the trophy. They both wore the no. 6 Springbok Rugby jersey. Commentators and social historians continue to argue whether such an occasion was a profound 'coming together' of South African warring factions or rather a cosmetic political sleight of hand and public relations posturing.

The 1999 World Cup was a Western European venture, with games held in Scotland, England, France and both Irelands. The most notable factor was not just that world Rugby was now fully professionalized, but that the game had become truly global. Seventy nations from six continents participated, including representatives from Central Europe (such as Latvia and Lithuania) and Africa (such as Botswana, Côte d'Ivoire, Kenya and Morocco). Many of these less well-known Rugby countries did not, however, succeed in getting a place in the final twenty teams.

In 1998, there was controversy regarding whether the new Millennium Stadium (built to replace the Cardiff Arms Park) would be ready in time. In fact, the original crowd capacity of 80,000 was cut to 72,500, and the inaugural game took place on June 26th, 1999, with the World Cup holders South Africa in attendance. The Cup was won by Australia, who convincingly beat France in the final.

References:

Sommerville, D., *The Encyclopedia of Rugby Union* (London: Aurum Press, 1997).

Further reading:

New York Times, 25 June 1995, p. 5.

See also:

Rugby Union

-Scott Crawford

Wrestling

Wrestling is one of the oldest and most basic of all human activities known to exist, having developed into its modern sporting form sometime in prehistory, when it became convenient to substitute death or serious injury for a more symbolic victory.

Wrestling existed in all early civilizations. At Beni-Hasan in Egypt, for example, wall paintings dating from 3,400 BC have been found, which depict over 200 wrestling scenes. However, it was in Ancient Greece that wrestling really developed into a sport, being included in the Olympic Games in 704 BC.

There are several different styles of wrestling, categorized into three basic types –

427

'belt-and-jacket' styles, in which the clothing of the wrestlers (belt, jacket or trousers) is used for grips; 'catch-hold' styles, in which the wrestlers are required to grip each other prior to, and usually throughout, the contest; and 'loose' styles, in which the wrestlers, who can take any grip apart from on clothing, are separated prior to the contest.

Wrestling styles can also be categorized according to five basic criteria required for victory – 'break-stance' involves forcing an opponent to relinquish a position; 'toppling' involves forcing an opponent to touch the ground with part of the body, apart from the feet; 'touch-fall' involves forcing an opponent into a specified position, usually supine, for a brief period; 'pin-fall' involves holding an opponent, once thrown, in a specified position for a period of time; and 'submission' involves forcing an opponent to admit defeat.

There are over eighty wrestling styles throughout the world. The most notable are *glima* from Iceland and *schwingen* from Switzerland, which are both belt styles, requiring toppling for victory; *kushti* from Iran, a catch-hold style, which requires a supine touch-fall; and *yagli* from Turkey, a loose style, which requires toppling.

In Britain, the most notable styles are 'Cornish wrestling', which is a jacket style, requiring toppling; and 'Cumberland and Westmorland wrestling', which is a catch-hold style, requiring toppling. The British Amateur Wrestling Association was established in 1969.

The international governing body for wrestling, the Fédération Internationale des Luttes Amateurs (F.I.L.A. – International Amateur Wrestling Federation), formed in 1921, recognizes three styles for competition. 'Freestyle' and 'Graeco-Roman' wrestling, the only styles fought in the modern Olympic Games, are both loose styles, requiring a touch-fall. The former allows any fair hold, throw or trip, whereas the latter does not permit holds below the hips, and grips with the legs. There are ten weight divisions in both styles – light flyweight, flyweight, bantamweight, featherweight, lightweight, welterweight, middleweight, light heavyweight, heavyweight and super heavyweight.

The third style recognized by F.I.L.A. is a synthesis of styles native to the former Soviet Union, called 'sambo' (an acronym taken from *samozash-chita*, meaning self-defence, and *bez oruzhiya*, meaning without weapons). Sambo is a combination of loose and jacket styles, requiring a submission for victory.

There are two further notable styles of wrestling. 'Inter-collegiate' wrestling, which is practised only in American colleges, is broadly similar to freestyle and Graeco-Roman styles, apart from the points system. 'Professional' wrestling, based on freestyle, is more a form of entertainment than sport, owing to its choreographed and theatrical moves.

The extensive media coverage of the sport, especially on I.T.V.'s *World of Sport* in the 1960s and 1970s, made many professional wrestlers, such as Big Daddy, Giant Haystacks, Mick McManus and Jackie Pallo, household names in Britain.

References:

Arlott, J. (ed.), *Oxford Companion to Sports and Games* (Oxford: Oxford University Press, 1976).

Kent, G., *A Pictorial History of Wrestling* (London: Spring Books, 1968).

Websites:

The British Amateur Wrestling Association – http://www.homeusers.prestel.co.uk/bawa/

-Michael Tripp

Y

Yachting (*see* Landyachting; Sailing)

Youth Sport Trust

The Youth Sport Trust is a national charity established in 1994 to build a brighter future for young people in sport. It was the brainchild of John L. Beckwith, who wanted to ensure that all young people received a quality introduction to sport. He was also keen to channel the energy of young people in a particular direction.

The Trust develops and implements, in close partnership with other organizations, quality physical education and sport programmes for all young people, aged eighteen months to eighteen years, in schools and the community. Key features of TOP programmes are illustrated resource cards, child-friendly equipment and quality training for teachers and deliverers. All of the programmes can be accessed by young disabled people.

To provide the best in education, training, research and development for the benefit of all young people, the Beckwith Chair of Youth Sport was established at Loughborough University in 1998.

By the end of 1999, the Trust had reached over 3 million young people through its TOP programmes.

Websites:
The Youth Sport Trust website – http://www.youthsport.net/

-Anna Windmill

429

Index

A

Abbagnale, Carmine 333
Abbagnale, Guiseppe 333
A.B.C. television 397
Aberdare Literary Prize 49
Aberdeen F.C. 169
Aberdeen Highland Games 177
Abide With Me 270
Aboyne Highland Games 176-77
Abrahams, Sir Adolphe 46, 375
Abrahams, Harold 7, 139, 369
A.C. Milan F.C. 109
Academy Ground, Edinburgh 343
Acrobatics 370-71, 399
Adam Shield 167
Adam, William 167
Addiscombe military college 25, 349
Admiral's Cup 1, 135
Advertising 2-3, 72
Advisory County Cricket Committee 83, 241
Aerobics 150
Aerobics for Women 150
Agasse, Jacques-Laurent 366
Agricultural Hall Society 353
Aida 270
Aikido 3
Aintree 3-4, 164, 190-91, 252
Aintree Racecourse Co. 4

Airth Highland Games 177
Aitken, G. G. 343
Ajax-Lewis, Dr Ifor 416
Akabusi, Kriss 13, 350
Albany Scottish society 177
Albert, Prince 353
Alcock, Charles William 6, 17-18, 86, 133
Alcohol 4-6
Aldaniti 163
Aldwych Skating Club 329
Alexander, Alexander 229
Alexander, Caroline 256
Alexander, Robert 212
Alfred McAlpine Stadium *see* McAlpine Stadium
Alfred, Prince (Duke of Edinburgh) 228
Alken, Henry 366
Ali, Mohammed 44, 247
All-England Badminton Championships 29-30
All England Championships (Tennis) *see* Wimbledon
All-England Croquet Club 93, 218-19, 421
All-England Eleven cricket team 82, 87
All England Jumping Course, Hickstead 175-76
All England Lawn Tennis and Croquet Club 217, 421 *see also* Wimbledon
All England Netball Association 150, 278-79
All England Women's Hockey Association 180-81

All I Want For Christmas Is The Dukla Prague Away Kit 269
All-Ireland Gaelic football series 143
Allardice, Captain Barclay 295
Allen, Gubby 130
Allen, Lauren 399-400
Allen, Terry 43
Allhusen, Derek 131
Alpine Club 256
Amalia, Queen 258
Amateur Athletic Association 6, 24, 26, 60, 70, 136, 238, 258, 291, 325-26, 401-03
Amateur Athletic Association Championships 24, 418
Amateur Athletic Supporters Association 318
Amateur Athletic Union of North America 148
Amateur Basket Ball Association of England and Wales 32
Amateur Boxing Association 42-43, 277
Amateur Championship (golf) 158, 160-61, 289
Amateur Diving Association 111
Amateur Fencing Association 137
Amateur Gymnastics Association 403
Amateur Rowing Association 6, 182-83, 270, 311, 331-32

Amateur Softball Association
of America 359
Amateur Swimming
Association 70, 111,
386-87, 389
Amateur Swimming Union
386
Amateur United Clay Pigeon
Association *see* Clay
Pigeon Shooting
Association
Amateur Volleyball
Association 411
Amateurism 6-7, 26, 67,
71-72, 81, 133-34
Ambush II 191
America's Cup 1, 347
American football *see*
Gridiron football
American Motorcycle
Association 255
American Pastoral 228
Ames, Leslie 85
Amos, Henry 224
Amsterdam Admirals 166
Anderson 295
Anderson, Carrick Crawford
256
Anderson, Lindsay 139
Andrews, Edward 311
Andrews, Richard 'Dick Ted'
416
Anfield 21, 363
Angelo, Harry 308
Anglia Television 396
Angling 8-11
see also Coarse fishing; Game
fishing; Sea fishing
Angus, Howard 321
Annalia Dubrensia 79
Anne, Princess 131, 247,
336, 405
Anne, Queen 11, 14, 186,
335
Announcers *see*
Commentators

Anquetil, Jacques 248
Ansell, Sir Michael 274
Ansell, Colonel Mike 183
Ansen, David 140
Anstey College 126
Anthony, Don 411
Anti-Gambling League 248
Apartheid 75-76, 91
Apollo House 306
Apperley, Charles ('Nimrod')
191
Applegarth, Willie 231
Archer, Fred 179, 249-50, 268
Archers' Hall 12
Archery 11-13, 324
Argyllshire Highland Games
176
Arkle 64, 191, 262, 264
Army, the 349
Army Gymnastic Staff *see*
Army Physical Training
Corps
Army Physical Training
Corps 13-14
Army School of Physical
Training 14, 137, 167
Army Sport Control Board 14
Arnold, Thomas 124, 260
Arrianus, Flavius 170
Arsenal F.C. 21, 104-05, 129
Art 49-51, 141-42, 365-67
Artillery Ground, Finsbury 85
Arts Council 146, 367
As 200
Ascari, Alberto 352
Ascham, Roger 12
Ascot 14-15, 186, 249, 335-36
Ashbourne Hall, Chelsea 23
Ashes 15-16, 88, 90, 263
Associated Metropolitan
Swimming Clubs 386
Association Football 6,
16-23, 56, 68, 72, 77-78,
104-05, 119-20, 133,
172, 214, 225, 282, 302,
305, 324, 361, 406-07

venues 20-23
Association Footballers'
Union 406
Association for the Protection
of Copyright in Sport
243, 396
Association Internationale
Medico-Sportive 375
Association of Masters of
Harriers and Beagles 170
Association of Organisers of
Physical Education 296
Association of Swedish
Physical Educationists *see*
Physical Education
Association
Association of Tennis Players
218
Astley Belt 24
Astley, Sir John 24
Aston Villa F.C. 18, 21, 283
Atherstone Hunt 191
Atherton, Michael 128
Athletic News 18, 200, 242,
244, 246
Athletics 7, 23-27, 317-18
indoor 23-25, 317-18
track and field 25-27
Atkins, Geoffrey 317
Atkins, Sue 44
Atlas Rounders Team 330
A.T.P. Council 218
A.T.P. Tour 218
Attendances *see* Record
crowds
Augee, Myrtle 415
Aureole 367
Austin, Bunny 215-17, 220
Australia cricket team 88,
90-91, 173, 398, 425-26
Australia Rugby League team
337-38, 426
Australia Rugby Union team
341-42, 404, 427
Australian Cricket Board 213
Australian Football League 27

Australian Rules Football 27
Auto-Cycle Union 253-54, 365

B

Bad Homburg 215
Baddeley, Herbert 216
Baddeley, Wilfred 216
Badminton 29-30
Badminton Association of England 29-30
Badminton Gazette 29
Badminton Horse Trials 31, 131
Badminton House 29-31
Badminton Library of Sports and Pastimes 31
Badminton Magazine 31
Bailey, Donovan 172
Bairner, Alan 49
Baker, Sir Herbert 233
Baker, Howard 78
Baker, Percy 39
Bala canoe course 58
Bale, John 49
Ball, Alan 324
The Ball Court, Nelson 417
Ball Court Inn, Merthyr Tydfil 416
Ball, John 256
Ball, John Junior 161
Ballater Highland Games 176
Balmat, Jacques 256
Balmoral 177
Bambra, Audrey 63
Bangor University 299
Banks, Mark 332
Bannerman, Charles 90
Bannister, Roger 7, 291, 370, 372
Barcelona Dragons 167
Barclay, C. 141
Barclay, Captain 308, 310
Barlow, Francis 365
Barna, Victor 392

Barnack, Oscar 367
Barnes, John 315, 370
Barra Highland Games 176
Barrington, Jonah 382
Barrow R.L.F.C. 281
Barry 75
Basketball 31-33
Bath Killer Bees 167
Bath R.F.C. 172, 343
Bathurst Cup (real tennis) 321
Batley R.L.F.C. 173, 338
Batten, Miriam 332
Bayern Munich F.C. 105
Baxter, Jim 369
Beacham, Margaret 25
Beattie, Joanne 323
Beaufort, Dukes of 29-31, 131
Beaufort House 26
Becher, Captain Martin William 163
Becher's Brook 163
Becker, Friedrich 215
Beckham, David 269
Beckham, Victoria 269
Beckwith, John L. 429
Bedford College 33, 126
Bedford Physical Education Old Students' Association 33
Bedser, Alec 85
Beesley, Abel 311
Bejtemen 226
Belcher, Jem 308-09
Beldham, William 84
Belfast Boy 269
Belfry, the 33-34, 160, 306
Bell, Ernest 224
Belle Vue speedway team 364
Bell's Life 16, 200, 242, 246-47
Ben Hur 139
Ben Nevis race 136
Benefit matches 34
Benetton 353
Benn, Nigel 44

Bennett, Phil 343
Benning, Derek 48
Benson and Hedges Cup 89, 263
Bentinck, Lord George 163
Bentley, John James 18, 244
Beresford, Lord 35
Berg, Jackie 44
Bergman, Martina *see* Österberg, Martina Bergman
Bergman Österberg Trust 102
Bergman Österberg Union 102
Bergmann, Richard 392
Berlin Lawn-Tennis-Turnier-Club 'Rot-Weiss' 217
Berlin Thunder 167
Best, George 140, 269, 370
Bethell, Andrew 114
Betting and Gaming Act (1960) 165
Bevan, Robert 366
Bexhill Speed Trials 381
Bey, F. D. Amr 382
Bibliography of British Sporting Artists 51
Bicknell, Reg 290
Bicycle Touring Club *see* Cyclists Touring Club
Bicycle Union *see* National Cyclists Union
Biddle, Stuart 307
Big Daddy 428
The Big Match 397
'Bill at Mount' 205
Birchfield Harriers Athletic Club 238
Birkenhead Great Float 229
Birkett, Jim 327
Birmingham Athletic Institute 35
Birmingham League (cricket) 82
Birmingham School Board Physical Exercises Committee 35

Birmingham speedway team
364
Birmingham University 35-36
Bisham Abbey 36, 60, 299,
302
Blackburn Olympic 17, 133,
178
Blackburn Rovers F.C. 172
Blackheath Hockey Club 180
Blackheath Rugby club 339
Blackpool F.C. 172
Blake, Peter 366
Blakiston, A. F. 343
Blankers-Koen, Fanny 287,
417
The Blaydon Races 268
Blazer 329
Bleackley, Edward 244, 246
Blenheim Horse Trials 131
Bligh, Hon. Ivo 15, 87, 90,
130
Bloomer, Steve 369
Blue Is The Colour 270
Bluebird 207-08
Board, Lillian 370
Board of Control 83, 241
Boardman, Chris 99
Boardman, Peter 257
Boat Race 56, 291, 331, 333,
408-09
Bobsleigh 36-37
Bodhidharma 205
Bodyline Series 91
Boehm, Joseph 367
Boer War 121, 126
Bogarde, Dirk 140
Bohinen, Lars 407
Boland, John Pius 220
Bolero 268
Bolton Wanderers F.C. 18,
21, 23, 78, 108-09, 133
Bonallack, Michael 159
Bond, Jack 153
Bonington, Chris 257
Borotra, Jean 223
Bosanquet, B. J. T. 130

Bosman ruling 119-20, 214
Botham, Ian 85-86, 173
Bournemouth (tennis venue)
218
Bowes 91
Bowls 37-40, 324
The Boxer 140
Boxiana 200
Boxing 40-44, 67, 324, 407
see also Pugilism
Boycott, Geoffrey 85
Boys Brigade 60
Boys' Own Book 330
Brabazon course, the Belfry 34
Brabham, Jack 252-53
Bradford City F.C. 109, 281,
338
Bradford League (cricket) 82
Bradford R.L.F.C. 173, 281
Bradley, Bill 250
Bradman, Don 91, 173
Braemar Highland Games
176-77, 336
Braemar Royal Highland
Society Gathering 177
Bragança, Catherine of 11
Bragança Shield 11
Braid, James 158, 305
Bramall Lane, Sheffield 86
Brando, Marlon 139
Brandon-Bravo, Martin 182
Brands Hatch 44-45, 252
Brands Hatch Leisure Group
290
Brasher, Chris 230-31
Breal, Michel 237
Brearley, Lee 400
Breeding see Horse-racing:
breeding
Breeze, Joe 255
Brian Johnston Film Theatre
264
Brigadier Gerard 264
Briggs, Barry 365
Brighton and Hove Albion
F.C. 23

Brighton University 358
British Aikido Association 3
British Amateur Gymnastics
Association 167-68, 226,
371
British Amateur Rugby
League Association 337
British Amateur Weight Lifters'
Association 36, 415
British Amateur Wrestling
Association 428
British American Football
Association 167
British Association for
Shooting and
Conservation 45-46, 421
British Association of
National Coaches 70
British Association of Road
Runners 325
British Association of Ski
Instructors 153
British Association of Sport
and Exercise Medicine
46-47, 375
British Association of Sport
and Exercise Sciences 47-
48, 306, 377-78
British Association of Sports
Scientists see British
Association of Sport and
Exercise Sciences
British Australian Rules
Football League 27
British Biathlon Union
Olympic Centre 153
British Bobsleigh Association
36
British Boxing Board of
Control 41-42, 211
British Broadcasting
Corporation 216, 243,
246, 278, 334, 396-98
Radio Five Live 245
Sports Personality of the
Year 247

British Canoe Association 58
British Canoe Union 58, 183
British Chartered Institute of Marketing 238
British Colleges Sports Association 52
British Collegiate American Football League 167
British Council of Physical Education 296
British Cycling Federation 98, 165
British Cyclo-Cross Association 100, 255
British Darts Council 103
British Darts Organisation 103
British Dressage 274
British Empire Exhibition 22, 417
British Empire Games Federation 73
British Endurance 274
British Equestrian Centre *see* National Equestrian Centre
British Federation of Sand and Land Yacht Clubs 208
British Field Sports Society 80
British Gay and Lesbian Sports Federation 148
British Golf Museum 262
British Grand Prix 3-4, 45, 53, 112, 251-53, 353
British Gymnastics 399
British Handball Association 170
British Hard Court Championships (tennis) 218
British Horse Society 183, 274, 333, 352
British Horse Trials Association 274

British Horseracing Board 188, 190
British Ice Hockey Superleague 195-96
British Institute of Sports Coaches 70, 273
British Journal of Physical Education 296
British Journal of Sports History 49
British Journal of Sports Medicine 47
British Jumping Derby 175
British Ladies Amateur Championship (golf) 161
British League of Racing Cyclists 98, 250
British Lions Rugby Union team 343
British Long Distance Swimming Association 388
British Longbow Society 12
British Medical Association 60, 149
British Motorcycle Grand Prix 112
British Mountaineering Council 299, 327
British Olympic Association 48, 70, 168, 284-85, 287, 403
British Orienteering Federation 290
British Parachute Association 293-94
British Polytechnics Sports Association 52
British Racing Motors 252
British Record (Rod Caught) Fish Committee 8
British Schools Cycling Association 165
British Show Jumping Association 183, 274, 352

British Society of One-Armed Golfers 106
British Society of Sport Psychology 306, 377
British Society of Sports History 48-49, 179
British Softball Federation 359
British Speedway Promoters' Association 365
British Sporting Art Trust 49-51, 264
British Sports Association for the Disabled 106
British Sports Trust 61
British Stock Car Racing Association 382
British Student American Football Association 167
British Students' Sports Federation 52
British Surfing Association 385
British Touring Car Championship 252, 290
British Trampoline Federation 399
British Triathlon Association 400
British Universities Sports Association 51-52
British Universities Sports Board 52
British Universities Sports Federation 51-52
British Volleyball Association 411
British Water Ski Federation 414
British Women's Cricket Association 150
Brittin, Janette 85
Broad, Neil 220
Broadbridge, James 84
Broadcasting Acts 243
Brookes, N. E. 422
Brookes, William 'Penny' 25-26, 257-59

435

Brooklands Automobile
Racing Club 53
Brooklands Circuit 52-53,
251, 254
Brooks, Shirley 15
Broome, Harry 308
Broughton, Jack 307, 368
Brown, Isla 167
Brown Jack 15
Brown, Jackie 44
Brown, Susan 409
Brownlie, Cyril 344
Bruce, Hon. Victor 319
Brunell, W. J. 319
Bruno, Frank 44, 59, 246,
269, 370
Bryant, David 39
BSkyB 155, 212, 243,
245-46, 337, 361, 398
Buchanan, Ken 43
Budd, Zola 76, 172
Budge, Donald 219
Budokwai Judo Club,
London 201
Budweiser League (basket-
ball) 32
Buffalo Scottish society
177
Bull, Phil 268
Bunbury, Sir Charles 69, 264
Bunn, Douglas 175, 334
Burgess, Thomas William 62
Burghley Horse Trials 131
Burke, Gillian 63
Burke, Jem 308
Burnden Park 21
1946 disaster 108
Burnley F.C. 19
Burns, Robert 95
Burrell, Sir Peter 87
Burton, Beryl 98
Busby, Sir Matt 13, 109
Buss, Miss 121
Bute family 59
Butler, E. M. 141
Butler, James 367

Byerley, Captain 185
Byerley Turk 185
Byles, J. B. 375
Byrd, Alton 166
Byron, Lord 308

C

Cae'r Castile School 75
Caesarewich horse-race 280
Cagney, Jimmy 139
Cahn, Sir Julien 368
Calcutta Cricket Club 82
Calcutta Cup 53, 266, 336,
340, 343-45, 404
Calcutta Football Club 55
Call, Ernest 281
Calzaghe, Joe 44
Camanachd see Shinty
Camanachd Association 351
Cambridge Pythons 167
Cambridge University 16, 25,
52, 55-56, 88, 195, 291,
304, 311, 317, 331, 340,
408-09
Cambridge University Boat
Club 56, 408
Cambridge University
Cricket Club 56
Cambridge University
Dampers Club 311
Cambridgeshire horserace
249, 280
Cameron, A. A. 269
Campaign for the Protection
of Hunted Animals 225
Campbell, Colin 231
Campbell, Donald 207-208
Campbell, Malcolm 207-08
Campbell, Mary 24
Campbell, Sue 273
Canmore, King Malcolm
135, 176
Canoe Camping Club 58
Canoe-polo 57
Canoe-sailing 57

Canoeing 57-58, 182-83
Canonero, Milena 139
Cantona, Eric 269
Cardiff Arms Park 58-59, 74,
341, 344, 427
Cardiff Athletic Club 59, 360
Cardiff Cricket Club 59
Cardiff Rugby Football Club
59, 341
Cardus, Neville 201
Carling, Will 245
Carlsson, Eric 319
Carlton Australian Rules
Football team 27
Carnegie, Andrew 116
Carnegie College 59-60, 273
Carnegie Trust 199
Carnoustie 160
Carpenter, John 285
Carroll, Lewis 226
Carter, Dick 135
Carter, Dr H. 35
Cartwright, John 16
Casuals F.C. 78
Cater, Gwyneth 63
Catford Cycle Club 178
Catkins, Sue see Atkins, Sue
Catton, J. A. H. 244
Caunt, Ben 308
Cavendish see Jones, Henry
Cayton 200
C.B.S. television 397
Celtic F.C. see Glasgow Celtic
F.C.
Celtic Park 21, 363
Central Council of Physical
Recreation 20, 36, 60-61,
122, 153, 168, 296, 302,
385
Central Council of Recreative
Physical Training see
Central Council of
Physical Recreation
Central Lancashire League
(cricket) 82
Central Park, Wigan 337

Centre Court, Wimbledon 218-19, 267, 421-22
Centre for Sports Studies, University of Stirling 179
CGU National League *see* Sunday League
The Chain 268
Challenge for the Silver Cup 156
Chamberlain, Neville 356
Chambers, Dorothea Katherine Douglass 223, 369
Chambers, John Graham 40
Chambers, Robert 161
Champion 140
Champion, Bob 140, 163
Champion Dabber 298
Champion Hurdle, Cheltenham 64, 191, 262
Chandos, Duke of 87
Channel Four television 397
Channel Swimming 61-63
Channel Swimming Association 63
Chaplin, Charlie 328
Chapman, Colin 252
Chariots of Fire 139, 369
Charles I, King 79
Charles II, King 11
Charlton, Bobby 109
Charterhouse School 16, 123
Chelsea College 63-64, 126
Cheltenham Hall of Fame 261-63
Cheltenham racecourse 64, 191, 262
Cheltenham School 123-24
Cheshire Tally-Ho Hare and Hounds 94
Chester regatta 333
Chester Roodee 65
Chester Vase 65
Chifney, Sam 368
Children 65-67
Children and their Primary Schools (1967) 122

Chilvers, Peter 423
Chipperfield, David 264
Christie, Linford 25, 370
Church, Bob 10
Chuter, P. 311
Civic pride 76-77
Civil Aviation Authority 294
Clarendon Commission (1864) 121
Claret Jug 288
Claridge, Steve 324
Clark, Ambrose 51
Clark, Jim 252-52, 353
Clarke, Barry 255
Clarke, William 34, 84, 86-87
Claro, Tom 407
Class 67-69, 81
Classics, the 69, 186, 280
Clay Bird Shooting Association 420
Clay pigeon shooting 419-20
Clay Pigeon Shooting Association 420
Clayton, Ed 74
Cleather, Colonel 13
Climbing *see* Rock climbing
Clothing *see* Costume
Club de Campo 33
Club Nautique de Gand (of Belgium) 174
Club U.K. sailing centre *see* U.K. Sailing Academy, Cowes
Coaching 69-71, 273-74
Coachwise 273
Coarse fishing 8-9
Cobb, John Rhodes 53, 207-08
Coca-Cola Cup *see* League Cup
Cock, Oliver 57-58
Coe, Sebastian 25, 369
Coleman, Thomas 190
Collings, Captain Tony 183
Collins, John 400

Collins, Peter 252
Collins, Tony 49
Come On You Reds 270
Commentators 371-72
Commercialism 71-73
Commission Internationale de Parachutisme 294
Commissions and reports 121-22, 424
Committee of Council on Education 121, 125
Commonwealth Games 30, 73-76
London 1934 74, 418
Cardiff 1958 74-75, 360
Edinburgh 1970 75
Edinburgh 1986 75-76
Commonwealth Weightlifting Federation 415
Community 76-77
Community Sports Leaders Award 61
Compton, Denis 84, 263, 370
Comrades Marathon, South Africa 325
Coniston Gullies 136
Conlon, Gerry 140
Connolly, Maureen 419
Conrad 163
Conteh, John 44
Contracts 120
Conway, Martin 257
Cook, Brenda 24
Cook, Captain 385
Cooke, Geoff 273
Cooley, Iris 30
Coope, Sarah 400
Cooper, Charles 252-53
Cooper, Charlotte (Chatty) 216, 220
Cooper, Henry 44, 247
Cooper, Jilly 228
Cooper, John 252-53
Cooper, John Astley 73

Cooper, Keith 227
Cooper, Kenneth H. 150
Corals bookmaker 145
Corbett, Jim 40
Corinthians F.C. 77-78
Cornish Gold 131
Cornishman 131
Cornwall Rugby Union team 343
Corporation of the Masters of Defence 137
Cosford see R.A.F. Cosford
Costume 78
Cotswold Games 25, 78-79, 171
Cottage Rake 64, 262
Cotton, G. E. L. 134
Cotton, Henry 159
Coubertin, Pierre de 259, 277, 283
Couch, Jane 42, 44, 211
Council for National Academic Awards 127
Council of the Royal Aero Club 294
Countryside Alliance 79-80
Countryside Business Group 80
Countryside Movement 80
County Championship (cricket) 88
A County Cricket Match 366
County Polo Association 304
Coursing 170-71, 414
Cousins, Robin 354
Coventry speedway team 364
Coventry University 236
Cowal Highland Games 176-77
Cowdray, Lord 304
Cowdrey, Colin 370
Cowes see U.K. Sailing Academy, Cowes
Cowley, Annette 76
Cox, Richard 48
Cracknell, James 332

Cram, Steve 369
Cramm, Gottfried von 219
Cranham, Gerry 367
Cranmer, Fred 112
Cranmer, Peter 344
Crawford, Jack 222, 421
Crawhall, Joseph 366
Cribb, Tom 308-10
Crick Run, the 93
Cricket 7, 15-16, 67, 80-93, 152-53, 173, 212-13, 324, 329-30, 361, 398-99, 407, 423-26
famous clubs and teams 87-88, 241-42
famous competitions 88-90
memorable events 90-91
personalities 84-85
terms and concepts 91-92
venues 85-87, 173, 232-33
Cricket 200
Cricket at Bedford Park 366
Cricket Council 83, 85, 241
The Cricket Match 366
Cricket Reporting Agency 200
Cricketers' Association 91
Critchley, Brigadier-General 165, 418
Croke Park, Dublin 144, 193
Croquet 93
Croquet Association 93
Cross Commission (1888) 121
Cross-country running 93-94, 400
Crowd disorder see Hooliganism; Spectators, fans and crowd disorder
Crowd safety 212
Crown green bowls 39
Crusader 208
Crystal Palace 22, 60, 94-95, 302
Crystal Palace speedway team 364

Crystal Palace table tennis club 391
Cumann Luthchleas Gael see Gaelic Athletic Association
Cumberland and Westmorland freestyle wrestling 164, 428
Curling 95-96
Curry, John 354
Curtis Cup 157, 161-62
Cusack, Cyril 140
Cusack, Michael 193
Cushman 295
Cycling 96-99, 165, 248, 250, 255-56, 400
Cyclists Touring Club 97-98
Cyclo-cross 99-100

D

Daily Citizen 200
Daily Express 201
Daily Herald 200, 243
Daily Mail 200
Daily Mirror 201
Daily Telegraph 201, 224
Daily Worker 200
Dallaglio, Lawrence 345
Dallas, John 344
Daltry, Roger 10
Daly, Chris 344
Dalzell, E. 164
Danzig, Allison 421
Darby, Newman 422
Darley Arabian 185
Darley, Thomas 185
Darlington F.C. 105
Darnley, Lord see Bligh, Hon. Ivo
Dartford College 101-02, 126, 279
Darts 102-03
Darwin, Bernard 159, 201
Darwin, Charles 82
Davies, C. T. M. 35

Davies, Dan 24
Davies, Gerald 343, 345
Davies, J. H. 282
Davies, Laura 159
Davies, Lee 417
Davies, W. J. A. 343
Davies, Wayne 321
Davis Cup 216-20, 223
Davis, Dwight Filley 220
Davis, Fred 357
Davis, Joe 357
Davis, Steve 357
Davison, Emily 303
Dawes, John 343
Dawn Run 64, 262
Dawson, Gerry 205
Day-Lewis, Daniel 140
Day School Code (1895)
    121, 126
De Blicksem 297
de Courcy Laffan, Reverend
    48
De Lillo 228
De Montfort University 33,
    236
De Saussure 256
de Silva, Aravinda 426
Deal golf-course 161
Dean, Christopher 247, 354,
    370
Dean, Dixie 369
Deans, Bob 344
Decies of Bolam, Lord 250
Decker, Mary 172
Decorated Hero 249
Deepdale Stadium, Preston
    263
Deer Act (1963) 104
Deer stalking 103-04
Deerfoot 295
Defoe, Daniel 93
Dell, the 21
Dempsey, Jack 41
Derby and District Motor
    Club 112
Derby County F.C. 23, 104

Derby Day 366
Derby, Lord 33, 69
Derby matches 104-05, 363
Derby, the 69, 127
Derbyshire County Cricket
    Club 88, 153, 173
Desborough, Lord 48, 307
Desert Orchid 191, 262
Desgoulieres 415
Detroit Scottish society 177
Dettori, Frankie 249, 268
Devizes to Westminster
    marathon canoe race 57
Devlin, Frank 30
Devon Loch 163
Dewar, Phyllis 74
Dewsbury R.L.F.C. 337
Diamond Lights 270
Diamond Sculls, Henley
    Regatta 174
Diary of a Manx Grand Prix
    Rider 237
Dickens, Charles 226
Diffident 249
Dinghy racing see Sailing
Disability Sport England 107
Disability sports 105-07, 383
Disabled Drivers Club 106
Disabled Living Foundation
    106
Disasters 107-110, 362
Disley, John 290
Diving 110-11
Dixon, Sir George (M.P.) 35
Dixon, Robin 36
Dobbin, Tony 163
Dobson, Edmund 250
Dod, Lottie 369
Doggett, Thomas 112
Doggett's Coat and Badge
    111-12, 333
Doherty, Ken 357
Doherty, Laurence 220, 222
Doherty, Reginald 220, 222
D'Oliveira, Basil 91
Doncaster racecourse 69, 186

Donington Park 112-13, 252
Dorling family 128
Douglas, Desmond 392
Douglas, J. W. H. T. 67
Dover, Robert 25, 78-79, 171
Downes, Terry 44
Drama 112-15
Driscoll, Jim 44
Drugs 115-16, 248
Dubai, Sheikhs of 187
Duckinfield, Chief
    Superintendent 110
Duckworth, George 85
Dudderidge, John 58
Duddingston Curling Society
    95
Duffy, Tony 367
Duke, Geoff 255
The Dumb Waiter: a Play in
    One Act 114
Duncan, Stanley 45
Duncan, Tony 237
Dunfermline College 116-17,
    126
Dunlop, John Byrd 97
Dunn 295
Dunn, Stacy 399
Dunning, Eric 359
Durham County Cricket
    Club 88, 153
Durham regatta 333
Dynamo Dykes 148
Dyson, G. H. G. 70

E

Eager, Patrick 367
East India Company College
    349
Eastbourne tennis venue 218
Eastham, George 214, 407
Eastman, George 366
Easy, Easy 270
E.C.B. 38-County
    Competition (cricket) 89
Eccentrics 367-68

Ecclestone, Bernie 253
Eclipse Stakes, Sandown 186
Economics 119-21
Ecurie Ecosse 253
Ederle, Gertrude 62
Edgbaston, Birmingham 86
Edge, S. F. 53
Edinburgh Academy Rugby
    club 339-40
Edinburgh, Duke of 276,
    304, 336
Edinburgh Highland Games
    177
Edinburgh Polo Club 259,
    341
Edinburgh Society of Bowlers
    38
Edinburgh University 117
Edinburgh University Rugby
    club 340
Education 65-67, 121-27
    see also individual colleges
    by name; Teacher train-
    ing
Education, Department of
    318
Edward I, King 137
Edward III, King 180
Edward VII, King 137, 163
Edward VIII, King 344
Edward, H. F. V. 231
Edwards, Eddie 'the Eagle'
    367
Edwards, Gareth 343, 369
Edwards, Lionel 366
Edwards, Phil 74
Egan, Pierce 200, 210, 308
Eglinton, Earl of 288
Eintracht Frankfurt F.C. 169
Elder, Verona 25
Elizabeth I, Queen 171, 186,
    335
Elizabeth II, Queen 75, 274,
    276, 335-36, 383
Elliot, Helen 392
Elliot, Launceston 415

Emmett 172
Empire Games see
    Commonwealth Games
Empire Pool, Wembley 24,
    74
Emus, Alan 58
The Encyclopedia of Sport 375
England and Wales Cricket
    Board 83, 85, 233, 241
England cricket team 88,
    90-91, 425-26
England Monarchs 166
England Rugby Union team
    340-45, 401, 403-04,
    427
English Basketball
    Association 32
English Board of Education
    121
English Bowling Association
    39
English Bowling Federation
    39
English Field Archery
    Association 12
English Hockey Association
    180
English Karate Board 203
English Karate Council 203
English Karate Governing
    Body 203
English Racing Automobiles
    112
English Table Tennis
    Association 391
English Troutmasters'
    National 10
English Volleyball Association
    411
English Winter Bowling
    Association 39
English Women's Bowling
    Association 39
Enstone, Wayne 141
Epsom racecourse 69,
    127-28, 186, 303, 336

L'Equipe 200
Essex County Cricket Club
    88
Ethics 128-30
Ethnicity 315
Eton College 121, 123-24,
    130, 134, 180, 310, 317,
    331
Eton Fives 141
Eton Fives Association 141
Eton Wall Game 124
Eubank, Chris 44
Euro 96 22
European Association for
    Sport Management 236
European Athletics
    Championships 25
European College of Sports
    Science 378
European Cup 22
European Cup (Rugby
    Union) 343
European Grand Prix 112,
    252
European Gymnastics Union
    168
European Ladies Professional
    Golf Association Tour
    158
European Showjumping
    Championships 175
European Volleyball
    Confederation 411
Evans, Godfrey 85
Evans, H. Roy 392
Evans, Justin 'Sheepy' 417
An Evening with Gary Lineker
    114
Eventing 130-32
Everton F.C. 21, 105
Exercise Medicine 46-47
Exercise Science 47-48
Exeter College, Oxford 25,
    94
Eye of the Tiger 269
Eyston, George E. T. 207

F

F.A. Cup 17-18, 22, 86, 129, 133, 172, 178, 324, 336, 363, 417
F.A. Premier League 23
Fair play 133-34
Fairbrother, Nicola 202
Fairfax-Blakeborough, Major 268
Faldo, Nick 159
Falkland Palace 320
Fallowfield, Bill 337
Fangio, Juan Manual 352
Fans *see* Spectators, fans and crowd disorder
Fanzines 244-45
Farr, Tommy 369
Farragut Boat Club, Chicago 359
Fastnet Force 10 135
Fastnet Race 1, 134-35
Fatefully 249
Faulkner, Max 368
Favonius 367
Federation Cup 218, 221
Fédération Aéronautique Internationale 293-94
Fédération Equestre Internationale 131, 352
Fédération Internationale de Bobsleigh et de Tobogganing 36
Fédération Internationale de Boxe Amateur 43
Fédération Internationale de Hockey 181-82
Fédération Internationale de Luttes Amateurs 428
Fédération Internationale de Médicine Sportive 375
Fédération Internationale de Motorcyclisme 237, 253-55, 349
Fédération Internationale de Natation Amateur 387

Fédération Internationale de Roller Skating 329
Fédération Internationale de Ski 355
Fédération Internationale de Tir à l'Arc 12
Fédération Internationale de Volleyball 411
Fédération Internationale des Sociétés d'Aviron 331-32
Federation of All Japan Karate-do Organisations 203
Federation of Artistic Roller Skating 329
Federation of Gay Games 148
Federation of Inline Speed Skating 329
Federation of International Competition Hockey 181
Federation of Roller Skating 329
Federation of Societies of Teachers in Physical Education 296
Fell Runners Association 136
Fell running 135-36
Fencing 136-38
Ferguson, Adam 358
Ferguson, Alex 78
Fernerley, John 366
Ferrari 353
Ferrari/Shell 353
Ferris, Sam 238
Festival of British Racing 15
Fever Pitch 179
The Field 200, 219, 246
Field hockey *see* Hockey
Field sports 138-39
F.I.F.A. 20, 227, 263, 277
F.I.F.A. Magazine 227
F.I.F.A. Museum Collection 263
Figure skating 353-54
Films 139-40
Finality 184

Finn, Ivor 368
Finnegan, Chris 43
Finsbury Archers 11
Fish, Ernie 175
Fisher Education Act (1918) 121
Fisher, Gary 255
Fishing *see* Angling
Fishmongers' Company 112
'Fitness for Services' courses 60
Fitzsimmons, Bob 43-44
Five Nations championship 342-43, 345
Fives 140-41
Fives Court and Tennis Court, London 40
Flack, Edwin 220
Flat-racing 186-87
Flatman, Nat 189
Fleetwood Mac 268
Flottbeck (Hamburg) Derby 175
Flower of Scotland 269
The Flying Dutchman 268
Fog On The Tyne 270
Fogarty, Carl 255
Foinavon 163
Football *see* Association Football
The Football and Sports Library 228
Football Association National School 226
Football Association, the 6-7, 17-20, 23, 60, 150, 226, 263, 277
Football In The Community schemes 305
Football League, the 6, 17-20, 23, 72, 225, 243, 263, 361, 406-07
Football Licensing Authority 212
Football (Offences) Act (1991) 212

Football Museum, Preston 263
Football Research Centre, University of Liverpool 179
Football Trust 22, 275
Foothold 148
Forbes, J. D. 256
Ford 228
Ford, Horace Alfred 12
Ford, John 140
Ford Sports tug-of-war team 401
Fordham, George 249
Forest Football Club 17
Forest Laws 103, 170
Formosa 69
Formula 1 252-53, 353
Formula 1 Constructor's Association 252
Formula 3 252, 290
Forrest Gump 139
Forsythe, Bill 114
Foster, Brendan 94
Foster, David 391
Foster, R. E. 77
Foster, Tim 332
Foster's Cup Australian Rules Football Series 27
Foul 244
Foulkes, Bill 109
Foundation for Sport and the Arts 141-42, 146, 275
Fountain, May 63
Fowler, R. St. L. 130
Fox, Colonel 13
Fox, Don 338
Fox-hunting 142
Fox, Ken 307
Fox, Richard 58
Foxhunter 175, 184
France Rugby League team 426
France Rugby Union team 342-43, 427
Francis, Dick 228

Francis, Joe 45
Francis, Roy 337
Frankfurt Galaxy 167
Freeman, E. M. 295
Freeman, 'Tich' 85
Freethy, Albert 344
French and Company 214, 222
Freshfield, Douglas 257
Frith, William Powell 128, 366
Frontrunners Club 148
Fry, C. B. 77, 369
Fry, Charles Burgess 291
Fujiyama Crest 249
Funakoshi, Gichin 203
Funden, Ove 365
Furlong, Beryl 48
Future Systems 233
Fylde International Sand Yacht Club 208

G

Gaelic Athletic Association 143-44, 170, 193, 277
Gaelic Football 143-44
Gallacher, Patsy 369
Gambling 68, 71, 144, 275
Game Act (1831) 146
Game fishing 9-10
Game laws 146-47
Game Licences Act (1860) 146
Game shooting 147-48
Gaming Act (1968)
Garnerin, Andre Jacques 293
Gascoigne, Paul 128, 270, 370, 380
Gathering of the Lonach Highland and Friendly Society 177
Gay Eurogames 148-49
Gay Games 148
Gay, L. H. 77
Gay sport 148-49

Gazetta 200
Gem, Harry 214
Gender 149-51, 425
General Stud Book 185, 188, 268
General Teaching Council for Scotland 127
Gennadius, J. 258
Gentleman's Magazine 16
Gentlemen versus Players cricket matches 89
Geography 151-52
George I, King of Greece 258
George IV, King 12
George V, King 219, 276, 303
George, Terry 140
George, Walter 7, 94
German Gymnastic Society 402
Germania of Frankfurt 174
Getty, John Paul 424
Giant Haystacks 428
Gibbons, Bill 308
Gibbs, Scott 345
Giddens, Anthony 359
Gilks, Gillian 30
Gillette Cup 89, 152-53, 263, 282
Gilpin, Sawrey 366
Girl Guides 60
Giro d'Italia race 99
Girton College, Cambridge 56
Glamorgan County Cricket Club 58-59, 88, 360
Glasgow Celtic F.C. 21, 104, 108-09, 155, 169, 244, 269, 316, 361-62, 380
Glasgow City Council 266
Glasgow Rangers F.C. 21, 104, 108-09, 155, 169, 244, 269, 316, 361-62, 380
Glasgow Tigers 167
Glendenning, Raymond 242
Gleneagles golf-course 160

Glenelg Highland Games 176
Glenmore Lodge 60, 153, 299
Gliding sports 153-54
Globalization 154-56
Gloucester Cathedral 180
Gloucestershire County Cricket Club 88
Glynne, Owen 327
The Go-Between 227
Godfree, Kathleen (Kitty) 220, 223, 369
Godfree, Leslie 219, 223
Godolphin Barb 185
Godophin, Earl of 185
Gold Cup (horse-racing) 15, 64, 163, 191, 262
Gold Cup (motor racing) 290
Gold Leaf tobacco company 253
Golden Miller 64, 191, 262
Goldwin, William 82
Golf 33-34, 156-62, 288-89, 305-06, 324, 345-46, 348
terms and concepts 162
Golf Foundation 158
Gooch, Graham 85, 263
Goodhew, Duncan 387
Goodison Park 21
Goodman, Bishop G. 79
Goodwood 162-63
Goodwood Cup 163
Goodwood Stakes 163
Goodyear, Charles 215
Gordon-Watson, Mary 131
Gore, A. W. 216
Gore, Spencer 219, 366
Gould, Arthur 369
Gousseau, Daniel 100
Government *see* Politics and government
Gower, David 85, 245
Grace, W. G. 2, 39, 84, 87, 90, 368-69, 424

Graff, Steffi 222
Graham, Judy 311
Grand Caledonian Curling Club 95
Grand Challenge Cup, Henley Regatta 173-74
Grand Golf Tournament 160
Grand Liverpool Steeplechase 163
Grand National Archery Society 12
Grand National, the 3, 163-64, 190-91
Grand National Tournament (golf) 157, 160-61
Grand Prix de Nations 98
Grand Slam (Rugby Union) 343-45
Grand Slam Cup 218
Grand Tour, the 256
Grandstand 243, 349, 396
Grandstand Association 128
Grandstand Media 183
Grant, Sir Francis 366
Grantham, William W. 384
Grasmere Guides race 136
Grasmere sports 164
Grass track racing 165
Great Britain Bulldogs 167
Great Britain Diving Federation 111
Great Britain Rugby League team 338, 426
The Great Escape 269
Great Ovation 131
Greaves, Alex 189
Green, Andy 207
Green, Lucinda 131
Green, Stephen 263
Greenop, J. 164
Gregg, Harry 109
Gregory IX, Pope 180
Gregory's Girl 114
Greig, Tony 212
Grenfel, William 311
Grey, Tanni 107

Greyhound racing 145, 165-66, 418
Greyhound Racing Association 165, 183, 418
Gridiron football 164-65
Griffiths, John 'Shoni Hugh' 417
Griffiths, William 'Wil o'r Wern' 416
Grimshaw, Nicholas 233
'Grind', the 94
Grinham, Judy 387
Grobler, Jürgen 332
Grovewood Securities Ltd 45
Grüning, Ed. 402
Guantanamera 269
Guard's Trophy 45
Guild of St George 11
Guillemard, A. G. 55
Guinness, Kenelm Lee 207
Gulley, John 308
Guttmann, Sir Ludwig 106, 383
Gwydyr, Baron 87
Gymnastics 167-68
see also Acrobatics; Rhythmic gymnastics

H

Hackett, Desmond 201
Hadow Report (1926) 121-22
Hagberg 111
Hailsham, Lord *see* Hogg, Quintin
Hailwood, Mike 255
Haines, W. 311
Haining, Peter 332-33
Hale, Edward 98
Halford, F. M. 10
Halifax Nova Scotia Scottish society 177
Halifax R.F.C. 173
Halifax R.L.F.C. 281

Halkirk Highland Games 177
Hall Walker, Colonel *see* Wavertree, Lord
Haller, Gordon 400
Halls of Fame *see* Museums and Halls of Fame
Halswelle, Wyndham 285
Hambledon Cricket Club 82, 87
Hamburg Lawn Tennis Guild 217
Hamed, Naseem 44
Hamilton, Archbishop 348
Hammersley, Jill 392
Hammond, Walter 84, 369
Hampden Park 22, 169, 261, 266, 362-63
Hampshire County Cricket Club 88, 90
Hampton Court 320
Handball 140-41, 169-70 *see also* Welsh handball
Hang-gliding153-54
Hankinson, Mary 296
Hanks, Tom 139
Hardaker, Alan 19-20
Hardy, Lew 307
Hare hunting and coursing 170-71
Hargreaves, Jenny 359
Harlem Globetrotters basketball team 281
Harlequins R.F.C. 341, 403
Harringay Arena 183
Harris, David 84
Harris, Reginald 98, 367
Harrow Football 124
Harrow School 123-24, 130, 141, 317, 381
Hartley, L. P. 227
Harvard rowing team 333
Hat trick 172
Hatton's Grace 64
Hawes, Mark 311
Hawke, Lord 130
Hawthorn, Mike 252

Hayes, Seamus 175
Hazlewood, Mike 414
Hazlitt 226
Head of River Race 332
Head, Patrick 253
Head to head 172
Headingley 86, 172-73, 337-38
Heald, Charles 375
Health Education Authority 377
Healy, Thomas 228
Hearn, George 387
Hearne, J. T. 173
Heath, Edward 1, 135
Heathcote, J. M. 215
Heenan, John Carmel 308-10
Hemery, David 291
Hendry, Leo 307
Henglers ice rink, London 195
Henley Royal Regatta 173, 265, 311, 331-33
Henman, Tim 217, 220, 395
Henry VIII, King 11, 137, 186, 320, 335
Herbert, Garry 332-33
Heritage Lottery Fund 263
Heroes 368-70
Herring, John Frederick Senior 366
Hertog, Fedor den 250
Heseltine, Herbert 367
Heyhoe-Flint, Rachel 85
Hibbit, Natasha 323
Hicks, B. 79
Hickstead 175-76, 334
Hide, 'Molly' 85
Higgins, John 357
High 327
Highbury 21
Highland Games 136, 165, 176-78
Higuita, Rene 367
Hill, A. V. 375
Hill, Albert 7, 231, 369

Hill climbing (motor car) 178
Hill, Damon 247, 252
Hill, Graham 252, 353
Hillary, Edmund 257
Hills bookmaker 145
Hillsborough disaster (1989) 21-23, 110, 363, 394
Hilton, John 392
Hird, Thora 140
Hirschmann 170
History 48-49, 178-80
History of Education Society 48
HK Foster Cup 317
Hoban, Barry 248
Hobbs, Elizabeth 414
Hobbs, Jack 84, 90, 369
Hockey 180-82
Hockey Association 180, 277
Hoddle, Glen 270
Hodge, Frank 30
Hogg, Miss 329
Hogg, Quintin (Lord Hailsham) 231, 302, 424
Holding, Michael 153
Holm, Ian 139
Holman, Fred 387
Holme Pierrepont Water Sports Centre 58, 60, 182-83, 414
Holmes, Kelly 13, 350
Holt, Jack 347
Holt, Richard 48
Homer 169
Hong Kong Sevens 342
Honourable Company of Edinburgh Golfers 156, 159, 288
Hooijdonk, Pierre Van 407
Hooliganism 68, 361-62
Hopkins, Michael 232
Hornby, A. N. 130
Hornby, Nick 179
Hornsted, L. G. 'Cupid' 207
Horse and Pony 228

Horse of the Year Show
    183-84, 352
Horse-racing 3-4, 14-15,
    64-65, 67, 69, 127-28,
    144-45, 162-64, 184-92,
    249, 279-80, 335-336,
    361
  American invasion 184
  breeding 184-85
  flat-racing 186-87
  governance and administra-
    tion 187
  jockeys 188-90
  National Hunt see National
    Hunt racing
  terminology 192
  see also individual venues by
    name
Horserace Betting Levy
    Board 188
Hoskins, Johnnie 364
Hotchkiss, Hazel see
    Wightman, Hazel
    Hotchkiss
Houlding, John 105
Howell, Denis 372
Howey, Kate 202
Howland, R. L. 74
Hoylake golf-course 160
Huddersfield and Lockwood
    Swimming Club 385
Huddersfield R.L.F.C.
    337-38
Huddersfield Town F.C. 23,
    243, 338
Hudson, Hugh 139
Hughes, David 282
Hughes, Justice R. Moelwyn
    108
Hughes, Thomas 228, 260
Hull Archers 12
Hull City F.C. 19
Hull R.L.F.C. 337
Hulley, John 228-29, 258
Hulton, Edward 244, 246
Hulton Press 247

Humphries, Richard 308-09
Hundeby, Chad 63
Hunt, James 252, 353
Hunt, John 257
Hunter, Fiona 167
Hunting 80, 103-04, 138-39,
    142, 170-71, 224-25
Hurling 192-93
Hurlingham Polo Association
    304
Hurlingham Polo Club 304
Hurst, Geoff 172, 266
A Hurting Business 228
Hutchinson '100' 45
Hutton, Captain 137
Hutton, Sir Leonard (Len)
    67, 84, 86, 369

I

I. M. March College,
    Liverpool 126
Ibbotson, Derek 24, 318, 350
Ibrox Park 21
  1902 disaster 21, 108
  1971 disaser 108-09
I.C.C. Cricket World Cup
    263
Ice hockey 195-96
Ice-skating see Figure skating
Iddison, Roger 87
Idsall School 226
Illustrated Sporting and
    Dramatic News 114
Imperial Cricket Conference
    83
In the Name of the Father 140
Inanimate Bird Shooting
    Association 420
Independence Day 228
Independent 201
Independent Television
    Authority 396
India cricket team 88, 425
Indoor athletics see Athletics:
    indoor

Indoor Tennis Initiative 218
Industry 373-74
The Informer 140
Injuries and Sport, a General
    Guide for the Practitioner
    375
Institute of Child Health,
    University of London
    377
Institute of Football Studies,
    University of Central
    Lancashire 179
Institute of Leisure and
    Amenity Managers 236
Inter-departmental
    Committee on Physical
    Deterioration 121
Intercalated Olympic Games
    (1906) 48
International Amateur
    Boxing Association 43
International Amateur
    Cycling Federation 100
International Amateur
    Handball Federation 170
International Association of
    Gay and Lesbian Martial
    Artists 148
International Badminton
    Federation 30
International Basketball
    Federation 32
International Board of the
    Amateur Swimming
    Association 413
International (later Imperial)
    Bowls Board 38
International Boxing
    Federation World
    Marathon
    Championships 42
International Canoe
    Federation 57
International Centre for Sports
    History and Culture, De
    Montfort University 179

International Cricket
Conference 83
International Cricket Council
83, 85, 212-13, 233,
241, 398
International Cricket Council
Trophy 425
International Cross-Country
Union 94
International Cyclist
Association 98
International Federation of
Women's Hockey
Associations 181
International Fund for
Animal Welfare 225
International Gymnastic
Federation 167-68, 323,
370
International Horse Show
352, 418
*International Journal of the
History of Sport* 49
International Judo Federation
202
International Lawn Tennis
Federation 216-18, 421
International Netball
Federation 279
International Olympic
Committee 115, 283,
285, 287, 332
International Orienteering
Federation 290
International Rowing
Federation 175, 182
International Rugby Football
Board 341, 403, 427
International Rules Board
(hockey) 181
International Society for
Advancement of
Kinanthropometry 378
International Sports
Acrobatics Federation
370

International Surfing
Association 385
International Table Tennis
Association 392-93
International Tennis Hall of
Fame, Rhode Island 224
International Trampoline
Federation 399
International Weightlifting
Federation 415
Into Thin Air 135
*Inventory of British Sporting
Art* 51
Inverleith ground, Edinburgh
341
Iomain *see* Shinty
I.R.A. 163
Ireland Rugby Union team
343-44, 401, 404
Irish Cricket Union 83
Irish Provincial
Championship (Rugby
Union) 343
Irish Rowing Union 331
Irish Rugby Union 340
Irish Tennis Association 218
Irvine (mountaineer) 257
Irvine (pedestrian) 295
Irvine Archers 288
Isle of Man T.T. Races
196-97, 254
Italy Rugby Union team 342
I.T.V. 243, 396-97, 428

J

Jacklin, Tony 159, 161
Jackson, Clement 291
Jackson, F. S. 130
Jackson, George 250
Jackson, John 'Gentleman'
308
Jackson, Norman A. 77
Jackson's Rooms 308
Jacobson, Stan 392
Jagger, Jackie 204

Jaguar 253
Jahn, Friedrich 125
Jaques, John 93, 391
James I, King 79
James, Mark 33
*James report on teacher train-
ing* (1972) 127
Jardine, Douglas 91
Jarrett, Keith 344
Jarvie, Grant 48, 359
Jarvis, John 387
Jayasuriya, Sanath 426
Jeet kune-do 205
Jenkins, Neil 345
Jesters Club 317
Jester's Cup 141
JJB Stadium, Wigan 337, 380
Jockey Club 4-5, 69, 128,
186-91, 211, 249, 279
Jockeys *see* Horse-racing:
jockeys
Johanneson, Albert 315
Johannson 111
John, Barry 343
John, Elton 269
John Paul II, Pope 417
John Peel 268
The John Player Special 252
Johns, Clara E. 39
Johnson, Ben 128
Johnson, Jack 140
Johnson, Martin 343
Johnson, Michael 172
Johnson, Tom 308
Johnston, Maurice 104
Joint Measurement Board
274
Jones, Ann 370
Jones, Bobby 161
Jones, Henry 215, 219
Jones, Dr Mike 58
Jones, Paul 404
Jones, Steve 231
Jones, Tommy 'Champ' 417
Jones, Vinnie 128
Jordan Mugen Honda 353

Jordanhill College 117, 199
Jose, Rebecca 323
Journal of School Hygiene and Physical Education 296
Journal of Sport Management 236
Journal of Sports Sciences 377
Journalism 199-201
Joy, Richard 415
Joyce, James 226
Judo 201-02
'Le Jumping', Paris 183

K

Kahanamoku, Duke 385
Kaiser 298
Kallicharran, Alvin 153
Kane, John 306
Kane, Peter 44
Kano, Professor Jigoro 201
Karate 203
Karrimor fell running event 136
Kashurin, Yuri 250
Kavanagh, Terry 230
Kearns, Jack 41
Kellogg's Tour of Britain *see* Tour of Britain
Kelly, Charlie 255
Kelner, Simon 201
Kelvin Hall, Glasgow 25, 318
Kelynack 295
Kempster, Michael 212
Kenji, Tomiki 3
Kennedy, E. S. 256
Kenneth Ritchie Wimbledon Library 267
Kennovan 295
Kenrik, George 35
Kent County Cricket Club 88, 90
Kent, Duke and Duchess of 336, 422
Kentucky Derby 69
Kenya 75

Kerr, Diana Rait 263
Kerr, Revd J.
Kershaw, C. A. 343
Khan, Hashim 382
Khan, Imran 213, 291
Khan, Jahangir 382
Kick boxing 204
Kilnsey Crag race 136
Kilwinning Papingo 11, 13
King George VI and Queen Elizabeth Stakes 15
King George VI Memorial Fund 299
Kings College, University of London 377
Kings Cross Steelers R.F.C. 148
Kingsby case (1912) 19
Kingsley, Charles 228
Kingston Canbury bowls club 39
Kingston, Patricia 63
Kinnaird Cup 141
Kinnaird Trophy 232
Kiralfy, Imre 418
Kirk Session Records of Glasgow 351
Kirkland, Geoff 298
Knapp, Barbara 35, 306
Knott, Alan 85
Knowles, Cyril 269
Knox, W. R. 70
Knur and Spell 204-05
Koch, Konrad 170
Koizumi, Gunji 201
Krakauer, Jon 135
Kristiansen, Ingrid 231
Kung Fu 205
Kwok Yuen 205
Kyle, Jack 343

L

Laban, Rudolf 117, 127
Ladbrokes 145
Ladies Alpine Club 257

Ladies Diving Association 111
Ladies' Football Association (Gaelic Football) 144
Ladies' Golf Union 157-58
Ladies Physical Training College, Southport 229
Ladies Professional Golf Association Championship 161
Lake Padarn 75
Lakeland sport 164
Laker, Jim 85-86, 263, 282
Lallemont, Pierre 96
Lambeth Baths, Liverpool 23
Lampkin, Duggie 349
Lancashire County Cricket Club 86, 88, 153, 282, 329-30
Lancashire League (cricket) 82
The Lancet 375
Land speed records 207-08
Landseer, Sir Edwin 366
Landyachting 208-09
Lang 295
Langton, Harry 266
Language 209-10
Lansbury, George 200
Lansdowne Road, Dublin 341
Lapize, Octave 100
Lara, Brian 91
Larwood, Harold 85, 91
The Last Horse Race Run Before Charles II 365
Laurel, Stan 328
Laurieston 131
Law 211-14
   Kerry Packer trial 212-13
   overseas players 213-14
   restraint of trade 214
   see also Game Laws
Law, Denis 369
Lawford, H. F. 216
Lawler, Ivan 58

Lawn tennis 214-24, 419,
421-22
  scoring system 215
  terms and concepts 221-22
Lawn Tennis Association 36,
216-18, 422
Lawrence 228
Lawrence, Stephen 315
Lawton, Tommy 369
Le Mans 24-hour race
252-53
Leach, Johnny 392
League Against Cruel Sports
224-25
League Cup 225
League of Tricyclists 98
Léautey, Paul 181
Lee, Bruce 205
Leeds Metropolitan
University 60
Leeds R.F.C. 173
Leeds R.L.F.C. 172-73, 338
Leeds United F.C. 133, 169,
244, 315
Leicester City F.C. 283, 324
Leicester R.F.C. 342
Leicester Swimming Club
368
Leicester University 358
Leicestershire County Cricket
Club 4, 88
Leitch, Archibald 108
Leitch, Cecil 159
Leith municipal bowling
green 38
Leloup, V. 349
Lenglen, Suzanne 215,
223-24, 421
Lennox, Colonel 87
Lessing, Simon 400
Lever, Sir Ashton 12
Levett 295
Levy, E. L. 403
Lewis, A. J. 368
Lewis, Cliff 'Sprinter' 417
Lewis, Lennox 44, 59, 247

Liddell, Eric 139, 369
Ligowoski, George 419
Lilienthal, Otto 154
Lilleshall Hall 60, 226, 299,
302
Lillie Bridge, London 26, 41,
304
Lillywhite, Frederick 84
Lillywhite, James 90
Lincoln City F.C. 109
Lindsay, Gillian 332
Lindsay, Maurice 337
Lineker, Gary 245
Ling Association see Physical
Education Association
Ling, Pehr Henrik 125-26
Lister, Moira 140
Lister, Noel 405
Lister Trust 405
Literature 226-28
A Little Pretty Pocketbook 330
Littlewoods 141, 145
Littlewoods Cup see League
Cup
Liverpool and Scottish
Rounders Association 330
Liverpool Athletic Club 229
Liverpool F.C. 21, 105, 110,
133, 225, 315, 394
Liverpool Gymnasium
228-29, 258
Liverpool John Moores
University 376
Liverpool Olympics 229-30
Llanelli R.F.C. 342-43
Llewellyn, Harry 175, 184
Lloyd, Cliff 305
Lloyd, Clive 425
Loader, Peter 173
Loates, Sammy 189
Lochangel 249
Locke-King, H. F. 52
Lockier, Ken 417
Lockley, Margaret 238
Logan, Dr Dorothy
Cochrane 63

Lombard R.A.C. Rally see
R.A.C. Rally
Lonach Highland Games
176-77
London Athletic Club 26, 70
London Canadians ice hock-
ey club 195
London Counties Golf
Professionals' Association
305
London Fencing Club 137
London Fire Brigade Sports
350
London Gun Club 419
London Marathon 230-31, 238
London Marathon Charitable
Trust 231
London Polytechnic see
Regent Street Polytechnic
London Prize Ring 308
London School Board 121,
126
London Scottish Drill Hall,
Buckingham Gate 29
London Swimming
Association 386
London to Brighton road
race 325
London Weekend Television
397
Loneliness of the Long Distance
Runner 139
Longmire, Thomas 164
Longstaff, Tom 257
Lonsbrough, Anita 370, 387
Lonsdale, Earl of 41, 164
Lord, Thomas 85, 87, 241,
264
Lord's Cricket Ground 85,
87, 232-33, 241, 263
Lothersdale race 136
Lottery (horse) 190
Lottery see National Lottery
Lotus 253
Loughborough School of
Sport and Games 70

Loughborough University
  233-34, 236, 358,
  376-77, 429
Louis, Joe 369
Lovelock, Jack 74
Lowe, Douglas 369
Lowerson, John 48
Lukic, Simona 42
Lunn, Arnold 355
Lunn, Henry 355
Lye, Tommy 189
Lyle, Sandy 159
Lynam, Desmond 267
Lynch, Benny 43, 369
Lyne-Dixon, Major 165
Lynn, William 3, 190, 414

M

McAlpine Stadium,
  Huddersfield 338, 380
McBride, Willie John 343
McCabe, Eamonn 367
McCall, Oliver 245
McCarthy, Jim 344
MacCartney, C. G. 173
McColgan, Liz 247
Macdonald, Arthur E. 207
MacDonald Bailey, E. 231
Mace, Jem 43
Macfie, A. F. 160
McGill University, Montreal
  195
McGowan, Walter 43
MacGregor, John 57
McGregor, William 18
McGrory, Jimmy 369
McGuigan, Barry 44, 140
Machell family 164
McIntosh, Peter 35, 48
McIntyre 196
Mack, G. S. B. 30
McKane, Kathleen see
  Godfree, Kathleen
McKane sisters 30
McKay, Bill 344

McKay, Heather 382
Mackay, Robert 317
McKenna, John 104
Mackenzie, Lois 157
Mackie, Laura 323
Mackinnon 172
McLaglen, Victor 140
McLaren 253
Maclaren, A. C. 130
Maclaren, Archibald 125
McLaren Mercedes 353
McManus, Mick 428
Macmillan, Harold 67
Macmillan, John Archie 368
Macmillan, Kirkpatrick 96
McNair, David 48
McNair, R. J. 217
McNair Report (1944) 127
Macpherson, G. P. S. 343
McTaggart, Dick 43
Madonna 417
Maguire, Joe 359
Maida Vale Lawn Tennis
  Club 215
Maindy Stadium 75
Major, John 275
Male, James 317
Mallin, Harry 43
Mallory 257
Malvern School 317
Management 235-37
Manchester City F.C. 105
Manchester Cricket Club 86
Manchester Guardian 201, 246
Manchester Storm ice hockey
  team 195
Manchester tennis venue 218
Manchester United F.C. 18,
  21, 78, 105, 133, 155,
  212, 261, 282-83
  Munich disaster (1958) 109
Mandela, Nelson 427
Mangan, Tony 48
Manningham 173, 338
Mansell, Nigel 247, 252
Manx Grand Prix 237

Many Memories 237
Marathon canoeing 57
Marathon racing 230-31,
  237-38, 324-26
Marca 200
Marina, Princess 336
Mark of Esteem 249
Marketing 238-40
Marks, Ivan 9
Marlborough College
  123-24, 134, 180
Marot, Veronique 231
Marquesse, Mark 49
Marsh, Irene 229
Marshall, Benjamin 366
Marshall, Julian 215
Marshall, Mary 295
Martin, Louis 415
Marylebone Cricket Club see
  M.C.C.
Mascots 240-41
La Mascotte 240
Mason, Lisa 168
Mason, Tony 48
*Master Digbie's Book of the Art
  of Swimming* 110
Master of Foxhounds
  Association 142
Masters of Basset Hounds
  Association 170
Match of the Day 243, 270,
  396
Matthews, Brian 141
Matthews, Stanley 108,
  369-70
Mauger, Ivan 365
Mauritzi 109
Maxwell, Robert 76
May, Peter 84, 370
M.C.C. 15-16, 60, 81-83,
  85, 87, 217, 232-33,
  241-42, 277
M.C.C. Museum 233,
  263-64
M.C.C. Trophy 89
Meade, Richard 131

Meadowbank Stadium,
    Edinburgh 75
Mealey, Charles 228
Mecca bookmaker 145
Media 242-48
Medicine 46-47, 374-75
Mellon, Paul 51
Mellor, David 245
Melly, Charles P. 229
Membership card scheme
    302
Mendel 185
Mendoza, Daniel 308-09
Men's International
    Professional Tennis
    Council see Men's Tennis
    Council
Men's Tennis Council 218
Merchiston Castle Rugby
    club 339
Meredith, Billy 305, 369
Merlin, Joseph 328
Metropolitan Diving School,
    London 389
Metropolitan Rowing
    Association 331
Metropolitan Swimming
    Association 386, 402
Meynell, Hugo 142
Michael, James 98
Michaux, Pierre 96
Mid-Cheshire Motor Club
    290
Middlesborough canoe course
    58
Middlesborough F.C. 23
Middlesex County Cricket
    Club 85, 88, 232
Middlesex Sevens 342, 403
Midland and East Anglia
    Bowling Association 39
Midland Counties A.A.A. 24,
    26, 318
Midlands Golf Association 305
Mikkola, Hannu 319
Milk Cup see League Cup

Milk Race 250
Mill Reef 264
Millar, Robert 99
Millennium Stadium, Cardiff
    see Cardiff Arms Park
Mills 295
Mills, Freddie 44
Millwall F.C. 23
Milnes, Simon 400
Milnes-Walker, Nicolette 368
Minardi 353
Ministry of Education 122
Minor Counties
    Championship (cricket)
    89
Minor Counties Cricket
    Association 83
Minshull, John 90
Mirror Group 247
Miss England II 208
Mitchell, Henry 35
Mitchell, William 38
Mohammed, Sheikh 247
Molineux, Tom 310
Monahan, Rinty 43
The Monarch of the Glen 366
Monaveen 191
Monckton, H. H. 217
Monday Night Football 397
Monmouthshire Polo Club
    304
Montagu, Ivor 391
Monte Carlo rally 319
Montgomerie, Colin 159
Moody, Helen Wills 223
Moore, A. W. 256
Moore, Ann 334
Moore, Bill 237
Moore, Brian 372
Moore, Jamie 400
Moores, John 145
Moorhouse, Adrian 387
Moray House Institute of
    Education 117, 199
Morecambe Cross Bay
    Swimming Association 388

Morgan, Bert 417
Morgan, Teddy 344
Morgan, William 411
Morley, David
Morning Cloud 1
Morpeth Olympic Games
    250-51
Morris, Tom 158, 161, 348
Morris, Tom Junior 158,
    288, 348
Mortensen, Stan 172
Mortimer, Angela 370
Morton, Alan 369
Morton, Lucy 387
Moss, Stirling 252, 290, 353
Motherwell 76
Moto-cross see Scrambling
Moto-cross des Nations 349
Motor (name of pigeon) 297
Motor boat racing 251
Motor racing 45, 52-53, 178,
    251-53, 290, 319,
    352-53, 380-83
Motorcycle racing 45,
    196-97, 237, 253-54,
    290, 363-65
Motson, John 78
Moulton, Alex 97
Mount Vernon Parade
    Ground 229
Mountain biking 255-56
Mountain Leader Training
    Board 299
Mountaineering 256-57
Much Wenlock Games 25,
    257-59
Muirfield 159-60, 288
Muirhead, Frank 282
Mullen, Karl 343
Mummery, A. F. 256
Munich disaster (1958) 109
Munn, Charles 165
Munnings, Sir Alfred 366
Munrow, A. D. 35
Murdoch, Elizabeth 63
Murdoch, John 176

Murdoch, Rupert 243, 245-46
Murphy, Kevin 63
Murrayfield 259-60, 341, 344-45
Muscular Christianity 115, 124, 134, 260, 322, 349
Museums and halls of fame 260-68
Museum of Rugby, Twickenham 265-66
Music 268-70
Musketeers 220
Mussabini, Sam 139
Musselburgh golf-course 160, 288-89
Muths, J. C. Guts 125
Mynn, Alfred 84, 369
Myths 270-71

N

Naismith, James 31
N.A.S.A. 154
Nash, Tony 36
National Academy of Sport, Lilleshall 226
National Agriculture Centre, Stoneleigh 274
National Amateur Playground Association of the United States 359
National Amateur Rowing Association 332
National Association for Stock Car Auto Racing 382
National Boxing Association 42
National Centre for Shooting, Bisley 393
National Centre for Water Skiing 414
National Club Championship (cricket) 89
National Coaching Foundation 70-71, 273-74, 306, 378

National Coaching Scheme 70
National Coursing Club 171, 414
National Cricket Association 83, 85, 241
National Curriculum 122, 125
National Cycling Strategy 99
National Cycling Union 70, 98
National Darts Association 102
National Equestrian Centre 274-75
National Exhibition Centre, Birmingham 274, 334
National Federation of Anglers 9
National Field Archery Society 12
National Football League (American Football) 166-67
National Football League (Gaelic Football) 143
National Horseracing Museum, Newmarket 51, 264
National Hunt Club 187
National Hunt Committee 190-91
National Hunt Festival, Cheltenham 64, 191
National Hunt racing 186, 190-92, 262
National Indoor Arena, Birmingham 25, 318
National Lottery 68, 99, 146, 275, 307, 372, 374, 378, 418
National Mountain Centre see Plas y Brenin
National Olympian Association 258, 402

National Olympian Games 258-59
National Olympian movement 26
National Olympic Committee 48
National Orienteering Centre 153
National Playing Fields Association 122, 275-76
National Rifle Association 393
National Rink Hockey Association 328
National Rounders Association 330
National Sailing Centre see U.K. Sailing Academy, Cowes
National Schools Regatta 183
National Sea Anglers' Federation 10
National Skating Association 329
National Sporting Academy 278
National Sporting Club 41
National Sports Centre at Lilleshall 226
National Sports Centre for Wales 60
National Sports Medicine Institute 47, 375
National Stadium, Wales 58-59
National Stoolball Association 384
National Stud 185, 280
National Union of Journalists 201
National Union of Teachers 60
National Village Championship (cricket) 89

National Water Sports
Centre, Holme
Pierrepont 58
National Youth Watersports
Centre *see* U.K. Sailing
Academy, Cowes
Nationalism 276-78
Nations Cup 352
NatWest Bank Trophy *see*
Gillette Cup
Navratilova, Martina 223
Naylor, Herbert 32
N.B.C. television 397
Nelson 76
Nessun Dorma 268
Netball 278-79
Neville, Ernest 325
New Cross speedway team
364
New Haw and Woodham
tug-of-war team 401
New York Athletic Club 402
New York City Scottish
society 177
New York Scottish society
177
New York State Athletic
Commission 42
New Zealand All Blacks
343-44, 404, 427
Newall, Sybil 'Queenie' 12
Newbolt, Sir Henry 260
Newcastle United F.C. 155,
214, 407
Newmarket 69, 185-87, 264,
279-80
Newmarket coursing club 414
Newmarket Library 264
Newnham College,
Cambridge 56
News Chronicle 325
News International Group
245
News of the World
Individual Darts
Championship 102

News of the World Match Play
Tournament (golf) 157,
160
Newsweek 140
Newton, Arthur 324
N.F.L. Europe League 165
N.F.L. World League *see*
N.F.L. Europe League
Nice One Cyril 269
Nicholls, E. Gwyn 343
Nicholson, John 251
Nicklaus, Jack 161
Nickson, Bill 250
Nickson, Robert 39
Nike 150, 155
'Nimrod' *see* Apperley,
Charles
1966 World Cup 22, 172,
266
Nissen, George 398
No Man's Land 114
No. 1 Court, Wimbledon
219, 422
Noble, Richard 207
Noel-Bruce Cup 317
Norfolk, Duke of 171
Norris, Sir Henry 104
North American Society for
Sport Management 236
North Kensington
Badminton Club 29
North London Collegiate
School 121
Northampton Town F.C. 23
Northamptonshire County
Cricket Club 88
Northern Championships
(tennis) 218
Northern Counties A.A.A. 26
Northern Rugby Football
Union (the Rugby
League) 5-6, 173, 336
see also Rugby League, the
Northumberland and
Durham Bowling
Association 38

Norwich Premier pigeon-
racing club 298
Nottingham City Regatta
183
Nottingham County Rowing
Association 182
Nottingham Forest F.C. 110,
225, 407
Nottingham International
Regatta 183
Nottingham (tennis venue)
218
Nottinghamshire County
Council 182
Nottinghamshire County
rowing team 333
Nottinghamshire Cricket
Club 34, 88, 173
NPFA Cymru 276
Nudd, Bob 9
Nuffield Trophy 112

O

Oaks d'Italia 69
Oaks, the 69, 127
Obolensky, Alexander 344
O'Brien, Des 344
O'Brien, Richard 140
O'Brien, Vincent 64
Odhams Press 248
Odsal Stadium 281, 337-38
Odyssey 169
Offside 281-82
Offside! exhibition 367
Old Etonians 178
Old Irish Brehon Laws 193
Old Rugbeian Society 271
Old Trafford cricket ground
86, 282
Old Trafford football stadium
21, 282-83, 363
O'Leary, Daniel 24
Olive Grove 21
Olsen, Ole 365
Olympia 333

Olympic Games 7, 36, 42-43, 48, 70, 111, 131, 137-38, 175, 181, 219-20, 223, 237-38, 241, 277-78, 283-88, 302, 323, 332-33, 353-54, 387, 402, 413, 415, 420, 423
London Games (1908) 48, 284-85, 418
London Games (1948) 22, 48, 58, 131, 285-87, 332, 417
Olympic bids 287-88
1972 massacre of Israeli athletes 114
On the Waterfront 139
Once a Jolly Swagman 140
One Flew Over the Cuckoo's Nest 139
100 Years of Wimbledon 224
One Thousand Guineas, the 69, 280
One Thousand Mile Trial rally 319
One Thousand Miles in the Rob Roy Canoe 57
Ooh Aaah Showab Khan 114
Open Championship (golf) 157-58, 160-61, 288-89
Orienteering 289-90
Orwell, George 324
Osborn, Samuel 375
Ossie's Dream 270
Österberg, Martina Bergman 101, 121, 126, 150, 279, 296
O'Sullivan, Ronnie 357
O'Sullivan, Tim 367
Oulton Park 290
Oval, the 22, 27, 86, 282, 380
Overseas players 213-14
Ovett, Steve 369
Owen, Bill 140
Owen, Michael 370

Owen, Robert 125
Oxford City regattas (1841 and 1842) 311
Oxford Magazine 220
Oxford University 25, 51, 56, 88, 174, 195, 291-92, 304, 311, 317, 331, 340, 408-09
Oxford University Charon Club 311
Oxfordshire County Cricket Club 153
Oxley, David 337

P

Paccard, Michel 256
Packer, Ann 370
Packer, Kerry 212-13, 398
Pakistan cricket team 88, 426
Pallo, Jackie 428
Palmer, Arnold 161
Palmer, Ronald Poulton 291
Papathanassiou, Vangelis 139
Parachuting 293-94
Paragliding 153-54
Paralympic Games 106-07, 138, 383, 411
Parker, Bridget 131
Parker, Jill *see* Hammersley, Jill
Parkinson, Michael 245
Parr, George 84, 87, 90
Parry, Nick 48
Pascoe, Alan 231
Paterson, Jackie 43
Patten, James 218
Peabody, Endicott 222
Pearce, Hen 308-09
Peat, Steve 256
Peberdy, Kathryn 371
Pedestrianism 23-24, 93-94, 295
Pelican Athletic Club, New Orleans 40
Pelota 214

Penhall, Bruce 365
The People 242
Pepys, Samuel 93
Pereira, Augurio 214
Perry, Bill 308
Perry, Fred 216, 220, 222-23, 369, 392, 395
Perry, Norah 30
Perth Golfing Society 157
Phelps, Brian 111
Philadelphia Scottish society 177
Philip, Prince 75
Philips, Lieutenant Mark 131
Phillips, Tom 417
Philp, Hugh 348
Physical Education Association 122, 279, 296-97
Pickwick Cycling Club 97
Pienaar, Francois 427
Pigeon racing 297-98
Piggot, Lester 264
Pilch, Fuller 84
Ping-Pong Association 391
Pinsent, Matthew 332
Pinter, Harold 114
Pinto, Antonio 231
Messrs Piper & Wheeler 402
Pirie, Gordon 94
Pissaro, Camille 366
Plas Menai 298-99
Plas y Brenin 60, 299
Plater, Alan 337
Platt, Joseph 337
Player violence 300-01
Plymton, James 328
Pockoke 256
Pointer 297
Poirer 349
Pok-tapok 31
Police Gazette 42
Police, the 349-50
Politics and government 301-03
Pollard, James 366

Polo 303-04
Polytechnic Harriers 232, 238
Polytechnic Marathon 232, 238
Pool Promoters Association 141
Pools 68
Popplewell enquiry 109, 212
Porritt, Sir Arthur 46, 375
Porter, E. 79
Portsmouth F.C. 324
'Posh Spice' 269
Powell, Foster 295
Premier League see F.A. Premier League
Premiership see F.A. Premier League
Prescott, Alan 338
President's Cup 352
Press Association 200
Preston North End F.C. 104, 243, 263, 315
Prestwick golf-course 160
Prestwick Golf Club 157, 288
Priestley, Sir Raymond 35
Primary Education in Scotland (1965) 122
Primary P.E. Focus 296
Prince of Wales Trophy (sailing) 347
Princes ice hockey club 195
Princess Royal see Anne, Princess
Princess Royal Challenge Cup 175
Prior Parker, Linda see Green, Linda
Prize fighting see Pugilism
Procter, C. J. 32
Procter, Mike 212
Professional Boxers' Association 407
Professional Cricketers Association 407

Professional Footballers' Association 214, 263, 305, 406-07
Professional Golfers Association 33, 157-58, 305-06
Professional Golfers Association European Tour 157-58, 160
Professional Southern League 17
Professionalism 6-7, 26, 67, 71-72, 81, 119
Prophetic Bell 246
Prost 353
Prudential Assurance Company 425
Prudential Tour (cycling) 99
Psychology 306-07
Public Order Act (1986) 301
Public schools 123-25, 134
Public Schools Alpine Sports Club 355
Puccini 268
Pugilism 40-41, 307-10
Pugilistic Benevolent Society 41
Pugilistic Club 308
Pullum, W. A. 415
Punchard, F. N. 199
Punting 310-11
Pygmalion 114

Q

Qualified Horses and Unqualified Riders 366
Que Sera Sera 269
Queen Alexandra Stakes 15
Queen Mother, the 191
Queen's Club 320
Queen's Park F.C. 22, 169
Queen's Park Rangers F.C. 418
Queensberry Amateur Championships 42

Queensberry, Marquess of 40-41
Quoits 313-14

R

R.A.C. Rally 319
R.A.C. T.T. 112
Race Relations Act (1976) 316
Racecourse Betting Control Board 188
Racecourse Holdings Ltd 4
Racing see Horse-racing
Racing Calender 188, 264, 268
Racing Post 247
Racism 315-16
Rackets (racquets) 316-17
Radio Five Live 245
Raeburn Place, Edinburgh 55, 340
R.A.F. 350
R.A.F. Cosford 24-25, 317-18, 350
R.A.F. Sports Board 318-19
R.A.F. Stanmore 317, 350
Raging Bull 139
Raitz, Karl B. 131
Rallying 319
Rampling, Godfrey 74
Ramsay, Revd J. 95
Rand, Mary 370
Ranelagh Harriers 94
Rangers F.C. see Glasgow Rangers F.C.
Rankov, Boris 409
Rate, Glen 400
Ravel 268
Ravenhill ground, Belfast 341, 344
Ravenstein, Ada 402
Ravenstein, E. R. 402
Ray, Tom 164
Read, Phil 255
Reading F.C. 23
Real tennis 214, 233, 316-17, 320-21

Record crowds 363
Red Bull Sauber Petronas 353
Red Rooster 135
Red Rum 191, 264
Red Star Belgrade F.C. 109
Redgrave, Steven 332, 370
Redknapp, Jamie 270, 367
Redknapp, Louise 270
Reebok Stadium, Bolton 380
Reeder, Annika 168
Referee 200
Regent Street Polytechnic 24, 231-32
Register of Exercise and Sports Care: U.K. 375
Reid, John Robertson 366
Reid, Sir Norman 51
Reiff, Lester 184
Reilly, Tom 377
Religion 321-23
Renshaw, Ernest 216, 219, 222
Renshaw, William 216, 219, 222
Reports *see* Commissions and reports
Repton School 123
Revie, Don 324
Reynolds, John 141
Reynoldstown 191
Rhein Fire 167
Rhodes, Wilfred 85
Rhythmic gymnastics 323
Richards, Gordon 249
Richards, Vivian 213, 282, 425
Richardson 328
Richardson, Tony 139
Richmond, Duke of 82, 87, 163
Richmond Park 304
Richmond Rugby club 339, 341, 403
Rickard, Tex 41
Ring, Siobhan 167
Risman, Gus 337
Ritual 324

River and Rowing Museum, Henley-on-Thames 264-65
Rivington Pike race 136
Road Race Advisory Committee 325
Road Runners Club 325
Road running 324-26
  see also Marathon racing
Rob Roy 57
Roberts, Charlie 305
Robertson, Allan 158, 161, 348
Robertson, George Stuart 220
Robbins, Jerome 139
Robbins Report (1963) 127
Robbins, William 285
Robert Dover's Games Society 79
Robinson 264
Robinson, Bobby 73
Rock climbing 326-28
Rocky 139
Roedean 150
Rogallo, Francis 154
Rogers, Annie 63
Roker Park 21
Roller hockey 328
Roller-skating 328-29
Rolling Stones 417
Rolls, Charles S. 207
Ronaldson, Chris 321
Ropidoux, Alain 357
'Rorke's Drift' test match 338
Rose, Billy 406
Rose, Ralph 285
Roses Matches 329-30
Roth 228
Rottenberg, S. 119
Rough-Stuff Fellowship 255
Roughshooting 45
Round Britain Race 251
Round, Dorothy 217, 369
Rounders 330-31
Rous, Admiral 187, 264

Rous, Sir Stanley 20
Rousmaniere, John 135
Rowe, Diane 392
Rowe, Rosalind 392
Rowell, Charles 24
Rowing 68, 111-12, 173-75, 182-83, 331-33, 384, 408-09
Rowlands, Fothergill (Fog) 191
Rowlandson, Thomas 366
Rowley Mile course, Newmarket 69
Royal Agricultural Hall, Islington 23-24
Royal Agricultural Society of England 274
Royal Air Force Sports Board *see* R.A.F. Sports Board
Royal and Ancient Golf Club 157-58, 288-89, 348
Royal Ascot *see* Ascot
Royal Automobile Club 178, 319, 381
Royal Birkdale 160
Royal British Bowmen 12
Royal Canoe Club 57
Royal Central Gymnastic Institute, Stockholm 101, 296
Royal Commission (1905) 127
Royal Company of Scottish Archers 11-12
Royal Deeside 177
Royal Engineers football team 133
Royal Engineers ice hockey team 195
Royal Horticultural Hall, Westminster 29
Royal Humane Society 387
Royal International Horse Show 333-34
Royal Life Saving Society 111, 388

Royal Liverpool Golf Club 157, 289
Royal Lytham and St Annes 160
Royal Navy 350
Royal Navy and Royal Marines Sports Control Board 334-35
Royal Ocean Racing Club 1
Royal patronage 335-36
Royal Pigeon Racing Association 298
Royal St Georges 160
Royal Society for the Prevention of Cruelty to Animals 225
Royal Toxophilite Society 12
Royal Troon 160
Royal Yachting Association 251, 423
Royle 172
Ruff's Guide to the Turf 268
Rugby Fives 141
Rugby Fives Association 141
Rugby Football Union, the 6, 17, 55, 60, 266, 277, 336, 340-41, 403-04, 408
Rugby League 7, 68, 173, 281-82, 336-39, 341, 361, 426
  concepts and terminology 338-39
Rugby League Challenge Cup 336-38
Rugby League Council 336
Rugby League Hall of Fame, Rothwell 261, 337
Rugby League International Board 337
Rugby League International Federation 336
Rugby League, the 6-7, 336-37
Rugby Museum, Twickenham *see* Museum of Rugby, Twickenham

Rugby School 16, 93, 123-24, 260, 271, 317, 339
Rugby sevens 342
Rugby Union 6-7, 16-17, 55, 58-59, 68, 173, 259-60, 271, 282, 336, 339-45, 361, 401, 407, 426-27
Rugby World Cup 341-42, 426-27
Rugby World Cup Sevens 342
Rühl, Joachim 48
Ruislip Lido water-skiing team 414
Rules of Golf Committee 157
Rumbelows Cup *see* League Cup
Running *see* Cross-country running
Rusedski, Greg 217
Russell, Alec 249
Ryder Cup 33-34, 157, 161, 345-46
Ryder, Samuel 345

S

Sabelli, B. 217
Safety of Sports Grounds Act (1975) 21-22, 109
Sailing 1, 134-35, 347-48
Sailor Prince 249
St Andrews 159, 161, 262, 288, 348
St Anne's golf-course 161
St Ann's Cricket Club, Barbados 82
St Fillans Highland Games 176
St George Swimming Club, Liverpool 385
St George's Golf Club, Sandwich 289
St Helens ground, Swansea 342

St Helens R.L.F.C. 173, 338
St John New Brunswick Scottish society 177
Saint Leger, General Anthony 69
Saint Leger, the 69, 190
St Mirin 179
St Paul's School 317
Salford R.L.F.C. 337
Salmon and Trout Association 10
Sam Maguire Cup 143
San Francisco Scottish society 177
Sanders, Doug 161
Sanderson, Tessa 370
Sandhurst military college 25, 349
Sandown Park 186
Sandyachting *see* Landyachting
Sandys family 164
Sang, Joe 49
Sangster, Robert 187
Sangster, Vernon 145
Sartorius, John Nost 366
Savannah Georgia Scottish society 177
Sayers, Tom 308-10
Sceptre 69
Schelenz, Dr Karl 170
Schockemohle, Paul 175
Schriver family 107
Schumacher, Michael 353
Science 47-48, 376-78
Scorton Arrow 13
Scotch Whisky Cup (curling) 96
Scotland Rugby Union team 340-41, 343-45, 401
Scott, Doug 257
Scott, Sir Walter 12, 95
Scottish Amateur Rowing Association 384
Scottish Avalanche Information Service 153

Scottish Bowling Association 38
Scottish Claymores 167, 260
Scottish Cricket Union 83
Scottish Cup 22
Scottish Federation of Sea Anglers 10
Scottish Football Association 108, 266
Scottish Football Association Museum 261, 266
Scottish Football Association Museum Trust 266
Scottish Games Association 177
Scottish Ice Hockey Association 195
Scottish Lawn Tennis Association 218
Scottish Mountain Leader Training Board 153
Scottish Professional Cycling Association 165
Scottish Rugby Union 259-60, 340-41
Scottish School of Physical Education *see* Jordanhill College
Scottish Sports Council 122, 153, 372
Scottish Tertiary Education Advisory Council 117, 199
Scottish Volleyball 411
Scotton, William 34
Scrambling 349
Scunthorpe United F.C. 23
Scwheitzer, Hoyle 423
Sea fishing 10-11
Searle, Greg 332-33
Searle, Jonny 332-33
Secker, J. H. 311
Second Eleven Championship (cricket) 89
Sefton, Earl of 3

Segrave, Sir Henry 207-08, 252
Senna, Ayrton 112
Services sport 349-50
Sevenoaks reserve 45
Sever, Hal 344
Severall Wayes of Hunting, Hawking and Fishing According to the English Manner 365
Seymour, James 366
Sharman, Liz 58
Shaw 114
Shawcross, Lord 364
Shearman, Montague 26
Sheene, Barry 255
Sheffield Independent 391
Sheffield Steelers ice hockey team 195
Sheffield United F.C. 86, 129
Sheffield Wednesday F.C. 5, 21, 172
Sheil Park Athletic Grounds 229
Sheilds, J. W. 112
Sherborne School 123
Sheridan, Jim 140
Sherman, Montague 291
Sherratt, Terry 298
Sherwood, Simon 262
Shindler, Colin 105
Shinty 350-51
Shooting 45-46, 80, 138-39, 147-48, 393, 419-21
Show classes 183-84
Showjumping 175-76, 183-84, 274, 333-34, 351-52
Shrewsbury, Arthur 84
Shrewsbury School 123
Shropshire Olympian Games 258
Shropshire Olympian Society 258
Shrubb, Alfred 94
Shuttleworth, Richard 112
Sillietoe, Alan 139, 226

Silverstone 45, 252, 352-53
Simms, W. 184
Simpson, Lynn 58
Simpson, Tommy 98, 248-49
Singing 324
Sir Norman Chester Centre for Football Research, University of Leicester 179
Six Nations championship 342
Skating, figure *see* Figure skating
Skating, speed *see* Speed skating
Ski Club of Great Britain 355
Skiing 355-56
Skues, G. E. M. 10
Sky Sports *see* BSkyB
Slade, Mr Justice 212
Slalom Canoeing 57
Slater, W. J. 35
Sloan, Tod 184, 209
Smith, Albert 256
Smith, Chris 367
Smith, G. O. 369
Smith, George 85
Smith, Harvey 334
Smith, I. S. 343
Smith, Joyce 238
Smith, Neil 317
Smithsonian Institute, Washington D.C. 298
Smyth, Paul 400
Smythe, Pat 175, 184
Snooker 356-57
Snow, John 85, 212
Snow, Julian 321
Snowdon Working Party 106
Society of Archer-Antiquaries 13
Society of St Andrews Golfers *see* Royal and Ancient Golf Club
Society of Sports Science 377

Sociology 357-59
Softball 359
Sole, David 344
Solent Swimming Club 388
Solheim Cup 157, 161
Solomons, Jack 41, 67
Somerset County Cricket
  Club 88-89
Somerset, Henry Charles
  Fitzroy 31
Sophia Gardens, Cardiff 75,
  360
South Africa 75-76
South Africa cricket team 88,
  91, 398
South Africa Rugby Union
  team 343, 403, 427
South African Non-Racial
  Olympic Committee 91
South Wales Daily News 401
Southampton F.C. 21, 78,
  133
Special Olympics 107
Spectators, fans and crowd
  disorder 360-63
Speed skating 354-55
Speedway 281, 363-65, 418
Speedway Control Board 365
Sphairistikè 214, 222
Sphere Cup 160-61
Spinks, Terry 43
Spofforth, F. R. 90, 172
Sponsorship 357, 379-80,
  397
*Sport and the Community: the
  Report of the Wolfenden
  Committee on Sport* 424
Sport England *see* Sports
  Council
Sport First 200
Sport 21 122
Sporting Chronicle 200, 244,
  246
Sporting League 248
Sporting Life 200, 246-47,
  308

Sporting Magazine 242
Sporting Times 15, 90
Sports acrobatics *see*
  Acrobatics
*Sports and Pastimes of the
  People of England* 16
Sports Biomechanics Study
  Group 377
Sports Council (now Sport
  England) 5, 60-61, 95,
  103, 115, 146, 150, 182,
  204, 273, 275, 278-79,
  299, 302-03, 372-73,
  376-78, 418, 424
Sports Council for Wales
  299, 360, 372
Sports Historian 49, 179
Sports History Publishing 49
Sports Illustrated 140, 200
Sports Lottery Fund 332
Sports Medicine *see* Medicine
Sports Medicine 375
Sports Personality of the Year
  247
Sports Report 245, 270
Sports science *see* Science
Sports Television Advisory
  Committee 243
Sportscar World
  Championship 112
Sportsman 200, 247-48
Sportsview 243, 396
Sportsweek 200
Spracklen, Mike 332
Springman, Sarah 400
Sprint canoe racing 58
Sprinting (motor car) 380-81
Squash 317, 381-82
Squash Rackets Association
  381
Sri Lanka cricket team 426
Stanley of Preston, Lord 195
Stansfeld, Margaret 33
Starley, James 96
Statham, Brian 85
Station, W. 329

Statutes of Galway (1527)
  193
Statutes of Kilkenny (1366)
  193
Steadman, G. 164
Stein 109
Stephen, Leslie 56, 123
Stephen(/s), William 82
Stephens, Edward 'Lumpy'
  84
Stewards Charitable Trust,
  Henley 175
Stewards' Cup (at
  Goodwood) 163
Stewart Grand Prix 353
Stewart, Jackie 252, 353
Stirling University 358
Stock-car racing 382-83
Stockport County F.C. 283
Stoke City F.C. 23, 108
Stoke Mandeville Games
  106, 383
Stoke Mandeville Hospital
  for the Spinal Injured
  106, 383
Stoke Mandeville Sports
  Stadium for the Paralysed
  and Other Disabled 383
Stoke Mandeville World
  Wheelchair Games 383
Stoneleigh Deer Park 274
Stoneleigh show ground
  274-75
Stonewall Revolt (1969) 148
Stoolball 383-84
Stoolball Association of Great
  Britain 384
Stopforth, Colleen 400
Storey, David 139
Stow, David 125
Stracey, John 44
Stradey Park, Llanelli 342
*Strategic Directions for Sports
  Science Research in the
  United Kingdom* 377
Strathclyde University 199

Strathclyde Water Park 384
Strathcona Cup (curling) 96
Street Betting Act 145
Streeter, Alison 63
Strikes *see* Unions and strikes
Strudwick, Herbert 85
Strutt, Joseph 16
Stuart, Nick 168
Stubbs, George 366
Stud *see* National Stud
Studd Trophy 231
Suffragette movement 303
Sugden, John 49
Sullivan, John L. 40
The Sun newspaper 110
Sunday Graphic 242
Sunday League cricket 89
Sunday Observance Act
    (1695) 193
Sunderland F.C. 21, 23,
    133
Sunderland Wearwolves 167
Sunningdale golf-course 160
Superstition 324
Surf canoeing 57
Surf Life Saving Association
    of Great Britain 385
Surfing 385
Surrey County Cricket Club
    6, 18, 86, 88, 90
Surtees, John 45, 252, 255
Sussex County Cricket Club
    88, 153
Sussex Stakes (at Goodwood)
    163
SUSTRANS 99
Sutcliffe, Charles Edward 19
Sutcliffe, Herbert 369
Sutherland, Duke of 226
Sutton, May 215, 223, 419,
    422
Swaffham coursing club 414
Swansea Leisure Centre 373
Swansea R.F.C. 342
Sward Trophy 232
Swaythling Cup 392

Swedish Amateur Boxing
    Association 43
Swedish gymnastics 296
Swimmers' Life Saving
    Society 388
Swimming 61-63, 385-89,
    400
Swimming Association of
    Great Britain 386, 413
Sydney to Hobart race 1
Syers, Florence 354
Synchronized swimming
    388-89

T

Taaffe, Pat 262
Table tennis 391-93
*Table Tennis and Pastimes
    Pioneer* 391
Table Tennis Association 391
Tagg, Henry 311
Talbot Handicap 39
Tani, Yukio 202
Tanner, Haydn 344
Tanzania 75
Target shooting 393
Tasker, Frank 298
Tasker, J. 257
Tate Gallery 51
Tate, Maurice 85
Tatler Cup 160-61
Taunton Commission (1868)
    121
Taylor, A. E. M. 217
Taylor, Andrew 305
Taylor, Bob 85
Taylor, Henry 387
Taylor, J. H. 158
Taylor, John 285
Taylor, John 345
Taylor Report 21-23, 212,
    260, 338, 361, 363,
    393-94
Teacher training 125-27, 199
Technology 394-96

Teddington Hockey Club
    180
Television 357, 396-98
Tennis *see* Lawn tennis
Tennis and Rackets
    Association 317, 320,
    381
Tennis Court Inn, Cardiff
    416
Tennis Wales 218
Tennyson, Lord 130
Tenzing 257
Terminology *see* Language
Terrance, Cuthbert *see*
    Tinling, Ted
Terson, Peter 114
Test and County Cricket
    Board 83, 85, 212-13,
    241
Test matches 398-99
Texaco Trophy (cricket)
    89-90
Thames Hare and Hounds
    94
Thames Punting Club 311
Thatcher, Margaret 244,
    301-02
Thelwell 228
This Time (We'll Get It Right)
    270
Thomas Cup 30
Thomas, F. 141
Thomas, Freddy Hall *see*
    Welsh, Freddy
Thomas, John Godfrey Parry
    207
Thompson, Daley 370
Thompson, William 308-09
Thorburn, Cliff 356
The Three Peaks race 136
This Sporting Life 139
Thrust SSC 207
Thrust 2 207
Tilden, Bill 216
Tillemans, Pieter 366
Timeform 268

The Times 201
Tingay, Lance 224
Tinling, Ted 224
Tinn, Jack 324
Tissue 246
Tom Brown's School Days 124, 260
Tomiki Aikido *see* Aikido
Tomkinson, Alan 359
Tonbridge School 123, 317
Tony Cornwell Memorial Trophy 298
Topham, Mirabel 3
Topham, Thomas 415
Torrance, Sam 161
Torvill, Jayne 247, 268, 354, 370
Tote, the 145-46, 187
Tottenham Hotspur F.C. 104-05, 133
Tottenham Hotspur (painting) 366
Tour de France 98, 100, 248
Tour of Britain (cycling) 98-99
Townley, Billy 172
Toxophilus 12
Track and field athletics *see* Athletics: track and field
Tragett, Margaret 30
Training of Young Athletes project 377
Trampolining 399-400
Traun, Friedrich Adolf 220
Treadwell, Peter 48
Tredgett, Mike 30
Trent Bridge, Nottingham 86
Triangular Tournament 91
Triathlon 400-01
Trinity College, Cambridge 173
Trinity Tales 337
Triple Crown 343-45, 401
Troon golf-course 161
Trueman, Fred 85
Trumper, Victor 262
Tuckett, Francis Fox 256

Tug of war 401-02
Tug-of-War Association 402
Tunnicliffe, Neil 337
Turnberry 160
Turnhalle, the 402-03
Turpin, Randolph 44
Twickenham 265-66, 341, 344, 403-04
Twickenham Rugby Club 403
Two Thousand Guineas, the 69, 280
TWR Arrows 253
Tyrrell 253, 353
Tysall, Walter 167
Tyson, Frank 85
Tyson, Mike 44

U

U.E.F.A. 20, 213
Ueshiba, Morihei 3
Uganda 75
Uist Highland Games 176-77
U.K. Athletics 325
U.K. Parachuting 294
U.K. Sailing Academy, Cowes 60, 405-06
U.K. Sport 273, 373
U.K. Sports Institute 36, 377-78
U.K. Sports Institute Wales 299
Umpire 200
Underworld 228
Union Cycliste Internationale 98, 100
Unions and strikes 406-08
United All-England Eleven cricket team 82, 87
United North of England cricket team 87
United South of England cricket team 87
United States Golf Association 157

United States Handball Association 417
United States National Lawn Tennis Association 217, 419
United States Olympic Committee 148
Universities 51, 307, 358
Universities Athletic Union 51-52
University Boat Race *see* Boat Race
University of Greenwich 102
University of London 377
Uphill Ski Club 153
Uppingham School 16, 123-23

V

Vale, David 237
Vale, Paul 237
Valley Parade disaster (1985) 109, 281
Vandervell, Tony 253
Vansittart family 36
Vansittart-Neale, Phyllis 36
Vanwall 252-53
Vardon, Harry 158
'Varsity' cricket match 88-89
'Varsity' Rugby Union match 291
Verity, Hedley 85, 173
Verity, Thomas 85, 232
Vernons 141, 145
Vestey, Edmund 51
Victoria County History 25
Victoria, Queen 177, 393
Villa Park 21
Villoresi, Luigi 353
Vincent, Sir Howard (M.P.) 48
Violence *see* Hooliganism; Player violence
Viollett, Dennis 109
Voce 91

Voigt, Charles Adolf 220
Volleyball 411
Voltiguer 268
Voyce, A. T. 343
Vuelta a Espana race 99

W

Waddell, Herbert 344
Waddell, Dr Tom 148
Waddle, Chris 270
Wade, Virginia Sarah 217, 223, 247, 370
Wagstaff, Harold 337-38
Wakefield Trinity R.L.F.C. 338
Wakefield, W. W. 343
Wales, Prince of 191, 308, 336, 344
Wales Rugby League team 337
Wales Rugby Union team 341, 343-45, 401, 403-04
Walker Cup 157, 161
Walker, Richard 9-10
Walker, Thomas 84
Wall Street 249
Wallace, A. C. 343
Walsall F.C. 23
Walsh, Shelsey 178
Wanderers Football Club 17, 133
Ward, James 366
Ward, Jem 308
Ward, Joe 308
Ward, Kirsty 399-400
Ward, Nick 308
Wareing, Mr 229
Waring, Thomas 12
Warner, Sir Pelham 241
Warren, B. R. 141
Warrington R.L.F.C. 281
Warwickshire County Cricket Club 86, 88, 153
Water polo 413

Water-ski jumping 183
Water-skiing 414
Water speed records 207-08
Waterloo Cup 171, 414
Waterloo Handicap 39
Watford F.C. 315
Watson, Alfred E. T. 31
Watson, Tom 161
Watt, Jim 43
Wattana, James 357
Waugh, Joe 250
Wavertree, Lord 185
We Are The Champions 269
Weatherby, James 185, 188
Weatherbys 188
Webb, Captain Matthew 61-62
Webb Ellis, William 271, 339
Webster, Jane 30
Weekly Dispatch 200
Weightlifting 414-16
Welford Road ground, Leicester 342
Welland, Colin 139
Wellington (N.Z.) Cricket Club 83
Wellington, Duke of 134, 260
Wellington School 123
Wells, H. G. 97
Welsh Badminton Union 30
Welsh, Freddy 43
Welsh handball 416-17
Welsh Handball Association 417
Welsh Institute of Sport 360
Welsh Rugby Union 59, 340
Welsh Yachting Association 299
Wembley Arena 183, 333, 352
Wembley Experience 266-67
Wembley Lions speedway team 364, 417

Wembley Stadium 22, 133, 266-67, 333, 337-38, 345, 363, 417-18, 426
Wenlock Agricultural Reading Society 257-58
Wenlock Olympian Class 257-58
Wenlock Olympian Games 258-59
Wenlock Olympian Society 258
Wentworth golf-course 160, 345
Wessex, Earl of 320
West Ham speedway team 364
West Ham United F.C. 5, 76, 133
West Indies cricket team 88, 173, 425
West, Jeremy 58
West Kirby Gymnastic Club 371
West London Rowing Club 23, 94
West, Reg 250
West Side Story 139
Westchester Cup (polo) 304
Westhall, Charles 295
Westminster School 123-24, 331
Westminster University 231
Westmorland Gazette 164
Weston, Edward Payson 24, 295
Wethered, Joyce 159
Whannel, Garry 359
Wharton, Arthur 315
Wheatcroft, Tom 112
Wheatley Report 109
Whitaker, John 184
Whitbread, Fatima 247, 370
Whitbread Gold Cup 187, 191
Whitbread Round the World Challenge 347
White, Bella 111

White City Stadium, London 74, 333-34, 350, 418
White Conduit Club 87
White, Jimmy 357
White, June 30
White-water canoe racing 57
Whitehead, Dr Nick 273
Whiting, John 306
Whitmore, Walter Jones 93
Whymper, Edward 256-57
Widdowson, Sam 78
Wide World of Sport 397
Wigan Athletic F.C. 23, 380
Wigan R.L.F.C. 172, 337-38
Wightman Cup 219-21, 419
Wightman, George 419
Wightman, Hazel Hotchkiss 220, 419
Wild Mammals (Protection) Act (1996) 225
Wild pigeon shooting 419-20
Wilde, Jimmy 43, 369
Wilde, Kerry 417
Wildfowl Trust 45
Wildfowlers Association of Great Britain and Ireland 45
Wildfowling 45, 420-21
Wildlife Guardian 225
Wilke, Dorette 63
Wilkie, David 387
Wilkie, Graham 355
Wilkinson, 'Wilkie' 253
William III, King 415
William IV, King 348
Williams 253, 353
Williams, Billy 403
Williams, Bleddyn 344
Williams, Dorian 334
Williams, Frank 253
Williams, J. P. R. 343
Williams, J. R. P. 375
Williams, Colonel V. D. S. 183
Willis, Bob 85-86, 173
Wills, Alfred 256
Wilson, Bob 372

Wilson, C.
Wilson, George 295
Wilson, John 337
Wilson, Peter 201
Wimbledon 216-19, 222-24, 267, 336, 421-22
Wimbledon F.C. 133
Wimbledon Lawn Tennis Museum 267-68
Wimbledon Professional Championships (1967) 219
Wimbledon speedway team 364
Winchester Fives 140
Winchester Football 124
Winchester School 123-24, 180, 317
Winchilsea, Lord 87
Windham 256
Windsurfing 422-23
Wingfield Sculls 333
Wingfield, Walter Clopton 214, 222
Wisden, John 84, 87, 423
Wisden Trophy 263
Wisden's Cricketers' Almanack 90, 200, 423-24
Wise, Bernard 291
Wolfenden Committee 35, 122, 424
Wolfenden, Sir John 424
Wolfenden Report 424-25
Wolffe, Jabez 62
Wolstenholme, Kenneth 210
Wolverhampton Wanderers F.C. 324
Women see Gender
Women's Amateur Athletic Association 24, 238
Womens' Army Rounders Team 331
Women's British Open Championship (golf) 161
Women's Cricket Association 83, 91

Women's International Boxing Federation 44
Women's League of Health and Beauty 389
Women's Road Racing Association 98
Women's Sports Foundation 150, 425
Womens' Teams Games Board 330
Women's Tennis Association 218, 224
Wood, Robin 58
Wood Treatment Bosley tug-of-war team 402
Woolley, Frank 369
Woolwich Common 304
Woolwich military college 25, 349, 356
Wootton, John 366
Worcestershire County Cricket Club 88
Workington Town R.L.F.C. 337
World Amateur Boxing Championships 43
World Bowls Board 38
World Boxing Association
World Boxing Council 42
World Boxing Organisation 42
World Canoe Sprint Championships 183
World Championship Tennis 218
World Cup (cricket) 90, 425-26
World Cup (football) 241
World Cup (Rugby League) 426
World Cup (Rugby Union) see Rugby World Cup
World Darts Federation 103
World Federation of Swimming 111
World Indoor Athletics Championships 25

World Karate Federation 203

World Marathon Canoeing Championships 183

World Mountain Bike Championship 256

World of Sport 243, 396-97, 428

World Rowing Championships 183

World Series Cricket 212-13, 398

World Slalom (canoe) Championships 183

World Squash Federation 381

World Student Games 52

World Union of Karate-do Organisations 203

Worrall, Fred 324

Worthington Cup *see* League Cup

Wrestling 164, 427-28

Wright brothers 154

Wright, Ian 370

Wyatt, Sir Myles 1

Wyatville, Sir Jeffry 226

Wyles, Charles 392

Y

Yachting *see* Sailing

Yachting World 347

Yankee Doodle Dandy 139

Yates, Aldeman Mrs 182

Yeovil Town F.C. 133

Y.M.C.A. 31-32, 60, 229, 411

York Racecourse 268

York Racing Museum 249, 268

Yorkshire County Cricket Club 86-88, 153, 172-73, 329-30

Yorkshire Rugby Union team 342

You'll Never Walk Alone 269

Young Men's Gymnastic Club, Cincinnati, Ohio 23

Younghusband, Francis 257

Youth Sport Trust 61, 429

Z

Zappas, E. 258

Zatopek, Emil 417

Zetters 141

Zigger Zagger 114

Zuoz Fives Club 141